MINN.
St. Paul ★

WIS.
Madison ★

MICH.
Lansing ★

ME.
Augusta ★

Concord
NH ★

Montpelier
VT. ★

MASS.
Boston ★

N. Y.
Albany ★

Providence
R. I. ★

CONN.
Hartford ★

IOWA
Des Moines ★

ILL.
Springfield ★

IND.
Indianapolis ★

OHIO
Columbus ★

PENN.
Harrisburg ★

Trenton
N. J. ★

DEL.
Dover ★

opeka ★

MISSOURI
Jefferson City ★

KY.
Frankfort ★

W.VA.
Charleston ★

Richmond ★

VA.

MD.
Annapolis ★

MA ★

oma City ★

ARK.
Little Rock ★

★Nashville
TENN.

N. C.
Raleigh ★

Columbia
S. C. ★

MISS.
Jackson ★

ALA.
Montgomery ★

Atlanta ★

GA.

LA.
Baton Rouge ★

★ Tallahassee

FLA.

STATE AND LOCAL GOVERNMENT

STATE AND LOCAL GOVERNMENT

Sixth Edition

Ann O'M. Bowman
University of South Carolina

Richard C. Kearney
East Carolina University

Houghton Mifflin Company   Boston New York

The sixth edition of State and Local Government *is dedicated to Joel: may his dreams come true.*

Vice President and Publisher: Charles Hartford
Sponsoring Editor: Katherine Meisenheimer
Development Editor: Terri Wise
Associate Project Editor: Teresa Huang
Editorial Assistant: Jake Perry
Senior Art and Design Coordinator: Jill Haber
Senior Photo Editor: Jennifer Meyer Dare
Senior Composition Buyer: Sarah Ambrose
Manufacturing Coordinator: Chuck Dutton
Executive Marketing Manager: Nicola Poser
Marketing Assistant: Kathleen Mellon

Cover image: © Wes Thompson/CORBIS.

Printed in the U.S.A.

Library of Congress Control Number: 2003110155

ISBN: 0-618-42947-6

23456789-MP-08 07 06 05

CONTENTS

Part Three: Local Governments . . . and the States

17   Social Welfare and Health Care Policy   481

18   Environmental Policy   506

PREFACE

This book is unabashedly pro-government—state and local government, that is. Despite the drumbeat of criticism of government and public officials in the mass media, we like politics and public service. We believe that government can be a force for good in society. We do acknowledge some of the concerns voiced by critics of government. Yes, there continue to be inefficiencies, and sure, there are some politicians who, once elected, seem to forget the interests of the people back home, not to mention what their parents taught them. But by and large, state and local governments work well. On a daily basis, they tackle some of the toughest problems imaginable—problems complicated recently by a slowing economy and fiscal stress. Still, states and localities design and implement creative and successful approaches to fight crime, house the poor, clean the air, educate children, and on and on.

In the sixth edition of our text, we attempt to capture the immediacy and vitality of state and local governments as they address the challenges facing the American people. A major goal is to foster continuing student interest and involvement in state and local politics, policy, and public service. Many of the students who read earlier editions of this text now work in state and local government. Some have run successfully for public office. We want readers of the sixth edition, too, to know that state and local government is a place where one person can still make a difference and serve a cause. For students who go on to graduate study in political science, public administration, or related fields, states and localities are fertile fields for research. And for students taking this course because they "have to" and who claim to dislike politics and government, we invite them to keep an open mind as they explore the contemporary world of politics at the grassroots.

THE THEME OF STATE AND LOCAL GOVERNMENT

This book revolves around a central theme: The increased capacity and responsiveness of state and local governments. In a way, this is yesterday's news. It has been decades since these levels of government were routinely dismissed as outmoded and ineffective. But state and local governments continue to be proactive, expanding their capacity to address effectively the myriad problems confronting their citizens. From Alabama to Wyoming, they are increasingly more responsive to their rapidly changing environment and the demands of citizens.

Our confidence in these governments does not blind us, however, to the varying capabilities of the fifty states and more than 88,000 units of local government. Some are better equipped to operate effectively than others. Many state and local governments benefit from talented leadership, a problem-solving focus, and an engaged citizenry. Others do not fare so well, and their performance disappoints. Still, as a group, states and localities are the driving forces—the prime movers—in the U.S. federal system. Even those jurisdictions perennially clustered at the lower end of various ratings scales have made quantum leaps in their capability and responsiveness.

FEATURES OF THE TEXT

The boxed features of *State and Local Government* supplement the themes of the book with compelling examples of nonnational governments in action. The boxes labeled "Breaking New Ground" identify states and localities on the leading edge of problem solving. Other boxes, titled "Debating Politics," raise questions for which the answers are more equivocal. More than half of the boxes are new to the sixth edition.

The **Breaking New Ground** boxes showcase some of the bold new actions states and localities are taking. New boxes address the battles between giant retailer Wal-Mart and local communities (Chapter 10) and the development of alternative-fuel "gas" stations (Chapter 18). Other compelling boxes focus on the issue of big money in political campaigns, efforts to get kids ready for school, the emergence of what are being called cool cities, and the phenomenon of the cyberjuror.

The **Debating Politics** boxes present differing points of view on current and controversial issues and highlight the different courses states have taken in tackling them. These boxes touch on key topics of interest to students to spark classroom discussion and foster engagement with state and local politics. For example, the new box in Chapter 4 considers the idea of lowering the voting age, the new box in Chapter 14 takes up the hot button issue of states dealing with the movement of jobs overseas, and the box in Chapter 17 brings students up-to-date on state efforts to provide prescription drugs to the growing ranks of the uninsured. Other boxes explore the definition of sexual harassment, running local governments like businesses, and standardized testing in schools.

Much effort has been invested in making this book accessible to the student. Each chapter opens with an outline and closes with a **Chapter Recap** to help structure student learning. The Chapter Recap sections are newly revised in this edition to better revisit important concepts and facts, providing a valuable study aid. Photographs provide visual images to bring the world of state and local government to life for the reader. Maps, tables, and figures provide recent information in an engaging format. Boxes throughout the chapters showcase the innovative, the unusual, and the insightful in state and local politics. Lists of states appear in each chapter and facilitate comparisons across the states. The sixth edition adds more **key terms,** all of which are boldfaced, defined in the margins of each chapter, and listed at the end of each chapter. References to web sites in the end-of-chapter **Surfing the Web** feature encourage student curiosity, engagement, and individual research. Students can access these sites independently and through the sixth edition web site.

THE CONTENT OF THE SIXTH EDITION

As in the first five editions, this book provides thorough and completely updated coverage of state and local institutions, processes, and policies. It is intended to be a core text.

In Chapter 1, we introduce the functions of nonnational governments and explore the theme of capacity and responsiveness. The contemporary controversy dubbed "culture wars" is featured in a new section of the chapter. Federalism's central importance is recognized in Chapter 2, which traces the twists and turns of the federal system, from the scribblings of the Framers to the Supreme Court's latest pronouncements on the Tenth Amendment. The chapter addresses these issues from the vantage point of states. The fundamental legal underpinnings of state governments—their constitutions—are discussed in Chapter 3. Chapter 4 explores citizen participation and elections (including the 2004 elections), focusing on the increased access of citizens and the demands they are making on government. Chapter 5, "Political Parties, Interest Groups, and Campaigns," gets at state politics—the real world of candidates, lobbyists, organizations, and money.

Coverage of the three branches of government—legislative, executive, and judicial—is updated and reflects the institutional changes each branch has undergone recently. Responses of state legislatures to the devolution revolution are illustrated in Chapter 6, and the institutional challenge posed by term limits is explored. Several new governors are featured in Chapter 7, and the issue of gubernatorial power is re-examined. Chapter 8, "Public Administration: Budgeting and Service Delivery," offers expanded coverage of privatization as a strategy for reinventing government and delivering public services, as well as new material on affirmative action policy. In Chapter 9, the policymaking role of judges is emphasized. In addition, new material is included on the application of computer technology in the criminal justice system.

Local governments are not treated as afterthoughts in this book. Two chapters focus solely on localities: Chapter 10 is devoted to the multiple types and structures of local government, and Chapter 11 to leadership and governance. Chapter 10 includes an updated discussion on city revenues and fiscal stress, while Chapter 11 examines new leadership approaches of mayors and city councils. Two other chapters consider localities within the context of the states: Chapter 12 focuses on the political issues linking the two levels and Chapter 13 emphasizes the growing interdependence of state and local financial systems. Chapter 12 specifically tackles the issue of urban sprawl, one of the hottest state–local issues of the early twenty-first century, while Chapter 13 offers a comprehensive synthesis of the principles and political economy of taxation and spending.

Five policy chapters illustrate the proactive nature of state and local governments in responding to change and citizen demands. The role of states and localities is different in each policy area. Chapter 14 examines economic development initiatives in the context of interstate and interregional competition for jobs and business. Chapter 15 focuses on the ever-important topic of public education; it includes examples of many of the most recent education reform efforts, including magnet schools and voucher plans, and provides up-to-date information on outcomes-based or performance-based education, homeschooling, and virtual schools. Coverage of the school choice controversy has been fully updated and expanded. Criminal justice policy is the subject of Chapter 16. Crime statistics have been updated, as have some of the early results of community policing initiatives, prison privatization, and "three strikes" laws. Social welfare and health care policy are featured in Chapter 17. The impact of federal welfare reform is discussed in light of state efforts designed to move former AFDC recipients from welfare to work, welfare traps are considered, and state programs aimed at plugging the gaps in the federal health system are examined. Finally, Chapter 18 has been rewritten to cover a wider range of environmental topics such as sustainability, ecoterrorism, and environmental justice. Of special interest are some of the success stories in "greening" states and localities.

ANCILLARY MATERIALS

The **Bowman/Kearney web site** makes a number of resources available to students and instructors. The site is accessible through the Houghton Mifflin Political Science home page at **politicalscience.college.hmco.com.** For students, an interactive U.S. map explores the similarities and differences among the states. Our Evolution of Devolution timeline illustrates how the capacity and responsibilities of state and local governments have increased over time. On-line chapter quizzes allow students to test their understanding of important concepts, and web links provide convenient access to research resources. New for the sixth edition, the student web site includes glossary flashcards to aid student review of key terms.

Instructors will benefit from the on-line **Instructor's Resource Manual,** written by Jeffrey Greene of the University of Montana. The manual features a sample syllabus, learning objectives, chapter overviews, suggested readings, and lecture topics. The instructor web site also features **PowerPoint slides,** the Evolution of Devolution timeline, an interactive U.S. map, and web links.

New to this edition is the **HMClassPrep CD-ROM.** This convenient resource brings together many of the instructor ancillaries in one place. It includes a computerized test bank, also written by Jeffrey Greene of the University of Montana, with multiple-choice questions, terms for identification, and essay questions. The HMClassPrep CD also contains the Instructor's Resource Manual and the PowerPoint slides.

ACKNOWLEDGMENTS

First, we thank the reviewers of the sixth edition, who provided us with many thoughtful observations and examples. We have incorporated their suggestions into this edition whenever possible.

William Kelley
Auburn University

Gilbert St. Clair
University of New Mexico

Richard Conboy
Lake Superior State University

Delmer Lonowski
South Dakota State University

We also extend our appreciation to the good folks at Houghton Mifflin, especially Katherine Meisenheimer, Terri Wise, Teresa Huang, and Nicola Poser. Gregory Plagens provided research assistance at the University of South Carolina; Jennie Koontz and John Deitle provided research assistance at East Carolina University. Finally, Carson, Blease, Kathy, and Joel contributed in many special ways to the final product, as usual. We assure them that they are not taken for granted.

A. O'M. B.
R. C. K.

NEW DIRECTIONS FOR STATE AND LOCAL GOVERNMENT

With appropriate oratorical flourishes, governors throughout the nation delivered their 2004 State of the State messages to their constituents. In capitol after capitol, a similar theme was heard: a lagging economy had created budget shortfalls that had forced policymakers to make difficult choices. But governors are inveterate "glass half-full" kind of people, so their speeches also contained upbeat exhortations and reassurances. Governor Janet Napolitano put it this way: "We have reawakened that trademark can-do spirit of Arizona."[1] A similar note was struck by Governor Tim Pawlenty: "The Minnesota Spirit. It's our legacy. It's our tradition. It's our future. It's made us different. It's made us great."[2] Governor Arnold Schwarzenegger, who had taken office after the rare recall of an incumbent governor, also voiced great optimism: "We have a new spirit, a new confidence. We have a new common cause in restoring California to greatness."[3] In Oklahoma, first-term governor Brad Henry evoked the image of the Sooner state: "We will confront the future with confidence and look to tomorrow with courage. The opportunities before us are as vast and brilliant as our wide-open Oklahoma skies."[4] These messages of action and optimism portray states and their local governments leading the country into the future. And, to hear the governors tell it, the future is bright.

STUDYING STATE AND LOCAL GOVERNMENT IN THE TWENTY-FIRST CENTURY

The study of state and local government has typically received short shrift in the survey of U.S. politics.[5] Scholars and journalists tend to focus on glamorous and imperial presidents, a rancorous and gridlocked Congress, and an independent and powerful Supreme Court. National and international issues capture the lion's share of media attention. Yet state and local politics are fascinating theater precisely because of their up-close and personal nature. True, a governor seldom gets involved in an international peace conference, and state legislatures rarely debate global warming. But the actors and institutions of states and localities are directly involved in our day-to-day lives. Education, welfare, health care, and crime are among the many concerns of state and local governments. And these issues affect all of us. Table 1.1 provides a sample of new state laws that took effect in 2004.

From Sewers to Science: The Functions of State and Local Governments

State and local governments are busy. They exist, in large measure, to make policy for and provide services to the public, and neither task is easy. Nonnational governments must operate efficiently, effectively, and fairly, and they must do so with limited financial resources. The high costs of inefficient government lead to higher taxes and thus to greater citizen displeasure with government, which in turn can lead to tax revolts and taxpayer exodus. A government performs effectively if it accomplishes what it sets out to do. Another expectation is that government function fairly—that its services be delivered in an equitable manner. It is no wonder, then, that state and local governments constantly experiment with new programs and new systems for delivering services, all the while seeking efficiency, effectiveness, and equity. For instance, the massive restructuring of Wyoming's state government was intended, according to the governor, to produce "a better method of delivering services from the state government to the citizens."[6]

Each year, the Ford Foundation sponsors Innovations in American Government awards to recognize the creativity that abounds in governments throughout the nation. Ten jurisdictions are selected for the prestigious and lucrative prize. The criteria for the awards are that the government's innovation be original, successful, and easily replicated by other jurisdictions. Among the semifinalists for the innovation award in 2004 were:

- Iowa's Project Resolve, which minimizes litigation in special education cases by subsidizing expert legal advice for the parents of children with disabilities and enabling a system of effective dispute resolution.

TABLE 1.1	A Sample of New State Laws Taking Effect in 2004
STATE	**DESCRIPTION OF THE LAW**
California	• Bans housing and job discrimination against transgendered people. • Allows spam recipients to sue for $1,000 for each unsolicited spam e-mail they receive.
Connecticut	• Allows crime victims to use substitute mailing addresses and keep home addresses secret to protect victims from potential stalkers or assailants.
Illinois	• Extends the amount of time, from six to ten years, that immigrant teachers have to obtain U.S. citizenship. • Prohibits tattoo shops from performing tongue-splitting procedures; doctors and dentists are allowed to perform them.
Louisiana	• Requires boat operators to complete a boating safety course.
New Hampshire	• Requires car safety seats for children under six years of age and less than four-and-a-half feet tall.
New Mexico	• Allows someone twenty-five years of age or older to possess a concealed, loaded firearm.
North Dakota	• Restricts merchants from printing receipts displaying a customer's entire credit card number.
Oregon	• Makes it a crime for drivers to fail to keep a safe distance from an emergency vehicle. • Requires people who dig for clams or harvest oysters and shrimp to obtain a $6.50 license.
Pennsylvania	• Expands eligibility for low-cost prescription drug benefits for the elderly.
Texas	• Requires pregnant women to wait twenty-four hours before they receive an abortion, during which time they will be given educational brochures.

SOURCES: Kathleen Murphy, "New Year Rings in Hundreds of New Statutes," www.Stateline.org (December 31, 2003); Sara B. Miller, "New State Laws Run Social Gamut," *Christian Science Monitor* (January 1–2, 2004), pp. 2–3; "Flood of New Laws in 2004," *Christian Science Monitor* (January 7, 2004), p. 16.

• Denver's use of goat herds to graze on weeds to help restore and reestablish native habitats in natural and open spaces in the city.
• A project of the Navajo Nation to train Native Americans as archaeologists and anthropologists in the workforce and in academia.
• An effort in Wayne County, Michigan, to encourage the rehabilitation of abandoned properties through creative use of nuisance abatement laws.
• The SEED Foundation in Washington, D.C., which established the first urban public boarding school to prepare disadvantaged students, both academically and socially, for success.[7]

Although some of the semifinalists' innovative projects are internal to government operations and carry the promise of increased efficiency, others have a policy goal, such as educational improvement or a stronger economy. The unifying characteristic is governmental willingness to try something new.

Our Approach

The argument of this book is that states and localities have the capacity to play central roles in the U.S. federal system. **Capacity** refers to a government's ability to respond effectively to change, make decisions efficiently and responsibly, and manage conflict.[8] Thus, capacity is tied to governmental capability and performance. In short, states and communities with capacity work better than those without it.

But what factors make one government more capable than another? Governmental institutions such as the bureaucracy matter. The fiscal resources of a **jurisdiction** and the quality of its leadership make a difference. Much of the research on capacity has focused on the administrative dimension of government performance, evaluating items such as financial management, information technology, and strategic planning. In a recent study of government performance, the highest overall state scores went to Michigan, Utah, and Washington. Forty counties were evaluated, with Fairfax, Virginia, and Maricopa, Arizona, earning the best grades. Among the thirty-five cities examined, Austin, Texas, and Phoenix, Arizona, were at the top of the list.[9] Generally, we would expect high-scoring states and cities to produce "better" government than low-scoring jurisdictions.

A survey in Iowa showed another side to governance. When asked about the characteristics of "good government," Iowans put trustworthiness, ethics, financial responsibility, and accountability at the top of the list.[10] Residents of the Hawkeye State are not unusual; all of us want our institutions and leaders to govern honestly and wisely. As political scientist David Hedge reminds us, better government is found in jurisdictions that are responsible and democratic.[11] But states and localities face significant challenges as they govern. Complex, often contradictory forces test the most capable of governments. State and local governments need all the capacity they can muster and maybe even a little bit of luck to meet those challenges.

Federalism, with its overlapping spheres of authority, provides the context for state and local action. (This topic is explored in depth in Chapter 2.) There are clear instances in which national government intervention in the affairs of a state or local government is defensible, even desirable. For example, the environmental problems of the 1960s and 1970s exceeded state and local governments' ability to handle them (see Chapter 18), so corrective action by the national government was generally welcomed. However, some federal actions are greeted less enthusiastically by states. For instance, No Child Left Behind, the education law promoted by President George W. Bush and enacted by the U.S Congress in 2002, is considered too intrusive by many state leaders.[12]

Our approach takes into account intergovernmental relations (that is, the relationships among the three levels of government)—particularly the possibilities

---

capacity

The ability of government to respond effectively to change, make decisions efficiently and responsibly, and manage conflict.

jurisdiction

The territorial range of government authority; "jurisdiction" is sometimes used as a synonym for "city" or "town."

federalism

A system of government in which powers are divided between a central (national) government and regional (state) governments.

for cooperation and conflict. Jurisdictions (national, state, or local) possess policymaking authority over specific, but sometimes overlapping, territory. They confront innumerable situations in which they must work together to accomplish an objective. This point was brought home most vividly in the wake of the September 11, 2001, terrorist attacks on the United States. Local governments were the first to respond, but before long, federal and state governments were heavily involved. However, cooperation in some cases is countered by conflict in other instances. Each level of government tends to see problems from its own perspective and design solutions accordingly. In sum, both cooperation and conflict define the U.S. federal system.

THE CAPACITY OF STATES AND LOCALITIES

With notable exceptions, states and their local governments in the 1950s and 1960s were havens of traditionalism and inactivity. Many states were characterized by unrepresentative legislatures, glad-handing governors, and a hodgepodge of courts. Public policy tended to reflect the interests of the elite; delivery of services was frequently inefficient and ineffective. According to former North Carolina governor Terry Sanford, the states "had lost their confidence, and people their faith in the states."[13] No wonder that, by comparison, the federal government appeared to be the answer, regardless of the question. In fact, political scientist Luther Gulick proclaimed, "It is a matter of brutal record. The American State is finished. I do not predict that the states will go, but affirm that they have gone."[14]

Those days are as outmoded as a black-and-white television. States and their local governments have proved themselves capable of designing and implementing "an explosion of innovations and initiatives."[15] As a result, even many national leaders have embraced the roles of states and localities as laboratories for policy experimentation.[16] A 2002 *New York Times* story with the headline, "As Congress Stalls, States Pursue Cloning Debate," is indicative of states pushing the policy envelope.[17]

The blossoming of state governments in the 1980s—their transformation from weak links in the federal chain to viable and progressive political units—resulted from several actions and circumstances.[18] In turn, the resurgence of state governments has generated many positive outcomes. During the 1990s, states and localities honed their capacity and became **proactive** rather than reactive. They faced hard choices and crafted creative new directions. A word of caution is necessary, however. Not all states enjoy the same level of capacity, and furthermore, fiscal stresses such as those endured by state governments in the early 2000s sorely test the ability of even the most capable states to function effectively.

proactive
An anticipatory condition, as opposed to a reactive one.

How States and Localities Increased Their Capacity

Among the factors that contributed to the resurgence of the states, two stand out: the reform of state constitutions and institutions, and the presence of state and local lobbyists at the national level.

State Reform State governments quietly and methodically reformed themselves by modernizing their constitutions and restructuring their institutions. During the past three decades, more than three-quarters of the states have ratified new constitutions or substantially amended existing ones. Formerly thought of as the "drag anchors of state programs" and as "protectors of special interests,"[19] these documents have been streamlined and made more workable. Even in states without wide-ranging constitutional reform, tinkering with constitutions is almost endless thanks to the amendment process. Almost every state general election finds constitutional issues on the ballot. (State constitutions are discussed in Chapter 3.)

States have also undertaken various internal adjustments intended to improve the operations of state governments.[20] Modernized constitutions and statutory changes have strengthened the powers of governors by increasing appointment and removal powers and by allowing longer terms, consecutive succession, larger staffs, enhanced budget authority, and the power to reorganize the executive branch.[21] Throughout the country, state agencies are staffed by skilled administrators.[22] The bureaucracy itself is more and more demographically representative of the public.[23] Annual rather than biennial sessions, more efficient rules and procedures, additional staff, and higher salaries have helped make reapportioned state legislatures more professional, capable, and effective.[24] State judicial systems have also been the targets of reform; examples include the establishment of unified court systems, the hiring of court administrators, and the creation of additional layers of courts.[25] (State institutions—legislatures, governors, state agencies, and courts—are addressed in Chapters 6 through 9.)

State and Local Presence in Washington, D.C. Nonnational governments have energized their lobbying efforts in the nation's capital. The three major state-level organizations are the National Governors' Association, the National Conference of State Legislatures, and the Council of State Governments. Major players for local governments are the National League of Cities, the National Association of Counties, the U.S. Conference of Mayors, and the International City/County Management Association. Beyond the "Big Seven," as they are known in Washington, D.C., are myriad others representing various state and local officials—for example, the Association of State Highway and Transportation Officials and the National Association of State Development Agencies. In addition, most states and a few of the largest cities have their own liaison offices in Washington.[26]

The intergovernmental lobbies serve an important function in watching out for the interests of their members in the nation's capital. Congress regularly solicits these organizations for information and advice on proposed legislation; through the State and Local Legal Center, nonnational governments are increasing their potential impact on the federal judiciary. Beyond lobbying, these groups provide a forum in which jurisdictions can learn from one another.

Increased Capacity and Improved Performance

Enhanced capacity has led to a resurgence of state and local governments and has generated a range of mostly positive results, which is evident in at least five endeavors: improved revenue systems, expanding scope of state operations, faster diffusion of innovations, more interjurisdictional cooperation, and increased national-state conflict. The ultimate outcome is better performance by states and localities.

Improved Revenue Systems The recession of the early 1980s and the wave of popularly sponsored taxation and expenditure limitations at state and local levels caused states to implement new revenue-raising strategies to maintain existing service levels. States also granted local governments more flexibility in their revenue systems. South Carolina, for example, now allows counties the option of providing property-tax relief to residents while increasing the local sales tax.

State governments first increased user charges, gasoline taxes, and so-called sin taxes on alcohol and tobacco; only then did they reluctantly raise sales and income taxes. Revenue structures were redesigned to make them more diversified and more equitable. State rainy day funds, legalized gambling through state-run lotteries and pari-mutuels, and extension of the sales tax to services are examples of diversification strategies. Exemptions of food and medicine from consumer sales taxes and the enactment of property-tax breaks for poor and elderly people characterize efforts at tax equity. These redesigned revenue structures helped states respond to the budget crises they confronted in 2002 and 2003.

States continue to tinker with their revenue-raising schemes. One successful foray into creative revenue raising has been the specialty license plate. Maryland, one of the first states to raise revenue this way, has generated hundreds of thousands of dollars with its Treasure the Chesapeake plate.[27] Monies generated by the plates are earmarked for special programs—in this case, water-quality monitoring and erosion control in the Chesapeake Bay. More than thirty states now offer specialty plates. In Florida, one can help an endangered marine mammal with a Save the Manatee license plate. And in New York, specialty plates allow fans to show their support for professional sports teams. Many states responded to the events of September 11, 2001, by marketing patriotic license plates. Michigan, for instance, charged $35.00 for its patriotic plate, with monies from this source designated for the Salvation Army and the American Red Cross.

Another effort of enterprising localities is to sell merchandise. Los Angeles County has marketed coroner toe tags as key chains; Portland and Tampa are among the cities that rent the entire outside surfaces of their buses to advertisers.[28] New York City, which loses thousands of street signs (Wall Street is especially popular) to souvenir-stealing tourists, now sells replicas. Baseball fans could purchase bricks ($19.95 each) from the old Comiskey Park at the City of Chicago Store. And in Seattle, gardeners welcome the opportunity to purchase "ZooDoo" for their shrubs and flowers, which allows the city to take in an extra

$20,000 a year.[29] As these examples show, states and localities are willing to experiment when it comes to revenue enhancement.

Expanding the Scope of State Operations Unlike the national government, which has shed functions like unwanted pounds, state governments are adding functions. In some instances, states are filling in the gap left by the national government's de-emphasis of an activity. Provision of state-sponsored low-income housing is one example of this behavior; increased state regulation of the trucking industry is another. Before the U.S. Congress reversed itself and enacted family-leave legislation, giving workers unpaid leave to care for newborn babies and ailing relatives, many states had already done so.[30] California, Hawaii, and Oregon were among the states enacting family-leave measures as early as 1991. In other cases, states have taken the initiative in ongoing intergovernmental programs by creatively utilizing program authority and resources. States, for example, led the way in welfare reform, establishing Workfare programs and imposing time limits on the receipt of welfare benefits. Carving out a major role for itself was the state of Wisconsin, whose plans to withdraw from the federal welfare system and create its own plan for public relief hastened federal welfare reform. States were also at the forefront of health care reform long before it landed on the national scene. In fact, proponents of national health care reform borrowed heavily from the approaches used by Hawaii, Minnesota, and Florida.[31]

The innovative behavior continues. As public outcry grew over the escalating cost of prescription drugs, Maine took action. In 2000, it became the first state to adopt legislation placing price controls on medications sold in the state. Seeking alternatives to parental tax credits and day care, Minnesota developed a program that subsidizes low-income parents who stay at home during their child's first year. Many governors now travel overseas to pitch their states' exports and suitability for foreign investment. In short, states are taking on the role of policy innovators and experimenters in the U.S. federal system—and in so doing, they are creating a climate for local government creativity and inventiveness.

Faster Diffusion of Innovations Among states, there have always been leaders and followers. The same is true for local governments. Now that states and localities have expanded their scope and are doing more policymaking, they are looking more frequently to their neighbors for advice, information, and models. As a result, successful solutions spread from one jurisdiction to another.[32] For example, the modernization of workers' compensation laws was begun by Pennsylvania in the early 1990s and, within five years, forty other states had enacted similar business-friendly provisions in their statutes.[33] Another fast-moving innovation was a Florida law that allowed consumers to stop unwanted telephone solicitations. By 1999, five more states had passed laws letting residents put their names on a do-not-call list for telemarketers. Seven additional states adopted similar legislation over the next two years before Congress enacted a national statute.[34]

Local-level innovations spread quickly, too. Dade County, Florida, was the first to try a controversial experiment by hiring a private company to run a public elementary school.[35] Other school districts, notably Baltimore and Minneapolis, followed the same example. Initial experiments in the privatization of public schools have spawned other innovations. Charter schools, designed in Minnesota, spread rapidly; by 2004, more than 2,500 were in operation around the country. In short, state and local governments learn from each other. Communication links are increasingly varied and frequently used. A state might turn to nearby states when searching for policy solutions. Regional consultation and emulation is logical: Similar problems beset jurisdictions in the same region, a program used in a neighboring state is politically more acceptable than one from a distant state, and organizational affiliations bring state and local administrators together with their colleagues from nearby areas.

Interjurisdictional Cooperation Accompanying the quickening flow of innovations has been an increase in interjurisdictional cooperation. States are choosing to confront and resolve their immediate problems jointly. A similar phenomenon has occurred at the local level with the creation of regional organizations to tackle areawide problems collectively.

Interjurisdictional collaboration takes many forms, including informal consultations and agreements, interstate committees, legal contracts, reciprocal legislation, and interstate compacts. For example, twenty-three states have a mutual agreement to aid one another when natural disasters such as hurricanes, earthquakes, and forest fires strike. Five states—Mississippi, Minnesota, West Virginia, Florida, and Massachusetts—were among the first to band together to share information and design tactics in their lawsuits against tobacco companies in the mid-1990s; by 1998, thirty-seven other states had joined in the successful effort to recover the Medicaid costs of treating tobacco-related diseases.[36] In the same year, twenty states filed an antitrust lawsuit against Microsoft Corporation, claiming that the firm illegally stifled competition, harmed consumers, and undercut innovation in the computer software industry. In 2000, twenty-eight states went after the world's five largest record labels and three largest music retailers, accusing them of fixing the prices of compact discs.[37] The states sought hundreds of millions of dollars in damages on behalf of consumers. By 2004, forty states had joined the Streamlined Sales Tax Project, an effort to craft an interstate agreement on the simplification of sales and use taxes. The intent is to make it easier for states to collect taxes on items purchased on the Internet. In each of these instances, the states worked together because they could see some benefit from cooperation.

Increased jurisdictional cooperation fosters a healthy climate for joint problem solving. In addition, when state and local governments solve their own problems, they protect their power and authority within the federal system. It appears that states are becoming more comfortable working with one another. The beginning of the twenty-first century was indeed historic: States were engaged in more cooperative interactions than ever before.[38]

Increased National-State Conflict An inevitable by-product of more capable state and local governments is intensified conflict with the national government.

One source of this trouble has been federal laws and grant requirements that supersede state policy; another is the movement of states onto the national government's turf. National-state conflict is primarily a cyclical phenomenon, but contention has increased in recent years. The issue of unfunded mandates—the costly requirements that federal legislation imposes on states and localities—has been particularly troublesome.[39] In an effort to increase the visibility of the mandates issue, several national organizations of state and local officials sponsored a National Unfunded Mandate Day in both 1993 and 1994. Making a strong case against mandates, Ohio governor George Voinovich stated, "Unfunded mandates devastate our budgets, inhibit flexibility and innovation in implementing new programs, pre-empt important state initiatives, and deprive states of their responsibility to set priorities."[40] Congress responded in 1995 by passing a mandate relief bill that requires Congress to consider the costs and benefits of proposed mandates; however, it contains some loopholes that have weakened its impact.

Conflict characterizes various policy areas: the removal of the exemption of local governments from federal antitrust laws (laws against business monopolies), disagreement over energy and water resources, the minimum drinking age, the speed limit on interstate highways, air- and water-quality standards, interstate trucking, severance taxes (fees imposed on the extraction of mineral resources from the earth), registration and taxation of state and municipal bonds, offshore oil drilling, land management and reclamation, and the storage and disposal of hazardous chemical wastes. Some of the disputes pit a single state against the national government, as in Nevada's fight to block the U.S. Energy Department's plan to build a nuclear fuel waste storage facility at Yucca Mountain, 100 miles northwest of Las Vegas. In other conflicts, the national government finds itself besieged by a coordinated, multistate effort, for example, when ten states sued the U.S Environmental Protection Agency in 2003 over the regulation of greenhouse gases.[41]

National-state conflicts are resolved (and sometimes made worse) by the federal judicial system. Cases dealing with alleged violations of the U.S. Constitution by state and local governments are heard in national courts and decided by national judges. Sometimes the rulings take the federal government into spheres long considered the purview of state and local governments. In Kansas City, Missouri, for instance, a federal district judge forced the local school board to increase taxes to pay for a court-ordered magnet plan. Although the rulings of the U.S. Supreme Court under Chief Justice William Rehnquist have been friendlier toward the states than other recent Courts have been, the national government still tends to have a higher winning percentage when it goes up against the states.[42]

Challenges Facing State and Local Governments

Increased capacity does not mean that all state and local problems have been solved. Nonnational governments face three tough challenges today: fiscal stress, interjurisdictional conflict, and political corruption.

Fiscal Stress The most intractable problem for states and localities involves money. Given the cyclical peaks and troughs in the national economy as well as the frequent fundamental changes in public finance, state and local finances remain vulnerable. Both the early 1990s and the early 2000s provide evidence of that vulnerability.

As the 1990s dawned, recessionary clouds hovered over the financial horizon, and state policymakers searched furiously for solutions. By the fall of 1991, thirty-one states had raised taxes by a combined $16.2 billion, and twenty-nine states had cut spending by $7.5 billion.[43] Others followed the California approach and tried to stave off fiscal imbalance by **downsizing** state agencies. As these tactics took effect and as the economy rebounded, states were able to enjoy revenue boomlets by the mid-1990s. By the end of the decade, states had amassed huge surpluses, and in legislature after legislature, cutting taxes, eliminating surcharges, and funding new programs became priorities.

However, states cannot afford to become complacent when it comes to revenues, as the events of the early twenty-first century demonstrated. Chapter 13 covers the recent economic downturn and its effect on states and localities in detail, but suffice it to say here that states were hit hard by fiscal stress. "Nearly every state faced budget gaps beginning in fiscal year 2002, and those gaps grew in fiscal 2003 and 2004."[44] As expected, states responded by drawing on their rainy day funds, using trust fund surpluses, and seeking special financing mechanisms. But these actions only went so far, and states were still forced to increase taxes (especially on tobacco products and alcohol), impose new fees, and cut spending.[45] Fiscal stress remains a serious threat, even for the most capable of states.

Increased Interjurisdictional Conflict Tension is inherent in a federal system because each of the governmental entities has its own set of interests along with a share of the national interest. Simply put, states are rivals. When one state's pursuit of its interests negatively affects another state, conflict occurs. And such conflict can become destructive, upsetting the continuation of state resurgence. In effect, states end up wasting their energies and resources on counterproductive battles among themselves.

Interjurisdictional conflict is particularly common in two policy areas very dear to state and local governments: natural resources and economic development. States rich in natural resources want to use these resources in a manner that will yield the greatest return. Oil-producing states, for instance, levy severance taxes that raise the price of oil. And states with abundant water supplies resist efforts by arid states to tap into these supplies. Often, it is among neighboring states where the most serious disputes erupt. In 2000, Georgia was fending off attacks from Alabama and Florida over the effect downstream of increased water consumption in metropolitan Atlanta.[46] In short, the essential question revolves around a state's right to control a resource that occurs naturally and is highly desired by other states. Resource-poor states argue that resources are in fact national and should rightfully be shared among states. The result is a series of seemingly endless battles often played out in the federal courts.

downsizing
To reduce the size and cost of something, especially government.

In the area of economic development, conflict is extensive because all jurisdictions want healthy economies. States try to make themselves attractive to business and industry through tax breaks, regulatory relaxation, even image creation. (The nearby *Breaking New Ground* box explores how states work to reverse negative images and to promote positive ones.) The conflict arises when they get involved in bidding wars—that is, when an enterprise is so highly valued that actions taken by one state are matched and exceeded by another. Suppose, for example, that an automobile manufacturer is considering shutting down an existing facility and relocating. States hungry for manufacturing activity will assemble a package of incentives such as below-cost land, tax concessions, and subsidized job training in an attempt to attract the manufacturer. The state that wants to keep the manufacturer will try to match these inducements. In the long run, economic activity is simply relocated from one state to another. The big winner is the manufacturer. (Chapter 14 explores economic development issues much more extensively.)

FIGURE 1.1   The Kansas State Quarter

SOURCE: United States Mint image.

 ## BREAKING NEW GROUND

Creating an Image

What image best captures a state's essential being? Ohio, for example, calls itself the Buckeye State, but most Americans don't know what a buckeye is (it's a shrub or tree of the horse chestnut family). Consider New Hampshire, which stamps the motto Live Free or Die on its license plates. A few years ago, some legislators advocated replacing the uncompromising phrase with the word *scenic*, arguing that the state needed a more caring image. And when a computer graphics software firm used the icon of an outhouse to designate West Virginia, protests by state officials led the company to change the icon to a more positive symbol: a mountain. (In 2004, West Virginia protested an Abercrombie & Fitch T-shirt that featured a map of the state and the phrase, "It's all relative in West Virginia.") The North Dakota legislature took the image issue to new heights when it seriously entertained a resolution that would have dropped the word *North* from the state's name. The name North Dakota was said to summon images of "snowstorms, howling winds, and frigid temperatures." Simply going with Dakota, a word that means "friend" or "ally" in the Sioux language, would project a warmer image of the state, supporters claimed. (The state senate ultimately defeated the name-changing resolution.)

Images are not trivial. They matter because they project and reflect public perceptions, which can be both accurate and inaccurate. They offer a shorthand understanding of a place, a slice of the whole. States and communities have become much more conscious of their images in recent years, and many have launched promotional campaigns to foster positive images.

Consequently, when Congress passed legislation to mint new varieties of quarters to commemorate states, the battle was on to decide what should appear on each state's quarter. George Washington had to remain on the heads side of the quarter; the tails side would feature the state symbol. And no two-headed coins would be allowed—the regulations prohibit an image of a person on the tails, or state's, side. The rules also barred "any frivolous or inappropriate designs." Five new coins are issued each year (the first set appeared in 1999) in the order that the states ratified the Constitution or were admitted to the Union. In each state, governors and legislators decide which ideas will be sent to the U.S. Department of the Treasury for its approval. Connecticut, one of the first five states, depicted the historically significant Charter Oak in Hartford on its coin. In New Jersey, also in the first group, some wags suggested whim-sically that a turnpike tollbooth should symbolize the state. Whimsy gave way to history and the image of George Washington crossing the Delaware graced the coin.

States used the quarter design and selection process to generate reflection about the state and its image. Like other states, Kansas sponsored a design competition to create a quarter emblematic of the state's "history, geography and rich heritage," but its process for selecting the winning design was different. In Kansas, the winner was chosen from a set of four finalists through a majority vote of all high school students in the state. The students selected the design that features a buffalo and sunflowers as their favorite, and it was submitted by the governor to the U.S. Mint to become the official Kansas quarter put into circulation in 2005 (see Figure 1.1.). The state quarter project has given states an opportunity to celebrate their unique histories and cultures, and to project positive images.

SOURCES: "Hey! It's 'the Mountain State,'" *Newsweek* (June 21, 1993), p. 24; Dale Wetzel, "Dakotans Consider Dropping 'North' to Thaw State's Image," *The Missoulian* (June 25, 2001), p. B4; Clare Nolan, "States Hark Back in Choice of Design for Quarters," www.Stateline.org (April 2, 2000); "Kansas State Quarter," www.ksgovernor.org/workgroups_quarter.html (April 22, 2004).

The pressure is great, even among jurisdictions that have agreed to forgo competitive behavior. Several years ago, the states of Connecticut and New Jersey, along with New York City, agreed not to engage in bidding wars over each other's businesses. However, the subsequent relocation of an international bank from the Big Apple to Connecticut unraveled the agreement. After one city official labeled the move "a shameless raid," New York City launched an advertising blitz in the Connecticut media aimed at nixing the deal.[47] The advertising campaign did not work and the city announced a new policy of offering incentives for Connecticut firms interested in relocating to New York City. So much for neighborliness.

Political Corruption Corruption exists in government, which is certainly no great surprise. Most political systems can tolerate the occasional corrupt official, but if corruption becomes commonplace, it undermines governmental capacity and destroys public trust. Public reaction ranges from cynicism and alienation (corruption as "politics as usual") to anger and action (corruption as a spur to reform). A survey found that the more extreme the corrupt act (a city clerk embezzling $100,000 versus a police officer accepting free food at a restaurant), the more harsh the public's judgment.[48] Even so, mitigating motives or circumstances tend to reduce the public's outrage (for example, a public official taking a bribe but using the money to pay his sick child's hospital bills). But governmental scandals have been linked tentatively to another negative effect—a slowdown in economic growth. Research on states found that federal corruption convictions are associated with declines in job growth primarily because, from a business perspective, corruption creates uncertainty and inflates costs.[49]

States and localities have taken great precautions to reduce the amount of wrongdoing occurring in their midst. Government is much more transparent than it has ever been, with more openness and more rules. But the statutes and policies are only as good as the people whose behavior they regulate. Thus, at any given time, examples of corrupt practices can be found, including these at the local level:

- Former mayors of two New Jersey cities, Camden and Paterson, were behind bars in 2003 on bribery convictions.
- Vincent (Buddy) Cianci, the long-serving mayor of Providence, Rhode Island, was credited with revitalizing the city, but he was convicted of racketeering in 2002 and sentenced to federal prison.
- In 2004, a city council member in Richmond, Virginia was found guilty of selling her vote and lying to the FBI; crimes that led to a prison sentence of nearly four years.
- In Los Angeles, investigations were launched into the city's contracting practices after allegations were made that some contractors doing business with the city were being pressured to donate to political campaigns.[50]

Corruption also occurs at the state level. In 2003, North Carolina's commissioner of agriculture received a four-year prison term after pleading guilty to extortion and conspiracy. Carnival companies had given her tens of thousands of dollars in illegal payments to be able to do business at the state's fairs, which she oversaw.[51] Former Illinois governor George Ryan was indicted in 2003 on federal charges of taking payoffs, gifts, and vacations in return for government contracts and leases while he was Illinois secretary of state. And in 2004, Connecticut governor John Rowland resigned from office just days before a legislative committee was to vote on his impeachment for accepting gifts and favors from state contractors. Corruption can be an issue in the judicial branch, as evidenced by the indictment of Mississippi Supreme Court Justice Oliver Diaz Jr. on charges of extorting money from litigants in return for favorable verdicts.[52]

As the preceding examples indicate, states and localities are certainly not corruption-free. What is reassuring, however, is that the amount of corruption is relatively low, given the vast number of public officials at nonnational levels of government. Still, even in states and communities with relatively clean government, the possibility of scandal is real; thus, it remains a potential drain on governmental capacity.

THE PEOPLE: DESIGNERS AND CONSUMERS OF GOVERNMENT

A book on state and local government is not only about places and governments; it is also about people—the public and assorted officeholders—and the institutions they create, the processes in which they engage, and the policies they adopt. Thus, this volume contains chapters on institutions, such as legislatures; processes, such as elections; and policies, such as those pertaining to education. But in each case, *people* are the ultimate focus: A legislature is composed of legislators and staff members who deal with constituents; elections involve candidates, campaign workers, and voters (as well as nonvoters); and education essentially involves students, teachers, administrators, parents, and taxpayers. In short, the word *people* encompasses an array of individuals and roles in the political system.

Ethnic-Racial Composition

More than 281 million people live in the United States. Some can trace their American heritage back to the *Mayflower,* whereas others look back only as far as a recent naturalization ceremony. Very few can claim indigenous (native) American ancestry. Instead, most Americans owe their nationality to some forebear who came here in search of a better life or—in the case of a significant minority, the descendants of slaves—to ancestors who made the journey to this country not out of choice but because of physical coercion. The appeal of the United States to economic and political refugees from other countries continues, with Mexicans, Central Americans, and eastern Africans among the most recent arrivals. News photographs of Haitians crowded aboard rickety boats in a desperate attempt to gain asylum in the United States remind us of the strength of the attraction.

The United States is a nation of immigrants, and therefore ethnic richness and cultural diversity abound. Current U.S. Census figures put the white population at 75 percent, the African American population and the Latino population each at 12 percent, and the Asian population at 4 percent.[53] (The numbers total more than 100 percent because of double-counting.) Large cities in which immigrants have found economic opportunity often have distinct ethnic enclaves—Greektown, Little Italy, Koreatown. The city of Miami, for instance, has become a stronghold for refugees from Latin America and the Caribbean. Some people continue to celebrate their ethnic background, referring to themselves as Polish Americans or Irish Americans. Use of the term *African American* in recognition of the cultural heritage of blacks has become the norm.

Ethnicity and culture still matter, despite the image of America as a melting pot. Researchers have found that a state's racial and ethnic diversity goes a long way in explaining its politics.[54] Looking toward the future, census projections for the year 2050 estimate a nation of approximately 420 million people, with the Anglo population dropping to 50 percent of the total, the African American population increasing slightly to 15 percent, the Latino population reaching 25 percent, and an Asian population of 8 percent.[55] If the trends hold, state policy in the twenty-first century will be affected.

Illegal immigration is putting the Statue of Liberty's motto (about "your poor, your huddled masses") to a severe test. Immigrants' demands for public services such as health care, education, and welfare have hit states like California and Florida hard. The governors of those states sued the federal government in 1994, arguing that it had failed to protect the nation's borders. California voters went a step further and overwhelmingly approved an anti-illegal immigration measure (called Save Our State) that would deny illegal immigrants access to education and to nonemergency medical services. In addition, public employees would be required to report any "apparent" illegal immigrants they encounter. Once passed, the Save Our State measure immediately met with a legal challenge in the courts, and in 1999 California dropped its effort to implement the law.

At the same time, states with an aging work force and slow population growth are encouraging immigration as a way to mitigate economic decline. Iowa, for example, recently enacted a series of immigrant-friendly policies, hoping to attract workers for its meatpacking plants. But the politics of immigration remain dicey. Even as the state took these actions, polls showed that 54 percent of Iowans opposed increasing immigration.[56]

Population Growth and Migration

As a whole, the United States grew by 13.2 percent from 1990 to 2000. Disaggregating the data by state reveals several trends. Reflecting the pattern of the previous decade, high rates of growth occurred in the western states; substantially slower growth rates characterized the Northeast and Midwest. (The map in Figure 1.2 displays the percentage change in each state's population from 1990 to 2000.) Nevada and Arizona continued to outpace the growth in other states, with rates of 66.3 percent and 40.0 percent, respectively. A strong labor market and an attractive, inexpensive lifestyle are among those states' features.

| FIGURE 1.2 | **Percentage Change in State Population, 1990–2000** |

SOURCE: http://www.census.gov/population/cen2000.

Sunbelt

An unofficial region of the United States, generally consisting of the South and the West.

Frostbelt

An unofficial region of the United States, generally comprising the Northeast and the Midwest. The label *Rustbelt* is sometimes used as a synonym.

None of the fifty states lost population during the 1990s, but two states had growth rates of less than 1 percent: North Dakota and West Virginia.[57] In percentage terms, Florida relinquished its role as the South's growth leader; Georgia grew at a faster clip. (In raw numbers, however, Florida outpaced Georgia with an increase of 3 million people compared to Georgia's 1.7 million.) California grew by 13.8 percent, similar to the national average, but that meant an increase of 4.1 million people in the Golden State.) The Census Bureau's projections for the year 2025 show Nevada, California, Arizona, and New Mexico with the largest population gains, much of the growth attributed to international immigration.

For cities, the population trends are equally compelling. Higher rates of growth are much more prevalent in cities in the **Sunbelt** region than in cities of the **Frostbelt.** Table 1.2 provides a snapshot of the pattern, showing population changes in a two-year time period, from 2000 to 2002, for cities of 100,000 or more. The top half of the table lists the cities with extremely high growth rates of 10 percent or more; the bottom half shows the cities with population losses of 2 percent or more. Western cities dominate the list of fast-growing places and are strikingly absent from the group of cities that lost population.

| TABLE 1.2 | **Estimated Population Changes in Cities of 100,000 or More, 2000–2002** |

CITY	2002 ESTIMATED POPULATION	PERCENTAGE CHANGE, 2000–2002
A. Cities with estimated population growth of 10% or more		
Gilbert, Arizona	135,005	22.8
North Las Vegas, Nevada	135,902	17.7
Henderson, Nevada	206,153	17.3
Chandler, Arizona	202,016	14.4
Peoria, Arizona	123,239	13.4
Irvine, California	162,122	13.3
Rancho Cucamonga, California	143,711	12.5
Chula Vista, California	193,919	11.7
Fontana, California	143,607	11.4
Joliet, Illinois	118,423	11.4
Corona, California	138,326	10.4
Cape Coral, Florida	112,899	10.4
B. Cities with estimated population loss of 2% or more		
Savannah, Georgia	127,691	-2.9
St. Louis, Missouri	338,353	-2.8
Detroit, Michigan	925,051	-2.8
Flint, Michigan	121,763	-2.5
New Orleans, Louisiana	473,681	-2.3
Cincinnati, Ohio	323,885	-2.2
Dayton, Ohio	162,669	-2.1
Evansville, Indiana	119,081	-2.1
Mobile, Alabama	194,862	-2.0
Cleveland, Ohio	467,851	-2.0
Pittsburgh, Pennsylvania	327,898	-2.0

SOURCE: U.S. Census Bureau, Population Estimates Program (July 2003).

Population growth and migration carry economic and political consequences for state and local governments. As a general rule, power and influence follow population. A state's representation in the U.S. Congress and its votes in the Electoral College are at stake. In 2000, Utah missed out on a new congressional seat by only 856 people. The seat went to North Carolina instead.[58] A city's legislative clout within its state is similarly affected by population shifts. Aware of the stakes, many cities and states took special efforts during the 2000 census to make certain that their residents were counted. For example, California spent millions of dollars on media advertisements encouraging its residents to mail in their census forms.[59]

Political Culture

political culture

The attitudes, values, and beliefs that people hold toward government.

One of the phrases that a new arrival in town may hear from long-time residents is "We don't do things that way here." When applied to government, the concept behind this statement is **political culture**—the attitudes, values, and beliefs that people hold toward government.[60] As developed by political scientist Daniel Elazar in the 1960s, the term refers to the way people think about their government and how the political system operates. Political culture is a soft concept—one that is difficult to measure—yet it has remained quite useful in explaining state politics and policy.[61]

According to Elazar, the United States is an amalgam of three major political cultures, each of which has distinctive characteristics. In an *individualistic political culture,* politics is a kind of open marketplace in which people participate because of essentially private motivations. In a *moralistic political culture,* politics is an effort to establish a good and just society. Citizens are expected to be active in public affairs. In a *traditionalistic political culture,* politics functions to maintain the existing order, and political participation is confined to social elites. These differing conceptions about the purpose of government and the role of politics lead to different behaviors. Confronted with similar conditions, officials in an individualistic community would resist initiating a program unless public opinion demanded it; leaders in moralistic areas would adopt the new program, even without pressure, if they believed it to be in the public interest; and traditionalistic rulers would initiate the program only if they thought it would serve the interests of the governing elite.

Political culture is a factor in the differences (and similarities) in state policy. Research has found that moralistic states demonstrate the greatest tendency toward policy innovation, whereas traditionalistic states exhibit the least.[62] In economic development policy, for example, political culture has been shown to influence a state's willingness to offer tax breaks to businesses.[63] Other research has linked political culture to state environmental policy and state expenditures on AIDS programs.[64]

Today, few states are characterized by pure forms of these cultures. The mass media have had a homogenizing effect on cultural differences; migration has diversified cultural enclaves. This process of cultural erosion and synthesis has produced hybrid political cultures. For example, Florida was once considered a traditionalistic state but now has many areas in which an individualistic culture prevails and even has a moralistic community or two. In an effort to extend Elazar's pioneering work, researcher Joel Lieske has used race, ethnicity, and religion to identify contemporary subcultures.[65] With counties as the building blocks and statistical analysis as the method, he identified ten distinctive regional subcultures. A state like Pennsylvania, which Elazar characterized as individualistic, becomes a mix of "heartland," Germanic, ethnic, and rural/urban counties in Lieske's formulation. Very few states are dominated by a single subculture, except perhaps Utah, by a Mormon subculture, and New Hampshire and Vermont, by an Anglo-French subculture.

Political culture is not the only explanation for why states do what they do, of course. Socioeconomic characteristics (income and education levels, for example) and political structural factors (the amount of competition between political parties) also contribute to states' and communities' actions. In fact, sorting out the cause-and-effect relationships among these variables is a daunting job.[66] For example, why do some states pass more laws to regulate handguns than other states do? Emily Van Dunk's study found several factors to be important, although the crime rate and partisanship, surprisingly, were not among them.[67] States with nontraditional political cultures adopt more handgun regulations, as do states with more women in the legislature and with populations that are more urbanized and nonwhite. In general, political factors, socioeconomic characteristics, and the particulars of a specific problem combine to produce government behavior.

Culture Wars

culture wars
Political conflicts that emerge from deeply held moral values.

In 2004, when San Francisco's mayor ordered city clerks to remove all references to gender on local marriage license applications, it opened the door for gay marriages to take place in the city. As gay activists and supporters celebrated, many politically conservative groups denounced the action and promised legal challenges and political repercussions for the mayor. This type of social conflict over morality issues is known informally as **culture wars,** or "morality politics." And these culture wars are defining the politics of many communities and states. Besides gay rights, battlegrounds in the culture wars include abortion, pornography, and prayer in schools. These issues tend to involve deeply held values, sometimes connected to religion, and they are less about economics than are many political issues. According to political scientist Elaine Sharp, culture wars have several distinctive features.[68] The issues are highly salient to people, eliciting passionate reactions; they mobilize people across different neighborhoods and racial and ethnic groups; and the ensuing political activism often takes unconventional forms, such as demonstrations. Throughout the country, battle lines have been drawn over issues such as more restrictive abortion laws and displaying the Ten Commandments in public buildings. But the most volatile culture war of 2004 involved gay marriage.

In 2003, the Massachusetts Supreme Court ruled that, under the state's constitution, same-sex couples were entitled to enter into marriages, a decision that angered the governor and many Bay State lawmakers. Generally, states bar gay and lesbian couples from marrying: nearly three dozen states have enacted defense of marriage acts (DOMAs) that prohibit gay marriage. But many of these states wanted to take it one step further and put a gay marriage ban into the state constitution. As of 2004, only a few states had moved in the opposite direction and taken actions supportive of gay marriage: Vermont recognizes marriage-like civil unions, while California, Hawaii, and New Jersey grant various rights to same-sex couples registered as domestic partners.[69] But no matter what decision a state makes, it leaves in its wake people who are extremely dissatisfied.

One particularly interesting skirmish with culture war overtones broke out in Hamtramck, Michigan, a suburb of Detroit, over the issue of Muslim prayer calls. The city, once dominated by people of Polish ancestry, has a growing Islamic population because immigrants from Bangladesh, Yemen, and Pakistan have settled there. Muslim leaders sought an amendment to the city's noise ordinance to allow the Muslim call to prayer to be broadcast over mosque loudspeakers five times a day. They contended it was a matter of religious freedom and tolerance. Opponents argued that it would be noise pollution; they vowed to circulate petitions to put the issue on the ballot for voters to decide and threatened to file a lawsuit challenging the city's action.[70] These hot-button issues can erupt into full-fledged culture wars, carrying the potential to divide states and localities.

LINKING CAPACITY TO RESULTS

State and local governments have become the new heroes of American federalism. Their ability to solve pressing problems is one of the reasons why. The interaction of three unique characteristics of our fifty-state system—diversity, competitiveness, and resiliency—makes it easier.[71] Consider the diversity of the United States. States and their communities have different fiscal capacities (some are rich, some are poor) and different voter preferences for public services and taxes (some are liberal, some are conservative). Along with the national government's reluctance to equalize intergovernmental fiscal disparities, these differences perpetuate diversity. As a result, citizens and businesses are offered real choices in taxation and expenditure policies across different jurisdictions.

Diversity is tempered, however, by the natural competitiveness of a federal system. No state can afford to be too far out of line with the prevailing thinking on appropriate levels of taxes and expenditures. During the 1970s, a high-tax state, Massachusetts, was labeled Taxachusetts, and a poor-service state like Mississippi was stigmatized as backward. Neither state could flourish by being at the extreme end of the scale. States with lower taxes became more attractive than Massachusetts; states with better services became more inviting than Mississippi. Citizens and businesses usually have the option of relocating. Eventually, the workings of government, through an attentive public and enlightened opinion leaders, brought Massachusetts's tax levels and Mississippi's service levels back into line with prevailing thinking. Such competition over taxes and expenditures stabilizes the federal system.

The third characteristic, resiliency, captures the ability of state governments to recover from adversity. The number of curves thrown at state government in the form of global economic shifts, national policy redirection, and citizen demands would confound even the most proficient of batters. State governments have shown a remarkable ability to hit the curve ball—perhaps not effortlessly, but certainly consistently. States are survivors. For example, to find the innovative approaches to environmental protection these days, look at the states, which have witnessed a veritable burst of activism in policy initiatives. Resiliency is the key.

It is unlikely that the days of unfettered national dominance will return. The federal government faces its own challenges in our increasingly global world. As one astute observer of the U.S. governmental scene has commented, "Over the past decade, without ever quite admitting it, we have ceased to rely on Congress (or the federal government, for that matter) to deal with our most serious public problems. . . . [T]he states have been accepting the challenge of dealing with problems that no other level of government is handling."[72] Return to the first page of this chapter and reread the governors' inspirational words. The twenty-first century began full of challenges, but states and their local governments are taking charge. That is what increased capacity is all about.

CHAPTER RECAP

- State and local governments are directly involved in our daily lives.
- The story of states and localities over the past two decades has been one of transformation. They have shed their backward ways, reformed their institutions, and emerged as capable and proactive.
- State resurgence is exemplified in improved revenue systems, the expanded scope of state operations, faster diffusion of innovations, more interjurisdictional cooperation, and increased national-state conflict.
- Several persistent challenges dog states and localities: fiscal stress, interjurisdictional competition, and political corruption.
- The United States is becoming more racially and ethnically diverse. The increase in population in Sunbelt states such as Nevada and Arizona outpaces the rest of the nation. Meanwhile states like North Dakota and West Virginia show negligible population growth.
- An outbreak of culture wars is redefining the politics of some communities and states.
- As a whole, the states are diverse, competitive, and resilient. With increased capacity to govern effectively, they are producing results.

Key Terms

capacity (p. 4)
jurisdiction (p. 4)
federalism (p. 4)
proactive (p. 5)
downsizing (p. 11)

Sunbelt (p. 17)
Frostbelt (p. 17)
political culture (p. 19)
culture wars (p. 20)

Surfing the Web

Originally, states were assigned the same (except for the two-letter state abbreviation) type of URL: **www.state.ak.us.** The suffix *gov* was reserved for the federal government. Some states such as Alaska still use this web address. Beginning in 2003, states were authorized to use *gov* and many states have switched to it. Alabama is an example: **www.alabama.gov.** Other states have opted to do something different, such as Florida's portal at **www.myflorida. com,** Montana's at **www.discoveringmontana.com,** or Oklahoma's at **www. youroklahoma.com.**

A web site that offers a wealth of policy information about the states, along with links to multistate organizations, national organizations of state officials, and state-based think tanks is **www.stateline.org,** established by the Pew Center on the States.

The web site of *Governing* magazine, **www.governing.com,** contains up-to-date, in-depth discussions of issues in states and localities.

At **www.census.gov,** the web site of the U.S. Bureau of the Census, you can find historical, demographic data on states and localities.

A comprehensive web site that will take you to the official web sites of states and local governments is **www.firstgov.com.**

FEDERALISM AND THE STATES

A single broad and enduring issue in American federalism transcends all others: What is the proper balance of power and responsibility between the national government and the states? The debate over this profound question was first joined by the Founders in pre-constitutional days and argued between the Federalists and Anti-Federalists. It continues today in the halls of Congress, the federal courts, and the state and local governments, over issues ranging from the profane to the presidential.

The immediate aftermath of the September 11, 2001, terrorist attack on the World Trade Center towers and the Pentagon provided stark evidence of the undisputed duties and responsibilities of the federal, state, and local governments. As corporate workers fled the towers for their lives, New York City police and firefighters mounted the stairways into the burning buildings. State and local emergency agencies quickly coordinated the on-the-scene response. National political leaders, for their part, focused on international relations, intelligence gathering, and military responses. Today, the response to the threats of terrorism is intergovernmentally complex, with roles still being sorted out.

Typically, in fact, role confusion reigns. For instance, which level of government should have the power to determine the right to die? Under Oregon's Death with Dignity Act, a terminally ill person, upon receiving the written agreement of two physicians, may ingest drugs to end his life. In a 1996 referendum, Oregon voters affirmed the controversial 1994 law by a 60 percent majority. More than ninety people had committed suicide under the law through November 6, 2001, when U.S. Attorney General John Ashcroft authorized the U.S. Drug Enforcement Administration to revoke the license of any physician who prescribed the suicide drugs. Oregon quickly obtained a stay of Ashcroft's order in federal court and sued Ashcroft, a social and religious conservative, in federal court. The critical issue: Did Ashcroft brazenly usurp state sovereignty and trample on states' rights, or can the Oregon-established legal right of a terminally ill person to choose the time and means of her own death be denied by the national government? U.S. district and federal appeals courts upheld Oregon's law, ruling that Ashcroft had overstepped his authority. The U.S. Supreme Court may have the final word.

However innocuous or enormous they may seem, these types of conflicts define U.S. federalism. As a system for organizing government, federalism has important consequences that often, in ways both direct and hidden, affect our political and personal lives.

THE CONCEPT OF FEDERALISM

In a nation—a large group of people organized under a single, sovereign government and sharing historical, cultural, and other values—powers and responsibilities can be divided among different levels of government in three ways: through a unitary government, a confederacy, or a federal system. To understand our federal system, we must know how it differs from the other forms of government.

Unitary, Confederate, and Federal Systems

unitary system
One in which all authority is derived from a central authority.

The great majority of countries (more than 90 percent) have a **unitary system**, in which most if not all legal power rests in the central government. The central government may create or abolish regional or local governments as it sees fit. These subgovernments can exercise only those powers and responsibilities granted to them by the central government. In France, the United Kingdom, Argentina, Egypt, and the many other countries with unitary systems, the central government is strong and the regional or local jurisdictions are weak. In the U.S., the states themselves function as unitary systems.

confederacy

A league of sovereign states in which a limited central government exercises few independent powers.

A **confederacy** is the opposite of a unitary system. In a confederacy, the central government is weak and regional governments are powerful. The regional jurisdictions establish a central government to deal with areas of mutual concern, such as national defense and a common currency, but they severely restrict the central government's authority in other areas. If they see fit, they may change or even abolish the central government. The United States began as a confederacy, and the southern states formed one following secession in 1861.

federal system

A means of dividing the power and functions of government between a central government and a specified number of geographically defined regional jurisdictions.

A **federal system** falls somewhere between the unitary and confederate forms in the method by which it divides powers among levels of government. It has a minimum of two governmental levels, each of which derives its powers directly from the people and each of which can act directly on the people within its jurisdiction without permission from any other authority. Each level of government is supreme in the powers assigned to it, and each is protected by a constitution from being destroyed by the other.[1] Thus, federalism is a means of dividing the power and functions of government between a central government and a specified number of geographically defined regional jurisdictions. In effect, people hold dual citizenship, in the national government and in their regional government.

In the U.S. federal system, the regional governments are called states. In others, such as Canada, they are known as provinces. Altogether there are approximately twenty federal systems in the world.

The Advantages and Disadvantages of Federalism

As it has evolved in the United States, federalism is a reasonably effective system of government. But it is not perfect, nor is it well suited to the circumstances of most other nations. Ironically, federalism's weaknesses are closely related to its strengths.

The advantages of federalism are as follows:

1. *A federal system helps manage social and political conflict.* It broadly disperses political power within and among governments. For example, the U.S. Senate represents the geographical diversity of the states, with two senators for each territorial unit, and the House of Representatives is apportioned on the basis of population. This system enables national as well as regional and subregional concerns to reach the central government. Local interests are expressed in state capitols through state legislatures and, of course, in city and county councils and other local legislative bodies. Many places exist for resolving conflicts before they reach the crisis stage. Also, federalism achieves unity through diversity. Ethnicity, color, language, religious preference, and other differences are not distributed randomly in the population; rather, people who share certain traits tend to cluster together spatially. And state and local governments represent such groups. For example, the large and growing Hispanic population of Texas is increasingly gaining representation in the state legislature and in mayoral and city council offices.

2. *Federalism promotes administrative efficiency.* The wide variety of services demanded by citizens are delivered more efficiently without a large central bureaucracy. From public elementary education to garbage collection, the government closest to the problem seems to work best in adapting public programs to local needs.

3. *Federalism encourages innovation.* States and localities can customize their policies to accommodate diverse demands and needs—and, indeed, such heterogeneity flourishes. New policies are constantly being tested by the more than 88,000 government "laboratories" that exist throughout the country, thus further encouraging experimentation and flexibility.

4. *A federal system maximizes political participation in government.* Citizens have opportunities to participate at all three levels of government through elections, public hearings, and other means. The local and state governments serve as political training camps for aspiring leaders, who can test the waters in a school board or county council election and, if successful, move on to higher electoral prizes in the state or national arena. The great majority of presidents and U.S. senators and representatives got their start in state or local politics. Through almost 1 million offices filled regularly in elections, citizens can have a meaningful say in decisions that affect their lives. And if one level of government is unable or unwilling to address citizen demands, two others are potentially available.

5. *A federal system helps protect individual freedom.* Federalism provides numerous potential points of opposition to national government policies and political ideology. James Madison argued that the numerous checks inherent in a federal system would control the effects of **factions**, making "it less probable that a majority of the whole will have a motive to invade the rights of other citizens."[2] Thus the states serve as defenders of democracy by ensuring that no national ideological juggernaut can sweep over the entire nation, menacing the rights of individual citizens.

factions

Any group of citizens or interests united in a cause or action that can threaten the rights or interests of the larger community.

Now we turn to a list of disadvantages:

1. *Federalism may facilitate the management of conflict in some settings, but in others it makes conflict more dangerous.* Federal experiments in Canada and the former Yugoslavia support this point. In Canada, the ethnically French province of Quebec fueled a secessionist movement during the 1970s that still simmers. Because of a civil war, the former Yugoslavia now consists of several ethnically based countries. Separatism in region/states

2. *Although provision of services through governments that are close to the people can promote effectiveness and efficiency, federalism can also hinder progress.* It is extraordinarily difficult, if not impossible, to coordinate the efforts of all state and local governments. Picture trying to get 88,000 squawking and flapping chickens to move in the same direction at once. Business interests level this criticism today as they increasingly encounter government regulations on products and services that vary widely across the United States.

3. *Not surprisingly, many governments lead to redundancy and confusion.* For example, fifty sets of law on banking and lending practices can make doing business across state lines tough for a financial firm.

4. *Federalism may promote state and local innovation, but it can also hinder national programs and priorities.* These many points of involvement can encourage obstruction and delay and can result in an ineffective national government. An obvious example is the successful opposition of the southern states to voting rights for African Americans for more than a hundred years.

5. *Broad opportunity for political participation is highly desirable in a democracy, but it may encourage local biases that damage the national interest.* For example, hazardous, radioactive, and solid wastes must be disposed of somewhere, but local officials and citizens are quick to protest, "Not in my back yard!"

THE HISTORY OF U.S. FEDERALISM

The men who met in Philadelphia during the hot summer of 1787 to draw up the U.S. Constitution were not wild-eyed optimists, nor were they revolutionaries. In fact, as we'll see in this section, they were consummate pragmatists whose beliefs shaped the new republic and created both the strengths and weaknesses of our federal system.

Early History

The Framers of the Constitution held to the belief of English political philosopher Thomas Hobbes that human beings are contentious and selfish. Some of them openly disdained the masses. For example, Gouverneur Morris of New York declared of the American people: "The mob begin to think and reason. Poor reptiles! . . . They bask in the sun, and ere noon they will bite, depend upon it."[3] Most of the Framers agreed that their goal in Philadelphia was to find a means of controlling lower forms of human behavior while still allowing citizens to have a voice in making the laws they were compelled to obey. The "philosopher of the Constitution," James Madison, formulated the problem in terms of factions, groups that pursue their own interests without concern for the interests of society as a whole. Political differences and self-interest, Madison felt, led to the formation of factions, and the Framers' duty was to identify "constitutional devices that would force various interests to check and control one another."[4]

Three practical devices to control factions were placed in the U.S. Constitution. The first was a system of representative government in which citizens would elect individuals who would filter and refine the views of the masses. The second was the division of government into three branches (executive, legislative, judicial). The legislative body was divided into two houses, each with a check on the activities of the other. Equal in power would be a strong chief executive, with the authority to veto legislative acts, and an independent judiciary. Finally, the government was structured as a federal system, in which the most dangerous faction of all—a majority—would be controlled by the sovereign states. Insurrection in one state would be put down by the others, acting through the national government.[5] Madison's ultimate hope was that the new Constitution would "check interest with interest, class with class, faction with faction, and one branch of government with another in a harmonious system of mutual frustration."[6]

Sometimes today there appears to be more frustration than harmony, but Madison's dream did come true. The U.S. federal system is the longest-lived constitutional government on earth. Its dimensions and activities are vastly different from what the Framers envisioned, but it remains a dynamic, adaptable, responsive, and usually effective system for conducting the affairs of government.

The Move Toward Federalism

The drive for independence by the thirteen American colonies was in large measure a reaction to "a history of repeated injuries and usurpations" (according to the Declaration of Independence) under a British unitary system of government. The Declaration of Independence proudly proclaimed the colonies' liberation from the "absolute tyranny" exercised over them by the English Crown.

The struggle for independence dominated political debate in the colonies, and there was little time to develop a consensus on the form of government best suited to the future needs of American society. Hence, the move toward federalism was gradual. The first independent government established in America was a confederacy; thus Americans tested two types of government—unitary and confederate—before deciding permanently on the third.

The Articles of Confederation   During the War for Independence, the colonies, now called states, agreed to establish a confederation. A unicameral (one-house) Congress was created to exercise the authority of the new national government. Its powers were limited to the authority to wage war, make peace, enter into treaties and alliances, appoint and receive ambassadors, regulate Indian affairs, and create a postal system. The states held all powers not expressly granted to the Congress. The governing document was the Articles of Confederation (effective from 1776 to 1787).

The inherent weaknesses of the confederacy quickly became apparent. The states had significant authority within their own borders, but the central government was unable to carry out its basic responsibilities because it did not have the power to force the states to pay their share of the bill. The central government had to rely on the good will of the states for all of its revenues and, therefore, often could not honor its financial obligations to private individuals, firms, or foreign governments. Bankruptcy was a chronic concern. The lack of national authority to regulate either domestic or international commerce led to discriminatory trade practices by the states, particularly through the use of protective tariffs. These and many other defects were important concerns. But the key event that brought together representatives of the states to draft a constitution for a new type of government was Shays' Rebellion. In 1786, Daniel Shays, a Revolutionary War officer, led an armed revolt of New England farmers who were fighting mad about debt and taxes. The weak central government had difficulty putting down the rebellion.

The Constitutional Convention How did the Framers create a long-lasting and successful system of government that seems to have the best features of both unitary and confederate forms? We could say, somewhat naively, that they carefully integrated the best theories of various political philosophers into a grand plan for government. And, indeed, they were familiar with the early developments in political and theological federalism in Europe and the ancient world. They were aware of tribal confederations among the Native Americans and, most important, the Framers were well informed by their own colonial experience.[7] Truly the Framers were learned men, well schooled in the theories of politics, and most of them did believe in designing a government that would serve the people and ensure justice. But above all they were pragmatists; they developed a practical compromise on the key issues of the day, including the proper role of the national government and the states. The reconciliation of the interests and powers of the states with the need for a strong national government, what Madison called a "middle ground," was an American invention. Today, the United States stands as the prototypical federal system. It is our most distinctive political contribution.

Delegates representing each of the states assembled at the constitutional convention. Here, the self-interest of the large states and small states diverged. The large states supported the Virginia Plan, introduced by Edmund Randolph, which proposed a strong central government spearheaded by a powerful bicameral Congress. Because representation in both chambers was to be based on population, larger states would be favored. The smaller states countered with the New Jersey Plan, which put forward a one-house legislature composed of an equal number of representatives from each state. There were other differences between the two plans (for example, the Virginia Plan had a single chief executive, whereas the New Jersey Plan had a multimember executive), but the issue of state representation was paramount.

The New Jersey Plan was defeated by a vote of 7 to 3, but the smaller states refused to give in. Finally, Connecticut moved that the lower house (the House of Representatives) be based on the population of each state and the upper house (the Senate) be based on equal state membership. This Great Compromise was approved, ensuring that a faction of large states would not dominate the small ones.

The Framers reached another important compromise by specifying the powers of the new central government. Those seventeen powers, to be exercised through Congress, included taxation, regulation of commerce, operation of post offices, establishment of a national court system, declaration of war, conduct of foreign affairs, and administration of military forces.

A third key compromise reached by the Framers concerned the question of who should resolve disputes between the national government and the states: Congress, the state courts, or the Supreme Court? The importance of the decision that the Supreme Court would be the final arbiter was understood only years later, when the Court established the supremacy of the national government over the states through several critical rulings.

State-Centered Federalism

Despite the fact that the new Constitution made the national government much stronger than it had been under the Articles of Confederation, the power of the states was still important. As James Madison wrote, "The powers delegated by the proposed Constitution to the federal government are few and defined. Those which are to remain in the State governments are numerous and infinite."[8]

The first decades under the new Constitution witnessed a clash between profoundly different views on governing. George Washington, John Adams, and their fellow Federalists favored national supremacy, or **nation-centered federalism.** Opposed to them were Thomas Jefferson and the Republicans, who preferred **state-centered federalism.** Much of the debate then, as today, concerned the meaning of the **reserved powers** clause of the **Tenth Amendment** to the Constitution. Ratified in 1791, the Tenth Amendment gave support to the states by openly acknowledging that "the powers not delegated to the United States by the Constitution, nor prohibited by it to the States, are reserved to the states respectively, or to the people." But in fact, the Tenth Amendment was an early omen of the eventual triumph of nation-centered federalism. As pointed out by constitutional scholar Walter Berns, if the states were intended to be the dominant federal actors, they would not have needed the Tenth Amendment to remind them.[9]

Those who defended the power of the states under the Constitution—that is, state-centered federalism—saw the Constitution as a *compact,* an agreement, among the sovereign states, which maintained their sovereignty, or the right of self-governance. The powers of the national government listed in the Constitution—the **enumerated (delegated) powers**—were to be interpreted narrowly, and the states were obliged to resist any unconstitutional efforts by the national government to extend its authority.[10]

This **compact theory** of federalism became the foundation for states' rights arguments. In particular, it became central to the fight of the southern states against what they considered discrimination by the North. During the 1820s, a national tariff seriously damaged the economy of the southern states. The slave-based agricultural economy of the South had already begun a protracted period of decline while the North prospered. The tariff, which placed high taxes on imported manufactured goods from Europe, hit the South hard because it produced few manufactured goods. Rightly or wrongly, the southerners blamed the "tariff of abominations" for many of their economic problems.

In 1828, Vice President John C. Calhoun of South Carolina asserted that the United States was composed of sovereign states united in a central government

nation-centered federalism

Theory in which the national government is dominant over the states.

state-centered federalism

Theory in which the national government represents a voluntary compact or agreement between the states, which retain a dominant position.

reserved powers

Those powers residing with the states by virtue of the Tenth Amendment.

Tenth Amendment

The amendment to the Constitution, ratified in 1791, reserving powers to the states.

enumerated (delegated) powers

Those expressly given to the national government, primarily in Article I, Section 8, of the Constitution.

compact theory

A theory of federalism that sees the Constitution as an agreement among the states.

through a compact. The powers of the national government had been entrusted to it by the states, not permanently handed over. Calhoun claimed that the states thus had complete authority to reinterpret or even reject (nullify) the law, making it invalid within that state's borders. Most important, Calhoun declared that if a large majority of the states sided with the national government, the nullifying state had the right to *secede*, or withdraw from the Union. (Indeed, until the Civil War, when Americans referred to "my country," they usually meant their state—not the United States.)

In 1832, Calhoun's theory had considerable impact. That year, after an additional tariff was enacted by the national government, South Carolina nullified it. President Andrew Jackson and the Congress threatened military action to force the state to comply with the law, and Jackson even threatened to hang Calhoun, who by this time had resigned from the vice presidency.[11]

Ultimately, eleven southern states (led by South Carolina) did secede from the Union, at which point they formed the Confederate States of America. The long conflict between state sovereignty and national supremacy, and the question of slavery as well, was definitively resolved by five years of carnage in such places as Manassas, Shiloh, and Gettysburg, and the eventual readmittance of the renegade states to the Union. The Civil War, often referred to in the South as The War Between the States, remains the single most violent episode in American history, resulting in more than 620,000 deaths (more than in all our other wars combined) and countless civilian tragedies.

The Growth of National Power Through the Constitution and the Judiciary

After the Civil War, a *nation-centered* concept of federalism evolved. For the most part, the national government has become the primary governing force, with the states and localities generally following its lead. The power of the states vis-à-vis the national government has also been eroded by the Supreme Court's interpretations of key sections of the Constitution.

national supremacy clause

Article VI of the Constitution, which makes national laws superior to state laws.

The National Supremacy Clause Article III of the Constitution established the U.S. Supreme Court. The supremacy of national law and the Constitution is constitutionally grounded in the **national supremacy clause** (Article VI), which provides that the national laws and the Constitution are the supreme laws of the land. Later decisions of the Supreme Court established its role as arbiter of any legal disputes between the national government and the states. For example, the Supreme Court has consistently struck down state laws that permit prayer in public schools and school-sponsored events, most recently in 2000.[12]

The Necessary and Proper Clause The fourth chief justice of the United States, John Marshall, was the architect of the federal judiciary during his thirty-four years on the bench. Almost single-handedly, he made it a coequal branch of government. Several of his rulings laid the groundwork for the expansion of national governmental power. In the case of *McCulloch* v. *Maryland* (1819), two issues were before the bench: the right of the national government to establish a national bank, and the right of the state of Maryland to tax that bank, once it was established.[13] The secretary of the treasury, Alexander Hamilton, had proposed a bill that would allow Congress to charter such a bank for depositing national revenues and facilitating the borrowing of funds. Those who wanted to limit the power of the national government, such as James Madison and Thomas Jefferson, argued that the Constitution did not provide the government with the specific authority to charter and operate a national bank.

> **necessary and proper clause**
>
> Portion of Article I, Section 8, of the Constitution that authorizes Congress to enact all laws "necessary and proper" to carry out its responsibilities.

The crux of the issue was how to interpret the **necessary and proper clause.** The final power delegated to Congress under Article I, Section 8, is the power "to make all laws which shall be *necessary and proper* for carrying into execution the foregoing powers, and all other powers vested by this Constitution in the Government of the United States" (emphasis added). Jefferson argued that *necessary* meant "indispensable," whereas Hamilton asserted that it meant merely "convenient." Hamilton argued that in addition to the enumerated powers, Congress possessed **implied powers.** In the case of the national bank, valid congressional action was implied through the powers of taxation, borrowing, and currency found in Article I, Section 8.

> **implied powers**
>
> Those that are not expressly granted by the Constitution but that are inferred from the enumerated powers.

Meanwhile, the state of Maryland had levied a tax on the new national bank, which was located within its borders, and the bank had refused to pay. The bank dispute was eventually heard by Chief Justice Marshall. Marshall was persuaded by the Hamiltonian point of view. He pointed out that the Constitution nowhere stipulates that the only powers that may be carried out are those expressly described in Article I, Section 8. Thus, he ruled that Congress had the implied power to establish the bank and that Maryland had no right to tax it. Significantly, *McCulloch* v. *Maryland* meant that the national government had an almost unlimited right to decide how to exercise its delegated powers. Over the years, Congress has enacted a great many laws that are only vaguely, if at all, associated with the enumerated powers and that stretch the phrase *necessary and proper* beyond its logical limits.

> **commerce clause**
>
> Part of Article I, Section 8, of the U.S. Constitution, which permits Congress to regulate trade with foreign countries and among the states.

The Commerce Clause Another important ruling of the Marshall Court extended national power through an expansive interpretation of the **commerce clause** (often referred to as the interstate commerce clause) of Article I, Section 8. The commerce clause gives Congress the power "to regulate commerce with foreign nations, and among the several states, and with the Indian tribes." In *Gibbons* v. *Ogden* (1824),[14] two important questions were addressed by Marshall: What *is* commerce? And how broadly should Congress's power to regulate commerce be interpreted?

The United States was just developing a national economy as the Industrial Revolution expanded. National oversight was needed, along with regulation of emerging transportation networks and of state activities related to the passage of goods across state lines (interstate commerce). The immediate question was whether New York could grant a monopoly to run a steamship service between

New York and New Jersey. Marshall's answer? No, it could not. He defined commerce broadly and held that Congress's power to regulate commerce applied not only to traffic across state boundaries but, in some cases, also to traffic of goods, merchandise, and people *within* a state. The Court further expanded the meaning of commerce in various rulings during the Nineteenth and Twentieth centuries.

general welfare clause

The portion of Article I, Section 8, of the Constitution that provides for the general welfare of the United States.

The General Welfare Clause   The **general welfare clause** of Article I, Section 8, states that "the Congress shall have power to lay and collect taxes, duties, imposts, and excises to pay the debts and provide for the common defense and *general welfare* of the United States" (emphasis added). Before the Great Depression of the 1930s, it was believed that poor people were responsible for their own plight and that it was up to private charity and state and local governments to provide limited assistance. The Great Depression inflicted massive unemployment and poverty throughout the country and made necessary a major change in the national government's attitude. Despite their best efforts, the states and localities were staggered by the tremendous loss of tax revenues and the need to help poor and displaced persons obtain food and shelter. Franklin D. Roosevelt, who won the presidency in 1932, set in motion numerous New Deal programs that completely redefined federal responsibility for the general welfare. These programs, such as Social Security, propelled the national government into a position of dominance within the federal system and extended into fields previously within the province of the states, the localities, and the private sector.

Fourteenth Amendment

Enacted in 1868, this amendment contains citizenship rights, due process, and equal protection provisions that states must apply to all citizens.

The Fourteenth Amendment   Ratified by the states in 1868, the **Fourteenth Amendment** had the effect of giving former slaves official status as citizens of the United States and of the state in which they lived. It included two other important principles as well: *due process* and *equal protection* of the laws: "No state shall make or enforce any law which shall abridge the privileges or immunities of the citizens of the United States; nor shall any state deprive any person of life, liberty, or property, without due process of law; nor deny to any person within its jurisdiction the equal protection of the laws." The federal courts have utilized the Fourteenth Amendment to increase national power over the states in several critical fields, especially civil rights, criminal law, and election practices.

The judiciary's application of the Fourteenth Amendment to state and local governments is illustrated by many contemporary cases that have, for example, ordered desegration of the public schools (*Brown* v. *Board of Education*), established the rights of a person accused of a crime (*Miranda* v. *Arizona*), forced states to reapportion their legislature (*Baker* v. *Carr*, *Reynolds* v. *Sims*), ordered local officials to hike property taxes to pay for school desegregation (*Missouri* v. *Jenkins*), and required formal hearings for welfare recipients before benefits are terminated (*Goldberg* v. *Kelly*).

The Growth of National Power Through Congress

The U.S. Supreme Court has not been the only force behind nation-centered federalism; Congress has worked hand in hand with the judiciary. The commerce clause represents a good example. Given the simple authority to control or eliminate state barriers to trade across state lines, Congress now regulates commercial activities within a state's boundaries as well, as long as these activities purportedly have substantial national consequences (examples include banking and corporate fraud). Congress has also used the authority of the commerce clause to expand national power into fields only vaguely related to commerce, such as protecting endangered species. The states have made literally hundreds of legal challenges to such exercise of the commerce power. Until recently almost all of these were resolved by the U.S. Supreme Court in favor of the national government.

Taxing and Spending Power Probably the most controversial source of the rise in national power in recent years has been the use of the *taxing and spending power* by Congress to extend its influence over the state and local governments. Under Article I, Section 8, Congress holds the power to tax and spend to provide for the common defense and general welfare. But the **Sixteenth Amendment,** which grants Congress the power to tax the income of individuals and corporations, moved the center of financial power from the states to Washington, D.C. Through the income tax, the national government raises huge amounts of money. A portion of this money is sent to the states and localities. Because Congress insists on some sort of accountability in how state and local governments spend these funds, attached to federal grants are various conditions to which the recipients must adhere if they are to receive the money. These conditions include requirements for recipient governments to match national dollars with some portion of state contributions. (The interstate highway program requires one state dollar for every ten federal dollars, for example.) The federal government also imposes mandates and regulations directly related to the purposes of the individual grant. For example, the Driver's Privacy Protection Act prohibits states from selling or releasing personal information on drivers' licenses to a private firm, upon penalty of loss of federal highway funds (South Carolina and Alabama challenged this mandate but lost in the Supreme Court).[15] Another bill, enacted in 2000, set a national blood-alcohol standard of .08 for drunk driving; again, noncomplying states (Delaware was the only hold out in 2004) would face the loss of federal transportation dollars.

Sixteenth Amendment

Enacted in 1913, this amendment grants the national government the power to levy income taxes.

Federal Pre-emption The national government has also seized power through the process known as **federal pre-emption.** The legal basis for pre-emption is Article VI of the Constitution, the national supremacy clause. Whenever a state law conflicts with a national law, the national law is dominant.

Congressional passage of a national law that supersedes existing state legislation is directly pre-emptive. An example is the Air Quality Act, which replaced state standards on permissible levels of air pollutants with minimum national standards. Another is the federal government's preemptive authority to regulate tobacco advertising. An extreme case of pre-emption is the Voting Rights Act of 1965, which enables the U.S. Justice Department to exercise an advance veto over changes in election procedures and jurisdictions in specified states and localities, and to substitute national voting registrars for local officials where

federal pre-emption

The principle that national laws take precedence over state laws.

abuses in voting rights have occurred. Congress also pre-empts state law when it passes legislation that gives administrators in federal agencies the power to veto programs, plans, and policies developed by state and local officials.

Smothering (Then Resuscitating) the Tenth Amendment Actions by the Congress and the federal courts have gradually undermined the Tenth Amendment, which reserves to the states all powers not specifically granted to the national government or prohibited to the states. In fact, it is extremely difficult to identify any field of state activity not intruded on by the national government today. Although the Tenth Amendment is a declaration of the original division of powers between nation and states under the Constitution, the configuration is hardly descriptive of American federalism today because the states have surrendered, usually unwillingly, more and more of their erstwhile rights and privileges.[16]

The Supreme Court has sent mixed signals on the relevance of the Tenth Amendment. A good example of the Court's fickle federalism involves the Fair Labor Standards Act (FLSA). Following forty years of case law that essentially relegated the Tenth Amendment to the basement of federalism, the Court surprisingly ruled in favor of state and local governments in the 1976 case of *National League of Cities* v. *Usery.* At issue was the constitutionality under the commerce clause of the 1974 amendments to the FLSA, which extended federal minimum wage and maximum hour requirements to state and local employees. In this case, the Court said that Congress did not have the constitutional right to impose wage and hour requirements on employees carrying out basic—or integral—functions, such as law enforcement or firefighting.[17]

But just nine years later, the Court reversed itself in *Garcia* v. *San Antonio Metropolitan Transit Authority.* A spate of litigation had not been able to resolve the issue of just which state and local activities are "integral." So the Court expressly overturned its findings in *Usery* and once again applied federal wage and hour laws to nonnational governments—in this specific instance, to a mass transit system run by the city of San Antonio.[18] What really offended the states was the written opinion of the Court, in which it excused itself from such future controversies involving state claims against congressional and executive branch power exercised under the commerce clause. Now Congress alone, with little or no judicial oversight, would be allowed to determine, through the political process, how extensively it would intrude on what had been state and local prerogatives. One dissenting Supreme Court justice wrote that "all that stands between the remaining essentials of state sovereignty and Congress is the latter's underdeveloped capacity for self-restraint."[19] In the view of some critics, the states were relegated to the status of any other special-interest group and the Tenth Amendment was irrelevant. Other critics more optimistically observed that the narrow 5-to-4 decision could be revisited by a more conservative Supreme Court at a later date.[20]

Sure enough, in 1995 the Court reaffirmed the Tenth Amendment in *U.S.* v. *Lopez* by recognizing a limit to Congress's power over interstate commerce. Ironically, this case also involved San Antonio, where a high-school student,

Alfonso Lopez, was arrested for bringing a handgun to school. He was charged with violating the Gun Free School Zones Act of 1990, which banned the possession of a firearm within 1,000 feet of a school. Here, the Court ruled that in this instance Congress had unconstitutionally extended its power to regulate commerce because there was no connection between the gun law and interstate commerce.[21] A 2000 decision of the Supreme Court[22] further restricted Congress's powers to regulate interstate commerce by finding that female rape victims cannot sue their attackers in federal court under the Violence Against Women Act; instead, they must pursue their claims in state court. (The argument was made that victims were deterred from travel, taking certain jobs, and other activities related to interstate commerce.)

The Court has continued to recalibrate the scales of power in favor of the states in a series of rulings beginning in 1997. State authority to incarcerate sexual predators in mental institutions once their criminal sentences have ended was upheld.[23] A section of the so-called Brady Bill that required local police to conduct background checks on people who want to purchase handguns was declared unconstitutional by the Court, which pronounced that Congress had offended "the very *principle* of separate sovereignty."[24] The Court then let stand a lower court ruling that upheld the constitutionality of California's Proposition 209, which banned race- or sex-based preferences in college admissions, hiring decisions, and government contracting.[25] The Court also upheld Oregon's Death with Dignity Act, which permitted doctor-assisted suicides,[26] granted states the freedom to restrict anti-abortion demonstrations outside health clinics,[27] and supported states' authority to temporally halt certain private uses of land.[28]

Recent rulings based on the Eleventh Amendment have revived the notion of the sovereign immunity of the states. According to this doctrine, which dates back to the Middle Ages, a king (the state) cannot be sued without his (its) consent (the Eleventh Amendment protects states from lawsuits by citizens of other states or foreign nations). Supreme Court decisions have upheld the sovereign immunity of the states from being sued in federal courts in cases involving lawsuits by Indian tribes,[29] patent infringement when a state ventures into commercial activities,[30] and discrimination against older employees[31] and disabled workers. The Court also protected the states against private complaints taken before federal agencies.[32]

A New Era of State Resurgence? The Rehnquist Court has clearly and undeniably positioned itself on the side of the states in most conflicts with the national government. However, the Supreme Court does not decide unilaterally in favor of the states in all cases, notwithstanding one justice's complaint that the majority has become "[a] mindless dragon that indiscriminately chews gaping holes in federal statutes."[33] For example, in 2000, the Court asserted that the states cannot infringe on the president's foreign policymaking role, declaring unconstitutional a Massachusetts law that restricted state purchases from firms doing business with the country of Myannar,[34] and overturned a law in Nebraska (and, by implication, in thirty-one other states) banning partial-term abortions.[35] In 2001, the Court limited the authority of the states to regulate tobacco advertising near playgrounds and schools.[36] Finally, the Court's willingness to overturn the Florida Supreme Court in issues concerning the ballot counting in the 2000 president's race indicates that ideology and partisanship sometimes trump federalism.[37]

A large majority of the Court's decisions in federalism cases have been by a fragile 5-to-4 margin. The five pro-state justices are all Reagan appointees, and three are more than seventy years old. The president elected in 2004 will likely have the opportunity to replace one or more justices, which could easily upset the balance.

American federalism, by its nature, is ambiguous: it "was born in ambiguity, it institutionalizes ambiguity in our form of government, and changes in it tend to be ambiguous, too."[38] Judicial intervention in the affairs of state and local governments has not rendered them mere administrative appendages or relics of the past. But federal intrusions into the affairs of state and local governments continue to be burdensome and unwelcome. For now, the Tenth and Eleventh Amendments are useful weapons for fending off federal encroachments on the power of state and local officials, but the strength of that club can be emasculated on the turn of a single Supreme Court appointment.

MODELS OF FEDERALISM

Perceptions of the role of the states in the federal system have shifted from time to time throughout our history. Those who study the federal system have generally described these perceptions through various models or metaphors, which attempt to present federalism's complexity in a form that is readily understandable. Such models have been used both to enhance understanding and to pursue ideological and partisan objectives. One complete inventory uncovered 326 models of federalism,[39] but only the best-known ones are reviewed here to demonstrate that the U.S. federal system and people's perceptions of it change over time.

Dual Federalism (1787–1932)

dual federalism

Model in which the responsibilities and activities of the national and state governments are separate and distinct.

The model of **dual federalism** holds that the national and state governments are sovereign and equal within their respective spheres of authority as set forth in the Constitution. The national government exercises those powers specifically designated to it, and the remainder are reserved for the states. The nation and the states are viewed as primarily competitive, not cooperative, in their relationships with one another. The metaphor is that of a layer cake, with two separate colored layers, one on top of the other.

Dual federalism, which has its roots in the compact theory, was dominant for the first 145 years of U.S. federalism, although the Civil War and other events led to substantial modifications of the model.[40] Until 1860, the functions of the national government remained largely restricted to the delegated powers. Federal financial assistance to the states was extremely limited. The states had the dominant influence on the everyday lives of their citizens, acting almost unilaterally in areas such as elections, education, economic development, labor relations, and criminal and family law.[41] After the Civil War shattered secession and dealt the compact theory of state-centered federalism a death blow, the nation-centered view became paramount.

Cooperative Federalism (1933–1964)

The selection of a specific date for the demise of dual federalism is rather subjective, but 1933, when Franklin D. Roosevelt became president, is as good a date as any. Roosevelt's New Deal buried dual federalism by expanding national authority over commerce, taxation, and the economy.

> **cooperative federalism**
>
> A model of federalism that stresses the linkages and joint arrangements among the three levels of government.

Cooperative federalism recognizes the sharing of responsibilities and financing by all levels of government.[42] Beginning with the Great Depression, the national government increasingly cooperated with states and localities to provide jobs and social welfare, develop the nation's infrastructure, and promote economic development.

The cooperative aspects of this era were measured in governmental finances. The national government spent huge amounts of money to alleviate the ravages of the Depression and to get the U.S. economic machinery back into gear. Total federal expenditures rose from 2.5 percent of the gross national product (GNP) in 1929 to 18.7 percent just thirty years later, far surpassing the growth in state and local spending during the same period. The number of federal grants-in-aid rose from twelve in 1932, with a value of $193 million, to twenty-six in 1937, with a value of $2.66 billion. A substantial amount of the federal aid was sent directly to local governments, particularly counties and school districts. The variety of grant programs also exploded, with grants for maternal and child health, old-age assistance, aid to the blind, fire control, treatment of venereal disease, public housing, road and bridge construction, and wildlife conservation.

Variations on Cooperative Federalism Since 1964

The broad theme of cooperative federalism has many variations. All of them stress intergovernmental sharing. Among these variations are creative federalism and new federalism.

> **creative federalism**
>
> A model of cooperative federalism in which many new grants-in-aid, including direct national-local financial arrangements, were made.

Creative federalism was devised by President Lyndon B. Johnson to promote his dream of a Great Society. Johnson sought to build the Great Society through a massive national government attack on the most serious problems facing the nation: poverty, crime, poor health care, and inadequate education, among others. The vehicle for the attack was the federal grant-in-aid. More than 200 new grants were put into place during the five years of Johnson's presidency. Johnson's policy of vast government spending bypassed the states in distributing funds for some seventy of the new programs, a major change. Federal disbursements went directly to cities and counties rather than through the states. Understandably, the states did not appreciate losing influence over how localities could spend their national dollars.

new federalism

A model that represents a return of powers and responsibilities to the states.

New federalism is a model that has been employed with separate but related meanings in four different presidencies. The new federalism initiated by President Richard Nixon was intended to restore power to the states and localities and to improve intergovernmental arrangements for delivering services. Among the major policy changes brought about by the Nixon administration were the establishment of ten regional councils to coordinate national program administration across the country, and the simplification and streamlining of federal regulations that apply to state and local government. States and localities were also given greater flexibility in program spending and decisionmaking through revenue sharing.

Ronald Reagan's brand of new federalism, like Nixon's version, sought to give more power and program authority to states and localities, at least in theory. However, Reagan's main goal—to shrink the size of the national government—soon became obvious. Reagan's new federalism initiative won congressional approval to merge fifty-seven categorical grants into nine new block grants and to eliminate another sixty categorical grants.[43] The states got more authority, but the funding for the new block grants decreased almost 25 percent from the previous year's allocation for the separate categorical grants.[44]

The president, and a Congress with an eye on deficit reduction, chipped away steadily at other grant programs in an effort to shrink the size of government. Reagan and his allies successfully terminated revenue sharing in 1986. Called *general revenue sharing* (GRS) when enacted during the Nixon administration, this program was highly popular with state and local officials. GRS provided funds, with no strings attached, to state and general-purpose local governments (cities, counties, towns, and townships). It was discontinued largely because of the mounting national budget deficit and Congress's desire to exert greater control over, and take more credit for, how federal monies were spent.

The Reagan legacy lived on with George Bush (senior) in the White House. Although the style was different—in the view of many state and local officials, the first Bush administration was more sympathetic—the substance remained the same.[45] The Bush administration continued emphasizing the sorting out of national, state, and local responsibilities in areas such as transportation and education.

President Clinton, the Republican Congress, and the "Devolution Revolution" By 1994, with the election of Republican majorities in the U.S. House and Senate and also the election of many new Republican governors, new federalism came back in style with impressive force. The new federalists, whose ranks included many Democrats as well, sought once again to sort out intergovernmental responsibilities. For the first time in recent history, the states and localities were basically united and working together through a coalition of government interest groups, including the National Governors' Association and the National League of Cities, to design smaller, more efficient government with greater program and policy flexibility for the states and localities.

devolution

The delegating of power and programs from the federal government to state and local governments.

This planned delegating of power from the federal to state and local governments is termed **devolution.** The constellation of supporters for devolution is impressive. The governors, acting as individuals and through the

National Governors' Association, have never been more active in Washington than they are now. During the Clinton administration, they found a sympathetic president and congressional majority to listen to their concerns, and a Supreme Court increasingly likely to rule in favor of state authority. Public opinion is in favor of greater state and local government authority. Public opinion polls consistently show that citizens believe the state and local governments do a better job than the national government in spending money and delivering services.[46] (A poll taken shortly after 9/11 showed a surge in support for the federal government, but this trend was likely to be a short-term phenomenon.) Together, these powerful forces for devolution are gradually reversing more than a century of centralizing tendencies in U.S. federalism. This trend has been so striking that is has been called the devolution revolution. The impact of devolutions are being registered in the states in social welfare and other areas, but apparently they have not yet made a significant policy impact in many local governments.[47]

The principal tool for devolving federal financial and programmatic authority and responsibility to the states is the block grant. In 1996, a major new block grant converted a sixty-one-year-old entitlement program, Aid to Families with Dependent Children (AFDC), into a block grant to the states. (See Chapter 17 for more detail on this change.) As one of the turnbacks supported by several previous presidents, the Personal Responsibility and Work Opportunity Reconciliation Act made AFDC a state responsibility, and it also consolidated several federal child-care programs into a previously enacted block grant. But serious discussion about additional turnbacks lost steam in the late 1990s, when conservative forces in Congress sought to usurp state authority over property rights and blood-alcohol limits, among other issues.[48]

George W. Bush and New Federalism The views of the latest president Bush (like Clinton, a former governor) were not clearly articulated, but initiatives of his administration and of Republican supporters in Congress sought to preempt state authority over school testing systems, override forty state laws that guarantee patient rights, obstruct state laws that permit the medical use of marijuana, and impose burdensome new homeland security requirements on the states. The predominance of business interests in Washington, D.C., appears to have stanched devolution in what one writer calls "the law of political physics—that for every flurry of state and local business regulations, there is an equal and opposite" effort by business to counter it in the nation's capitol.[49]

INTERGOVERNMENTAL RELATIONS

Cooperative federalism demands positive interactions among governments at all levels. Devolution of responsibilities to states and localities may be a long-term trend, but cooperative activities are constantly increasing among the national, state, and local governments. For that matter, so are relationships between the states and Native American tribes.

Tribal Governments

With the arrival of the Europeans, the estimated 7 to 10 million people who lived in what is now the United States soon was severely depleted by warfare, disease, and famine. Hundreds of treaties, statutes, and other agreements notwithstanding, the Native Americans were eventually deprived of their traditional lands and isolated on reservations. Today, some 2.5 million people identify themselves as Native American; there are 557 recognized tribes. About one-third of them continue to live on tribal reservations, mostly in the western portion of the United States. The Navajo Nation, for instance, has a population of more than 250,000 and covers some 17 million acres extending from northwest New Mexico to northeast Arizona and southeast Utah. At the other extreme of the tribal spectrum are the Mashantucket Pequots. Registering just thirty-five to forty members with "only the barest trace of Indian descent"[50] when officially recognized by the federal government in the 1990s, the Pequots occupy several hundred acres in Connecticut, where they operate Foxwoods Casino and Resorts. On average, Native Americans are the poorest and least healthy group in the United States.

Tribes are semisovereign nations exercising self-government on their reservations. They are under the authority and supervision of Congress and are subject to the federal courts, but their legal relationship with the states is complex. Tribal governments are permitted to regulate their internal affairs, hold elections, and enforce their own laws under congressional supervision. States are prevented from taxing or regulating tribes or extending judicial power over them. Off the reservation, however, Native Americans are subject to the same laws as any other state residents. They have the right to vote in both federal and state elections.

Recently, the tribes have been engaged by the federal government and some states in a more consultative role. The federal government has granted additional waivers for various tribal activities. States and tribes cooperate to pursue certain common interests, such as fishing and hunting rights and regulation of reservation gaming. The highly lucrative gaming enterprises of some tribes have advanced tribal political interests and clout by providing financial resources.[51] Interactions among tribal governments, the state, and nearby local governments are occasionally testy. Tribal actions concerning land use may conflict with local zoning or state environmental policy. The tax-free sale of gasoline and alcohol and tobacco products on the reservation diminishes state sales tax revenues. And tribal casinos have been highly contentious in some settings. When conflicts arise, states and tribal governments may sort out their differences through compacts. Compacts between tribes and states are required by federal law before casinos can be operated on tribal land, but in several states, casinos have been run without state authorization. During such conflicts, Congress may be asked to enter the fray.

Interstate Cooperation

Cooperation Under the Constitution Four formal provisions exist for cooperation among the states.

1. *The full faith and credit clause* of the Constitution binds every citizen of every state to the laws and policies of other states. This means, among other things, that a person who has a legitimate debt in North Dakota will be made to pay even if he moves to Montana. Crossing a state boundary does not alter a legal obligation. The courts have interpreted full faith and credit to apply to contracts, wills, divorces, and many other legal issues. The clause does not, however, extend to criminal judgments. An interesting test of the full faith and credit clause results from a Massachusetts Supreme Court decision in 2004 that allows "same sex marriages." Hundreds of gay and lesbian couples did so right away. The Massachusetts legislature voted to ban same-sex marriage shortly after the state supreme court decision, and Governor Mitt Romney issued an executive order forbidding them, but several Massachusetts municipalities began issuing marriage licenses anyway. What should transpire when a same-sex married couple from Massachusetts seeks to have their status recognized in Alabama or one of the thirty other states that have enacted laws denying recognition to same-sex marriages? And when a gay couple united in Massachusetts wants to get a divorce, can another state grant it?

2. *The interstate rendition clause* begins where full faith and credit leaves off, covering persons convicted of criminal violations. Governors are required to extradite (return) fugitives to the state in which they were found guilty or are under indictment (although in certain cases they refuse).

3. *The privileges and immunities clause* states that "the citizens of each state shall be entitled to all privileges and immunities of citizens in the several states." This clause was intended by the Framers to prevent any state from discriminating against citizens of another state who happen to be traveling or temporarily dwelling outside their own state's borders. Of course, states do discriminate against nonresidents in matters such as out-of-state tuition, hunting and fishing license fees, and residency requirements for voting. The Supreme Court has upheld these and other minor discrepancies, as long as the fundamental rights of nonresidents are not violated. Such rights include the right to conduct business, have access to state courts, and receive the same welfare benefits as long-term residents.

4. Finally, the *interstate compact clause* authorizes the states to negotiate compacts, which are binding agreements between two or more states that address important cross-boundary issues. Early interstate compacts were used to settle boundary disputes. More than 120 are in effect today in various areas, including shared water resources, pest control, riverboat gambling, and education.

Informal Cooperation Among the States Interstate cooperation can be facilitated through several informal methods. One example is the establishment of regional interstate commissions such as the Appalachian Regional Commission (ARC), which was created by national legislation in 1965 to attack poverty in the states of Appalachia. Another example is found in the Mississippi Delta region, where several states adopted a ten-year economic development plan to help pull the area out of its own cycle of poverty.

In addition, states have developed uniform laws to help manage common problems ranging from child support to welfare cheating. Interstate cooperation also occurs through information-sharing among elected and appointed officials and the organizations to which they belong, such as the National Governors' Association and the National Conference of State Legislatures. And it may take place in legal actions, as demonstrated by state attorneys general who joined together in the late 1990s to sue the tobacco companies for driving up medical costs. Or one state may contract with another for a service, as Hawaii does with Arizona for a health care management system.

Of course, interstate relations do not always go smoothly; occasionally, the states get into serious (and not so serious) conflicts and disagreements. Those that the states cannot settle themselves are taken directly to the U.S. Supreme Court for resolution. One conflict recently resolved by the Court involves which state owns Ellis Island, where millions of immigrants landed just offshore from New York City between 1892 and 1954. Originally the island was comprised of only three acres, but landfill projects expanded it to 27.5 acres. In 1998, after about 200 years of dispute, the Court decided that New York will retain sovereignty over little more than the original three acres, while New Jersey gains control of the remaining landfill area. With a nod to the biblical King Solomon, the Court divided the Great Hall, where some 12 million immigrants were processed, equally between the states.[52]

The Supreme Court recently ruled that Ellis Island lies mostly in New Jersey. New York can lay claim to only part of the island's 27.5 acres.
SOURCE: AP/Wide World of Photos.

Intergovernmental Financial Relations

revenues

Monies raised by governments from taxes, fees, enterprises, and payments from other levels of government.

expenditures

Outlays or disbursements of government monies.

grant-in-aid

An intergovernmental transfer of funds or other assets, subject to conditions.

revenue sharing

A no-strings form of financial aid from one level of government to another.

categorical grants

A form of financial aid from one level of government to another to be used for a narrowly defined purpose.

block grants

A form of financial aid from one level of government to another for use in a broad, functional area.

formula grant

A funding mechanism that automatically allocates monies based on conditions in the recipient government.

project grant

A funding mechanism that awards monies based on the strength of an applicant government's proposal.

Money has always been important to government, although the word *money* is seldom used. Instead, the talk is of revenues and expenditures. **Revenues** are the funds that governments have at their disposal. They are derived from taxes, fees and charges, and transfers from other levels of government. **Expenditures** are the ways in which the governmental revenues are disbursed. Governments spend money to operate programs, build public facilities, and pay off debts.

The **grant-in-aid** is the primary mechanism for transferring money from the national to the state and local governments. The national government makes grants available for several reasons: to redistribute wealth, to establish minimum policy standards, and to achieve national goals. But grants are primarily designed to help meet the needs of state and local governments, including environmental protection, transportation, community and regional development, education, and health care. Federal grant outlays totaled some $350 billion in 2002.

Discretion of Recipients Grants differ in two major ways: the amount of discretion (independence) the recipient has in determining how to spend the money, and the conditions under which the grant is awarded. Imagine a spectrum running from maximum discretion to minimum discretion. The grant labels that correspond to these end points are **revenue sharing** and **categorical grants,** respectively. Under revenue sharing, states and communities are allocated funds that they may use for any purpose. A categorical grant, in contrast, can be used by the recipient government only for a narrowly defined purpose, such as removing asbestos from school buildings or acquiring land for outdoor recreation.

Located between revenue sharing and categorical grants on the discretion spectrum are block grants. **Block grants** are *broad-based grants;* that is, they can be used anywhere within a functional area such as transportation or health care. The difference between categorical and block grants is that the recipient government decides how block grants will be spent. For instance, a local school system can decide whether the purchase of personal computers is more important than buying microscopes for the science laboratory. More than 625 grants are in existence today, including 17 block grants. Block grants give nonnational governments considerable flexibility in responding to pressing needs and primary goals. This grant mechanism assumes that state and local governments can make rational choices among competing claims.

Conditions for Grants Grants also vary in the manner in which they are awarded. A **formula grant** makes funding available automatically, based on state and local conditions such as poverty level or unemployment rate. A **project grant** is awarded to selected applicants based on administrative assessments of the strength of competing proposals. Block grants are distributed on a formula basis; categorical grants can be either formula- or project-based.

Recognition of these two characteristics—the amount of discretion enjoyed by the recipient jurisdiction and the manner in which the grant is awarded—is important for understanding the grant system. Another, less prominent factor also affects intergovernmental financial relations: the existence of *matching requirements.* Most federal grants require that the recipient government use its own resources to pay a certain percentage of program costs. This arrangement is designed to stimulate state and local spending on programs deemed to be in the national interest and to discourage nonnational governments from participating in a program simply because money is available. For example, if a state government wants funding through the Boating Safety Financial Assistance program administered by the U.S. Department of Transportation, it must contribute 50 percent itself. And for a local government to participate in the U.S. Interior Department's Urban Parks program, it must provide from 15 percent to 50 percent of the costs. In each case, the recipient government's commitment to boating safety or urban parks is likely to be higher because of the joint funding.

FEDERAL PURSE STRINGS

Federalism today turns less on theory and more on money. The distribution of intergovernmental monies and the conditions attached to them define the distribution of governmental power and authority. Federalism is a matter not only of which level of government will do what, but also of which level will pay for it. Some have called this a period of fend-for-yourself federalism, with each jurisdiction essentially on its own in a Darwinian struggle for financial survival.

The Importance of Federal Funds

Figure 2.1 provides a historical look at national grant-in-aid expenditures. It is important to remember that the data in this figure have not been adjusted for inflation; the $91.4 billion spent in 1980 was worth vastly more than it would be today. The amounts also do not take into account the increase in population since 1980. The second set of bars in Figure 2.1 documents the variable proportion of national dollars in the expenditures of state and local governments, reflecting the fact that aid to states and localities consumes a relatively small share of the federal government's budget.

Although the Washington-funded portion of state and local government expenditures is only around one-third, it represents an important source of revenue for nonnational governments. Grants to state and local governments averaged approximately $1,037 per person in fiscal year 2002. However, the funds were not spread evenly across the country (see Table 2.1). Alaska and Wyoming received the most per capita. Federal grants poured into these states at the rate of $4,876 and $2,281, respectively. In last place is Nevada, where federal grant monies averaged just $854 per person.

States battle in Congress over their share of grant allocations, which are affected by factors such as military installations in the state and social welfare needs. They attempt to influence competitive project grant awards, and they lobby Congress to adjust the weighing of certain factors in formula grants in their favor. State and local influence is wielded by their representatives sitting in Congress and through various actions by elected state and local officials and their Washington lobbyists.

| FIGURE 2.1 | **Historical Trends in Federal Grant-in-Aid Outlays** |

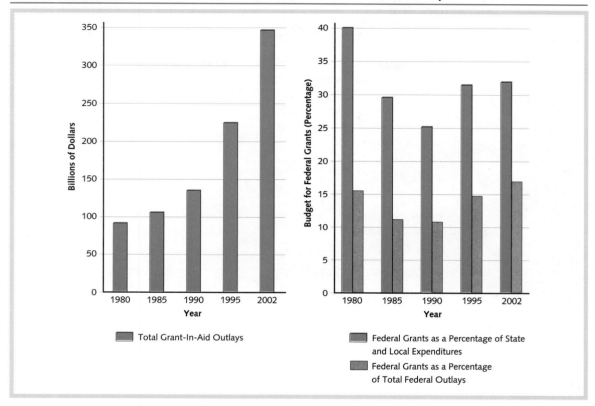

SOURCE: U.S. Office of Management and Budget, The Budget of the United States Government, Fiscal Year 2002, Historical Tables, and www.access.gpo.gov/usbudget/fy2003/pdf/hist.pdf.

National expenditures in nongrant forms also affect state and local economies substantially. In the nongrant category are payments to individuals (representing 64 percent of total federal grants today, up from 36 percent in 1980), notably through Social Security; Medicaid; purchases by the national government; and wages and salaries of federal workers, most of whom work outside Washington, D.C. In this sense, federal expenditures emphasize people more than places.

Here's the Check and Here's What to Do with It: Mandates, Pre-emptions, Set-Asides, and Cost Ceilings

Although many voices are crying, "Let the states and localities do it," Congress continues to impose mandates and pre-empt the states. In addition, Congress includes set-asides and cost ceilings in block grants. Old habits die hard, and one of Congress's oldest habits is to place requirements and conditions on the states.

TABLE 2.1	Federal Grants to State and Local Governments in 2002, in Rank Order

STATE	GRANTS PER CAPITA	STATE	GRANTS PER CAPITA
Alaska	$4,876	Idaho	1,375
Wyoming	2,481	California	1,374
North Dakota	2,245	Oregon	1,372
New York	2,219	Washington	1,371
New Mexico	2,138	South Carolina	1,365
Montana	2,105	Nebraska	1,356
Vermont	2,081	Wisconsin	1,336
South Dakota	1,981	Michigan	1,323
Rhode Island	1,962	North Carolina	1,319
Massachusetts	1,922	Ohio	1,301
West Virginia	1,831	Minnesota	1,296
Mississippi	1,759	New Hampshire	1,284
Maine	1,757	New Jersey	1,263
Louisiana	1,660	Georgia	1,232
Kentucky	1,553	Arizona	1,230
Connecticut	1,528	Kansas	1,206
Tennessee	1,497	Illinois	1,190
Arkansas	1,495	Utah	1,169
Missouri	1,488	Maryland	1,160
Oklahoma	1,465	Texas	1,147
Pennsylvania	1,462	Indiana	1,133
Alabama	1,415	Colorado	1,056
Delaware	1,393	Florida	983
Iowa	1,383	Nevada	854

SOURCE: The Tax Foundation, "Special Report: Federal Tax Burdens and Expenditures by State," no. 124 (July 2003).

Washington-based politicians may claim to support state power in principle, but when it conflicts with other priorities, devolution takes a back seat.

federal mandate

A requirement that a state or local government undertake a specific activity or provide a particular service.

Federal mandates are especially burdensome when they are unfunded—that is, when the national government requires the states and localities to take action but does not pay for it, and the states and localities must foot the bill. Recent federal mandates require the states to establish rigorous school-testing programs, impose stringent new standards on drinking water, lower the blood-alcohol limit for drunken driving from .10 to .08, make Viagra available to Medicare recipients, and spend millions of dollars yearly to implement school testing and other requirements under No Child Left Behind. The total cost of these mandate millstones hanging round the necks of states and localities to-taled $29 billion in 2003.[53] Mounting opposition to mandates without money finally convinced Congress to enact the Unfunded Mandate Reform Act of 1995, which provides that any bill imposing a mandate of more than $50 million on a state or local government must include a cost estimate. If passed, the legislation is supposed to include sufficient funds to pay for the mandate. Indications are that proposed laws containing unfunded mandates are facing tougher scrutiny in Congress than before and that Congress is taking a more consultative approach with state and local elected officials. However, members of Congress still seize opportunities to revert to their mandating ways.

As noted earlier, *pre-emption* represents another intrusion of the national government into the state sphere. It takes two forms: *total* pre-emption, whereby the national government seizes all regulatory authority for a given function from states and localities; and *partial* pre-emption, whereby the national government establishes minimum national standards for state-implemented programs. Both forms prevent states from doing what they want. An example of a totally pre-emptive action is the Americans with Disabilities Act, which requires states and localities to make physical and occupational accommodation for disabled persons. Many partial pre-emptions involve environmental protection, whereby states may regulate pollution emissions as long as state standards are at least as stringent as those of the federal government. A new concern of global pre-emption was raised by the terms of the 1994 General Agreement on Tariffs and Trade (GATT), which permits foreign corporations to challenge state laws that unfairly discriminate against them in the World Trade Organization (WTO).

Thus, when mandates and pre-emptions are taken into consideration, a less optimistic picture of intergovernmental relations emerges. To the states and localities, it seems that the country has shifted from cooperative federalism to coercive federalism. In the words of Nebraska governor Ben Nelson, "shift and shaft" federalism has demoted the governors from significant policymakers to branch managers "of a behemoth national government."[54]

set-asides

Requirements in block grants that assign a certain percentage of an expenditure for a particular activity.

Set-asides offer an alternative mechanism through which policymakers in Washington, D.C., can influence the behavior of distant governments. Set-asides are provisions in block grants that designate a certain minimum percentage expenditure on a particular activity. For example, the Alcohol, Drug Abuse, and Mental Health Block Grant contains requirements that states spend at least 50 percent of the funds on services to intravenous (IV) drug users. Congress reasoned that the sharing of hypodermic needles among addicts was contributing to the spread of the AIDS virus and that states were not doing enough to address the problem. But state leaders, although they admitted AIDS was a national priority, argued that the problem was not uniformly spread around the country. Why should Montana spend the same proportion of its funds on IV drug users as New York? Perhaps Montana should spend its drug abuse funds on adolescent alcohol abusers. In any case, the issue is clear: Who should decide how federal funds are to be spent—the government allocating the funds or the government implementing the program?

THE FUTURE OF FEDERALISM

Of the past five presidents, four have been governors. None has been particularly sensitive to the needs and perspectives of the states. George W. Bush assumed office in 2001 after having promised a bipartisan approach to governing. Soon, however, he became embroiled in a growing number of disputes with Democrats in Congress and in the states. Clearly, the world looks quite different from the White House.

For the states and localities, national political gridlock has meant a golden opportunity to reverse more than a century of centralizing forces. They have taken up the slack in the federal system, busily innovating—developing and implementing policies in a great variety of fields, from social welfare and health care to education and economic development. Public opinion polls consistently show greater trust in state and local government than in the federal government. As laboratories of democracy, states have designed and experimented with numerous policies that later have served as models for other states and for Congress. For instance, states have recently pioneered policy initiatives in children's issues, unwanted telemarketing calls, a patient's bill of rights, campaign finance, and education and welfare reform, among many other fields.[55] The high level of policy activity in the states has attracted to state capitols a horde of lobbyists representing interests such as tobacco, gun control, and the insurance industry. Lobbyists who once focused their attentions on Washington, D.C. spent nearly $890 million to woo state legislators in 2003.

Journalists and many citizens have routinely referred "to 'the government' as if there were only one—the Big One."[56] But the United States is a nation of many governments, and Washington is not the best location for addressing all the nation's complex policy problems. As one observer puts it, Washington, D.C., represents a "mainframe government in a PC world."[57] Whereas centrally designing and implementing policies and programs was once believed to be the best approach, today it implies wasteful and ineffective one-size-fits-all government. The clear trend in government, as well as in business, is to decentralize decisionmaking to the lowest feasible level of the organization. For the U.S. federal system, that means sending decisionmaking to the states and localities and even, in some instances, to nonprofit organizations and citizens' groups.

At the very time that the state and local governments are most needed as policy leaders and problem solvers, certain social and economic forces seriously threaten state and local government capability. The economic recession of 2001–2002 severely reduced state and local revenues. High levels of births to unmarried women and teenage girls have left millions of children in poverty. Illegal drugs and gang activity, homelessness, and a flood of immigrants present seemingly impossible challenges for the cities. Finally, the growing disparity of wealth and income threatens our great reservoir of political and social stability: the middle class.

For its part, the federal government is provoking growing criticism for tying the hands of the states and localities with mandates, pre-emptions, and confused and conflicting policy directives. Most state and local governments *want* to become more creative, but they are also being *forced* to, so that they can figure out how to implement and pay for federally mandated requirements. This conflicted, ambiguous federalism is something less than empowerment.[58] When the president or Congress takes actions to squash innovative programs such as legalization of medical marijuana in California (see the accompanying *Debating Politics* box) or assisted suicide in Oregon, they profess to do so for purposes of the national interest or high moral principles. But some think the issue is also about money and power and, perhaps at the most basic level, the need for Congress to justify its existence in an increasingly state and local political world.

At first thought, the tragic events of September 11, 2001, and the war on terrorism might seem to create a centralizing phenomenon in American federalism. Shouldn't the response involve strong national government actions and top-down hierarchical controls? The U.S.A. PATRIOT Act did have centralizing implications, including surveillance provisions and the consolidation of federal agencies into a new Department of Homeland Security. But in fact, homeland security calls for *more*—not less—intergovernmental relations.[59] State and local governments play critical roles in all four key functions of homeland security: prevention, preparedness, response, and recovery.[60] Local governments are the first responders to disasters of all sorts, for example, sending police, firefighters, and other emergency personnel to the site. States provide crisis management, emergency services, and coordination, and steer recovery efforts.

Effective homeland security means improved cooperation across and within levels of government, and with nonprofits and firms as well. Multiple jurisdictions, agencies, and other organizations must mobilize and respond jointly to crises. Volatile circumstances call for adaptation on and around the scene, not rigid, top-down decisionmaking.

At a fundamental level, multiple actors must be able to talk to one another to acquire and exchange information. This means expensive investments in communications equipment and technology. Indeed, enhanced homeland security commands a high financial cost. State and local governments in 2003–2004 were in the grip of a profound financial crisis that threatened significant cutbacks in basic services. The addition of homeland security, in this sense, came at the worst possible time, threatening to push the nonnational governments further into the danger zone. President Bush and the national government promised $3.5 billion in homeland security aid shortly after the terrorist attacks, but two years later, only $1.5 billion had been delivered. Cities alone were estimated to be spending $70 million a week on new homeland security activities.

Both financially and operationally, homeland security represents a profound challenge to American federalism. The effectiveness of the American response to this unprecedented challenge depends heavily on the quality of federal, state, and local relations.

In homeland security and almost all other fields, what the states and localities are demanding is cooperative, consultative relationships and flexible or facilitative federalism, in which the national government helps them through selective funding for technical assistance—a federalism in which they are treated as partners in governance, not as just another self-absorbed interest group. What they want, in a word, is empowerment.

Decriminalizing Medical Marijuana

Ten states (California, Colorado, Arizona, Hawaii, Maine, Nevada, Oregon, Vermont, Washington, and Alaska) have enacted laws permitting the legal purchase of marijuana for medicinal purposes, mainly through citizen initiatives. These actions directly contradict federal drug policy and regulations, which forbid any possession and use of the herb and assess a fine of up to $10,000 and up to one year in prison for mere possession of one reefer.

Decriminalization originated with California's Proposition 215, approved by the voters in 1997. Proposition 215 permits cultivation and possession of marijuana by patients and their caregivers if its use is prescribed by a physician. Arizona's Proposition 200 went a huge step further by also decriminalizing stronger drugs for the ill, including heroin, methamphetamines, and lysergic acid diethylamide (LSD), if recommended by two doctors.

These state actions reflected widespread public dissatisfaction with a flawed and failed federal drug enforcement policy. And at least as far as marijuana is concerned, the decriminalization recognized increasing evidence of the medical uses of marijuana for treating several conditions, including glaucoma (an eye disease) and neurological diseases such as multiple sclerosis. Marijuana also has been found to stimulate the appetite and suppress nausea for AIDS sufferers and for cancer patients on chemotherapy and radiation treatment.

Predictably, the new laws have encountered vehement opposition from political and social conservatives and from the U.S. Food and Drug Administration (FDA), which is responsible for enforcing federal drug laws. For example, the California initiative was initially blocked by a federal district court judge who applied a federal law prohibiting the use of marijuana since 1937. The U.S. Supreme Court ruled in 2001 that the medical necessity exception is not allowed under the federal law. Both the Clinton and Bush administrations threatened doctors who recommended marijuana to their patients with criminal prosecution and the loss of their right to prescribe all prescription drugs for Medicare and Medicaid patients. In 2003, the Justice Department prosecuted a case in federal court against a fifty-eight-year-old man who was acting as a so-called officer of the city of Oakland, California, in growing marijuana plants for distribution to seriously ill people in the San Francisco Bay area. He was convicted under federal law and sentenced to a minimum of five years in prison. Later that same year, the Supreme Court let stand a lower court decision that refused to permit the Justice Department to punish doctors for recommending marijuana to their patients.

Although other states are certain to consider the issue, a majority continue to outlaw all use of marijuana. Tremendous variability exists in state laws for possession, cultivation, and sale. Eleven states may impose maximum penalties of thirty years or more incarceration. In ten states, the maximum penalty is five years or less. In other states and localities, marijuana violations are routinely overlooked by law enforcement personnel.

The marijuana issue had important economic dimensions as well. In addition to enormous criminal justice expenditures for enforcing marijuana laws and the loss of productivity from incarcerating tens of thousands of people, the economic benefits of growing marijuana are substantial. It represents a vast, untaxed black market crop in West Virginia, Kentucky, North Carolina, California, Vermont, Hawaii, and many other states. Legalization could significantly boost tax revenues. A large and growing commercial market for industrial hemp (essentially the same plant but with minuscule levels of the psychoactive ingredient THC). Legally grown in much of the world for thousands of years, industrial hemp is used to manufacture rope, textiles, paper, cosmetics, animal feed, and thousands of other products.

Marijuana presents a multifaceted issue that raises numerous legal, ethical, and economic questions. From the perspective of federalism, consider the following: Does the federal government have the statutory, regulatory, and constitutional powers to overrule public opinion and law in the states? If a majority of Californians or Alaskans want doctors to be able to prescribe marijuana for medical purposes, should the federal government stand in their way? What about the responsibilities of the states to respond to citizen demands, even if their preferences are out of favor with the president and a majority in Congress? Is medicinal marijuana an issue properly resolved by the states, or should there be a more uniform national policy? What about recreational use and the lessons of legalization for America's youth?

SOURCES: "Marijuana as Medicine: How Strong is the Science?" *Consumer Reports* 62 (May 1997): 62–63; *United States v. Oakland Cannabis Buyer's Cooperation*, No.000151, 2001; and various articles of the *New York Times*, 1997–2004.

Of course, some states, including California, Massachusetts, Oregon, and Wisconsin, consistently rank high as policy initiators. But others predictably bring up the rear. Counting as policy laggards are Alabama, Mississippi, and South Carolina.[61] Why are some states more innovative than others? A host of factors come into play, including political culture, the presence of policy entrepreneurs, levels of population and population growth, urbanization, and state wealth. And while all states achieve policy breakthroughs at one time or another, most are also guilty of occasional boneheaded decisions. California, for instance, made a hugely expensive mess out of electricity deregulation in 2000–2001.

In fairness to the national government, remember that much federal intervention has been in response to state failures to govern effectively and fairly. Corruption, racial prejudice and exclusion, and rampant parochialism, among other shortcomings, have prompted presidential, congressional, and judicial interventions that have, on the whole, helped the states move to the much higher plane they inhabit today.

The states, now prepared to govern responsibly, are determined to oppose further federal pre-emptions of their powers and responsibilities. They have fought to protect the health, safety, and physical environment of their citizens, often with standards and a level of commitment that far exceed those of the federal government. They have continued to serve as political laboratories for experiments in service delivery and other fields in spite of severe reductions in federal financial support and expensive, federally imposed spending requirements. As the burdens of governing more than 290 million Americans have grown, the limitations of the national government have become evident. Effective federalism in the United States today demands a cooperative partnership among nation, states, and localities.

The question of the balance of power and responsibility in U.S. federalism is no less important now than it was when the representatives of the colonies met in Philadelphia's Independence Hall, first to draft the Articles of Confederation and later to design the Constitution. The focus of the debate has shifted, however, to a pragmatic interest in how the responsibility of governing should be sorted out among the three levels of government. As pointed out by an insightful observer of U.S. government, "[t]he American federal system has never been static. It has changed radically over the years, as tides of centralization and decentralization have altered the balance of power and the allocation of functions among the different levels of government."[62] The pendulum marking the balance has swung to and fro over the two centuries of U.S. federalism. Today it swings in the direction of the state and local governments.

CHAPTER RECAP

- U.S. federalism is an ongoing experiment in governance.
- A fundamental question is, What is the proper balance of power and responsibility between the national government and the states?

- Actions of the courts, Congress, and the executive branch have expanded powers of the national government.
- Until recently, the trend has been generally in the direction of a stronger national government. Beginning in the early 1980s, however, there has been a resurgence of the state and local governments as political and policy actors.
- The power relationships among the three levels of government are described by various models, including dual and cooperative federalism. The operative model is cooperative federalism, under the variant known as new federalism.
- A key concept in federalism is intergovernmental relations, particularly financial relationships among the three levels of government.
- The national government imposes certain controversial requirements on grants-in-aid, including mandates and pre-emptions.

Key Terms

unitary system *(p. 25)*
confederacy *(p. 26)*
federal system *(p. 26)*
factions *(p. 27)*
nation-centered federalism *(p. 31)*
state-centered federalism *(p. 31)*
reserved powers *(p. 31)*
Tenth Amendment *(p. 31)*
enumerated (delegated) powers *(p. 31)*
compact theory *(p. 31)*
national supremacy clause *(p. 32)*
necessary and proper clause *(p. 33)*
implied powers *(p. 33)*
commerce clause *(p. 33)*
general welfare clause *(p. 34)*
Fourteenth Amendment *(p. 34)*
Sixteenth Amendment *(p. 35)*

federal pre-emption *(p. 35)*
dual federalism *(p. 38)*
cooperative federalism *(p. 39)*
creative federalism *(p. 39)*
new federalism *(p. 40)*
devolution *(p. 40)*
revenues *(p. 45)*
expenditures *(p. 45)*
grant-in-aid *(p. 45)*
revenue sharing *(p. 45)*
categorical grants *(p. 45)*
block grants *(p. 45)*
formula grant *(p. 45)*
project grant *(p. 45)*
federal mandate *(p. 48)*
set-asides *(p. 49)*

Surfing the Web

Examples of unfunded mandates are found on a Heritage Foundation web page at **www.regulation.org/states.html.**

Federalism decisions by the U.S. Supreme Court may be reviewed at The Council of State Governments' web site at **www.statesnews.org.** This site also includes other items related to federalism.

For current information on relationships among the three levels of government, see **governing.com.**

www.census.gov has comparative data on the states and localities, particularly state and local finances.

STATE CONSTITUTIONS

The Evolution of State Constitutions
The First State Constitutions • Legislative Supremacy • The Growth of
Executive Power

Weaknesses of Constitutions
Excessive Length • Problems of Substance

Constitutional Reform
The Essential State Constitution • Constitutions Today

Methods for Constitutional Change
Informal Constitutional Change • Formal Constitutional Change

State Responsiveness and Constitutional Reform

Alabama's 1901 constitution is a monument to the traditionalistic political culture. It enshrines the power of the "Big Mules" (agriculture, timber, and steel), disenfranchised blacks and many poor whites, and protected the powerful elite from paying their fair share of taxes. It hobbled the authority of local governments to govern themselves, ensured an impoverished system of public K–12 education, and in general guaranteed a dysfunctional state government.

The reformers, spearheaded (improbably) by conservative Republican Governor Bob Riley (a former three-term member of Congress who prided himself on never voting for a tax increase), sought voter approval for a constitutional convention in 2002 to revise the tax structure, remove racist and sexist language, and simplify the document. Entrenched opponents of constitutional change, including timber and agriculture interests, taxophobes, and extreme elements of the religious right (alleging revision "would bring new taxes in and throw God out"), attacked Riley's convention proposal. But the legislature approved sending a package of twenty-three amendments to the voters in a

September 9, 2003, referendum for an up or down vote. Riley's overall plan: to expand the state income tax base and rate and tax personal wealth (intangible assets), while spending an estimated $1.2 billion in new revenues to improve the state's woeful school system, educate its underqualified work force, provide significant tax relief to low-income people, and attract high-wage business. A proud son of the Bible Belt, Riley pitched his reform in religious terms: "If the New Testament teaches me anything, it teaches me not only to love thy neighbor but also to help those who are least among us."[1]

By a 2 to 1 margin, the voters of Alabama rejected Riley's plan. Ironically, even low-income voters overwhelmingly rejected the amendments that would have benefited them most. Faced with a $675 million budget deficit, Riley called a special session of the legislature to cut outlays for education, prisons, and state agencies. The first step was to cut state agency budgets by 18 percent, lay off state employees, and begin the release of at least 5,000 prison inmates. For now, Alabama remains bound to the past, but new efforts to reform the archaic state constitution are inevitable. In a sense, the struggle over constitutional tradition and change in Alabama represents a battle for the economic and political future of the state and its people.

In Alabama and the other forty-nine states, constitutions both distribute and constrain political power among groups and regions. They set forth the basic framework and operating rules for government, allocate power to the three branches, limit the scope of governmental authority, and protect individual rights.[2] Constitutions represent the **fundamental law** of a state, superior to statutory law. They provide a set of rules for running state government, and those who master the regulations and procedures have a distinct advantage over novices. Everything that a state government does and represents is rooted in its constitution. Constitutions do not describe the full reality of a political system, but they do provide a window to perceive its reality. Only the federal Constitution and federal statutes take priority over state constitutions, which is why the constitution is called the fundamental law.

To most people, however, constitutional law still means the federal document. State constitutions are often neglected in secondary school and college courses in history and political science. One national survey discovered that 51 percent of Americans were not aware that their state had its own constitution.[3]

In the U.S. system of *dual constitutionalism,* in which there are both national and state constitutions, the national government is supreme within the spheres of authority specifically delegated to it in the U.S. Constitution. Powers granted exclusively to the national government are denied to the states. But the national Constitution is incomplete. It leaves many key constitutional issues to the states, including local finance, public education, and the organization of state and local government.[4] In theory, state constitutions are supreme for all matters not expressly within the national government's jurisdiction or pre-empted by federal constitutional or statutory law. In practice, however, congressional actions and federal court interpretations have expanded the powers of the national government and, in some cases, eroded the powers of the states. And in reality many

fundamental law

The basic legal and political document of a state; it prescribes the rules through which government operates.

concurrent powers, such as taxing, spending, and protecting citizens' health and safety, are shared by all levels of government.

The earliest state constitutions were simple documents reflecting an agrarian economy, single-owner businesses, and horse-and-buggy transportation. As American society and the economy changed, the rules of state government also required transformation. Constitutional reform has been a regular theme throughout the U.S. experiment in federalism.

Constitutions are, in their essence, political documents, products of history, culture, events, economics, and above all the clash of interests. Some reforms have reflected changing political fortunes. Newly powerful groups have pressed to revise the state constitution to reflect their interests, or one or another political party has gained control of state government and sought to solidify its power. Constitutional reforms have promoted different views of politics and the public interest, as when Progressive reformers rallied for honest and efficient government in the late nineteenth and early twentieth centuries.[5] Since the 1960s, constitutional revisions have concentrated power in the governor's office; unified court systems; and generally sought to make state government more efficient, effective, and responsive to shifting social and economic forces. The fact that constitutions are subject to change also recognizes that human judgment is fallible, and that human understanding is imperfect.[6] In 2000, for instance, Alabama voters finally removed a long-ignored prohibition against miscegenation (mixed-race marriage). Through such constitutional reform, states can elevate their role as democratic laboratories and respond to the changing needs and opinions of citizens. This capacity for change is in sharp contrast to the seldom-amended federal Constitution.

THE EVOLUTION OF STATE CONSTITUTIONS

When the states won their independence from Great Britain more than two hundred years ago, there was no precedent for writing constitutions. A constitution called the Great Binding Law existed for the Five Nations of the Iroquois, but it was oral and not particularly appropriate for consideration by the people in the colonies.[7] The thirteen colonial charters provided the foundation for the new state constitutions. These documents were brief (around five pages each); the British Crown had granted them to trading companies and individuals to govern settlements in the new territories. As the settlements became full colonies, the charters were expanded to incorporate the "rights of Englishmen"—political and civil rights first enumerated by the Magna Carta in 1215. For territories too remote from their native country to be governed by its laws, these charters also laid down some basic principles of colonial government.[8]

In a sense, the existence of these documents helped fuel the fires of independence. In what was to become Connecticut, early settlers escaping the oppressive rule of the Massachusetts Bay Colony took matters of governance into their own hands. Under the leadership of Thomas Hooker, these ambitious farmers established an independent government free from references to the Crown. The Fundamental Orders of 1639 contended that "the choice of the public magistrates belongs unto the people by God's own allowance. The privilege of election belongs to the people . . . it is in their power, also, to set and limit the bounds and limitations of the power [of elected officials]."[9] Years later, a representative of King James II was sent to take possession of the Fundamental Orders and unite the New England colonies under the Crown. In a night meeting, as the Orders were laid out on a table before the king's men, the candles suddenly were extinguished. When they were relighted, the document had disappeared. According to legend, a patriot had hidden the Orders in a nearby hollow tree, later to be known as the Charter Oak. Infuriated, the king's men dissolved the colony's government and imposed autocratic rule that lasted many years. But they never found the Fundamental Orders, which essentially governed Connecticut until the Constitution of 1818 was adopted.[10]

The First State Constitutions

Following the War of Independence, the former colonies drafted their first constitutions in special revolutionary conventions or in legislative assemblies. With the exception of Massachusetts, the new states put their constitutions into effect immediately, without popular ratification. The making of the first state constitutions was not a casual or simple affair. Critical questions had to be answered in constitutional conventions, including the structure of the new government, how and when elections would be held, and how land once owned by the Crown would be distributed. Territorial integrity was not well defined. For example, in what is now known as Kentucky, people frustrated with Virginia's rule met in 1784 and petitioned the Congress for statehood. It took six years and nine constitutional conventions before Kentucky became a state. Complicating factors causing delay involved the "necessity of communicating across the mountains, the change from the Articles of Confederation to the Constitution of the United States, Indian attacks, [and] the revelation of a plot to have Kentucky secure independence and join Spain."[11]

In content, most of these documents simply extended the colonial charters, removing references to the king and inserting a bill of rights. The constitutions of Connecticut and Rhode Island, for example, differed only slightly from those states' colonial charters. All the documents incorporated the principles of limited government: a weak executive branch, the separation of powers, checks and balances, a bill of rights to protect the people and their property from arbitrary government actions, and (except for Pennsylvania) a bicameral legislature.[12] The earliest constitutions were not truly democratic. Essentially, they called for government by an aristocracy. Officeholding and voting, for instance, were restricted to white males of wealth and property.[13]

Only one of the thirteen original state constitutions, that of Massachusetts, survives (although it has been amended 120 times). It is the oldest functioning constitution in the world. Its longevity can be attributed in large part to the foresight of its drafter, John Adams, who grounded the document in extensive research of governments that took him all the way back to the ancients

This painting illustrates the signing of the Massachusetts state constitution, which is the oldest active constitution in the world.

SOURCE: Photo courtesy of the Massachusetts Archives.

and the Magna Carta. Even after many amendments, the Massachusetts constitution reflects a composite of the wisdom of the foremost political philosophers of the eighteenth century: John Locke, Jean-Jacques Rousseau, and the Baron de Montesquieu.[14] In this enduring document, Massachusetts establishes itself as a commonwealth (from the words *common weal,* meaning "general well-being"), on the principle that its citizens have a right to protect and manage their collective interests. (Kentucky, Pennsylvania, and Virginia are also commonwealths.)[15]

Legislative Supremacy

The first state constitutions reflected the Framers' fear and distrust of the executive—a result of their experiences with the colonial governors. The governors were not all tyrants, but because they represented the British Crown and Parliament, they became a symbol of oppression to the colonists. As a result, the guiding principle of the new constitutional governments was **legislative supremacy,** and the legislatures were given overwhelming power at the expense of governors. Most governors were to be elected by the legislature, not the people, and were restricted to a single term of office. State judiciaries also were limited in authorized powers; judges, like governors, were to be elected by the legislature. The

legislative supremacy
The legislature's dominance of the other two branches of government.

pre-eminence of legislative power was so great that an English observer, Lord James Bryce, was moved to remark: "The legislature . . . is so much the strongest force in the several states that we may almost call it the government and ignore all other authorities."[16]

The Growth of Executive Power

Disillusionment with the legislatures soon developed, spreading rapidly through the states during the early 1800s. There were many reasons for disenchantment, including the legislatures' failure to address problems caused by rapid population growth and the Industrial Revolution; the growing amount of legislation that favored private interests; and a mounting load of state indebtedness, which led nine states to default on their bonds in a single two-year period.

Gradually the executive branch began to accumulate more power and stature through constitutional amendments that provided for popular election of governors, who were also given longer terms and the authority to veto legislative bills. The constitutions of states admitted to the Union during the early 1800s established stronger executive powers at the outset. This trend toward centralization of power in the executive branch continued during the 1830s and 1840s, the so-called Jacksonian era; however, the Jacksonian principle of popular elections to fill most government offices resulted in a fragmented state executive branch. The governor now had to share authority with a lieutenant governor, an attorney general, a treasurer, and other popularly elected officials, as well as with numerous agency heads appointed by the legislature. Although the growth of the governor's powers continues today, the divided nature of the executive branch still makes it difficult for an individual to exercise those powers.

As executive power grew, public confidence in state legislatures continued to erode. This trend was reflected in the process of constitutional revision. One delegate at Kentucky's 1890 constitutional convention proclaimed that "the principal, if not the sole purpose of this constitution which we are here to frame, is to restrain the legislature's will and restrict its authority."[17] Also affecting constitutional change were broader social and economic forces in the United States, such as the extension of suffrage and popular participation in government, the rise of a corporate economy, the Civil War and Reconstruction, the growth of industry and commerce, the process of urbanization, and a growing movement for government reform. States rapidly replaced and amended their constitutions from the early 1800s to 1920 in response to these and other forces. The decade immediately after the Civil War saw the highest level of constitutional activity in U.S. history, much of it in the southern states; between 1860 and 1870, twenty-seven constitutions were replaced or thoroughly revised as Confederate states ratified new documents after secession, then redrew the documents after Union victory to incorporate certain conditions of readmission to the United States.

Constitutional change after Reconstruction was driven by the Populist and Progressive reform movements. During the late 1800s, the Populists championed the causes of the "little man," including farmers and laborers. They sought to open the political process to the people through constitutional devices such as the initiative, the referendum, and recall (see Chapter 4). The Progressives, who made their mark during 1890–1920, were kindred spirits whose favorite targets were concentrated wealth, inefficiencies in government, machine politics, corruption, and boss rule in the cities. Reformers successfully promoted constitutional reforms such as regulation of campaign spending and party activities, replacement of party conventions with direct primary elections, and selection of judges through nonpartisan elections.

WEAKNESSES OF CONSTITUTIONS

Despite the numerous constitutional amendments and replacements enacted during the nineteenth and twentieth centuries, by 1950, the states were buffeted by a rising chorus criticizing their fundamental laws. Ironically, many states were victims of past constitutional change, which left them with documents that were extravagantly long, frustratingly inflexible, and distressingly detailed. In general, state constitutions still provided for a feeble executive branch because they granted limited administrative authority to the governor, permitted the popular election of numerous other executive branch officials, and organized the executive into a hodgepodge of semiautonomous agencies, boards, and commissions. State judiciaries remained uncoordinated and overly complex, whereas legislatures suffered from archaic structures and procedures. Statutory detail, outdated language, local amendments (those that apply only to designated local governments), and other problems contaminated the documents and confined state government.

Excessive Length

From the first constitutions, which averaged 5,000 words, state documents had expanded into enormous tracts averaging 27,000 words by 1967. (The U.S. Constitution contains 8,700 words.) Some of this increase resulted from growing social and economic complexity, and from a perceived need to be extremely specific about what the legislatures could and could not do. The states did have to delineate their residual powers (those powers not delegated to the national government), identify the scope of their responsibility, and define the powers of local governments. In addition, state constitutions are much easier to amend than the federal Constitution. But some constitutions went too far. Louisiana's exceeded 253,000 words. Georgia's contained around 583,500 words, surpassing Tolstoy's *War and Peace* in length. Even today the constitution of South Carolina limits local government indebtedness but lists seventeen pages of exceptions. Maryland's constitution devotes an article to off-street parking in Baltimore. Oklahoma's sets the flash point for kerosene at 115 degrees for purposes of illumination,[18] and California's addresses a compelling issue of our time—the length of wrestling matches. A 2002 constitutional initiative in Florida prohibits "cruel and unusual confinement of pigs during pregnancy." The dubious prize for the most verbose constitution today goes to Alabama. An estimated 70 percent of the amendments to its 340,136-word document apply to only one county.[19] Table 3.1 provides an overview of the fifty state constitutions, including each one's length.

Not surprisingly, lengthy state constitutions tend to be plagued by contradictions and meaningless clauses. Article II, Section 13, of Pennsylvania's constitution states that "the sessions of each House and of committees of the whole shall be open, unless when the business is such as ought to be kept secret." Other constitutions suffer from superfluous formality, legal jargon, redundancy, and poor grammar. Some constitutions address problems that are no longer with us, such as the regulation of steamboats[20] or the need to teach livestock feeding in Oklahoma public schools.

TABLE 3.1   State Constitutions*

STATE	NUMBER OF CONSTITUTIONS	EFFECTIVE DATE OF PRESENT CONSTITUTION	ESTIMATED NUMBER OF WORDS	NUMBER OF AMENDMENTS SUBMITTED TO VOTERS	ADOPTED
Alabama	6	Nov. 28, 1901	340,136	1,028	746
Alaska	1	Jan. 3, 1959	15,988	40	28
Arizona	1	Feb. 14, 1912	28,876	240	133
Arkansas	5	Oct. 30, 1874	59,500	186	89
California	2	July 4, 1879	54,645	848	507
Colorado	1	Aug. 1, 1876	56,944	299	143
Connecticut	4	Dec. 30, 1965	17,256	30	29
Delaware	4	June 10, 1897	19,000	†	136
Florida	6	Jan. 7, 1969	51,456	127	96
Georgia	10	July 1, 1983	39,526	81	61
Hawaii	1	Aug. 21, 1959	20,774	119	100
Idaho	1	July 3, 1890	24,232	204	117
Illinois	4	July 1, 1971	16,510	17	11
Indiana	2	Nov. 1, 1851	10,379	75	43
Iowa	2	Sept. 3, 1857	12,616	57	52
Kansas	1	Jan. 29, 1861	12,296	122	92
Kentucky	4	Sept. 28, 1891	23,911	74	40
Louisiana	11	Jan. 1, 1975	54,112	184	124
Maine	1	March 15, 1820	16,276	201	169
Maryland	4	Oct. 5, 1867	46,600	254	218
Massachusetts	1	Oct. 25, 1780	36,700	148	120
Michigan	4	Jan. 1, 1964	34,659	61	23
Minnesota	1	May 11, 1858	11,547	213	118
Mississippi	4	Nov. 1, 1890	24,323	157	122
Missouri	4	March 30, 1945	42,600	162	103
Montana	2	July 1, 1973	13,145	49	27

TABLE 3.1 *(continued)*					
STATE	NUMBER OF CONSTITUTIONS	EFFECTIVE DATE OF PRESENT CONSTITUTION	ESTIMATED NUMBER OF WORDS	NUMBER OF AMENDMENTS SUBMITTED TO VOTERS	ADOPTED
Nebraska	2	Oct. 12, 1875	20,048	330	219
Nevada	1	Oct. 31, 1864	31,377	216	131
New Hampshire	2	June 2, 1784	9,200	284	143
New Jersey	3	Jan. 1, 1948	22,956	69	36
New Mexico	1	Jan. 6, 1912	27,200	277	148
New York	4	Jan. 1, 1895	51,700	290	216
North Carolina	3	July 1, 1971	16,532	39	31
North Dakota	1	Nov. 2, 1889	19,130	257	144
Ohio	2	Sept. 1, 1851	48,521	266	160
Oklahoma	1	Nov. 16, 1907	74,045	329	165
Oregon	1	Feb. 14, 1859	54,083	499	235
Pennsylvania	5	1968‡	27,711	36	30
Rhode Island	2	May 2, 1843	10,908	105	59
South Carolina	7	Jan. 1, 1896	22,300	670	484
South Dakota	1	Nov. 2, 1889	27,675	217	112
Tennessee	3	Feb. 23, 1870	13,300	59	36
Texas	5	Feb. 15, 1876	80,000	605	432
Utah	1	Jan. 4, 1896	11,000	154	103
Vermont	3	July 9, 1793	10,286	211	53
Virginia	6	July 1, 1971	21,319	46	38
Washington	1	Nov. 11, 1889	33,564	168	95
West Virginia	2	April 9, 1872	26,000	119	70
Wisconsin	1	May 29, 1848	14,392	181	133
Wyoming	1	July 10, 1890	31,800	116	91

*The information in this table is current through January 1, 2004. The constitutions referred to include those Civil War documents customarily listed by the individual states.

†Proposed amendments are not submitted to the voters in Delaware.

‡Certain sections were revised in 1967–1968.

SOURCE: "State Constitutions," from *The Book of the States 2003*. Reprinted by permission of The Council of State Governments.

Verbose constitutions, such as those of Alabama, Oklahoma, and Texas, fail to distinguish between the fundamental law and particularistic issues that properly should be decided by the state legislature.[21] Excessive detail leads to litigation because the courts must rule on conflicting provisions and challenges to constitutionality; hence, the courts are often burdened unnecessarily with decisions that should be made by the legislature. Once incorporated into a constitution, a decision becomes as close to permanent as anything can be in politics. In contrast to a statute, which can be changed by a simple legislative majority, constitutional change requires an extraordinary majority, usually two-thirds or three-fourths of the legislature. This requirement hampers the legislature's ability to confront problems quickly and makes policy change more difficult. Too many amendments may also deprive local governments of needed flexibility to cope with their own problems. For instance, a 2002 Oklahoma amendment exempts storm shelters from local property taxes. Indeed, too much detail generates confusion, not only for legislatures and courts but also for the general public. It encourages political subterfuge to get around archaic or irrelevant provisions and breeds disrespect or even contempt for government.

State constitutions are political documents and, contrary to the admonitions of reformers, may sometimes be used to address some of the most controversial issues in politics, such as abortion rights, gay rights, and even smokers' rights. Many detailed provisions favor or protect special interests, including public utilities, farmers, timber companies, religious groups, and many others.

There is enormous variance in the length of state constitutions (see Table 3.1). What accounts for such disparity? Studies by political scientists find, not surprisingly, that interest groups play an important role. In states with only one strong political party, where legislative outcomes tend to be unpredictable because of dissension among members of the majority party, interest groups try to insulate their favorite agencies and programs from uncertainty by seeking protective provisions for them in the constitution.[22] Also, research indicates that long, detailed documents tend to become even longer because their very complexity encourages further amendment, until they finally become so cumbersome that political support develops for a simpler version. Finally, the easier it is to amend a constitution, the higher the amendment rate.[23]

Problems of Substance

In addition to the contradictions, anachronisms, wordiness, and grants of special privilege found in state constitutions, their *substance* has drawn criticism. Specific concerns voiced by reformers include the following:

- *The long ballot.* Because elected executive branch officials are not accountable to the governor for their jobs, the governor has little or no formal influence on their decisions and activities. Reformers who seek to maximize the governor's powers would restrict the executive branch ballot to only two elected leaders: the governor and the lieutenant governor.
- *A glut of executive boards and commissions.* This reform of the Jacksonian period was intended to expand opportunities for public participation in state government and to limit the powers of the governor. Today, it leads to fragmentation and a lack of policy coordination in the executive branch.
- *A swamp of local governments.* There are some 88,000 municipalities, counties, and special-purpose districts in the states. Sometimes they work at cross-purposes, and nearly always they suffer from overlapping responsibilities and an absence of coordination.

- *Restrictions on local government authority.* Localities in some states have to obtain explicit permission from the state legislature before providing a new service, tapping a new source of revenue, or exercising any other authority not specifically granted them by the state.
- *Unequal treatment of racial minorities and women.* Constitutional language sometimes discriminates against African Americans, Latinos, and women by denying them certain rights guaranteed to white males. (Although a few holdouts remain, such as New Hampshire, most states have now adopted race- and gender-neutral language).

CONSTITUTIONAL REFORM

Shortly after World War II, problems of constitutional substance began to generate increasing commentary on the sorry condition of state constitutions. One of the most influential voices came in 1955 from the U.S. Advisory Commission on Intergovernmental Relations, popularly known as the Kestnbaum Commission. In its final report to the president, the commission stated that

> the Constitution prepared by the Founding Fathers, with its broad grants of authority and avoidance of legislative detail, has withstood the test of time far better than the constitutions later adopted by the States. . . . The Commission believes that most states would benefit from a fundamental review of their constitutions to make sure that they provide for vigorous and responsible government, not forbid it.[24]

Model State Constitution

An ideal of the structure and contents of a state constitution that emphasizes brevity and broad functions and responsibilities of government.

Another important voice for constitutional reform was the National Municipal League, which developed a **Model State Constitution** in 1921 that is now in its sixth version.[25]

Thomas Jefferson believed that each generation has the right to choose for itself its own form of government. He suggested that a new constitution every nineteen or twenty years would be appropriate. Between 1960 and 1980, it seems that the states took his remarks to heart. Every state altered its fundamental law in some respect during this period, and new or substantially revised constitutions were put into operation in more than half the states. During the 1970s alone, ten states held conventions to consider changing or replacing their constitution. One such state was Louisiana, which set a record by adopting its eleventh constitution; Georgia is in second place with ten.

positive-law tradition

A state constitutional tradition based on detailed provisions and procedure.

higher-law tradition

A state constitutional tradition based on basic and enduring principles that reach beyond statutory law.

Two state constitutional traditions are evident today.[26] The newer **positive-law tradition** is represented by the detailed and lengthy documents of states such as Alabama, New York, and Texas. Detailed provisions tend to usurp the lawmaking powers of state legislatures by locking in rigid procedures and policies that typically favor strong political or economic interests. The original **higher-law tradition** is represented by the U.S. Constitution and the National Municipal League's Model State Constitution. It is embodied in brief documents that put forward basic and enduring framework principles and processes of government and recognizes that public policy choices are the proper responsibility of legislatures. Of course, no constitutional formula can be suitable for all the states because they differ too much in history, society, economics, and political culture. The best constitutions strike a balance between the need for stability and the requirement for enough flexibility to deal with emerging problems. Today the higher-law tradition is once again in favor in those states whose constitutions have become briefer, more readable, and simple enough for the average citizen to understand. In others, however, continued conflicts between special interests are often resolved through constitutional change.

The Essential State Constitution

The Model State Constitution has twelve basic articles, which are embodied to a greater or lesser extent in the various state constitutions today. The following subsections provide brief descriptions of each article and the ways in which its contents are changing.

Bill of Rights Individual rights and liberties were first protected in state constitutions. They closely resemble, and in some cases are identical to, those delineated in the first eight amendments to the U.S. Constitution. For example, all state constitutions protect citizens from deprivation of life, liberty, and property without due process of law. Originally, the national Bill of Rights protected citizens only from actions by the U.S. government. State constitutions and courts were, arguably, the principal guardians of civil liberties until the Supreme Court's interpretation of the Fourteenth Amendment extended the protective umbrella of the national courts over the states in 1925.[27] U.S. Supreme Court rulings also applied the U.S. Bill of Rights to the states, especially during the Warren Court beginning in 1953. Some states had failed to uphold their trust, particularly those that perpetuated the unequal treatment of women and minorities.

In the 1980s, however, activist states began to reassert guarantees of individual rights under state constitutions. At a minimum, all state constitutions must protect and guarantee those rights found in the U.S. Bill of Rights. But state constitutional provisions may guarantee additional or more extensive rights to citizens. Seventeen states now have equal rights amendments that guarantee sexual equality and prohibit sex-based discrimination. The U.S. Constitution does not guarantee a right of privacy, but ten states do guarantee it. And thirteen states give constitutional rights to crime victims. Some constitutional provisions border on the exotic. Californians enjoy the right to fish, residents of New Hampshire hold the right to revolution, and clean air and pure water are rights guaranteed to all Pennsylvanians. To deter animal rights activists, North Dakotans added—by an overwhelming vote in 2000—a statement that hunting, fishing, and trapping are "a valued part of our heritage" that must "be forever preserved for the people." The good citizens of Rhode Island "shall continue to enjoy and freely exercise all the . . . privileges of the shore . . . (including) the gathering of seaweed (and) leaving the shore to swim in the sea."

The major reason for the rebirth of state activism in protecting civil liberties and rights has been the conservatism of the U.S. Supreme Court since the 1970s. One commentator accused the Supreme Court of having abdicated its role as "keeper of the nation's conscience."[28] The states' power to write and interpret their constitutions differently from the U.S. Constitution's provisions in the area of protecting civil rights and liberties has been upheld by the Supreme Court, as long as the state provisions have "adequate and independent" grounds.[29] Increasingly, civil rights and liberties cases are being filed by plaintiffs in state rather than federal courts, based on state bill of rights protections. (See Table 3.2 for selected excerpts from state bills of rights.)

Power of the State This very brief article states simply that the powers enumerated in the constitution are not the only ones held by the state—that, indeed, the state has all powers not denied to it by the state or national constitutions.

Suffrage and Elections This article provides for the legal registration of voters and for election procedures. Recent extensions of voting rights and alterations in election procedures have been made in response to U.S. Supreme Court decisions and to national constitutional and statutory changes. Generally, states have improved election administration; liberalized registration, voting, and office-holding requirements; and shortened residency requirements. Some states have amended this article to provide for partial public financing of election campaigns; others have adopted provisions designed to count ballots more accurately.

The Legislative Branch This article sets forth the powers, procedures, and organizing principles of the legislature. In a pair of decisions in the 1960s, the U.S. Supreme Court ordered that state legislatures be apportioned on the basis of one

TABLE 3.2   **Excerpts from State Bills of Rights**
Alabama: "The legislature may hereafter, by general law, provide for an indemnification program to peanut farmers for losses incurred as a result of Aspergillus flavus and freeze damage in peanuts."
Alaska: "Public schooling shall always be conducted in English."
Illinois: "The equal protection of the laws shall not be denied or abridged on account of sex by the State or its units of local government."
Montana: "Human dignity is inviolable."
New York: "Every citizen may freely speak, write, and publish his sentiments on all subjects. . . ."
North Carolina: "Secret political societies shall not be tolerated."
Pennsylvania: "The people have a right to clean air, pure water, and to the preservation of the natural, scenic, historic and esthetic values of the environment. Pennsylvania's public natural resources are the common history of all the people, including generations yet to come. . . ."
Rhode Island: "The power of the state and its municipalities to regulate and control the use of land and waters in the furtherance of the preservation, regeneration, and restoration of the natural environment, and . . . of the rights of the people to enjoy and freely exercise the rights of fishery and the privileges of the shore . . . shall be liberally construed, and shall not be deemed a public use of private property."

person, one vote. That is, legislators must represent approximately the same number of constituents—House members the same as other House members and senators the same as other senators. District lines must be redrawn every ten years (most recently in 2002), after the national census has revealed population changes. Nineteen states have placed term limits on their elected officials in this article.

On the basis of this article, states have taken numerous actions to approach greater conformity with the Model State Constitution, including increasing the length and frequency of legislative sessions and streamlining rules and procedures. Instead of stipulating specific dollar amounts for legislators' pay and fringe benefits (which are soon rendered inappropriate by inflation), most state constitutions now establish a procedure to determine and occasionally adjust the compensation of legislators.

For many years, the Model State Constitution recommended a unicameral legislature as a means to overcome complexity, delay, and confusion. In its most recent revision, the National Municipal League tacitly recognized the refusal of the states to follow this suggestion (only Nebraska has a single-house general assembly, as discussed in the nearby *Debating Politics* box) by providing recommendations appropriate for a bicameral body.

The Executive Branch The powers and organization of the executive branch, which are outlined in this article, have seen many notable modifications. Essentially, executive power continues to be centralized in the office of the governor. Governors have won longer terms and the right to run for re-election. Line item vetoes, shorter ballots, the authority to make appointments within the executive branch, and the ability to reorganize the state bureaucracy have also increased gubernatorial powers (see Chapter 8). Several states have opted for team election of the governor and lieutenant governor.

The Judicial Branch All states have substantially revised not only their courts' organization and procedures but also the election of judges. A large majority of the states have also unified their court systems under a single authority, usually the state supreme court. Court procedures have been modernized. Many states now select judges through a merit plan rather than by gubernatorial appointment, legislative election, or popular election (see Chapter 10). The states have also established means to investigate charges against judges and to recommend discipline or removal from the bench when necessary.

Finance This article consists of provisions relating to taxation, debt, and expenditures for state and local government. A wave of tax and expenditure limitations swept across the states during the late 1970s and 1980s, and in many states tax relief has been granted to senior citizens, veterans, and disabled people.

Local Government Here, the authority of municipalities, counties, and other local governments is recognized. Most states have increased local authority through home rule provisions, which give localities more discretion in providing services. Local taxing authority has been extended. In addition, mechanisms for

DEBATING
POLITICS

The Unicameral Legislature

Forty-nine states have bicameral legislatures, with upper and lower houses and election of representatives through ballots that identify the candidates' political party. But a bold—even radical—constitutional amendment was adopted by the voters of Nebraska in 1934. Nebraska's unicameral, nonpartisan legislature stands alone among the states' ongoing experiments in democracy. First recommended by a legislative joint committee in 1915, the unicameral design was defeated four times before its adoption by a margin of 286,000 to 193,152 in a popular initiative to amend the state constitution. It is allowable under the U.S. Constitution, Article IV, which permits each state to determine its own government structure.

Why Nebraska? Apparently several events were at least partly responsible for what Nebraskans have come to call "Unicam." For one thing, it was on the same statewide ballot with two other popular initiatives: repeal of Prohibition and approval of pari-mutuel horse racing. In addition, the bicameral body had been suffering increasing criticism for its apparent inability to conduct the state's business efficiently and effectively. But the key factor was the unrelenting preaching of the evils of bicameralism and the virtues of unicameralism by influential and popular U.S. Senator George W. Norris. Norris "wore out two sets of tires and two windshields" driving around on Nebraska's dusty back roads to make the case for Unicam.

Norris and other supporters argued that unicameralism has several virtues. It would eliminate conference committees, which Norris considered not only too secretive and inefficient but also apt to develop laws that nobody really wanted. By facilitating compromise between the house and the senate, Norris explained, these committees encourage the two houses to pass the buck to one another, each

hoping the other would deal with the tough or complicated issues. In short, the Unicam would be more efficient because legislation would be enacted more quickly and less expensively. The Unicam would be small (it numbers forty-nine representatives, the smallest legislature among the states). And because the Unicam is nonpartisan, representatives would be likely to focus more on the important business of the state than on national issues of partisan significance.

Critics, including the press, called the proposal dangerous and "un-American." They believed it would be an embarrassing failure. Supporters were confident that Unicam would serve as a model for the other states to follow. Both were wrong. From most reports, Unicam gets high marks for efficiency, simplicity, and effectiveness. And it remains popular except for its nonpartisan feature. The major complaint is that nonpartisanship depresses voter interest and turnout in elections because voters do not have party identification as a voting cue.

As for other states that have entertained the notion of a unicameral legislature, bills have been introduced, amended, and then pigeonholed. Predictably, legislators are loath to vote themselves out of a job. If the unicameral model is to be adopted outside Nebraska, a state authorizing a constitutional initiative that bypasses the legislature is the best bet.

Should your state (or, if you are a Cornhusker—a Nebraskan—, other states) adopt a unicameral legislature? Why or why not? What groups would you expect to favor change? Obviously, the present legislature is likely to be opposed to this change. What other groups might be expected to oppose it?

SOURCES: www.governor.state.mn.us/unicameral.html; Pat Wunnicke, "Fifty Years Without a Conference Committee: Nebraska's Unicameral Legislature," *State Legislatures* 13 (October 1987): 20–23; Jack Rodgers, Robert Sittig, and Susan Welch, "The Legislature," in Robert Miewald, ed., *Nebraska Government and Politics* (Lincoln: University of Nebraska Press, 1984), pp. 57–86.

improved intergovernmental cooperation, such as consolidated city and county governments and regional districts to provide services, have been created.

Public Education On the basis of this article, the states establish and maintain free public schools for all children. Higher-education institutions, including technical schools, colleges, and universities, are commonly established in this section.

Civil Service The Model State Constitution sets forth a *merit system* of personnel administration for state government, under which civil servants are to be hired, promoted, paid, evaluated, and retained on the basis of competence, fitness, and performance instead of political party affiliation or other such criteria.

Intergovernmental Relations As recommended by the Model State Constitution, some states stipulate specific devices for cooperation among various state entities, among local jurisdictions, or between a state and its localities. They may detail methods for sharing in the provision of certain services, or they may list cost-sharing mechanisms such as local option sales taxes.

Constitutional Revision In this article, the methods for revising, amending, and replacing the constitution are described. Generally, the trend has been to make it easier for the voters, the legislature, or both to change the constitution.

Constitutions Today

In general, state constitutions today conform more closely to the higher-law tradition and the Model State Constitution than did those of the past. They are shorter, more concise, and simpler, and they contain fewer errors, anachronisms, and contradictions. They give the state legislatures more responsibility for determining public policy through statute, rather than through constitutional amendment. The two newest states, Alaska and Hawaii, have constitutional documents that follow the Model State Constitution quite closely.

However, much work remains to be done. Some state constitutions are still riddled with unnecessary detail because new amendments have continually been added to the old documents, and obsolete provisions and other relics can still be found. But more important deficiencies demand the attention of legislators and citizens in states whose constitutions inhibit the operations of state government and obstruct the ability to adapt to change. In some jurisdictions, the governor's formal powers remain weak; a plethora of boards and commissions makes any thought of executive management and coordination a pipe dream; local governments chafe under the tight leash of state authority; and many other problems persist. Constitutional revision must be an ongoing process if the states are to cope with the changing contours of American society and stay in the vanguard of innovation and change. The opening anecdote on the fight for constitutional change in Alabama illustrates this point.

METHODS FOR CONSTITUTIONAL CHANGE

There are only two methods for altering the U.S. Constitution. The first is the constitutional convention, wherein delegates representing the states assemble to consider modifying or replacing the Constitution. Despite periodic calls for a national constitutional convention, only one has taken place—in Philadelphia, more than 200 years ago. Two-thirds of the states must agree to call a convention; three-fourths are required to ratify any changes in the Constitution.

The second means of amending the U.S. Constitution is through congressional initiative, wherein Congress, by a two-thirds vote of both houses, agrees to send one or more proposed changes to the states. Again, three-fourths of the states must ratify the proposals.

Since 1787, more than 1,000 amendments have been submitted to the states by Congress. Only twenty-seven have been approved (the most recent one, in 1992, limits the ability of members of Congress to increase their pay), and the first ten of these were appended to the Constitution as a condition by several states for ratification. Note that neither method for amending the U.S. Constitution requires popular participation by voters, in sharp contrast to the citizen participation requirements for state constitutional change, as we shall see in the next section.

Informal Constitutional Change

interpretation

An informal means of revising constitutions whereby members of the executive, legislative, or judicial branch apply constitutional principles and law to everyday affairs.

One informal and four formal methods for amending state constitutions exist. The informal route is **interpretation** of constitutional meaning by the state legislature, executive branch, courts, or attorneys general, or through usage and custom. Governors issue executive orders; courts and attorneys general produce advisory opinions on meanings of specific provisions; state agencies make decisions that affect policy. But the force of habit can be a powerful influence, specific constitutional provisions notwithstanding. It is a good bet that one or more antiquated or unrealistic constitutional provisions are ignored in every state. A common example is the requirement that all bills be read, in their entirety, three times in each house for enactment. Another is the list of requirements for holding political office, such as a belief in God.

judicial review

The power of the U.S. Supreme Court or state supreme courts to review and declare invalid or unconstitutional not only actions of the executive and legislative branches but also decisions of lower courts.

State supreme courts play the most direct role in changing constitutions through interpretation. In large measure, a constitution is what the judges say it is in their decisions from the bench. Judicial interpretation of constitutions may be based on various standards, including strict attention to the express language of the document and to the original intent of the Framers or authors of amendments, deference to legislative enactments or executive actions, precedent, policy considerations, and individual rights. The power of the state supreme courts to review executive actions, legislative actions, and decisions of lower courts is known as **judicial review.** This power evolved in the states much as it did on the national level—through the courts' own insistence that they hold this authority. During recent years, as the U.S. Supreme Court has become more conservative and less activist in its interpretations of the law, some state courts have moved in the opposite direction and earned reputations as judicial activists. By ruling in 2004 that gay couples have full marriage rights under the constitution, Massachusetts' Supreme Judicial Court confirmed its status as an activist court.

We have already noted that state supreme courts have the authority to interpret and apply state guarantees of civil rights and liberties more broadly than the U.S. Supreme Court's interpretation of the Bill of Rights in the U.S. Constitution. In 2003, for instance, the New Hampshire Supreme Court extended the right to privacy to household garbage, even when it is placed at the curb for collection. The U.S. Supreme Court does not review state court decisions that are clearly and properly based on state constitutional provisions.[30] In practice, however, state supreme courts are often guided by constitutional rulings of the U.S. Supreme Court and high courts in other states. Because courts apply similar constitutional language to many common issues, it is natural for them to share their experiences in legal problem solving.[31] Of course, the national courts are supreme under the U.S. Constitution and will strike down any serious constitutional contradictions between the nation and the states, but for about two decades now, the U.S. Supreme Court has shown "a studied deference to the work of the state judiciaries."[32]

Formal Constitutional Change

ratification

The formal approval of a constitution or constitutional amendment by a majority of the voters of a state.

The four formal procedures for constitutional change are legislative proposal, initiative, constitutional convention, and constitutional commission. All involve two basic steps: initiation and **ratification.** The state legislature, or in some cases the voters, propose (initiate) a constitutional change. Then the proposed amendment is submitted to the voters for approval (ratification).

legislative proposal

The most common means of amending a state constitution, wherein the legislature proposes a revision, usually by a two-thirds majority.

Legislative Proposal Historically, **legislative proposal** is the most common road to revision. More than 90 percent of all changes in state constitutions have come through this method, which is permitted in all fifty states (see Table 3.3).

The specifics of legislative proposal techniques vary, but most states require either two-thirds or three-fifths of the members of each house to approve a proposal before it is sent to the voters for ratification. Twelve states require two consecutive legislative sessions to consider and pass a proposed amendment. The procedure can become quite complicated. For instance, South Carolina's legislative proposal must be passed by two-thirds of the members of each house; then it is sent to the people during the next general election. If a majority of voters approve, the proposal returns to the next legislative session, in which a majority of legislators have to concur.

Almost all states accept a simple majority for voter ratification of a proposed revision. In New Hampshire, however, two-thirds of the voters must approve the proposal. And Tennessee requires approval by a majority of the number of citizens who cast a vote for governor.

Legislative proposal is probably best suited to revisions that are relatively narrow in scope. However, some legislatures, such as South Carolina's, have presented a series of proposals to the voters over the years and thereby have

| TABLE 3.3 | **State Constitutional Changes and Methods of Initiation, Selected Years** |

	METHOD	1982–1983	1990–1991	2002–2003
TOTAL PROPOSALS	All methods	345	266	175
	Legislative proposal	330	197	154
	Initiative	15	29	21
	Constitutional convention	0	0	0
	Constitutional commission	0	0	0
TOTAL ADOPTED	All methods	258	145	118
	Legislative proposal	255	134	109
	Initiative	3	11	9
	Constitutional convention	0	0	0
	Constitutional commission	0	0	0
PERCENT ADOPTED	All methods	75%	63%	67%
	Legislative proposal	77	67	71
	Initiative	20	38	43
	Constitutional convention	–	–	0
	Constitutional commission	–	–	89

SOURCE: "State Constitutional Changes and Methods of Initiation," from *The Book of the States 2003*. Reprinted by permission of The Council of State Governments.

significantly revised the constitution. The disadvantage to such a strategy is that it tends to result in a patchwork of amendments that can conflict with or overlap other constitutional provisions. This circumstance spawns additional revisions, which in turn lead to increased litigation in the state supreme court.

Initiative Eighteen states permit their citizens to initiate and ratify changes in the constitution and thus bypass the legislature (see Table 3.4). Only five of these initiative states are east of the Mississippi River, thus reflecting the fact that the initiative was a product of the Progressive reform movement of the early 1900s. Most of the territories admitted as states during this period chose to permit the **initiative** (known as constitutional initiative in some states). Twenty-three states also authorize the initiative for enacting statutory change (see Chapter 4).

initiative

A proposed law or constitutional amendment that is placed on the ballot by citizen petition.

The initiative is used much less often than legislative proposal in amending constitutions (see Table 3.3), although it has been attempted more frequently during the past two decades. The later adopters, including Florida, Illinois, and Mississippi, are more restrictive in permitting initiatives than early adopters, such as Oregon, California, or Colorado. It is also less successful in terms of the percentage of amendments that are adopted by the voters. On average, about 45 percent of all initiatives have been written into state constitutions in recent years.

| TABLE 3.4 | States Authorizing Constitutional Amendment by Citizen Initiative | |

STATE	YEAR ADOPTED	NUMBER OF SIGNATURES REQUIRED ON INITIATIVE PETITION
Arizona	1910	15% of total votes cast for all candidates for governor at last election.
Arkansas	1909	10% of voters for governor at last election.
California	1911	8% of total voters for all candidates for governor at last election.
Colorado	1910	5% of total legal votes for all candidates for secretary of state at last general election.
Florida	1972	8% of total votes cast in the state in the last election for presidential electors.
Illinois*	1970	8% of total votes cast for candidates for governor at last election.
Massachusetts†	1918	3% of total votes cast for governor at preceding biennial state election (not less than 25,000 qualified voters).
Michigan	1908	10% of total votes for all candidates at the gubernatorial election.
Mississippi	1992	12% of total votes for all candidates for governor at last election.
Missouri	1906	8% of legal voters for all candidates for governor at last election.
Montana	1904	10% of qualified electors, the number of qualified electors to be determined by the number of votes cast for governor in the preceding general election.
Nebraska	1912	10% of total votes for governor at last election.
Nevada	1904	10% of voters who voted in entire state in last general election.
North Dakota	1914	4% of population of the state.
Ohio	1912	10% of total number of electors who voted for governor in last election.
Oklahoma	1907	15% of legal voters for state office receiving highest number of voters at last general state election.
Oregon	1902	8% of total votes for all candidates for governor in last election, when the governor was elected for a four-year term.
South Dakota	1898	10% of total votes for governor in last election.

*Only Article IV, the Legislature, may be amended by initiative petition.

†Before being submitted to the electorate for ratification, initiative measures must be approved at two sessions of a successively elected legislature by not less than one-fourth of all members elected, sitting in joint session.

SOURCE: "States Authorizing Constitutional Amendment by Citizen Initiative," from *The Book of the States 2003*. Reprinted by permission of The Council of State Governments.

The number of signatures needed for the initiative petition to be valid varies widely: Arizona requires 15 percent of total votes cast in the last gubernatorial election, whereas Massachusetts requires 3 percent (see Table 3.4).[33] Eight states specify that the petition signatures must be collected widely throughout the state as a means of ensuring that an initiative that favors one region does not become embodied in the constitution.

In general, a petition for constitutional amendment is sent to the office of the secretary of state for verification that the required number of registered voters have signed their names. Then the question is placed on a statewide ballot in

direct initiative

A procedure by which the voters of a jurisdiction propose the passage of constitutional amendments, state laws, or local ordinances, bypassing the legislative body.

indirect initiative

Similar to the direct initiative, except that the voter-initiated proposal must be submitted to the legislature before going on the ballot for voter approval.

the next general election. Ratification requires a majority vote of the people in most states.

It is usually easy enough to collect the required number of signatures to place a proposed amendment on statewide ballot. But actual passage of the initiative is much more difficult, once it receives a close public examination and opposing interests proclaim their objections. If the legislature is circumvented altogether and propositions are placed directly on the general-election ballot by citizens, the procedure is called a **direct initiative.** If a legislature participates by voting on the citizen proposal, as in Massachusetts and Mississippi, the procedure is known as an **indirect initiative.** (In Florida, the state supreme court must review every amendment.)

The initiative is useful in making limited changes to the state constitution and, in recent years, has addressed some controversial issues that state legislatures refuse to confront. Colorado voters, for example, adopted an initiative to prohibit the use of public funds for abortions. A recent Massachusetts initiative severely limited bilingual public education. Other controversial proposals have included those for legalized gambling, gun control, school vouchers, and medical use of marijuana.

A major advantage of the initiative is that it permits the people's will to counter a despotic or inertia-ridden legislature. For instance, Illinois voters in 1978 reduced the size of the House of Representatives from 177 to 118 after the legislature voted itself a huge pay raise during a period of economic hardship. Another advantage is that this method appears to enhance citizen interest and participation in government.

However, the initiative can also be abused by special interests with selfish motives who seek to gain privileges, and under crisis conditions it can result in ill-conceived, radical changes to the constitution. Indeed, the initiative can result in just the kind of excessive detail and poorly drafted verbiage that is so widely condemned by constitutional scholars and reformers.[34] It can also make doing routine business extremely difficult. In California, for example, an initiative prevents local governments from hiking taxes without two-thirds approval of the electorate.

constitutional convention

An assembly of delegates chosen by popular election or appointed by the legislature or the governor to revise an existing constitution or to create a new one.

Constitutional Convention Legislative proposals and initiatives are quite specific about the type of constitutional change that is sought. Only those questions that actually appear on the ballot are considered. In contrast, a **constitutional convention** assembles delegates who suggest revisions or even an entirely new document, then submit the proposed changes to the voters for ratification. The convention is especially well suited to consider far-reaching constitutional changes or a new fundamental law.

The convention is the oldest method for constitutional change in the states and is available in all fifty of them. The process begins when the electorate or the legislature decides to call for a constitutional convention. In fourteen states, the question of calling a convention must be regularly voted on by the electorate, but most convention calls have been routinely rejected since the 1980s. Alaskans and Iowans hold an automatic convention call every ten years; in New York and

Maryland, the convention issue is submitted to the voters every twenty years. Except in Delaware, proposals emerging from the convention must be ratified by the voters before they become part of the constitution.

Delegates to a convention are usually elected on a nonpartisan ballot by the voters from state house or senate districts. Conventions are usually dominated by professionals, educators, and businesspeople. This delegate composition is not surprising because convention calls are strongly supported by higher socioeconomic groups in urban areas.

The characteristics of a delegate pool are important for several reasons. First, the delegates need knowledge of and experience in state government and politics if they are to contribute meaningfully to the debate and drafting of proposed amendments. It is usually not too difficult to attract qualified people for service; the experience is important, unique, and a privilege, and it is not as time consuming as running for and serving in the legislature. Second, the delegates should represent a cross section of the state's population as much as possible. If the delegate pool does not reflect gender, racial, regional, ethnic, and other salient characteristics of the population, the fruit of its labor may lack legitimacy in the eyes of substantial numbers of voters. Finally, partisanship should be avoided where possible. Partisan differences can wreck consensus on major issues and destroy the prospects for voter ratification of amendments suggested by the convention.

All conventions experience some divisions, partisan or not. The basic conflict is frequently between those who favor comprehensive constitutional change—reformers—and supporters and protectors of the status quo. Splits can also develop between urban and rural interests, among regional interests, and between blacks and whites.

Voter approval of convention proposals is problematic. If partisan, racial, regional, or other disagreements dominate media reports on the convention, voter approval is difficult to obtain. People naturally tend to be skeptical of suggestions for sweeping changes in the basic structures and procedures of government. If they have not been regularly involved with and informed of the progress of the convention, they may be reluctant to give their approval to the recommendations.

Delegates usually understand these dynamics and are sensitive to how their proposed changes may affect the general public. For example, they must carefully consider how to present the proposed amendments for ratification. There are two choices: the all-or-nothing strategy of consolidating all changes in a single vote, and the piecemeal strategy, which presents each proposal as a separate ballot decision. In recent years, voters have tended to reject inclusive packages. Each suggested change is certain to offend some minority, and when all the offended minorities coalesce, they may well constitute a majority of voters.[35]

constitutional commission

A meeting of delegates appointed by the governor or legislature to study constitutional problems and propose solutions.

Constitutional Commission Often called a *study commission,* the **constitutional commission** is usually established to study the existing document and to recommend changes to the legislature or to the voters. Little or no citizen participation is associated with this method of constitutional change. Depending on the mandate, the constitutional commission may examine the entire constitution with a view toward replacement or change, focus on one or more specific articles or provisions, or be given the freedom to decide its own scope of activity. Commission recommendations to the legislature and/or governor are only advisory, thus helping to account for this method's popularity with elected officials, who sometimes prefer to study a problem to death rather than face it head on. Some or all of the recommendations may be submitted to the voters; others may be completely ignored. Only in Florida can a commission send its proposals directly to the voters.[36]

A constitutional commission operated in 1998 in Florida. Utah's revision commission functions permanently. Service on a constitutional commission can be a thankless task because legislators sometimes ignore the commission's recommendations or employ them as a symbolic device for relieving political pressure. For example, Kentucky's 1987–1988 Revision Commission recommended seventy-seven changes to the constitution, but only one was referred by the legislature to the voters as a proposed amendment.[37] When used properly, however, commissions can furnish high-quality research both inexpensively and relatively quickly.

STATE RESPONSIVENESS AND CONSTITUTIONAL REFORM

Each state's constitution is designed specifically to meet the needs of that state. The rich political culture, history, economics, values, and ideals of the state community are reflected in its constitutional language. Through their constitutions, the states experiment with different governmental institutions and processes. As passionate patriot Thomas Paine observed more than two hundred years ago, "It is in the interest of all the states, that the constitution of each should be somewhat diversified from each other. We are a people founded upon experiments, and . . . have the happy opportunity of trying variety in order to discover the best."[38]

State constitutions were the original guardians of individual rights and liberties, with their own bills of rights preceding those of the U.S. Constitution by many years. They are again assuming their rightful position in American government today as independent state constitutional law develops further. Yet few tasks in government are more difficult than modernizing a constitution. The process requires "sustained, dedicated, organized effort; vigorous, aggressive and imaginative leadership; bipartisan political support; education of the electorate on the issues; judicious selection of the means; and seemingly endless patience."[39] In the words of constitutional scholar W. Brooke Graves, "The advocate of constitutional reform in an American state should be endowed with the patience of Job and the sense of time of a geologist."[40] The solemn duty of framing the original state constitutions, which was so effectively discharged by our predecessors, must be matched by the continuous oversight of present and future generations. Changes are necessary to adjust state governments to the vagaries of the future.

The constitutional changes enacted in the states since the 1955 Kestnbaum Commission report have generally resulted in documents in the higher-law tradition, documents that "are shorter, more clearly written, modernized, less encumbered with restrictions, more basic in content and have more reasonable amending processes. They also establish improved governmental structures and contain substantive provisions assuring greater openness, accountability and equity."[41] The states have made a great deal of progress in modernizing their governments. As state constitutional scholar Richard Leach has put it, "There are not many constitutional horrors left."[42]

Old-style constitutions were "the drag anchors of state programs, and permanent cloaks for the protection of special interests and points of view."[43] These constitutions held back progress and delayed the states' resurgence as lead players in the drama of U.S. federalism. Recent constitutional amendments have responded to, and indeed caused, profound changes in state government and politics. Since the genesis of modern reform in the mid-1960s, some forty states have adopted new constitutions or substantially amended existing ones. Problems persist, and future constitutional tinkering and replacements will be necessary. But in most states, the constitutional landscape is much cleaner and more functional than it was a generation ago.

CHAPTER RECAP

- Constitutions are the fundamental law of a state, superior to statutory law.
- State constitutions evolved from the original colonial charters. From an original basis of legislative supremacy, they have gradually increased executive power.
- Some constitutions continue to suffer from excessive length and substantive problems.
- Constitutional reform has modernized the documents and made them conform more closely to present challenges of governance.
- Methods for changing constitutions include interpretation and judicial review, legislative proposal, initiative, constitutional convention, and constitutional commission.

Key Terms

fundamental law *(p. 56)*
legislative supremacy *(p. 59)*
Model State Constitution *(p. 65)*
positive-law tradition *(p. 65)*
higher-law tradition *(p. 65)*
interpretation *(p. 71)*
judicial review *(p. 71)*

ratification *(p. 72)*
legislative proposal *(p. 72)*
initiative *(p. 73)*
direct initiative *(p. 75)*
indirect initiative *(p. 75)*
constitutional convention *(p. 75)*
constitutional commission *(p. 76)*

Surfing the Web

For full texts of state statutes and constitutions see individual state web sites (for example, **www.state.fl.us**).

Most state constitutions can also be accessed through Findlaw at **www.findlaw.com/11stategov/indexconst.html**, **www.law.cornell.edu/statutes**, or **www.constitutions.org.**

The Alaska constitution draws heavily on the Model State Constitution. It is located in the State of Alaska Documents Library at **www.law.state.ak.us.**

For everything you want to know about Unicam in Nebraska, go to **www.unicam.state.ne.us.**

A useful site is the Center for State Constitutional Studies at **www.camlaw.rutgers.edu/statecon/.**

4

CITIZEN PARTICIPATION AND ELECTIONS

Participation
Why and How People Participate • Nonparticipation • The Struggle for the Right to Vote • Voting Patterns

Elections
Primaries • Runoff Elections • General Elections • Recent State Elections • Nonpartisan Elections

Election-Day Lawmaking
The Initiative • The Recall • The Special Case of California

Citizen Access to Government
Open Meeting Laws • Administrative Procedure Acts • Advisory Committees • E-Government

Volunteerism as Participation

The Effects of Citizen Participation

Throughout the country, communities are casting about for ways to increase citizen participation in governance. Although some of their efforts catch fire, many simply fizzle because they do not effectively engage the public. The city of Philadelphia offers an example of a successful venture in rekindling the citizen–government link. An experiment in political conversation, called Citizen Voices, was launched by the local newspaper, *The Philadelphia Inquirer.* Through a series of dialogues, citizens identified and discussed issues that mattered to them. In Philadelphia, five issues repeatedly rose to the surface: schools and education, quality of life, jobs, government reform, and crime. Eventually, the dialogues were widened to include candidates for local public office. Instead of delivering canned speeches, the candidates found themselves engaged in unscripted conversations with citizens. But the project did not end when the campaign was over. After the election, participants in the project got together and created an agenda for the city of Philadelphia—a to-do list that was presented to the new mayor and city council when they took office.[1] In the City of Brotherly Love, it was *citizens* who were setting the agenda.

PARTICIPATION

participation

Actions through which ordinary members of a political system attempt to influence outcomes.

Democracy assumes citizen **participation**—taking action to influence government. Persistent evidence indicates that citizens are not much interested in participation. We have grown accustomed to reports of low voter turnout and public hearings that few attend. In his influential book, *Bowling Alone,* political scientist Robert Putnam documented this gradual disengagement of people from all sorts of community activities and organizations.[2] On the surface, government works just fine with limited participation: The interests of the active become translated into public policy, and those who are inactive can be safely ignored because they do not vote. If, however, some traditional nonvoters (such as low-income, less educated citizens) went to the polls, then vote-seeking candidates would be forced to pay more attention to their interests, and public policy might be nudged in a different direction. In this light, it is important to understand both why many people do participate and why others do not. This chapter addresses individual citizen involvement in government; Chapter 5 takes up collective participation (that is, participation by political parties and interest groups).

Why and How People Participate

In a representative democracy, voting is the most common form of participation. For many citizens, it is a matter of civic responsibility. It is a fundamental facet of citizenship—after all, it is called "the right to vote." Citizens go to the polls to elect the officials who will govern them. But there are other methods of participation. Consider the citizen who is unhappy because the property taxes on her home have increased substantially from one year to the next. What options are available to her besides voting against incumbent officeholders at the next election? As shown in Figure 4.1, she can be either active or passive; her actions can be either constructive or destructive. Basically, she has four potential responses: loyalty, voice, exit, and neglect.[3]

According to this formulation, voting is an example of *loyalty,* a passive but constructive response to government action. Specifically, this response reflects the irate taxpayer's underlying support for her community despite her displeasure with specific tax policies. An active constructive response is *voice:* The aggrieved property owner could contact officials, work in the campaign of a candidate who promises to lower tax assessments, or (assuming that others in the community share her sentiments) participate in anti-tax groups and organize demonstrations.

| FIGURE 4.1 | **Possible Responses to Dissatisfaction in the Community** |

Each of these participatory options affects public policy decisions in a community. Citizens who choose the voice option frequently find themselves in the thick of things.

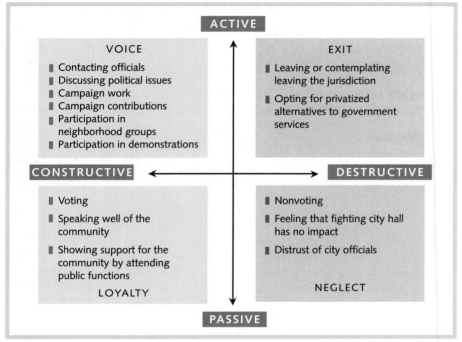

SOURCE: "The Organization of Political Space and Citizen Responses to Dissatisfaction in Urban Communities: An Integrated Model," by William E. Lyons and David Lowery, *Journal of Politics* 48, no. 2 (1986): 321–45, Figure 1. Reprinted by permission of Blackwell Publishing Ltd.

Destructive responses (those that undermine the citizen–government relationship) are similarly passive or active. If the citizen simply shrugs and concludes that she can't fight city hall, she is exhibiting a response termed *neglect*. She has nearly given up on the community and does not participate. A more active version of giving up is to *exit*—that is, to leave the community altogether (a response often referred to as voting with your feet). The unhappy citizen relocates in a community that is more in line with her tax preferences.

Every citizen confronts these participatory options. It is much healthier for the political system if citizens engage in the constructive responses, but some individuals are likely to conclude that constructive participation is of little value to them and opt for neglect or, in more extreme cases, exit.

Nonparticipation

What motivates the citizens who choose neglect as their best option? One explanation for nonparticipation in politics is socioeconomic status. Individuals with lower levels of income and education tend to participate less than wealthier, more educated individuals do.[4] Tied closely to income and education levels is occupational status. Unskilled workers and hourly wage earners do not participate in politics to the same degree that white-collar workers and professionals do. Individuals of lower socioeconomic status may not have the time, resources, or civic skills required to become actively involved in politics.

Other explanations for nonparticipation have included age (younger people have participated less than middle-aged individuals have), race (blacks have participated less than whites have), and gender (women have participated less than men have). Of these factors, however, only age continues to affect political activity levels. African American political participation actually surpasses that of whites when socioeconomic status is taken into consideration,[5] and the gender gap in the types and levels of political participation has disappeared.[6] In the 2000 elections, persons between eighteen and twenty-four years of age constituted only a small percentage of the voting public, but they accounted for a much larger percentage of the nonvoters. Alarmed by this trend, groups such as Kids Voting USA have developed programs to socialize children about political affairs.[7] The underlying assumption is that children who get into the habit of citizen participation at an early age will be more politically active as adults. Another factor that exerts an independent effect on participation is where one lives. Big-city dwellers (those who live in places with a population of 1 million or more) are less likely than people in small communities (less than 5,000 inhabitants) to participate in various civic activities, including contacting local officials, attending community meetings, and voting in local elections.[8]

The explanation for nonparticipation does not rest solely with the individual. Institutional features—the way the political system is designed—may suppress participation. For example, local governments that have instituted nonpartisan elections, in which candidates run without party affiliation, have removed an important mobilizing factor for voters. Voter turnout tends to be lower in these elections than in partisan contests. Some state governments still have not modernized their voter registration procedures to make the process quick and easy, thus discouraging potential registrants. City council meetings scheduled at 10:00 a.m. put a tremendous strain on workers who must take time off from their jobs if they want to attend; consequently, attendance is low. And local governments in which it is difficult for citizens to contact the appropriate official with a service request or complaint are not doing much to facilitate participation. Features like these play an often unrecognized role in dampening participation.

Nonparticipants typically have lower levels of interest in politics and tend to be weakly connected to their communities.[9] In many communities, the media have launched efforts to boost participation in civic life. Television stations convene forums and town meetings on the issues of the day, and local newspapers report the views of ordinary citizens on current events. Called public or civic journalism, the idea is to reconnect people with the democratic process and, in doing so, to make them active participants in public life. This is just one effort at restoring some of the **social capital** that Putnam found lacking in contemporary communities. In the language of Figure 4.1, greater social capital leads to more constructive forms of citizen participation.

social capital

A dense network of reciprocal social relations that promotes greater civic engagement.

The Struggle for the Right to Vote

State constitutions in the eighteenth and early nineteenth centuries entrusted only propertied white males with the vote. They did not encourage public involvement in government, and the eventual softening of restrictions on suffrage did not occur without a struggle. Restrictions based on property ownership and wealth were eventually dropped, but women, blacks, and Native Americans were still denied the right to vote.

In an effort to attract women to its rugged territory, Wyoming enfranchised women in 1869. The suffragists—women who were actively fighting for the right to vote—scored a victory when Colorado extended the vote to women in 1893. Gradually, other states began enfranchising women, and in 1920 the Nineteenth Amendment to the U.S. Constitution, forbidding states to deny the right to vote "on account of sex," was ratified.

Even after the Fifteenth Amendment (1870) extended the vote to blacks, some southern states clung defiantly to traditional ways that denied blacks and poor people their rights. Poll taxes and literacy tests prevented the poor and uneducated from voting. Southern Democrats designed the white primary to limit black political influence. In the one-party South, the Democratic primary elections, in which candidates for the general election were chosen, were the scene of the important contests. The general election amounted to little more than ratification of the party's choices because so few elections were contested by the Republicans. Thus, blacks were still barred from effective participation because they could not vote in the primaries. In *Smith* v. *Allwright* (1944), the U.S. Supreme Court ruled that since primaries were part of the machinery that chose officials, they were subject to the same nondiscriminatory standards as general elections, and the days of the white primary came to an end.

Although most states expanded the franchise, segregationists in some parts of the South continued to erect elaborate barriers to participation.[10] Even as the number of black voters increased steadily during the mid-twentieth century, substantial discrimination remained. The outlawing of the white primary forced racists to resort to more informal methods of keeping blacks from the polls—including physical intimidation. National enactments such as the Civil Rights Act of 1964 and the Twenty-fourth Amendment (1964), which made poll taxes unconstitutional, were important in helping African Americans gain access to the voting booth.

Voting Rights Act of 1965

The law that effectively enfranchised racial minorities by giving the national government the power to intercede in state and local electoral operations when necessary.

The **Voting Rights Act of 1965** finally broke the back of the segregationists' efforts. Under its provisions, federal poll watchers and registrars were dispatched to particular counties to investigate voter discrimination. To this day, counties covered under the Voting Rights Act (all of nine southern states and parts of seven other states) must submit to the U.S. Department of Justice any changes in election laws, such as new precinct lines or new polling places. Over time, judicial interpretations, congressional actions, and Justice Department rules have modified the Voting Rights Act. One of the most important modifications has been to substitute an effects test for the original intent test. In other words, if a governmental action has the effect of discouraging minority voting, whether intentionally or not, the action must be rejected. Civil rights activists welcomed this change because proving the intent of an action is much more difficult than simply demonstrating its effect.

Voting Patterns

Voter turnout is affected by several factors. First, it varies according to the type of election. A presidential race usually attracts a higher proportion of eligible voters than a state or local election does; therefore, turnout is higher when a presidential contest is on the ballot than in off-years, when many state races occur. In 2004, with a presidential race under way, turnout was approximately 60 percent. As Table 4.1 shows, 1970 was the last time that turnout in a nonpresidential election year exceeded 40 percent of the voting-age population. (What helps explain the before- and after-1970 trends? The voting age was lowered from twenty-one to eighteen years of age in 1971. Read the nearby *Debating Politics* box to learn about lowering the voting age even further.) Second, popular candidates running a close race seem to increase voter interest. When each candidate has a chance to win, voters sense that their vote will matter more than in a race with a sure winner. Third, not only partisan competition but party ideology affects voter turnout.[11] When parties take distinctive ideological stances in competitive elections, the incentive for party-identifiers to vote increases.

There are noteworthy differences among states in terms of the proportions of both voting-age population registered and voter turnout. Nationally, more than 76 percent of the voting-age population was registered to vote in 2000. But when we look at the figures for individual states, wide variations appear. Compare two states with similar voting-age populations: Nebraska, with 1.23 million, and Nevada, with 1.39 million. Eighty-eight percent of the voting-age population in Nebraska was registered; in Nevada, the comparable figure was 64.6 percent.[12] Registration matters because people who are registered tend to vote, and votes translate into political power. Thus, groups anxious to increase their electoral clout will launch registration drives among their membership. The recent efforts of groups such as the Council of American Islamic Relations to register Muslims are but one example.[13]

TABLE 4.1	**Voter Turnout in Off-Year Elections (as a percentage of voting-age population)**

YEAR	VOTER TURNOUT	YEAR	VOTER TURNOUT
1962	47.3%	1986	36.4%
1966	48.4	1990	36.5
1970	46.6	1994	38.8
1974	38.2	1998	36.4
1978	37.2	2002	39.0
1982	39.8		

SOURCE: U.S. Federal Election Commission, www.fec.gov/pages/2000turnout/reg&tto00.htm (April 22, 2004).

DEBATING POLITICS

Voting: It's Not Just for Old People

The company Urban Outfitters got itself into hot water with some folks when it started selling a T-shirt with the statement "Voting is for old people" printed on it. In fact, the Institute of Politics at Harvard contacted the retailer and asked its representatives to reconsider selling the shirt, arguing that it sent the wrong message. However, there is an element of truth in the statement. In 1972, the turnout of eighteen- to twenty-four-year-old voters was 52 percent; by 2000, it had dropped to 38 percent. These youthful voters once comprised 15 percent of the active electorate, but by 2000, they accounted for only 8 percent. Among older voters, turnout has remained relatively high.

Why is America's youth not voting at the same rate as other age groups? Some contend it is because political parties have failed to energize young voters; others argue that candidates and their messages have not had a youthful focus. Many believe that a step in the right direction would be to utilize youth-oriented media more effectively, such as MTV's Rock the Vote. Another suggestion is a more skillful use of cyberspace, which was former Vermont governor Howard Dean's tactic. He relied on the Internet to build his base of support among college students during his 2004 bid for the Democratic presidential nomination.

Perhaps the most controversial solution offered for this problem comes from California, where four legislators have proposed giving fourteen- to seventeen-year-olds the right to vote. Not a whole vote, but a partial one. Fourteen- and fifteen-year-olds would be given one-quarter of a vote; their sixteen- and seventeen-year-old counterparts would be allowed one-half of a vote. The idea is that if young people had a sort of electoral apprenticeship, it would raise their consciousness about the importance of voting. Before dismissing this as just another wacky idea, consider that parts of Germany and Austria already allow sixteen-year-olds to vote, and Great Britain is considering a similar proposal. The California proposal would amend the state's constitution and requires a two-thirds majority of both houses before it could be put on the ballot for voters to decide.

Some have embraced the idea as sensible, arguing that American youths are far more sophisticated than they used to be, with access to much more information. They would take their enfranchisement seriously and exercise a thoughtful vote. Youth rights groups are supportive, claiming that lowering the voting age would reduce some of the alienation felt by teens. After all, young people are affected by government's actions, why not let them have some say via the voting booth? However, not all supporters of the measure like the idea of fractional votes. They contend that if the vote is extended to younger people, it ought to be a full vote, not a partial one. Many are just plain opposed to the whole idea, seeing it as conferring a measure of adulthood on children who should be enjoying childhood. They say that it burdens children too soon with adult responsibilities and opens the door for other actions such as redefining criminal statutes that differentiate between youthful and adult offenders. What do you think: Would California's "Training Wheels for Citizenship" boost participation and make the Urban Outfitters T-shirt a collector's item?

SOURCES: Robert Weiner and Amy Rieth, "The Dwindling Youth Vote: Where Will It Be in 2004?" *Christian Science Monitor* (June 23, 2003), p. 9; "Voting Is for Old People," *Christian Science Monitor* (March 8, 2004), p. 8; Daniel B. Wood, "Should 14 Year Olds Vote? OK, How About a Quarter of a Vote?" *Christian Science Monitor* (March 12, 2004), pp. 1–2.

States can also be differentiated according to voter turnout rates (see Figure 4.2 for voter turnout levels in 2000). In 2004, the highest turnout rate was recorded in Minnesota, where 77 percent of the voting-age population voted. Arizona, with 42 percent voting, garnered the dubious distinction of being the state with the lowest voter turnout in 2004.[14] States with moralistic political cultures typically experience higher voter turnout than do states with traditionalistic political cultures. States with competitive political parties (as opposed to states where one party dominates) tend to have elections with a higher proportion of voters participating; each party needs to mobilize individuals who identify with it in order to win. Finally, states can affect turnout by the way in which they administer the registration and election processes.

Registering to vote is getting easier. All but two states permit voters to register by mail.[15] Passage of the National Voter Registration Act in 1993 means that individuals can register to vote when they apply for a driver's license, welfare benefits, or unemployment compensation, or when they register their automobile. Many states, such as Florida, have taken another step by allowing on-line voter registration; any computer terminal with an Internet connection can be a registration site. And some states have moved the closing date for registration

FIGURE 4.2 **State Voter Turnout, 2000**

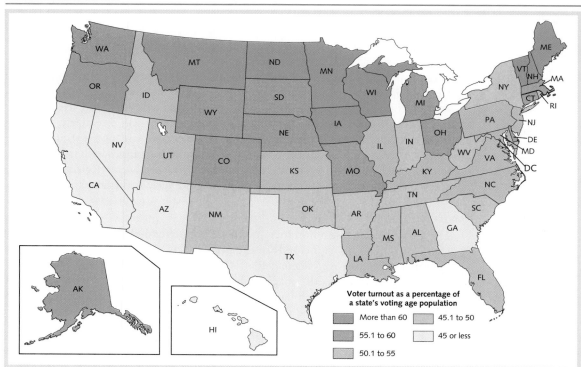

SOURCE: U.S. Federal Election Commission, "Voter Registration and Turnout 2000," www.fec.gov.

nearer to the actual date of the election, giving potential voters more time to register. This factor is important because campaigns tend to heighten the public's interest in the election. Most states now close their registration books fewer than thirty days before an election, and Idaho, Maine, Minnesota, New Hampshire, Wisconsin, and Wyoming allow registration on election day.[16] North Dakota is the only state in the nation that does not require voter registration.

Absentee balloting has also been made easier than it was in the past. Most states still require a voter applying for an absentee ballot to supply an acceptable reason, such as being away on business or at school, but some have lifted these restrictions and allow any voter to vote in absentia. Arizona, California, Colorado, Iowa, Nevada, Tennessee, and Texas are among the states that allow early voting. Voters can cast in-person absentee ballots before election day at satellite polling stations.[17] Sixteen states have statutes authorizing mail-ballot elections under certain conditions, such as special elections and nonpartisan elections.[18] Oregon conducted its 2000 general election almost entirely by mail. Analysis of the Beaver State's elections shows that vote-by-mail elections can increase the turnout rate by as much as 15 percent.[19] In short, the notion of election *day* is gradually giving way.

ELECTIONS

Elections are central to a representative democracy. Voters choose governors and legislators, and in most states, lieutenant governors, attorneys general, secretaries of state, and state treasurers; in some, they also choose the heads of the agriculture and education departments and the public utility commissioners. At the local level, the list of elected officials includes mayors and council members, county commissioners, county judges, sheriffs, tax assessors, and school board members. If state and local governments are to function effectively, elections must provide talented, capable leaders. But elections are not just about outcomes; they are also about the process itself. Florida's troubles with ballot design, voting machines, and recount rules in the 2000 presidential election underscored the need for elections to be administered fairly and transparently.

Primaries

For a party to choose a nominee to put on the general-election ballot, potential candidates must be winnowed. In the pre-Jacksonian era, party nominees were chosen by a legislative caucus—that is, a conference of the party's legislators. Caucuses gave way to the mechanism of state party conventions, which were similar to national presidential nomination conventions but without most of the spectacle; popularly elected delegates from across a state convened to select the party's nominees. Then the Progressive movement made an effort to open up the nomination process and make it more democratic. Political parties adopted the **primary system,** whereby voters directly choose from among several candidates to select the party's nominees for the general election. The use of primaries has effectively diminished the organizational power of political parties.

primary system
The electoral mechanism for selecting party nominees to compete in the general election.

Thirteen states still allow for party conventions in particular instances, such as nominations for lieutenant governor and attorney general (Michigan) and selection of nominees by third parties (Kansas). Connecticut, the last state to adopt primaries, operates a unique challenge system, whereby party nominees for various state offices are selected at a convention; but if a contest develops at the convention and a second candidate receives as much as 15 percent of the votes, the convention's nominee and the challenger square off in a primary.[20]

closed primary

An election in which only voters registered in the party are allowed to participate.

open primary

Voters decide which party's primary they will participate in.

Primaries can be divided into two types: closed and open. The only voters who can participate in a **closed primary** for a particular party are those who are registered in that party; an **open primary** does not require party membership. However, even this basic distinction lends itself to some variation. States differ, for example, in terms of the ease with which voters can change party affiliation and participate in the closed primary of the other party. In thirteen states, a voter is an enrolled member of one party (or is an Independent and may or may not be eligible to vote in either party's primary) and can change that affiliation only well in advance of the primary election.[21] New Mexico and Pennsylvania are two of the states that conduct completely closed primaries. Fifteen other closed-primary states (Iowa and Wyoming are examples) allow voters to change their party registration on election day, thus accommodating shifts in voters' loyalties.

Open primaries account for (and perhaps contribute to) fleeting partisan loyalties among the public. The key difference among states with open primaries is whether a voter is required to claim publicly which party's primary he is participating in. Eleven states, including Alabama and Indiana, require voters to request a specific party's ballot at the polling place. Ten other open-primary states make no such demand; voters secretly select the ballot of the party in which they wish to participate. Idaho and Wisconsin are examples of states in which primaries are truly open.

blanket primary

A primary in which a voter can choose from among candidates of both parties in a single election.

For many years, California and Washington operated a **blanket primary** in which voters could vote in the primaries of both parties in a single election. It allowed voters to cross over from one party's primary ballot to the other's primary ballot. A voter could select from among Democratic candidates for governor and among Republican candidates for the legislature, in effect participating in both primaries. Federal court rulings in 2000 (California) and 2003 (Washington) put an end to blanket primaries. California opted for a semi-closed primary; Washington for an open primary.

runoff election

A second election pitting the top two vote-getters from a first election in which no candidate received a majority of the votes cast.

Louisiana does something completely different: the Pelican State uses a single nonpartisan primary for its statewide and congressional races. Voters can choose from among any of the candidates, regardless of party affiliation. If a candidate receives a majority of votes in the first round of voting, she is elected to office; if she does not, the top two vote-getters face each other in a **runoff election.** The nonpartisan, or "unitary" primary is particularly disruptive to political party power. Washington flirted with a Louisiana-style primary as an alternative to its blanket primary, but Governor Gary Locke vetoed the nonpartisan primary bill passed by the legislature in 2004.[22] In New York City, Mayor Michael Bloomberg, arguing that local party machines had "a chokehold on ballot access," fought unsuccessfully to change the city's charter to allow nonpartisan primaries.[23] The chief opposition to his proposal came from the Big Apple's Democratic and Republican parties.

The distinction between closed and open primaries obviously affects party influence in elections, but does it have any impact on the outcome? In other words, if we had completely open primaries, would different candidates win? There are no definitive answers to these questions, but preliminary research on presidential primaries offers compelling evidence that primary structure does not seem to affect electoral outcomes dramatically.[24] One possible but not too likely upset would occur if voters of one party overwhelmingly voted in the other party's primary election, which happened in the 1986 Democratic gubernatorial primary in Alabama and resulted in an unexpected winner.

Runoff Elections

A runoff election is a second election that is held if none of the candidates for an office receives a majority of votes in the primary. Runoffs have become a controversial topic because of the contention that different people win than would win in a system without runoff elections.

Primary election runoffs have a distinct regional flavor to them. They are used by parties in nine states: Alabama, Arkansas, Florida, Georgia, Mississippi, North Carolina, Oklahoma, South Carolina, and Texas. (Kentucky and South Dakota use primary runoffs but only in certain instances.) In the past, these states were one-party (Democratic) states, so the greatest amount of competition for an office occurred in the Democratic Party's primaries, in which as many as ten candidates might enter the race. In these states, a candidate must receive more than 50 percent of the votes in the primary to become the party's nominee. (North Carolina recently lowered the winning primary percentage to 40 percent; Georgia has a cutoff of 45 percent for some offices.) When many candidates compete, it is quite probable that no one will be able to receive a majority of the votes, so the top two vote-getters face each other in a runoff election. This process ensures that the party's nominee is preferred by a majority of the primary voters. And in the old days, the Republican Party offered only token opposition in the general election, therefore winning the Democratic runoff was tantamount to being elected to office.

Theoretically, the rationale for the runoff primary is majority rule. But political circumstances have changed since several southern states adopted the runoff primary system in the 1920s, and the Democratic Party no longer dominates in the region. In fact, in many southern states, the Republican Party has overtaken the Democrats, a subject we will cover in Chapter 5. This raises an important question: Has the runoff primary outlived its usefulness? It is often difficult for a party to mobilize its voters for the second election, and voter participation in the runoff drops, on average, by one-third.[25]

General Elections

Primaries and runoffs culminate in the general election, through which candidates become officeholders. General elections typically pit candidates of the two major political parties against one another. The winner is the candidate who re-

plurality

The number of votes (though not necessarily a majority) cast for the winning candidate in an election with more than two candidates.

fusion

A state election provision that allows candidates to run on more than one party ticket.

coattail effect

The tendency of a winning (or losing) presidential candidate to carry state candidates of the same party into (or out of) office.

ceives more votes, that is, a majority of the votes cast. In a race where more than two candidates compete (which occurs when an Independent or a third-party candidate enters a race), the winner may not receive a majority but instead receives a **plurality.** A few states allow candidates to run under the label of more than one party, which is called **fusion.** In New York in 2002, for instance, Carl McCall was the candidate for governor of the Democratic and Working Families parties.

Political parties have traditionally been active in general elections, mobilizing voters in support of their candidates. Their role has diminished over time, however, because general-election campaigns have become more candidate centered and geared to the candidate's own organization.[26] One new twist in the past decade has been the emergence of legislative party caucuses as major factors in general elections. In large states with professionalized legislatures, the funds distributed to their party's nominees by legislative party caucuses run into the millions of dollars. For example, Vern Riffe, who was speaker of the Ohio house of representatives for twenty years, hosted an annual birthday party to raise campaign funds for house Democrats.[27] Attendance at the event came at a high price: $500 per ticket. With lobbyists and political action committees purchasing blocs of tickets, the speaker was able to raise a substantial campaign war chest for his party's candidates.

Most states schedule their statewide elections in off-years, that is, in years in which no presidential election is held. Only eleven states elected governors during the presidential election year of 2004; forty-one held their statewide races in other years. (The number sums to 52 because New Hampshire and Vermont limit their governors to two-year terms, thereby holding gubernatorial elections in both off- and on-years.) Among those forty-one off-year states, five—Kentucky, Louisiana, Mississippi, New Jersey, and Virginia—have elections that take place in odd-numbered years. Off-year elections prevent the presidential race from diverting attention from state races and also minimize the possible **coattail effect,** by which a presidential candidate can affect the fortunes of state candidates of the same party. By holding elections in off-years, races for governor may serve instead as referenda on the sitting president's performance in office. Generally, however, the health of a state's economy is a critical issue in gubernatorial elections.[28]

Recent State Elections

The stakes were high for the 2002 state elections, with thirty-six governors' seats on the ballots. Republicans, holding seven of the governorships in the ten largest states, wanted to keep them—and, if possible, win the biggest prize of all: the governorship of California. Democrats, buoyed by their victories in the only two governors' races held in 2001 (New Jersey and Virginia), wanted to extend their winning streak. The changing demographics of the nation, especially the increase in the Latino population, and the economic slowdown, factored heavily in campaign strategies.

The results of the 2002 gubernatorial elections left both Democrats and Republicans smiling. The Democratic Party was able to increase its share of governors' seats, but not by enough to gain a majority of them. The Democrats retained the governorship of California and, for the first time in many years, counted Arizona, Illinois, Michigan, Pennsylvania, and Wisconsin in their column. Republicans relished their incumbents' victories in the large states of Texas, New York, Florida, and Ohio. GOP gubernatorial candidates were also successful in some traditionally Democratic states such as Georgia, Hawaii, Maryland, and Massachusetts. Alabama provided a reminder that every vote does matter: the margin of victory in the disputed governor's race was less than half of a percentage point. The results were mixed for women's bids for the top job in state government. Carrying a major party's banner in nine states, women won in four of them: Arizona, Hawaii, Kansas, and Michigan.

Only three gubernatorial elections were scheduled in 2003, and Republicans won two of them (in Kentucky and Mississippi) and Democrats won one (in Louisiana). The most dramatic state-level political event of 2003 was the recall election of California Governor Gray Davis (a Democrat) and the election of Arnold Schwarzenegger (a Republican) to take his place. By the end of the year, the partisan balance in governors' offices was firmly Republican, with the GOP holding twenty-eight seats to the Democrats twenty-two. In 2004, with eleven seats up for grabs (six held by Democrats, five held by Republicans) and a presidential election on tap, partisan maneuvering was in full swing. Although voters turned out in record high numbers throughout the country, the partisan mix in governor's offices was unchanged by the 2004 election: six Democrats and five Republicans were elected.[29] Four incumbent governors won reelection, two were defeated: the Democrat in Indiana and the Republican in New Hampshire.

Nonpartisan Elections

A **nonpartisan election** removes the political party identification from the candidate in an effort to depoliticize the electoral campaign. Elections that have been made nonpartisan include those for many judicial offices and for many local-level positions. The special task of judges—adjudicating guilt or innocence, determining right and wrong—does not lend itself to partisan interpretation. The job of local governments—delivering public services—has also traditionally been considered nonideological. Nonpartisan local elections are likely to be found in municipalities and in school districts and special districts (see Chapters 10 and 11).

Under a nonpartisan election system, all candidates for an office compete in a first election; if there's no majority winner, a second election (runoff) is held. Although approximately three-quarters of cities use nonpartisan elections, some regional variation exists in their usage. The prevalence of nonpartisanship is somewhat lower in the Northeast and Midwest than it is in western cities.[30] Large cities are no more likely to conduct partisan elections than smaller ones are; however, those that do, such as New York City and Philadelphia, tend to attract attention.

Most studies have concluded that nonpartisanship depresses turnout in municipal elections that are held independent of state and national elections. The figures are not dramatic, but in what are already low-turnout elections, the difference can run as high as 10 percent of municipal voters.[31] Nonpartisan elections seem to produce a city council that is somewhat elite by socio-economic standards and a greater number of officeholders who consider them-selves Republicans. One fascinating finding is that, although the nonpartisan election structure seems to result in a different type of city council, the policy outcomes appear unaffected.[32] In terms of policies, city councils elected in nonpartisan elections are not noticeably different from those elected in parti-san elections.

What does it take to get elected? In the absence of political parties, candi-dates are forced to create their own organizations to run for office. They raise and spend money (much of it their own), and they seek the endorsements of newspapers and business and citizen groups. Money matters, and according to new studies of city elections in Atlanta and St. Louis, so do incumbency and newspaper endorsements.[33] In some communities, **slating groups** function as unofficial parties because they recruit candidates and finance their cam-paigns.[34] (Slating groups are nonpartisan organizations that actively support a slate of candidates.) Citizens' groups can also be an important factor in local elections.[35]

slating groups

Nonpartisan political or-ganizations that endorse and promote a slate of candidates.

ELECTION-DAY LAWMAKING

What happens when the government does not respond to the messages that the people are sending? More and more frequently, the answer is to transform the messages into ballot propositions and let the citizens make their own laws. As explained in Chapter 3, *initiatives* are proposed laws or constitutional amend-ments that are placed on the ballot by citizen petition, to be approved or re-jected by popular vote. An initiative lets citizens enact their own laws and thus bypass the state legislature. This mechanism for legislation by popular vote was one of several reforms of the Progressive era, which lasted roughly from 1890 to 1920. Other Progressive reforms included the popular referendum and the re-call. The **popular referendum** allows citizens to petition to vote on actions taken by legislative bodies. It provides a means by which the public can overturn a legislative enactment. (A popular referendum is different from a general **refer-endum**—a proposition put on the ballot by the legislature that requires voter approval before it can take effect. Constitutional amendments and bond issues are examples of general referenda.) The **recall,** another citizen-initiated process, requires elected officials to stand for a vote on their removal, before their term has expired. Recall provides the public with an opportunity to force an official out of office.

The key characteristic shared by initiative, popular referendum, and recall is that they are actions begun by citizens. The Progressives advocated these mech-anisms to expand the role of citizens and to restrict the power of intermediary institutions such as legislatures, political parties, and elected officials.[36] Their efforts were particularly successful in the western part of the United States, probably because of the difficulty of amending existing state constitutions in

popular referendum

A special type of refer-endum whereby citizens can petition to vote on actions taken by legisla-tive bodies.

referendum

A procedure whereby a governing body submits proposed laws, constitu-tional amendments, or bond issues to the vot-ers for ratification.

recall

A procedure that allows citizens to vote elected officials out of office before their term has expired.

Chanting slogans and holding signs, members of this family make their views known on California's Proposition 54 and on the gubernatorial recall.
SOURCE: David McNew/Getty Images.

the East and an elitist fear of the working class (namely, the industrialized immigrants in the Northeast and the rural black sharecroppers in the South). The newer western states, in contrast, were quite open, both procedurally and socially. In 1898, South Dakota became the first state to adopt the initiative process. And the initiative was actually used for the first time in Oregon in 1902, when citizens successfully petitioned for ballot questions on mandatory political party primaries and local option liquor sales. Both of the initiatives were approved.

Today, twenty-four states allow the initiative for constitutional amendments, statutes, or both; Mississippi is the most recent addition, having adopted it in 1992. A few of the twenty-four states use the indirect initiative, which gives the legislature an opportunity to consider the proposed measure. If the legislature fails to act or if it rejects the measure, the proposal is put before the voters at the next election. Popular referendum is provided in twenty-five states, and recall of state officials is provided in eighteen. These figures understate the use of such mechanisms throughout the country, however, because many states without statewide initiative, popular referendum, and recall allow their use at the local government level.[37] Table 4.2 shows in which states citizens can and cannot influence government through initiatives and recalls.

The Initiative

The first step in the initiative process is the petition. A draft of the proposed law (or constitutional amendment) is circulated along with a petition for citizens to sign. The petition signature requirement varies by state but usually falls between 5 and 10 percent of the number of votes cast in the preceding statewide election. To ensure that a matter is of statewide concern and that signatures have been gathered beyond a single area, some states set geographic distributional requirements. In Montana, for example, signature requirements must be met in at least one-third of the legislative districts; in Nebraska, in two-fifths of the counties. Door-to-door canvassing is one way to gather signatures, as is dispatching supporters to shopping malls and sporting events. Initiative organizers are relying more and more on direct mail: Petition forms are simply mailed to a preselected, computer-generated list of likely signers.

The Return of Initiatives Initiatives emerged as a potent force in the 1970s, thanks primarily to the activism of three types of groups: environmental activists, consumer advocates, and tax-limitation organizations. One of the most influential modern initiatives was California's Proposition 13 (1978), which rolled back property taxes in the state and spawned an immediate wave of tax-reduction propositions across the land.

The increased popularity of initiatives has at least two explanations: (1) Some observers believe that wavering public confidence in government has led citizens to take matters into their own hands. The attitude seems to be that if government can't be trusted to do the right thing, citizens will do it themselves. (2) New methods of signature collection have brought the initiative process within the reach of almost any well-financed group with a grievance or concern. An example from Massachusetts makes the point. When then-governor Paul Celluci could not get the legislature to pass his tax-cut proposals, he took the issue straight to the voters. Using donations from supporters, he paid a company to collect sufficient signatures on petitions, and he got his issue on the 2000 ballot.[38] And the voters approved it. These two factors explain why the current climate is ripe for election-day lawmaking. The contemporary return of the initiative and its durability have led some researchers to conclude that the country is experiencing a resurgence of populism, a modern-day progressivism.[39]

Recent Initiatives If ballot questions are any indication of the public's mood, then the public has had quite an attitude lately. Table 4.3 offers some indication of the range of subjects covered by the initiatives on the ballot in 2002 and 2003. Drug policy reform, animal rights, education quality, election reform, gaming, and taxes were the most prevalent citizen-initiated ballot measures.

| TABLE 4.2 | Citizen Influence in State Government | | |

REGION/ STATE	CAN CITIZENS CHANGE THE CONSTITUTION THROUGH PETITION?	CAN CITIZENS CHANGE STATE LAWS THROUGH PETITION?	CAN CITIZENS FORCE A RECALL ELECTION THROUGH PETITION?
New England			
Connecticut	NO	NO	NO
Maine	NO	YES (Indirectly)	NO
Massachusetts	YES (Indirectly)	YES (Indirectly)	NO
New Hampshire	NO	NO	NO
Rhode Island	NO	NO	YES
Vermont	NO	NO	NO
Middle Atlantic			
New Jersey	NO	NO	YES
New York	NO	NO	NO
Pennsylvania	NO	NO	NO
South Atlantic			
Delaware	NO	NO	NO
Florida	YES	NO	NO
Georgia	NO	NO	YES
Maryland	NO	NO	NO
North Carolina	NO	NO	NO
South Carolina	NO	NO	NO
Virginia	NO	NO	NO
West Virginia	NO	NO	NO
South Central			
Alabama	NO	NO	NO
Kentucky	NO	NO	NO
Mississippi	YES (Indirectly)	NO	NO
Tennessee	NO	NO	NO
Midwest			
Illinois	YES	YES	NO
Indiana	NO	NO	NO
Michigan	YES	YES (Indirectly)	YES
Ohio	YES	YES	NO
Wisconsin	NO	NO	YES
Northern Plains			
Iowa	NO	NO	NO
Kansas	NO	NO	YES

TABLE 4.2	*(continued)*		

REGION/ STATE	CAN CITIZENS CHANGE THE CONSTITUTION THROUGH PETITION?	CAN CITIZENS CHANGE STATE LAWS THROUGH PETITION?	CAN CITIZENS FORCE A RECALL ELECTION THROUGH PETITION?
Minnesota	NO	NO	YES
Missouri	YES	YES	NO
Nebraska	YES	YES	NO
North Dakota	YES	YES	YES
South Dakota	YES	YES	NO
Southwest			
Arizona	YES	YES	YES
Arkansas	YES	YES	NO
Louisiana	NO	NO	YES
New Mexico	NO	NO	NO
Oklahoma	YES	YES	NO
Texas	NO	NO	NO
Mountain			
Colorado	YES	YES	YES
Idaho	NO	YES	YES
Montana	YES	YES	YES
Nevada	YES	YES	YES
Utah	NO	YES	NO
Wyoming	NO	YES (Indirectly)	NO
Pacific			
Alaska	NO	YES (Indirectly)	YES
California	YES	YES	YES
Hawaii	NO	NO	NO
Oregon	YES	YES	YES
Washington	NO	YES	YES

SOURCE: *The Book of the States 2000–01* (Lexington, Ky.: Council of State Governments, 2000), pp. 233, 248, 249. Reprinted by permission of The Council of State Governments.

Florida voters demonstrated their commitment to funding public education when they approved measures requiring high-quality pre-kindergartens for all four-year-olds and setting relatively low maximum class sizes. Efforts to liberalize drug policies experienced setbacks in several states, as did measures designed to reform election laws. More popular, however, were initiatives dealing with animal rights and with gaming. As is typically the case, more initiatives went

TABLE 4.3	A Sampling of Ballot Initiatives, 2002 and 2003	
STATE	**DESCRIPTION OF INITIATIVE**	**RESULT**
Arizona	Legalizing marijuana for medicinal purposes	Failed
California	Increasing state funds for before- and after-school programs	Passed
Colorado	Authorizing same-day voter registration	Failed
Florida	Banning the use of gestational crates for pregnant pigs	Passed
Idaho	Abolishing legislative term limits	Passed
Maine	Requiring the state to pay a greater share of public education	Passed
Massachusetts	Abolishing the state's income tax	Failed
Nevada	Legalizing marijuana for recreational use	Failed
North Dakota	Allowing the state to join a multistate lottery	Passed
Ohio	Treating rather than jailing nonviolent drug offenders	Failed
Oklahoma	Outlawing cockfighting	Passed

SOURCE: M. Dane Waters, "2002 Initiatives and Referenda," *The Book of the States 2003* (Lexington, Ky.: Council of State Governments, 2003), pp. 281–85; www.iandrinstitute.org (April 2, 2004).

down to defeat than passed. Historically, the approval rate for statewide initiatives is approximately 41 percent.[40] One of the most unusual initiatives appeared on Denver's 2004 ballot. It was unusual due to its focus (banning circus animal acts from the city) and its sponsor (Youth Opposed to Animal Acts, an organization of high school students).[41]

Questions About the Initiative In the 2002 elections, there were fifty-three citizen-initiated questions on the ballots, in nineteen states—and 2002 was not a particularly busy year. Oregon led the way, with seven initiatives on its ballot; Colorado and Florida had five each. These numbers raise questions about the use of initiatives in particular and the wisdom of direct democracy more generally. By resorting to initiatives, citizens can bypass (or, in the case of indirect initiatives, prod) an obstructive legislature. And initiatives can be positive or negative; that is, they can be used in the absence of legislative action or they can be used to repudiate actions taken by the legislature. But is the initiative process appropriate for resolving tough public problems? Seldom are issues so simple that a yes-or-no ballot question can adequately reflect appropriate options and alternatives. A legislative setting, in contrast, fosters the negotiation and compromise that produce workable solutions. Legislatures are deliberative bodies, not instant problem solvers.

A related concern is whether the public is too ill informed to make intelligent choices or to avoid susceptibility to emotional appeals. Ballot questions are considered low-information elections: Facing little information or conflicting claims, voters respond to readily available cues.[42] Although they do not always win, well-financed business and religious groups have used the initiative process to their advantage. And the campaign costs associated with ballot initiatives remain high. In 2000, for instance, California campaign contributors spent over $80 million to promote and fight two initiatives.[43] Some initiative states have enacted laws requiring clear identification of financial sponsors of initiatives, on the assumption that the public is being hoodwinked by some initiatives. But, at the same time, initiatives have positive effects on the electoral process. For one, they seem to stimulate more citizen participation. Research has found that voters with frequent exposure to ballot questions are more likely to vote and to donate money to political campaigns.[44]

Legislators are of two minds when it comes to direct citizen involvement in policymaking. On the one hand, having the public decide a controversial issue such as abortion or school prayer helps legislators out of tight spots. On the other hand, increased citizen lawmaking intrudes on the central function of the legislature. Given the popularity of initiatives, legislators must proceed cautiously with actions that would make them more difficult to use. So far, efforts to increase the signature requirements, as Oklahoma legislators tried to do in 2002, or to reduce the amount of time citizens and groups have to get petitions signed, a change that Florida lawmakers considered in 2004, have been unsuccessful. A citizenry accustomed to the initiative process does not look kindly on its weakening. A survey of Oregon citizens found 81 percent agreeing with this statement: "Ballot initiatives enhance the democratic process in Oregon by allowing voters to decide important policy issues."[45]

Passage of the initiative is not the final step in the process. The new law has to be implemented and, as research has shown, "under normal conditions, legislatures, bureaucrats, or other government officials will work to alter a winning initiative's impact on public policy."[46] Direct democracy enthusiasts should heed the words of political scientist Valentina Bali who studied local compliance with a California initiative intended to dismantle bilingual education programs: ". . . the large number of constraints suggests that the final policy outcome of an initiative can be quite limited after the initiative's implementation."[47]

The Recall

Recalls, too, were once a little-used mechanism in state and local governments. Only eighteen states provide for recall of state officials, and in seven of them, judicial officers are exempt. City and county government charters, even in states without recall provisions, typically include mechanisms for recall of local elected officials. In fact, the first known recall was aimed at a Los Angeles city council member in 1904.[48] Recalls have a much higher petition signature requirement than initiatives do; it is common to require a signature minimum of 25 percent of the votes cast in the last election for the office of the official who is the subject of the recall. Kansas, for example, requires a 40 percent minimum.

Recall efforts usually involve a public perception of official misconduct. On occasion, however, simply running afoul of citizen preferences is enough to trigger a recall, as former state senator George Petak of Wisconsin discovered. Petak, a Republican, had promised his constituents that he would vote against a regional sales tax to fund a new stadium for the Milwaukee Brewers.[49] In the heat of legislative debate and partisan pressure, however, he voted *for* the tax. His vote was all it took. A successful petition drive put him into a recall election, which he lost. (The recall had further implications: Because a Democrat defeated Petak, Republicans lost their one-seat control of the state senate.)

In a few states, such as Wisconsin, the recall ballot resembles an election ballot. The name of the official who is the subject of the recall appears on the ballot, as do the names of challengers. To continue in office, the official must receive the most votes. In other states, the ballot includes no candidates but contains wording such as "Should Official X be recalled on the following charges?" (A brief statement of the charges would follow.) A majority vote is required to remove an official, and the vacancy created by a successful recall is filled by a subsequent special election or by appointment.

The rationale for the recall process is straightforward: Public officials should be subject to continuous voter control.[50] As the organizer of the successful campaign to recall a mayor stated, "We've shown you can fight city hall."[51] Whether it is used or not, the power to recall public officials is valued by the public. A national survey several years ago indicated that two-thirds of those polled favored amending the U.S. Constitution to permit the recall of members of Congress.[52]

Initiatives and recalls have helped open up state and local government to the public. Yet ironically, increased citizen participation can also jam the machinery of government, thus making its operation more cumbersome. Advocates of greater citizen activism, however, would gladly trade a little efficiency to achieve their goal.

The Special Case of California

California is a special case when it comes to election-day lawmaking. In terms of citizen initiatives, the Golden State ranks second only to Oregon in its use of the process: it put more than 265 initiatives on the ballot during the twentieth century. All sorts of fundamental issues have been addressed via the initiative process, including the state's property-tax rate, legislative term limits, the provision of public services to undocumented immigrants, comprehensive environmental protection, and school choice.

But California did something nearly unprecedented in 2003 when it recalled its governor, Gray Davis. It had been eighty years since a governor had been recalled: North Dakota's Lynn Frazier was removed from office amid charges that he abused power and misused state funds. In Governor Davis's case, the complaints were less about wrongdoing and more about leadership: how to resolve a massive budget crunch and how to fix energy deregulation.[53]

In a sense, the recall process began when Davis narrowly won re-election to a second term as governor and opponents sensed his vulnerability. In assessing the situation at the time, a California historian commented that, "There is a massive disconnect between many voters and the state government."[54] Republican strategists were quick to fan the flames of discontent as Davis's approval rating among the public dropped to around 25 percent. To force a recall, 986,874 signatures on petitions—12 percent of the number voting in the last gubernatorial election—were required.[55] When a sufficient number of signatures was collected, a recall election was scheduled. The ballot contained two sections: the recall question (a yes-or-no choice) and a list of candidates vying to replace the incumbent if the yeses prevail. (The recall question requires a majority vote, the replacement vote requires a simple plurality.)

After a seventy-seven-day campaign, 61.2 percent of the state's registered voters turned out to recall Davis by a 55 to 45 percent margin. There was a regional pattern to the vote, with Los Angeles County and the San Francisco Bay area opposing the recall, and much of the rest of the state voting to oust the governor.[56] The winning candidate, a body-builder/movie star, Arnold Schwarzenegger, captured 49 percent of the vote in a 135-candidate race. A social moderate and fiscal conservative with substantial charisma and financial resources, Republican Schwarzenegger was able to mobilize the GOP base and attract sufficient support from some typically Democratic-leaning groups such as women, union members, and Latinos.

Californians had mounted gubernatorial recall attempts thirty-one times over the years but all of them failed to get enough signatures to make it onto the ballot.[57] But in 2003, voters had had enough. It is unlikely, however, that California's success will trigger a rash of recalls because most states with recall provisions require higher signature thresholds and allow less time to collect signatures.[58] In Nevada in 2003 for instance, an effort to force a gubernatorial recall election fell well short of the necessary 25 percent of voters. But the recall of Governor Davis did give many incumbents pause because citizens used one of the participatory means at their disposal to effect change.

CITIZEN ACCESS TO GOVERNMENT

As we saw in Figure 4.1, citizens have opportunities to participate in government in many nonelectoral ways. Because state and local governments have undertaken extensive measures to open themselves to public scrutiny and stimulate public input, citizen access to government has been increased. Many of these measures are directly connected with the policymaking process. At the least, they enable government and the citizenry to exchange information, and thus they contribute to the growing capacity of state and local governments. At most, they may alter political power patterns and resource allocations.[59]

An example of a local jurisdiction that has embraced citizen participation extensively is Tacoma, Washington, a city of nearly 200,000 people and with a land area of 49 square miles. Table 4.4 lists six different participatory venues, ranging from a twenty-four-hour voice-mail line that records citizen suggestions and complaints to more structured neighborhood council meetings. Through citizens' forums and the CityLine call-in talk show, Tacoma has worked to engage citizens and policymakers in meaningful conversations.

Many of the accessibility measures adopted by state and local governments are the direct result of public demands that government be more accountable. Others have resulted from an official effort to involve the public in the ongoing work of government. Four types of official access are discussed in the following sections.

TABLE 4.4	How to Participate in City Government	
The City of Tacoma believes its citizens rate as the most valuable asset of Tacoma. The city offers many ways for citizens to participate in government. Citizens are invited to attend all public meetings. Disabled persons who need special accommodations should contact the City Clerk's Office— at 253-591-5171— forty-eight hours before the scheduled meeting time.	**CITIZENS' FORUM**	Citizens' Forum takes place at the first city council meeting of every month. During Citizens' Forum, citizens may address the council on any issue. Citizen's Forum begins at approximately 6:00 p.m.
	VISION LINE	The city manager maintains a twenty-four-hour voicemail line to record ideas, suggestions, issues and concerns from citizens. Call 253-591-2020 to leave a message. The city manager's office will respond and/or forward the message to the appropriate department.
	CITYLINE	CityLine is aired live Thursday at noon. TV Tacoma produces this one-hour, live, call-in talk show discussing issues related to city government. Viewers may call in at 253-591-5168 during the show to participate in the discussion.
	NEIGHBORHOOD COUNCILS	The city council established the neighborhood council program in 1993 to provide a link between neighborhoods and city government. The neighborhood councils serve as advisory bodies to the city council and city staff on neighborhood matters. Call 253-591-5229.
	TACOMA CARES	Tacoma CARES (Tacoma Cleanup And Revitalization EffortS) brings together several city services to help with clean-up efforts in Tacoma's neighborhoods. It involves immediate steps to work with neighbors to clean up garbage and debris, and involves a long-range plan to revitalize, improve, and maintain city neighborhoods. Call 253-591-5001.
	CITY COUNCIL MEETINGS	Meetings are held Tuesdays at 5:00 p.m. in the council chambers, first floor of the Tacoma Municipal Building, 747 Market Street, Tacoma, Washington. TV Tacoma airs the meetings live and replays them during the following week on TV Tacoma, Channel 12.

SOURCE: City of Tacoma, Mayor Bill Baarsma, Deputy Mayor Bill Evans, Council Members Julie Anderson, Connie Ladenburg, Mike Lonergan, Spiro Manthou, Kevin Phelps, Rick Talbert, and Tom Stenger. Used by permission; www.cityoftacoma.org/55involved/.

Open Meeting Laws

open meeting laws

Statutes that open the meetings of government bodies to the public.

Florida's 1967 sunshine law is credited with sparking a surge of interest in openness in government, and today **open meeting laws** are on the books in all fifty states. These laws do just what the name implies: They open meetings of government bodies to the public, or, in Florida's terminology, they bring government "into the sunshine." Open meeting laws apply to both the state and local levels and affect the executive branch as well as the legislative branch. Basic open meeting laws have been supplemented by additional requirements in many states. Advance public notice of meetings is required in all states; most insist that minutes be kept, levy penalties against officials who violate the law, and void actions taken in meetings held contrary to sunshine provisions. These "brighter sunshine" laws make a difference. Whether a meeting is open or closed is irrelevant if citizens are unaware that it is occurring. If no penalties are assessed for violation, then there is less incentive for officials to comply.

Some states remain relatively resistant to the sun's rays. In the late 1990s, Rhode Island failed to adopt a package of tougher open meeting laws despite extensive media attention and public pressure. At the same time, North Dakota legislators strengthened the state's open meeting law but exempted themselves from most of the provisions.[60] In general, however, the trend is toward more openness. For example, the advent of electronic mail—making cyberspace meetings possible—led Colorado to expand its open-records laws. Now, the stored e-mail files of the state's politicians are open to the public.

Administrative Procedure Acts

After state legislation is passed or a local ordinance is adopted, an administrative agency typically is responsible for implementation. This process involves the establishment of rules and regulations and hence constitutes powerful responsibility. In practice, agencies often have wide latitude in translating legislative intent into action. For example, if a new state law creates annual automobile safety inspections, it is the responsibility of the state's Department of Motor Vehicles to make it work. Unless the law specifies the details, bureaucrats will determine the items to be covered in the safety inspection, the location of inspection stations, and the fee to be charged. These details are just as important as the original enactment.

administrative procedure acts
Acts that standardize administrative agency operations as a means of safeguarding clients and the general public.

To ensure public access to this critical rulemaking process, states have adopted **administrative procedure acts,** which usually require public notice of the proposed rule and an opportunity for citizen comment. All states provide for this notification and comment process, as it is known. In addition, some states give citizens the right to petition an administrative agency for an adjustment in the rules.

Advisory Committees

advisory committee
An organization created by government to involve members of the public in studying and recommending solutions to public problems.

Another arena for citizen participation that is popular in state and especially local governments is the **advisory committee,** in the form of citizen task forces, commissions, and panels. Regardless of name, these organizations are designed to study a problem and to offer advice, usually in the form of recommendations. People chosen to serve on an advisory committee tend to have expertise as well as interest in the issue and, in most cases, political connections. But not always. One of the first efforts to make the advisory process more inclusive occurred in 1991 when Oregon's governor Barbara Roberts invited a random cross section of Oregonians to attend interactive, televised meetings at one of thirty sites. The governor went live (via cable television) to each of the sites to ask citizens to assess the performance of their governments. She got an earful. But she also received invaluable input.[61]

Citizen advisory committees provide a formal structure for citizen input. Many cities have created community boards like Tacoma's neighborhood councils to provide a channel for communication between neighborhoods and city government. If officials heed public preferences, citizen advice can become the basis for public policy. Citizen advisory organizations also provide elected officials with a relatively safe course of action. In a politically explosive situation, a governor can say, "I've appointed a citizen task force to study the issue and report back to me with recommendations for action." The governor thus buys time, with the hope that the issue will gradually cool down. Another benefit of these organizations is that they ease citizen acceptance of subsequent policy decisions because the governor can note that an action "was recommended by an impartial panel of citizens." This is not to suggest that citizen advisory committees are merely tools for manipulation by politicians, but they do have uses beyond citizen participation.

E-Government

The Internet has the potential to bring state and local government into citizens' homes in a way earlier technology could not. States and localities have already incorporated electronic communications into their daily operations. Web sites and e-mail communications abound. People can click on a city's home page and find an array of useful information, such as the agenda for the next city council meeting, the minutes of previous council sessions, the city budget, the comprehensive plan, and the like. States have created elaborate web sites that link the user to vast data bases and information resources. In a clever twist, Pennsylvania was the first state to promote its web address by emblazoning it across the bottom of its vehicle license plates.

Now the task for states and localities is to expand their use of the Internet in dealing with the public. Jurisdictions have begun to see the Internet's potential beyond simple information provision. It started with the downloading of public reports and generic forms and has moved into more highly individualized interaction such as filing taxes, applying for licenses and permits, and accessing personal information. In the nearby *Breaking New Ground* box, several innovative e-government programs are highlighted.

The Internet also offers an efficient way for government to gauge public opinion and preferences. This aspect of e-government was put to good use in 2003 when Maine's new governor confronted a $1 billion deficit. Clearly, cuts would have to be made, but in which programs? Governor John Baldacci came up with a novel idea: create a budget-balancing game that Pine Tree state residents could play on the state's web site.[62] (The look of the game's web page is displayed in Figure 4.3.) State programs, their costs, and their funding sources were listed. The simulation forced players to choose which programs to cut and which taxes to increase as they tried to whittle away at the deficit and achieve a balanced budget. Players were encouraged to e-mail the governor with their suggestions once they made their way through the thicket of competing programs.

One of the major concerns as the push toward e-government grows is that the so-called technology have-nots will be left behind. Low-income Americans lag far behind middle- and upper-income groups regarding access to the Inter-

BREAKING NEW GROUND

E-Z Access to Government... and the Ballot Box

The states are valued in the federal system for their role as "laboratories of democracy," in Supreme Court Justice Louis Brandeis's famous phrase. States are places where creative new solutions to society's problems can be tried out. If they are successful, other states will adopt them. If they are unsuccessful, they will be abandoned. In that spirit, state officials and agencies have embraced the Internet, harnessing its speed and power. The comptroller for the state of Texas, Carole Keeton Rylander, launched a new program in 2000 called e-Texas that led the way in making many state transactions available on-line twenty-four hours a day. In the same vein, the state of Utah passed the Digital State Act in 2000; it required all state agencies to provide their services on-line within three years. Other states have taken similar actions; localities have gone electronic, too. When Baltimore's mayor was deciding whether a new bridge should be painted red or green, he put the question on the city's web site to let the public select the color scheme. (Red was more popular with the e-voters.) Seattle, San Francisco, Indianapolis, Charlotte, and Denver are among the cities leading in the use of participatory e-technologies such as on-line surveys and conversation forums.

Being able to pay parking tickets or review real-estate records has become standard on-line offerings. But the biggie is voting. Internet voting debuted modestly in the 2000 elections in presidential primaries in Thurston County, Washington, and three Alaska house districts. These voting experiments were nonbinding; the first binding election for public office using the Internet was Arizona's Democratic presidential primary. About half of the voters participating in the primary chose the electronic method. Later, in the November 2000 election, the federal government funded a pilot program in four states that allowed 250 military personnel stationed overseas to vote on-line.

Many were optimistic that the 2004 elections would bring e-voting into wider use. The federal government passed the Help America Vote Act (HAVA), which provided funds so that states could upgrade their election equipment (and replace punch-card voting systems that had caused irregularities in Florida in 2000). Many states purchased electronic-voting devices such as touch screens, but voting via the Internet remained limited. More than 40,000 Michigan Democrats were able to cast their ballots over the Internet in the presidential primary, but they were the only voters able to do so. The U.S. Department of Defense's plans to join with states to allow military personnel stationed abroad to register and vote over the Internet were put on hold. The reason for the caution lay in a report that Internet voting was not sufficiently secure to prevent hackers from tampering with the system. The sticky problems of security and reliability mean that widespread Internet voting will have to wait for awhile.

SOURCES: Maureen Cosgrove, "E-Voting: States Better Get Ready, Experts Say," www.stateline.org (January 24, 2000); Christopher Swope, "E-Gov's New Gear," *Governing* 17 (March 2004): 40–42; "Internet Voting Gains, Loses Ground in 2004," *State Government News* 47 (February 2004): 5.

net. This digital divide has led many communities to install personal computers in libraries as well as in government information kiosks located in shopping malls and transit stations. In an effort to get its rural communities wired, North Dakota spent over $3 million to connect more than sixty communities to a broadband network.[63] Other concerns involve security and privacy. Fear that hackers might break into government computers or that personal information might be misused tempers some public enthusiasm for e-government.

| FIGURE 4.3 | **An E-Game: Balancing a State Budget** |

The Budget

My first priority as Governor is the state budget. As I begin my term, Maine faces a projected shortfall of $1 billion over the next two years. I submitted a balanced budget to the Legislature on February 7th that eliminates this shortfall without raising taxes. This tool will allow you to view the most current budget projections and to send me your own balanced budget proposal.

The Budget Balancing Education Tool

The Budget Balancing Tool was created without any General Fund spending, through an innovative partnership between the state and the Information Resource of Maine (InforME). InforME has been self-funding since its inception in 1999 and does not draw any money from the state's General Fund budget.

Expenditures [Adjust]
$ 6,062,483,500

Revenue [Adjust]
$ 4,983,926,555

The projected budget creates a deficit by spending more money than the state is taking in. Click 'Adjust' and change the numbers to see if you can balance the budget.

When you are done adjusting, click 'Compare Budgets' to see how your budget stacks up against the projections and to send your suggestions to the Governor.

[Reset]   Deficit   [Compare Budgets]
$ -1,078,556,945

SOURCE: Office of the Governor, State of Maine, www.maine.gov/governor/baldacci/issues/budget/index.html (April 30, 2004).

VOLUNTEERISM AS PARTICIPATION

volunteerism

A form of participation in which individuals or groups donate time or money to a public purpose.

Voluntary action is another constructive participatory activity unrelated to the ballot box. People and organizations donate their time and talents to supplement or even replace government activity. **Volunteerism** is a means of bringing fresh ideas and energy, whether physical or financial, into government while relieving some of the service burden. Washington created the first statewide volunteerism office in 1969, and within twenty years all states had volunteer programs in place.

One highly visible example of volunteerism is the Adopt a Highway program. Over the past fifteen years, the number of local businesses and civic clubs willing to pick up litter along designated stretches of state highways has skyrocketed. You have probably noticed the Adopt a Highway signs, with the names of volunteering groups listed on the signs. The state saves money, the roadsides stay cleaner, and the volunteering groups share good feelings and free advertising. Figure 4.4 displays the particulars of adopting a highway as part of Minnesota's Don't Waste Our State anti-littering campaign. Groups that volunteer have to agree to work at least three times a year on a specific stretch of highway for a minimum of two years. In return, the state supplies equipment to the volunteers and handles removal of the filled trash bags.

Successful volunteer programs like Adopt a Highway are emblematic of the concept of social capital, as mentioned earlier in this chapter. Stephen Knack's 2002 study showed a positive relationship between several indicators of social capital, especially the percentage of the public engaged in volunteerism, and state governmental quality.[64] States with a greater propensity toward volunteerism scored higher on several performance measures, including financial management, capital management, and information technology.

| FIGURE 4.4 | **Volunteering in Minnesota** |

Adopt-a-Highway is a public service program for volunteers to pick up litter along Minnesota's highways. Community groups, churches or businesses adopt a highway by picking up litter on both sides for at least two years.

How does it work? Adopt-a-Highway groups agree to:

- Adopt a highway for a minimum of two years.
- Select an available segment of highway at least two miles in length.
- Pick up litter at least three times a year.

SOURCE: Minnesota Department of Transportation, "Don't Waste Our State: Adopt A Highway," www.dot.state.mn.us/adopt/index.html (April 28, 2004). Reprinted courtesy of Minnesota Department of Transportation.

Local governments use volunteers in various ways. Generally, volunteerism is most successful when citizens can develop the required job skills quickly or participate in activities they enjoy, such as library work, recreation programs, or fire protection.[65] In addition to providing services to others, volunteers can be utilized for self-help; that is, they can engage in activities in which they are the primary beneficiaries. For example, some New York City neighborhoods take responsibility for the security and maintenance of nearby parks. Residential crime-watch programs are another variety of self-help. In both these instances, the volunteers and their neighborhoods benefit. Overall, studies show that volunteerism is especially successful in rural areas and small towns.[66] An important supplement to government volunteer programs are those of the nonprofit sector. Members of local faith-based groups and civic organizations, for example, often volunteer their time in support of community improvement projects such as Habitat for Humanity, Meals on Wheels, and Sistercare. The emphasis on volunteerism received a boost in the aftermath of 9/11, when the president established the Citizen Corps, volunteers who work within their communities to prevent and respond to terrorism.[67]

THE EFFECTS OF CITIZEN PARTICIPATION

Consider again the four quadrants of Figure 4.1. Constructive participatory behaviors, whether active or passive, invigorate government. The capacity of state and local governments depends on several factors, one of which is citizen participation. Underlying this argument is the implicit but strongly held belief shared by most observers of democracies that an accessible, responsive government is a legitimate government.

An active public, one that chooses the *voice* option in Figure 4.1, has the potential to generate widespread change in a community. The mobilization of lower-class voters, for instance, is linked to more generous state welfare policies.[68] From the perspective of government officials and institutions, citizen participation can be a nuisance because it may disrupt established routines. The challenge is to incorporate citizen participation into ongoing operations. A noteworthy example is Dayton, Ohio, where neighborhood-based priority boards shape city services and policies. As a Dayton official noted, "Citizen participation in this city is just a way of life."[69] Citizen involvement may not be easy or efficient, but in a democracy, it is the ultimate test of the legitimacy of that government.

Recent research raises the stakes for citizen participation. Political scientists Tom Rice and Alexander Sumberg developed measures to reflect the civic culture of each state, looking at, among other things, the level of citizen involvement and the amount of political equality.[70] Vermont and Massachusetts were found to be the most civic states, Mississippi and Louisiana the least civic. More important, however, is the impact of a state's civic culture on the performance of its government. According to Rice and Sumberg, a state's civic culture is "a powerful predictor of government performance."[71] Statistical analysis shows that the more civic the state, the more innovative and effective its government. Figure 4.5 displays the states' positions when civic culture and government per-

| FIGURE 4.5 | **Civic Culture and Government Performance** |

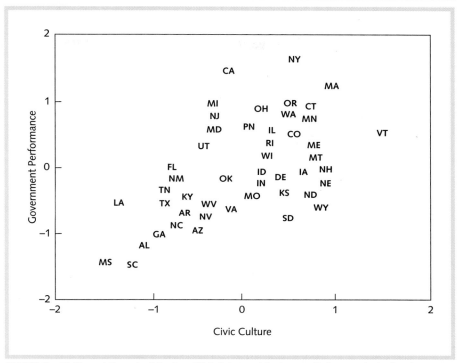

SOURCE: Tom W. Rice and Alexander F. Sumberg, "Civic Culture and Government Performance in the American States," *Publius: The Journal of Federalism* 27 (Winter 1997): 110. Reprinted by permission.

formance are considered simultaneously. The closer a state is to the upper right corner, the better it is on both indicators. Conversely, states landing near the lower left corner score poorly on both factors. The lesson? Citizen participation matters, not only for the individual but also for the government.

CHAPTER RECAP

- Citizen participation in the community can be active or passive, constructive or destructive. Local governments have devoted much time and energy to encouraging active, constructive participation among the citizenry.
- Voter turnout rates vary dramatically from one state to another, and the reasons have to do with the political culture of the state, the competitiveness of the political parties, and the way elections are administered.
- Republicans control more governorships than Democrats do. As a result of the 2004 elections, the GOP edge remained twenty-eight to twenty-two seats. The Democratic Party regained control of several state legislative chambers in the 2004 election.

- Almost half of the states have an initiative process and in those that do, it has become an important tool for policymaking.
- Although it is difficult to mobilize the public in support of a statewide recall, it happened in California in 2003 when Governor Gray Davis was recalled from office.
- E-government is on the rise, with states and localities adopting more and more high-tech ways of interacting with citizens. This trend holds tremendous potential for increasing citizen participation in government.
- Volunteerism is a way of bringing fresh ideas and energy into government and helps connect citizens to their community.
- State and local governments continue to encourage their citizens in meaningful participation. Doing so seems to make government work better.

Key Terms

participation *(p. 81)*
social capital *(p. 83)*
Voting Rights Act of 1965 *(p. 84)*
primary system *(p. 88)*
closed primary *(p. 89)*
open primary *(p. 89)*
blanket primary *(p. 89)*
runoff election *(p. 89)*
plurality *(p. 91)*
fusion *(p. 91)*

coattail effect *(p. 91)*
nonpartisan election *(p. 92)*
slating groups *(p. 93)*
popular referendum *(p. 93)*
referendum *(p. 93)*
recall *(p. 93)*
open meeting laws *(p. 102)*
administrative procedure acts *(p. 103)*
advisory committee *(p. 103)*
volunteerism *(p. 106)*

Surfing the Web

The web site of the Federal Election Commission, **www.fec.gov,** contains information about U.S. elections, including laws, voter turnout, and results.

The League of Women Voters, a well-respected organization that encourages informed and active participation of citizens in government, maintains a web site at **www.lwv.org.**

A nonpartisan, nonadvocacy web site providing up-to-the-minute news and analysis on election reform can be found at **electionline.org.**

The organization found at **www.americaspromise.org** encourages volunteers to create "communities of promise" in their home towns.

An interactive site that allows users to vote yes or no on current hot-button issues is **www.vote.org.** For example, before the 2004 election, the site polled e-public opinion on this question: "Should the U.S.A. Patriot Act be renewed before parts of the law expire in 2005?" The site is maintained by a former aide to President Clinton and a former public interest lobbyist.

You can find just about anything you want to know about ballot measures at **www.iandrinstitute.org** and **www.ballot.org.**

5 POLITICAL PARTIES, INTEREST GROUPS, AND CAMPAIGNS

Political Parties
Political Parties in Theory and in Reality • Party Organization • The Two-Party System • Interparty Competition • Is the Party Over?

Interest Groups
Types of Interest Groups • Interest Groups in the States • Local-Level Interest Groups • Techniques Used by Interest Groups

Political Campaigns
A New Era of Campaigns • The Impact of Mass Media • Campaign Finance

I n 2003, Republican Haley Barbour was elected governor of Mississippi by a 53 to 46 percent edge over the Democratic candidate.[1] Although electing a GOP governor is an infrequent occurrence in the Magnolia State, the 2003 process was much more routine than the previous one. In the 1999 gubernatorial elections, the Democrat was slightly ahead of the Republican in the popular vote (49.5 to 48.6 percent), but the two candidates had evenly split the electoral votes. According to the Mississippi constitution, to be elected governor, a candidate must win a majority of both the popular vote and the electoral vote. As prescribed by the state constitution, the election was thrown into the Mississippi House of Representatives for resolution. In a straight party-line vote, the house selected Ronnie Musgrove, the Democratic candidate, over the Republican candidate.[2] Mississippi's rules for selecting a governor may seem odd, but the larger point is this: State rules cut a wide swath through the electoral process and produce some interesting politics.

POLITICAL PARTIES

political parties
Organizations that nominate candidates to compete in elections.

The two major **political parties,** the Democratic Party and the Republican Party, offer slates of candidates to lead us. Candidates campaign hard for the glamorous jobs of governor, state legislator, mayor, and various other state and local positions. In some states, even candidates for judicial positions compete in partisan races. But party involvement in our system of government does not end on election day—the institutions of government themselves have a partisan tone. Legislatures are organized along party lines; governors offer Republican or Democratic agendas for their states; county commissioners of different ideological stripes fight over the best way to provide services to local residents. Through the actions of their elected officials, political parties play a major role in the operation of government.

The condition of contemporary American political parties has been described with words such as *decline, decay,* and *demise*. In some ways, the description is accurate, but in other ways, it is overstated. True, the number of people who identify themselves as members of one of the two major parties is only about 60 percent of the electorate, while the number of people calling themselves independents is nearly 40 percent.[3] Furthermore, campaigns are increasingly candidate-centered rather than party-centered, and they rely on personal organizations and political consultants. But at the same time, the party organization has become more professionalized, taking on new tasks and playing new roles in politics and governance. Parties have more financial and technological resources as their disposal.[4] Thus, to some observers, political parties are enjoying a period of *revitalization* and *rejuvenation*. It seems clear that political parties have undergone a *transformation* during the past twenty-five years and that they have proven to be quite adaptable.

Political Parties in Theory and in Reality

responsible party model

A theoretical ideal in which political parties are issue oriented, candidates toe the party line, and voters respond accordingly.

One ideal against which political party systems can be measured is called the **responsible party model,** which has several basic principles:

1. Parties should present clear and coherent programs to voters.
2. Voters should choose candidates according to the party programs.
3. The winning party should carry out its program once in office.
4. At the next election, voters should hold the governing party responsible for executing its program.[5]

According to this model, political parties carve out identifiable issue positions, base their campaign appeals on them, and endeavor to enact them upon taking office. Voters select candidates who represent their preferences and hold officeholders accountable for their performance.

But even a casual observer would recognize that U.S. political parties fall somewhat short of the responsible party model. For example, U.S. political parties take on different issues in different places, so a single, coherent program is unworkable. Although Democratic politicians tend to be more liberal than their Republican counterparts, it would be difficult to find an abundance of liberals in a Democratic-controlled southern state legislature. Voters also display a remarkable penchant for **ticket splitting**—that is, voting for a Democrat for one office and a Republican for another in the same election. Many voters are fond of saying that they "vote for the person, not the party."

ticket splitting

Voting for candidates of different political parties in a general election.

Parties in the United States function as umbrella organizations that shelter loose coalitions of relatively like-minded individuals. A general image for each party is discernible: The Republicans typically have been considered the party of big business, the Democrats the party of workers. On many of the social issues of the day—gay rights, abortion, pornography, and prayer in schools—the two parties tend to take different positions. By 2003, each party could claim about 30 percent of the voting-age public for itself. (See Figure 5.1, which tracks party identification during the recent past.) The geographical distribution of partisan loyalties has produced some interesting patterns. The South, where conservative political attitudes predominate, is no longer the Democratic stronghold it was forty years ago. In fact, it has become a region of so-called red states, that is, states that vote Republican in presidential elections. Other red states are found in the plains region and the Rocky Mountain west. States that are more reliably Democratic in presidential elections—usually the Northeastern region, the Pacific Coast, and the upper Midwest—are designated "blue" states. (The labels "red" and "blue" refer to the color coded maps that television broadcasters use to show election returns.) States with greater partisan diversity have been called "purple" by some pollsters.[6] It is important not to over-generalize from these colorful, but simple, descriptors of state-level partisanship. Within an individual state, various partisan configurations exist, as research on presidential voting at the county level has shown.[7]

As noted, the responsible party model does not aptly describe politics and

| FIGURE 5.1 | **Party Identification in the United States, 1990–2003** |

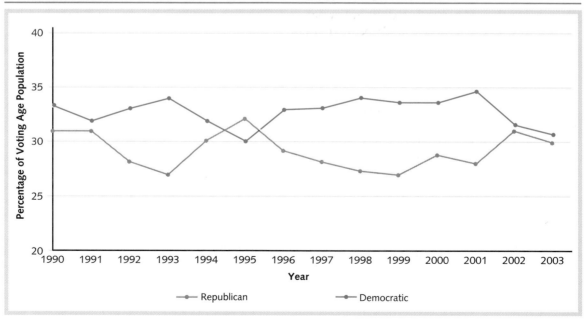

Partisan identification among the voting-age public has fluctuated somewhat in the recent past.

SOURCE: "The 2003 Political Landscape," Pew Research Center for the People and the Press, http://people-press.org/ reports/display.php3?PageID=750 (May 1, 2004). Reprinted by permission of The Pew Research Center For The People & The Press.

governance in the states. Therefore, does it matter which party controls the institutions of state government? One can reasonably conclude that it does matter because the parties vary in their ideological composition. Americans have grown more ideologically conservative and, at present, conservatives outnumber liberals in every state. However, states with proportionately higher numbers of liberals tend to have a more liberal direction to their public policies.[8] And although ideology and partisanship are not completely interchangeable, the link is strong. States with proportionately more liberals are more likely to vote for Democrats; conservatives tend to favor Republicans. In the past, the South would stand as an exception to the rule; however, as mentioned, conservative southerners are now finding a home in the Republican Party. For the Democrats, the increasing conservatism of the public has forced the party to move more toward the center of the ideological spectrum. The emergence of candidates who refer to themselves as "New Democrats" and speak the language of **pragmatism** is evidence of that movement.

pragmatism
A practical approach to problem solving, a search for "what works."

Party Organization

Political parties are decentralized organizations, with fifty state Republican parties and fifty state Democratic parties. Each state also has local party organizations, most typically at the county level. Although they interact, each of these units is autonomous, a situation that promotes independence but is not so helpful to party discipline. Specialized partisan groups, including the College Democrats, the Young Republicans, Democratic Women's Clubs, Black Republican Councils, and so on, have been accorded official recognition. Party organizations are further decentralized into precinct-level clusters, which bear the ultimate responsibility for turning out the party's voters on election day. Figure 5.2 shows a typical state party organization.

State Parties State governments vary in how closely and how vigorously they regulate political parties. In states with few laws, parties have more discretion in their organization and functions.[9] Each state party has a charter or by-laws to govern its operation. The decisionmaking body is the state committee, sometimes called a central committee, which is headed by a chairperson and is composed of members elected in party primaries or at state party conventions. State parties (officially, at least) head their party's push to capture statewide elected offices. Although they may formulate platforms and launch party-centered fundraising appeals, their value to candidates is in the services they provide.[10] In many states, parties host seminars for party nominees about campaigning effectively, they conduct research into the public's mood, and they advertise on behalf of their candidates. For example, in 2000, Indiana's Democratic Party assisted the incumbent governor, who was seeking reelection, by sending campaign advertising to targeted households, staffing phone banks, distributing bumper stickers and yard signs, and handling absentee ballot applications.[11]

State party organizations vary widely in their organizational vitality and resources. In nonelection years, the parties operate with limited staff and revenue; in election years, however, they employ, on average, nine full-time staffers and

| FIGURE 5.2 | **Typical State Party Organization** |

Most political party organizations look something like this.

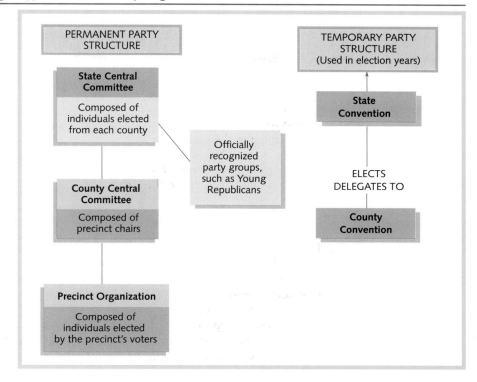

seven part-timers, and their funds increase dramatically.[12] For example, in the 2002 election cycle, state parties had more than $800 million to spend. On average, Republican organizations generally outstrip Democratic ones in measures of organizational strength. In each state, the two major parties and even some of the third parties maintain web sites, but many of the home pages are not very detailed or up-to-date. Although partisan volunteers still canvass neighborhoods, knocking on doors and talking to would-be voters, these activities are increasingly supplemented by Web-based and e-mail appeals for funds and votes. To a candidate, one of the most valuable services the state party can provide is access to its data base of party voters.[13]

Local Parties County party organizations are composed of committee members chosen at the precinct level. These workers are volunteers whose primary reward is the satisfaction of being involved in politics. But the work is rarely glamorous. Party workers are the people who conduct voter registration drives, drop off the lawn signs for residents' front yards, organize candidate forums, and stand at the polls and remind voters to vote Democratic or vote Republican.

Local party organizations, come election time, kick into high gear. On behalf of the party's candidates, they distribute campaign literature, organize fund-raising events, make telephone calls to voters, and run newspaper advertisements. But what impact do these activities have on the campaign? From the perspective of local party leaders, these actions provide a vital service to candidates. State legislative candidates report that local parties are most helpful when providing traditional grassroots services such as rounding up volunteer workers and getting voters to the polls on election day.[14]

Local parties are less professionally organized than state parties. Although many local organizations maintain campaign headquarters during an election period, few operate year-round offices. County chairpersons report devoting a lot of time to the party during election periods, but otherwise the post does not take much of their time. Most chairpersons lead organizations without any full-time staff, and vacancies in precinct offices are common.

Factions Political parties frequently develop *factions*—that is, identifiable subsets. They can be ideologically based, such as the struggle between moderates and liberals for control of state Democratic parties. They can be organized around particular political leaders, or they can reflect sectional divisions within a state. When factions endure, they make it difficult for a party to come together in support of candidates and in support of policy. Persistent intraparty factions create opportunities for the opposing party.

A factional challenge to local Republican parties has come from evangelical Christian activists who want to move the party to a more conservative stance. In Minnesota, for instance, the state Republican Party's tradition was one of moderately progressive social policies and fiscal restraint. The emergence of the Christian right, with its conservative social agenda, rocked the party.[15] And not just in Minnesota. By 1994, the Christian coalition was sufficiently organized to dominate many local Republican Party conventions. In Texas, the religious right took over precinct meetings, gained control over many party committees, and was able to dictate platform positions. Thus, in socially liberal Travis County, the GOP convention adopted an anti-abortion, anti-gay, prayer-in-schools platform.[16] Minnesota and Texas reflect a near-national trend. The publication *Campaigns & Elections* reported that in eighteen states, the Christian right dominated the Republican Party governing organization; in thirteen states, their influence was considered substantial.[17]

Political parties continually face the problem of factions. The challenge for party leadership is to unite the factions into a winning force.

The Two-Party System

General elections in the United States are typically contests between candidates representing the two major political parties. Such has been the case for the past century and a half. The Democratic Party has been in existence since the 1830s, when it emerged from the Jacksonian wing of the Jeffersonian party.[18] The Republican Party, despite its label as the Grand Old Party (GOP), is newer; it developed out of the sectional conflict over slavery in the 1850s.

Why Just Two? There are numerous reasons for the institutionalization of two-party politics. Explanations that emphasize sectional dualism, such as East versus West or North versus South, have given way to those focusing on the structure of the electoral system. Parties compete in elections in which there can be only one winner. Most legislative races, for example, take place in single-member districts in which only the candidate with the most votes wins; finishing second or third offers no reward. Hence, the development of radical or noncentrist parties is discouraged. In addition, laws regulating access to the ballot and receipt of public funds contribute to two-party politics by creating high start-up costs for third parties. Another plausible explanation has to do with tradition. Americans are accustomed to a political system composed of two parties, and that is how we understand politics.

Third Parties The assessment of former Alabama governor George Wallace that "there ain't a dime's worth of difference between Democrats and Republicans" although exaggerated, raises questions about the need for alternative parties. Third parties (also called nonmajor or minor parties) are an unsuccessful but persistent phenomenon in U.S. politics. The two major parties may not differ substantially, but for the most part their positions reflect the public mood. When third-party options are presented to voters in national elections, voters tend to stick to the two major parties. Third parties also suffer because the two established parties have vast reserves of money and resources at their disposal; new parties can rarely amass the finances or assemble the organization necessary to make significant inroads into the system. Third parties receive scant attention from the news media, and without it, credibility wanes.[19]

Third parties have enjoyed limited electoral success at the state level. The Socialist Party elected a few state representatives in New York in the early 1900s, and the Progressive Party of Robert La Follette in Wisconsin and the Farmer Labor Party in Minnesota strongly influenced the politics of those states before World War II. In the eight years from 1976 to 1984, third-party candidates and independents captured less than 1 percent of the vote in state legislative races.[20] And only in five states (led by New York, with 9.2 percent) did nonmajor party candidates receive more than 2 percent of the vote. By 2002, third-party candidates were faring better, at least in terms of getting their nominees on state ballots. The Libertarian Party was the most successful, running gubernatorial candidates in twenty-three states. Only in Wisconsin (11 percent) and Oregon (5 percent) were the Libertarian gubernatorial candidates somewhat competitive; in most states, the party garnered support from a mere 2 percent of the electorate.

Still, the public remains interested in partisan alternatives. One national survey reported that 53 percent of the electorate believed that there should be a third major political party.[21] Many indicated that their estrangement from the Democratic and Republican parties had reached the point that they would willingly affiliate with a third party that reflected their interests. This sentiment makes it easier to understand why, in 1998, a third party, the Reform Party, was successful in its quest for the governorship of Minnesota. The nearby *Debating*

Politics box discusses three minor parties that are attracting adherents and winning some local offices.

Interparty Competition

Although the amount of meaningful two-party electoral competition has increased over time, there is still variation across the states. A recent study ranked states according to the amount of competition for legislative seats.[22] It combined the percentage of the popular vote given the winning candidate, the margin of victory, and the relative safeness of the seat. Topping the list with relatively high levels of competition for the legislature were North Dakota and Oregon; clustered at the bottom of the list were Arkansas, Georgia, and Mississippi. In these three southern states, as many as 60 percent of their legislative seats go uncontested; thus, incumbents are returned to office again and again.[23]

The extension of interparty competition to states that had lacked it in the past is a healthy development in American politics. Citizens who are dissatisfied with the performance of the party in power have another choice. And there is an interesting twist to increased party competition and more choices for voters. Research has found that the amount of competition for legislative seats appears to be related to the policy outputs of the legislatures. States with higher levels of electoral competition tend to adopt more liberal policies than do states with less competitive legislative elections. To be sure, the relative strength of the two parties also affects the relationship.[24]

Patterns of Competition Beyond electoral competition, an important consideration is which party controls the major policymaking institutions in the state: the governor's office and the state legislature. Generally, there is a link between the partisan composition of the electorate and partisan control of a state's institutions. For instance, in Utah in 2003, the Republican Party had a voter registration advantage over the Democratic Party of more than 2 to 1. Not surprisingly, in the Utah legislature, Republicans outnumbered Democrats by a 3 to 1 margin, and a Republican occupied the governor's office. But the electorate–institution relationship is not a simple one. Consider Maryland and Massachusetts, two of the states in which voter registration patterns give the Democratic Party a strong advantage. Both states elected Republicans to the governor's office in 2002 but sustained the Democratic dominance in the legislature. In Maryland and Massachusetts, and in many other states, voting produced an institutional outcome called **divided government.**

In 2004, the Republican Party controlled the governor's office and both houses of the legislature in twelve states; the Democratic Party had institutional control of eight states. But **unified government** was not the norm: in twenty-nine states, divided government prevailed. Figure 5.3 shows the state-by-state patterns.

Consequences of Competition Two-party competition is spreading at a time when states are becoming the battleground for the resolution of difficult policy issues. Thirty-one states have competitive two-party systems.[25] As governors set

divided government
One party controls the governor's office; the other party controls the legislature.

unified government
Both houses of the legislature and the governor's office are controlled by the same party.

DEBATING POLITICS

Third Parties: Also-Rans or Real Contenders?

The two major parties still rule the roost, but candidates of third parties are making more credible bids for public office throughout the country. Third parties run the ideological gamut, and since the 1990s, they have enjoyed increased electoral success.

Consider three third parties—the Green Party, the Libertarian Party, and the New Party. Each has a formal platform, is recognized nationally, and has state chapters that are actively recruiting candidates and challenging the established parties. The Green Party, which grew out of the environmental movement, emphasizes citizen involvement. Citizen involvement, according to the Green platform, should be encouraged through proportional representation and grassroots organizations. The grassroots Greens call for the decentralization of government and the expansion of the power of local boards. Given this orientation, it is not surprising that the Green Party has had most of its success on the local level. By 2004, there were 202 Greens holding local offices in twenty-seven states, including city council positions in cities such as Santa Monica, California; Chapel Hill, North Carolina; and Madison, Wisconsin. In the coastal town of Arcata, California, Greens actually held a majority of seats on the city council, leading some to dub the town Ecotopia.

While the Green Party would restructure government, the Libertarian party seeks to reduce the government's size. Another difference between the two parties is the Libertarian emphasis on the freedom of the individual rather than on the importance of community. The message of the Libertarian platform is that our current government is hopelessly defective

and needs a major overhaul. For example, Libertarians advocate abolishing the income tax and most federal programs, including Social Security. They believe that schools should be left to parental choice, reasoning that lower taxes will allow them to afford to send their children to private or home schools. By 2004, Libertarians had been elected to 600 local offices in thirty-seven states, with their impact greatest in California, New Hampshire, and Pennsylvania.

The New Party calls itself a progressive party and advocates a revolution to transfer power to the American people. Promoting equality, freedom, and prosperity, the New Party stresses the importance of the community in achieving its goals. A unique component of the party's platform is the call for a guaranteed minimum income, or social wage, and a shorter workweek to reach full employment. Women and people of color figure prominently in the New Party. Although its impact is not as extensive as the Green and Libertarian parties, the New Party has found some success in local elections in states such as Arkansas, Montana, and Wisconsin.

Third parties offer alternatives, and a growing number of Americans like what they have to offer. What do you think: Should the two major parties be looking over their shoulders? Should states make it easier for third parties to get on the ballot? And what about Independents? They reject all parties, major and minor. Are we headed toward a partyless future?

SOURCES: The Green Party, www.gp.org (May 1, 2004); the Libertarian Party, www.lp.org (May 1, 2004); the New Party, www.newparty.org (May 1, 2004); Scott Lasley, "Explaining Third Party Support in American States," paper presented at the annual meeting of the American Political Science Association, Washington, D.C. (1997); William Poole, "Inside Ecotopia," *Sierra* (January/February 1998): 30–33.

their agendas and legislatures outline their preferences, cries of partisan politics will undoubtedly be heard. But in a positive sense, such cries symbolize the maturation of state institutions. Partisan politics will probably encourage a wider search for policy alternatives and result in innovative solutions.

In the view of many, two parties are better than one. Heated partisan competition turns a dull campaign into a lively contest, sparking citizen interest and increasing voter turnout. In governance, however, many believe that unified

| FIGURE 5.3 | **Party Control of State Government, 2004** |

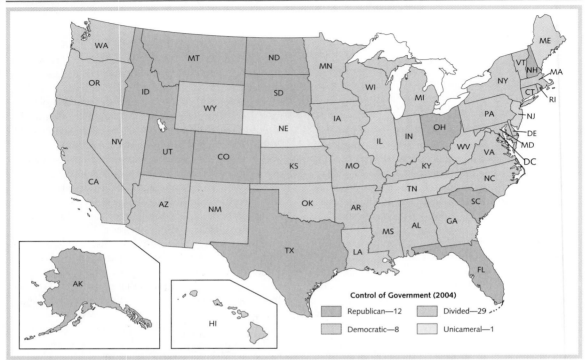

Control of Government (2004)

- Republican—12
- Democratic—8
- Divided—29
- Unicameral—1

SOURCE: "2004 Political Landscape," *State Legislatures* (January 30, 2004): 4. Reprinted with permission from the January 2004 issue of *State Legislatures.* Copyright © 2004 by The National Conference of State Legislatures.

party control is preferable to divided government. When competitive elections produce unified party control of government institutions, the ideal of the responsible party model seems almost within reach.

Is the Party Over?

This impertinent question is intended to spark debate. Have political parties, as we know them, outlived their usefulness? Should they be cast aside as new forms of political organization and communication emerge?

As some have argued, a more educated populace that can readily acquire political information via the Internet is likely to be less reliant on party cues.[26] Today's generation is less loyal to political parties than its grandparents were and is not so likely to vote along party lines. The trend toward **dealignment,** or weakening of individual partisan attachments, slowed for a period but has begun to pick up again. For example, from 1992 to 2004, the number of registered voters in New York increased from 8 million to 11 million. Democrats enjoy a 42 to 28 percent margin in registration, but more than 1 million of the new voters rejected the major parties and registered as unaffiliated or as Independence Party members.[27] These nonmajor party identifiers are difficult to categorize in

dealignment

The weakening of an individual's attachment to political parties.

ideological terms. According to one political consultant, "A large group of the electorate tends to be socially tolerant and more receptive to fiscally conservative methods. They don't have a home in either party."[28] This trend is not good news for the two major parties.

The Democratic and Republican parties are not sitting idly by as their role in the political system is challenged. Party organizations are making their operations more professional and have more money to spend and more staff to spend it. The past several years have seen the development of party-centered advertising campaigns and a renewed commitment to get-out-the-vote drives.[29] In a few states that have publicly funded campaigns, parties as well as candidates have been designated as recipients of funds. All in all, parties are doing their best to adapt to the changing environment.

INTEREST GROUPS

interest groups

Organizations of like-minded individuals who desire to influence government.

Interest groups have become powerful players in our democratic system. Joining a group is a way for individuals to communicate their preferences—their interests—to government. Interest groups attempt to influence governmental decisions and actions by pressuring decisionmaking bodies, for example, to put more guidance counselors in public schools, restrict coastal development, keep a proposed new prison out of a neighborhood, or strengthen state licensing of family therapists. Success is defined in terms of getting the group's preferences enacted. In certain states, interest groups actually dominate the policymaking process.

In considering the role of groups in the political system, we must remember that people join groups for reasons other than politics. For instance, a teacher may be a member of a politically active state education association because the group offers a tangible benefit such as low-cost life insurance, but he may disagree with some of the political positions taken by the organization. In general, motivations for group membership are individually determined.[30]

Types of Interest Groups

Interest groups come in all types and sizes. If you were to visit the lobby of the state capitol when the legislature was in session, you might find the director of the state school boards association conversing with the chairperson of the education committee, or the lobbyist hired by the state hotel-motel association exchanging notes with the representative of the state's restauranteurs. If a legislator were to venture into the lobby, she would probably receive at least a friendly greeting from the lobbyists and at most a serious heart-to-heart talk about the merits of a bill. You would be witnessing efforts to influence public policy. Interest groups want state government to enact policies that are in their interest or, conversely, not to enact policies at odds with their interest.

The interests represented in the capitol lobby are as varied as the states themselves. One interest that is well represented and powerful is business. Whether a lobbyist represents a single large corporation or a consortium of businesses, when he or she talks, state legislators listen. From the perspective of business groups (and other economically oriented groups), legislative actions can cost or save their members money. Therefore, the Chamber of Commerce, industry groups, trade associations, financial institutions, and regulated utilities maintain a visible presence in the state capitol during the legislative session. Table 5.1 documents the influential nature of business interests at the state level. Of course, business interests are not monolithic; occasionally they even find themselves on opposite sides of a bill.

Other interests converge on the capitol. Representatives of labor, both established AFL-CIO unions and professional associations such as the state optometrists' group or sheriffs' association, frequent the hallways and committee meeting rooms to see that the legislature makes the "right" decision on the bills

TABLE 5.1 The Twenty Most Influential Interests in the States

RANK	INTEREST	NUMBER OF STATES IN WHICH THE INTEREST WAS SEEN AS VERY EFFECTIVE
1	General business organizations (chambers of commerce, etc.)	40
2	Schoolteachers' organizations (NEA and AFT)	37
3	Utility companies and associations (electric, gas, water, telephone/telecommunications)	24
4	Insurance: general and medical (companies and associations)	21
5	Hospital/nursing home associations	21
6	Lawyers (predominately trial attorneys and state bar associations)	22
7	Manufacturers (companies and associations)	18
8	General local government organizations (municipal leagues, county organizations, etc.)	18
9	Physicians/state medical associations	17
10	General farm organizations (state farm bureaus, etc.)	16
11	Bankers associations	15
12	Traditional labor associations (predominantly the AFL-CIO)	13
13	Universities and colleges (institutions and employees)	13
14	State and local government employees (other than teachers)	11
15	Contractors/builders/developers	13
16	Realtors' associations	13
17	K–12 education interests (other than teachers)	9
18	Individual labor unions (Teamsters, UAW, etc.)	8
19	Truckers and private transport interests (excluding railroads)	9
20	Hunting and fishing groups (includes anti–gun control groups)	9

NOTE: The ranking is determined by more than the "very effective" score.
SOURCE: Clive S. Thomas and Ronald J. Hrebenar, "2002 State Interest Group Power Update: Results and Tables," manuscript (June 12, 2003), pp. 1, 2. Reprinted by permission of Comparative State Politics.

before it. For example, if a legislature were considering a bill to change the licensing procedures for optometrists, you could expect to find the optometrists' interest group immersed in the debate. Another workers' group, schoolteachers, has banded together to form one of the most effective state-level groups. In fact, as Table 5.1 indicates, schoolteachers' organizations are ranked among the most influential interest groups in thirty-seven states.[31]

Many other interest groups are active (but not necessarily influential) in state government, and a large number are ideological in nature. In other words, their political activity is oriented toward some higher good, such as clean air or fairer tax systems or consumer protection. Members of these groups do not have a direct economic or professional interest in the outcome of a legislative decision. Instead, their lobbyists argue that the public as a whole benefits from their involvement in the legislative process. Penn PIRG, for instance, describes itself as a nonprofit, nonpartisan watchdog group working on behalf of consumers, the environment, and good government in Pennsylvania. The group's motto, and that of other public interest research groups (PIRGs), is "get active, speak out, make a difference."

Looking at a specific state reveals a mix of active, effective interest groups. The list of leading lobbying organizations in Minnesota includes an array of economic interests: professional sports, telecommunications, energy, the alcoholic beverage industry, the Chamber of Commerce, among others.[32] The column of figures in Table 5.2 shows how much each group spent to lobby the legislature, state agencies, and metropolitan government in 2001–2002. The big-spending ways of the Minnesota Twins reflect the organization's persistent pursuit of a new, publicly funded baseball stadium. The range of interests represented among the top fifteen groups is extensive: not only businesses, such as Qwest, but also taxpayers and environmentalists, cities and nonprofits.

Interest Groups in the States

Although states share some similarities, the actual interest group environment is different from one state to another. Variation exists not only in the composition of the involved groups but also in the degree of influence they exert. Research by political scientists Clive Thomas and Ronald Hrebenar, along with a team of researchers throughout the country, provides fresh insights into the interest group scene. Table 5.3 classifies states according to the strength of interest groups vis-à-vis other political institutions in the policymaking process. Groups can dominate other political institutions such as political parties, they can complement them, or they can be subordinate to them.[33] As Table 5.3 shows, interest groups are dominant in five states—that is, they wield an overwhelming and consistent influence on policymaking. There are no states in which interest groups are completely subordinate, but interest groups are comparatively weak in a cluster of three states. Interest groups enjoy complementary, somewhat balanced relationships with other political institutions in sixteen states. The pattern is less stable in the twenty-six states in the dominant/complementary category. In those states, more flux in the system is likely as group power ebbs and flows.

For the most part, interest group politics is defined by its state context.[34] First

| TABLE 5.2 | Big-Spending Lobbying Organizations in Minnesota |

LOBBYING ORGANIZATION	AMOUNT SPENT LOBBYING 2001–2002
Minnesota Twins	$826,489
Qwest	305,251
Xcel Energy Services, Inc.	304,461
Minnesota Licensed Beverage Association	296,800
Minnesota Chamber of Commerce	274,428
Minnesota Credit Union Network	238,057
Minnesota Business Partnership, Inc.	226,346
Minnesota Association of Realtors	181,893
Coalition of Greater Minnesota Cities	166,083
Medica	130,812
Taxpayers League of Minnesota	127,752
Education Minnesota	113,515
Greate River Energy	112,733
Minnesota Council of Nonprofits	102,024
Izaak Walton League of America	100,126

SOURCE: Table, "Big-Spending Lobbying Organizations in Minnesota," *Star Tribune*, September 28, 2002. Copyright 2004 Star Tribune. Republished with permission of Star Tribune, Minneapolis-St. Paul. No further republication or re-distribution is permitted without the written consent of Star Tribune.

of all, interest groups and political parties have evolving, multidimensional relationships. Typically, in states where political parties are weak, interest groups are strong; where political parties are strong, interest groups tend to be weaker.[35] Strong parties provide leadership in the policymaking process, and interest groups function through them. In the absence of party leadership and organization, interest groups fill the void, becoming important recruiters of candidates and financiers of campaigns; accordingly, they exert tremendous influence in policymaking. Although the inverse relationship between parties and groups generally holds true, the politics in a state like New York offers an interesting variation. In the Empire State, groups are active and can be influential, but they work with the established party system in a kind of symbiotic relationship.[36]

A second, related truth adds a developmental angle to interest group politics. As states diversify economically, their politics are less likely to be dominated by a single interest.[37] Thus, we find that the interest group environment is becoming more cluttered, resulting in *hyperpluralism,* or a multiplicity of groups. As states increasingly become the arena in which important social and economic policy decisions are made, more and more groups go to statehouses hoping to find a receptive audience.

TABLE 5.3	**Interest Group Impact**

STATES IN WHICH THE OVERALL IMPACT OF INTEREST GROUPS IS:			
DOMINANT (5)	DOMINANT COMPLEMENTARY (26)	COMPLEMENTARY (16)	COMPLEMENTARY SUBORDINATE (3)
Alabama	Alaska	Colorado	Michigan
Florida	Arizona	Connecticut	Minnesota
Montana	Arkansas	Delaware	South Dakota
Nevada	California	Hawaii	
West Virginia	Georgia	Indiana	
	Idaho	Maine	
	Illinois	Massachusetts	
	Iowa	New Hampshire	
	Kansas	New Jersey	
	Kentucky	New York	
	Louisiana	North Carolina	
	Maryland	North Dakota	
	Mississippi	Pennsylvania	
	Missouri	Rhode Island	
	Nebraska	Vermont	
	New Mexico	Wisconsin	
	Ohio		
	Oklahoma		
	Oregon		
	South Carolina		
	Tennessee		
	Texas		
	Utah		
	Virginia		
	Washington		
	Wyoming		

SOURCE: Clive S. Thomas and Ronald J. Hrebenar, "2002 State Interest Group Power Update: Results and Tables," manuscript (June 12, 2003), Table 2B, pp. 1–3. Reprinted by permission of Comparative State Politics.

Local-Level Interest Groups

Interest groups also function at the local level. Because so much of local government involves the delivery of services, local interest groups devote a great deal of their attention to administrative agencies and departments. Groups are involved in local elections and in community issues, to be sure, but their major focus is on the *actions* of government: policy implementation and service delivery.[38]

National surveys of local officials have indicated that although interest groups are influential in local decisionmaking, they do not dominate the process.[39] As is true at the state level, business groups are considered to be the most influential. Business-related interests, such as the local Chamber of Commerce or a downtown merchants' association, usually wield power in the community. An increasingly influential group at the local level is the neighborhood-based organization. Newer groups at the local level include women's organizations, ideological groups, and homosexual-rights groups. Thus far, these groups have not achieved the degree of influence accorded business and neighborhood groups.

Neighborhood organizations deserve a closer look. Some have arisen out of issues that directly affect neighborhood residents—a local school that is scheduled to close, a wave of violent crime, a proposed freeway route that will destroy homes and businesses. Others have been formed by government itself as a way of channeling citizen participation. For example, St. Paul, Minnesota, is divided into district councils; Portland, Oregon, uses district coalition boards to pull neighborhood representatives together. Research has shown that these arrangements not only empower citizens but also make local government more responsive to public preferences.[40]

direct action

A form of participation designed to draw attention to a cause.

Neighborhood groups, as well as others lacking a bankroll but possessing enthusiasm and dedication, may resort to tactics such as **direct action,** which might involve protest marches at the county courthouse or standing in front of bulldozers clearing land for a new highway. Direct action is usually designed to attract attention to a cause, and it tends to be a last resort, a tactic employed when other efforts at influencing government policy have failed. A study of citizen groups in seven large cities found that 34 percent of the groups engaged in protests or demonstrations at least occasionally.[41]

Techniques Used by Interest Groups

Interest groups want to have a good public image. It helps a group when its preferences can be equated with what is good for the state (or the community). Organizations use slogans like "What's good for the timber industry is good for Oregon" or "Schoolteachers have the interests of New York City at heart." Some groups have taken on the label *public interest groups* to designate their main interest as that of the public at large. Groups, then, invest resources in creating a positive image.

Being successful in the state capitol or at city hall involves more than a good public image, however. For example, interest groups have become effective at organizing networks that exert pressure on legislators. If a teacher pay-raise bill is in jeopardy in the senate, for instance, schoolteachers throughout the state may be asked by the education association to contact their senators to urge them to vote favorably on the legislation. To maximize their strength, groups with common interests often establish coalitions. For example, several years ago, eighteen environmental groups in Arkansas formed an umbrella organization, the Environmental Congress of Arkansas, to get their message out. Sometimes related groups carve out their own niches to avoid direct competition for members and support.[42] For example, gay and lesbian groups, relatively new to state politics, focus on narrow issues such as ending prohibitions on same-sex marriages rather than broad concerns.[43] This targeting strategy allows more groups to flourish. Interest groups also hire representatives who can effectively promote their cause. To ensure that legislators will be receptive to their pressures, groups try to influence the outcome of elections by supporting candidates who reflect their interests.

Several factors affect the relative power of an interest group. In their work, Thomas and Hrebenar have identified ten characteristics that give some groups more political clout than others:

- The degree of necessity of group services and resources to public officials.
- Whether the group's lobbying focus is primarily defensive or offensive.
- The extent and strength of group opposition.
- Potential for the group to enter into coalitions.
- Group financial resources.
- Size and geographical distribution of group membership.
- Political cohesiveness of the membership.
- Political, organizational, and managerial skills of group leaders.
- Timing and the political climate.
- Lobbyist-policymaker relations.[44]

No single interest group is on the "high end" of all ten of these characteristics all of the time. Many of the groups listed in Table 5.1, for example, possess quite a few of these factors. An indispensable group armed with ample resources, a cohesive membership, and skilled leaders, when the timing is right, can wield enormous influence in the state capitol, especially when the group has taken a defensive posture—that is, when it wants to block proposed legislation. On the other hand, victory comes less easily to a group lacking these characteristics.

lobbying

The process by which groups and individuals attempt to influence policymakers.

Lobbying Lobbying is the attempt to influence government decisionmakers. States have developed official definitions to determine who is a lobbyist and who is not. A common definition is "anyone receiving compensation to influence legislative action." A few states, such as Nevada, North Dakota, and Washington, require everyone who attempts to influence legislation to register as a lobbyist (even those who are not being paid), but most exclude public officials, members of the media, and people who speak only before committees or boards from this definition. Because of definitional differences, comparing the number of lobbyists across states raises the proverbial apples-and-oranges problem. But with that in mind, some cautious comparisons can be made. As of 2003, Arizona, Connecticut and New York had more than 3,400 registered lobbyists. Smaller interest group universes are found in Delaware, Hawaii, and Wisconsin each with fewer than 300 registered lobbyists.[45]

In most states, lobbyists are required to file reports indicating how and on whom they spent money. Concern that lobbyists would exert undue influence on the legislative process spurred states to enact new reporting requirements and to impose tougher penalties for their violation. Maine and New Jersey, for instance, require lobbyists to report their sources of income, total and categorized expenditures, the names of the individual officials who received their monies or gifts, and the legislation they supported or opposed. Despite stringent disclosure laws, legislator–lobbyist scandals have caused many states to clamp down even harder. For example, in the wake of scandals in Kentucky, lobbyists and their employers are prohibited from giving *anything* of value (with the exception of meals) to legislators or their immediate family. Public employees in South Carolina and Wisconsin are prohibited from accepting a gift of value from lobbyists, even if it is no more than a cup of coffee.[46]

As state government has expanded and taken on more functions, the number of interests represented in state capitals has exploded.[47] The increase in the number of lobbyists has a simple but important cause: Interests that are affected by state government cannot afford to be without representation. An anecdote from Florida makes the point. Legislators supported a new urban development program that Florida cities had lobbied for but about which they could not agree on a funding source. After much debate, they found one: a sales tax on dry cleaning. Because the dry-cleaning industry did not have a lobbyist in Tallahassee, there was no one to speak out on its behalf. Indeed, since their views were not represented in the debate over funding sources, dry cleaners were an easy target. (The dry-cleaning industry learned its lesson and hired a lobbyist a few days after the tax was enacted.)[48]

To influence legislators in their decisionmaking, lobbyists need access, so they cultivate good relationships with lawmakers. In other words, they want connections; they want an in. There are many ways of establishing connections, such as entertaining, gift giving, and contributing to campaigns. Lawmakers want to know how a proposed bill might affect the different interests throughout the state and in their legislative districts, and what it is expected to achieve. And lobbyists are only too happy to oblige. Social lobbying—wining and dining legislators—still goes on, but it is being supplemented by another technique: the provision of information. A study of western states has revealed a new breed of lobbyists trained as attorneys and public relations specialists, skilled in media presentation and information packaging.[49]

An analysis of the lobbying environment in three states—California, South Carolina, and Wisconsin—identified the kinds of techniques that lobbyists rely on. Table 5.4 lists the techniques that more than 80 percent of the 595 lobbyists surveyed said they used. Providing information is clearly a large part of a lobbyist's role, but a few of the techniques, such as having influential constituents contact a legislator's office, tend toward more of a leaning-on approach. Notice that lobbying is not confined to the legislative process. Lobbyists regularly attempt to shape the implementation of policies after they are enacted.

The influence of lobbyists specifically and of interest groups generally is a subject of much debate. The popular image is one of a wheeler-dealer lobbyist whose very presence in a committee hearing room can spell the fate of a bill. But, in fact, his will is done because the interests he represents are considered vital to the state, because he has assiduously laid the groundwork, and because legislators respect the forces he can mobilize if necessary. Few lobbyists cast this long a shadow, however, and their interaction with legislators is seldom this mechanical. Much contemporary interest group research suggests that patterns of influence are somewhat unpredictable and highly dependent on the state context.[50]

grassroots lobbying

Group mobilization of citizens to contact public officials on behalf of shared public policy views.

A not so new tactic that is enjoying a resurgence is **grassroots lobbying**—"the planned and orchestrated demonstration of public support through the mobilization of constituent action."[51] Since lobbying reforms have changed the political landscape, groups increasingly rely on their members to communicate with legislators (translation: bombard with mail, faxes, and telephone calls) on behalf of the group's issue. Grassroots lobbying is not just a technique for outsiders. A recent study shows that citizen groups, unions, religious/charitable groups, corporations, and trade and professional associations all use grassroots techniques.[52] This trend has given rise to the term *astroturfing,* or bogus grassroots lobbying.

political action committees (PACs)

Organizations that raise and distribute campaign funds to candidates for elective office.

Political Action Committees Political action committees (PACs) made extensive inroads into state politics in the 1980s. Narrowly focused subsets of interest groups, PACs are political organizations that collect funds and distribute them to candidates. PACs serve as the campaign financing arm of corporations, labor unions, trade associations, and even political parties. They grew out of long-standing laws that made it illegal for corporations and labor unions to contribute directly to a candidate. Barred from direct contributions, these organizations set up political action subsidiaries to allow them legal entry into campaign

TABLE 5.4	**The Most Popular Techniques Used by Lobbyists**
1.	Testifying at legislative hearings.
2.	Contacting government officials directly to present a point of view.
3.	Helping to draft legislation.
4.	Alerting state legislators to the effects of a bill on their districts.
5.	Having influential constituents contact legislator's office.
6.	Consulting with government officials to plan legislative strategy.
7.	Attempting to shape implementation of policies.
8.	Mounting grassroots lobbying efforts.
9.	Helping to draft regulations, rules, or guidelines.
10.	Shaping government's agenda by raising new issues and calling attention to previously ignored problems.
11.	Engaging in informal contacts with officials.
12.	Inspiring letter-writing or telegram campaigns.

SOURCE: Anthony Nownes and Patricia Freeman, "Interest Group Activity in the States," *Journal of Politics* 60 (February 1998): 92. Reprinted by permission of Blackwell Publishing Ltd.

finance. Probably one of the oddest PACs in recent years was 21st Century Vote, organized by a Chicago street gang called the Gangster Disciples.[53] In 1994, this PAC raised money on behalf of certain candidates in the Windy City and, with a membership of 30,000, even engaged in grassroots lobbying.

The impact of PACs on state politics is just beginning to become clear. Some Michigan legislators, for example, consider PACs a potentially dangerous influence on state politics because their money "buys a lot of access that others can't get."[54] And access can mean influence. Research on tobacco industry PACs suggests that their campaign contributions affect legislative behavior: "As legislators [in California, Colorado, Massachusetts, Pennsylvania, and Washington] received more tobacco industry campaign contributions . . . legislators were more likely to be pro-tobacco industry."[55]

States have responded to the proliferation of PACs by increasing their regulation. In New Jersey, for instance, PACs are required to register and to provide information regarding their controlling interests. In Kentucky, a candidate's total PAC contributions are limited to 35 percent of receipts or $5,000, whichever is larger.[56] One likely possibility is that an independent interstate network of groups with money to spend could emerge as a real threat to political parties as a recruiter of candidates and a financier of campaigns. As a harbinger of tighter regulation of PACs, Washington enacted a law that restricts contributions from out-of-state PACs.

POLITICAL CAMPAIGNS

Political parties and interest groups bump into each other all the time, especially in political campaigns. Political campaigns aren't what they used to be. State and local campaigns are no longer unsophisticated operations run from someone's dining room table. The new era of campaign technology and financing makes information accessible to almost everyone through television, the mailbox, and most recently the Internet. But despite the sophisticated technologies, the goal remains the same: attracting enough voters to win the election. Figure 5.4 diagrams the voting configuration in a hypothetical election district. This district typically splits its vote evenly between Democrats and Republicans. Thus, in any given election, each party can count on about 25 percent of the vote (labeled the "base" in the diagram), with another 17 percent that is fairly likely to vote for the party's candidate (the "soft" partisan vote). That leaves about 16 percent of the vote up for grabs (the toss-up vote).[57] The toss-up vote and the soft partisan vote comprise what is typically referred to as the swing vote. Candidates target their energies on the swing vote, the size of which varies with the distribution of the partisan base vote. It is important to remember that most districts are not as evenly divided in their partisan loyalties as the hypothetical district.

A New Era of Campaigns

Campaigns of the past conjure up images of fiery oratory and county fairs. But campaigns orchestrated by rural courthouse gangs and urban ward bosses have

FIGURE 5.4   The Voting Configuration of a Hypothetical Election District

Candidates rely on their partisan base and compete for the swing vote.

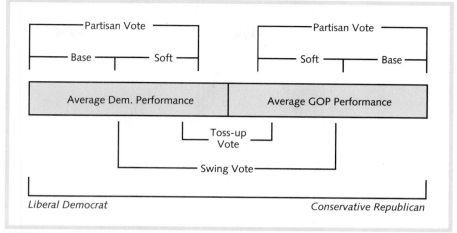

SOURCE: Daniel M. Shea and Michael John Burton, *Campaign Craft: The Strategies, Tactics, and Art of Political Campaign Management* (Westport, Conn.: Praeger, 2001), p. 77.

given way to stylized video and electronic campaigning, which depends on the mass media and political consultants. Direct contact with potential voters still matters, of course. Candidates for state legislative seats, for example, devote time to door-to-door canvassing, neighborhood drop-ins, and public forums. Yet more and more, they rely on direct mail and electronic media to deliver their messages to voters and on political consultants to help them craft the message.[58]

Negative Campaigning The level of negativism in political campaigns, especially in advertising, has increased. Yet, nationwide, the public is registering its disapproval of mudslinging, take-no-prisoners campaigns. The strident tone projected in campaigns seems to have fueled cynicism about both government and politics and may have the effect of reducing voter turnout. Tired of the unrelenting nastiness, states are exploring different ways of controlling negative campaigning.

Negative campaign advertising comes in three flavors: fair, false, and deceptive. A fair ad might emphasize some embarrassing aspect of an opponent's voting record or some long-forgotten indiscretion. A false ad, as the label implies, contains untrue statements. More problematic are deceptive advertisements. These misleading ads distort the truth about an opponent. The difficulty for states is to regulate negative campaign advertising without violating free-speech guarantees of the U.S. Constitution. False advertising that is done with actual malice can be prohibited by a state, but deceptive ads, replete with accusation and innuendo, are more difficult to regulate.[59]

Louisiana
gubernatorial
candidate, Bobby
Jindal, enlists the
support of his wife
and daughter as he
campaigns on
election day 2003.
SOURCE: © J. Becker Hill/
CORBIS.

Twenty states have enacted laws prohibiting false campaign statements; candidates who use false ads against their opponents can be fined. One of the problems with these laws is that the damage is done long before the remedy can be applied. Fining a candidate after the election is akin to latching the barn door after the horse has fled. Nine states have adopted a fair campaign practices code. These codes typically contain broad guidelines such as "do not misrepresent the facts" or "do not make appeals to prejudice based on race or sex." The limitation of the codes is that compliance is voluntary rather than mandatory.

In addition to government action, many newspapers have begun to report regularly on the content, presentation, and relative accuracy of campaign advertising. Ad watches or truth boxes, as they are often called, occasionally have led to the retraction or redesign of ads. Despite the efforts of government and the media, negative campaign advertising persists because many candidates believe that, if done cleverly, it can benefit their campaigns. After all, people may not like negative ads, but they certainly seem to remember them.

Political Consultants Along with increased use of the media, a new occupational specialty sprang up during the 1970s and 1980s: political consulting. Individuals with expertise in polling, direct mail, fund-raising, advertising, and campaign management sign on to work for political campaigns, in which the use of new campaign technology makes their expertise invaluable. The occupation is undoubtedly here to stay, and several colleges and universities now offer degree programs in practical politics and campaign management.

Consultants form the core of the professional campaign management team assembled by candidates for state offices. They identify and target likely voters, both those who are already in the candidate's camp and need to be reminded to vote *and* those who can be persuaded to vote for the candidate. They use survey research to find out what the public is thinking. They carefully craft messages to appeal to specific voters, such as the elderly, home owners, and environmentalists. Advertising on cable television and through direct mail are two popular means of getting a candidate's message to subsets of potential voters (see Table 5.5).

Any number of factors can influence the result of an election, such as the presence of an incumbent in a race and the amount of funds a challenger has accumulated, but one significant factor is the ability to frame or define the issues during the campaign. Even in a quietly contested state legislative race, district residents are likely to receive mailings that state the candidates' issue positions, solicit funds, and perhaps comment unfavorably on the opposition. The candidate who has an effective political consultant to help set the campaign agenda and thereby put her opponent on the defensive is that much closer to victory. Research on legislative elections indicates that the use of campaign professionals is especially valuable to challengers who are hoping to unseat incumbents.[60]

The Impact of Mass Media

The mass media, especially television, are intrinsic aspects of modern statewide campaigns. Even candidates for local offices are increasingly using the mass media to transmit their messages. Campaigners can either buy their time and newspaper space for advertising or get it free by arranging events that reporters are

| TABLE 5.5 | **What Political Consultants Do for Candidates** |

SERVICE	PERCENTAGE
Survey research	92.2
Cable television advertising	86.7
Direct mail	86.7
Newspaper advertising	82.2
Direct voter contact	82.2
Radio advertising	75.6
Precinct walking	73.3
Broadcast advertising	71.1
Phone banks	57.8
Internet sites	44.4
Press secretary	40.0

SOURCE: "What Political Consultants Do for Candidates," adapted from Stephen J. Stambough and David McCuan, "Political Cable Advertising and the Future of Political Campaigns," *Comparative State Politics* 20 (December 1999): 19. Reprinted by permission from Comparative State Politics, University of Illinois at Springfield.

likely to cover. These events range from serious (a candidate's major policy statement) to gimmicky (a candidate climbing into the ring with a professional wrestler to demonstrate his "toughness"); either way, they are cleverly planned to capture media attention.

A candidate seeking free media attention needs to create visual events, be quotable, and relentlessly attack opponents or targeted problems. But as the magazine *Campaigns & Elections* advises, he or she must integrate gimmicks with a message that appeals to the electorate. In one of its issues, this magazine contained articles, aimed at candidates, about "making a name for yourself," "nailing the opposition," and "effective targeting."[61] Televised debates offer another opportunity for free media time. In 2002, the Democratic candidates for governor in Texas debated twice during the primary election campaign. Their debating twice was not particularly unusual; the distinction lay in that one of the debates was conducted in Spanish, an indicator of just how important the Latino vote has become, and not only in Texas.[62]

Free media time is seldom sufficient. Candidates, particularly those running for higher-level state offices and for positions in large cities, rely on paid advertisements to reach the public. Paid media advertisements seem to be of two distinct varieties: negative (as discussed earlier) and generic. Generic advertisements include:

1. *The sainthood spot,* which glorifies the candidate and her accomplishments.
2. *The testimonial,* in which other people (celebrities, average citizens) attest to the candidate's abilities.
3. *The bumper-sticker policy spot,* which emphasizes the campaign's popular and noncontroversial themes (good schools, lower taxes, more jobs).
4. *The feel-good spot,* which identifies and capitalizes on the spirit of a place and its people (for example, "Vermont's a special place" or "Nobody can do it better than Pennsylvania").[63]

Media advertising is important because it is frequently the only contact a potential voter has with a candidate. A candidate's personal characteristics and style—important considerations to an evaluating public—are easily transmitted via the airwaves. And, indeed, advances in communications technology offer new options to enterprising candidates. For instance, more candidates are now using cable television to cut media costs and to target audiences. One candidate for the Maryland House of Delegates distributed homemade videotapes to 7,000 targeted households in his district. Curious VCR-equipped voters could tune into the candidate whenever they wanted, pause the spiel, rewind the tape, and play it again.[64]

As former Vermont governor Howard Dean's bid for the Democratic presidential nomination in 2004 showed, the Internet can be a powerful campaign tool. It can disseminate the candidate's message to far-flung audiences, mobilize potential supporters, and serve as a vehicle for attracting contributions. To many observers, the Internet has the potential to transform campaigning just as television did fifty years ago. By 2002, all of the major candidates for gubernatorial offices were maintaining campaign web sites, some rudimentary, others much more elaborate. Several statewide candidates pioneered the use of campaign e-cards (the electronic equivalent of chain letters) so that supporters could contact people in their e-mail address books about the candidate. One of the keys for the future is the creation of interactive web sites that engage Web surfers and keep them coming back. The value of the Internet in campaigns has only just begun to be explored, but an example from Denver underscores its potential. In a preemptive move, a Denver politician bought the domain names of his rivals in an effort to keep them off the Web.[65] It is a far cry from the old days when a candidate's biggest worry during the campaign season was whether an opponent was stealing his yard signs!

Campaign Finance

To campaign for public office is to spend money—a lot of money. How do you define "a lot"? Return to the 2002 Democratic primary for governor of Texas mentioned earlier. The victorious candidate, Tony Sanchez, spent more than $20 million for the chance to face (and ultimately, lose to) the Republican incumbent in the general election.[66] Much of the money came from Sanchez's own personal fortune. Thirty-six governors' seats were up for election in 2002 and, all told, campaign spending topped $839 million.[67] This represented a near doubling of the expenditure totals from the gubernatorial campaigns just four years earlier. And big spending is not confined to gubernatorial contests. Spending in state legislative races was higher than ever in 2002, topping the half-million dollar mark in a few hotly contested races. The same year, more than $6 million was spent in the campaigns for two seats on the Ohio Supreme Court. Spending by issue-advocacy groups in support or opposition to the judicial candidates pushed total spending in the court races closer to $12 million.[68] By 2004, the figures for spending on campaign advertising alone soared to $1.3 billion, much of that money spent, of course, in the presidential race that headed the ballot.[69]

Just how important is money? One knowledgeable observer concluded: "In the direct primaries, where self-propelled candidates battle for recognition, money is crucial. Electronic advertising is the only way to gain visibility. Hence the outcome usually rewards the one with the largest war chest."[70] This trend does not bode well for an idealistic but underfunded potential candidate. Winning takes money, either the candidate's or someone else's. If the latter, it may come with a string or two attached. And as noted earlier, that stipulation is the real concern: To what extent do campaign contributions buy access and influence for the contributor?

Recent research has confirmed several long-standing truths about the costs of campaigning.[71] For instance, close elections cost more than elections in which one candidate is sure to win because uncertainty regarding the outcome is a spur to spending. A candidate quickly learns that it is easier to get money from potential contributors when the polls show that she has a chance of winning. Also, elections that produce change—that is, in which an incumbent is unseated or the out-of-office party gains the office—typically cost more. Taking on an existing officeholder is a risky strategy that drives up election costs. And an open race in which there is no incumbent represents an opportunity for the party out of office to capture the seat, thus triggering similar spending by the in-office party in an effort to protect the seat. It is no wonder that campaign costs are exploding.

Major candidates, especially incumbents, do not have to look too hard to find campaign money. As mentioned earlier, PACs loom larger and larger as heavy funders of state election campaigns. Data from legislative races in seventeen states show that PACs contribute heavily to incumbents.[72] In Utah, incumbent legislators rely on PACs for approximately 70 percent of their campaign funds; in Kansas, they rely on PACs for 66 percent. In Minnesota, however, PAC funding accounts for only 11 percent of an incumbent's funds.

State Efforts at Campaign Reform Concern over escalating costs and the influence of wealthy special interests in campaigns has led reform groups such as Common Cause to call for improved state laws to provide comprehensive and timely disclosure of campaign finances, impose limitations on contributions by individuals and groups, create a combined public-private financing mechanism for primaries and general elections, and establish an independent commission to enforce tough sanctions on violators of campaign finance laws.

States have performed impressively on the first of these recommendations; in fact, all states have some sort of campaign financing reporting procedure. In response to the fourth recommendation, twenty-six states have established independent commissions to oversee the conduct of campaigns, although they have found it somewhat difficult to enforce the law and punish violators.

The other recommendations have proved more troublesome. States have grappled with the issue of costly campaigns but have made only modest progress in controlling costs. A 1976 decision by the U.S. Supreme Court in *Buckley* v. *Valeo* made these efforts more difficult; the Court ruled that governments cannot limit a person's right to spend money on spreading his views about particular issues and candidates. In essence, then, a candidate has unlimited power to spend his own money on his own behalf, and other individuals may spend to their hearts' content to promote their own opinions on election-related issues. In 1996, in a lawsuit from Colorado, the Court decided that **independent spending** by political parties, so-called **soft money,** also could not be limited. The 2002 federal Bipartisan Campaign Reform Act, typically referred to as the McCain-Feingold law, aims at controlling the flow of soft money. (The nearby *Breaking New Ground* box takes up the issue of soft money and state campaign finance reform.) What the Court let stand, however, were state limits on an individual's contributions to candidates and parties; it also ruled that if a candidate accepts public funds, then he is bound by whatever limitations the state may impose.

Some states have established specific limits on the amount of money that organizations and individuals can contribute to a political race. In New York, for example, corporations are limited to a contribution maximum of $5,000 per calendar year, and individuals (other than official candidates) are restricted to $150,000. Florida allows corporations, labor unions, and PACs to contribute a maximum of $500 per candidate. The same limits apply to individuals, excluding the candidate's own contributions. Some states, such as Arizona, Connecticut, North Dakota, Pennsylvania, and Rhode Island, have gone even further by prohibiting contributions from corporations and labor unions.[73] But a totally different philosophy pervades the politics of several states that continue to op-

independent spending

Spending that is not tied to specific candidates but promotes activities such as voter registration and turnout.

soft money

Unregulated funds contributed to national political parties and nonparty political groups.

BREAKING NEW GROUND

Rethinking Campaign Finance

Money is a necessary evil in campaigns, and efforts to reform campaign financing have frustrated the states. But states continue to persevere. Maine voters approved the Clean Elections Act initiative in 1996, which gave candidates the option of privately or publicly financed campaigns. The new law also clamped down on contributions by corporations and PACs, limiting their donations to a maximum of $250. Vermont passed its own Clean Elections Act in 1997; voters in Arizona and Massachusetts followed suit and adopted similar reforms in 1998; Oregon did so in 2000. The Arizona program has an unusual funding source: a 10 percent surcharge is levied on criminal and civil penalties to generate funds for it. But the "free" money comes with some conditions. Candidates who accept public funds have to agree to certain spending limits and lower contribution levels. The Arizona program has grown in popularity; in 2002, for example, nearly 50 percent of the eligible candidates selected the public financing option. That same year, Governor Janet Napolitano became the first governor to be elected with full public financing of her campaign.

These new campaign finance laws have to adjust to the changing rules regarding soft money. "Soft money" refers to unregulated funds that, prior to the passage of the federal Bipartisan Campaign Reform Act, were contributed to national political parties and then redistributed to state parties. In fact, in 2002, soft money made up more than one-quarter of the funds at state parties' disposal. These funds can be used for promotional activities such as voter registration efforts, get-out-the-vote drives, issue advertising, and events that benefit all candidates. Once parties were banned from receiving soft money, nonparty political organizations (called 527s, after a section of the U.S. tax code) sprang up and began receiving and disbursing soft money. (America Coming Together is a pro-Democratic group; Americans for a Better Country is a pro-Republican 527.)

Soft money weakens a state's campaign finance laws. For example, groups that may be prohibited by state law from providing funds directly to candidates can give their money to a 527 organization. This organization then spends the money in the state on a candidate's behalf. State political parties and many candidates, on the other hand, welcomed soft money and were unhappy to see the rules changed. In the 2004 elections, even with 527 organizations playing a big role, much spending was "hard money," that is, subject to contribution limits and required to be disclosed. As the impact of the federal law became clear, states began a new round of legislation aimed at regulating campaign finance.

SOURCES: Alan Greenblatt, "That Clean-All-Over Feeling," *Governing* 15 (July 2002): 40–42; Ronald D. Michaelson, "Trends in State Campaign Financing," *The Book of the States 2003* (Lexington, Ky.: Council of State Governments, 2003), pp. 270–80.

---

erate their election systems without any limitations on contributions. In Illinois, Missouri, and Virginia, to name just a few, organizations and individuals can contribute as much as they wish.

States have also considered the other side of the campaign financing equation: expenditures. Almost all states require candidates and political committees to file reports documenting the expenditure of campaign funds. Although a few states continue to impose limits on a candidate's total expenditures, many have followed Hawaii's lead and set voluntary spending limits. Colorado, for example, has adopted a nonbinding $2 million spending cap for gubernatorial candidates. But legal challenges wait in the wings. For instance, Missouri's system for voluntary expenditures was recently ruled unconstitutional. Michigan takes a different approach: Publicly funded candidates (governor and lieutenant governor) are restricted to $2 million per election, with additional spending allowable in certain circumstances. Florida and Kentucky have similar systems in place for candidates receiving public funds. In just over half of the states, however, candidates campaign without any spending limits.

Public Funding as a Solution   Almost half the states have adopted some sort of public funding of campaigns. Individuals voluntarily contribute to a central fund, which is divided among candidates or political parties. The system is fairly easy to administer and is relatively transparent for citizens. In most of the public-funding states, citizens can use their state income tax form to earmark a portion (a dollar or two) of their tax liability for the fund. A check-off system of this sort does not directly increase taxpayers' tax burden. In a few states, the public fund is amassed through a voluntary surcharge, or additional tax (usually $1.00, although California allows surcharges of $5.00, $10.00, and $25.00). Indiana has opted for a different approach: Revenues from the sale of personalized motor vehicle license plates support the fund.

In addition to check-offs and surcharges, some of the public-funding states, including Minnesota and Ohio, offer taxpayers a tax credit (usually 50 percent of the contribution, up to a specific maximum) when they contribute to political campaigns. A more popular supplement to public funding is a state tax deduction for campaign contributions, an approach used in Hawaii, Oklahoma, and North Carolina. A final though not widely explored approach is direct state appropriation of funds. Maryland, for instance, does not use check-offs or surcharges but relies on a direct state appropriation to candidates for governor and lieutenant governor.[74]

Public campaign financing is supposed to rid the election process of some of its evils. Proponents argue that it will democratize the contribution process by freeing candidates from excessive reliance on special-interest money. Other possible advantages include expanding the pool of potential candidates, allowing candidates to compete on a more equal basis, and reducing the cost of campaigning. In Maine, a Green Party gubernatorial candidate turned down PAC money and large contributions, relying instead on nearly $900,000 in public funds. (He finished third with 9 percent of the vote.)[75]

By contributing to the fund, average citizens may feel that they have a greater stake in state elections. Although more research needs to be done, studies suggest that public financing produces at least some of the benefits its supporters claim. For instance, an analysis of gubernatorial campaigns indicated that the use of public funds by incumbents and challengers holds down overall spending. It also narrows the expenditure gap between them.[76] As the *Breaking New Ground* box suggested, public financing continues to be an important weapon in the state struggle to reform and control the influence of money in campaigns.

CHAPTER RECAP

- Even though voter loyalties have weakened, political parties have proved remarkably resilient and have taken on new roles in politics and governance.
- Each major party can claim about 30 percent of the voting-age public for itself. The rest of the electorate is considered independents, with a small fraction affiliated with third parties.
- Interparty competition has increased over time. One result has been a rise in divided government.
- Interest groups exert a powerful force in state government, with business lobbyists and teachers' groups the most influential in the majority of states.
- The state interest group system is changing: A more diverse set of interests lobbies at the state capital; meanwhile, state governments have tightened their regulation of lobbyists.
- Groups are involved in local elections and in community issues, but their major focus is on the *actions* of government: policy implementation and service delivery.
- Campaigns for state office still involve door-to-door canvassing, neighborhood drop-ins, and public forums, but they increasingly use direct mail, electronic media, and political consultants.
- Running for public office can be an expensive proposition. To try to level the playing field and diminish the role of private money, most states limit contributions and many provide public financing.

Key Terms

political parties *(p. 111)*	interest groups *(p. 121)*
responsible party model *(p. 112)*	direct action *(p. 126)*
ticket splitting *(p. 112)*	lobbying *(p. 127)*
pragmatism *(p. 114)*	grassroots lobbying *(p. 129)*
divided government *(p. 118)*	political action committees (PACs) *(p. 129)*
unified government *(p. 118)*	independent spending *(p. 136)*
dealignment *(p. 120)*	soft money *(p. 136)*

Surfing the Web

The major political parties have official web sites: **www.democrats.org** and **www.rnc.org.**

At the state level, illustrative web sites are Hawaii's at **www.hawaiidemocrats. org** and Ohio's at **www.ohiogop.org.**

An interesting state-level, third-party web site, **www.cagreens.org,** is the site for the Green Party of California.

Common Cause has a web site, **www.commoncause.org/states,** that tracks the activities of its thirty-six state offices and the progress of campaign finance reform.

Another group devoted to cleaning up elections is Public Campaign. Their web site is **www.publicampaign.org.**

Different perspectives are reflected in the web sites of the American Civil Liberties Union, **www.aclu.org,** and the Christian Coalition, **www.cc.org.**

www.flchamber.com and **www.ilchamber.org** are the web sites for the chambers of commerce for Florida and Illinois, respectively. Other state chambers use similar URLs.

The Texas State Teachers' Association at **www.tsta.org** is an example of a state school teachers organization. A different but related perspective is provided by the Oregon Congress of Parents and Teachers Associations at **www.oregonpta. org.**

Other examples of state-level interest groups include The West Virginia Association of Realtors at **www.wvrealtors.com** and the Arizona Hospital and Healthcare Association at **www.azhha.org.**

STATE LEGISLATURES

These days, channel surfers may encounter unusual images as they check out one television channel after another. There, amid *Survivor* and *American Idol,* is an actual reality show: the state legislature. Twenty-nine states have made provisions to televise some or all of their legislative proceedings. Debate on the floor, testimony in committees, and reports of the staff are just some of the programming features. States vary: Is the coverage gavel-to-gavel (as in Minnesota) or limited to certain hours (as in Oregon), live (as in New Jersey) or tape-delayed (as in Nevada), produced by the legislature (as in California) or contracted out (as in Hawaii), or supplemented by streaming video over the Internet (as in Florida) or not (Massachusetts)? Regardless of the variations, the legislature is making its way into citizens' living rooms.

The rationale behind the programming is simple: to make the work of the legislature accessible to the public.[1] Thus, the public can decide for itself whether its elected representatives and the legislature are performing up to expectations.

THE ESSENCE OF LEGISLATURES

The new year dawns quietly in Boise, Idaho, Jefferson City, Missouri, and Harrisburg, Pennsylvania, but it does not remain quiet for long: State legislators are set to converge on the state capitol. Every January (or February or March in a few states; every other January in a few others), state legislatures reconvene in session to do the public's business. More than 7,000 legislators hammer out solutions to intricate and often intransigent public problems. They do so in an institution that is steeped in tradition and governed by layers of formal rules and informal norms.

Legislative Functions

Legislatures engage in three principal functions: *policymaking, representation,* and *oversight.* The first, policymaking, includes enacting laws and allocating funds. The start of the twenty-first century found legislators debating issues such as e-commerce, tax relief, and growth control. These deliberations resulted in the revision of old laws, the passage of new laws, and changes in spending, which is what policymaking is all about. Legislatures do not have sole control of the state policymaking function; governors, courts, and agencies also determine policy, through executive orders, judicial decisions, and administrative regulations, respectively. But legislatures are the dominant policymaking institutions in state government. Table 6.1 lists the issues that attracted legislative attention in 2004.

In their second function, legislators are expected to represent their constituents—the people who live in their district—in two ways. At least in theory, they are expected to speak for their constituents in the legislative chamber—to do the will of the public in designing policy solutions. This task is not easy. On quiet issues, a legislator seldom has much of a clue about public opinion. And on noisy issues, constituents' will is rarely unanimous. Individuals and organized groups with different perspectives may write to or visit their legislator to urge her to vote a certain way on a pending bill. In another representative function, legislators act as their constituents' facilitators in state government. For example, they may help a citizen deal with an unresponsive state agency. This kind of constituency service (or casework, as it is often called) can pay dividends at re-election time because voters tend to look favorably on a legislator who has helped them.

The oversight function is different from the policymaking and representation functions. Concerned that the laws they passed and the funds they allocated frequently did not produce the intended effect, lawmakers began to pay more attention to the performance of the state bureaucracy. Legislatures have

TABLE 6.1	Popular Legislative Issues in 2004
ISSUE	**WHAT IT'S ALL ABOUT**
Budget shortfalls	Even amid signs of economic recovery, most state budget situations are tenuous. States must cut spending and find revenue—a particularly ticklish task in an election year.
Health care coverage	The escalating cost of health insurance affects states as employers and as Medicaid administrators. States look for ways to lower costs and insure more people.
Education standards	States are trying to meet educational goals set in the federal No Child Left Behind Act. Major efforts aim at improving teacher quality and assisting failing schools.
Prescription drugs	Costs for prescription drugs consume a large part of a state's health care expenditures. Legislatures are considering drug-purchasing pools and discounted drugs.
Business climate	In an effort to attract new jobs and spur economic development, legislatures are debating tax incentives and changes to worker's compensation systems.
Tax reform	The primary issues are the distribution of the tax burden and whether the tax system is sufficiently robust.
Energy	The 2003 blackouts left concerns in their wake, especially the reliability of the energy grid, the prices for natural gas, and power line placement.
Insurance	Two major issues in this policy area: medical malpractice insurance (capping damage awards) and life insurance (streamlining the approval process).
Air quality	Northeastern states seek remedies for pollution from midwestern facilities. Many states are investigating alternative-fuel vehicles.
Gay marriage	Massachusetts court ruling allows gay marriage. Two-thirds of the states have laws defining marriage as between a woman and a man.

SOURCE: Adapted from Melissa Conradi, "Ten Legislative Issues to Watch," *Governing* (January 2004): www.governing.com. Reprinted by permission of *Governing*.

adopted several methods for checking on agency implementation and spending. The oversight role takes legislatures into the administrative realm. Not surprisingly, this role is little welcomed by agencies, although legislatures see it as a logical extension of their policymaking role.

A History of Legislative Malfunction

Early in the twentieth century, state legislatures were in poor shape, and they continued to languish well into the 1960s. Malfunctioning legislatures were the result of three conditions: not enough pay, not enough time, and not enough help.[2] Until the mid-1960s, pay was so low that legislative service attracted only the independently wealthy, the idle, and young careerists on the rise. For example, lawyers who were just beginning their practice often campaigned for the legislature as a way of getting their names known, in the hope that it might bring some business their way. Annual legislative salaries ranged from $100 in New Hampshire to $10,000 in New York. Serving in the legislature was a part-time vocation, and most members had to supplement their salaries with other jobs. Some collected unemployment compensation. Others sought income from legal fees; retainers from corporations, public utilities, or interest groups; or outright payoffs from lobbyists for votes or other assistance in the legislative process.

The length and frequency of legislative sessions were additional problems. Some were restricted to as few as thirty-six days in session (in Alabama, for example), and most met on a biennial basis. For instance, the Texas constitution required the legislature to meet once every two years for 140 days. (Critics have suggested that the constitution really meant for the legislature to meet once every 140 years for two days.) As the policy problems confronting state government became more numerous and complex, legislators found themselves overburdened with work and without the time to give much more than cursory examination to most of the proposed legislation that crossed their desks.

As for help, legislatures in the early 1960s were woefully understaffed and poorly equipped to process information, study problems, or respond to the needs of citizens. Many states did not make transcripts of committee hearings or floor debates and thus had no formal legislative history. Some states turned to organizations such as the state bar association for assistance in drafting bills. Without enough staff, legislatures lacked an independent research capability. It was almost impossible for them to accumulate information and systematically analyze possible solutions to contemporary problems. Instead, they tended to rely on the governor and the executive branch as well as on lobbyists for special interests, who set the policy agenda and controlled the flow of information.

State legislatures could not function as effective policymaking institutions under these conditions. Despite the pervasive sense that matters had to improve, it took two factors to shake legislatures out of their lethargy: first, the federal court decisions in *Baker v. Carr* (1962) and *Reynolds v. Sims* (1964), which resulted in the reapportionment of both the lower and upper houses of state legislatures (compliance with these rulings eventually changed the composition of legislatures); second, the activities of private reform groups of the 1960s such as the Committee on Economic Development and the Citizens' Conference on State Legislatures, which promoted the modernization of state legislatures to make them more capable institutions. The success of the reformers has produced legislative assemblies that are far more professional than they were in the past. (Reapportionment and legislative reform are discussed in depth later in this chapter.)

LEGISLATIVE DYNAMICS

State legislative bodies are typically referred to as the legislature, but their formal titles vary. In Colorado, it is the General Assembly that meets every year; in Massachusetts, the General Court; and in Oregon, the Legislative Assembly. The legislatures of forty-four states meet annually; in only six states (Arkansas, Montana, Nevada, North Dakota, Oregon, and Texas), they meet every two years. (Kentucky had been among the biennial sessions group until 2000, when voters approved a switch to annual legislative sessions.) The length of the legislative session varies widely. For example, the New York legislature convened on

Length

Define

day

90 days

January 8, 2003, and did not adjourn until December 31 of that year—a total of 359 calendar days in session. In Utah, by contrast, the legislature gathered in Salt Lake City on January 20, 2003, and was out of town by March 5, 2003, for a total of forty-five calendar days in session.[3]

The length of a state's legislative session can be a sensitive issue. In 1997, the Nevada legislature met for 169 days—the longest, most expensive session in its history.[4] Nevadans showed their displeasure the following year, when they passed a measure limiting future legislative sessions to 120 days. Voters in the Silver State apparently believe that it should not take more than four months—every two years—to conduct their state's business.

The Senate and the House

State legislatures have two houses or chambers, similar to those of the U.S. Congress. Forty-nine state legislatures are bicameral. (As noted in Chapter 3, the exception is Nebraska, which in 1934 established a unicameral legislature). Bicameralism owes its existence to the postcolonial era, in which an upper house, or senate, represented the interests of the propertied class, and a lower house represented everyone else. Even after this distinction was eliminated, states stuck with the bicameral structure, ostensibly because of its contribution to the concept of checks and balances. It is much tougher to pass bills when they have to survive the scrutiny of two legislative houses. Having a bicameral structure, then, reinforces the status quo. Unicameralism might improve the efficiency of the legislature, but efficiency has never been a primary goal of the consensus-building deliberative process.

In the forty-nine bicameral states, the upper house is called the senate; the lower house is usually called the house of representatives. The average size of a state senate is forty members; houses typically average about 100 members. As with most aspects of state legislatures, chamber size varies substantially—from the Alaska senate, with twenty members, to the New Hampshire house, with 400 representatives. Chamber size seldom changes, but in 2001 Rhode Island began implementing a voter mandate that by 2003 had reduced its 150-member legislature by one-fourth.

For senators, the term of office is usually four years; approximately one-quarter of the states use a two-year senate term. In many states, the election of senators is staggered. House members serve two-year terms, except in Alabama, Louisiana, Maryland, Mississippi, and North Dakota, where four-year terms prevail. The 2004 state legislative sessions found Republicans in control of both chambers in twenty-one states, the Democratic Party controlling both houses in seventeen states, and split control in the remaining eleven states.

There are 7,382 state legislators in this country: 1,971 senators and 5,411 representatives. The number of Democrats and Republicans is almost tied: at just under and just over 50 percent, respectively; men outnumber women 77.5 to 22.5 percent. States with the highest percentage of women legislators are listed in Table 6.2. Washington is at the top of the list, as it has been in other years. Legislatures are becoming more racially and ethnically diverse. African Americans occupy 8 percent of all legislative seats, Latinos 3 percent, Asian

Americans 1 percent, and Native Americans one-half of a percent. Yet even these small proportions of women and racial-ethnic minorities represent a substantial increase, relative to their near absence from most pre-1970s legislatures. In terms of occupations, attorneys remain the single largest occupational category (16 percent). Full-time lawmakers constitute the next largest category (15 percent), followed by businessowners (10 percent), farmers (8 percent), educators (8 percent), real estate or insurance agents (8 percent), and retirees (7 percent).[5]

Legislative Districts

Legislators are elected from geographically based districts. Each district has approximately the same number of inhabitants. In Nebraska, for instance, each member of the unicameral legislature represents 32,210 people, more or less. Dividing or apportioning a state into districts is an intensely political process. These decisions affect the balance of power in a state. In the 1960s, for example, the less-populated panhandle area of Florida was overrepresented in the legislature at the expense of the heavily populated southern areas of the state. The balance of power lay with the northern rural regions. Therefore, despite Florida's rapid urbanization during that period, public policy continued to reflect the interests of a rurally based minority.

multimember districts
Legislative districts containing more than one seat.

Eight states, including Minnesota and the Dakotas, continue to use **multimember districts** containing more than one lower house seat.[6] In multimember districts, candidates compete for specific seats, and voters in the district vote in as many races as there are seats in the district. Once elected, the legislators represent the entire area.

malapportionment
Skewed legislative districts that violate the one person, one vote ideal.

Malapportionment **Malapportionment,** or unequal representation, has characterized many legislative bodies. For example, in the past, some states allocated an equal number of senators to each county. (This system calls to mind the U.S. Senate, which has two senators per state.) Because counties vary in population size, some senators were representing ten or twenty times as many constituents as their colleagues were. New Jersey offered one of the most extreme cases. In 1962, one county contained 49,000 residents and another had 924,000, yet each

TABLE 6.2	**Leading States in the Percentage of Women Legislators, 2004**		
STATE	PERCENTAGE OF WOMEN	STATE	PERCENTAGE OF WOMEN
Washington	36.7	New Mexico	29.5
Colorado	34.0	Connecticut	29.4
Maryland	33.5	Delaware	29.0
Vermont	31.1	Oregon	28.9
California	30.0	Nevada	28.6

SOURCE: Center for the American Woman and Politics, www.cawp.rutgers.edu/Facts/Officeholders/cawpfs.html (May 10, 2004).

county was allotted one senator, and each senator had one vote in the senate.[7] This kind of imbalance meant that a small group of people had the same institutional power as a group that was nineteen times larger. Such disproportionate power is inherently at odds with representative democracy, in which each person's vote carries the same weight.

Until the 1960s, the federal courts ignored the legislative malapportionment issue. It was not until 1962, in a Tennessee case in which the malapportionment was especially egregious (house district populations ranged from 2,340 to 42,298), that the courts stepped in. In *Baker* v. *Carr,* the U.S. Supreme Court ruled that the Fourteenth Amendment guarantee of equal protection applies to state legislative apportionment.[8] With this decision as a wedge, the Court ruled that state legislatures should be apportioned on the basis of population. Two years later, in *Reynolds* v. *Sims* (1964), Chief Justice Earl Warren summed up the apportionment ideal by saying, "Legislators represent people, not trees or acres."[9] Accordingly, districts should reflect population equality: one person, one vote. In the aftermath of this decision, which overturned the apportionment practices of six states, a **reapportionment** fever swept the country, and district lines were redrawn in every state.

Reapportionment provided an immediate benefit to previously underrepresented urban areas, and increased urban representation led to a growing responsiveness in state legislatures to the problems and interests of cities and suburbs. Where reapportionment had a partisan effect, it generally benefited Republicans in the South and Democrats in the North. Other effects of reapportionment have included the election of younger, better-educated legislators and, especially in southern states, better representation of blacks.[10] All in all, reapportionment is widely credited with improving the representativeness of American state legislatures.

Redrawing District Lines State legislatures are reapportioned following the U.S. Census, which is taken every ten years. Reapportionment allows population fluctuations—growth in some areas, decline in others—to be reflected in redrawn district lines. Thirty-six legislatures **redistrict** themselves; twelve states attempt to depoliticize the process by using impartial commissions to develop their redistricting plans.[11] In two states, Alaska and Maryland, the governor plays a dominant role in redistricting.

In states where the legislature redistricts itself (and the state's congressional districts), the party controlling the legislature controls the redistricting process. Therefore, district lines have traditionally been redrawn to maximize the strength of the party in power. The art of drawing district lines creatively was popularized in Massachusetts in 1812, when a political cartoonist for the *Boston Gazette* dubbed one of Governor Elbridge Gerry's district creations a **gerrymander** because the district, carefully configured to reflect partisan objectives, was shaped like a salamander. Gerrymandering has not disappeared. Political parties poured record sums of money into the 2000 state legislative elections, in large part because of looming reapportionment. When the Republicans gained control of the Kentucky senate, the Republican chair of the redistricting committee

---

reapportionment

The reallocation of seats in a legislative assembly.

redistrict

The redrawing of legislative district lines to conform as closely as possible to the one person, one vote ideal.

gerrymander

The process of creatively designing a legislative district, usually to enhance the electoral fortunes of the party in power.

Republican state senators in Texas meet with the press in 2003 to explain their side of the hotly contested, highly partisan redistricting process. *SOURCE:* Bob Daemmrich/ The Image Works.

stated his philosophy this way: "Any party that's in control, charity begins at home."[12]

Redistricting has become a sophisticated operation in which statisticians and geographers use computer mapping to assist the legislature in designing an optimal districting scheme. Although one person, one vote is the official standard, some unofficial guidelines are also taken into consideration. Ideally, districts should be geographically compact and unbroken. Those who draw the lines pay close attention to traditional political boundaries such as counties and, as noted, to the fortunes of political parties and incumbents. As long as districts adhere fairly closely to the population-equality standard (if a multimember district contains three seats, it must have three times the population of a single-member district), federal courts tolerate the achievement of unofficial objectives. But redistricting does occasionally produce some oddly shaped districts resembling lobsters, spiders, and earmuffs.[13] Dividing Montgomery County, Maryland, into legislative districts after the 2000 census produced the shapes displayed in Figure 6.1.

Legislatures have to pay more and more attention to the effects of their redistricting schemes on racial minority voting strength. In fact, amendments to the Voting Rights Act and subsequent court rulings instructed affected states to create some districts in which racial minorities would have majority status. After years of designing districts to minimize the political power of blacks, legislatures were forced by the courts to change their ways. States throughout the South spent the 1990s drawing and redrawing district lines to satisfy the courts.

The intentional creation of districts more favorable to the election of African Americans had an unintentional partisan consequence. "Packing" blacks into

| FIGURE 6.1 | **State Legislative Districts in Montgomery County, Maryland** |

Although the districts have similar population sizes, their shapes and territorial sizes vary.

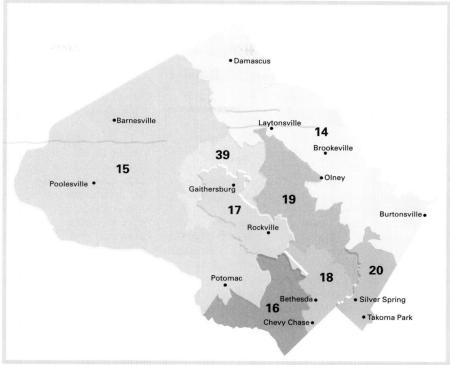

SOURCE: www.777vote.org/images/legis02.gif.

districts diluted the Democratic vote of nearby districts, thereby allowing Republicans to win. For instance, Florida drew thirteen heavily African American state house districts, leaving the other 107 districts with relatively few black voters. Some observers contended that this situation made it easier for Republicans to win sixty-five of those seats and thus control the house.[14]

The courts have not spoken with crystal clarity on the question of reapportionment.[15] Yes, the racial composition of districts should be taken into account, but no, racial considerations should not be the sole criterion. In their decision in *Easley* v. *Cromartie* (2001), the Supreme Court ruled that reliance on partisan considerations remains an appropriate redistricting option. As one expert, political scientist Ronald Weber, put it, the strategy for line-drawers is "to determine the best way to waste the vote of the partisans of the other party."[16] Thus, the practice of redrawing district lines in response to population shifts is an intensely political process, as a recent study of the Kansas legislature demonstrated.[17] Deals are made, interests are protected, coalitions are built, all in an effort to craft an acceptable map, one that the legislature will adopt and the courts will uphold. The story of Texas Democratic senators in 2003, retold in the

DEBATING POLITICS

Redistricting Politics in Texas: The Democrats Head for the Border

The redistricting process is intensely political, as the discussion in this chapter has indicated. But in 2003 in Texas, where Republicans controlled both houses of the legislature for the first time since Reconstruction, it took a turn toward the bizarre. Locked in a partisan battle during the spring over redistricting congressional seats, more than fifty Democratic legislators crossed the border into Oklahoma, thus preventing a **quorum** from being present in the chamber to conduct business. In the not-in-session house, some Republican legislators killed time by pasting photographs of the missing legislators on milk cartons. The Republican governor called the action by Democrats "cowardly and childish" and dispatched a law enforcement unit, the Texas Rangers, to track them down, but the legislative session was effectively over.

In July 2003, when the governor called a second session of the legislature to take up redistricting, eleven Texas senators took off for New Mexico, where they stayed for six weeks to keep the Senate from having a quorum. What raised the Democrats' ire in both May and July was the effort of the speaker of the U.S. House of Representatives, Texas Republican Tom DeLay, to have the state's congressional districts redrawn in a way that would greatly benefit Republican candidates. (In 2003, Democrats held an edge over Republicans, 17 to 15, in congressional seats.) Congressman DeLay defended his actions as a way of bringing the Texas congressional delegation in line with the political philosophy of the state; Democrats saw his action as a meddlesome power grab. The charges and countercharges flew fast and furiously. The media both within the state and beyond had a field day with the legislative imbroglio.

In early September, one Democrat was persuaded to return to the Senate, thus insuring a quorum when the governor called a third session. The other ten headed back to Austin, Texas, where they found that Republicans had revoked their parking privileges at the Capitol and imposed $57,000 in fines on each of them. The new redistricting plan passed, and the Democrats filed a lawsuit in federal court charging the GOP with violating their constitutional rights and the provisions of the Voting Rights Act.

Did the Democratic senators act appropriately when they left the chamber and the state? Has the redistricting process become too partisan and political, as incumbent legislators unabashedly draw lines to reward friends and punish enemies? Should a group other than legislators themselves make redistricting decisions? Given the rapid population changes in some states, should redistricting occur more frequently than once every ten years?

SOURCES: David Barboza with Carl Hulse, "Texas Republicans Fume; Democrats Remain AWOL," *New York Times* (May 14, 2003), www.nytimes.com/2003/05/14/national; Nick Madigan, "On the Lam, Texas Democrats Rough It," *New York Times* (August 1, 2003), www.nytimes.com/2003/08/01/national; Lee Hockstader, "Texas Governor Orders Session," *Washington Post* (September 10, 2003), p. A2; "Gerrymuddling in Texas," *Christian Science Monitor* (January 9, 2004), p. 10.

---

quorum
The minimum number of legislators who must be present to transact business.

Debating Politics box, gives meaning to the phrase *an intensely political process.* Concern that partisan gerrymandering has gotten out of hand was the basis for a legal challenge in Pennsylvania in 2004. However the U.S. Supreme Court ruling in *Vieth* v. *Jubelirer* gave a green light to the continuation of the partisan practice, at least for now.

Legislative Pay

Legislative compensation has increased handsomely in the past three decades, again with some notable exceptions. Before the modernization of legislatures, salary and per diem (money for daily expenses) levels were set in the state constitution and thus were impossible to adjust without a constitutional amendment. The lifting of these limits puts most legislatures, as the policymaking branch of state government, in the curious position of setting their own compensation levels. Recognizing that this power is a double-edged sword (the legislators can vote themselves pay raises and the public can turn around and vote them out of office), almost half the states have established compensation commissions or advisory groups to make recommendations on legislative remuneration. Arizona carries it a step further, requiring that a commission-recommended pay raise for legislators be submitted to the voters for approval—or rejection.

As of 2003, annual salaries of legislators (excluding per diem) ranged from a low of $200 in New Hampshire to a high of $99,000 in California.[18] Seventeen states paid their legislators more than $30,000 annually. Compare these figures with the more modest pay levels of legislators in Georgia ($16,200), Idaho ($15,646), and Nebraska ($12,000). As a general rule, states paying a more generous compensation typically demand more of a legislator's time than do low-paying states. New Mexico legislators cannot be accused of seeking elective office for the money. There, legislators receive no salary. What is their financial reward for legislative service? One hundred forty-five dollars per day for living expenses while in Santa Fe during the session, plus a travel allowance.

Legislative pay is but a fraction of the cost of operating a legislature. Legislative staff salaries consume a large chunk of the expenditures, as do building maintenance and technological improvements. Large states such as California and New York spend the most on their legislatures. However, when legislative costs are calculated on a per capita basis, Alaska is at the top, followed by Hawaii and Rhode Island.[19]

Legislative Leadership

Legislatures need leaders, both formal and informal. Each chamber usually has four formal leadership positions. In the senate, a president and a president pro tempore (who presides in the absence of the president) are in charge of the chamber; in the house, the comparable leaders are the speaker and the speaker pro tempore. These legislative officials are chosen by the members. (In some states, the post of senate president is occupied by the lieutenant governor.) Both houses have two political party leadership positions: a majority leader and a minority leader.

The leaders are responsible for making the legislature, a relatively decentralized system, run smoothly and seeing that it accomplishes its tasks. In a typical chamber, the presiding officer appoints committee members, names committee chairs, controls the activity on the floor, allocates office space and committee budgets, and (in some states) selects the majority leader and the holders of other majority-party posts.[20] The actual influence of the leadership varies from one chamber to another. One factor that affects leaders' power is whether the positions are rotated or retained. Leaders who have the option of retaining their position can build power bases. In the case of rotation, however, one set of leaders is replaced with another on a regular basis, so the leaders are lame ducks when they assume the posts. On average, today's leaders are different from the caricatured wheeler-dealers of the past. Successful leaders are those who adapt as the membership changes and the institution evolves.[21] The nearby *Breaking New Ground* box focuses on a new trend in legislative leadership: an increase in the number of women in the top jobs.

Leadership in legislatures is linked to political parties. Voting to fill leadership posts follows party lines. For example, the Florida senate began one term with twenty Democrats and twenty Republicans. Each time the chamber voted to select its president, the balloting was tied 20 to 20. To break the deadlock, the senators negotiated a novel solution: Split the term into two one-year segments, with a Republican president the first year and a Democratic president the second year. The Michigan house of representatives, also operating with partisan equality, opted for a different power-sharing arrangement. There, lawmakers decided to use cospeakers and co-committee chairs. The speakership rotated monthly between the Republican leader and the Democratic leader; the committee chairs did likewise.

As political parties become more competitive in the states, legislative behavior and decisions take on a partisan cast. There are Democratic and Republican sides of the chamber and Democratic and Republican positions on bills. The parties meet in caucuses to design their legislative strategies and generate camaraderie. In states where one political party continues to dominate, partisanship is less important. In one-party settings, the dominant party typically develops splits or factions at the expense of party unity. When the outnumbered minority party begins to gain strength, however, the majority party usually becomes more cohesive.

In many states, legislative leaders have embraced a new function: fundraising. Leaders tap interest groups and lobbyists for money and divide it among their party's candidates for legislative seats. California has led the way, with multimillion-dollar war chests. The amount of money thus raised is not as great in other states, of course, but it has become a significant source of campaign funding. Lobbyists find it difficult to say no to a request for funds from the leadership. The leaders allocate the funds to candidates who need them most—candidates in close races. If they are victorious, their loyalty to party leaders pays legislative dividends.

Legislative Committees

The workhorse of the legislature is the committee. Under normal circumstances, a committee's primary function is to consider bills—that is, to hear testimony, perhaps amend the bills, and ultimately approve or reject them. A committee's action on a bill precedes debate in the house or senate.

All legislative chambers are divided into committees, and most committees have created subcommittees. Committees can be of several types. A *standing committee* regularly considers legislation during the session. A *joint committee* is made up of members of both houses. Some joint committees are standing; others are temporary (sometimes called ad hoc or select) and are convened for a specific purpose,

token

Member of a small minority in a majority organizational culture.

BREAKING NEW GROUND

Women Legislative Leaders

A T-shirt popular at women's political rallies in the 1980s read: "A woman's place is in the House . . . and in the Senate." In most states, the slogan has become reality. By 2004, 22.5 percent (1,661 legislators) of the country's state legislators were women, and 18.4 percent of the female lawmakers (305 legislators) were women of color. Thirty years earlier, the number of female legislators had been 4 percent. Though far from achieving gender parity in the legislature, women are now a more visible and forceful presence than ever before. Every state has female legislators, with the percentages ranging from a low of 9.4 percent in South Carolina to a high of 36.7 percent in Washington. And even in states where women have merely **token** presence, research shows that they have the potential to affect the direction of public policy.

The membership percentages don't tell the whole story, however; more impressive has been the movement of women into leadership roles in state legislatures. Ascending to positions of leadership signals the full inclusion of women into the legislative system. The Alaska legislature achieved a first in 1995 when women took over both of the top leadership positions: speaker of the house and president of the senate. During the 2003

legislative sessions, women held 13.6 percent of the top legislative leadership positions, including five lower house speakers and three senate presidents. In addition, women chaired 18.9 percent of the standing committees, with California (where 42.6 percent of its legislative committees are headed by women) leading the way.

A recent study sought to determine why women are more successful in reaching leadership ranks in some states than in others. Only one state characteristic was shown to be statistically significant: the level of urbanization. The more urbanized the state, the higher the proportion of female legislative leaders. A state's education level, ideological bent, and regional location were inconsequential. Two other factors related to women becoming leaders were the amount of legislative turnover and the historic success of women leaders. In other words, turnover creates opportunities for women to rise in the ranks. And if women had been selected for legislative leadership posts before—if they had broken the ice, so to speak—there were more women leaders in that state.

Once women legislators reach positions of leadership within a chamber, they operate differently from their male counterparts. For instance, research on legislative leaders in twenty-two states found that women's leadership styles tended toward coordination or

consensus-building rather than the more traditional command style. Catherine Hanaway, the new speaker of the Missouri house, said prior to the 2003 session that she would not adopt the "cajoling and bullying" style of someone like Lyndon Johnson, who had used those methods to become an extremely effective leader in the U.S. Senate. Instead, Speaker Hanaway vowed a different approach. She would get to know the members of the House, regardless of their party affiliation, learning their backgrounds, where they stood on issues, and what their districts needed. That approach, she contended, would be the key to legislative success.

Women are no longer unusual in the legislature. Indeed, as the public becomes more disenchanted with politics as usual, female legislators stand a good chance of increasing their numbers. And not just in the rank and file.

SOURCES: Susan J. Carroll, "Women in State Government: Historical Overview and Current Trends," Center for the American Woman in Politics, www. cawp.rutgers.edu (May 5, 2004); Jocelyn Elise Crowley, "When Tokens Matter," *Legislative Studies Quarterly* 29 (February 2004): 109–36; Cindy Simon Rosenthal, "Determinants of Collaborative Leadership," *Political Research Quarterly* 51 (December 1998): 847–68; Rebecca E. Deen and Thomas H. Little, "Getting to the Top: Factors Influencing the Election of Women to Positions of Leadership in State Legislatures," *State and Local Government Review* 31 (Spring 1999): 123–34; Rob Gurwitt, "New Day Under the Dome," *Governing* 16 (January 2003): 26–30.

such as investigating a troubled agency or a particularly challenging public policy problem. A *conference committee* is a special type of joint committee. Most states use *interim committees* during the period when the legislature is not in session to get a head start on an upcoming session. The number of committees varies, but most senates and houses have standing committees on the issues listed in Table 6.3. Most of these committees, in turn, have professional staffs assigned to them.

A substantive standing committee tends to be made up of legislators who have expertise and interest in that committee's subject matter.[22] Thus, farmers would be assigned to the agriculture committee, teachers to the education committee, small businessowners to the commerce committee, lawyers to the judiciary committee, and so on. These legislators bring knowledge and commitment to their committee assignments; they also may bring a certain bias because they tend to function as advocates for their career interests.

The central concern of a standing committee is its floor success—getting the full chamber to accede to its recommendations on a bill. Several plausible explanations exist for a committee's floor success.[23] A committee with an ideological composition similar to that of the chamber is likely to be more successful than one whose members are at odds with the chamber. The leadership takes this situation into account when it makes committee assignments; thus, very few committees are ideological outliers.[24] Also, committees full of legislatively experienced members generally have more floor success than committees composed of legislative novices. And committees that have a reputation for being tough have more floor success with their bills than committees that are easy and pass everything that comes before them.

TABLE 6.3   Standing Committees of the Legislature

Both houses of state legislatures typically have standing committees dealing with these substantive issues:

Agriculture	Government operations
Banking/financial institutions	Health
Business and commerce	Insurance
Communications	Judiciary and criminal justice
Education	Local affairs
Elections	Public employees
Energy rules	Environment and natural resources
Social/human services	Ethics
Transportation	

In addition, both houses have standing committees that address the raising and allocating of state funds. These committees may have different names in different chambers:

Appropriations	Finance and taxation
Ways and means	

LEGISLATIVE BEHAVIOR

Legislatures have their own dynamics, their own way of doing things. Senate and house rulebooks spell out what can and cannot be done, in the same way that an organization's by-laws do. Legislatures function as self-regulating institutions for the most part; it is especially important, therefore, that participants know what is expected of them. To make certain that the chamber's rules are understood, most legislatures conduct orientation sessions for new members.

Legislative Norms

An understanding of the legislature involves not only knowledge of formal structures and written rules but also awareness of informal norms and unwritten policies. For example, nowhere in a state's legislative rules does it say that a freshman legislator is prohibited from playing a leadership role, but the unwritten rules of most legislatures place a premium on seniority. A primary rule of legislative bodies is that you must go along to get along, a phrase that emphasizes teamwork and paying your dues. Legislators who are on opposite sides of a bill to regulate horse racing might find themselves on the same side of a bill outlawing the use of cell phones while operating a motor vehicle. Yesterday's opponent is today's partner. For this reason, a legislator cannot make bitter enemies in the legislature and expect to flourish.

Those who aspire to rise from rank-and-file legislator to committee chairperson and perhaps to party leader or presiding officer find consensus-building skills quite useful. These skills come in handy because many norms are intended to reduce the potential for conflict in what is inherently a setting full of conflict. For instance, a freshman legislator is expected to defer to a senior colleague. Although an energetic new legislator might chafe under such a restriction, one day he will have gained seniority and will take comfort in the rule. Legislators are expected to honor commitments made to each other, thus encouraging reciprocity: "If you support me on my favorite bill, I will be with you on yours." A legislator cannot be too unyielding. Compromises, sometimes principled but more often political, are the backbone of the legislative process. Few bills are passed by both houses and sent to the governor in exactly the same form as when they were introduced.

The internal organization of legislatures varies, as emphasized in a study of three legislatures—in New York, Connecticut, and California.[25] New York has a stable organizational system in which seniority is the major criterion for advancement. Empire State legislators tend to be careerists who expect a long tenure in office. In Connecticut, where an unstable system prevails and few career incentives exist, members stay in the legislature a short time and then return to private life. California has an unstable system that is not seniority oriented, and talented legislators can advance quickly; therefore, California legislators tend to be politically ambitious, and the system allows them to act as entrepreneurs. The informal rules in these three legislatures are quite different, and the institutions tend to attract different types of legislators. The New York legislature is considered career oriented, Connecticut's legislature a dead end, and California's a springboard.[26]

Informal rules are designed to make the legislative process flow more smoothly. Legislators who cannot abide by the rules find it difficult to get along. They are subjected to not-so-subtle behavior-modification efforts, such as powerful social sanctions (ostracism and ridicule) and legislative punishment (the bottling up of their bill in committee or their assignment to an unpopular committee), actions that promote adherence to norms.

Legislative Cue-Taking

Much has been written about how legislators make public policy decisions, and several explanations are plausible. Legislators may adopt the policy positions espoused by their political party. They may follow the dictates of their conscience—that is, do what they think is right. They may yield to the pressures of organized interest groups. They may be persuaded by the arguments of other legislators, such as a committee chairperson who is knowledgeable about the policy area or a trusted colleague who is considered to be savvy; or they may succumb to the entreaties of the governor, who has made a particular piece of legislation the focus of her administration. Of course, legislators may also attempt to respond to the wishes of their constituents. On a significant issue—one that has received substantial media attention—they are likely to be subjected to tremendous cross-pressures.

A legislator reflecting on his years in the Massachusetts house tells this revealing story. During one session, he voted yes on corporate tax break legislation that he was opposed to because the speaker of the house favored the bill and wanted him to vote yes. Why was the speaker's position so compelling? Because the legislator's favorite bill was due to be voted on later and he wanted the speaker's support on it.[27] Another remarkably candid assessment of how legislators make public policy decisions was offered by a freshman in the Tennessee house of representatives. He identified two often unspoken but always present considerations: "Will it cost me votes back home?" and "Can an opponent use it against me [in the] next election?"[28] These pragmatic concerns intrude on the more idealistic notions of decisionmaking. They also suggest a fairly cautious approach to bold policy initiatives.

Assuming that legislators are concerned about how a vote will be received back home, it seems logical that they would be particularly solicitous of public opinion. Some research on the subject has shown, however, that state legislators frequently hold opinions at odds with those of their constituents.[29] They occasionally misperceive what the public is thinking; at such times, it is difficult for them to act as mere **delegates** and simply fulfill the public's will. To improve the communications link, some legislators use questionnaires to poll constituents about their views; others hold town meetings at various spots in the district to assess the public's mood.

It is quite probable that first-term legislators feel more vulnerable to public pressure than legislative veterans do. Hence, the new legislator devotes more time to determining what the people want, whereas the experienced legislator "knows" what they want (or perhaps knows what they need) and thus functions

delegate
A legislator who functions as a conduit for constituency opinion.

trustee

A legislator who votes according to his or her conscience and best judgment.

as a **trustee**—someone who follows his or her own best judgment. Since the vast majority of legislators are returned to office election after election, it appears that there is some validity to this argument. Research on Oklahoma and Kansas legislators, for example, found that the members' personal values were consistently important in their decision choices.[30]

In the final analysis, the determining factor in how legislators make decisions depends on the issue itself. On one hand, "when legislators are deeply involved with an issue, they appear to be more concerned with policy consequences" than with constituency preferences.[31] In this situation, the legislators are focused on a goal other than re-election. On the other hand, if the legislators are not particularly concerned about an issue that is important to their constituents, they will follow their constituents' preference. In that sense, they act as **politicos,** adjusting as the issues and cues change.[32]

politico

A legislator who functions as either a delegate or a trustee, as circumstances dictate.

HOW A BILL BECOMES LAW

A legislative bill starts as an idea and travels a long, complex path before it emerges as law. It is no wonder that of the 5,920 bills introduced in the Illinois legislature in 2003, only 600 had become law by the end of the session.[33] A legislative session has a rhythm to it. Minor bills and symbolic issues tend to be resolved early, whereas major, potentially divisive issues take a much longer time to wend their way through the legislative labyrinth. With the clock ticking at the end of the session, legislators try to broker compromises and build coalitions to get key bills passed.[34] The budget or appropriations bill is typically one of the last matters that the legislature debates during the session. And if legislatures cannot get their work completed, they may end up back in the state capitol at a later date in a special session. In 2001, for example, forty-six special legislative sessions were called; some states held more than one extra session.

The lawmaking process has been described in many ways: a zoo, a circus, a marketplace. Perhaps the most apt description is casino because there are winners and losers, the outcome is never final, and there is always a new game ahead.[35] Figure 6.2 illustrates a typical lawmaking process, showing at just how many points a bill can get sidetracked.

The diagram of the legislative process in Figure 6.2 cannot convey the dynamism and excitement of lawmaking. Ideas for bills are everywhere: with constituents, interest groups, and state agencies. Legislators may turn to other states for ideas or to their staffs. **Policy entrepreneurs,** people who are knowledgeable about certain issues and are willing to promote them, abound. Introducing a bill—"putting it in the hopper," in legislative parlance—is just the beginning.

policy entrepreneur

A person who brings new ideas to a policy-making body.

A bill does not make it through the legislative process without a lot of effort and even a little luck. A bill's chances of passage rise as more legislators sign on as cosponsors, and if the cosponsors are legislative leaders, even better. Assignment of the bill to a favorable committee improves the likelihood that the bill will be scheduled for a hearing in a timely manner. Many bills get bottled up in

| FIGURE 6.2 | **How a Bill Becomes Law** |

At each of the stages in the process, supporters and opponents of a bill clash. Most bills stall at some point and fail to make it to the end.

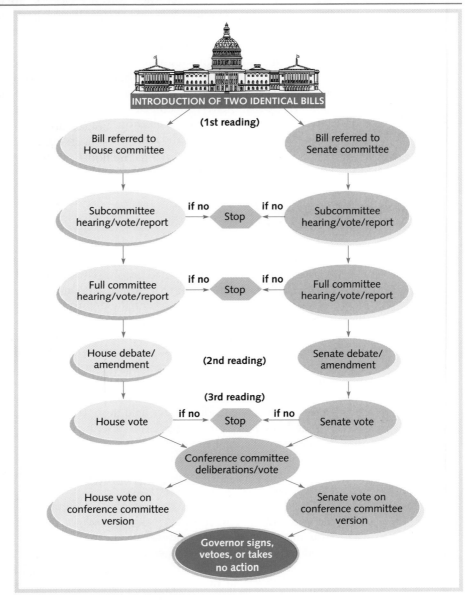

INTRODUCTION OF TWO IDENTICAL BILLS

(1st reading)

Bill referred to House committee — Bill referred to Senate committee

Subcommittee hearing/vote/report — **if no** → Stop ← **if no** — Subcommittee hearing/vote/report

Full committee hearing/vote/report — **if no** → Stop ← **if no** — Full committee hearing/vote/report

House debate/amendment — (2nd reading) — Senate debate/amendment

(3rd reading)

House vote — **if no** → Stop ← **if no** — Senate vote

Conference committee deliberations/vote

House vote on conference committee version — Senate vote on conference committee version

Governor signs, vetoes, or takes no action

committee and never receive a hearing. Strong support from key interest groups is a powerful advantage, as is the emergence of only weak opposition to the bill. Sometimes bill passage is a matter of fortuitous timing. For example, a spectacular prison break from an overcrowded state penitentiary would help garner support for passage of a prison construction bill.

Controversial issues such as abortion raise the stakes. The former speaker of the Wisconsin Assembly, Tom Loftus, described abortion politics in his state as trench warfare in which compromise was almost impossible. Leadership on the issue came from legislators who felt strongly about the matter and who held safe seats. (In this instance, "safe" meant that taking a position was not likely to cost them too many votes or generate too many serious challengers when they ran for re-election.) As anti-abortion bills were introduced, battle lines were drawn. According to the speaker, the pro-choice side, which included the Democratic leadership, tried to keep the bill in committee, and the pro-life side, through political pressure on the Republicans and conservative Democrats, tried to pull it out so the whole assembly could vote on it on the floor of the chamber. If the pro-life forces could get the bill to the floor for a vote, they would win. To accomplish this end, they needed to gain supporters from the pivotal middle group of legislators, usually moderates of both parties from marginal districts.[36]

The powerful anti-abortion group, Wisconsin Citizens Concerned for Life, pressured vulnerable legislators. These legislators were in a tough position because they knew "regardless of how you voted, you were going to make a slew of single-issue voters mad."[37] Their strategy became one of parliamentary maneuvering and delay.

While bills are making their way (some quickly, some slowly, some not at all) through the legislative labyrinth, other events intervene. The Texas Bankers Association (TBA), the interest group representing bankers in the Lone Star State, pushed a home equity lending bill during one session. As the house was debating the bill, some banks around the state announced new surcharges on automatic teller machine (ATM) fees. The angry public reaction was heard by lawmakers and despite TBA's attempt to defuse the issue, unfavorable amendments were attached to the home equity bill.[38]

Even if a bill is successful in one chamber, potential hurdles await in the other chamber. Representatives and senators may see the same issue in very different terms. In Ohio in 1997, everyone agreed that the state's system for funding public education needed reform. (The Ohio Supreme Court had found the state's school-funding system unconstitutional and had given the legislature one year to devise a new system.) But initial efforts derailed when the house and senate could not agree on a plan. The senate approved a funding package that would have increased the sales tax, provided debt financing, and allowed local school boards to propose property tax increases.[39] The house, dominated by Republicans who had signed an anti-tax pledge the preceding year, approved a bill that did not include tax hikes. Each chamber rejected the other's plan. Hammering out a compromise agreeable to both chambers took a long time, even with the court's order as a spur to action.

Once conference or concurrence committees resolve differences and agreement is secured in both chambers, then the bill is enrolled (certified and signed) and sent to the governor. The governor may do one of three things: (1) sign the act (once passed, a bill is called an act) into law, (2) veto it (in which case the legislature has a chance to have the last word by overriding the veto), or (3) take no action. If the governor does not take action and the session has ended, then in most states the act will become law without the governor's signature. Why not simply sign it if the act will become law anyway? Sometimes it is a matter of political symbolism for the governor. In approximately one-third of the states, if the governor does not sign or veto the act and the legislature has adjourned, the act dies (a circumstance called a pocket veto).

During its 2003 session, the Illinois General Assembly passed only 10.1 percent of the bills that were introduced. Is this a sign of success or failure? Illinois's figures are lower than those of most states—20 to 25 percent is a common passage rate—but not necessarily a cause for alarm. Not all bills are good ones, and the inability to generate sufficient consensus among legislators may reflect that condition.

Colorado tried something new for one of its sessions: a process called "Getting to Yes."[40] A task force representing groups involved in education—teachers and their unions, administrators, school board members, business leaders, and legislators—met before the session to develop bills on procedures for evaluating and dismissing teachers. Participants agreed beforehand to focus on goals, not turf. Although the process was not conflict-free, it did produce two bills that participants could agree on.

LEGISLATIVE REFORM AND CAPACITY

It was not easy to get state legislatures where they are today. During the 1970s, fundamental reforms occurred throughout the country as legislatures sought to increase their capacity and to become more professional. And, even though these reforms have had a substantial impact, the modernization process never really ends.

The Ideal Legislature

In the late 1960s, the Citizens' Conference on State Legislatures (CCSL) studied legislative performance and identified five characteristics critical to legislative improvement.[41] Ideally, a legislature should be functional, accountable, informed, independent, and representative; the acronym is FAIIR.

The *functional* legislature has almost unrestricted time to conduct its business. It is assisted by adequate staff and facilities and has effective rules and procedures that facilitate the flow of legislation. The *accountable* legislature's operations are open and comprehensible to the public. The *informed* legislature manages its workload through an effective committee structure, legislative activities between sessions, and a professional staff; it also conducts regular budgetary review of executive branch activities. The *independent* legislature runs its own affairs, independent from the executive branch. It exercises oversight of agencies, regulates lobbyists, manages conflicts of interest, and provides adequate compensation for its members. Finally, the *representative* legislature has a diverse membership that effectively represents the social, economic, ethnic, and other characteristics of the constituencies.

The fifty state legislatures were evaluated and scored by CCSL according to the FAIIR criteria. For the first time ever, the rankings offered a relatively scientific means of comparing one state legislature with another. Overall, the most effective state legislatures were found in California, New York, Illinois, Florida, and Wisconsin. The worst, in the assessment of CCSL, were those in Alabama, Wyoming, Delaware, North Carolina, and Arkansas.

The CCSL report triggered extensive self-evaluation by legislatures around the country. Most states launched ambitious efforts to reform their legislatures. The results are readily apparent. In terms of the CCSL criteria, states have made tremendous strides in legislative institution building. The evidence of increased professionalism includes more staff support, higher legislative compensation, longer sessions, and better facilities. Many legislatures revamped their committee systems, altered their rules and procedures, and tightened their ethics regulations. The consequences of these actions are state legislatures that are far more FAIIR now than they were thirty years ago.

The Effects of Reform

Today's legislative institutions are different, but are they better? Initial research suggested that legislative professionalism had an independent, positive effect on social welfare policy.[42] In other words, policymaking in professional legislatures seemed to be more responsive to the needs of lower-income citizens. However, subsequent research arrived at a different conclusion: Professionalized legislatures did not seem to affect the direction of state public policy.[43] More recent studies have sought to clarify the relationship between the characteristics of a legislature and its public policy outputs. They have led to the recognition that legislative characteristics *and* various other factors, such as a state's socioeconomic conditions and executive branch strength, affect policy decisions.[44] Recent analysis has confirmed the link between reform and legislative capacity. Legislatures that are closer to the FAIIR standards appear to have greater capacity than the less FAIIR institutions do.[45] Furthermore, if the CCSL study were repeated today, the gap between the most effective legislature and the least would have narrowed considerably.

But the legislative reform picture is not unequivocally rosy. Political scientist Alan Rosenthal, who has closely observed legislative reform, warns that "the legislature's recent success in enhancing its capacity and improving its performance may place it in greater jeopardy than before."[46] This prospect certainly was not an intended effect of the reform efforts. Rosenthal's argument is that a constellation of demands pulls legislators away from the legislative core. That is, the new breed of legislators becomes caught up in the demands of re-election, constituent service, interest groups, and political careerism and thus neglects institutional matters such as structure, procedure, staff, image, and community. The legislature as an institution suffers because it is not receiving the necessary care and attention from its members. Minnesota, with a highly reformed legislature, exhibited relatively poor performance in the mid-1990s, described as a period of bitter partisanship and personal scandal. Some observers blame reform.[47]

Consider the idea of a citizen-legislator, one for whom service in the legislature is a part-time endeavor. Since the onset of reform, the proportion of legislators who are lawyers, businessowners, or insurance or real-estate executives has dropped, and the number of full-time legislators has risen. In states such as Michigan, Pennsylvania, and Wisconsin, roughly two-thirds of the lawmakers identify themselves as legislators, with no other occupation. The critical issue is whether the decline of the citizen-legislator is a desirable aspect of modernization. Should a state legislature represent a broad spectrum of vocations, or should it be composed of career politicians? One perspective is this: "If I'm sick, I want professional help. I feel the same way about public affairs. I want legislators who are knowledgeable and professional."[48] Another view is represented by a Michigan legislator, who believes that his careerist colleagues have lost touch with their constituents: "When you spend all your time in Lansing, you're more influenced by the lobbyists than by your constituents."[49]

In effect, state legislatures are becoming more like the U.S. Congress. Legislators are staying in the legislature in record numbers. Modernization has made the institution more attractive to its members, so turnover rates are declining. But do we really want fifty mini-Congresses scattered across the land? Today's legislatures are more FAIIR than in the past, but reform has also brought greater professionalization of the legislative career, increased polarization of the legislative process, and more fragmentation of the legislative institution.[50] Figure 6.3 shows the pattern of citizen, professional, and hybrid state legislatures throughout the land.

FIGURE 6.3   Legislatures: Three Flavors

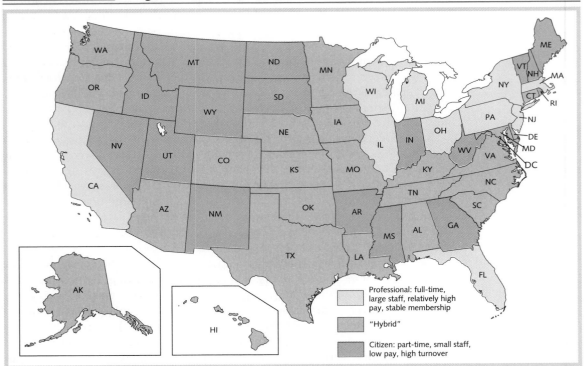

Professional: full-time, large staff, relatively high pay, stable membership

"Hybrid"

Citizen: part-time, small staff, low pay, high turnover

SOURCE: National Conference of State Legislatures; as appeared in Charles Mahtesian, "The Sick Legislature Syndrome," *Governing* 10 (February 1997): 20. Copyright The Council of State Governments. Reprinted with permission.

Change continues in state legislatures, but much of it is cloaked in an anti-reform guise. Term limits (discussed below) are, of course, a major component in the effort to limit the legislature. Other attempts to chip away at reform include Louisiana's approval of a constitutional amendment in 1993 to cut the length and limit the focus of even-year legislative sessions in that state. Now, in even-numbered years, the legislature is restricted to a thirty-day session that addresses only fiscal issues.[51] North Dakota took a different tack and tried to improve its legislature without sacrificing its part-time citizen legislative tradition.

To some analysts, the reforms of the past decades have produced a legislative monster. Richard Nathan, a veteran observer of the states, argues that the key to increased government productivity is the empowerment of the governor.[52] Therefore, the legislative Godzilla must be contained. Nathan advocates term limits, unicameral legislative bodies, rotation of committee memberships, and reduction of legislative staff and sessions as a means of reining in the legislature vis-à-vis the governor. If adopted, Nathan's recommendations would undo thirty years of legislative reform. And the governor's political power would be significantly strengthened. The legislative–gubernatorial nexus is the subject of a later section of this chapter.

Term Limits

In September 1990, Oklahoma voters took an action that has sent state legislatures reeling. Oklahomans overwhelmingly approved a ballot measure limiting the tenure of state legislators and statewide officers. And, as it turned out, limiting terms was not just a "Sooner" thing. Within two months, voters in California and Colorado had followed suit. With only a close defeat in Washington State slowing it slightly, the term-limits movement swept the country. In Oregon, a group called Let Incumbents Mosey into the Sunset (LIMITS) grew out of a tax-limitation organization. In Wisconsin, a coalition known as Badgers Back in Charge took up the term-limitation cause. And political activists of many stripes—populists, conservatives, and libertarians—found a home in the term-limitation movements in Florida, Michigan, and Texas.[53] In time, twenty-one states slapped limits on state legislative terms. And they gradually bore the intended fruit: More than 380 legislators in eleven states were barred from seeking re-election in 2000. Table 6.4 compares the term-limits provisions of the states where legislative term limits remained in force in 2004. Note that Nebraska voters had approved term limits three times prior to the 2000 initiative, but the courts had invalidated the measures.

In most states, the measures limit service in each chamber separately. In Maine, for example, a legislator is limited to eight years in the house and eight years in the senate. It is quite possible, then, that an individual could serve a total of sixteen years in the legislature under this plan. In a few states, the restriction is on total legislative service. In Oklahoma, for instance, the limitation is twelve years, whether in the house, the senate, or a combination of the two. Some term limits are for a lifetime (as in Arkansas and Nevada), some simply limit the number of consecutive terms (as in Ohio and South Dakota).

Limiting legislative terms captured the fancy of a public angry with entrenched

TABLE 6.4	Term Limits in the States, 2004					
STATE	YEAR ADOPTED	SENATE	HOUSE	YEAR LAW TAKES EFFECT	REFERENDUM VOTE	BALLOT STATUS
Arizona	1992	8	8	2000	74 to 26	Initiative
Arkansas	1992	8	6	2000/1998	60 to 40	Initiative
California	1990	8	6	1998/1996	52 to 48	Initiative
Colorado	1990	8	8	1998	71 to 29	Initiative
Florida	1992	8	8	2000	77 to 23	Initiative
Louisiana	1995	12	12	2007	76 to 24	Referendum
Maine	1993	8	8	1996	67 to 33	Indirect Initiative
Michigan	1992	8	6	2002/1998	59 to 41	Initiative
Missouri	1992	8	8	2002	74 to 26	Initiative
Montana	1992	8	8	2000	67 to 33	Initiative
Nebraska	2000	8	—	2008	56 to 44	Initiative
Nevada	1994	12	12	2006	70 to 30	Initiative
Ohio	1992	8	8	2000	66 to 34	Initiative
Oklahoma	1990	12	12	2002	67 to 33	Initiative
South Dakota	1992	8	8	2000	63 to 37	Initiative

SOURCE: State Legislative Term Limits (2004), http://www.termlimits.org and the Council of State Governments, *The Book of the States 2003* (Lexington, Ky.: Council of State Governments, 2003). Updated by the authors.

politicians. The measure offers voters a chance to strike back at an institution that they perceive as self-serving and out of touch. In California, for example, power brokers like Willie Brown—at that time, the speaker of the assembly and self-described ayatollah of the legislature—became symbols of legislative arrogance. But not everyone favors limiting legislative terms. Opponents offer several arguments against them. On a theoretical level, they argue that term limits rob voters of their fundamental right to choose their representatives. In a related vein, they contend that these measures unfairly disqualify a subset of the population—legislators—from seeking office. And, finally, they claim that term limits are unnecessary, that sufficient legislative turnover occurs without them.

Term limits were expected to produce several consequences:

- Ending the domination of a chamber by powerful, entrenched veteran legislators.
- Increasing the proportion of first-term legislators in any given session.
- Increasing representation by groups underrepresented in the legislature, especially women and minorities, because of the guarantee of open seats.[54]
- Shifting power from the legislature to the governor and to lobbyists.

Term limits have changed the nature of the legislative process in affected states. The first two expected consequences have indeed come to pass. The exodus of veteran legislators and the influx of inexperienced members have some observers shaking their heads in dismay. Data from term-limit states like Maine, Oregon, and California reflect procedural difficulties, a slower-working institution, and less deliberation in committees.[55] One solution has been to increase the amount of training new legislators receive; another has been to increase the role of legislative staff. Clearly, replacing the lost institutional experience is a critical issue. The expectation that terms limits would produce greater representation of underrepresented groups has not been borne out, at least not yet. The number of women in term-limited legislatures has actually decreased slightly, and the increase in racial and ethnic minorities may be due more to their increased voting strength rather than to term limits.[56] As for shifting power to other actors, consensus seems to exist among researchers that governors, agency heads, legislative staff, and interest groups have benefited at the expense of the term-limited legislature.[57] In sum, limiting the terms of legislators has consequences beyond simply forcing incumbents out of office.

Popular as they may be with the public, term limits may have already reached their zenith. As Table 6.4 indicates, citizen initiatives are the primary vehicle through which the term-limits question has been placed before the voters. And the issue has just about run the gamut of states that allow initiatives. (The Utah legislature imposed term limits on itself in 1994, but it had a change of heart and repealed the law in 2003.) Court challenges have undone legislative term limits in Massachusetts, Oregon, Washington, and (in 2004) Wyoming. And in a surprising move, the Idaho legislature, bowing to an array of political pressures, repealed the term-limits law that was adopted via the initiative process in 1994.[58] (In Idaho, term limits were statutory, not constitutional; thus, the repeal was within the legislature's purview. The governor vetoed the legislature's action, but the House and Senate overrode the veto.) Angry Idahoans gathered a sufficient number of signatures to place a question on the 2002 ballot asking whether the legislature's action should be upheld. After a heated campaign, the Repeal the Repeal question was defeated, thus ending term limits in Idaho before they took effect.

RELATIONSHIP WITH THE EXECUTIVE BRANCH

In Chapter 7, you will read about strong governors leading American states boldly in the twenty-first century. In this chapter, you have read about strong legislatures charting a course for that same century. Do these institutions ever collide in their policymaking? Of course, conflict exists between the legislature and the governor in a state. In the words of one observer, "Conflict is the chief manifestation of a new calculus of political and institutional power in state government today."[59]

Interinstitutional tension is inevitable, but it is not necessarily destructive. It is inevitable because both governors and legislators think that they know what is best for the state. It is not necessarily destructive because, during the posturing, bargaining, and negotiating that produces a consensus, governors and legislators may actually arrive at the best solution.

Dealing with the Governor

The increased institutional strength of the legislature and its accompanying assertiveness have made for strained relations with a governor accustomed to being the political star. Institutional conflict is exacerbated under conditions of divided government, that is, when a legislature is controlled by one party and the governor is of the other party. The result of divided government is often gridlock, accompanied by finger pointing and accusations of blame. As the Republican governor of Mississippi, Haley Barbour, said to the Democratic-controlled legislature in his first State of the State address, "As Governor of Mississippi you have two choices . . . you can work with the Legislature, or you can fail. Well, I'm not into failure, so I look forward to working with each of you to make sure we all succeed."[60] As Governor Barbour quickly learned, that is much easier said than done. Figure 6.4 tracks the incidence of divided government over a fifty-five-year period. The trend is clear: Divided government is more prevalent now than it was in the 1940s and 1950s.

FIGURE 6.4   **Divided Government in the States, 1946–2002**

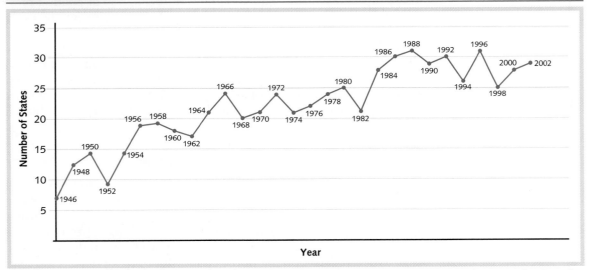

SOURCE: Data for 1946–1958 adapted from Morris Fiorina, "Divided Government in the States," in *The Politics of Divided Government*, Gary Cox and Samuel Kernell, eds. (Boulder, Colo.: Westview, 1991), p. 180. Data for 1960 to the present calculated by National Conference of State Legislatures. States with nonpartisan elections (Minnesota prior to 1972 and Nebraska) are excluded. States with odd-year elections are included in the succeeding even-numbered year. Updated by the authors.

A governor and a legislature controlled by the same party does not necessarily make for easy interbranch relations either. Especially in states where the two parties are competitive, legislators are expected to support the policy initiatives of their party's governor. Yet the governor's proposals may not mesh with individual legislators' attitudes and ambitions.

Governors have a media advantage over deliberative bodies such as a legislature. The governor is the visible symbol of state government and, as a single individual, fits into a media world of thirty-second sound bites. The Colorado senate president offered an explanation from a distinctly legislative perspective: "We never win in Colorado in the public's eye. We, the legislature, are always the bad guys, and the governor is the white hat, and he has been very successful in making that appeal to the public through the news media."[61] In contrast, media images of the legislature often portray dealmaking, pork barrel politics, and general silliness. To be sure, those images can be quite accurate. In an effort to project a more positive image of the legislature in action, the leadership of the California Assembly in 2004 pledged to bring "a new decorum to the often-rowdy lower house."[62] "Gotcha" journalism, the term for media efforts to catch public officials in seemingly questionable situations, certainly complicates legislative life.

Another weapon of the governor is the veto. In 1995, the Republican governor in New Mexico vetoed 200 bills out of the 424 bills that were passed: 47 percent. A political novice, the governor was thought by some legislators to be "ignorant of the political process."[63] But Governor Gary Johnson's use of the veto was strategic. He might not be able to get the legislature to embrace his agenda, but he could block their priorities by wielding his veto power. The governor alienated the Democratic majority in the legislature, but New Mexico's voters applauded his actions, returning him to office in 1998 by a comfortable margin. During his two terms, Governor Johnson vetoed 752 enactments and suffered only two overrides.[64]

Sometimes governors who have previously served as legislators seem to have an easier time dealing with the lawmaking institution. For example, former governor Madeleine Kunin of Vermont assumed the office after three terms in the legislature and one term as lieutenant governor "knowing the needs of legislators, the workings of the legislative process, the sensitivities of that process."[65] Usually about two-thirds of the governors have had legislative experience, although the proportion has recently declined. In 2002, for example, just over half of the fifty governors had put in time in the legislative ranks.

The legislature is not without its weapons. If the legislature can muster the votes, it can override a gubernatorial veto. Legislatures have also enacted other measures designed to enhance their control and to reduce the governor's flexibility in budgetary matters.[66] For example, some states now require the governor to obtain legislative approval of budget cutbacks in the event of a revenue shortfall. Others have limited the governor's power to initiate transfers of funds among executive branch agencies. These actions reflect the continuing evolution of legislative–executive relations.

Overseeing the Bureaucracy

Legislative involvement with the executive branch does not end with the governor. State legislatures are increasingly venturing into the world of state agencies and bureaucrats, with the attitude that after authorizing a program and allocating funds for it, they should check on what's happened to it. Legislative oversight involves four activities: policy and program evaluation, legislative review of administrative rules and regulations, sunset legislation, and review and control of federal funds received by the state.[67]

Policy and Program Evaluation Legislatures select auditors to keep an eye on state agencies and departments (in a few states, auditors are independently elected officials). Auditors are more than super-accountants; their job is to evaluate the performance of state programs with respect to their efficiency and effectiveness (a task sometimes known as the postaudit function). Specifically, they conduct periodic performance audits to measure goal achievement and other indicators of progress in satisfying legislative intent, a process that has been credited with both saving money and improving program performance.[68] In this respect, Virginia's Joint Legislative Audit and Review Commission (JLARC), regarded as a model for the rest of the country, was reinventing government before it became fashionable.[69] Throughout its thirty-year history, JLARC has conducted hundreds of evaluations of state programs and saved the state millions of dollars. The key to a useful auditing function is strong legislative support (even in the face of audits that turn up controversial findings) and, at the same time, a guarantee of a certain degree of independence from legislative interference.

Legislative Review of Administrative Rules All state legislatures conduct reviews of administrative rules and regulations, but they vary in their methods. They may assign the review function to a special committee (such as a rule review committee) or to a specific legislative agency, or they may incorporate the review function in the budgetary process.

Legislative review is a mechanism through which administrative abuses of discretion can be corrected. Legislative bills frequently contain language like the following: The Department of Youth Services shall develop the necessary rules and regulations to implement the provisions of this act. Such language gives the agency wide latitude in establishing procedures and policies. The legislature wants to be certain that, in the process, the agency does not overstep its bounds or violate legislative intent. If it is found to have done so, then the legislature can overturn the offending rules and regulations through modification, suspension, or veto, depending on the state.

This issue is a true gray area of legislative–executive relations, and court rulings at both the national and state levels have found the most powerful of these actions, the **legislative veto,** to be an unconstitutional violation of the separation of powers. For example, in 1997, the Missouri Supreme Court ruled that the legislature's rule-review process was an unconstitutional intrusion into the functions of the executive branch.[70] Legislatures continue to use the budgetary

legislative veto

An action whereby the legislature overturns a state agency's rules or regulations.

process to review (and sanction) agency behavior. Increasingly, legislatures are requiring state agencies to furnish extensive data to justify their budget requests, and they can use their financial power to indicate their displeasure with agency rules and regulations.[71]

Sunset Legislation Half the states have established **sunset laws** that set automatic expiration dates for specified agencies and other organizational structures in the executive branch. An agency can be saved from termination only through an overt renewal action by the legislature. Review occurs anywhere from every four years to every twelve years, depending on individual state statute, and is conducted by the standing committee that authorized the agency or by a committee established for sunset review purposes (such as a government operations committee). The reviews evaluate the agency's performance and its progress toward achieving its goals.

During the 1970s, sunset legislation was widely hailed as an effective tool for asserting legislative dominion over the executive branch, but more than thirty years' experience with the technique has produced mixed results, and some states have repealed their sunset laws. Agency reviews tend to be time-consuming and costly. And the process has become highly politicized in many states, involving not only agencies and legislators but lobbyists as well. One Texas representative commented that she "never saw so many alligator shoes and $600 suits as when some agency is up for sunset review."[72] On the positive side, sunset reviews are said to increase agency compliance with legislative intent. Statistics show that, nationwide, only about 13 percent of the agencies reviewed are eventually terminated, thus making termination more of a threat than an objective reality.[73]

Review and Control of Federal Funds Since the early 1980s, legislatures have played a more active role in directing the flow of federal funds once they have reached the state. Before this time, the sheer magnitude of federal funds and their potential to upset legislatively established priorities caused great consternation among legislators. The executive branch controlled the disposition of these grant funds almost completely by designating the recipient agency and program. In some cases, federal money was used to fund programs that the state legislature did not support. Federal dollars were simply absorbed into the budget without debate and discussion, and legislators were cut out of the loop. By making federal fund disbursement part of the formal appropriations process, however, legislators have redesigned the loop.

If legislatures are to do a decent job in forecasting state priorities, some control of federal funds is necessary. In the face of reduced federal aid to states, it is critical for legislators to understand the role that federal dollars have played in program operation. When funding for a specific program dries up, it is the legislature's responsibility to decide whether to replace it with state money.

How effectively are legislatures overseeing state bureaucracies? As with so many questions, the answer depends on who is asked. From the perspective of legislators, their controls increase administrative accountability. A survey of legislators in eight states found legislative oversight committees, the postaudit function, and sunset laws to be among the most effective bureaucratic controls available.[74] Another effective device, and one that legislatures use in special circumstances, is legislative investigation of an agency, an administrator, or a program. But from the perspective of the governor, many forms of legislative oversight are simply meddling and as such, they undermine the separation of powers.[75]

LEGISLATURES AND CAPACITY

State legislatures are fascinating institutions. Although they share numerous traits, each maintains some unique characteristics. Houses and senates have different traditions and styles, even in the same state. And across states, the variation in legislative systems is notable. As Alan Rosenthal writes, "Legislatures are interwoven in the fabric of their states."[76] As institutions, legislatures are dynamic; amid the layers of traditions and rules, they change and evolve.

The demands placed on state legislatures are unrelenting. Challenges abound. The ability of the legislatures to function effectively depends on institutional capacity. The extensive modernization that almost all legislatures underwent in the 1970s is evidence of institutional renewal. Structural reforms and a new breed of legislator have altered state legislatures and are sending them in the direction of increased capacity. How ironic then that, with all their institutional success, reformed legislatures continue to struggle with their public image.[77]

One real concern is that the legislatures of some states are being marginalized through a citizen-empowering mechanism, the initiative, and an institution-weakening provision, term limits. It is no wonder then that, in several states, legislators have mounted efforts to increase public knowledge of and respect for the legislative process. For instance, in its 2003 session, the leadership of the New Jersey Assembly bundled bills into topic areas to be taken up on various theme days.[78] Some days were devoted to "Advocating for Consumers," seven others were devoted to other topics, including Defending Our Families and Protecting Our Seniors. Theme days were preceded by public forums around the state on the upcoming topics. These forums were designed to increase public understanding of how the assembly conducts its business. Was it worth the time and energy? The speaker of the assembly summed it up this way: "The ultimate bottom line for any legislature is the quality of laws it enacts."[79]

CHAPTER RECAP

- The three principal functions of legislatures are policymaking, representation, and oversight.
- Reapportionment is a battleground for state legislatures because drawing district lines is a partisan process.
- Legislatures operate with their own formal and informal rules. Violations of institutional norms result in sanctions.

- The lawmaking process is a complex one, with multiple opportunities for delay and obstruction. Most bills never make it through; those that do seldom look like they did when they were introduced.
- Although legislatures perform more effectively than they used to, in 2004, fifteen states had term limits in effect. Term limits create open seats and thus increase competition for legislative seats. But when legislative terms are limited, other institutional actors such as the governor gain power.
- Legislators vie with governors in the policymaking process. Governors have the power to veto, but legislators have the power to override a gubernatorial veto. In addition, the legislature plays several oversight roles with regard to the bureaucracy.
- Legislative capacity has increased but at the same time, legislatures risk becoming marginalized in states with the initiative process and term limits.

Key Terms

multimember districts *(p. 146)*
malapportionment *(p. 146)*
reapportionment *(p. 147)*
redistrict *(p. 147)*
gerrymander *(p. 147)*
quorum *(p. 150)*
token *(p. 152)*

delegate *(p. 156)*
trustee *(p. 157)*
politico *(p. 157)*
policy entrepreneur *(p. 157)*
legislative veto *(p. 168)*
sunset laws *(p. 169)*

Surfing the Web

To find out what's up in state legislatures, visit the web site of the National Conference of State Legislatures at **www.ncsl.org.**

Most states have web sites that allow citizens to follow the progress of legislation during the session. See, for example, the legislative sites for Iowa and West Virginia at **www.legis.state.ia.us** and **www.legis.state.wv.us,** respectively.

The web site, **www.vote-smart.org,** tracks the performance of political leaders, including state legislators.

To learn about model state laws, see the National Conference of Commissioners on Uniform State Laws at **www.nccusl.org.**

An advocacy web site, **www.termlimits.org,** provides up-to-date coverage of the term-limits issue.

A watchdog organization that scrutinizes and regularly criticizes government, including state legislatures, maintains a web site at **www.publicintegrity.org.**

7

GOVERNORS

Just a few years ago the nation's governors were either routinely ignored by Congress or treated like any other of the many supplicants who appear regularly in Washington, D.C., appealing for congressional largess. Today, however, the governors speak with voices of authority on important national policy issues. Although they do not always agree on what they want, the governors have recently been influencing Congress and president as never before in our history. For example, the Republican governors played a leading role in nominating and electing Texas governor George W. Bush as president in November 2000. About a year earlier, at the annual Republican National Convention in Philadelphia, twenty-one of thirty Republican governors decided to endorse Bush, giving him a huge fund-raising advantage over other candidates. During the primary and general elections, all twenty-nine Republican governors (not counting candidate Bush himself) actively supported and campaigned for Bush, and were credited with delivering several closely contested states to his win column.

The governors have asserted themselves more and more frequently as a righteous third force in U.S. politics. Speaking through the National Governors' Association (NGA), they played a major role in shaping federal welfare reform, education reform, and Medicaid reform. While Congress feuds along partisan and ideological lines on almost all significant issues, the governors have preached—and practiced—partisan peacemaking to reach common policy ground with their own legislatures. As one respected capitol commentator observed, "The senators and representatives talk about bills they are trying to pass or defeat, the governors about things they have actually done."[1]

Members of Congress and leaders of the national Democratic and Republican parties have developed a new respect for the governors, for their ideas, and for their practical knowledge of policies and problems and of how federal actions play out at the state and local levels. Indeed, it is no longer unusual for governors to sit at the table to help congressional committees draft laws that are of special consequence to the states.[2] In the nation's time of need after 9/11, President Bush sought out a sitting governor, Tom Ridge of Pennsylvania, to head a new cabinet-level agency on homeland security. With strong odds that gridlock will continue to snarl a Congress divided closely along partisan lines the governors continue to serve as catalysts for positive national policy change. This challenging task was made even more complicated than usual by the states' financial problems of the early 2000s—the worst since the Great Depression. Faced with a voting public with no stomach for raising taxes and state budgets in which some three-fourths of expenditures are dedicated to education, health care, and local government, the governors have had to make some tough choices. Some advanced tax hikes, in spite of public opposition; others imposed brutal spending cuts on prisons, Medicaid, and education.

The governors' enhanced visibility and performance in national politics is a tribute to their policymaking capacity and responsiveness to common problems affecting the citizens of their respective states. It is also recognition of the policy leadership of the states in the U.S. federal system.

THE OFFICE OF GOVERNOR

It has been said that the American governorship was conceived in mistrust and born in a straitjacket. Indeed, because the excesses of some colonial governors appointed by the English Crown resulted in strong dislike and distrust of executive power by the early American settlers, the first state constitutions concentrated political power in the legislative branch.

History of the Office

Early governors were typically elected by the legislature rather than by the voters, were restricted to a single one-year term of office, and had little authority.[3] Two states, Pennsylvania and Georgia, even established a plural (multimember) executive. Slowly the governorships became stronger through longer terms, popular election, and the power to veto legislation, but power did not come easily. The movement for popular democracy during the Jacksonian era led to the election of other executive branch officials, and reaction to the excesses of Jacksonian democracy resulted in numerous independent boards and commissions in the executive branch. Although governors did gain some power, they were not able to exercise independent authority over these executive boards and commissions.

In the early 1900s, along with their efforts to democratize national politics and clean up the corrupt city political machines, Progressive reformers launched a campaign to reform state government. Their principal target was the weak executive branch. Efforts to improve the state executive branch have continued throughout the twentieth century. The essential goal has been to increase the governor's powers to make them more commensurate with the increased duties and responsibilities of the office. As a result, constitutional and statutory changes have fortified the office of the chief executive, reorganized the executive branch, and streamlined the structure and processes of the bureaucracy. The capacity of governors and the executive branch to apply state resources to the solution of emerging problems has thus been greatly enhanced.[4] And, as observed at the beginning of this chapter, the governors have become eminent players in national policymaking.

Today's Governors

Today, being governor is a high-pressure, physically demanding, emotionally draining job. As political scientist Larry Sabato states, "Governors must possess many skills to be successful. They are expected to be adroit administrators, dexterous executives, expert judges of people, combative yet sensitive and inspiring politicians, decorous chiefs of state, shrewd party tacticians, and polished public relations managers."[5] The job is also hard on the governor's private life. It consumes an enormous number of hours, at the expense of family activities; hobbies; and, in some cases, more significant moneymaking opportunities in law, consulting, or business.

Fortunately, governorships are attracting well-qualified chief executives who are a far cry from the figureheads of the eighteenth and nineteenth centuries and the stereotypical back-slapping, cigar-smoking wheeler-dealers of the early twentieth century. Today's governors are better educated and better prepared for the job than their predecessors were. The average age has declined somewhat—fifty-five years is the average. (The legal minimum age ranges from eighteen in California, Ohio, Rhode Island, Vermont, Washington, and Wisconsin to thirty-one in Oklahoma; it is thirty in most states.) Formal education averages around eighteen years (the general population averages 13.4 years), and a large proportion of the governors have held law degrees. Most of today's governors paid their political dues in state legislatures, gaining an understanding of important issues confronting the state, a working familiarity with influential figures in government and the private sector, and a practical knowledge of the legislative process and other inner workings of state government (see Table 7.1). Twenty-seven were born in the states they serve. About one-third of governors have served previously as elected state executive branch officials, and six have a background in law enforcement, having served as attorney general. Six were once mayors. Seven came straight from the private sector, including California Governor Arnold Schwarzenegger, elected to replace Gray Davis in a 2003 recall. The attractiveness of the governorship is evident in the fact that nine current chief executives left a congressional seat to take office. Why would someone desert the glamour of the nation's capital for the statehouse in Boise, Augusta, or Columbia? For political power and the opportunity to make a difference in one's own state. Simply put, being a state chief executive is just more fun. As John Ashcroft, a former two-term Missouri governor serving as U.S. attorney general in the Bush

TABLE 7.1	**Background Data on Selected Governors**				
NAME	STATE	PARTY	YEAR ELECTED	AGE FIRST ELECTED	PREVIOUS PUBLIC SERVICE
Ruth Ann Minner	DE	Democrat	2000	65	Lieutenant governor; state representative; state senate.
Jeb Bush	FL	Republican	2002	45	Secretary of commerce, governor (1998–2002).
Sonny Perdue	GA	Republican	2002	55	State legislature.
Dirk Kempthorne	ID	Republican	2002	51	U.S. senator; mayor; governor (1998–2002).
Kathleen Sebelius	KS	Democrat	2002	54	State insurance commissioner.
Jennifer Granholm	MI	Democrat	2002	43	State attorney general.
Tim Pawlenty	MN	Republican	2002	42	State legislature.
George Pataki	NY	Republican	2002	49	Governor (1994–2002); mayor; state senate.
Ed Rendell	PA	Democrat	2002	59	Mayor; district attorney.
Rick Perry	TX	Republican	2002	50	Lieutenant governor, governor (2000–2002).
Kathleen Blanco	LA	Democrat	2003	61	Lieutenant governor; legislator.

SOURCE: "Background Data on Selected Governors." Reprinted by permission of The Council of State Governments.

administration, puts it, "Anyone who tells you that being senator is as much fun as being governor will lie to you about other things, too."[6]

Though still predominantly white and male, today's governors are more representative of population characteristics than former chief executives were. Several Hispanics have served as governors in recent years, including Tony Anaya of New Mexico and Bob Martinez of Florida. In 1989, the first African American was elected governor—L. Douglas Wilder of Virginia. Gary Locke, the first Asian American governor not from Hawaii was elected governor of Washington in 1996. In earlier years, several women succeeded their husbands as governor, but since 1974 a growing number have won governorships on their own, including active governors Ruth Ann Minner (Delaware), Jennifer Granholm (Michigan), Kathleen Sebelius (Kansas), Linda Lingle (Hawaii), Janet Napolitano (Arizona), Kathleen Blanco (Louisiana), Judy Martz (Montana), and Olene Walker (Utah).

The path to the governorship of Delaware's Minner makes a compelling rags-to-riches story. She had to drop out of school at sixteen to work on a tenant farm. At seventeen she was married. Widowed with three children when her husband died at age thirty-two of a heart attack, Minner worked two jobs, earned her high school equivalency degree, and eventually graduated from college. She remarried and took a job as a secretary for former Delaware governor Sherman Tribbet. A few years later, she won a seat in the state house, and later moved to the state senate and the lieutenant governorship. On January 3, 2000, Ruth Ann Minner, former governor's secretary, became chief executive of Delaware.

Getting There: Gubernatorial Campaigns

If anyone ever said that running for governor was easy, they were profoundly wrong. The campaign is both expensive and humbling. As North Carolina Governor Mike Easley observed during his successful race in 2000, "My mama taught me never to think I was better than anybody else, never to brag and never to ask for money. So you get into politics, and what do you do? Tell people you're better than someone else, brag about your accomplishments and ask for money."[7]

Certainly, the lure of the governorship must be weighed against the financial costs. Campaigning for the office has become expensive. Because candidates no longer rely on their political party to support them, they must continuously solicit great sums of money from donors to pay for campaign costs—political consultants, opinion polls, air travel, advertisements in the print and broadcast media, telephone banks, direct mailings, web sites, and interactive video links. The growing attractiveness of the office has led to more competitive (and costlier) primary and general election races. To date, the most expensive governor's race was the 2002 election in New York, in which $146.8 million was spent by three candidates. Loser Thomas Golisano spent $76.3 million; the winner, George Pataki, spent only $44.2 million. These official figures do not include in-kind donations, such as free transportation, telephones, door-to-door canvassing, and other contributions from supporters. Generally, elections tend to cost more when they are close, are held in a nonpresidential election year, involve a partisan shift (that is, when a Democrat succeeds a Republican, or vice versa), and are held in highly populated and geographically large states (for example, Florida, Texas, California, and New York).[8] On a cost-per-vote basis, races in states with a widely scattered population or hard-to-reach media markets, such as Alaska or Nevada, tend to be the most expensive. Cost per vote in 2002 gubernatorial elections ranged from $42.77 in New Hampshire to only $2.54 in Kentucky.[9] In the 1998 California Democratic gubernatorial primary, candidate Al Checchi spent $40 million of his own money—$59.00 per vote—only to lose to Lieutenant Governor Gray Davis, who spent only $5.00 per vote received. In 2002, Davis spent $64.2 million to win re-election, only to be recalled by the voters the following year.

Money may be the single most important factor in winning a governorship, but it doesn't mean everything. As one veteran of political campaigns has reflected, "Everyone knows that half the money spent in a political campaign is wasted. The trouble is that nobody knows which half."[10] The rate of increase for the cost of governors' races is escalating. In the 2002 elections, the average amount spent per vote was about $12.50.[11]

Other factors important in candidate success are state party strength and candidate profile, including incumbency. The strongest influence is the strength of the candidate's political party in the state electorate[12] because party identification usually translates into votes for a party's candidate. Party can also matter in the legislature, as Mississippi's former Democratic governor Mike Musgrove discovered in 1999 when he collected 49.6 percent of the popular vote, compared with the 48.5 percent his opponent received. Because a handful of votes for a third candidate prevented a majority outcome, the election was determined in the state house of representatives. Fortunately for Musgrove, Democrats held a large majority of the seats.

High-profile candidates stand an excellent chance of being elected because they possess campaign skills, political experience, and other characteristics that help them raise needed campaign funds to get their message and persona across to the electorate. Of course, being independently wealthy doesn't hurt either.

Incumbency is a particularly important aspect of a candidate's profile. An incumbent governor running for re-election stands an excellent chance of victory; about three-quarters of incumbents have retained their seats since 1970. Incumbents enjoy several important advantages, including the opportunity while in office to cultivate popularity with the voters and collect campaign donations from interest groups. However, re-election is no sure thing. Budget and tax woes can lead voters to toss chief executives out of office, particularly those who, as candidates, pledged not to raise taxes but then do so after election to their first term. From 1970 to 2003, one-fourth of sitting governors eligible for re-election chose not to run, in most cases because of a poor state economy or voter antipathy to tax increases during their term.[13]

BEING GOVERNOR: DUTIES AND RESPONSIBILITIES

In performing the duties of the office, the governor wears the hats of top policy-maker, chief legislator, chief administrator, ceremonial leader, intergovernmental coordinator, economic development promoter, and political party leader. Sometimes several of these hats must be balanced atop the governor's head at once. These roles make the governorship one of the most difficult and challenging, yet potentially most rewarding, job in the world.

Developing and Making Policy

One of the 1990s' most successful governors, Tommy Thompson of Wisconsin, said, "I have a million ideas. I get about 100 ideas a day. One [of them] is good."[14] Transforming that good idea from concept to practice is an exciting but extraordinarily difficult challenge for governors. A governor is the leading formulator and initiator of public policy in his state, from his first pronouncements as a gubernatorial candidate until his final days in office. The governor's role as chief policymaker involves many other players, including those in the legislature, bureaucracy, courts, interest groups, and voting public, but few major policies that the governor does not initiate are enacted, and success or failure depends largely on how competent the governor is in framing the policy and developing public support for it. The governor must also follow through to see that adopted policies are put into effect as originally intended.

Some issues are transitory, appearing on the agenda of state government and disappearing after appropriate actions are taken. These issues are often created by external events, such as a federal court decision that mandates a reduction in prison overcrowding; a new national transportation law requiring states to alter highway maintenance practices; or an act of nature such as a tornado, flood, or forest fire. Examples include abortion rights, affordable health care, taxation of e-commerce, and preservation of open space.

Most policy issues, however, do not emerge suddenly out of happenstance. Perennial concerns face the governor each year: education, corrections, social welfare, the environment, and economic development. Cyclical issues also appear, increase in intensity, and slowly fade away. Examples of the latter type are consumer protection, ethics in government, reapportionment, and budget deficits. Of course, national policy issues sometimes absorb the governors' time as well, such as preparing for and responding to acts of terrorism, providing health care insurance to children and the working poor, and dealing with proposals to drill for oil and gas in national parks or in areas adjacent to state shorelines.

Several factors have contributed to stronger policy leadership from the state chief executives in recent years, including larger staffs with more able personnel who are knowledgeable in important policy fields; a more integrated executive branch with department heads appointed by the governor; strengthened formal powers of the office, such as longer terms and the veto and budget powers; and the assistance of the NGA, which offers ideas for policy and program development. Of no small importance is the high caliber of individuals who have won the office in recent years. Among the most entrepreneurial and innovative gubernatorial policy leaders of today are George Pataki (New York), Bill Richardson (New Mexico), and Ed Rendell (Pennsylvania). These governors are defining and developing national policies.

Of course, unforeseen events can disrupt any governor's policy agenda. The immensity of state fiscal problems caught many new governors by surprise when they assumed office in January 2003. Added to the fiscal problems were rising Medicaid and homeland security costs. New initiatives quickly take a back seat when severe budget problems assume center stage and legislative debate dwells on tax hikes or proposed service and spending reductions.

Marshaling Legislative Action

This gubernatorial role is closely related to that of policymaker because legislative action is required for most of the chief executive's policies to be put into effect. In fact, the governor cannot directly introduce bills; party leaders and policy supporters in the state house and senate must put the bills in the hopper. Dealing with legislators is a demanding role for a governor, consuming more time than any other role and representing for many the single most difficult aspect of the job.

Executive–Legislative Tensions Developing a positive relationship with the legislature requires great expenditures of a governor's time, energy, and resources. Several factors hinder smooth relations between the chief executive and the legislature, including partisanship and personality clashes. Even the different natures of the two branches can cause conflict. Governors are elected by a statewide constituency and therefore tend to take a broad, comprehensive, long-range view of issues, whereas legislators represent relatively small geographical areas and groups of voters, and are more likely to take a piecemeal, parochial approach to policymaking.

According to one study, the amount of strife between the two branches is influenced by three factors: the size of the majority and the minority parties, the personalities of the governor and legislative leaders, and the nearness of an election year.[15] Following the 2003 elections, there were twenty-six Republican and twenty-four Democratic governors. Before the 1970s, it was common for a single party to control the governorship and the legislature. In a majority of the states today, however, the governor has to deal with a one- or two-house majority from the opposing political party. When the opposition party is strong, the governor must seek bipartisan support to get favored legislation passed. Often a governor facing a large legislative majority from the opposing party has only the veto and the possibility of mobilizing public support as weapons against the legislature. Independent governors don't even have a minority party to count on, but this situation doesn't preclude success. Former governor Angus King of Maine asserted that not having a party affiliation brought some advantages. For instance, he says, "I have no automatic friends in the legislature, but I have no automatic enemies. I have 186 skeptics."[16] On another occasion, he observed that "Golden opportunities often come disguised as insurmountable obstacles."[17]

A governor who ignores or alienates members of the opposing political party can quickly find himself in the desert without a drink of water. Republican Governor Gary Johnson of New Mexico took office proudly proclaiming his intention not to compromise his lofty principles with "a bunch of careerist Democratic officeholders who had brought the curse of bloated government upon the Land of Enchantment."[18] The result was overridden vetoes, failed policy initiatives, an ineffective administration, and an exhausting shouting contest between Johnson and the legislature that continued into a second administration. Altogether, Johnson vetoed 752 bills during his two terms, quite possibly a national record. Former governor Gray Davis of California antagonized legislators by insisting that their responsibility was "to implement my vision. That is their job."[19] Such conflicts typically erupt during budget time, when critical spending decisions are at hand.[20] But in Wisconsin, former governor Tommy Thompson's bipartisan, pragmatic approach to making government work was widely acclaimed and produced major legislative triumphs in education and welfare policy reform.

The approach of statewide elections can also bring gubernatorial–legislative deadlock because incumbents in both branches of government may be extremely cautious or overtly partisan in their efforts to please (or at least not to offend) the voters while discrediting their opponents. Gridlock may result. These three conflict-producing factors of partisanship, personalities, and proximity of an election are intensified during debates on the budget, when the principal policy and financial decisions are made.

Even in states where the governor's own party enjoys a large majority in both houses of the legislature, factions are certain to develop along ideological, rural–urban, geographical, institutional (house versus senate), or other divisions. Ironically, a large legislative majority can create the greatest problems with factionalism primarily because a sizable opposition doesn't exist to unite the majority party. Apparently a legislative majority of 60 to 70 percent helps a governor; anything more than that percentage and the majority party tends to degenerate into intraparty rivalries beyond the governor's control. As one Democratic governor lamented in the face of a 4-to-1 majority of his own party in the legislature, "You've got Democrats, you've got moderate Democrats, you've got suburban Democrats, you've got urban Democrats, you've got rural Democrats . . ."[21]

Executive Influence on the Legislative Agenda Despite the difficulties in dealing with the legislature, most governors dominate the policy agenda, usually by working hand in hand with legislative leaders. The governor's influence begins with the State of the State address, which kicks off each new legislative session and continues in most states with the annual budget message. In 2004, governors stressed fiscal problems and education improvements. During the legislative session itself, the governor might publicly threaten to veto a proposed bill or appeal directly to a particular legislator's constituency.

Most of the drama, however, takes place behind the scenes. The governor might promise high-level executive branch jobs or judgeships (either for certain

pork barrel

Favoritism by a governor or other elected official in distributing government monies or other resources to a particular program, jurisdiction, or individual.

legislators or for their friends) to influence legislative votes. Or she might offer some sort of **pork barrel** reward, such as arranging funding for a highway project in a legislator's district or approving an appropriation for the local Strawberry Festival. Private meetings or breakfasts in the governor's mansion flatter and enlist support from individuals or small groups of legislators. Successful governors can usually relate to representatives and senators on a personal level. Many of the more effective governors have a history of personal experiences with state legislators, so they know which strings to pull to win key supporters.

In addition, all governors have one or more legislative liaisons who are assigned to lobby for the administration's program. Members of the governor's staff testify at legislative hearings, consult with committees and individuals on proposed bills, and even write floor speeches for friends in the legislature. Some governors designate a floor leader to steer their priorities through the legislature.

Most governors, however, are careful not to be perceived as unduly interfering in the internal affairs of the legislature. For example, chief executives generally do not become involved in legislative elections for majority and minority leadership positions—or if they do, they act only in a quiet and selective way.[22] Too much meddling in legislative affairs can bring a political backlash that undermines a governor's policy program. Thus, the role of chief legislator requires a balancing act that ultimately determines the success or failure of the governor's agenda.

Administering the Executive Branch

As chief executive of the state, the governor is (in name, at least) in charge of the operations of numerous agencies, departments, boards, and commissions. In the view of many voters, the governor is directly responsible not only for pivotal matters such as the condition of the state's economy but also for mundane concerns such as the number and depth of potholes on state highways. Most governors are sensitive to their chief administrative responsibilities and spend a great amount of time and energy attending to them. Constitutional and statutory reforms, including the concentration of executive power in the office of the governor and the consolidation of numerous state agencies, have considerably strengthened the governor's capacity to manage the state. (See Chapter 8 for additional discussion of public administration.) If governors are diligent in expeditiously appointing talented and responsive people to policymaking posts, they should feel no compulsion to micromanage the state's day-to-day affairs. Instead, they can focus their energies on leadership activities such as identifying goals, marshaling resources, and achieving results.

In many respects the governor's job is comparable to that of the chief executive officer of a large corporation. Governors must manage thousands of workers, staggering sums of money, and complex organizational systems. They must establish priorities, handle crises, and balance contending interests. But there are also important differences. Governors are not paid comparably for their responsibilities. In terms of expenditures and employees, most states are as big or bigger than *Fortune* 500 companies, whose chief executive officers typically earn tens of millions of dollars a year in salary, stock options, and other forms of remuneration. Governors average only about $110,000 in salary per year. (The highest paid is the governor of New York, at $179,000; the lowest is Maine's, at $70,000.[23]) In addition to being woefully underpaid, today's governors experience high levels of stress from constant media attention to every possible misstep, interest group carping and criticism, legislative sniping, and extraordinarily long hours on the job. Arkansas Governor Mike Huckabee and his First Lady even endured the ignominy of living in a manufactured home, or trailer, while the mansion underwent much-needed repairs and refurbishing. Plagued with unforgiving budget problems, South Carolina Governor Mark Sanford was planning to shut down the governor's mansion and move his family out until a group of business supporters saved the day with a bailout.

Restraints on Management Reforms of the executive branch have allowed far more active and influential gubernatorial management, but significant restraints still exist. For example, the separation-of-powers principle dictates that the governor share his or her authority with the legislature and the courts, either or both of which may be politically or philosophically opposed to any given action. Changes in state agency programs, priorities, or organization typically require legislative approval, and the legality of such changes may be tested in the courts. The governor's ability to hire, fire, motivate, and punish is severely restricted by the courts; merit-system rules and regulations; collective bargaining contracts; independent boards and commissions, with their own personnel systems; and other elected executive branch officials, who pursue their own administrative and political agendas. Thus, most employees in the executive branch are outside the governor's formal sphere of authority and may challenge that authority almost at will. Career bureaucrats, who have established their own policy direction and momentum over many years of seeing governors come and go, usually march to their own tune. In sum, governors must manage through third parties and networks in the three branches of government as well as in the private and nonprofit sectors. They have little unilateral authority.

One of the most critical functions of the governor's role as chief administrator is crisis management. Immense problems may come crashing down on the chief executive as a result of natural or humanmade disasters. Some governors are unfortunate enough to have a series of crises, none of their own making, befall the state during their administration. For instance, during Pete Wilson's eight years in office (1990–1998), California suffered the worst drought in decades, followed by earthquakes, fires, floods, and the deadly 1992 Los Angeles riots. Wilson could be forgiven for feeling like a biblical victim of God's holy wrath. When catastrophic events like these occur, governors typically demonstrate personal concern, reallocate money, and exercise their power to call out the state National Guard.

Governors as Managers Some governors minimize their managerial responsibilities, preferring to delegate them to trusted staff and agency heads. Others provide strong administrative and policy leadership in state government. A popular former governor known for his management abilities was Utah Republican Mike Leavitt. Leavitt, a former insurance executive, utilized a collaborative decisionmaking style to attain remarkable gains in economic development and other areas. His state was named the nation's "best managed" by *Financial World* magazine.[24]

The constraints on the governor's managerial activities are not likely to lessen nor are the potential political liabilities. The governors who courageously wade into the bureaucratic fray must invest a great deal of time and scarce political resources, yet they risk embarrassing defeats that can drag their administrations into debilitation and disrepute. After all, claiming to have reorganized the state bureaucracy hardly resonates with the voters on a campaign bumper sticker. Meanwhile, in the face of social, economic, and technological changes, the management of state government has become increasingly complex, and the need for strong administrative leadership is more critical than ever before.

Master of Ceremonies

Some governors thrive on ceremony and others detest it, but all spend a large portion of their time on it. Former governors remember ceremonial duties as the second most demanding of the gubernatorial roles, just behind working with the legislature. Cutting the ribbon for a new highway, celebrating the arrival of a new business, welcoming potential foreign investors, receiving the queen of the Collard Green Festival, announcing Be a Good Neighbor Week, opening the state fair, and handing out diplomas are the kind of ceremonial duties that take a governor all over the state and often consume a larger portion of the workweek than does any other role.[25] George A. Aiken, the late governor of Vermont, dreaded having to pin the ribbon on the winner of the Miss Vermont contest because he couldn't figure out how to put the pin in without getting his hand under the bathing suit.

Coordinating Intergovernmental Relations

Governors serve as the major points of contact between their states and the president, Congress, and national agencies. For example, following Hurricane Isabel's foray into North Carolina in 2003, Governor Mike Easley coordinated relief efforts with the Federal Energy Management Agency, the Armed Forces, nonprofit organizations, and local governments. State-to-state relations to settle disputes over cross-boundary water or air pollution and other environmental concerns are carried out through the governor's office. At the local level, governors are involved in allocating grants-in-aid, promoting cooperation and coordination in economic development activities, and various other matters. Governors also provide leadership in resolving disputes with Native American tribes involving casino gambling and related issues.

The role of intergovernmental coordinator is most visible at the national level, where governors are aided by the NGA and the state's Washington office. In the 1960s, the NGA was transformed from a social club into an organization providing lobbying, information, and research services with a staff of more than

100. It now meets annually in full session to adopt policy positions and to discuss governors' problems and policy solutions. The governors also meet in separate regional organizations. (C-SPAN covers national meetings of the governors.) The NGA's staff analyzes important issues, distributes its analyses to the states, offers practical and technical assistance to the governor, and holds a valuable seminar for new governors. The NGA has recently come under fire, however, from conservative Republicans, who object to the organization's perceived tax-and-spend agenda, even when it benefits their own states. In fact, in 2003, Republican governors of Texas and Hawaii withdrew from the NGA over this concern.

More than thirty-two states have established Washington offices to fight for their interests in Congress; the White House; and, perhaps most important, the many federal agencies that interact with states on a daily basis. A governor's official inquiry can help speed up the progress of federal grant-in-aid funds or gain special consideration for a new federal facility. Washington offices are often assisted by major law and lobbying firms under contract to individual states.

The governor's role as intergovernmental coordinator is becoming more important with each passing year. It reflects the elevated position of the states in the scheme of American federalism and the increasing state importance in national and international affairs. Acting together and as individuals, the governors have exercised national policy leadership on critical issues such as taxation of Internet sales, public education, welfare and health care reform, economic development, and urban sprawl. When the national government confronts a policy problem, it turns more and more often to the states for solutions.

Promoting Economic Development

Unfairly or not, governors are held responsible by the voters for their state's economic health.[26] As promoter of economic development, a governor works to recruit business and tourists from out of state and to encourage economic growth from sources within the state (see Chapter 14). Governors attend trade fairs; visit the headquarters of firms interested in locating in the state; telephone, write, and e-mail promising business contacts; and welcome business leaders. The role may take the governor and the state economic development team to Mexico, Korea, or Germany as well as to other states, but development mostly entails making the state's climate good for business through improving infrastructure, arranging tax and service deals, and other strategies designed to entice out-of-state firms to relocate and encourage in-state businesses to expand or at least stay put. New Mexico Governor Bill Richardson proudly boasts that he calls corporate chief executive officers (CEOs) daily and "sucks up to them."[27]

When a state enjoys success in economic development, the governor usually receives (or at least claims) a major portion of the credit. Sometimes the personal touch of a governor can mean the difference between an industrial plum and economic stagnation; success stories include the cases of BMW's selection of South Carolina and Mercedes-Benz's and Honda's choice of Alabama as locations for new vehicle assembly facilities. The economic development policies of Michigan Governor Engler helped turn "[a] listing industrial behemoth into a technically sophisticated . . . competitor."[28] West Virginia Governor Bob Wise promised, "In five years, West Virginia will be the Silicon Valley of biometrics."[29] Wise has taken tangible actions to improve his state's human capital, as described in the nearby *Breaking New Ground* box.

Leading the Political Party

By claiming the top elected post in the state, the governor becomes the highest-ranking member of his or her political party. This role is not as significant as it was several decades ago, when the governor controlled the state's party apparatus and legislative leadership and had strong influence over party nominations for seats in the state legislature and executive branch offices. Primaries have replaced party conventions and put nominations in the hands of the voters. And legislative leaders constitute a much more independent breed than they were,

BREAKING NEW GROUND

A Vision Shared

West Virginia has been economically stagnant for decades. State per-capita income is only 70 percent of the national average. The state ranks fourth highest in the proportion of the population living in poverty, at 16.4 percent. West Virginia ranks last in the percentage of people who have graduated from high school, and only 16.3 percent of the residents are college graduates (the national average is 24.4 percent). Young people have been abandoning their home state for better opportunities elsewhere, pushing West Virginia past Florida as the "oldest" state with the most senior citizens. Still distressingly dependent on heavy industry (20 percent of all jobs are related to coal mining), the state desperately needed a new strategy for economic development.

Governor Bob Wise took office in 2001 with that new plan, which he named A Vision Shared. To advance the economy and overcome a tradition of labor strife, Wise relied on leadership skills honed in the state senate and U.S. Congress to promote business–labor collaboration, working hard to bring the two traditional adversaries together to attract new business. Wise spends hours each week—an estimated one-third of his time—making personal phone calls to corporate CEOs, telling them how eager the Mountaineer State is to serve as a business location. He touts the state's new tax breaks and other incentives, which replaced a confusing, failed mix of incentives geared to an old-style economy. He also boasts of cheap utilities, plenty of water, and nearly $1 billion in bonds and private investment to improve infrastructure. Wise even gives out his personal phone number and e-mail address to prospects who want to contact him directly. The governor also succeeded in convincing the legislature to fund the PROMISE program, which provides a full tuition scholarship to all graduates of West Virginia high schools with a 3.0 GPA and 1000 combined SAT score who enroll in a public university in that state.

Slowly, help is arriving from high-tech enterprises, which are locating along a thirty-five-mile corridor between Clarksburg and Morgantown. More firms are considering West Virginia and sharing Wise's vision. More of West Virginia's brightest students are staying home for college and, Wise hopes, future employment.

SOURCES: Alan Ehrenhart, "Moving Mountains," *Governing* (December 12, 2002): 36–39; www.State.wv.us/governor (October 22, 2003); and www.wv.gov (October 22, 2003).

for example, in Illinois, when Governor Richard Ogilvie (1969–1973) brought up the need for income tax legislation during a breakfast meeting at the mansion. Senate president Russ Arrington angrily asked, "Who is the crazy son of a bitch who is going to sponsor this thing?" The governor calmly replied, "Russ, you are."[30] And he did. Such an order is unlikely these days. Still, some governors get involved in legislative elections through campaign aid, endorsements, or other actions. If the governor's choice wins, he or she may feel a special debt to the governor and support him on important legislation.

The political party remains at least marginally useful to the governor for three principal reasons.[31] Legislators from the governor's own party are more likely to support the chief executive's programs. Communication lines to the president and national cabinet members are more likely to be open when the president and the governor are members of the same party. Finally, the party remains the most convenient means through which to win nomination to the governor's office.

A growing number of states have highly competitive political parties, and governors find that they must work with the opposition if their legislative programs are to pass. For Independent governors, a special challenge exists: how to govern without a party behind you to organize votes and otherwise push proposed laws through the convoluted legislative process. Maine's Independent governor, Angus King, demonstrated a talent for working with shifting legislative coalitions on various major issues. Reform party governor (and former Navy Seal and professional wrestler) Jesse Ventura did not experience the same level of success with the Minnesota legislature.

FORMAL POWERS OF THE GOVERNOR

formal powers

Powers of the governor derived from the state constitution or statute.

Several powers are attached to the governor's office. A governor's **formal powers** include the tenure of the office, power of appointment, power to veto legislation, responsibility for preparing the budget, authority to reorganize the executive branch, and the right to use professional staff in the governor's office. These institutional powers give governors the potential to carry out the duties of office as they see fit. The formal powers vary considerably, however, from state to state. Some governors' offices (Illinois, New York) are considered strong and others (Georgia, Alabama) weak. Also, the fact that these powers are available does not mean that they are used effectively. Equally important are the **informal powers** that governors have at their disposal. Informal powers are potentially empowering features of the job or the person that are not expressly provided in the law. Many of the informal powers are associated with personal traits on which the chief executive relies to carry out the duties and responsibilities of the office. They are especially helpful in relations with the legislature.

informal powers

Powers of the governor not derived from constitutional or statutory law.

Both sets of powers have increased over the past several decades. Indeed, governors are more influential than ever before because of their enhanced formal powers and the personal qualities they bring to the state capital. The most successful governors are those who employ their informal powers to maximize the formal powers. The term for this concept is *synergism,* a condition in which the total effect of two distinct sets of attributes working together is greater than the sum of their effects when considered together. Thus, an influential governor is one who can skillfully combine formal and informal powers to maximum effectiveness. Counting among the most effective governors in recent years are Michael Leavitt (Republican, Utah), Zell Miller (Democrat, Georgia), and Tommy Thompson (Republican, Wisconsin). The nearby *Debating Politics* box poses a conundrum that calls for exercising both types of powers.

Tenure

The governor's tenure power has two characteristics: the duration (number of years) of a term of office and the number of terms that an individual may serve as governor. Both have slowly but steadily expanded over the past two centuries. From the onerous restriction of a single one-year term of office placed on ten of the first thirteen governors, the duration has evolved to today's standard of two or more four-year terms (only New Hampshire and Vermont restrict their governors to two-year terms). In addition, gubernatorial elections have become distinct from national elections now that thirty-nine states hold them in nonpresidential election years. This system encourages the voters to focus their attention on issues important to the state rather than allowing national politics to influence state election outcomes.

DEBATING POLITICS

What Should the Governor Do?

Here is the situation: You have served successfully as governor for the past three years. With your re-election campaign just kicking off, however, you are facing what could be your greatest challenge: what to do about a $500 million shortfall (about 5 percent of the state's budget).

You have already ordered emergency cuts in state expenditures on Medicaid and other programs, laid off 250 prison guards and 1,200 other state workers, signed off on a 20 percent tuition hike by public universities, and withheld state aid to local governments. The cries of economic anguish are becoming deafening, and you can't find anything else to cut.

Raising new revenues appears to be the only alternative. Yet you were elected to office on a platform that promised no new taxes. In the legislature, support is growing for a one-penny sales tax increase. If the trend continues, you are quite likely to have a sales tax bill placed on your desk for signature or veto. A majority in the state senate has already committed to passing it.

You have mixed feelings about a tax hike. On one hand, it would solve the budget problems for at least the next few years, and in your heart you feel it is the optimal solution. On the other hand, negative taxpayer reaction could cost you re-election.

The speaker of the state house of representatives, a member of your own political party and someone with whom you have a good working relationship, has scheduled an appointment with you for tomorrow at 10:00 A.M. to discuss the proposed tax bill. You know that he personally favors it but that the floor vote is too close to call.

What will you do? What formal and informal powers are at your disposal to help resolve this dilemma?

The importance of longer consecutive terms of office is readily apparent. A two-year governorship condemns the incumbent to a perpetual re-election campaign. As soon as the winner takes office, planning and fund-raising must begin for the next election. For any new governor, the initial year in office is typically spent settling into the job. In addition, the first-term, first-year chief executive must live with the budget priorities adopted by his or her predecessor. A two-year governorship, therefore, does not encourage success in matters of legislation or policy. Nor does it enable the governor to have much effect on the bureaucracy, whose old hands are likely to treat the governor as a mere bird of passage and make him almost a lame duck when his term begins. As Governor Alfred E. Smith of New York observed after serving four two-year terms during the 1920s, "One hardly has time to locate the knob on the Statehouse door."[32]

In contrast, Virginia's governor, the only one who is restricted to a single four-year term, is a bit less confined in carrying out his responsibilities. He really has only two years to put his programs and priorities in place, sandwiched on one side by the initial learning year and on the other by the lame-duck period. The incumbent needs another four-year term to design new programs properly, acquire the necessary legislative support to put them into place, and get a handle on the bureaucracy by appointing competent political supporters to top posts. Eight years in office also enhances the governor's intergovernmental role, particularly by giving him or her sufficient time to win leadership positions in organizations such as the NGA. The record of an eight-year chief executive stands on its own, untainted by the successes or failures of the office's previous inhabitant.

The average time actually served by governors has grown steadily since 1955 as a result of fewer restrictions on tenure. The gubernatorial graybeard is Illinois Governor Jim Thompson, who stepped down after serving his fourth consecutive term in 1990—a twentieth-century record. (North Carolina's Jim Hunt served two, nonconsecutive four-year terms, 1980–1988 and 1992–2000.) Long periods in office strengthen the governor's position as policy leader, chief legislator, chief administrator, and intergovernmental coordinator, as shown by the policy legacies left in Illinois by Thompson and in North Carolina by Hunt.[33] Another sort of gubernatorial record was set by Cecil H. Underwood, who in 1956 became West Virginia's youngest governor at the age of thirty-four. He was re-elected for a second term in 1996 as the state's *oldest* governor at seventy-four years of age but lost in another bid for office in 2000.

Some resistance to unlimited tenure still exists. More than one re-election creates fears of political machines and possible abuses of office. And, pragmatically speaking, a long period of a safe governorship can result in stagnation and loss of vigor in the office. Even in states that do not restrict governors to two consecutive terms, the informal custom is to refrain from seeking a third term.

Appointment Power

Surveys of past governors indicate that they consider appointment power to be the most important weapon in their arsenal when it comes to managing the state bureaucracy. The ability to appoint one's supporters to top positions in the executive branch also enhances the policy management role. When individuals who share the governor's basic philosophy and feel loyal to the chief executive and her programs direct the operations of state government, the governor's policies are more likely to be successful. Strong appointment authority can even help the governor's legislative role. The actual or implicit promise of important administrative and especially judicial positions can generate a surprising amount of support from ambitious lawmakers.

Unfortunately for today's governors, Jacksonian democracy and the long ballot live on in the **plural executive.** Most states continue to provide for popular election of numerous officials in the executive branch, including insurance commissioners, public utility commissioners, and secretaries of agriculture. Proponents of popular election claim that these officials make political decisions and therefore should be directly responsible to the electorate. Opponents contend that governors and legislators can make these decisions more properly, based on the recommendations of appointed executive branch professionals who are not beholden to special interests.

Perhaps appointment authority should depend on the office under consideration. Those offices that tend to cater to special interests, such as agriculture, insurance, and education, probably should be appointive. Less substantive offices such as secretary of state or treasurer probably should be appointive as well. It makes sense to elect an auditor and an attorney general, however, because they require some independence in carrying out their responsibilities. (The auditor oversees the management and spending of state monies; the attorney general is concerned with the legality of executive and legislative branch activities.)

Many governors are weakened by their inability to appoint directly the heads of major state agencies, boards, and commissions. These high-ranking officials make policy decisions in the executive branch, but if they owe their jobs in whole or in part to legislative appointment, the governor's authority as chief executive is diminished significantly. Though nominally in charge of these executive branch agencies, the governor is severely constrained in her ability to manage them. Such an arrangement would be unthinkable in a corporation.

The fragmented nature of power in the executive branch diminishes accountability and frustrates governors. Former Oregon governor Tom McCall once lamented that "we have run our state like a pick-up orchestra, where the members meet at a dance, shake hands with each other, and start to play."[34] When the assorted performers are not selected by the chief conductor, their performance may lack harmony, to say the least. And elected statewide offices provide convenient platforms for aspiring governors to criticize the incumbent.

Most reformers interested in "good government" agree on the need to consolidate power in the governor's office by reducing the number of statewide elected officials and increasing the power of appointment to policy-related posts in the executive branch. Most states have expanded the number of policymaking, or unclassified, positions in the governor's staff and in top agency line and staff positions. But the number of elected branch officials has remained almost the same since 1965. Table 7.2 shows the range and number of separately elected officials. The largest number is in North Dakota, where twelve statewide offices are filled through elections: governor, lieutenant governor, secretary of

plural executive
A system in which more than one member of the executive branch is popularly elected on a statewide ballot.

state, attorney general, agricultural commissioner, chief state school officer, treasurer, labor commissioner, tax commissioner, two insurance commissioners, and utility commissioner. At the bottom of the list are the reformer's ideal states: Maine, New Hampshire, and New Jersey, which elect only the governor. The average number of elected officials is about eight.

Why has it been so difficult to abolish multiple statewide offices? The main reason is because incumbent education superintendents, agricultural commissioners, and others have strong supporters in the electorate. Special-interest groups, such as the insurance industry, benefit from having an elected official—the insurance commissioner—representing their concerns at the highest level of state government. Such groups fiercely resist proposals to make the office appointive. Additional resistance may come from many citizens who simply like having an opportunity to vote on a large number of executive branch officials.

patronage

The informal power of a governor (or other officeholder) to make appointments on the basis of party membership, and to dispense contracts and other favors to political supporters.

Professional Jobs in State Government The vast majority of jobs in the states are filled through objective civil service (merit-system) rules and processes. Governors are generally quite content to avoid meddling with civil service positions (see Chapter 8), and a few have actually sought to transfer many **patronage** appointments—those based on personal or party loyalty—to an independent, merit-based civil service.[35] Gubernatorial sacrifice of patronage power is under-

TABLE 7.2	**Separately Elected State Officials**

OFFICE	NUMBER OF STATES ELECTING
Governor	50
Lieutenant governor	42
Attorney general	43
Treasurer	40
Secretary of state	37
Education (superintendent or board)	14
Auditor	25
Secretary of agriculture	13
Controller	9
Public utilities commissioner	7
Insurance commissioner	11
Land commissioner	5
Labor commissioner	4
Mines commissioner	1
Adjutant general (National Guard)	1

SOURCE: Adapted from *The Book of the States 2004* (Lexington, Ky.: Council of State Governments, 2004), Table 2.10. Reprinted by permission of The Council of State Governments.

standable in view of the time and headaches associated with naming political supporters to jobs in the bureaucracy. The possibility of embarrassment or scandal is a factor if the governor accidentally appoints a person with a criminal record, a clear conflict of interest, or a propensity for sexual harassment, or someone who causes harm through simple incompetency. One former governor recalled that "I was appointing people I didn't know to boards and commissions I never heard of."[36] Those who are denied coveted appointments are likely to be angry. Another governor is quoted as stating: "I got into a lot of hot water because I refused to appoint some of the more prominent Democrats around the state." According to another, who was about to name a new member of a state commission, "I now have twenty-three good friends who want [to be] on the Racing Commission. [Soon] I'll have twenty-two enemies and one ingrate."[37] A governor benefits from a stable, competent civil service that hires, pays, and promotes on the basis of knowledge, job-related skills, and abilities rather than party affiliation or friendship with a legislator or other politician.

The Power to Fire The power of the governor to hire is not necessarily accompanied by the power to fire. Except in cases of extreme misbehavior or corruption, it is very difficult to remove a subordinate from office, even if it is constitutionally permitted. For instance, if a governor attempts to dismiss the secretary of agriculture, he can anticipate an orchestrated roar of outrage from legislators, bureaucrats, and farm groups. The upshot is that the political costs of dismissing an appointee can be greater than the pain of simply living with the problem. In settings where the governor indirectly appoints top officials, it may be nearly impossible to sack an undesirable employee. For example, in Missouri, the governor appoints eight members of the State Board of Education, who then choose a commissioner of education. The governor cannot sanction or remove the commissioner except through the state board. In the case of merit-selected civil servants, formal dismissal procedures bypass the chief executive entirely.

Several U.S. Supreme Court rulings have greatly restricted the governor's power to dismiss or remove from office the political appointees of previous governors. In the most recent case, *Rutan et al.* v. *Republican Party of Illinois* (1990), the Court found that failure to hire, retain, or promote an individual because of his or her political or party affiliation violates that person's First Amendment rights.[38]

A good appointment to a top agency post is the best way for a governor to influence the bureaucracy. By carefully choosing a competent and loyal agency head, the governor can more readily bring about significant changes in the programs and operations of that agency. Where appointment powers are circumscribed, the chief executive must muster her informal powers to influence activities of the state bureaucracy or rely on the seasoned judgment of professional civil servants.

Veto Power

A veto can be purposeful, instructive, or punitive. A bill may be vetoed because its contents are contrary to a governor's principles. A veto accompanied by an explanation makes a powerful symbolic statement or can instruct the legislature about how the bill might be amended for the governor's signature. A veto can also punish offending legislators or state agencies who were counting on approval of a favored program. Often the mere threat of a veto is enough to persuade a recalcitrant legislature to see the governor's point of view and compromise on the language of a bill. Vetoes are not easy to override. Most states require a majority of three-fifths or two-thirds of the legislature, depending on the type of veto the governor has employed.

package veto

The governor's formal power to veto a bill in its entirety.

line item veto

The governor's formal power to veto separate items in a bill instead of the entire piece of proposed legislation.

pocket veto

The governor's power to withhold approval or disapproval of a bill after the legislature has adjourned for the session, in effect vetoing the measure.

executive amendment

A type of veto used by the governor to reject a bill, and also to recommend changes that would result in the governor's approval of the bill.

Types of Vetoes The veto can take several forms. The **package veto** is the governor's rejection of a bill in its entirety. All governors hold package veto authority. The package veto is the oldest form available to governors, having been adopted in the original constitutions of New York and Massachusetts.

The **line item veto** allows the governor to strike out one or more objectionable sections of a bill, permitting the remaining provisions to become law. Only Nevada, North Carolina, and five other states forbid this gubernatorial power. Several states permit a hybrid form of line item veto in which the governor may choose to reduce the dollar amount of a proposed item to hold down state expenditures or cut back support for a particular program. In some states, the line item veto is permitted only in appropriations bills.

The **pocket veto,** which is available in fifteen states, allows the governor to reject a bill by refusing to sign it after the legislature has adjourned. In three states (Hawaii, Utah, and Virginia), the legislature can reconvene to vote on a pocket veto; otherwise, the bill dies. A governor might use the pocket veto to avoid giving the legislature a chance to override a formal veto or to abstain from going on record against controversial legislation.

A fourth type of veto is the **executive amendment,** formally provided in fifteen states and informally used in several others. With this power, a governor may veto a bill, recommend changes that would make the bill acceptable, and then send it back to the legislature for reconsideration. If the legislature concurs with the suggestions, the governor signs the bill into law.

Use of the Veto The actual use of the veto varies by time, state, and issue. Some states, such as California and New York, often record high numbers of vetoes, whereas others, like Virginia, report few. On average, governors veto around 4 percent of the bills that reach their desks.[39] The variation among states reflects the tensions and conflicts that exist between the governor and the legislature. The largest number of vetoes typically occurs in states with divided party control of the executive and legislative branches. Occasionally, the governor stands as the last line of defense against a flawed bill backed by the legislature because of powerful interest groups. Occasionally legislators may secretly ask the governor to veto a questionable bill they have just passed because the bill itself is politically popular.[40]

Although the overall rate of veto utilization has remained steady, the proportion of successful legislative overrides increased in the past two decades. This trend is an indication of the growing strength and assertiveness of state legislatures, the increase in conflict between the executive and legislative branches, and the prevalence of split-party government. Differences in party affiliation between the governor and the legislative majority probably provoke more vetoes than any other factor, especially when party ideology and platforms openly clash.

Conversely, when mutual respect and cooperation prevail between the two branches, the governor rarely needs to threaten to use or actually use the veto. Most governors interact with the legislature throughout the bill-adoption process. Before rejecting a bill, the governor will request comments from key legislators, affected state agencies, and concerned interest groups. He may ask the attorney general for a legal opinion. And before vetoing proposed legislation, the governor usually provides advance notification to legislative leaders, along with a final opportunity to make amendments.

The veto can be a powerful offensive weapon that may be used to obtain a legislator's support for a different bill dear to the governor's heart, particularly near the end of the legislative session. The governor may, for instance, hold one bill hostage to a veto until the legislature enacts another bill that he favors. Former Arizona governor Bruce Babbitt once threatened to veto a popular highway bill unless a teacher salary increase was passed—"No kids, no concrete." The legislature capitulated in the end.[41] In another instance, former Wisconsin governor Tommy Thompson's creative use of the line item veto inspired a legislative revolt. Thompson applied the veto on some 1,300 occasions during a contentious six-year period, even striking out certain words and letters to radically change the meaning of text.

Budgetary Power

Whether one is a conservative Republican or a liberal Democrat, spending money is fun. By developing the executive budget, the governors effectively set the legislative agenda at the beginning of each session. By framing the important policy issues and attaching price tags to them, the governor can determine the scope and direction of budgetary debates in the legislature and ensure that they reflect his overall philosophy on taxing and spending. All but a handful of governors now have the authority to appoint (and remove) the budget director and to formulate and submit the executive budget to the legislature. In Mississippi and Texas, budget authority is shared with the legislature or with other elected executive branch officials. And in these two states, two budgets are prepared each year, one by the governor and one by a legislative budget board.

Because full budgetary authority is normally housed in the office of the chief executive, the governor not only drives the budgetary process in the legislature but also enjoys a source of important leverage in the bureaucracy. The executive budget can be used to influence programs, spending, and other activities of state agencies. For example, uncooperative administrators may discover that their agency's slice of the budget pie is smaller than expected, whereas those who are attentive to the concerns of the governor may receive strong financial support. Rational, objective criteria usually determine departmental budget allocations, but a subtle threat from the governor's office does wonders to instill a cooperative agency attitude.

The governor's budget requests are rarely, if ever, enacted exactly as put forward. Rather, they are usually argued and debated thoroughly in both houses of the legislature. A legislature dominated by the opposing political party is nearly certain to scorn or disparage the governor's budget, and governors who are elected statewide, must appeal to a large and diversified electorate. Legislatures must please localized geographic constituencies.[42] Ultimately, "the governor may propose, but the legislature disposes." In fact, no monies may be appropriated without formal action by the legislature. (The budget process is discussed further in Chapter 8.) During the state budget crises of the early 2000s, governors and legislatures struggled over the question of who would assume primary responsibility for reducing state expenditures or hiking taxes. Usually, governors take the heat, and even light the match, by unilaterally cutting agency budgets or introducing tax increases.[43] Such bold actions, though fully appropriate, are not taken without due caution by the governor because the electoral consequences can be direct and extremely negative.

Reorganization Power

Reorganization power refers to the governor's ability to create and abolish state agencies, departments, and other offices and to reallocate administrative responsibilities among them. Reorganizations are usually aimed at the upper levels of the bureaucracy in an effort to streamline the executive branch and thereby make it work more efficiently and effectively. The basic premise is that the governor, as chief manager of the bureaucracy, needs the authority to alter administrative structures and processes to meet changing political, economic, and citizen demands. For instance, serious and recurring problems in coordinating the delivery of social services among several existing state agencies may call for a consolidated human services department with expanded powers. A governor with strong reorganization power can bring about such a department without approval of the legislature.

Traditionally, legislatures have been responsible for the organization of state government, and in the absence of a constitutional amendment to the contrary or a statutory grant of reorganization power to the governor, they still are. But today, twenty-one states specifically authorize their chief executive to reorganize the bureaucracy through **executive order.** Through an executive order, the governor can make needed administrative changes when she deems it necessary. All governors are permitted through constitution, statute, or custom to issue directives to the executive branch in times of emergency, such as during natural disasters or civil unrest.[44]

Administrative reorganization today takes place under the assumption that streamlined government improves bureaucratic performance by cutting down on duplication, waste, and inefficiency. Achieving a more efficient and user-friendly government is a top priority of most governors. Reinventing-government initiatives aim to make government more flexible and responsive by changing incentive systems for state employees, privatizing certain operations, reducing layers of bureaucracy, and decentralizing human resource management agency activities. Florida Governor Jeb Bush outsourced to private contractors a large

executive order

A rule, regulation, or policy issued unilaterally by the governor to change executive branch operations or activities.

portion of the state's human resource management activities. Governor Mitt Romney won legislative approval to reorganize health and human services in Massachusetts in 2003 but saw his other reorganization proposals collapse in the legislature. Former Montana governor Marc Racicot won legislative approval to abolish two departments and reorganize several others, saving the state an estimated $1.1 million. Ohio's former governor George Voinovich eliminated two departments and 3,200 state employees, saving $900 million.

Executive branch reorganization is widely practiced, but its actual benefits may be ephemeral. Reorganization typically achieves modest financial savings, if any at all.[45] Political scientist James K. Conant's analysis of reorganizations in twenty-two states indicates that such actions are not a cure for state fiscal ills. However, executive branch reorganization may help to provide a clearer focus on a particular problem or to contain administrative costs, and it may serve various political purposes, such as rationalizing the pain of employee layoffs.[46]

The Politics of Reorganization Reorganization is a politically charged process. Mere talk of it sounds alarms in the halls of the legislature, in the honeycombs of state office buildings, and in the offices of interest groups. Reorganization attempts usually spawn bitter controversy and conflict both inside and outside state government as assorted vested interests fight for favorite programs and organizational turf. Reorganization proposals are frequently defeated or amended in the legislature, or even abandoned by discouraged chief executives. One study of proposed state reorganizations discovered that almost 70 percent resulted in rejection of the plan either in part or in its entirety.[47] Even when enacted, reorganizations may generate extreme opposition from entrenched interests in the bureaucracy and, in the final analysis, be judged a failure. In the memorable words of former Kansas governor Robert F. Bennett:

> In the abstract, [reorganization] is, without a doubt, one of the finest and one of the most palatable theories ever espoused by a modern-day politician. But in practice . . . it becomes the loss of a job for your brother or your sister, your uncle or your aunt. It becomes the closing of an office on which you have learned to depend. . . . So there in many instances may be more agony than anything else in this reorganization process.[48]

Most governors who have fought the battle for reorganization would concur. Perhaps this fierce opposition helps explain the rarity of far-reaching executive branch restructuring in the past several years.

Staffing Power

The governor relies on staff for policy analysis and advice, liaison with the legislature, and assistance in managing the bureaucracy. Professional staff members are significant components of the governor's team, comprising a corps of political loyalists who help the governor cope with the multiple demands of the office. From the handful of political cronies and secretaries of several decades ago, the staff of the governor's office has grown in number, quality, and diversity with respect to gender and race. The average number of professional and clerical staff members is approximately fifty-seven today. In the larger, more highly populated states, staff members number well over 100 (Florida lists 310).[49] The principal staff positions of the governor's office may include the chief of staff, legislative liaison, budget director, planning director, public relations director, legal counsel, press secretary, and intergovernmental coordinator. Some governors have also established strong offices of policy management.

A question of serious concern, especially in the states whose governors have large staffs, is whether too much power and influence is being placed in the hands of nonelected officials. Clearly, professional staff members have been highly influential in developing and promoting policies for the governor in some states, particularly in states where the governor lacks a coherent set of priorities and lets the staff have free rein. In other states, the chief executive is clearly in charge, relying on staff primarily for drafting bills and providing technical information.[50] Given their physical and intellectual proximity to the governor, staff members are in a highly advantageous position to influence their boss. In their role as the major funnel for policy information and advice, they can affect the governor's decisions by controlling the flow of information and individuals into his office.

The Relevance of the Formal Powers

In Table 7.3, the states are scored according to the strength of the governor's formal powers of office. As noted, governors have won stronger powers during the past three decades. But how helpful are the formal powers? In spite of the major transformation of the governor's office, governors remain relatively weak because of the setting of state government. They must function within a highly complex and politically charged environment with formal authority that is quite circumscribed by the legislature, the courts, and constitutional and statutory law. Because of the nature of our federal system, the national government effectively strips them of control over many policy and administrative concerns. The business of state government is carried out in a fishbowl, open to regular scrutiny by the media, interest groups, talk-show hosts, and other interested parties. Notwithstanding the continued constraints on the exercise of their authority, however, today's governors as a group are more effective than their predecessors were in carrying out their varied responsibilities. Today, the formal powers of the office are substantially strengthened, and highly qualified people are serving as chief executives.

In theory, governors with strong formal powers, such as the governors in Illinois, New York, and Utah, should be more effective than their counterparts in Alabama and North Carolina. In practice, that is usually true—but not always. The potential for power and influence must not be confused with action. A governor with strong formal powers enjoys the capacity to serve effectively, but she may choose not to do so or, for various reasons, be unable to utilize the formal powers properly. This point is indirectly confirmed by a study that finds that formal gubernatorial power does not translate into greater success for incumbent governors seeking re-election.[51] Alternatively, a governor with weak formal powers can nonetheless be an effective, strong chief executive if she actively and skillfully applies the levers of power available in the constitution and in the statutes.

TABLE 7.3					**Relative Power of the Offices of Governor**									
WEAK					**MODERATE**						**STRONG**			
2.7	2.8	2.9	3.0	3.1	3.2	3.3	3.4	3.5	3.6	3.7	3.8	3.9	4.0	4.1
AL	RI	AZ	AR	LA	MO	OR	CA	ID	MI	NE	SD	ND	AK	NY
	NC		NV	MS	NH		MA	DE	MT	HI	CO	NJ	MN	IL
	VT			IN	VA		FL		IA	NM	CT	OH	WV	UT
	GA			OK	WA		KS		WI	PA	ME	TN		PN
				SC			KY		WY		MD			
				TX										
U.S. average 3.5														

NOTE: The scale varies from 2.7 to 4.1. Seven measures of power are assigned points for strength: tenure, appointment, removal power, budget control, veto power, whether governor and legislature belong to the same party, and number of other statewide elected officials.

SOURCE: Virginia Gray and Russell L. Hanson, eds., *Politics in the American States: A Comparative Analysis,* 8th ed. (Washington, D.C.: CQ Press, 2003), Table 7.5. Copyright © 2003 CQ Press, a division of Congressional Quarterly Inc. Reprinted by permission of the publisher, CQ Press.

INFORMAL POWERS

No doubt a governor with strong formal powers has an advantage over one without them. But the exploitation of the informal powers of the office is at least equally important for a successful governorship. These powers carry authority and influence that are not directly attached to the governorship through statute or constitution but rather are associated with the human being who happens to occupy the governor's mansion. Governors who can master these powers can be highly effective, even in the absence of strong formal powers.

The informal powers help transform the capacity for action into effective action. They react in synergy with the formal powers to create a successful governorship. An incumbent chief executive in the strong-governor state of New York will be hopelessly weak unless he also uses his personal assets in performing the multiple roles of the office. Alternatively, a chief executive in a weak-governor state such as Georgia can be remarkably successful if he fully employs his informal powers to become a change agent—one who excels in persuading the people in the state to adopt new ideas.[52] The informal powers are not as easy to specify as the formal powers are; however, they generally include tools of persuasion and leadership traits (such as popular support, prestige of the office, previous electoral experience, special sessions, public relations and media skills, negotiating and bargaining skills, pork barrel and patronage) and personal characteristics (such as youth, ambition, experience, and energy).

Tools of Persuasion and Leadership

Popular support refers to public identification with and support for the governor and his or her program. It may be measured in terms of the margin of victory in the primary and general elections or in terms of the results of public opinion polls. Governors can parlay popular support into legislative acceptance of a policy mandate and influence over bureaucratic behavior, and otherwise channel the pressures of public opinion to their advantage.[53]

But popular support may erode when governors' actions alienate the voters. California governor Gray Davis experienced the wrath of the voters when he was recalled in 2003, a mere one year after they had re-elected him to a second term. He was the first governor to be recalled since Lynn J. Frazier of North Dakota in 1921. Davis was generally considered unlikable, venal, and incompetent, but he was not believed to be guilty of any specific crime or flagrant misbehavior. The recall was largely a partisan affair, with Republicans attempting to remove the Democratic governor. Davis's opponents tapped into widespread dissatisfaction with California's massive budget deficit, seriously failed energy policy deregulation, and Davis's overall job performance. The recall campaign could have been filmed as a bad Hollywood comedy. Among the 135 candidates were a porn star whose platform consisted of a breast implant tax, former child actor Gary Coleman, a man who sought to legalize the ownership of ferrets, a self-described smut peddler, and the actor who played Father Guido Sarducci on *Saturday Night Live*. When the votes were counted, Davis was recalled and actor Arnold Schwarzenegger, who invested over $10 million of his own funds, had won the race.

The *prestige of the office* helps the governor open doors all over the world that would be closed to an ordinary citizen. National officials, big-city mayors, corporate executives, foreign officials, and even the president of the United States recognize that the governor sits at the pinnacle of political power in the state, and they treat her accordingly. The governors of California, New York, and Texas—the largest states—almost automatically assume roles of national prominence. Within the state, the governor typically uses the prestige of the office by inviting important individuals for an official audience, or perhaps to a special meal or celebration at the governor's mansion.

The governor's power to call the legislature into *special session* can be employed to focus public and media attention on a particular part of the legislative program or on a pressing issue. In this situaton, the governor can delineate the topics that will be considered, thereby forcing the legislature's hand on divisive or controversial matters, such as insurance reform or a tax increase. In conjunction with popular support and with media and public relations skills, this informal power can work effectively to bend legislative will.

Previous electoral experience is a valuable asset. Those who have made their way up the state's political ambition ladder by serving in the state legislature or serving as attorney general or lieutenant governor have learned how to find their way through political briar patches and avoid tar pits.[54] They can also take advantage of political friends and allies they cultivated along the way.

Other informal powers may be defined in terms of leadership skills. *Public relations and media skills* help the governor command the "big mike": the captive attention of the press, radio, and television. Any governor can call a press conference at a moment's notice and get a substantial turnout of the state's major media representatives, an advantage enjoyed by precious few legislators. Some chief executives appear regularly on television or radio to explain their policy positions and initiatives to the people. Minnesota Governor Tim Pawlenty offers a weekly radio call-in show featuring special celebrity guests. Others write a weekly newspaper or Web column for the same purpose. Frequent public appearances, staged events, telephone calls, correspondence, and even state-funded advertisements delivered by the governor can also help develop and maintain popular support. Governors such as Mike Leavitt of Utah have used such techniques to attain statewide voter approval ratings of 85 percent and above.[55] The ability to improvise in unpredictable, chaotic situations doesn't hurt. Maryland Governor Parris Glendening listened with astonishment as his transportation secretary delivered the governor's speech at a public event rather than his own. But Glendening took the podium, ad-libbed, and no one except his speech writer noticed the difference. Spontaneity may serve the governor well, but one must also weigh his words carefully before speaking. Outgoing Oklahoma Governor Frank Keating observed that "[t]he biggest mistake I made was saying things I thought were cute or funny, and very few other people did. Keep it to your wife and children."[56]

Indeed, the media can be a strong ally in carrying out the governor's programs and responsibilities. Effective governors know this instinctively and cultivate the press "like a backyard garden." But media relations are a two-way street. The media expect the governor to be honest, forthright, and available. If he instills respect and cooperation, observes political scientist Coleman B. Ransome, Jr., the governor's media relations can be "of incalculable value in his contest for the public eye and ear."[57] After all, most or all of what the public knows about the governor comes from the media.[58] Jesse Ventura, for example, was elected Reform party governor of Minnesota in 1998. The six-foot, four-inch, ex-Navy Seal, pro wrestler, radio personality, and actor captivated the voters with his unconventionality and straight talk. His approval ratings soared as Minnesota's roaring economy permitted a $1.3 billion tax rebate. But following a *Playboy* interview in which he dismissed organized religion as a sham and made other controversial statements, Ventura's popular support plummeted. Without strong popularity to help push his policy ideas through a legislature containing no partisan allies, Ventura's clout diminished significantly.[59] In addition to his poorly received *Playboy* interview, Ventura suffered from a hostile relationship with the media. Once, when attempting to escape persistent reporters to go on a hunting trip, a microphone was thrust in front of his face. The reporter inquired, "Mr. Ventura, what are you going to be hunting today?" Ventura replied, "Media people. You got a ten second head start."[60]

Negotiating and bargaining skills are leadership tools that help the governor to convince legislators, administrators, interest groups, and national and local officials to accept his point of view on whatever issue is at hand. These skills are of tremendous assistance in building voting blocs in the legislature, particularly in divided-power settings where hyperpluralism (which is prevalent in national politics) must be avoided. They also help persuade new businesses to locate in the state and help the governor effectively represent a state's interests before the national government. Two former governors who showed a special knack for finding common ground and brokering deals between warring parties were Roy Romer of Colorado and George W. Bush of Texas. Bush took great pride in his ability to bring contending elements of his legislature together. Weak in institutional powers, Bush was willing to spend much time and energy negotiating the details of an agreement, eventually brokering a compromise through his powers of persuasion.[61] Romer helped to develop federal–state accords on rangeland management in the West and to settle bitter teacher strikes.[62]

Pork barrel and patronage are aspects of the seamier side of state politics. Although they are utilized much less frequently now than they were before the civil service reforms of the first half of this century, governors are still known to promise jobs, contracts, new roads, special policy consideration, electoral assistance, and other favors to influential citizens, legislators, and other politicians in return for their support. All governors have discretionary funds with which to help out a special friend who has constituents in need. And although patronage appointments are now severely limited in most jurisdictions, a personal telephone call from the governor can open the door to an employment opportunity in state government.

Characteristics of a Successful Governor

The *personal characteristics* of an effective governor are nearly impossible to measure. Research by political scientists indicates that age and personality are statistically significant predictors of gubernatorial performance: Younger governors and those with a strong desire to influence others have been more successful than older, less power-driven ones.[63] As indicated earlier, however, leadership is generally agreed to be a vital quality of effective governors. Leadership traits are difficult to define, but former Utah governor Scott Matheson identified the best governors as "men and women who have the right combination of values for quality public service—the courage to stick to their convictions, even when in the minority, integrity by instinct, compassion by nature, leadership by perception, and the character to admit wrong and when necessary, to accept defeat."[64]

A successful governor—one who enjoys success in discharging the activities of the office and in achieving his objectives—blends these qualities with the formal and informal powers of office. For example, following the political campaign to win the election, the governor must conduct a never-ending campaign to win the loyalty and support of her cabinet, state employees, the legislature, and the people if she is to be effective.[65] Sixteen-hour work days are not uncommon.

Successful governors, particularly those in weak-governor states, know how to limit their policy agendas. Realizing that to try to do everything is to accomplish nothing, they focus on a few critical issues at a time and marshal their formal and informal resources behind them. Eventually, the determined governor can wear down opponents. But more important, the successful governor exercises leadership by convincing the public that he is the person to pursue their vision and their interests. He prevails in the legislature by applying the pressure of public opinion and by building winning blocs of votes, and he leads the bureaucracy by personal example. Above all else, the successful governor must be persuasive.

In short, the formal powers of the office are important to any governor, but even strong formal powers do not guarantee success. As noted earlier, they must be combined with the informal powers to be effective. Whatever approach the governor chooses as chief executive, his or her individual skills are probably more important than formal powers.[66] Evidence of this conclusion is provided by governors who have won and held their state's top job and successfully pursued their policy agendas in the face of significant partisan opposition. Notable examples are Zell Miller of Georgia and Bush of Texas, who combined the politics of pragmatism with outstanding interpersonal skills in exercising leadership. Those who are antagonistic toward the legislature or who lack appropriate individual skills are unlikely to leave a policy legacy.

REMOVAL FROM OFFICE

After leaving office, the vast majority of governors simply continue their public service in another venue. Four out of the last five presidents were ex-governors. Five former governors were appointed to cabinet-level positions by President George W. Bush. Former California governor Jerry Brown was elected mayor of Oakland, and Colorado's Roy Romer took on the challenge of serving as superintendent of Los Angeles, California, public schools. Eleven former governors are serving in the U.S. Senate.

But sometimes a seriously flawed individual wins the governorship. Because state chief executives are held to higher standards today than ever before and are constantly under the microscope of the media and watchdog groups, illegal actions or conflicts of interest are likely to be discovered and prosecuted.

All states but one provide in their constitutions for the impeachment of the governor and other elected officials (in Oregon, they are tried as regular criminal offenders). Impeachment proceedings are usually initiated in the state house of representatives, and the impeachment trial is held in the senate. A two-thirds vote is necessary for conviction and removal of the governor in most states. Of the more than 2,100 governors who have held office, only 18 have been impeached and 11 actually convicted and removed from office.

The most recent impeachment was of Connecticut Governor John Rowland in 2004. During his third term, Rowland then resigned in a cavalcade of allegations, including accepting gifts for favors granted to friends and political supporters, and the gathering force of a federal criminal investigation. Another recent impeachment and conviction occurred in 1993 in Alabama. The case involved Republican governor Guy Hunt, a Primitive Baptist (fundamentalist) preacher and farmer. Hunt's troubles began in 1991 when the state ethics commission ruled that Alabama's first Republican governor in 112 years had violated the ethics law by using the state's executive jet to fly to preaching engagements out of state and by accepting "love offerings" from his flock. The elected Democratic attorney general of Alabama investigated and prosecuted Hunt on this and twelve other charges. Following indictment by a grand jury, the governor was convicted for illegally using his inaugural fund to channel $200,000 for personal use, including payment of his home mortgage and the purchase of cattle feed, a riding lawn-mower, and a marble shower stall for his home.[67]

Other modern governors have left office under a cloud of criminal allegations. In 1988, Arizona Republican Governor Evan Mecham was impeached and convicted by the senate of misusing state money and trying to stop an investigation of a murder threat against one of his aides. In 1997, another Arizona governor, Fife Symington, was forced to resign after being convicted of fraud. Former Democratic governor of Rhode Island, Edward DiPrete, pleaded guilty to bribery, extortion, and racketeering in 1998. One of the most sordid governorships in recent years was Ray Blanton's in Tennessee. Blanton was convicted of conspiracy, extortion, and mail fraud and charged with numerous additional offenses, including the selling of liquor licenses to restaurant and bar owners and of pardons to state prison inmates. The most recent was New Jersey Governor James McGreevey, who resigned from office during a press conference in which he disclosed that he had been having a homosexual affair with a staffer.

But the handful of fallen governors are the gubernatorial black sheep—the oddities of contemporary state government who make interesting reading in the scandal sheets. They deflect proper attention from the vast majority of hardworking, capable, and honest chief executives who typify the American state governorship today.

When governors die or are removed from office for misconduct, they are normally succeeded by the lieutenant governor. For example, Lieutenant Governor Jody Rell replaced John Rowland in Connecticut when Rowland resigned from office, Utah Governor Olene Walker stepped up to assume her state's top job when Mike Leavitt became head of the U.S. Environmental Protection Agency in 2003, and Lieutenant Governor Joe Kernan took office in Indiana after the death of Governor Frank O'Bannon in 2003. States lacking the office of lieutenant governor specify alternative arrangements, such as succession by the president of the senate (West Virginia) or by other executive branch officials such as the secretary of state (Arizona).

OTHER EXECUTIVE BRANCH OFFICIALS

The states elect more than 450 officials to their executive branches, not counting the fifty governors. These positions range from attorneys general and treasurers to railroad commissioners. The four most important statewide offices are described here.

Attorney General

The attorney general (AG) is the state's chief legal counsel. The AG renders formal written opinions on legal issues, such as the constitutionality of a statute, administrative rule, or regulation, when requested to do so by the governor, agency heads, legislators, or other public officials. In most states, the AG's opinions have the force of law unless they are successfully challenged in the courtroom.

State Attorney General Eliot Spitzer has successfully reached financial settlements for the people with the music industry, giant investment firms, and Microsoft, among other firms.
SOURCE: Stephen Chernin/Getty Images.

The AG represents the state in cases where the state government is a legal party, and he conducts litigation on behalf of the state in federal and state courts. The AG can initiate civil and criminal proceedings in most states. AGs have represented their states more and more often in legal actions contesting national government statutes and administrative activities in controversial fields such as hazardous waste, nuclear waste, and business regulation. Activist AGs such as New York's Eliot Spitzer have initiated actions to protect consumers against mail fraud, Medicaid fraud, misleading advertisements, and overpriced compact disks, among many other consumer ripoffs. AGs recently took on the tobacco industry, winning huge ($200 billion) reimbursements for state funds spent to provide Medicaid-related health care for residents with smoking-related illnesses. These highly competent, aggressive attorneys often work together under the auspices of the National Association of Attorneys General to assert and protect the role of the states in U.S. federalism. Their collective actions are helping to reform corrupt corporate behavior and to shift business regulation from the national government to the states. The AGs increasingly cooperate with federal officials in sharing information and coordinating law enforcement actions. Predictably, the AGs' activism has spawned a growing corporate backlash that includes intense interest and participation in AG elections.

Lieutenant Governor

The office of lieutenant governor was originally created by the states for two major reasons: to provide for orderly succession to a governor who is unable to fill out a term because of death or other reasons, and to provide for an official to assume the responsibilities of the governor when the incumbent is temporarily incapacitated or out of the state. Eight states do not see the need for the office: Arizona, Maine, New Hampshire, New Jersey, Oregon, Tennessee, West Virginia, and Wyoming. Others attach little importance to it, as indicated by an extremely low salary or the absence of official responsibilities. The historical reputation of the lieutenant governor was that of a do-nothing on a death watch. One former occupant of the office in Nevada characterized his major responsibility as "checking the obituaries to see if I should be in Carson City."[68] Indeed, several of today's governors rose to the top office from that of lieutenant governor, although only one, Joseph Kernan of Indiana, became governor because of his predecessor's death.

Over the past twenty-five years, however, the lieutenant governorship in the majority of states has become a more visible, demanding, and responsible office. This trend is likely to continue as state governance grows increasingly complex and as additional states adopt the team election of governor and lieutenant governor. Many lieutenant governors hold important powers in the state senate, including serving as presiding officer and assigning bills to committees. Half can break a tie vote in the senate. They are official members of the cabinet or of the governor's top advisory body in twenty-five states.[69] And almost all lieutenant governors accept special assignments from the chief executive, some of which are quite visible and important. For example, Indiana's lieutenant governor acts as the state's commissioner of agriculture. In general, lieutenant governors' salaries, budget allocations, and staff have grown markedly during the past two decades.

A lingering problem is that nineteen states continue to elect the governor and lieutenant governor independently. This system can result in conflict when, for example, the chief executive is out of state and the two officeholders are political rivals or members of opposing political parties. On several recent occasions, a lieutenant governor, after assuming command, has proceeded to make judicial appointments, veto legislation, convene special sessions of the legislature, and take other actions at odds with the governor's wishes.

To avoid partisan bickering and politicking in the top two executive branch offices, twenty-four states now require team election. New York was the first to adopt this innovation, in 1953. In addition to avoiding embarrassing factionalism, team election has the advantages of promoting party accountability in the executive branch, making continuity of policy more likely in the event of gubernatorial death or disability, and ensuring a measure of compatibility and trust between the two state leaders. But it doesn't entirely preclude problems. Lieutenant Governor Betsy McCaughey Ross shocked New York Republican Governor George Pataki by changing her party stripes to Democrat a year before Pataki's first term expired. Needless to say, she was dropped from the Republican ticket.

Treasurer

The treasurer is the official trustee and manager of state funds. He or she collects revenues and makes disbursements of state monies. (The treasurer's signature is on the paycheck of all state employees and on citizens' state tax refunds.) Another important duty is the investment of state funds, including state employee pension monies. The failure to make profitable investments can cost the treasurer his or her job. West Virginia Treasurer A. James Manchin was impeached by the House of Delegates for losing $279 million in state funds through bad investments. Other treasurers have been criticized for taking lucrative private-sector jobs in the middle of their terms (Connecticut, New Jersey), accepting gifts from financial firms (Massachusetts), or using their post to raise large sums of money from investment companies for their next election (nearly all states in which the treasurer is elected rather than appointed).

Secretary of State

In a majority of states, the duties of the secretary of state are rather perfunctory. For the most part, they entail record-keeping and election responsibilities. Secretaries of state typically register corporations, securities, and trademarks, and commission people to be notary publics. In their election-related responsibilities, they determine the ballot eligibility of political parties and candidates, receive and verify initiative and referendum petitions, supply election ballots to local officials, file the expense papers and other campaign reports of candidates, and conduct voter registration programs. The typical secretary of state also maintains state archives, registers drivers' licenses, files agency rules and regulations, publishes statutes and copies of the state constitution, and registers lobbyists.

THE CAPABILITY OF U.S. GOVERNORS

The states have reformed their executive branches to enhance the capability of the governor as chief executive and to make the office more efficient, effective, accountable, and responsive. Indeed, the reforms discussed in this chapter not only have extended the formal powers and capacity of the office but also have improved the contemporary governor's performance in his many demanding roles.

In addition, today's governors are better educated, more experienced in state government, and more competent than their predecessors. Never before has the strength and policy influence of the governors been surpassed. They are better able to employ the informal powers of their office in meeting multiple and complex responsibilities. In sum, the governorships have displayed greater *capability* and *vigor* than ever before.

CHAPTER RECAP

- The American governorship historically was institutionally weak, with limited formal powers.
- Today's governors are better qualified, better educated, and better prepared for the office than governors of the past. But winning the office is increasingly expensive.
- Duties of the governors include making policy, marshaling legislative action, administering the executive branch, serving as master of ceremonies, coordinating intergovernmental relations, promoting economic development, and leading their political party.
- Formal powers of the office, which have strengthened over time, are tenure, appointment, veto, budgeting, reorganizing the executive branch, and staffing.
- To be successful, a governor must master the informal powers of the office and integrate them with the formal powers. Among the informal sources of power are tools of leadership and persuasion, such as public relations skills and negotiating and bargaining skills.
- Governors who violate the law may be removed from office through impeachment.
- Other key executive branch officials are the attorney general, lieutenant governor, treasurer, and secretary of state.

Key Terms

pork barrel *(p. 181)*	package veto *(p. 192)*
formal powers *(p. 186)*	line item veto *(p. 192)*
informal powers *(p. 186)*	pocket veto *(p. 192)*
plural executive *(p. 189)*	executive amendment *(p. 192)*
patronage *(p. 190)*	executive order *(p. 194)*

Surfing the Web

The governors have their own web sites in each state, which can be located through the state home page or from links at **www.nga.org.**

The NGA's web page is located at **www.nga.org.** It features, among other items, governors' biographies, the latest State of the State addresses, and a subject index on various state and local issues, including welfare reform.

For information about western governors, see **www.westgov.org.**

8

PUBLIC ADMINISTRATION: BUDGETING AND SERVICE DELIVERY

bureaucracy

The administrative branch of government, consisting of all executive offices and their workers.

Bureaucracy is a paradox. On one hand, bureaucracy is portrayed as the problem with U.S. government at all levels. From the ponderous Department of Social Services, to the department of motor vehicles, to the county tax assessor's office, it is depicted as all-powerful, out of control, inefficient, wasteful, and drowning in red tape. Bureaucrats are often seen as insensitive and uncaring, yet they stay in their jobs forever. Nearly everyone, from elected officials—presidents, governors, mayors, and legislators at all levels—to talk-show commentators, television and film script writers, and even product advertisers have stridently bashed the bureaucrats, blaming them for all imaginable sins of omission and commission (and all too often for their *own* personal shortcomings). The answer to the problem is no less than bureaucratic liposuction to "get the fat out."

On the other hand, bureaucracy can be beautiful.[1] Bureaucratic organization is indispensable to public administration. Legislative bodies and chief executives enact public policies through vague laws and depend on various state and local agencies to deal with the specifics, such as operationally defining key components of the policies and putting the policies into effect. Some bureaucracies make our lives more difficult, but others help the quality of our existence by enforcing the laws and punishing the criminals, putting out the fires, repairing and maintaining the roads, and helping the poor and disadvantaged among us. Who can forget, as corporate workers fled the burning twin towers in New York City on September 11, 2001, the police and firefighters who rushed into the buildings to assist the survivors, only to perish when the towers collapsed?

A theme of this chapter is that state agencies and local departments (the public administration) should not be treated as scapegoats for all the social, economic, and political maladies that befall society. The quality and capacity of public administration have improved markedly in the vast majority of the country's states, municipalities, and counties during the past twenty-five years in terms of the characteristics of employees and the efficiency, effectiveness, and professionalism with which they perform their duties. In fact, studies comparing public employees with cohort groups in the private sector find no important differences between them. Government workers are just as motivated, competent, and ethical as private-sector workers. And public employees tend to be more sensitive to other human beings, and more highly educated, than their counterparts in business and industry.[2] See Table 8.1 for a comparison of public- and private-sector employees.

State and local employees are responding to citizen demands by providing a wider range of services, in greater quantities, to more people than ever before, and publicly provided services are perceived to be just as good as the same services provided by private firms.[3] Public employees are much more accountable and responsive to political actors and to the public than they are popularly perceived to be. And contrary to popular opinion, government work is not always a sunny day in the park. Public employees perform some of the most unpleasant (but necessary) tasks imaginable, from taking abused or threatened children away from their parents and investigating charges of sexual abuse to caring for the mentally ill and guarding prisoners who hurl feces at them. They act, sometimes heroically, as our first—and continuing—responders to disasters and terrorist events.

On those rare occasions when someone fouls up, a public outcry is raised and a media investigation is launched; praise for consistency and excellence in public-service delivery is seldom heard. In truth, dedicated public servants who work for the people should be saluted, not castigated, for jobs well done under difficult conditions. When government fails to perform effectively, blame can occasionally be laid at the feet of public employees. But more often than not, good government workers are the scapegoats for vague and poorly designed statutes and policies, failed political leadership, and other factors beyond the control of

TABLE 8.1	Comparing Public- and Private-Sector Employees

An extensive analysis of published studies on the characteristics of public- and private-sector employees debunks certain stereotypes.

CHARACTERISTIC	ADVANTAGE
Motivation	Equal
Work habits	Equal
Competence	Equal
Education	Public employees have higher levels of educational achievement.
Sentiments of civic duty and public service	Public employees
Compassion and self-sacrifice	Public employees
Ethics	Public employees
Helping other people	Public employees

SOURCE: Adapted from J. Norman Baldwin, "Public Versus Private Employees: Debunking Stereotypes," *Review of Public Personnel Administration* 11 (Fall 1990–Spring 1991): 1–27; James L. Perry, "Antecedents of Public Service Motivation," *Journal of Public Administration Research and Theory,* 7(2) (1997): 181–97; Gene A. Brewer, Sally Coleman Selden, and Rex L. Facer, II, "Individual Conceptions of Public Service Motivation," *Public Administration Review* 60 (May/June 2000): 254–64.

civil servants. It must also be pointed out that occasional lapses in government administrative ethics pale in comparison to corporate scandals such as recent ones involving Enron, WorldCom, and Arthur Anderson.

PUBLIC EMPLOYEES IN STATE AND LOCAL GOVERNMENT: WHO THEY ARE, WHAT THEY DO

More than 18.3 million employees work for states and localities. Their numbers have grown steadily since accurate counts were first compiled in 1929. The distribution of government employees is also of interest. The percentage of civilian national government employment has declined from its World War II high of 51.5 percent in 1944 to only 12.8 percent today. Correspondingly, the state and local proportions have inched upward, to around 24 percent and 63 percent, respectively (see Figure 8.1). Government work tends to be labor-intensive. As a result of this fact and because of inflation, personnel expenditures for states and localities have risen even faster than the number of workers. Total payroll costs for state and local governments exceed $600 billion.

Of course, the number of employees varies greatly among jurisdictions. Generally, states and localities with large populations and high levels of per-capita income provide more services and thus employ larger numbers of workers than do smaller, less affluent jurisdictions. California, for instance, has some 2.1 million state and local employees on its payroll, compared with only 49,500 in Vermont. Employment figures are also influenced by the smaller number and scope of programs undertaken by governments (as compared with those

FIGURE 8.1	**Distribution of Public Employment, 1929–2003**

Since the end of World War II, the percentage of state and local employees, as a proportion of the total government work force, has increased.

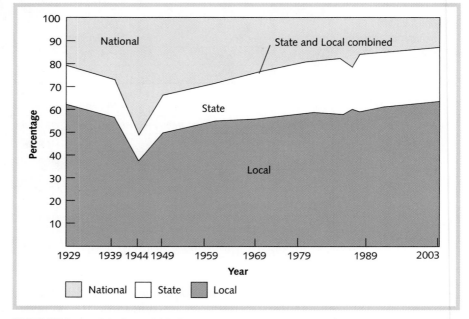

SOURCE: U.S. Bureau of the Census, *Public Employment,* selected years, Series GE 84 (Washington, D.C.: U.S. Government Printing Office) and www.census.gov.

provided by nonprofit organizations or private firms) and by the distribution of functions and service responsibilities between states and their local jurisdictions. A state government may have hundreds of agencies, boards, and commissions. A municipality or county may have dozens of departments, boards, and commissions.

But such figures do not adequately represent the real people who work for states, cities, counties, towns, townships, and school districts. These workers include the police officer on patrol, the welfare worker finding a foster home for an abandoned child, the eleventh-grade English teacher, the state trooper, and even your professor of state and local government in public institutions. (See the nearby *Debating Politics* box.) Their tasks are as diverse as their titles: sanitation engineer, animal-control officer, heavy-equipment operator, planner, physician, and so on. The diversity of state and local government work rivals that of the private sector, although important distinctions are made in the nature of the work (see Table 8.2). From the sewer maintenance worker to the director of human services, all are public servants—often known as bureaucrats. Approximately one of every six working Americans is employed by government at some level. If bureaucrats are the enemy, we have met them and they are us.

DEBATING POLITICS

Damned If You Do. . .

Welfare caseworkers are staffing the frontlines of the states' and localities' efforts to change the welfare system and its culture. Many of these individuals are highly educated and trained, with Master of Social Work (MSW) degrees and casework certificates. But sometimes they are called on to intervene or provide counseling in terribly difficult situations.

Put yourself in the following situation. You are a county welfare caseworker who specializes in the well-being of children who live in troubled households. Your office has received two telephone calls from the neighbors of a welfare mother complaining that her two young children (ages two and four) appear to have suffered bruises on their bodies, and that they are frequently heard crying when their mother's boyfriend is in their apartment. You visit the welfare mother's apartment, and the children look fine, except for a couple of minor bruises. The mother assures you that they are not in any danger from the boyfriend or from anyone else. Obviously, however, the children are not in an entirely healthy environment. Trash is strewn around the apartment, the children are not well clothed, and the older child

seems to be a bit slow or retarded. You tell the mother that you will be back next week to check on the situation and that she should let you know immediately if they are endangered in any way. She agrees.

Three days later, you receive a call from your department head. The boyfriend has disappeared, and the four-year-old is dead. The mother claims he fell down the stairs, but a neighbor reports that she heard the boyfriend, who appeared to be high on drugs, screaming at and then beating the child.

Media reaction is immediate. Some are calling for your dismissal; others criticize departmental policy that did not encourage you to remove the child from his mother and place him in a foster home as soon as you heard allegations of trouble (departmental policy encourages caseworkers to give the benefit of the doubt to the family, so that the child can remain with his relatives).

In hindsight, did you make the right decision? Should you have acted differently? What principles of ethics or decisionmaking should guide you in such decisions? How would you have handled criticism from the mother and welfare groups insisting that families be kept together?

TABLE 8.2	**Public Management and Private Management: What Are the Distinctions?**

Public- and private-sector management differs in terms of constraints, clients, accountability, and purpose.

	PUBLIC MANAGEMENT	PRIVATE MANAGEMENT
CONSTRAINTS	Politics, public opinion, resources.	Markets, resources.
CLIENTS	Citizens, legislatures, chief executives.	Customers who purchase products or services.
ACCOUNTABILITY	To citizens and elected and appointed officials.	To customers, boards of directors, and shareholders.
PURPOSE	To serve the public interest and the common good.	To make profits and grow the organization.

BUDGETING IN STATE AND LOCAL GOVERNMENT

The budget is the lifeblood of government bureaucracy. Without a budgetary appropriation, state and local organizations would cease to exist. The monies are allocated (usually on an annual basis) by legislative bodies, but the politics of the budgetary process involves all the familiar political and bureaucratic players: chief executives, interest and clientele groups, other government employees, the general public, and—of course—the recipients of legislative appropriations: the state highway department, the municipal police department, the county sanitation office, firms and industries, and so on. In a phrase, budgeting is a highly charged political poker game with enormous stakes. To understand public organization, one must have a grasp of budgetary politics.

An often-quoted definition of politics is Harold Lasswell's famous line: "Politics is who gets what, when, where, and how."[4] The budget document provides hard dollars-and-cents data in answer to this question. It is a political manifesto—the most important one you will find in state and local government. It is a policy statement of what government intends to do (or not do) for the next year (or two), detailing the amount of the taxpayers' resources that it will dedicate to each program and activity. The outcomes of the budgetary process represent the results of a zero-sum game—for every winner there is a loser—because public resources are limited. An extra million dollars for corrections can mean that much less for higher education; an expensive new fleet of sanitation trucks requires higher taxes or fees from home owners.

The Budget Cycle

The process of governmental budgeting is best understood as a cycle with overlapping stages, five of which can be identified: preparation, formulation, adoption, execution, and audit (see Figure 8.2). Several stages are taking place at any single time. For example, while the 2005 budget is being executed and revenues and expenditures are being monitored to guard against an operating deficit, the governor and the legislature are developing the 2006 budget. Meanwhile, the 2004 budget is being audited to ensure that monies were properly spent and otherwise accounted for.

Budgets are normally based on a *fiscal* (financial) *year* rather than on the calendar year. Fiscal years for all but three states run from July 1 through June 30 (the exceptions are Alabama, Michigan, and Texas). Twenty-one states, including Oregon, Indiana, and Kentucky, have biennial (two-year) budget cycles. Most local governments' fiscal years also extend from July 1 to June 30.

The initial phase of the budget cycle involves demands for slices of the budget pie and estimates of available revenues for the next fiscal year. State and local agency heads join the chorus of interest groups and program beneficiaries seeking additional funding. (With no concern for profits, agencies have little incentive to ask for less funding instead of more.) Large state agencies are typically represented by their own lobbyists, or public information specialists. State and local administrators develop estimates of revenues based on past tax receipts and

| FIGURE 8.2 | **The Budget Process** |

The budget process has built-in checks and balances because all spending is approved or audited by more than one agency or branch.

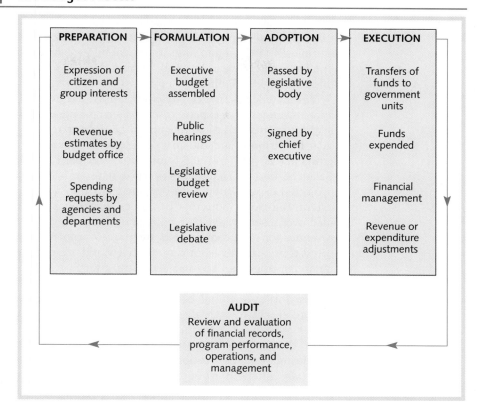

PREPARATION	FORMULATION	ADOPTION	EXECUTION
Expression of citizen and group interests	Executive budget assembled	Passed by legislative body	Transfers of funds to government units
Revenue estimates by budget office	Public hearings	Signed by chief executive	Funds expended
Spending requests by agencies and departments	Legislative budget review		Financial management
	Legislative debate		Revenue or expenditure adjustments

AUDIT
Review and evaluation of financial records, program performance, operations, and management

expected economic conditions, and they communicate them to their respective state agencies or municipal departments, which then develop their individual spending requests for the fiscal year. Such spending requests may be constrained by legislative and executive guidance, such as agency or program dollar ceilings and program priorities.

Formulation, or initial development, of the budget document is the responsibility of the chief executive in most states and localities. Exceptions include states in which the balance of power rests with the legislature (such as Arkansas, Mississippi, and South Carolina) and local governments in which budgeting is dominated by a council or commission. The executive budget of the governor or mayor is prepared by budget office staff (for example, the staff at an office of management and budget) and submitted to the chief executive for the final touches.[5] The executive budget is then presented to the appropriate legislative body for debate, review, and modification. (In many New England local governments, budgets are approved by citizens attending a town meeting or through a public referendum.) The lengthy review process that follows allows agencies, departments, interest groups, and citizens to express their points of view. Finally, the amended budget is enacted by the legislative body. Usually the budget moves forward in accordance with mandated deadlines. Sometimes, however, fiscal crisis or political disputes delay budget passage. For various reasons, New York is chronically tardy in adopting its annual budget, having missed its April 1 deadline for eighteen straight years. During the 2003 fiscal crisis, another six states missed budget deadlines.

The state legislature or city council must ensure that the final document balances revenues with expenditures. Balanced-budget requirements are contained in the constitutions or statutes of forty-eight states and operate through precedent in Vermont and Indiana.[6] These requirements usually apply to local governments as well and are found in municipal ordinances in many localities. Balanced-budget requirements force state and local governments to balance projected expenditures with revenues, but they may be circumvented to some extent. Big-ticket items may be funded in a capital budget with payments scheduled over several years. One popular device is the off-budget, in which costs and revenues for public enterprises such as government corporations or for special projects are exempt from central review and are not included in budget documents and figures. Another accounting tactic is to borrow money from employee pension funds or next year's revenues to cover the current year's deficit. Before the budget bill becomes law, the chief executive must sign it. Last-minute executive–legislative interactions may be needed to stave off executive vetoes or to override them. Once the chief executive's signature is on the document, the budget goes into effect as law, and the execution phase begins.

During budget execution, monies from the state or local general fund are periodically allocated to agencies and departments to meet payrolls, purchase goods and materials, help average citizens solve problems ranging from a rabid raccoon in the yard to a raging forest fire, and generally achieve program goals. Accounting procedures and reporting systems continually track revenues and outlays within the agencies. If revenues have been overestimated, the chief executive or legislative body must make adjustments to keep the budget in the black. They may draw on a rainy day fund to meet a shortfall (see Chapter 13) or, if the deficit is a large one, order service reductions, layoffs, or spending cuts. In a crisis the governor may call the legislature into special session, or the mayor may request a tax increase from the city council.

Budgeting during 2003–2004 illustrates the difficulty of making ends meet when revenues are declining and expenditure demands are rising. During the late 1990s, states contributed to their own future fiscal problems by slashing taxes and boosting spending. Then the terrorist assaults of 9/11 hit state and local budgets hard. The national economy slipped into recession and millions of jobs were lost. Shortly thereafter, economic growth rates plummeted across the country, even as new spending on security measures and personnel at key facilities shot up rapidly. By 2004, states had suffered an estimated three-year cumulative budget deficit of $40 billion. Most states had to raise taxes, reduce expenditures, cut services, or use some combination thereof to balance the budgets—unpopular choices all (see Table 8.3). During the initial response to

TABLE 8.3	**Typical Budget Balancing Actions During the 2002–2004 Fiscal Crisis**

CUT	*Spending*	K–12 and higher education
		Highway and road construction and maintenance
		Parks and recreation
		Libraries
		The arts
REDUCE		Reserve funds
		State and local employment
		Medicaid rolls
		Prison and jail populations
		State aid to higher education students
		Financial aid to higher education students
		Service levels (for example, health care, school buses, garbage pickup, etc.)
HIKE	*Taxes*	Sales
		Income
		Property
		Tobacco
		Alcohol
	Fees	Parks
		Motor vehicles
		Fishing and hunting
		Tuition and fees at colleges and universities

the economic reversal, governors imposed various money-saving measures, including hiring and travel freezes, layoffs, furloughs, and across-the-board spending reductions. Rainy day funds were tapped as well. Local governments implemented similar strategies, including spending reductions, tax or fee hikes, short-term borrowing, and delayed or canceled capital expenditures.

The final portion of the budget cycle involves several types of audits, or financial reviews—each with a different objective. Fiscal audits seek to verify that expenditure records are accurate and that financial transactions have been made in accordance with the law. Performance audits examine agency or department activities in relation to goals and objectives. Operational and management audits review how specific programs are carried out and assess administrators' performance. The auditors may be employed by either the executive or the legislative branch. Some jurisdictions retain professional auditors from the private sector to ensure complete objectivity.

The Actors in Budgeting

Four main actors participate in the budget process: interest groups, agencies, the chief executive, and the legislative body. Interest groups organize testimony at budget hearings and pressure the other three actors to pursue favored policies and programs. The role of the agency or department is to defend the base—the amount of the last fiscal year's appropriation—and to advocate spending for new or expanded programs. Agency and department heads are professionals who believe in the value of their organization and its programs, but they often find themselves playing Byzantine games to get the appropriations they want (see Table 8.4).

The late political scientist Aaron Wildavsky described the basic quandary of agency and departmental representatives as follows:

> Life would be simple if they could just estimate the costs of their ever-expanding needs and submit the total as their request. But if they ask for amounts much larger than the appropriating bodies believe is reasonable, their credibility will suffer a drastic decline. . . . So the first decision rule for agencies is: do not come in too high. Yet the agencies must also not come in too low, for the assumption is that if the agency advocates do not ask for funds they do not need them.[7]

What agency heads usually do is carefully evaluate the fiscal-political environment. They take into consideration what happened last year, the composition of the legislature, the economic climate, policy statements by the chief executive, the strengths of clientele groups, and other factors. Then they put forward a figure somewhat larger than they expect to get.[8]

The chief executive has a much different role in the budget process. In addition to tailoring the budget to his program priorities as closely as possible, he acts as an economizer. Individual departmental requests must be reconciled, which means that they must be cut because the sum of the requests usually greatly exceeds estimated revenues. Of course, an experienced governor or mayor recognizes the games played by administrators; he knows that budget requests are likely to be inflated in anticipation of cuts. In fact, various studies on state and local budgeting indicate that the single most influential participant is the chief executive.[9] Not surprisingly, astute administrators devote time and other resources to cultivating the chief executive's support for their agency's or department's activities.

The role of the legislative body in the initial stage of the budget cycle is essentially to respond to and modify the initiatives of the chief executive. The governor, mayor, or city manager proposes, and the legislature or council reacts. Later in the budget cycle, the legislative body performs another important function through its review of agency and department spending and its response to constituents' complaints.

Pervasive Incrementalism

In a perfect world, budgeting would be a purely rational enterprise. Objectives would be identified, stated clearly, and prioritized; alternative means for accomplishing them would be considered; revenue and expenditure decisions would be coordinated within the context of a balanced budget. That is how budgeting

TABLE 8.4	**The Games Spenders Play**

The following are tactics used by state and local officials to maximize their share of the budget during negotiations and hearings with governors, local chief executives, and the legislative body.

MASSAGE THE CONSTITUENCY	Locate, cultivate, and utilize clientele groups to further the organization's objectives. Encourage them to offer committee testimony and contact legislative members on your behalf.
ALWAYS ASK FOR MORE	If your agency or department doesn't claim its share of new revenues, someone else will. The more you seek, the more you will receive.
SPEND ALL APPROPRIATED FUNDS BEFORE THE FISCAL YEAR EXPIRES	An end-of-year surplus indicates that the elected officials were too generous with you this year; they will cut your appropriation next time.
CONCEAL NEW PROGRAMS BEHIND EXISTING ONES	Incrementalism means that existing program commitments are likely to receive cursory review, even if an expansion in the margin is substantial. An announced new program will undergo comprehensive examination. Related to this game is *camel's nose under the tent,* in which low program start-up costs are followed by ballooning expenses down the road.
"HERE'S A KNIFE; CUT OUT MY HEART WHILE YOU'RE AT IT"	When told that you must cut your budget, place the most popular programs on the chopping block. Rely on your constituency to organize vigorous opposition. Alternatively, state that all your activities are critically important so the elected officials will have to decide what to cut (and answer for it to voters).
A ROSE BY ANY OTHER NAME	Conceal unpopular or controversial programs within other program activities. And give them appealing names (for instance, call a sex education class "Teaching Family Values").
"LET'S STUDY IT FIRST" (AND MAYBE YOU WON'T BE RE-ELECTED)	When told to cut or eliminate a program, argue that the consequences would be devastating and should be carefully studied before action is taken.
SMOKE AND MIRRORS	Support your requests for budget increases with voluminous data and testimony. The data need not be especially persuasive or even factual, just overwhelming. Management writer James H. Boren calls this "bloatating" and "trashifying."
A PIG IN A POKE	Place an unneeded item in your budget request so you can gracefully give it up while protecting more important items.
END RUN	If the chief executive initiates a budget cut, run quickly to friends in the legislature.
EVERY VEIN IS AN ARTERY	Claim that any program cut would so completely undermine effectiveness that the entire program would have to be abandoned.

should be done. But state and local officials have to allocate huge sums of money each year (they spend more than a quadrillion dollars a year) in a budgetary environment where objectives are unclear or controversial and often conflict with one another. It is nearly impossible to prioritize the hundreds or thousands of policy items on the agenda. Financial resources, time, and the capacity of the computers—not to mention the human brain—are severely stretched.

To cope with such complexity and minimize political conflict over scarce resources, decisionmakers "muddle through."[10] They simplify budget decisionmaking by adopting decision rules. For example, instead of searching for the optimal way to address a public policy problem, they search only until they find a feasible solution. As a result, they sacrifice comprehensive analysis and rationality for **incrementalism,** in which small adjustments (usually an increase) are made to the nature and funding base of existing programs. Thus, the policy commitments and spending levels of ongoing programs are usually accepted as a given—they become the base for next year's funding. Decisions are made on a small proportion of the total budget: the increments from one fiscal year to the next. If the budget has to be cut, small percentage adjustments are subtracted from the base. In this way, political conflict over values and objectives is held to a minimum.

The hallmarks of incremental budgeting are consistency and continuity: The future becomes an extension of the present, which is itself a continuation of the past. Long-range commitments are made and then honored indefinitely. We do not mean to say that state and local budgeting is a simple affair. On the contrary, it is as tangled and intricate as the webs of a thousand spiders on amphetamines.

incrementalism

A decisionmaking approach in the budgetary process in which last year's appropriations are used as a base for this year's budget figures.

Types of Budgets

A budget document can be laid out in various ways, depending on the purposes one has in mind: control, management and planning, or performance. Historically, *control,* or fiscal accountability, has been the primary purpose of budgeting, incrementalism the dominant process, and the line item budget the standard document.

line item budget

A budget that lists detailed expenditure items such as personal computers and paper, with no attention to the goals or objectives of spending.

Control Through Line Item Budgets The **line item budget** facilitates control by specifying the amount of funds each agency or department receives and monitoring how those funds are spent. Each dollar can be accounted for with the line item budget—which lists every object of expenditure, from police uniforms to toilet paper—on a single line in the budget document. Line item budgets show where the money goes and track the annual incremental changes, but they do not tell how effectively the money is spent. They do not inform us on important matters such as the impact of police spending on crime rates.

Budgeting for Management and Planning Budget formats that stress *management* and *planning* are intended to help budget makers move beyond the narrow constraints of line items and incrementalism toward more rational and flexible decisionmaking techniques that focus on program results. Chief executives and agency officials seek to ensure that priorities set forth in the budget are properly carried out by organizational units—the management aspect of budgeting. Formal program and policy evaluations are necessary steps in ensuring proper performance and public accountability. The planning part involves orienting the budget process toward the future by anticipating needs and contingencies. A budget format that emphasizes planning is one that specifies objectives and lays out a financial plan for attaining them.

Several techniques permit budgeting for management and planning, but the most important today is performance budgeting. In **performance budgeting,** the major emphasis is on services provided and program results. The idea is to focus attention on how efficiently and effectively work is done rather than on what is acquired. Whereas line item budgets are input oriented, performance budgets are output and outcome oriented. Governments decide what they want to accomplish and then measure these accomplishments versus expenditures. For example, the performance of a state highway department can be evaluated through an examination of the unit costs of resurfaced highways or rebuilt bridges. For a fire department, the focus might be on response times to emergency calls and the extent to which fires are contained after the fire company's arrival on the scene. By focusing on program objectives and work performance, performance budgets can assist, and even link, managers, elected officials, and citizens in assessing the efficiency of government operations.[11]

> **performance budgeting**
>
> Budgeting organized to account for the outcomes of government programs.

Capital Budgets The budget formats described above apply to operating budgets, whose funds are depleted within one (annual budget) or two (biennial budget) years. Capital outlays are made over a longer period of time and are composed of big-ticket purchases such as hospitals, university buildings, libraries, highways, and information systems. They represent one-time, nonrecurring expenditures that call for special funding procedures, or a **capital budget.** Because such items cannot be paid for within a single fiscal year, governments borrow the required funds, just as most individuals borrow when buying a house or an expensive automobile. The debt, with interest, is paid back in accordance with a predetermined schedule.

> **capital budget**
>
> A budget that plans large expenditures for long-term investments, such as buildings and highways.

Capital projects are funded through the sale of general obligation or revenue bonds. *Bonds* are certificates of debt sold by a government to a purchaser, who eventually recovers the initial price of the bond plus interest (see Chapter 13). *General obligation bonds* are paid off with a jurisdiction's regular revenues (from taxes and other sources). In this instance, the full faith and credit of the government is pledged as security. *Revenue bonds* are usually paid off with user fees collected from use of the new facility (for example, a parking garage, auditorium, or toll road). Payments for both types of bonds are scheduled over a period of time, which usually ranges from five to twenty years. The costs of operating a new facility, such as a school or recreation area, are met through the regular operating budget and/or user fees.

Capital budgets lend themselves to a more rational approach than do operating budgets. Payments must be scheduled years in advance, and most state and local governments have constitutional or statutory limitations on how much they can borrow. Thus, capital purchases must be anticipated and prioritized well into the future by agency heads, program administrators, and elected officials.

Budget Reform

State and local budgeting has undergone remarkable changes during the past two and a half decades. Prompted by taxpayer resistance and concern about how their tax dollars are spent, state and local governments have launched various reforms intended to make budgeting more transparent, performance-based, understandable, and responsive to the public. For their part, states have also endeavored to deregulate municipal and county budgeting, thus permitting more discretion for local officials to develop budget solutions adapted to local circumstances. Much remains to be done to bring some state and local governments up to speed, but on the whole, budgeting today is greatly improved.

HUMAN RESOURCE MANAGEMENT POLICY IN STATE AND LOCAL GOVERNMENT: FROM PATRONAGE TO MERIT

Whether the tasks of state and local government are popular (fighting crime, educating children), unpopular (imposing and collecting taxes and fees), serious (saving a helpless infant from an abusive parent), or mundane (maintaining the grass on municipal sports fields), they are nearly always performed by public employees. The 5 million state workers and 13.3 million city, county, and town employees are the critical links between public policy decisions and how those policies are implemented. Agencies and departments must be organized to solve problems and deliver services effectively, efficiently, and reliably. Human resource management rules and procedures must determine how public employees are recruited, hired, paid, and fired.

National laws and court decisions help determine the parameters within which personnel policies can be set. Although such national influence is important, policy innovations are more likely to come from state and local jurisdictions.

In the nation's first decades, public employees came mainly from the educated and wealthy upper class and, in theory, were hired on the basis of fitness for office. During the presidency of Andrew Jackson (1829–1837), who wanted to open national government jobs to all segments of white, male society, the *patronage* system was adopted to fill many positions. Hiring could depend on party affiliation and other political alliances rather than on job-related qualifications.

Patronage became entrenched in many states and cities, where jobs were awarded almost entirely on grounds of partisan politics, personal friendships, family ties, or financial contributions. This system made appointees accountable to the governor, mayor, or whoever appointed them, but it did nothing to ensure honesty and competence. By the beginning of the Civil War, the spoils system permeated government at all levels, and the quality of public service plummeted.

The Merit System

merit system

The organization of
government personnel
to provide for hiring and
promotion on the basis
of knowledge, skills, and
abilities rather than
patronage or other
influences.

The concept of the **merit system** is usually associated with the campaign to pass the Pendleton Act of 1883. Two key factors led to its passage. First, Anglo-Saxon Protestants were losing political power to urban political machines dominated by new Americans of Irish, Italian, and Polish descent. Second, scandals rocked the administration of President Ulysses S. Grant and spawned a public backlash that peaked with the assassination of President James Garfield by an insane attorney seeking a political appointment. The Pendleton Act set up an independent, bipartisan civil service commission to make objective, merit-based selections for federal job openings.

The *merit principle* was to determine all personnel-related decisions. Those individuals best qualified would receive a job or a promotion based on their knowledge, skill, and abilities. Far from perfect, the merit system was thoroughly overhauled by the Civil Service Reform Act of 1978. But as a result of the Pendleton Act, the negative effects of patronage politics in national selection practices were mostly eliminated. **Neutral competence** became the primary criterion for obtaining a government job, and public servants are expected to perform their work competently and in a politically neutral manner.

neutral competence

The concept that public
employees should
perform their duties
competently and
without regard for
political considerations.

During the period of national human resource management reform, the state and local governments were also busy. New York was the first state to enact a merit system, in 1883, the year of the Pendleton Act, and Massachusetts followed its example in 1884. The first municipal merit system was established in Albany, New York, in 1884; Cook County, Illinois, became the first county with a merit system, in 1895. (Ironically, both Albany and Cook County [Chicago] were later consumed once again by machine politics and spoils-ridden urban governance.)

Many states and numerous local governments enacted merit-based civil service systems on their own. Congressional passage of the 1939 amendments to the Social Security Act of 1935 gave additional impetus to such systems. This legislation obligated the states to set up merit systems for employees in social service and employment security agencies and departments that were at least partly funded by national grants-in-aid under the Social Security Act. Thus, all states are now required to establish a merit system for a sizable segment (around 20 percent) of their work force; most of them have in fact developed comprehensive systems that encompass almost all state employees. Common elements of these modern personnel systems include recruitment, selection, and promotion according to knowledge, skills, and ability; regular performance appraisals; and employee incentive systems.

Some merit systems work better than others. In a handful of states and localities, they are mere formalities around which a shadowy world of patronage, spoils, favoritism, and incompetence flourishes.[12] Such conditions came to public attention when terrorists boarded and hijacked two commercial aircraft at Boston's Logan Airport on 9/11. For years, gubernatorial patronage appointees with little or no experience in security or law enforcement had run Logan's security operations.[13] Rigid personnel rules, a lack of training programs, and inadequate salaries continue to plague some jurisdictions. Political control over merit-system employees is limited everywhere because most cannot be fired without great difficulty.

State and Local Advances

On balance, state and local personnel systems have been greatly improved, and the process continues. Nonnational governments are experimenting with recruitment and testing innovations, pay-for-performance plans and other incentive systems, participative management innovations, new performance-appraisal methods, comprehensive training programs, the decentralization of personnel functions, and many other concepts. Almost every state is reforming its civil service in some way.[14] General public dissatisfaction with government at all levels, combined with increasing needs for government to become more sophisticated and responsive to its clients, means that efforts to reinvent human resource management are certain to grow.

These reforms are designed to make the executive branch leaner and more responsive to the chief executive; to improve service efficiency and effectiveness; and, through decentralization of authority, to enhance flexibility for chief executives, agency heads, city managers, and other officials.[15] Reformers remain dedicated to the principle of protecting the civil service from unnecessary and gratuitous interference by politicians with patronage considerations in mind. But they also want to increase the capacity of government executives to manage programs and people in their organizations and to achieve desired results.

Merit-System Controversies

As we shall see, state and local governments have taken the lead in addressing controversial questions that involve merit-system principles and practices, including affirmative action, sexual harassment, and labor unions.

representative bureaucracy

The concept that all major groups in society should participate proportionately in government work.

Affirmative Action This controversial policy is related to another key concept— **representative bureaucracy.** The concept of representative bureaucracy suggests that the structure of government employment should reflect major sexual, racial, socioeconomic, religious, geographic, and related components in society. The assumptions behind this idea are that (1) a work force representative of the values, points of view, and interests of the people it governs will be responsive to their special problems and concerns, and (2) a representative bureaucracy provides strong symbolic evidence of a government "of the people, by the people, and for the people." These assumptions have been widely debated. For example, empirical research indicates that the specific agency a person works for and the profession she belongs to are better predictors of public policy preferences than racial, sexual, and other personal characteristics.[16] But we do know that the symbolic aspects of representative bureaucracy are important. A government that demonstrates the possibility of social and occupational mobility for all sorts of people gains legitimacy in the eyes of its citizens and expands the diversity of views taken into account in bureaucratic decisions.

A controversial question is, How do we *achieve* a representative work force, particularly at the upper levels of government organizations, without sacrificing the merit principle? *Equal employment opportunity (EEO)*—the policy of prohibiting employment practices that discriminate for reasons of race, sex, religion, age, disability, or other factors not related to the job—is mandated by federal law. This policy has been the law for well over 100 years, yet progress was slow until the past thirty years or so, when **affirmative action** policies were adopted throughout government.

affirmative action

Special efforts to recruit, hire, and promote members of disadvantaged groups to eliminate the effects of past discrimination.

Affirmative action recognizes that equal opportunity has not been sufficient because employment discrimination persists. Governments must take proactive steps to hire and retain those categories of workers, legally defined as "protected classes," who have suffered discrimination in the past. These measures may be adopted voluntarily, but they are required under certain conditions specified by the U.S. Equal Employment Opportunity Commission (EEOC), the regulatory body created to enforce EEO. The measures include goals, timetables, and other preferential selection and promotion devices intended to make the work forces of public and private organizations more representative of the racial, sexual, and other characteristics of the available labor pool.

Under affirmative action, the absence of overt discrimination in employment is not sufficient; organizations typically implement preferential recruitment, hiring, and promotion schemes to redress existing imbalances. The legitimacy of affirmative action policies imposed on employers by the EEOC was seriously questioned in a series of U.S. Supreme Court decisions during the past two decades and by state legislative actions and referendums.[17]

Affirmative action remains highly controversial. Establishing specific numerical goals and timetables for hiring and promoting minorities does not necessarily correspond with selection or promotion of the best person for the job. In other words, affirmative action appears to conflict with the merit principle. It has also alienated many white males, who feel that they have become victims of reverse discrimination.

Legal clashes among the federal courts, Congress, and the states and localities continue but have not produced a coherent interpretation of affirmative action's legal standing. Three examples illustrate the complexity of the issues surrounding affirmative action policy. The first concerns a 1992 lawsuit against the University of Texas Law School, filed by four white applicants (three men and a woman), who alleged that they had not been admitted despite having LSAT scores higher than those of black and Hispanic applicants who were accepted. The first federal judge to hear this case, in *Hopwood* v. *Texas*, ruled against the white applicants.[18] On appeal, however, the Fifth Circuit Court judges agreed that the university had violated the students' constitutional rights. According to the court, the use of race as a selection criterion "is no more rational . . . than would be choices based upon the physical size or blood type of applicants." The Fifth Circuit Court's decision applied to universities in Texas, Louisiana, and Mississippi.

Texas attorney general Dan Morales appealed to the U.S. Supreme Court, which refused to hear the case and thus kept the circuit court's ruling in effect.

Yet to the astonishment of Texans, the U.S. Department of Education warned the state, in an official letter, that Texas could lose all federal financial aid if it ended its affirmative action programs as ordered by the courts! After a furious reaction by the state's powerful congressional delegation, the Department of Education backed down. But the effects of federal court intrusion into Lone Star affirmative action were soon registered at the University of Texas Law School, where black and Hispanic admission fell precipitously.

National confusion and uncertainty about affirmative action are also illustrated by the 1996 passage of Proposition 209 in California, which amended the state constitution by prohibiting race and gender consideration in contracting decisions and in hiring for state and local jobs. The initiative was approved by nearly 55 percent of the voters. Soon, however, a federal judge blocked enforcement on grounds that Proposition 209 was discriminatory and therefore unconstitutional. About six months later, judges for the Ninth Circuit Court of Appeals reinstated Proposition 209, an action that was upheld by the U.S. Supreme Court. The debate in California presaged similar conflicts elsewhere. In 1998, Washington voters approved an anti–affirmative action initiative, and in 2000, Governor Jeb Bush of Florida eliminated racial preferences in college admissions in his state through an executive order.

The third example of confusion and complexity involves a pair of U.S. Supreme Court rulings in 2003 on the admissions procedures at the University of Michigan. The Court invalidated a point system, used to select undergraduates, that awarded additional points for minority status, but it upheld the law school's consideration of race as a nonquantified plus in its admission decisions.[19]

Despite such confusion and ugly political invective, substantial progress toward representative bureaucracy has been made, especially in recruiting and hiring protected-class individuals for entry-level positions. Minorities and women continue to bump against a glass ceiling as they try to penetrate the upper levels of state and local agencies,[20] as well as glass walls that restrict their access to certain agencies, departments, or occupations.[21] But gradual progress is being seen even with respect to this final barrier to representative bureaucracy, as indicated both by descriptive data (for instance, the number of female city managers rose from around 100 in 1986 to 435 in 1997, and the percentage of Hispanic professionals in state and local government has grown dramatically in recent years) and by scholarly research on improvements in and attitudes toward minority employment. Female and minority employment at all levels of state and local government exceeds that in the private sector. Indeed, state and local governments today widely recognize the need to recruit, motivate, and manage a work force that reflects an increasingly diverse general population. When employees working together differ in terms of gender, color, religion, customs, and other characteristics, misunderstandings and miscommunications are inevitable. The astute public manager helps employees recognize and accept such differences while maintaining and even raising levels of organizational productivity and effectiveness.[22]

Sexual Harassment Sexual harassment has long been a problem in public and private employment, but it has only recently gained widespread recognition. Sexual harassment can consist of various behaviors: unwanted touching or other physical contact of a sexual nature, implicit or overt sexual propositions, or (in one of its worst forms) extortion of a subordinate by a supervisor who demands sexual favors in return for a promotion or a raise. A "hostile working environment" that discriminates on the basis of gender also constitutes sexual harassment.[23] Examples in this category include repeated leering, sexual joking or teasing, or lewd calendars or photographs at the workplace. An emerging issue with implications is the legal responsibility of teachers and school administrators to prevent flagrant sexual harassment of one student by another.

Sexual harassment is common in the workplace: Surveys of women discover that at least half of the respondents report being a victim.[24] Approximately 15 percent of men have experienced sexual harassment. Such behavior subverts the merit principle when personnel decisions such as hiring or promotion are influenced by illegal or discriminatory considerations of a sexual nature, or when an employee cannot perform his or her assigned duties because of sexual harassment. Sexual harassment can exact a high price on organizational productivity. Unfortunately for the recipient of unwanted sexual attention, there are seldom any witnesses. The matter becomes one person's word against another's. And when one of the parties is the supervisor of the second party, a formal complaint may be decided in favor of the boss. Sexual harassment is illegal according to federal and state law, a form of punishable employee misconduct under civil service rules. It is increasingly being prosecuted in the courts. (See the *Debating Politics* box for a glimpse at its definitional complexity.)

Much of the official activity aimed at stopping sexual harassment has been concentrated in the states, with local governments rapidly following suit. Michigan was the first, in 1979, to adopt a sexual harassment policy; since then nearly every state has adopted a statewide sexual harassment policy through legislation or executive order. States offer employee training programs that help workers and supervisors identify acts of sexual harassment, establish procedures for effectively addressing it, and enforce prompt, appropriate disciplinary action against offenders.

The consequences of sexual harassment go far beyond the personal discomfort, stress, or injury suffered by victims. The problem also results in significant financial costs to organizations whose employees lose productive work time.[25] Such misconduct is unacceptable today in a national work force that is almost 50 percent female.

Unions Nearly always controversial in government, *public-employee unions* present a potentially serious threat to the merit principle. They usually insist on seniority as the primary criterion in personnel decisions, they often seek to effect changes in merit-system rules and procedures, and they regularly challenge management authority. They aggressively seek higher pay and benefits, threatening to drive up the costs of government and, in some instances, prompting tax increases.

DEBATING POLITICS

Is This Sexual Harassment?

A woman employed by the county school district meets with two male employees to assess written evaluations of applicants for a job opening. At the meeting, one of the men reads aloud a statement about one of the female applicants that alludes to her physical attributes. One says to the other, "What about you, Bob, what do you look for in a woman?" Both men laugh. The woman, Ms. Lewis, does not find the remarks amusing at all.

Lewis complains about the incident to the two men right there, and then later, to other school district personnel. Unhappy with the response, she then files complaints with the district Equal Employment Opportunity Office and the state Equal Rights Commission, and sues the school district in federal court for sexual harassment.

Soon, Lewis learns in a conversation with a fellow employee that the assistant superintendent is considering transferring her to another job. Lewis then amends her lawsuit to allege that the school district is retaliating against her for her complaints and legal action. Subsequently, she is, indeed, transferred.

Public employees such as Lewis are protected from sex discrimination by Title VII of the Civil Rights Act of 1964 and by federal court rulings that have determined that sexual harassment is a form of sex discrimination. Title VII also prohibits retaliation or discrimination against an employee who alleges sex discrimination. The courts have identified two types of sexual harassment: *quid pro quo,* which involves a demand for sexual favors in return for a favorable employment decision, such as a promotion; and *hostile working environment,* which refers to a workplace in which verbal abuse or physical conduct of a sexual nature is pervasive and unwelcome.

Does the behavior of the two male colleagues represent sexual harassment? Why or why not? Is Lewis's assertion that her transfer was made in retaliation for filing a lawsuit a legitimate claim?

Until the 1960s, the growth and development of unions in the United States was a private-sector phenomenon, boosted by national legislation in the early 1930s. This legislation protected the rights of workers in industry to organize and engage in **collective bargaining** with their employers over wages, benefits, and working conditions. Workers then organized in record numbers. By the late 1950s, however, private-sector union growth had halted. A slow but steady decline in the percentage of organized employees continues for several reasons, including the shift in the U.S. economy from manufacturing to services and the globalization of labor markets.

Unionization in state and local government developed and flourished in the 1960s and 1970s, some thirty years after the heyday of private-sector unionism. During the 1960s, the number of public-employee union members more than tripled. Why the sudden growth? In retrospect, several reasons are apparent.

First, the rise of unionism in government was spurred by the realization by state and local employees that they were underpaid and otherwise mistreated in comparison to their counterparts in the private sector, who had progressed so well with unionization and collective bargaining. Second, the bureaucratic and impersonal nature of work in large government organizations encouraged unionization to preserve the dignity of the workers. A third reason for the rise of state and local unionism was the employees' lack of confidence in many civil

collective bargaining

A formal arrangement in which representatives of labor and management negotiate wages, benefits, and working conditions.

service systems. Not only were pay and benefits inadequate, but grievance processes were controlled by management; employees had little or no say in setting personnel policies; and merit selection, promotion, and pay were often fraught with management favoritism.

Perhaps most important, the growth of unions in government was promoted by a significant change in the legal environment of labor relations. The rights of public employees to join unions and bargain collectively with management were guaranteed by several U.S. Supreme Court rulings, state legislation, local ordinances, and various informal arrangements that became operative during the 1960s and 1970s. Wisconsin was the first state, in 1959, to permit collective bargaining for state workers. Today, forty-two states specifically allow at least one category of state or local government employees to engage in collective bargaining.

The extent of unionization and collective bargaining is greatest in the states of the industrial Midwest and Northeast—the same areas so fertile for the growth of private-sector unions. A handful of traditionalistic states, including Arizona, Mississippi, Utah, Virginia, and the Carolinas, continue to resist the incursion of state and local unions (see Figure 8.3). Public employees in these jurisdictions have the legal and constitutional right to join a union, but their government employers do not have a corresponding duty to bargain with them over wages, benefits, or conditions of work.

FIGURE 8.3   **Public Employee Collective Bargaining Rights in the States**

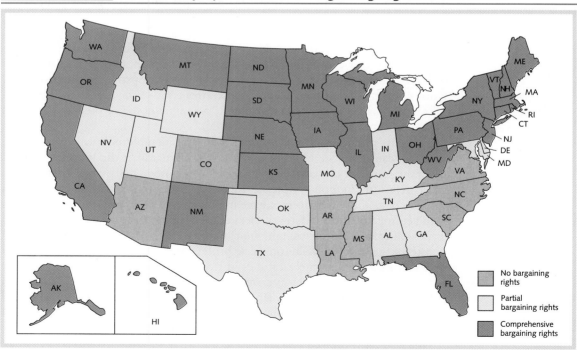

Approximately 31 percent of state and 43 percent of local government workers belong to unions, compared with only about 8.5 percent of workers in private industry. The highest proportions of union workers are found in education, highway departments, public welfare, police protection, fire protection, and sanitation.[26]

The surge in the fortunes of state and local unions was partially arrested by the taxpayer revolt of the late 1970s, and by President Reagan's successful effort to "bust" a federal air traffic controllers' union. Additional resistance to unions developed in the 1990s and continues today as governments downsize and privatize, and seek greater efficiencies. Taxpayer resistance has helped stiffen the backbones of public officials, who had been criticized in some jurisdictions for giving the unions too much.

As a result of these factors, unionism in state and local government has leveled off and even declined in some jurisdictions. Substantial gains in membership and bargaining rights are not likely in the near future; indeed, signs of reversals have appeared in some states. Nonetheless, unions remain an important and highly visible component of many state and local government personnel systems.

What is the impact of collective bargaining in state and local government? The outcomes of bargaining between a union and a firm in the private sector are largely determined by market forces, such as profit levels and the supply and demand for labor. In government, political factors are much more important. The technical process of negotiating over wages and other issues is similar in business and government. But the setting makes government labor relations much more complex, mostly because the negotiating process culminates in the political allocation of *public* resources.

Four factors make government labor relations highly political. First, public officials are under greater pressure than private employers to settle labor disputes. Public services are highly visible and often monopolistic in nature; for example, other convenient suppliers of police and fire protection do not exist. Thus, elected officials who confront a controversial labor dispute in an essential service may fear that negative developments will derail their opportunity for re-election.

Similarly, public-employee unions wield considerable political clout. Their members can influence election outcomes, particularly at the local level. A recalcitrant mayor or city council member who opposes a hefty wage increase may suffer defeat at the polls in the next election if the municipal union members vote as a bloc. Unions actively engage in politics by raising money, writing letters to the editor about candidates, knocking on doors to get out the vote, formally endorsing candidates, or using any of the other electoral techniques employed by interest groups. Many unions have professional lobbyists and negotiators to represent them at the state capitol or in city hall.

A third politicizing factor in government labor relations is the symbiotic relationship that can develop between unions and elected officials. In exchange for special consideration at the bargaining table and perhaps elsewhere, the unions can offer public officials two valued commodities: labor peace and electoral support.

Finally, a hard-pressed union can use the strike or a related job action (such as a slowdown or a picket line) as a political weapon. In the private sector, a strike is not likely to have widespread public repercussions unless it involves goods or services that the nation relies on for its economic well-being (such as air transportation, coal mining, or communications). In government, however, a strike can directly involve the health and safety of all the citizens of a jurisdiction. For instance, a nine-day strike by 3,300 city garbage workers left Chicago with stinking, rat-infested piles of trash in October 2003. A general strike involving police officers, firefighters, and sanitation workers has the potential to turn a city into filthy, life-threatening anarchy. At a minimum, the public is inconvenienced. Simultaneous strikes by 4,300 bus and train drivers of the Metropolitan Transportation Authority and 42,000 Los Angeles County employees in 2000 provide a case in point. Nearly half a million commuters had to make other arrangements to get to work. Thousands of residents encountered delays in health clinics and other facilities because of travel problems for employees.

Strikes and other job actions by public employees are illegal in most jurisdictions, although twelve states permit work stoppages by nonessential workers under strictly regulated conditions. However, teachers, health care workers, firefighters, and others sometimes walk off the job anyway. The nightmare of a defenseless populace terrorized by acts of violence during a police strike, or by a crazed arsonist during a firefighter strike, has convinced many an elected official to seek prompt settlement of government–labor impasses.

Given these politicizing factors, one might expect unions in government to be extravagantly successful at the bargaining table, but quite the opposite is true. Public-employee unions have raised wages and salaries an average of 4 to 8 percent, depending on the service, place, and time period under consideration (for example, teachers earn around 5 percent more and firefighters around 8 percent more if represented by a union). These figures are much lower than the union-associated wage effects identified in the private sector.[27] Greater success has come in the form of better benefits, particularly pensions and health care insurance. Note that union-driven wage and benefit hikes in the private sector are absorbed through profits, layoffs, or higher product prices. In government, by contrast, the choices are to raise taxes or fees, cut services, increase productivity, or contract out to a private firm.

Certain personnel effects have also been associated with collective bargaining in government. Clearly, unions have gained a stronger employee voice in management decisionmaking. All personnel-related issues are potentially negotiable, from employee selection and promotion procedures to retention in the event of a reduction in force. Civil service rules, regulations, and procedures have been altered by many employers as a result of collective bargaining. In heavily unionized jurisdictions, two personnel systems coexist uncomfortably—the traditional civil service system and the collective bargaining system.[28] Certainly the rights of public employees have been strengthened by unions.

Generally, governments and collective bargaining have reached an uneasy accommodation. The principle of merit in making personnel decisions is still largely in place, and it is usually supported by the unions as long as seniority is fully

Teachers picket in Eveleth, MN, threatening a strike unless a new collective bargaining contract is reached.
SOURCE: Kim Kalish/CORBIS.

respected as an employment decision rule. In an increasing number of jurisdictions, unions are cooperating with management to increase productivity in government services through participative decisionmaking techniques, labor–management partnerships, and worker empowerment programs.

THE POLITICS OF BUREAUCRACY

In an ideal democracy, political officials popularly elected by the people would make all decisions regarding public policy. They would delegate to public administrators in the executive branch the duty of carrying out these decisions through the agencies of state and local government. In the real world of bureaucratic politics, however, the line dividing politics and administration is transparent. Politicians frequently interfere in administrative matters, for example, when a legislator calls an agency head to task for not treating a constituent favorably. Administrators play politics at the state capitol and in city hall by participating in and influencing policy formulation decisions.

Joining Administration and Politics

Bureaucrats are intimately involved in making public policy, from the design of legislation to its implementation. Government workers are often the seedbed for policy ideas that grow to become law, in large part because they are more familiar with agency, departmental, and clientele problems and prospective solutions than anyone else in government. It is not unusual, for instance, for law enforcement policy to originate with police administrators or higher education policy to be the brainchild of university officials.

Once a bill does become law, state and local employees must interpret the language of the legislation to put it into effect. Because most legislation is written in general terms, civil servants must apply a great deal of **bureaucratic discretion** in planning and delivering services, making rules for service delivery, adjudicating cases and complaints, and otherwise managing the affairs of government. All states have legal systems for hearing and acting on disputes over agency rules and regulations; one example is the application of regulations for local drinking water and sewage treatment. These administrative procedures permit individuals, firms, and local governments to challenge agency rules and regulations before an administrative law judge, who issues an order settling the dispute. In a real sense, the ultimate success or failure of a public policy depends on the administrators who are responsible for its implementation. Experienced legislators and chief executives understand this situation, and they bring relevant administrators into the legislative process at an early stage. The knowledge and expertise of these administrators is invaluable in developing an appropriate policy approach to a specific problem, and their cooperation is essential if a policy enacted into law is to be carried out as the lawmakers intend.

Thus, bureaucratic power derives from knowledge, expertise, information, and discretionary authority. It also comes from external sources of support for agency activities—that is, from the chief executive, legislators, and interest groups. Those who receive the benefits of government programs—the clientele, stakeholders, or customers—are also frequently organized into pressure groups. All government programs deliver benefits to some interest—tourism policy benefits the business community; public assistance policy benefits the poor; education policy benefits parents, students, teachers, and administrators—and these **clientele groups** are often capable of exerting considerable influence in support of policies that benefit them. Their support is critical for securing the resources necessary to develop and operate a successful government program. They serve as significant political assets to state agencies and municipal and county departments that are seeking new programs or additional funding from legislative and executive bodies, and they can become fearsome political in-fighters when their program interests are threatened.[29] Often, clientele and other concerned interest groups align with relevant government agencies and legislative committees to dominate policymaking and implementation in a particular policy field. These iron triangles, or subgovernments, may be found in fields ranging from health care policy to public education.

The problem of politics and administration thus has two dimensions. First,

bureaucratic discretion

The ability of public employees to make decisions interpreting law and administrative regulations.

clientele group

A group that benefits from a specific government program, such as contractors and construction firms in state highway department spending programs.

elected officials have the duty of holding administrators responsible for their decisions and accountable to the public interest, as defined by the constitution and by statute. Second, political oversight and intrusion into administrative activities should be minimized so that administrative decisions and actions are grounded in objective rules and procedures—not in the politics of favoritism. For example, legislators have the duty of ensuring that decisions by a state department of environmental protection guard the public from the harmful effects of pollution while also treating polluting companies fairly. Nevertheless, state representatives should not instruct agency employees to go easy on a favored business constituent. Most government agencies discharge their tasks competently and professionally, and therefore require little direct oversight. Occasionally, however, a rogue agency or department head may strike out in the wrong direction and require reining in.

An example of the proper balance of politics and administration is the attempt by legislators to influence public administrators, which typically occurs when legislators and council members perform casework for members of their constituency. Although the legislator may occasionally seek favorable treatment that borders on illegality, the bulk of legislative casework comprises responses to citizens' inquiries or complaints, or requests for clarification of administrative regulations.[30] Such legislative casework is useful because it promotes both feedback on the delivery of services and helpful exchanges of information with elected officials. If inquiries determine bias in the means by which services are delivered, corrective political actions can be taken.

In sum, state and local politics are intricately joined with administration. Public policy is made and implemented through the interaction of elected officials, interest groups, and public administrators. Nonetheless, the vast majority of administrative decisions are based on the neutral competence and professionalism of public employees. When the municipal transportation department must decide which streets to repave, for example, a formula is applied that takes into account factors such as the date of the last repaving, intensity of public usage, and the condition of the road.

We do not mean to imply that such decisions are never made on the basis of political favoritism. Sometimes political pressures influence bureaucratic discretion. For example, black elected officials are associated with an increase in black municipal employment.[31] Black members of school boards tend to select black administrators, who are likely to hire black teachers; black teachers tend to provide black students with improved access to educational opportunities.[32] And race and social class can influence the way in which police officers treat both victims and perpetrators of crimes. On the whole, however, state and local services are provided in an unbiased fashion through applying professional norms and standards. An important question remains: Are administrators responsive to the public interest in their decisionmaking?

The Public Interest

Everyone agrees that government programs should be conducted in accordance with the public interest. The dilemma for state and local administrators lies in defining the concept of public interest. In fact, numerous public interests compete with no clear set of priorities among them. Public administrators may be expected to respond to the general interest of the people, but who has the power (or presumption) to identify it? Administrators also must listen to their immediate superiors, elected and appointed officials at all levels, clientele groups, and interest groups, and they must be aware of national and state constitutional, statutory, and administrative law.

Often various publics make demands all at once. Take the case of the county animal-control officer. Her job is to keep stray and unattended animals off the streets. Citizens call to complain about stray cats and barking dogs. Owners criticize her for making them pay to retrieve their animals. To have adequate space and to stay within the budget on feeding and maintenance expenses, she has to destroy unclaimed animals, prompting regular outcries from the local animal rights groups. Yet failure to destroy the animals means a budget fight with the county administrator or county council, or a rabies epidemic that could involve state health department officials.

The point is that public administrators are required to identify and balance various interests in carrying out their responsibilities. For practical purposes, a single, clearly identifiable public interest does not exist, nor should one exist. In a sense, public administration plays an important role in integrating political demands made from various interests within U.S. government.[33] This task is accomplished largely by applying professional values, expertise, and common sense to the formulation of standard operating procedures, decision rules, and work routines. Citizens' quality of life in the United States depends on it.

REINVENTING GOVERNMENT

State and local government employment has burgeoned since the 1960s at a rate much faster than that of population growth. In Texas, the number of state workers jumped from 112,000 in 1970 to 306,398 in 2001. In New Jersey during the same period, the increase was from 58,000 to 153,708. The total state and local government payroll exceeds $600 billion per year. Explanations for this huge expansion in the size and costs of government are numerous, including federal mandates, public-employee unionization, partisan politics, and the power of incremental budgeting.[34]

Are the quantity and quality of services better than ever? Not according to most citizens, as we pointed out at the beginning of this chapter. Instead, taxpayer ire and criticism of government are high at all levels. Approval of government began rising in 2001, however, when the heroic actions of public employees and military personnel in response to terrorist attacks helped citizens regain an understanding of the value of civil service. Innovations that make government more efficient, effective, and responsive have also played a role.

The most all-encompassing approach is called reinventing government, and it is based on a widely read book with the same name, written by David Osborne and Ted Gaebler.[35] According to these authors, governments today are preoccupied with rules, regulations, and hierarchy; their bureaucracies are bloated, inefficient, and altogether poorly suited for meeting the demands made on them. The solution is for governments to tap the powers of entrepreneurialism and market competition to design and provide efficient and effective services to state and local customers. In short, governments should "steer, not row," by stressing a facilitative or cooperative approach to getting services to citizens rather than delivering all services directly. Among the alternative service-delivery systems described by the authors are public–private partnerships, volunteerism, voucher plans, and technical assistance. Once transformed, the governments would be enterprising, mission driven, outcome oriented, focused on the needs of their customers, and prepared to do more with less.

Osborne's and Gaebler's book was met with great enthusiasm by many people in government. President Clinton and Vice President Gore commissioned a national performance review to make recommendations on reinventing the federal government. But critics soon appeared like ants at a picnic. First, one or two came forward, then a horde of academics and practitioners emerged to question and even ridicule the assumptions and examples associated with reinventing government. Among the formidable obstacles to such profound change in government activities and behavior are service-intensive tasks (for example, teaching, policing) that do not lend themselves to labor-saving technology; rule-bound civil service systems, which tend to discourage risk taking; the inevitable inertia that plagues public organizations that have no bottom line and few market-driven incentives; the difficulties of innovating in organizations created essentially to regulate; the need for politicians to buy into and support the movement, which implies greater autonomy and discretion for administrative agencies but also more risks and more mistakes; and the certain opposition by powerful vested interests, such as public-employee unions, that feel threatened by change. Undeterred by the carping critics and maligning malcontents, many state and local governments have adopted a reinventing attitude in tackling various problems. Principally, they have placed their bets on the privatization of government services and on e-government.

Privatization

Privatization shifts government functions to private or nonprofit organizations through service arrangements such as vouchers, franchises, public-private partnerships, and contracting out. It is a widely heralded reform that garners much support today, especially among conservatives, Republicans, and others who want to see a businesslike approach to government. Almost any government service is a candidate for contracting out (outsourcing), from jails to janitorial work, teaching to trash collection. (In theory, most government facilities could even be sold to private interests and operated as businesses; airports and bridges are examples.) The purported benefits of privatization include cost savings, higher-quality services, the acquisition of highly specialized skills, and more efficient service delivery, making it an increasingly popular strategy for reducing service costs. To date, privatization has been used most frequently to outsource vehicle towing, solid waste collection, building security, street repair, ambulance services, printing, data processing, personnel tasks, and social welfare services.[36]

In choosing the privatization route to reinventing government, Massachusetts has contracted out mental health care, prison health care, various highway maintenance functions, and operations of interstate highway rest stops, among many other functions. New York has contracted out the processing of state personal income tax returns. Riverside, California, has privatized operations of its public libraries, while Chicago outsources window washing, sewer cleaning, and compost processing. Privately built and operated toll roads and bridges operate in a growing number of states.

Still, privatization isn't as easy as it sounds, and it doesn't guarantee savings.[37] It usually elicits virulent opposition from public-employee unions, who fear the loss of their jobs. Unless governments carefully negotiate and then monitor the quality and effectiveness of privatized services, performance may decline and costs may actually rise. Contracts that are vague or filled with loopholes, and insufficient contract oversight on the part of some jurisdictions, have resulted in cost overruns, shoddy services, and fraud or corruption by the contractors. Such problems were evident recently in California with utility deregulation and a huge, $95 million sole-source contract with Oracle Corporation for database software that has been seldom used since the purchase. Service disruptions have occurred when a firm's workers have walked off the job. Indeed, successful outsourcing requires not only careful government planning, design, and analysis of what the jurisdiction and its citizens need and want to have done, but also recognition that government accountability cannot be negotiated. The state, county, or city must remember that ultimately *it* will be held accountable for successful, reliable delivery of a service. Government officials—not the private provider—will be blamed and held responsible for mishaps. Successful contract monitoring requires careful inspections, comprehensive performance reports, and assiduous investigations of citizen complaints.

To keep contractors honest, some governments use multiple, competing firms, and public and nonprofit organizations to deliver the same service to different state agencies or localities. Phoenix, Arizona, for instance, devised a garbage-collection plan that permitted the city public works department to compete against private collectors for long-term contracts in five service districts. The city workers were consistently noncompetitive in their bids. But after garbage-truck drivers redesigned routes and work schedules and adopted one-person collection vehicles, the public works department eventually won back all five district contracts. In this case, government, prodded by managed competition or competitive contracting, was able to do more with less and achieved greater operating efficiencies than private firms could.[38] Arizona state employees compete head-to-head with a national firm in administering public assistance programs. Inspired by pioneers such as Phoenix and Indianapolis, Indiana, other jurisdictions have developed public–private partnerships. Such collaboration among governments, nonprofit organizations, and private firms saved Indianapolis some $100 million in four years through negotiated arrangements in waste-water treatment, recycling, sewer billing, street sweeping, and many other services.[39]

Is privatization worthwhile? Research indicates that it saves cities and states up to about 20 percent for some jurisdictions and service categories, but little or nothing for others. Local officials believe that outsourcing improves service delivery in most cases, but privatization has often failed, and studies of the alleged benefits of privatization have been criticized on methodological and statistical grounds.[40] It is not a cure-all for the problems besetting states and local governments, but it does represent one potentially useful alternative for reinventing government.

E-Government

e-government

The use of information technology to simplify and improve interactions between governments and citizens, firms, public employees, and other entities.

E-government is reinventing and re-engineering the way various government activities are conducted, and making the face of government more efficient and user-friendly. Some improvements are rather mundane and commonsensical. For instance, most states permit on-line tax filing and renewal of auto licenses and registrations. Seattle, Washington, Miami, Florida, Little Rock, Arkansas, Scottsdale, Arizona, and other cities have established "little city halls" in major neighborhoods to make local government more convenient for residents. Other improvements are more futuristic. Arizonans can vote in primary elections on the Web and view live proceedings of the state legislature in their state's "digital democracy." New York City and Washington State have mounted computer-coordinated attacks on crime that electronically track incidents and suspects, spot emerging crime patterns, and coordinate some crime-fighting activities with other state and local jurisdictions. Management of personnel systems has been vastly improved in Wisconsin through on-line job bulletins, walk-in testing services, and rapid hiring of employees for hard-to-fill positions. Long Beach, California, provides free Wi-Fi Internet access downtown to attract visitors and firms.

We are well on the road to electronic government. Nearly 97 million "hits" were registered on government web sites in 2003, a 50 percent leap from 2002.[41] "Virtual offices" operating through the Internet are establishing new, convenient, twenty-four-seven connections among citizens, businesses, nonprofit organizations, and their governments. From a home or office personal computer (PC) or a conveniently located PC in the neighborhood kiosk or library, citizens can obtain everything from English-language lessons on-line in Boston to legal aid from Victor, the cyber-lawyer in Arizona. Massive filing systems for documents and other hard copy are no longer needed. Instead, paperless offices use imaging technology to scan, store, and access important records from marriage licenses, birth certificates, death certificates, business licenses, and a host of other documents. The nearby *Breaking New Ground* box explains how govern-

BREAKING NEW GROUND

Re-engineering Government with Geographic Information Systems

Geographic information systems (GISs) are rapidly transforming the land-based policies and operations of state and local governments through computer-generated geographical mapping technology. The California Department of Fish and Game uses GIS to track and monitor endangered species of plants and animals; Georgia's Department of Natural Resources uses GIS to inventory wetlands and land cover for improved environmental management decisions; police in Denver, Colorado, use it to track neighborhood crime trends throughout the city. Phoenix, Arizona, applies GIS to model the effects of urban sprawl. GIS is also used to redraw election districts; track bills; settle planning and zoning disputes; map incidents of child abuse and domestic violence; route garbage trucks efficiently; direct police, fire, and emergency medical personnel in response to 911 calls; field and track citizen complaints by neighborhood; and beam traffic reports directly to commuters.

GIS consists of computer hardware and software, a data base, and an electronic base map. Visual data on police stations, transportation routes, water and sewer lines, and other physical factors are depicted on maps and linked with descriptive data (words and numbers) to help government employees analyze information visually and make decisions more easily and less expensively. In addition to automating repetitive labor-intensive tasks, GIS facilitates interagency and interlocal cooperation on issues from land-use planning to social welfare services. Best of all, GIS turns abstract information into understandable visual displays.

State and local spending on GIS has increased dramatically. GIS technology is rapidly evolving and is now accessible by handheld electronic devices and wireless laptops; thus, it promises even greater applications in the years ahead.

SOURCES: Anya Sostek, "Bringing Sprawl to Life," *Governing* (December 2001): 31–32; Christopher Swope, "Working Without a Wire," *Governing* (June 2002): 32–34.

---

ment is being re-engineered in several states using geographic information systems (GISs).

Telecommuting permits county employees throughout Los Angeles and in an increasing number of other state and local jurisdictions to work at home several days a week, saving workers commuting time, enhancing productivity, and cutting down on air pollution. Customer relationship call centers in Des Moines, Iowa, Houston, Texas, and New York City categorize and analyze calls to the cities' complaint lines to identify and respond to developing situations in specific parts of the city. Welfare case-processing activities are being re-engineered in many jurisdictions. In Minnesota, New Jersey, and Wisconsin, for instance, welfare recipients use specially coded smart cards to draw monthly benefits, thereby reducing the number of stolen checks, paperwork and fraud, and program administration costs. To cut down even more on fraud, Connecticut, Texas, and other states use finger-imaging systems to establish the identification of welfare recipients. Information technology is still on a steep learning curve, with new developments announced almost daily.

Despite such enthusiastic rhetoric, at least three hurdles are slowing the diffusion of e-government: the enormous investments required to pay for the computer hardware and trained personnel required; unresolved legal questions of liability, privacy, and security, especially with wireless networking;[42] the difficulty of integrating software across multiple agencies and departments; and the fact that many citizens do not have ready access to personal computers. But the potential of e-government to make government more accessible, understandable, and efficient is enormous.

Is the move toward reinventing government simply a fad? Definitely not. Responsive states and localities have been reinventing their operations and services since they were created, and they will continue to do so for as long as they exist. In the short run, some governments will be reinvented or at least changed in fundamental ways, but others will continue to run the old way. Change is politically risky, and inertia is a powerful force. Ultimately, it is the responsibility of citizens and the elected officials who represent them to bring about change and reforms.

THE QUALITY OF PUBLIC ADMINISTRATION

Despite the quantity of criticism hurdled at government agencies, departments, and workers by the popular media, elected officials, and others, the quality of public administration in state and local government has improved markedly. Of course, considerable variance in capability exists among jurisdictions; that capacity generally is of a higher quality in affluent, highly educated, industrialized, and urban jurisdictions.

Results of a two-year study of state government administrative performance are found in Table 8.5. The Government Performance Project, conducted by the Maxwell School of Citizenship and Public Affairs at Syracuse University and *Governing* magazine, examined state performance in five key administrative areas: financial management, capital management, human resources, managing for results, and information technology.

Administrative quality is a critical factor in the revitalization and responsiveness of states and localities. State and local governments, particularly through partnership with private and nonprofit organizations, have the capacity to accomplish more on a grander scale than ever before, and this trend is continuing through the movement to reinvent government. The basics of providing services, from disposing of dead animals to delivering healthy human babies, will continue to depend on government employees for high standards of performance and professionalism.

TABLE 8.5	State Administrative Report Card					

STATE	FINANCIAL MANAGEMENT	CAPITAL MANAGEMENT	HUMAN RESOURCES	MANAGING FOR RESULTS	INFORMATION TECHNOLOGY	AVERAGE GRADE
Alabama	D+	D-	C-	F	D	D
Alaska	C	C+	C-	C-	C-	C
Arizona	B-	D+	C+	B-	D+	C
Arkansas	B-	C	C+	D	D	C-
California	C-	C-	C-	C-	C+	C-
Colorado	C	C	B	C	C	C+
Connecticut	C-	C+	C-	D+	D+	C-
Delaware	A-	B	B	B	B	B
Florida	B	C	C+	B	C-	C+
Georgia	C+	C	B-	C+	C	C+
Hawaii	C-	B-	C-	C-	F	C-
Idaho	B-	B-	C	C-	D+	C
Illinois	B+	B-	B	C	D+	B-
Indiana	B	C	C+	C	C	C+
Iowa	A-	B-	B+	B+	C+	B
Kansas	B-	B	B+	C	C+	B-
Kentucky	B+	A-	B	B	C+	B
Louisiana	B-	B	C+	B	C-	B-
Maine	B-	C-	C+	C	C	C
Maryland	A-	A-	B	B-	C	B
Massachusetts	B	B+	C+	C	C	B-
Michigan	A-	B+	B+	B	B+	B+
Minnesota	A-	A-	C+	B	B	B
Mississippi	B	B	C+	C	C-	C+
Missouri	A-	A	B	A-	B+	A-
Montana	B	B+	B-	C	B-	B-
Nebraska	B+	A-	B-	B-	C+	B
Nevada	B	B+	D	C	C	C+
New Hampshire	B-	C	B	D+	C	C+
New Jersey	B-	B+	C-	B-	B-	B-
New Mexico	C-	D	B-	D+	C	C-
New York	D+	C-	C	D+	C	C-
North Carolina	B	B+	B+	B-	C	B
North Dakota	B	B+	B-	D	B-	B-

(cont. on next page)

TABLE 8.5

STATE	FINANCIAL MANAGEMENT	CAPITAL MANAGEMENT	HUMAN RESOURCES	MANAGING FOR RESULTS	INFORMATION TECHNOLOGY	AVERAGE GRADE
Ohio	B+	B	B	C+	B	B
Oklahoma	B-	C	C-	D+	C-	C
Oregon	B	B-	C+	B+	C+	B-
Pennsylvania	A-	B	B	B-	B	B
Rhode Island	B-	C+	F	C	D	C-
South Carolina	B+	B-	A-	B-	B	B
South Dakota	B+	B	C+	D	B	B-
Tennessee	B	B-	C+	C	B+	B-
Texas	B	C	B	B+	B	B
Utah	A	A	B+	B+	B+	A-
Vermont	B	B	B-	B-	C	B-
Virginia	A	A	B	A-	A-	A-
Washington	A-	A	B+	B+	A	A-
West Virginia	B	C+	C+	C	C	C+
Wisconsin	C+	A-	B+	C	B	B
Wyoming	C+	C+	B-	C	D+	C
U.S. average	B	B-	B-	C+	C+	

NOTE: *Definitions:* **Financial management:** managing a state's financial resources, including cash management, cost accounting, and rainy day fund. **Capital management:** managing large-scale projects, upkeep on buildings. **Human resources:** managing people, personnel policies, procedures, and pay systems. **Management for results:** strategic planning, performance measurement. **Information technology:** data management, information planning, procurement, and training; use of information technology to transmit information to citizens and stakeholders.
SOURCE: Adapted from Katherine Barrett and Richard Greene, "Grading the States," *Governing* (February 1999): 17–90.

CHAPTER RECAP

- The quality and capacity of public administration have greatly improved in the great majority of the states and local governments.
- State and local government employment has grown rapidly.
- State and local operating budgets must be balanced each year.
- Interest groups, agencies, the chief executive, and the legislative body are the four principal actors in the budgetary process.
- Budgets tend to expand (or contract) incrementally.
- The trend in accounting for revenues and expenditures is performance-based budgeting.
- Most state and local jobs are part of a merit system; they are filled based on knowledge, skills, and experience.

- Affirmative action has led to gains in the advancement of minorities and women in state and local employment, but it is a controversial issue.
- States are addressing the problem of sexual harassment in public agencies.
- Unions and collective bargaining present special challenges to many state and local governments.
- Bureaucratic discretion makes public employees important actors.
- The movement to reinvent government through privatization, e-government, and other steps is a major development.

Key Terms

bureaucracy *(p. 207)*
incrementalism *(p. 218)*
line item budget *(p. 218)*
performance budgeting *(p. 219)*
capital budget *(p. 219)*
merit system *(p. 221)*
neutral competence *(p. 221)*

representative bureaucracy *(p. 222)*
affirmative action *(p. 223)*
collective bargaining *(p. 226)*
bureaucratic discretion *(p. 231)*
clientele group *(p. 231)*
e-government *(p. 236)*

Surfing the Web

Most major municipalities and all states have web pages. Many provide links to jobs, reinventing government initiatives, service-provision information, and other data. For careers in state and local government, see individual state, county, and municipal human resource management web sites. Also see **www.govtjob.net.** Innovative, award-winning web sites are Indianapolis's "Electronic City Hall" at **www.indygov.org/,** Service Arizona at **www.servicearizona.ihost.com,** NC@YourService at **www.ncgov.com,** and AccessWashington at **www.access.wa.gov.**

An Internet-based clearinghouse on GIS is maintained by the Center for Technology in Government at **www.ctg.albany.edu/gisny.html.** Another interesting site on technology and government is located at **www.govtech.net.**

An informative public-employee union web site is AFSCME's at **www.afscme.org.**

For publications and information on public-private partnerships, see **www.ncppp.org/.**

For a step-by-step illustration of a state budget process, see **www.state.ny.us/dob/citizen/process/process.html.**

You can play a budget simulation for New York City at **www.gothamgazette.com/budgetgame/budgetgame.html.**

To view streaming videos of public meetings in Indiana, visit **www.stream. hoosier.net/cats.**

The National Center for Productivity offers research, cases, and a course on government performance at **www.andromeda.rutgers.edu/~ncpp/curriculum.**

Information on the Government Performance Project is found at **www. maxwell.syr.edu/campbell/gpp.html.**

9

THE JUDICIARY

In the case of *Barnes* v. *Glen Theatre Inc.* (1991), a prudish U.S. Supreme Court ruled that nude dancing, being dangerous to "order and morality," is not protected as free expression under the First Amendment of the U.S. Constitution. This case, which arose in Indiana, was tried in the federal courts under national constitutional law.

Yet in Boston, Massachusetts, a city once known for banning all manner of objects and activities deemed to be immoral, totally naked women grind, bump, and pirouette at tacky cabarets, fully confident that their activity is legal. In Massachusetts, the voluntary display of a naked body has been protected under the *state* constitution as a form of expression since the state supreme court ruled it so in 1984.[1] As the U.S. Supreme Court has become increasingly conservative, from Chief Justice Earl Warren (1953–1969) to today's Rehnquist Court,

New York City has cracked down on the sex business, forcing strip clubs and other businesses to move at least 500 feet away from residences, schools, churches, and graveyards.
SOURCE: Stephen Ferry/Getty Images.

state courts have become more popular with individuals and groups advocating liberal causes such as civil rights, free speech, and freedom of expression. All sorts of conflicts and problems find their way to state and local courts, from the profound (abortion rights) to the profane (nude dancing). Decisions of state courts have a weighty "impact on the overall distribution of wealth and power in the United States and on the daily well-being of the citizens."[2] And courts at this level are busy; 99 percent of the nation's cases are filed in state courts. New York State's cases alone outnumber those filed in all federal courts by a factor of 9 to 1. Once castigated for being slow, congested, inefficient, and tolerant of unfit and unqualified judges, today's state courts have been transformed through reorganization, management reforms, new judicial selection systems, and other changes. Many are innovative in their decisionmaking and administration, and they are far more accessible to the people and responsive to their concerns than are the federal courts.

State supreme courts sometimes act as policymakers. As the third branch of government, the judiciary is, after all, the final authority on the meaning of laws and constitutions and the ultimate arbiter of disputes between the executive and legislative branches. It also makes public policy through rulings on questions of political, social, and economic significance and may serve as the last chance for minority interests to defend themselves from the decisions of the majority. As noted in Chapter 3, state courts have become more active policymakers in recent years and have increasingly based important decisions on state constitutions rather than on the national constitution. As with the other branches of state government, their structures and processes have been greatly reformed and modernized. In our lifetimes, nearly all of us will experience the judicial branch in the role of juror, plaintiff, defendant, or witness. At times, the courts are more accessible to us than are the other branches of government. Disputes that cannot be resolved through ordinary legislative, executive, and political processes frequently wind up before a judge, as litigation.

The work of the fifty state court systems is divided into three major areas: civil, criminal, and administrative. In **civil cases,** one individual or corporation sues another over an alleged wrong. Occasionally, a governmental body is party to a civil action. Typical civil actions are divorces, property disputes, and suits for damages arising from automobile or other accidents. **Criminal cases** involve the breaking of a law by an individual or a corporation. The state is usually the plaintiff; the accused is the defendant. Murder, assault, embezzlement, and disorderly conduct are common examples. **Administrative cases** concern court actions such as probating wills, revoking driver's licenses, or determining custody of a child. Some administrative cases involve administrative law judges and quasi-judicial (less formal) proceedings. A government entity is usually a party to an administrative case.

State courts adjudicate (take actions to administer justice) by interpreting state statutes, the state and federal constitutions, and **common law.** In developing and deciphering the common law, courts are concerned with the legal rules and expectations that have developed historically through the citizens' custom, culture, and habits, and that have been given standing through the courts. The most important applications of common law today concern enforcing contracts (contract law), owning and selling property (property law), and establishing liability for death or injuries to people as well as damage to property (tort law).

civil case

A case that concerns a grievance involving individuals or organizations, not the breaking of a law.

criminal case

A case that involves the breaking of a law.

administrative case

A legal dispute not involving a civil suit or a criminal matter. Usually, it is a case in which a government agency applies rules to settle the dispute.

common law

Unwritten law based on tradition, custom, or court decisions.

THE STRUCTURE OF STATE COURT SYSTEMS

State courts have evolved in response to changes in their environment. In colonial days, they developed distinct difference because they were influenced by local customs and beliefs. Because of a shortage of trained lawyers and an abiding distrust of English law, the first judges were laypeople who served on a part-time basis. It did not take long for the courts to become overwhelmed with cases: Case overloads were reported as long ago as 1685.[3] More than three centuries later, case backlogs still plague our state judiciaries.

As the population and the economy grew, so did the amount of litigation. Courts expanded in number and in degree of specialization. Their development was not carefully planned, however, and new courts were added to existing structures. The results were predictably complex and confusing, with overlapping, independent jurisdictions and responsibilities. For instance, Chicago offered an astounding array of jurisdictions, estimated at one time to number 556.[4] State court systems were beset not only by numerous overlapping and independent jurisdictions but also by a host of other serious problems, including administrative inefficiency, congestion, and excessive delays. In short, the American system of justice left much to be desired.

The organization of the state courts is important because it affects the quality and quantity of judicial decisions and the access of individuals and groups to the legal system. It also influences how legal decisions are made. An efficiently organized system, properly staffed and administered, can do a better job of deciding a larger number of cases than a poorly organized system can. Court structure is of great interest to those who make their living in the halls of justice, namely, lawyers and judges. It can also be an issue of concern to citizens who find themselves in court.

The Two Tiers of Courts

limited jurisdiction trial courts

Those courts with original jurisdiction over specialized cases such as juvenile offenses or traffic violations.

Most states today have a two-tiered court structure: trial courts and appellate courts. Each tier, or level, has a different range of authority. Trial courts, which comprise the lower tier, include (1) minor courts of limited jurisdiction and (2) major trial courts of general jurisdiction. **Limited jurisdiction trial courts** handle minor, specialized cases, such as those involving juveniles, traffic offenses, and small claims. Most states have three to five courts of limited jurisdiction, with names that reflect the type of specialized case: traffic court, police court, probate court, municipal court, and so on. Criminal cases here are usually restricted by law to misdemeanor violations of municipal or county ordinances that are punishable by a small fine, a short jail term, or both. Additional courts of limited jurisdiction, sometimes called boutique courts, have been created to deal with special types of cases or circumstances. For example, some states have created drug courts, with the dual aims of processing drug-related offenses more efficiently and reducing the recidivism rates of drug offenders on probation or parole. Water courts have been established in Colorado and Montana to hear disputes over water rights. And in Charleston, South Carolina, a livability court convenes regularly to hear complaints against those accused of damaging the quality of life, including barking dogs, those with unkempt lawns, and parking violators.[5]

Present in almost all states are *small claims courts,* which offer a relatively simple and inexpensive way to settle minor civil disputes without either party having to incur the financial and temporal burdens of lawyers and legal procedures. Small claims courts are usually divisions of county, city, or district trial courts. In cases before small claims courts, the plaintiff (the person bringing the suit) asks for monetary recompense from the defendant (the individual or firm being sued) for some harm or damage. Claims are limited to varying amounts, usually around $1,000. The proceedings are informal. Each party presents to a judge the relevant facts and arguments to support his or her case. The party with the preponderance of evidence on his or her side wins. Most disputes involve tenant–landlord conflicts, property damage, or the purchase of goods (for example, shoddy merchandise or the failure of a customer to pay a bill).

The plaintiff usually wins in small claims court. About half the time, defendants do not show up to plead their case and thereby lose by default. In contested cases, plaintiffs win around 80 percent of the time. Unfortunately for the plaintiff, winning a case is often easier than collecting from the defendant. It's the plaintiff's responsibility to get written court permission to extract the amount due from the debtor's wages, bank account, or other assets, and to retain the local sheriff or constable to deliver and enforce the court order.

major trial courts

Courts of general jurisdiction that handle major criminal and civil cases.

The second type of trial court is the **major trial court,** which exercises general authority over civil and criminal cases. Most cases are filed initially under a major trial court's original jurisdiction. However, trial courts also hear cases on appeal from courts of limited jurisdiction. Major trial courts are often organized along county or district lines. Their names (for example, circuit courts, superior courts, district courts, courts of common pleas) vary widely.

supreme court

The highest state court, beyond which there is no appeal except in cases involving federal law.

intermediate appellate court

A state appellate court that relieves the case burden on the supreme court by hearing certain types of appeals.

The upper tier of the two-tiered state court system consists of appellate courts: **supreme courts** (sometimes called courts of last resort) and, in most states, **intermediate appellate courts.** Oklahoma and Texas have two supreme courts: one for criminal cases and the other for civil disputes. Thirty-eight states have intermediate appellate courts (Alabama, Oklahoma, Oregon, Texas, Pennsylvania, and Tennessee have two, typically one each for criminal and civil cases). Most intermediate appellate courts are known as courts of appeals. Their work generally involves cases on appeal from lower courts. Thus, these courts exercise appellate jurisdiction by reviewing a trial court's interpretation and application of the law. By contrast, state supreme courts have original jurisdiction in certain types of cases, such as those dealing with constitutional issues, as well as appellate jurisdiction.

Intermediate appellate courts constitute the most notable change in the structure of the state court system during the past thirty years. They are intended to increase the capability of supreme courts by reducing their caseload burden, speeding up the appellate process, and improving the quality of judicial decisionmaking. The bulk of the evidence points to moderate success in achieving each of these objectives.[6] Case backlogs and delays have been reduced, and supreme court justices are better able to spend an appropriate amount of time on significant cases. Counteracting this positive trend, however, is the growing number of mandatory appeals, such as for death penalty cases, which now make up over 60 percent of the caseload.[7]

If a state supreme court so chooses, it can have the final word on any state or local case except one involving a federal constitutional question, such as First Amendment rights. Some cases can be filed in either federal or state court. For example, a person who assaults and abducts a victim and then transports him across a state line can be charged in state court with assault and in federal court with kidnapping. Some acts violate nearly identical federal and state laws; possession or sale of certain illegal drugs is a common example. Other cases fall entirely under federal court jurisdiction, such as those involving treason, theft of mail, or violation of currency laws.

Thus, there is a *dual system* of courts in the United States, sometimes referred to as *judicial federalism.* Generally, state courts adjudicate, or decide, matters of state law, whereas federal courts deal with federal law. The systems are separate and distinct; however some jurisdictional overlap or competition exists. Following the arrests of Beltway snipers John Muhammad and Lee Malvo in 2003, Virginia, Maryland, Alabama, Louisiana, and the federal justice department all sought to bring the multiple murder case to trial first (six victims were killed in Maryland, three in Virginia, and one in the District of Columbia; additional crimes were alleged in Alabama and Louisiana). Although state courts cannot overturn federal law, they can base certain rulings on the federal constitution. Recently, state courts have decided cases governed by both state and federal law in hate crimes, the right to die, and gay rights. It is unusual for a case decided by a state supreme court to be heard by the U.S. Supreme Court or any other federal court. Such a dual hearing occurs only when the case involves a federal question, that is, an alleged violation of federal constitutional or statutory law. Judicial federalism also comes into play when a state supreme court applies U.S. Supreme Court rulings.

Because facts, issues, and other case patterns differ, state court judges exercise significant discretion in interpreting the Constitution in cases before them. Research indicates that state courts are generally faithful to the spirit of the Supreme Court rulings. However, state judges sometimes choose to interpret Supreme Court decisions liberally or even to ignore them altogether. Because the Supreme Court exercises no control over the selection, retention, or pay of judges in the states, its capacity to oversee and ensure compliance is extremely limited.[8] A recent exception to Supreme Court reticence to trespass on the grounds of state supreme courts occurred in the aftermath of the 2000 presidential election. In an extremely tight election whose outcome would determine who would be the next president of the United States, the Florida Supreme Court, overturning a decision of the Florida secretary of state, ordered manual recounting of ballots in three counties. Acting with unusual dispatch, the U.S. Supreme Court overturned the Florida court decision, effectively awarding the presidency to George W. Bush.

Structural Reforms

The court reform movement that swept across the states in the 1960s and 1970s sought, among other things, to convert the state courts into more rational, efficient, and simplified structures. A driving goal was to increase the capacity and responsiveness of state and local judicial systems. One important legacy of that movement is the *unified court system*.

Although the two tiers of state courts appear to represent a hierarchy, in fact they do not. Courts in most states operate with a great deal of autonomy. They have their own budgets, hire their own staff, and use their own procedures. The decisions of major and specialized trial courts usually stand unchallenged. Only around 5 percent of lower-court cases are appealed, mostly because great expense and years of waiting are certain to be involved.

Unified court systems consolidate the various trial courts with overlapping jurisdictions into a single administrative unit and clearly specify each court's purpose and jurisdiction. The aim of this arrangement, which includes centralized management and rulemaking, is to make the work of the courts more efficient, save time and money, and avoid confusion. Instead of a system whereby each judge runs her own fiefdom, rulemaking, recordkeeping, budgeting, and personnel management are standardized and centralized, usually under the authority of the state supreme court.

Such centralization relieves judges from the mundane tasks of day-to-day court management so that they can concentrate on adjudication. Additional efficiencies are gained from *offices of court administration,* which exist in all states. Some of these offices do little more than collect and disseminate statistics, but court administration in an increasing number of states involves actively managing, monitoring, and planning the courts' resources and operations.

Computer technology provides tremendous improvement in how the courts manage their business. Integrated justice information systems link data from various state agencies and local governments, thus allowing improved coordination and less paperwork. In Los Angeles County, which has the largest local government justice system in the country, Consolidated Criminal History Reporting System (called "Cheers") consolidates the data bases of fifty law enforcement agencies, twenty-one prosecutor's offices, twenty-four municipal courts, and sixty-two other authorities. Judges and other law enforcement authorities have instant access to the case histories of defendants, as well as to computerized fingerprint-matching technology. A lack of communications between justice agencies in New Jersey once enabled convicted felons to pay homeless persons to serve their sentences. Correctional institutions had no effective means of verifying inmate identity. Today, New Jersey's criminal-identification system is state of the art and networked statewide.[9] Responsiveness to the public is also growing. An increasing number of state courts are electronically disseminating court documents; judicial rulings; and general information such as instructions for jury duty, maps showing directions to the courthouse, and answers to commonly asked questions about the courts. Some even display photographs and biographies of judges, and many permit interested citizens to ask questions via e-mail. (See Surfing the Web at the end of the chapter.)

Despite consolidation and centralization, court structures and processes continue to vary widely among the states, as shown in Figure 9.1. Generally, the most modern systems are found in the western states, including Alaska and Hawaii, and some of the most antiquated are situated in southern states. Additional improvements could be made in most states, but the staggering number of changes made in state court structures and procedures in recent years has produced a system that would hardly have been recognizable in the 1950s.[10]

HOW JUDGES ARE SELECTED

The quality of a state court system depends heavily on the selection of competent, well-trained judges. According to the American Bar Association (ABA), the leading professional organization for lawyers, judges should be chosen on the basis of solid professional and personal qualifications, regardless of their political views and party identification. Judges should have "superior self-discipline, moral courage, and sound judgment."[11] They should be good listeners. They should be broadly educated and professionally qualified as lawyers. An appellate

FIGURE 9.1   Simplicity and Complexity in State Court Systems

State court systems can vary from the simple to the complex, as illustrated by Alaska and Georgia, respectively.

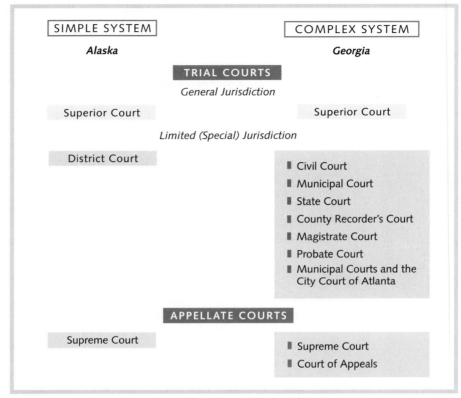

SIMPLE SYSTEM
Alaska

COMPLEX SYSTEM
Georgia

TRIAL COURTS

General Jurisdiction

Superior Court

Superior Court

Limited (Special) Jurisdiction

District Court

■ Civil Court
■ Municipal Court
■ State Court
■ County Recorder's Court
■ Magistrate Court
■ Probate Court
■ Municipal Courts and the City Court of Atlanta

APPELLATE COURTS

Supreme Court

■ Supreme Court
■ Court of Appeals

SOURCE: State Court Organization, 1998, Washington, D.C.: U.S. Bureau of Justice Statistics.

or general trial court judge should also have relevant experience in a lower court or as a courtroom attorney.

For a great many years, however, controversy has swirled over the selection of state judges. Should they be elected by popular vote? Should they be appointed by the governor? By the legislature? Many critics insist that judicial selection should be free from politics and interest group influences. Others claim that judges should regularly be held accountable to a majority of the people or to elected officials for their decisions.

The conflict between judicial independence and accountability is manifest in the types of selection systems used in the states: legislative election, partisan popular election, nonpartisan popular election, merit plan, and gubernatorial appointment. Most states use a single selection system for all appellate and major trial court judges, but some states take separate approaches to selecting judges, depending on the tier. Figure 9.2 shows the popularity of these selection techniques for appellate and major trial courts. Categorization is complicated by intricacies in selection systems. Oklahoma, for example, utilizes a merit plan for the supreme court and court of criminal appeals, nonpartisan elections for its other appellate courts and district courts, and city council appointment of municipal judges.

Legislative Election

This method is found in only two states, both of them original colonies. In South Carolina and Virginia, the legislature elects judges from among announced candidates by majority vote. Not surprisingly, the vast majority of judges selected under this plan are former legislators; in South Carolina, the proportion has been close to 100 percent.[12] In these two states, a judgeship is viewed as a highly valued reward for public service and a prestigious cap to a legislative career.

Few people other than legislators approve of legislative election. Indeed, the method is open to criticism. The public has no role in either choosing judges or re-electing them, so democratic accountability is minimal. The judges may be independent, but because the major criterion for selection is service as a legislator, they often lack other qualifications. Legislative service has little connection to the demands of a judgeship.

| FIGURE 9.2 | **State Appellate and Major Trial Court Selection Plans** |

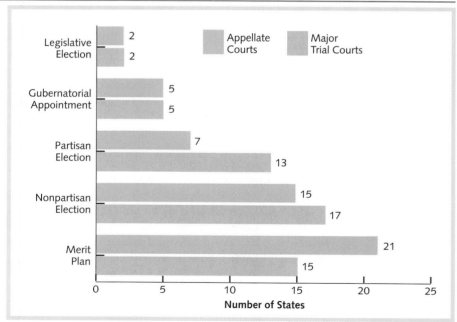

NOTE: Kansas and Missouri select some major trial court judges through a merit plan and others through partisan elections. New Mexico has a mix of elections and a merit system.
SOURCE: Adapted from State Court Organization 1998, Bureau of Justice Statistics, 1999, Tables 4 and 5. Updated to January 1, 2004.

Popular Election

About 87 percent of all state court judges attain or keep their offices through some sort of popular election. Judges on one or more courts face elections in thirty-nine states. Some are listed on the ballot by party identification; others are not. In theory, elections maximize the value of judicial accountability to the people. Judges must run for office on the same ticket as candidates for other state offices. Like other candidates, they must raise and spend money for their election campaigns and publicly deal with political issues.

Partisan Popular Election Partisan popular election is a plan that enjoyed enormous popularity during the Jacksonian era as a way to create a judiciary answerable to the voters. More than half of the partisan election states are located in the South; Mississippi was the first, in 1832, to adopt this system.

Nonpartisan Popular Election Nonpartisan popular election won favor during the first half of the twentieth century, when reformers sought to eliminate party identification in the election of judges and certain other officials in state and local government. Political parties are prohibited from openly taking sides in nonpartisan judicial elections. In reality, however, they sometimes play a covert role in such contests. Approximately 95 percent of all judges have a political party preference.[13] Most list it in the official biographies that are available to interested voters during campaigns. A disadvantage of nonpartisan elections is that they tend to reduce voter participation because incumbent judges are less likely to be challenged and party identification is an important voting cue for many citizens.

The Problems with Popular Elections Voter turnout is extremely low in most judicial elections, whether partisan or nonpartisan. This fact is a long-standing criticism of both methods of electing judges: The winners are not truly accountable to the people, which is the principal advantage commonly associated with elections. Low rates of voter interest and participation combine with low-key, unexciting, and issueless campaigns to keep many incumbent judges on the bench as long as they run for re-election. One recent study indicates that less than 10 percent are defeated.[14]

Two more complicated problems have become increasingly troublesome: the politicization of judicial races and the creeping realization that campaign donations influence decisions from the bench. The American Bar Association Code of Judicial Conduct forbids judicial campaigning on legal issues, but this prohibition is increasingly overlooked in close contests and in elections where crime-related concerns, such as the death penalty or an accused murderer freed on a legal technicality, claim voters' attention. As in other electoral contests, negative campaigning is on the rise in judicial elections. Judicial candidates today energetically sling mud at their opponents for allegedly letting drug abusers free, corruption, laziness, and acting soft on crime. Several states have moved to restrict aggressive judicial politicking through new ethics rules and other limitations. When challenged in federal or state courts, however, such restrictions are usually overturned as intrusions on the candidates' First Amendment rights to free speech.[15]

Even more serious is the problem that occurs when judges elected on a partisan ballot are accused of pandering to special interests during election campaigns and of favoring them in court decisions. In Texas, for instance, supreme court justices deciding a $10.5 billion judgment against Texaco in favor of Pennzoil were criticized for accepting huge campaign contributions from both parties. Nonpartisan elected judges have been open to similar charges, especially because political action committees (PACs) have boosted their contributions to candidates for state court judgeships. Recent research by political scientist Madhavi McCall found systematic empirical evidence that judicial decisions have followed dollars. Similar conclusions have been drawn from research on judicial decisionmaking in Alabama and Ohio.[16]

In addition, popular elections are criticized for the growing amount of money necessary to win a state judgeship. In some cases, the implication is that judges have sacrificed their independence and professionalism for crass electoral politics. Following the trend set in executive and legislative contests, judicial campaign spending has skyrocketed in states that elect judges. In 2000 elections, judicial candidates raised and spent more than $15 million in Michigan and $13 million in Alabama.[17] An estimated $6.2 million was spent on only two supreme court races in Ohio. The largest campaign contributors are usually trial lawyers and other groups with a stake in judges' decisions, such as labor unions; business interests; and various professions, such as insurance or medicine.[18]

It looks as though judges running for election are forfeiting their independence in certain legal disputes while offering accountability only to the highest bidders instead of to the general public. If indeed this trend is the case, neither independence nor accountability is achieved and faith in the legal system is eroded. According to the president of the Ohio State Bar Association, "The people with money to spend who are affected by court decisions have reached the conclusion that it's a lot cheaper to buy a judge than a governor or an entire legislature, and he can probably do a lot more for you."[19]

If it is unethical for a judge to rule on a case in which he or she has accepted money from one or more of the interested parties, then it would be difficult to bring together enough judges to hear cases in some states. The general sentiment is that judges should be both qualified and dignified, and that elections do not further either objective. But states are beginning to take action. North Carolina launched public financing for judges' campaigns in 2004 to help contain spiraling costs.

Merit Plan

Dissatisfaction with the other methods for selecting judges has led to the popularity of the so-called *merit plan*. Incorporating elements of gubernatorial appointment and elective systems, the merit plan attempts to provide a mechanism for appointing qualified candidates to the bench while permitting the public to evaluate a judge's performance through the ballot box.

First recommended by the ABA in 1937 and strongly supported today by almost the entire legal community, the merit plan has been adopted by nearly all of the states that have changed their selection systems since 1940. Missouri became the initial adopter in 1940. Since then, another twenty-two states have adopted the merit plan, and others are considering merit selection.

Three Steps Commonly referred to as the Missouri plan, the basic merit plan involves three steps:

1. A judicial nominating commission meets and recommends three or more names of prospective judges to the governor. Members of this bipartisan commission usually include a sitting judge (often the chief justice), representatives chosen by the state bar association, and laypersons appointed by the governor. The nominating commission solicits names of candidates, investigates them, chooses those it believes to be the best-qualified individuals, and then forwards three or more names and the corresponding files to the governor.

2. The governor appoints the preferred candidate to the vacant judgeship.

3. A retention election is held, usually after one or two years, in which the newly appointed judge's name is placed before the voters on a nonpartisan ticket. The voters decide whether or not the judge should be retained in office. If he is rejected by a majority vote, the judicial nominating commission begins its work anew. Subsequent retention elections may be held every eight or twelve years, depending on the merit plan's provision.

Various hybrids of the basic plan are also in use. For example, the California plan for choosing appellate judges begins when the governor identifies a candidate for a vacancy on the bench and sends that person's name to the Commission on Judicial Appointments. The commission, composed of two judges and the attorney general, hears testimony regarding the nominee and votes to confirm or reject. The new judge is then accepted or rejected in a retention election in the next regularly scheduled gubernatorial contest. Thus, although the governor appoints, the new judge is subject to confirmation by both the Commission on Judicial Appointments and the voters. In New Mexico's multistage merit plan, a judge is nominated by a commission and appointed by the governor. During the next general election, the judge must run in a partisan election. If she wins, she must run unopposed in a nonpartisan retention election on the next general-election ballot.

The object of the merit plan is to permit the governor some appointive discretion while removing politics from the selection of judges. If it works as intended, election or direct gubernatorial appointment (which are highly politicized procedures) is replaced with a careful appraisal of candidates' professional qualifications by an objective commission. The process is intended to ensure both the basic independence of judges and their accountability to the people.

The Politics of Merit Selection The merit plan looks great on paper, but in practice it has not fulfilled its promise. First, it certainly has not dislodged politics from judicial selection. A judgeship is too important a political office in any state to be completely immune from politics. It is a prized job and an important point of judicial access for numerous individuals, firms, and interest groups, especially the powerful state bar association.

Studies of judicial nominating commissions show that politics is rampant in the review and nomination of candidates.[20] For better or worse, the legal profession often dominates the process. Counting the judge who presides over the nominating commission, lawyers make up a majority of the commission in most of the states. Bar-association lobbying is often the prime reason that merit plans are adopted in the first place. However, the legal profession is not monolithic in its politics: it is often divided into two camps: plaintiff's attorneys and defendant's attorneys.

The governor's influence can be exceptionally strong. The laypersons he appoints to the nominating commission may hold the judge in awe, but they are there to represent the governor's point of view and sometimes to promote specific candidates or the agenda of the governor's political party. In six states, the majority of commission members are laypersons. The judge may also respect the governor's preferences, particularly if he owes his appointment to that chief executive.

A second criticism of the merit plan is that the procedure intended to ensure judicial accountability to the people—the retention election—rarely generates voter interest and seldom results in the departure of an incumbent judge from office. Turnout in retention elections is normally low. Fewer than 3 percent of incumbent judges have been voted out in retention elections—only a handful of judges in nearly sixty years. In effect, merit selection has been a lifetime appointment in most states. However, voter backlashes have occurred against judges whose decisions are distinctly out of step with public opinion. In 1986, California Chief Justice Rose Bird and two associate justices were swept from the state supreme court by large margins in retention elections because voters reacted negatively to a series of supreme court rulings that significantly expanded the rights of the accused and of convicted felons. Bird had voted to overturn all sixty-one capital-punishment cases brought to the court during a period when polls showed 80 percent of the public supported the death penalty in California.[21] Tennessee Supreme Court Justice Penny White was rejected in a 1996 retention election for failing to support the death penalty for the perpetrator of a particularly heinous crime.[22]

The final charge leveled against the merit plan is that, despite reformers' claims to the contrary, it does not result in the appointment of better-qualified judges or of more women and minorities. When background, education, experience, and decisionmaking are taken into account, judges selected through the merit plan are comparable to those selected through other plans. A large majority are white males. Most leave private practice for the bench in their forties and stay on the bench until retirement. Some come from a family in which the father or grandfather held political office (often a judgeship). And a substantial majority were born, raised, and educated in the state in which they serve.

Gubernatorial Appointment

All gubernatorial appointment states are former colonies, a fact that reflects the early popularity of the plan. As a method per se, gubernatorial appointment rates fairly high on independence because the judge is appointed without an election, but it is weak on accountability because the judge is generally beholden to only one person for his or her job.

Although only five states formally recognize it, gubernatorial appointment is in fact the most common method for selecting a majority of appellate and major trial court judges in the United States. Judges in states with popular elections or merit plans often resign or retire from office just before the end of their term. Under most state legal systems, the governor has the power to make interim appointments to vacant seats until the next scheduled election or the commencement of merit-plan selection processes. The governor's temporary appointee then enjoys the tremendous advantage of running as an incumbent for the next full term. Gubernatorial appointment is also used to replace a judge who dies before the expiration of her term.

What criteria does a governor apply in making appointments to the bench? Political considerations usually come first. The governor can use the appointment to reward a faithful legislator, shore up support in certain regions of the state, satisfy the demands of party leaders and the state legal establishment, or appeal to women's groups or to racial or ethnic groups. Of course, a poor choice can sometimes backfire politically, so governors must pay close attention to the judge's background, education, experience, and legal philosophy.

Which Selection Plan Is Best?

The ongoing debate over which selection plan is best among the five formal selection systems is unlikely to be decided convincingly. Legislative election and gubernatorial appointment are probably the least desirable because judges selected under these systems tend to come from a rather specific political occupation (the legislature), and the general public has little opportunity to hold them accountable. Some research shows that women are significantly more likely to attain a state supreme court seat when appointment is made by the governor (particularly a Democratic governor);[23] however, none of the three remaining systems produces better-qualified judges. And minorities have not done particularly well under any selection plan. Hispanics and blacks fill only about 5 percent of state court seats. Gubernatorial appointment and legislative election apparently increase the selection opportunities for African American judges, but significant gains probably await development of a larger pool of Hispanic and black attorneys and creation of new courts (and judgeships).[24]

Politics, of course, is what raises all judges into office, regardless of the selection method. Research by political scientists finds that what matters is the path a judge takes to the bench. Those chosen through elective systems tend to view the judiciary in more political—as opposed to juridical—terms than those who reach the bench through gubernatorial or merit appointment systems. Elected judges also tend to be more activist in their decisionmaking, and they are more likely to dissent from other judges in their opinions than are appointed judges.[25] Voter preferences carry extra weight in the decisionmaking of judges facing competitive elections, particularly with respect to issues of crime and criminal justice.[26] Those in merit-plan states have less to fear from an angry electorate and can be guided more by personal ideological preferences. In other words, judges who attain their jobs through electoral politics tend to behave like elected officials in the executive and legislative branches of state government by emphasizing political, rather than legal, factors in their decisionmaking.[27]

Removal of Judges

Like anyone else, judges can and do break the law or become physically incapable of carrying out their responsibilities. If a judge displays serious deficiencies, he or she must be removed from the bench. Forty-five states provide for impeachment, wherein charges are filed in the state house of representatives and a trial is conducted in the senate. Other traditional means for removing justices include the legislative address and popular recall. In the legislative address, both houses of the legislature, by two-thirds vote, must ask the governor to dismiss a judge. Popular recall requires a specified number of registered voters to petition for a special election to recall the judge before the term has expired. These traditional mechanisms are slow, cumbersome, and uncertain, and hence are seldom used.

Today, states generally use more practical methods to remove judges. Problems related to senility and old age are avoided in at least thirty-seven states by a mandatory retirement age (generally seventy years) or by the forfeiture of pensions for judges serving beyond the retirement age. Such measures have the added benefit of opening the courtrooms to new and younger judges, even in situations where advancing age does not impair performance. Most states have established special entities to address behavioral problems. *Courts of the judiciary,* whose members are all judges, and *judicial discipline and removal commissions,* composed of judges, lawyers, and laypersons, are authorized to investigate complaints about judges' qualifications, conduct, or fitness. These entities may reject allegations if they are unfounded, privately warn a judge if the charges are not serious, or hold formal hearings. Hearings may result in dismissal of the charges; recommendation for early retirement; or, in some states, outright suspension or removal.[28]

The discipline, suspension, or removal of state court judges is uncommon, but it becomes necessary in all states at one time or another. Judges have been found guilty of drunkenness and drug abuse, sexual misconduct with witnesses and defendants, soliciting and accepting bribes, buying and selling verdicts, and just about every other kind of misconduct. Sometimes judicial ethics seem to be in short supply. In Rhode Island, a state seldom celebrated as a paragon of political virtue, two consecutive supreme court chief justices vacated the bench when faced with impeachment. One resigned in 1986 following allegations and testimony that he associated with criminals and had adulterous relations with two women in a Mafia-linked motel, among other allegations. In 1994, another pleaded guilty to using court money to pay for personal expenses, assigning $45,000 in court work to a legal partner, fixing friends' and relatives' speeding tickets, and ordering his secretary to destroy financial records.[29] Two Ohio supreme court justices settled an argument (over an unflattering press report in 1991) with a wrestling match in which one combatant's ribs were cracked. In New York, Chief Justice Sol Wachtler was awarded thirteen months in prison for making harassing telephone calls to a former girlfriend and threatening to kidnap her child.[30] In 2003, Alabama Chief Justice Roy Moore was removed by the Court of Judiciary for defying orders by the state supreme court and a federal district court to haul away a two-and-a-half-ton Ten Commandments monument he had installed in the state judicial building. Despite the publicity surrounding such aberrant behavior, only a tiny proportion of state judges have been involved in activities that warrant removal.

JUDICIAL DECISIONMAKING

What factors influence the rulings of state court judges? Why are some judges and supreme courts widely recognized as liberal (California, Hawaii) and others as tough on crime (Arizona, Mississippi)? Why does a prosecutor judge shop, preferring to file a case before one judge rather than another? Isn't justice supposed to be blind, like its symbol of the woman holding the scales?

Judges, alas, are mortal beings like the rest of us. The legal formalities and mumbo jumbo of the courtroom tend to mask the fact that judges' decisions are no less discretionary and subjective than the decisions of a governor, legislator, or agency head. Before we examine the factors that affect judicial decisionmaking, however, we must distinguish between the legal settings of appellate courts and trial courts.

In and Out of the Trial Court

It is estimated that 90 percent of all civil and criminal cases are resolved outside the courtroom or through guilty pleas. In many civil cases, the defendant never appears in court to defend himself, and so he implicitly admits his guilt and loses the case by default. Other civil cases are settled in a pretrial conference between the defendant and the plaintiff (where, for instance, payments on an overdue debt might be rescheduled).

plea bargaining

Negotiation between a prosecutor and a criminal defendant's counsel that results in the defendant pleading guilty to a lesser charge or pleading guilty in exchange for a reduced sentence.

The process of settling criminal cases out of court at the discretion of the prosecutor and the judge is called **plea bargaining.** Although some defendants plead guilty as originally charged, acknowledging guilt for a lesser charge is more typical in criminal proceedings. With the possible exception of the victim and the general citizenry, all parties in a criminal case benefit from plea bargaining, which helps explain its extensive use. The accused gets off with lighter punishment than she would face if the case went to trial and she lost. The defense attorney frees up time to take on additional legal work. The prosecuting attorney increases his conviction rate, which looks good if he has political ambitions. The judge helps cut back the number of cases awaiting trial. Even police officers benefit by not having to spend time testifying (and waiting to testify) and by raising the department's clearance rate (the number of cases solved and disposed of).

Out-of-court settlements through plea bargaining are negotiated in an informal atmosphere in the judge's chamber, between attorneys in the halls of the court building, or over drinks in a neighboring pub. This casual negotiating is a disturbingly casual way to dispense justice. The process is secretive and far removed from any notion of due process. The prosecuting (district) attorney enjoys enormous discretion in making deals. Often her propensity to settle depends on the length of her court docket or her relationship with the attorney representing the accused, not on the merits of the case. All too often an innocent person pleads guilty to a lesser offense for fear of being wrongly convicted of a more serious offense, or because he cannot post bail and doesn't want to spend any unnecessary time behind bars. Equally disturbing, particularly to a victim, is the fact that plea bargaining can soon put a guilty person back on the streets, perhaps to search for another victim.

Nonetheless, plea bargaining is widely practiced. It is almost inevitable when the prosecutor's case hinges on weak evidence, police errors, a questionable witness, or the possibility of catching a bigger fish. Negotiation of a guilty plea for a lesser offense can occur at any stage of the criminal justice process. Sometimes it is abetted by a judge, who promises a light sentence in exchange for a guilty plea.

If the accused is unable to reach a compromise with the prosecuting attorney, he faces either a bench trial by a single judge or a trial by jury. Both involve a courtroom hearing with all the legal formalities. In some jurisdictions and for certain types of cases, the defendant has a choice. In other situations, state legal procedures specify which trial format will be utilized. For murder cases, a jury is always mandatory.

bench trial

Trial by a single judge, without a jury.

trial by jury

A trial in which a jury decides the facts and makes a finding of guilty or not guilty.

In a **bench trial,** the judge alone hears all arguments, determines the facts, and makes rulings on questions of law. **Jury trials** depend on a panel of citizens who decide the facts of the case; the judge instructs the jury on the applicable law. The uncertainty introduced by twelve laypersons is usually great enough to convince a defendant to choose a bench trial. Fewer than 1 percent of all cases are resolved by jury trial.

Attorneys seek to limit the unpredictable nature of juries by extensively questioning individuals in the jury pool. Each side in the dispute has the right to strike the names of a certain number of potential jurors without giving a specific reason. Others are eliminated for cause, such as personal knowledge of the case or its principals. In high-stakes cases, the jury-selection process involves public opinion surveys, individual background investigations of potential jurors, and other costly techniques. The nearby *Breaking New Ground* box shows what some states are doing to make prospective jurors more comfortable and jury-dodgers decidedly uncomfortable.

Inside the Appellate Court

Appellate courts are substantially different from trial courts: no plaintiffs, defendants, or witnesses are present; no bargaining or pre-decision settlement is allowed. The appeal consists of a review of court records and arguments directed by the attorneys, who frequently are not the same lawyers who originally represented the parties. Appellate court rulings are issued by a panel of at least three judges. State supreme courts sit *en banc,* with all of the judges collectively reviewing each case to decide if legal errors have occurred. Unlike decisions in most trial courts, appellate court decisions are written and published. The majority vote prevails. Judges voting in the minority have the right to make a formal, written dissent that justifies their opinion.

BREAKING NEW GROUND

Cyberjuror

In Passaic County, New Jersey, fourteen citizens were recently collected by the sheriff's department and brought before a judge at the county courthouse. Their offense? Refusing to respond to multiple notices to report for service as jurors. Their punishment? Fines up to $500 and assignment to jury duty.

The keystone of the U.S. justice system is the right to a trial by a jury of one's peers. Many courts have experienced serious problems in getting people to perform their civic duty. Only one out of four adults has served as a juror, and jury avoidance is at an all-time high. It is not uncommon for trials to be delayed because too few jurors are available. When juries are finally constituted, they are often made up of a large proportion of senior citizens, who have more time on their hands than the average citizen.

Most juries continue to number twelve individuals, although six jurors are sometimes used. Most jury decisions must be unanimous—anything short of that leads to a hung jury and either retrial or dismissal. Potential jurors are summoned by the court for assignment to a jury pool. Jurors usually must be U.S. citizens eighteen years of age or older. Questioning by the judge, prosecuting attorney, and defense attorney—known as *voir dire*—disqualifies individuals with potential conflicts of interest, bias,

or other factors germane to the case. Once selected, the juror may be required to give a day or two to service, or months for the occasional long, complex trial. Remuneration is minimal, ranging from $5.00 a day in California and New Jersey to $40.00 in South Dakota and New York.

Why has jury-dodging become a problem? First, some individuals suffer a loss of income from not being able to work. Employers may be required to keep employee-jurors on their payroll and are prohibited from firing them for serving jury duty, but abuses occur. For the self-employed, jury duty can be a serious hardship, and the same is true for potential jurors with small children and no day-care arrangement. Other burdens of jury duty include time spent away from one's job, family, or leisure activities. Jurors in tough criminal cases can suffer psychological disturbances. A relatively minor—but annoying—problem is the uninviting, uncomfortable surroundings of many jury waiting rooms.

All states have provisions (such as old age, disability, undue hardship, extreme inconvenience, and military duty) for excusing or postponing service for people selected for duty. For those who ignore their summons, judges may respond with punishment, like the Passaic County judge did. In Grant County, Washington, two randomly picked jury scofflaws are regularly brought before the judge. In North Dakota, New Jersey, and

other states, their names are published in the local newspaper. A judge in Baltimore once placed nonreporting jurors in jail for several hours. A kinder approach is to improve the quality of jury duty, for instance, by installing computer workstations, libraries, and other amenities in the jury lounges. Arizona's 2003 jury reform law imposed a filing fee on civil cases that significantly hiked juror pay, and promised jurors they would only serve one day every two years unless picked for a trial. Those who do not cooperate may be fined up to $500.00.

Gradually, courts are incorporating information technology to create a *cyberjuror*. Basic touchtone telephone systems inform members of the jury pool whether they will be needed the next day. On-line, twenty-four-hour, interactive systems that qualify potential jurors by administering an electronic *voir dire*, make specific assignments, and process excuse and postponement requests. Postage savings alone can be substantial, and the new cyberjurors appreciate the convenience.

SOURCES: Ellen Perlman, "Calling All Jury-Dodgers," *Governing* (January 1999): 16; www.ncsc.dni.us; J. Eric Oliver and Raymond E. Wolfinger, Tara D. Trolio, "Arizona Reengineers Its Juror Panels," *Governing* (August 2003): 50; Susan Carol Losh, Adina W. Wasserman, and Michael A. Wasserman, "What Summons Responses Reveal About Jury Duty Attitudes," *Judicature* 83 (May/June 2000): 304–9.

Marked variation exists in the dissent rates of state appellate courts. Some courts maintain a public aura of consensus on even the most controversial matters by almost always publishing unanimous opinions. Other courts are rocked by public disputes over legal questions. Personal, professional, partisan, political, and other disagreements can spill over into open hostility over casework. Supreme courts in states such as California, New York, Michigan, and Mississippi have a history of contentiousness, whereas others, like those in Rhode Island and Maryland, are paragons of harmony. Dissent rates appear to be positively related to state socioeconomic and political complexity, such as urbanization and partisan competition. More dissent occurs in courts with a large number of justices. The same is true in states with intermediate appellate courts that relieve the courts of last resort of some of their caseload.

On the average, state appellate court dissent rates are much lower than those in federal courts. The finding reflects the tradition of unanimity in some states, the similar backgrounds of state justices, and the way in which cases are managed. For example, it is common to manage heavy caseloads by making one judge responsible for writing the opinion on each case. In such instances, the other judges tend to concur without careful independent review, which results in a unanimous decision.

Influence of the Legal System

In addition to the facts of the case itself, judicial decisionmaking is influenced by factors associated with the legal system, including institutional arrangements, accepted legal procedures, caseload pressures, and the ease with which certain interested parties gain access to the legal process.

1. *Institutional arrangements.* When court organization includes an intermediate appellate court, supreme court judges have more time and discretion to consider important cases. The level, or tier, of court is another structural characteristic that influences decisionmaking. Trial court judges enforce legal norms and routinely *apply* the law as it has been written and interpreted over the years. The trial court permits direct interpersonal contacts among the judge, the jury, and the parties (usually individuals and small businesses). Divorce cases, personal injury cases, and minor criminal cases predominate in trial courts.

   Appellate courts are more apt to interpret the law and create public policy. State constitutional issues, state–local conflicts, and challenges to government regulation of business are the kinds of issues likely to be found in appellate courts. Cases typically involve government and large corporations. A particular case in a high court sometimes has an enormous impact on public policy, for example, when judges depart from established precedent or offer new interpretations of the law. In 2003, the Wisconsin supreme court essentially overturned a 1998 constitutional amendment guaranteeing the right to carry a concealed weapon, the supreme court of Massachusetts legalized same-sex marriages, and the Nevada supreme court nullified a state constitutional provision that two-thirds of the legislature approve tax increases.

Another important institutional arrangement is selection procedures for judges. For instance, judicial decisions may be influenced by partisan electoral competition. Especially when a judge facing re-election must vote on an issue highly salient to voters, public opinion can affect the judge's ruling.[31] Death penalty cases provide a good example of this point. In a study of judicial decisionmaking in Texas, North Carolina, Louisiana, and Kentucky, political scientist Melinda Gann Hall found that judges seeking re-election tend to uphold death sentences. In these traditionally conservative states, a decision in support of the death penalty helps to avoid unwanted pre-election criticism from political opponents and angry voters.[32]

precedent

The legal principle that previous similar court decisions should be applied to future decisions.

2. *Legal procedures and precedent.* On the basis of **precedent,** the principles and procedures of law applied in one situation are applied in any similar situation. In addition, lower courts are supposed to follow the precedents established by higher courts. An individual decision may seem unimportant, but when it is made in the context of other, similar cases, it helps judicial policy evolve. Through this practice, the doctrine of equal treatment before the law is pursued. When lower-court judges refuse to follow precedent or are ignorant of it, their decisions can be overturned on appeal. Of course, several conflicting precedents may relate to a case; in such instances, a judge is permitted to choose among them in justifying his ruling. In this regard, precedent can be a misleading explanation for judicial decisionmaking.

Where do judges find precedent? Within a state, supreme court decisions set the norms. Supreme courts themselves, however, must scan the legal landscape beyond state boundaries. In the past, decisions of the U.S. Supreme Court heavily influenced them. Increasingly, however, state supreme courts are practicing doctrinal diversity and looking to one another for precedent.[33] State appellate judges borrow from the experiences of other states. They especially tend to rely on the more professional, prestigious supreme courts, such as those of Massachusetts and New York. State courts also tend to network with courts in the same region of the country, where cultural and other environmental factors are similar.[34]

3. *Caseload pressures.* Caseload affects the decisions of judges. The number of cases varies in accordance with crime rates, socioeconomic characteristics of the jurisdictions, state laws, the number of judges, and many other variables. It stands to reason that the quality of judicial decisionmaking is inversely related to caseload. Judges burdened by too much litigation are hard-pressed to devote an adequate amount of time and attention to each case before them.

4. *Access to the system.* The final legal-system characteristic affecting judicial decisions is the access of individuals, organizations, and groups to the court system. Wealthy people and businesses are better able to pay for resources (attorneys, legal research, alternative dispute settlement, and so on) and therefore enter the legal system with a great advantage over poorer litigants. Special-interest groups also enjoy certain advantages in influencing judicial decisions. They often have specialized knowledge in areas of litigation, such

as environmental or business regulation. Lobbying by interest groups is much less prominent in the judicial branch than in the legislative and executive branches, but groups can affect outcomes by providing financial aid to litigants in important cases and by filing *amicus curiae* ("friend of the court") briefs supporting one side or the other in a dispute.

The states have implemented several reforms to increase access to the judicial system for those who are at a disadvantage. For example, court interpreter training is now available in states with large Hispanic populations. Physical and communication barriers are being removed so that persons with disabilities can participate fully in all aspects of the legal system. Racial, ethnic, and gender biases against attorneys, plaintiffs, defendants, witnesses, and other court participants are being addressed. Night courts remain open past closing hours for people who have difficulty getting off their day jobs to appear in court. And day care is being provided for children of plaintiffs, defendants, witnesses, and jurors. Gradually, the state courts are responding to changes in society.[35]

Most of the legal-system factors influencing judicial decisionmaking are subject to manipulation by elected officials, who can add judges, pass laws, alter procedures, boost or deplete court budgets and judicial pay, and ease caseloads through various reforms. However, the second set of factors related to decisionmaking in the courts—judges' values, attitudes, and characteristics—is rather immutable.

Personal Values, Attitudes, and Characteristics of Judges

Simply put, judges do not think and act alike. Each is a product of his or her individual background and experiences, which in turn influence decisions made in the courtroom. Studies of state court justices have found that decisions are related to the judges' party identification, political ideology, prior careers, religion, ethnicity, age, and sex. In other words, personal characteristics predispose a judge to decide cases in certain ways.

For example, Democratic judges tend to favor the claimant in civil rights cases, the government in tax disputes, the employee in worker's compensation cases, the government in business regulation cases, the defendant in criminal contests, the union in disagreements with management, and the tenant in landlord-tenant cases. Republicans tend to support the opposite side on all these issues. Female judges, who now occupy one of four seats on supreme courts, are more supportive of women on feminist issues; more likely to favor the accused in obscenity and death penalty cases; and, in general, are more liberal than their male colleagues.[36] The judge's race appears to have little effect on the sentences handed down to black and white defendants, although African American judges, according to one study, tend to be tougher when sentencing all defendants than white judges are.[37] Obviously, these distinctions do not hold in all situations, but the point is that *justice* is a complex concept subject to individual interpretation and discretion. No wonder attorneys try to shop around for the most sympathetic judge before filing a legal action.

NEW JUDICIAL FEDERALISM

During the 1950s and 1960s, the U.S. Supreme Court was the leading judicial actor in the United States. Under Chief Justice Earl Warren (1953–1969) and his liberal majority, the Court handed down a long series of rulings that overturned racial segregation, mandated legislative reapportionment, extended voting rights, and expanded the rights of the accused. Significant reversals of state court decisions were commonplace.

Beginning with Chief Justice Warren Burger (1969–1986) and a growing faction of conservative justices, however, the Supreme Court changed direction in the 1970s and 1980s. Since 1988, a conservative majority has been in control. The Court has been less intrusive in state and local affairs and has, through its caution, flashed a green light to state courts inclined to activism (see Chapter 2). The result is **New Judicial Federalism,** in which state courts look first to state constitutional and statutory law in rendering legal judgments on important state and local issues, which were once addressed mostly by the federal courts.

New Judicial Federalism

A trend in which state constitutional and statutory law is consulted and applied before federal law.

judicial activism

Judges' making of public policy through decisions that overturn existing law or effectively make new laws.

Judicial Activism in the States

Judicial activism is a value-laded term with ideological dimensions.[38] When associated with politically liberal Court decisions, it is decried by conservatives. However, some conservative judges are also tagged as activists. Activist judges can be either liberals or conservatives, but all tend to show strong ideological tendencies.

Thus, an objective definition of judicial activism points to court-generated change in public policy that is perceived as illegitimate by opponents who favor the status quo. Judicial activism is in the eye of the beholder; it holds a pejorative association for some people and a positive one for others, depending on the issue at hand.

Regardless of one's feelings on the matter, state supreme courts have clearly become *more* activist by expanding into new policy areas. They are more likely to be involved in the policymaking process by making decisions that affect policy in the executive branch, and many even appear to pre-empt the lawmaking responsibility of the legislature when, in exercising the power of judicial review, they invalidate a statute based on constitutional grounds. State supreme courts are increasingly engaging policy issues in prison overcrowding, public school financing, gay rights, and treatment of the mentally ill. Vermont's supreme court is one of the most activist, having recognized the legal rights of gay couples and thrown out the state's system for funding public schools.

Some of the most spectacular examples of state court activism have taken certain minimum standards established by the federal Supreme Court and expanded them within the jurisdiction and judicial primacy of the states. Examples of this judicial federalism include the following:

- California, Connecticut, and Massachusetts courts have expanded a woman's right to abortion on demand and the right to financial aid from the state for abortions. (Virginia, on the other hand, requires parental consent before an abortion for a woman under the age of eighteen.)

- Although the U.S. Supreme Court has upheld state sodomy prohibitions, courts in New York, Pennsylvania, and other states have struck down sodomy laws as violations of the right to privacy, as spelled out in the state constitution. And, as noted above, Massachusetts and Vermont have recognized the state constitutional rights of gay couples.
- The Oregon supreme court has rejected a U.S. Supreme Court decision that provided guidelines for declaring certain printed and visual materials to be obscene. The Oregon court notes that its state constitution had been authored "by rugged and robust individuals dedicated to founding a free society unfettered by the governmental imposition of some peoples' views of morality on the free expression of others." The court went on to declare, "In this state, any person can write, paint, read, say, show or sell anything to a consenting adult even though that expression may generally or universally be considered 'obscene.'"[39]
- The supreme courts of California and other states have upheld the use of medical marijuana, despite federal opposition.

How can the state courts override the decisions of the highest court in the United States? The answer is that they are grounding their rulings in their own constitutions instead of in the national constitution. The bill of rights protections of many states are more precise and broader in scope than the rights set forth in the first ten amendments to the U.S. Constitution. In several decisions, the U.S. Supreme Court has upheld the right of the states to expand on the minimum rights and liberties guaranteed under the national document. Of course, when an irreconcilable conflict exists between state and federal law, the latter prevails.

Current Trends in State Courts

The new wave of state court activism is not carrying all the states with it; many state supreme courts remain caught in the doldrums, consistently endorsing—rather than repudiating—U.S. Supreme Court decisions. Some of them are so quiet, as one wag suggested, "that you can hear their arteries harden." But even traditionally inactive courts in states such as Wisconsin and North Carolina have been stirred into independent actions recently, and the trend is continuing. The U.S. Supreme Court is likely to have a conservative majority for many years, permitting the state courts to explore the legal landscape further. State court activism seems to be contagious when courts utilize their own information and case networks instead of those of the Supreme Court.

Of course, with rare exceptions, judges cannot seize issues as governors and legislators can; they must wait for litigants to bring them to the courthouse. Although judges can issue rulings, they must depend on the executive and legislative branches to comply with and enforce those rulings. Nonetheless, many state supreme courts are becoming more active in the policymaking process. A case in point is the supreme court of New Jersey, which has clearly departed from several U.S. Supreme Court rulings on issues including free speech, search and seizure, mandatory drug testing, and public financing of abortion rights for poor women. The reluctance of the federal courts to address important and controversial issues comprehensively has resulted in more cases for state supreme courts to decide.

State court activism does have some disadvantages. First, some courts may overstep their authority and go too far in policymaking, intruding into the proper domain of executive and legislative actors—not to mention that of the voters. The Nevada supreme court's nullification of a two-thirds legislative majority for tax increases is a rather extreme example. One problem is that judges have little expertise in the substance of public policy or in the policymaking process. They have no specialized staff to perform in-depth policy research on particular policy issues, and they cannot realistically depend on lawyers to conduct policy research for them. After all, lawyers are trained and practiced in legal reasoning, not social science or political science. Second, state courts are increasingly issuing policy decisions that have significant budgetary implications. Court rulings on school finance, prison overcrowding, and treatment of the mentally ill have stretched state budgets. Such court actions rarely take into account the financial effects. A third problem is that in the context of state constitutional rights, geography is destiny. A state-by-state approach may not be appropriate for policies in areas such as civil rights or clean air, which should be equal for all citizens.

ADMINISTRATIVE AND ORGANIZATIONAL IMPROVEMENTS IN STATE COURTS

We have already discussed several important judicial reforms: intermediate appellate courts, court unification and consolidation, merit-selection plans for judges, more practical means for disciplining and removing judges, and administrative and organizational improvements. This last category remains important, as we will discuss next.

Financial Improvements

The exorbitant costs of some trials can bankrupt local jurisdictions if state financial assistance is not forthcoming. For example, one child molestation case in Los Angeles County lasted two and a half years and carried a tab of $15 million. (Neither of the two defendants was convicted.) The price tag for a murder trial and subsequent appeals can also be counted in the millions. Given such contingencies, more than half of the states have assumed full financial responsibility for the operation of state and local courts.

Another financial reform, centralized budgeting (also called *unified court budgeting*), has been adopted by more than half of the states. This capacity-enhancing reform entails a consolidated budget for all state and local courts, prepared by the chief administrative officer of the state court system, that details all personnel, supplies, equipment, and other expenditures. It is intended to enhance financial management; equitably distribute resources among the courts; and help maintain judicial independence from the executive and legislative branches, which lose their authority to alter the judiciary's budget. A unified court system, centralized management and financing, and unified budgeting are all similar because they share the objective of bringing a state's entire court system under a single, authoritative administrative structure.

Dealing with Growing Caseloads

Recently, court reformers have recognized the need to deal more effectively with case backlogs. State courts confront more than 100 million new cases each year. Some judges hand down more than 300 opinions annually. Delays of two years or more have not been uncommon for appellate court hearings, and the unprecedented pressure is growing.

Excessive caseloads are caused by numerous factors, including the greater propensity of losing parties to appeal lower-court decisions, the tremendous growth in litigation, huge increases in drug-related and drunk-driving cases, and poor caseload-management procedures. Exacerbating the problem is the sheer number of lawyers in the United States, which accounts for nearly two-thirds of all the lawyers in the world. Calls for tort reform are common. (See the nearby *Debating Politics* box.)

The paramount concern is that long delays thwart the progress of justice. The quality of evidence deteriorates as witnesses disappear or forget what they saw, and victims suffer from delays that prevent them from collecting damages for injuries incurred during a crime or an accident. Even accused (and perhaps innocent) perpetrators can be harmed by the experience of being held in prison for long periods while awaiting trial.

Reducing excessive caseloads is not a simple matter. Common sense dictates establishing intermediate appellate courts and adding new judgeships. But much like a new highway draws more traffic, intermediate appellate courts, by their very existence, tend to attract more appeals. Although additional judges can speed up the trial process in lower courts, they may also add to appellate backlogs. Expanding the number of judges in an appellate court is also problematic; hearings may take longer because of more input or factional divisions among judges.

The stubborn persistence of case backlogs has led to some promising new approaches.

1. *Alternative dispute resolution.* Almost all states today use mediation, arbitration, or other techniques to help settle litigation prior to or between formal courtroom proceedings. Mediation involves a neutral third party who tries to help the opponents reach a voluntary agreement; arbitration consists of a binding ruling by a neutral participant in favor of one party or the other. In some states, including California and Washington, civil litigants in search of timely settlement have hired private judges to arbitrate their disputes.

2. *Fines against lawyers and litigants.* New laws or court rules allow judges to levy monetary fines against lawyers and litigants guilty of delaying tactics or frivolous litigation, or of violating standards that require cases to be heard within a specified time period.

3. *Case management systems.* Although individual systems vary widely, a typical approach is multitracking, or *differentiated case management,* which distinguishes

DEBATING POLITICS

Tort Reform

In Houston, a woman who scalded herself with hot coffee purchased at McDonald's sued the fast-food chain and won $2.9 million (later reduced to $480,000). In Maine, a woman golfer hit a shot that bounced off an obstacle and struck her in the face. She sued the country club and won $40,000. In Connecticut, a twelve-year-old Little League baseball player uncorked a wild throw that conked a woman in the stands, who promptly sued the player and the local government. In New York City, several prison inmates somehow shot themselves in the foot and then sued the city for negligence.

Such stories seem to be increasingly common as 950,000 lawyers in the United States seek to justify their existence (more and more often through advising clients on how to avoid expensive lawsuits) and citizens look for an easy dollar instead of a sense of personal responsibility (trial lawyers assert that they turn away as many clients as they take because of poor cases). The results are a transfer of financial assets from individuals and organizations to attorneys, personal and corporate financial tragedies, and local governments that must hike taxes to cover legal fees and liability settlements.

The biggest problem is that of torts, the suits for damages for product liability, personal injury, medical malpractice, and related claims. Throughout the twentieth century, state courts gradually eliminated restrictions on tort liability and substituted legal doctrines favoring plaintiffs over defendants. For example, nearly all states have a strict liability rule for product safety, which means that manufacturers of defective products (or even very hot coffee) may be held fully liable for damages caused by their product, whether or not the manufacturer was negligent.

Today, the state legislatures are actively engaged in tort reform that shifts the balance more toward defendants. Punitive damages have been capped in Alabama, New Jersey, Illinois, Texas, and other states. Laws protecting local governments and their employees from exorbitant liability awards have been adopted in several states. Business interest in judicial elections in California and other states has surged; judges known for generous tort decisions have come under electoral attack and, in some cases, have been ousted.

Aligned against tort reform are the powerful trial lawyers, for whom product liability and personal injury suits are their bread and butter, and with certain consumer groups, which see unlimited tort liability as a fundamental right for injured citizens and a way to hold individuals and firms accountable for shoddy and dangerous practices and merchandise. Opponents of reform are fighting against insurance companies, manufacturers, professional associations, and others in the courtrooms and in the state capitols. In several recent instances (for example, Indiana, Ohio, and Oregon), state supreme courts have overturned court reforms.

Should monetary limits, or caps, be set on tort liability? Why or why not? If so, at what level should they be set? Who should determine the limits of tort liability? The individual states, the federal government, the courts? Should the voters of individual states decide this issue through referendums? If tort liability were capped at, say, $100,000 for defective consumer goods or medical malpractice, which interests or individuals would win and which would lose?

SOURCES: Sarah Whitmire, "Torts Pit Lawmakers Versus Courts," *State Government News* (February 2000): 14–17; André Henderson, "Damming the Lawsuit Flood," *Governing* 8 (September 1995): 37–38; Henry R. Glick, "Courts: Politics and the Judicial Process," in Virginia Gray and Russell L. Hanson, eds., *Politics in the American States*, 8th ed. (Washington, D.C.: CQ Press, 2004).

between simple and complex cases, and between frivolous and potentially significant cases, and treats them differently. Complex and significant cases are waved on down the traditional appellate track. Simple and frivolous cases take a shorter track, usually under the direction of staff attorneys. In Vermont, this case management system is referred to as a rocket docket. Experiments with multitracking have been successful in reducing case delays in Arizona, Maine,

New Hampshire, and several other states. Another case management innovation designed to speed the wheels of justice is *boutique courts,* in which environmental law disputes, drug cases, or others with special characteristics are heard by judges in specialized courts.

4. *New technology.* Technological innovations are also improving the quality and quantity of court operations. Electronic data bases (for example, LEXIS and WESTLAW) are used to store case information and legal research and to transmit information from law offices to courts. Electronic filing of court documents and on-line access to court information for attorneys and citizens saves the courts money and staff time. Automation helps track child support payments, court administrative systems, and traffic tickets. Videotaping of witnesses' testimony is becoming common. Arraignment procedures, during which suspects are formally charged, are also videotaped to save time or to prevent potential problems from a disruptive defendant. Video courtrooms, in which trials are filmed by TV cameras, create a more accurate trial record and cost much less than a written transcript by a court stenographer. Lawyers in high-tech courtrooms speed up proceedings by using PowerPoint presentations, video clips, and Internet technology, all displayed on individual flat-screen monitors. Audiovisual technology permits hearings, motions, pleas, sentencing, and other proceedings to be conducted long distance, between the jail and the courthouse, thereby saving money and enhancing security.

5. *Performance standards.* The National Center for State Courts has developed twenty-two performance standards for state trial courts to aid self-assessment and improvement.[40] A growing number of states are not only adopting quantitative indicators of the speed with which cases are processed but are also trying to measure broader concerns such as access to justice, fairness and integrity, public trust and confidence, and the quality of judges' decision-making. One finding is that case processing depends partly on the local legal culture—the norms shared by judges, attorneys, clerks, and others involved in the legal process.

Compensating the Judges

At first glance, judicial salaries seem high. State supreme court judges earn an average of approximately $121,000.[41] The variation is great, however; California justices make $170,319, and their counterparts in Montana are paid only $89,381. Trial court judges are paid 10 to 20 percent less. However, these amounts are substantially below what an experienced, respected attorney can expect to make. A successful lawyer who gives up private practice for the bench must be willing to take a considerable cut in income. Unlike legislators, state judges are permitted little outside income. Therefore, it is reasonable to ask whether the best legal minds will be attracted to judgeships when judicial compensation is relatively low. This dilemma exists at all levels and in all branches of public service, from the municipal finance officer to the highway patrol officer, because most state and local government compensation lags behind pay for comparable jobs in the private sector. If we expect our judges, law enforcement officers, and other public employees to be honest, productive, and highly qualified, they must be compensated adequately. Recent salary increases for state judges seem to reflect this principle.

State Courts Enter the Modern Age

Like the other two branches of government, the state judiciary has been reformed significantly. Court systems have been modernized and simplified, intermediate appellate courts have been added, processes have been streamlined, judicial selection has been moved toward the merit ideal, and case delays have been reduced. Disciplinary and removal commissions now make it easier to deal with problem judges. As a result, courts are striving for greater independence from political pressures and favoritism and for more accountability for their actions. Justice may still appear to be an ephemeral ideal, (and an expensive one at that), but it is more likely to be approximated in state judicial decisions today than ever before.

Although the changes in state court systems during the past quarter-century have not gone far enough in some instances, one can't help but be amazed that so much has happened in so short a period of time to a conservative, slow-moving institution of government. The courts, like the rest of society, are no longer immune to the technological age and its prime tool, the computer. New innovations and approaches will follow the recommendations of commissions in states now studying the needs of state judicial systems in the twenty-first century.

Court modernization and reform have been accompanied by increased judicial activism. The new state courts have far surpassed the federal courts in public policy activism. They sometimes blatantly disagree with federal precedents and insist on decisions grounded in state constitutional law rather than in the national constitution. In short, the state courts are actively responding to public concern about crime and the administration of justice.

CHAPTER RECAP

- State courts are organized into two tiers: appellate courts and trial courts.
- Structural reforms such as unified court systems have sought to make the courts more efficient and effective.
- The five methods for selecting judges are legislative election, partisan election, nonpartisan election, merit plan, and gubernatorial appointment. Each selection plan has certain advantages and disadvantages—none of them is perfect.
- Many factors influence judicial decisionmaking, including institutional arrangements; legal procedures; case precedent; caseload pressures; access to the legal system; and the personal values, attitudes, and characteristics of judges.
- Judicial federalism is related to increased capability and judicial activism in many state courts.
- Efforts to reform state courts include financial improvements, better caseload management, and improved compensation for judges.

Key Terms

civil case *(p. 245)*

criminal case *(p. 245)*

administrative case *(p. 245)*

common law *(p. 245)*

limited jurisdiction
    trial courts *(p. 246)*

major trial courts *(p. 247)*

supreme court *(p. 247)*

intermediate appellate court *(p. 247)*

plea bargaining *(p. 258)*

bench trial *(p. 259)*

trial by jury *(p. 259)*

precedent *(p. 262)*

New Judicial Federalism *(p. 264)*

judicial activism *(p. 264)*

Surfing the Web

The National Center for State Courts (NCSC) maintains a list of courts and their web addresses. NCSC's web site at **www.ncsc.dni.us/** is a rich source of information on the courts. State court decisions may also be accessed at the NCSC web site.

Interesting state sites include the following: California at **www.courtinfo. ca.gov/**, Florida at **www.flcourts.org,** and Alaska at **www.alaska.net/~akctlib/ homepage.htm.**

The American Bar Association's web site at **www.abanet.org/** provides an analysis of current controversial cases and other legal information.

The Law Forum Legal Resources site at **www.lawforum.net** has links to all on-line state and local courts.

For a detailed examination of all states' judicial selection systems, see **www. ajs.org/select11.html.**

To watch live performances of Florida's Ninth Judicial Circuit Court, see **www.dascom-systems.com/Iowa%20Supreme%20Court.htm.**

The Iowa Supreme Court may be viewed at **www.governmentvideo. com/2001/0901/presentation_0901.shtml.**

THE STRUCTURE OF LOCAL GOVERNMENT

I n 1999, America's second largest city, Los Angeles, did something that it
had not done for three-quarters of a century: It rewrote its charter. The
charter, which sets out the city's structure and functions, had been amended
400 times in its history and had grown to an unwieldy and complicated 700
pages. The mayor had little real authority over the nearly 500-square-mile city,
sharing power with the city council, boards of commissioners, and professional
general managers. In essence, the city's structure was a blueprint for failure. The

citizens of Los Angeles had grown increasingly weary of dealing with an unresponsive city government. The dissatisfaction provided sufficient impetus for the mayor to sponsor a charter-reform effort. It was a long, drawn-out, conflictual process, with most of the city council in opposition. But when the reformed charter was put to the voters, they endorsed it, 60 to 40 percent.[1]

No sooner had this new era in Los Angeles government begun when another challenge emerged: the potential secession of a portion of the city located in the San Fernando Valley. Feeling that the area did not receive its fair share of city services, leaders of Valley VOTE spearheaded a movement to create an independent city in 2002. After Los Angeles voters defeated the secession ballot question (it passed in the Valley section), the city tried to make nice by creating neighborhood councils and establishing satellite city halls. The lesson to city government? Pay attention to the citizenry.

American local governments were not planned according to some grand design. Rather, they grew in response to a combination of citizen demand, interest group pressure, and state government acquiescence. As a consequence, no rational system of local governments exists. What does exist is a collection of autonomous, frequently overlapping jurisdictional units. The number of local governments varies from state to state. Consider the case of Pennsylvania and its 5,031 local jurisdictions. The state contains sixty-six counties, 1,018 cities, 1,546 townships, 1,885 special districts, and 516 school districts.[2] Nevada, on the other hand, has a grand total of 210 local governments.

What do citizens want from local governments? The answer is, to be governed well. They want jurisdictions with adequate capacity to resolve the tough public problems of our times. But as this chapter demonstrates, "governed well" is hard to achieve. Even with improved capacity, local governments confront a series of challenges. As the Los Angeles example shows, just as soon as they solve one problem, another crops up.

ORIENTATIONS TO COMMUNITIES

Communities and their governments can be discussed in many different ways. Theoretically, at least three different orientations have some appeal. When you move from the theoretical realm to legal realities, five types of local governments can be differentiated.

Theoretical Orientations

In the early days of the United States, communities were idealized as *civic republics*.[3] In a civic republic, community government is based on the principle of mutual consent. Citizens share fundamental beliefs and participate in public affairs. Their motivation for civic involvement is less materialistic self-interest than altruistic concern for community welfare. Although this idea continued to have theoretical appeal, its reality was threatened by the growing and diverse nineteenth-century populace, which preferred to maximize individual liberty and accumulation of wealth. An economically inspired conception of community, that of the *corporate enterprise,* gradually emerged. Economic growth and the ensuing competition for wealth sparked extensive conflict.[4] With the guidance of state government, local governments adopted policies and juggled the clashing interests.

These two theoretical orientations, the community as a civic republic and the community as a corporate enterprise, remain viable. A new orientation has emerged, however—one that portrays the community as a *consumer market.*[5] In a consumer market, citizens are consumers of public services and governments are providers. This idea places increased emphasis on quality of life and cost-effectiveness. Individuals make choices about where they will live—in the heart of the city, a suburban jurisdiction, or a rural portion of the county. In each of these locales, the individual will encounter government, or more accurately, *governments.* The range of government services and their cost vary from one place to another. Informed consumers seek communities that are in line with their preferences. You say that you want to live in the Los Angeles area? You have many jurisdictional choices: Twenty-one cities share a border with Los Angeles. Each one provides a different package of services, in terms of type, quality, and cost—a consumer market, indeed.

Five Types of Local Governments

Local governments are special because they are close to the people they serve. Local government is the level of government that fights crime, extinguishes fires, paves streets, collects trash, maintains parks, provides water, and educates children. Some local governments provide all of these services; others, only some. Native American reservations are not a type of local government, even though they perform many local government functions. And they are most definitely *not* creatures of the states in which they are located, as local governments are. (Chapter 2 discusses the national-tribal-state relationship in more detail.) **Metropolitan areas,** which are comprised of a central city and its surrounding county (or counties), are not local governments either. The label *metropolitan statistical area (MSA)* is used by the federal government to designate urban areas that have reached a certain population threshold. As of the 2000 census, the United States counted more than 280 MSAs.

There are five types of local governments: counties, municipalities, towns and townships, special districts, and school districts. A useful way of thinking about local governments is to distinguish between general-purpose and single-purpose local governments. **General-purpose local governments** perform a wide range of governmental functions and include three types of local governments: counties, municipalities, and towns and townships. **Single-purpose local governments,** as the label implies, have a specific purpose and perform one function. School districts and special districts are single-purpose governments. Typically, single-purpose local governments coexist with the general-purpose local governments covering the same territory. For example, the boundaries of a school district may be coterminous with the county, they may cover smaller portions of the county, or even extend over sections of two or more counties. In the United

metropolitan area
A central city of at least 50,000 people and its surrounding county (or counties); often called an urban area.

general-purpose local government
A local government that provides a wide range of functions.

single-purpose local government
A local government, such as a school district, that performs a specific function.

States, the number of local governments exceeds 87,800. Figure 10.1 shows the number of local governments at two points in time: 1952 and 2002. Among general-purpose local governments, the number of counties and towns and townships decreased slightly over the fifty-year period as the number of municipalities increased. In terms of single-purpose local governments, the trends are more dramatic. From 1952 to 2002, nearly 80 percent of America's school districts were abolished or consolidated with surrounding districts; in the same period, special districts have tripled in number.

Regardless of the purpose of a local government, we must remember that it has a lifeline to state government. In short, state government gives local government its legal existence. This relationship is not quite the equivalent of a hospital patient hooked up to a life-support system, but it is a basic condition of the local–state link. Local citizens may instill a community with its flavor and its character, but state government makes local government official. Over time,

FIGURE 10.1 **Numbers of Local Governments, by Type of Government: 1952 Versus 2002**

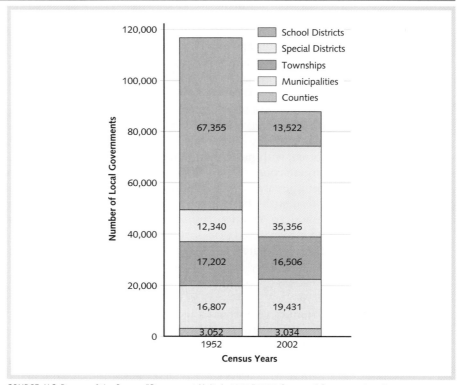

SOURCE: U.S. Bureau of the Census, "Government Units in 2002," 2002 *Census of Governments*, p. 8.

home rule

A broad grant of power from the state to a local government.

most states have gradually relaxed their control over localities through grants of **home rule,** which give local governments more decisionmaking power.

Being so close to the people offers special challenges to local governments. Citizens know almost immediately when trash has not been collected or when libraries do not carry current bestsellers. They can contact local officials and attend public hearings. And they do. A recent survey asked a national sample of Americans about their interaction with government. Over 40 percent said that they had contacted an elected official or attended a community meeting.[6] The interactive nature of local government makes the questions of capacity and responsiveness all the more critical.

COUNTY GOVERNMENT

State governments have carved up their territory into 3,034 discrete subunits called counties (except in Louisiana, where counties are called parishes, and Alaska, where they are called boroughs). Counties exist everywhere, with only a few exceptions: Connecticut and Rhode Island, where there are no functional county governments; Washington, D.C., which is a special case in itself; municipalities in Virginia that are independent jurisdictions and are not part of the counties that surround them; and cities like Baltimore and St. Louis, which are not part of a county because of past political decisions. Also, some jurisdictions—Philadelphia and San Francisco, for example—are considered cities but are actually consolidated city-county government structures.

Not All Counties Are Alike

Counties can be differentiated according to their urban/rural nature. Urban, or metropolitan, counties contain one or more large cities and surrounding suburbs and serve as the employment hubs for the area. Los Angeles County, California, with more than 9 million residents—and larger than most states—is the largest county. Even though most Americans live in metropolitan areas, most counties are actually nonmetropolitan; that is, they contain one or more small cities, with the rest of the area sparsely settled. More than three-fourths of American counties have fewer than 100,000 inhabitants. Counties that contain no incorporated places with more than 2,500 residents are the most rural of all. Loving County, Texas, with fewer than 100 people spread over its 673-square-mile territory, is an example.

The Role of County Government

Counties were created by states to function as their administrative appendages. In other words, counties were expected to manage activities of statewide concern at the local level. Their basic set of functions traditionally included property tax assessment and collection, law enforcement, elections, recordkeeping (pertaining to matters such as land transactions, births, and deaths), and road maintenance.[7] The county courthouse was the center of government.

The twin pressures of modernization and population growth placed additional demands on county governments. As a result, their service offerings have expanded. In addition to their traditional responsibilities, counties today handle health care and hospitals, pollution control, mass transit, industrial development, social services, and consumer protection.[8] Examples of the old and new functions of counties appear in Table 10.1. The more new services a county provides, the more it is delivering city-type services to its residents and

| TABLE 10.1 | **County Government Functions** |

FUNCTION	TRADITIONAL FUNCTION	NEW FUNCTION
Building and housing code enforcement		X
Disaster preparedness		X
Water supply/sewage disposal		X
Parks and recreation		X
Judicial administration	X	
County jail maintenance	X	
Planning and land use control		X
Record keeping: land transactions births, deaths, marriages	X	
Airports		X
Public hospitals		X
Law enforcement	X	
Local roads and bridges, construction and maintenance	X	
Consumer protection		X
Mass transit		X
Property tax assessment and collection	X	
Election administration	X	
Natural resource preservation		X
Welfare and social service programs	X	
Libraries		X
Stadiums, convention and cultural centers		X
Pollution control		X
Public health, including clinics		X
Community development and housing		X

SOURCES: David R. Berman, *County Governments in an Era of Change* (Westport, Conn.: Greenwood Press, 1993); Tanis J. Salant, "Overview of County Governments," in Roger L. Kemp, ed., *Forms of Local Government* (Jefferson, N.C.: McFarland, 1999).

businesses.[9] As a result, counties are increasingly regarded less as simple functionaries of state government than as important policymaking units of local government. State governments have awarded greater decisionmaking authority and flexibility to counties through home rule. By 2000, thirty-seven states had adopted home rule provisions for at least some of their counties.[10] This has made it easier for counties to change their organizational structures and reform their practices.

Even with their gradual empowerment, counties, like other local governments, continue to chafe at the traditionally tight reins of state government control. In a recent survey, county officials blamed "state requirements without state funding" for many of the problems plaguing their government.[11] Also ranking high on their list of complaints were "state limits on authority." The issue of empowerment is unlikely to fade during the remainder of the decade.

How County Governments Are Organized

The traditional structure of county government is based on an elected governing body, usually called a board of commissioners or supervisors, which is the central policymaking apparatus in the county. The board enacts county ordinances, approves the county budget, and appoints other officials (such as the directors of the county public works department and the county parks department). One of the board members acts as presiding officer. This form of government has been the most popular; more than half of U.S. counties use it, although its predominance is decreasing. A typical county commission has three or five members and meets in regular session twice a month.

The board is not all-powerful, however, because several other county officials are also elected, forming a plural executive structure. In most places, these officials include the sheriff, the county prosecutor (or district attorney), the county clerk (or clerk of the court), the county treasurer (or auditor), the county tax assessor, and the coroner. These officials can become powerful political figures in their own right by controlling their own bureaucratic units. Figure 10.2 sketches the typical organizational pattern of county government.

There are two primary criticisms of the traditional county organizational structure. First, it has no elected central executive official, like the mayor of a city or the governor of a state. County government is run by a board. Second, it does not have a single professional administrator to manage county government, the way a city manager does in a municipality. Elected officials are responsible for administering major county functions.

These criticisms have led to calls for reform of the structure of county government. Two alternative county structures have grown in popularity over the past two decades. In one, called the *county council–elected executive plan,* the voters elect an executive officer in addition to the governing board. The result is a clearer separation between legislative and executive powers—in effect, a two-branch system of government. The board still has the power to set policy, adopt the budget, and audit the financial performance of the county. The executive's role is to prepare the budget, administer county operations (in other words, implement the policies of the board), and appoint department heads.

FIGURE 10.2   **Traditional Organization of County Government**

The most common form of county government lacks a central executive.

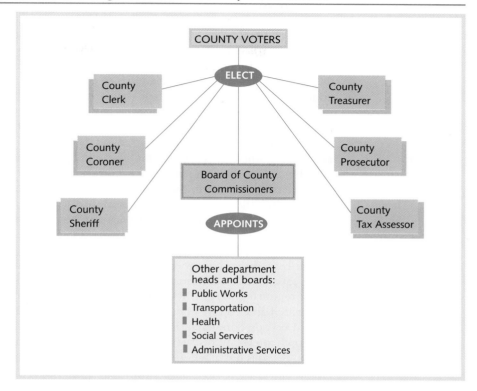

Just under 400 counties have adopted this arrangement. In the other alternative structure, the *council-administrator plan,* the county board hires a professional administrator to run the government. The advantage of this form of government is that it brings to the county a highly skilled manager with a professional commitment to efficient, effective government. Approximately 1,000 counties have variations of the council-administrator structure.

Determining the most effective structural arrangements for county government is an ongoing issue. Defections from the long-standing commission form of county government and experimentation with alternatives continue, especially in the most populous counties.[12] Does structure matter? If results from new research in Florida counties can be extended to other states, the answer is yes. Among fast-growing counties in the Sunshine State, the adoption of a reformed structure led to an expansion of the counties' services to its residents.[13]

The Performance of County Government

The last word on counties has not been written. Since the 1970s, they have been described as improving, modernizing, or exhibiting some other positive behavior.

Granted, counties are now more prominent than they were in the old days, when they were considered the shadowy backwaters of local governments. As urban populations spill beyond the suburbs into the unincorporated territory of counties, the pressure on local governments grows.[14] The county–state relationship is rocky, primarily because of spiraling costs of state-imposed mandates for programs such as indigent services and long-term health care. In addition, counties are expected to tackle tough dilemmas of affordable housing and environmental compliance at the same time that they are expanding their services to include growth management, refugee resettlement, and trash recycling. And county government, when compared with the cities located within its boundaries, often fares poorly. A story, "Good Government, Bad Government," in a state and local magazine, *Governing,* makes that point. The good government featured in the story was the city of Phoenix, Arizona; the bad government was Maricopa County, Arizona. Management in the city was described as "orderly, innovative and efficient," while the county was characterized as "chaotic, hidebound and wasteful."[15] In the ensuing five years, Maricopa County took the criticisms to heart, made extensive changes in its operation, and by 2002 was earning A and B grades in management from the Government Performance Project.[16]

Concerned that county governments were overwhelmed by these pressures, the speaker of the California assembly introduced legislation in 1991 to create a tier of regional governments in his state.[17] Under the proposal, California would be divided into seven regions that would be governed by thirteen-member elected boards. These regional "supergovernments" would assume many of the development and infrastructure functions currently assigned to county governments. Although the bill did not pass, the performance of county government remains an issue in other parts of the nation. In Massachusetts, where cities and towns provide most local services, the state legislature has abolished several counties as functioning governments, contending that they were superfluous in the Bay State.[18] (The *Debating Politics* box in Chapter 12 addresses the Massachusetts case in greater detail.) Although these threats to county survival are isolated, county governments must continue to modernize and focus on the big picture or run the risk of being bypassed.

MUNICIPAL GOVERNMENT

Municipalities are cities; the words are interchangeable because each refers to a specific, populated territory, typically operating under a charter from state government. Cities differ from counties in terms of how they were created and what they do. Historically, they have been the primary units of local government in most societies—the grand enclaves of human civilization. Augustine wrote of a city of God and Cotton Mather of a heavenly city; later formulations labeled cities as ungovernable[19] and unheavenly.[20] Cities today are encouraged to be entrepreneurial.[21] Whatever the appropriate image, they are fascinating places.

Creating Cities

A city is a legal recognition of settlement patterns in an area. In the most common procedure, residents of an area in a county petition the state for **incorporation.** The area slated for incorporation must meet certain criteria, such as population or density minimums. In Alabama, for instance, 300 people is the population threshold necessary for incorporation; in Arizona, the number is 1,500. In most cases, a referendum is required. The referendum enables citizens to vote on whether they wish to become an incorporated municipality. Frequently, citizens are also asked to vote on the name of the municipality and its form of government. If the incorporation measure is successful, then a **charter** is granted by the state, and the newly created city has the legal authority to elect officials, levy taxes, and provide services to its residents. Not all cities have charters, however. Most California cities, for example, operate under general state law.

New cities are created every year. For instance, during one six-year period, 145 places incorporated (and thirty-three cities disincorporated, or ceased to exist as official locales).[22] Although most new cities tend to be small, some begin with sizable populations. Two new cities—Lakewood, Washington, and Taylorsville, Utah—had populations of more than 55,000 and 50,000, respectively, when they incorporated.

Like counties, cities are general-purpose units of local government. But unlike counties, they typically have greater decisionmaking authority and discretion. Most states have enacted home rule provisions for cities, although in some states, only cities that have attained a certain population size can exercise this option. (One of the few states without home rule for cities, New Hampshire, sought to provide it through a constitutional amendment in 2000. The measure was defeated by voters.) In addition, cities generally offer a wider array of services to their citizenry than most counties do. Police and fire services, public works, and parks and recreation are standard features, supplemented in some cities by publicly maintained cemeteries, city-owned and -operated housing, city-run docks, and city-constructed convention centers. City government picks up garbage and trash, sweeps streets, inspects restaurants, maintains traffic signals, and plants trees.

City Governmental Structure

City governments operate with one of three structures: a mayor–council form, a city commission form, or a council–manager form. In each structure, an elected governing body, typically called a city council, has policymaking authority. What differentiates the three structures is the manner in which the executive branch is organized.

Mayor–Council Form In the mayor–council form of government, executive functions such as the appointment of department heads are performed by elected officials. This form of government can be subdivided into two types, depending on the formal powers held by the mayor. In a **strong-mayor–council structure,** the mayor is the source of executive leadership. Strong mayors run city hall like governors run the statehouse. They are responsible for daily administrative

incorporation

The creation of a municipality through the granting of a charter from the state.

charter

A document that sets out a city's structure, authority, and functions.

strong-mayor–council structure

The mayor is empowered to perform the executive functions of government and has a veto over city council actions.

activities, the hiring and firing of top-level city officials, and budget preparation. They have a potential veto over council actions. The strong-mayor–council structure grew out of dissatisfaction in the late nineteenth century with the **weak-mayor–council structure.** The weak-mayor–council structure limits the mayor's role to that of executive figurehead. It has its roots in the colonial period of American history. The council (of which the mayor may be a member) is the source of executive power (and legislative power). The council appoints city officials and develops the budget, and the mayor has no veto power. He performs ceremonial tasks such as speaking for the city, chairing council meetings, and attending ribbon-cutting festivities. A structurally weak mayor can emerge as a powerful political figure in the city, but only if he possesses informal sources of power. Figure 10.3 highlights the structural differences between the strong- and weak-mayor–council forms of city government.

weak-mayor–council structure

The mayor lacks formal executive power; the city council (of which the mayor may be a member) is the source of executive and legislative power.

| FIGURE 10.3 | **Mayor–Council Form of Government** |

The primary difference between these two structures concerns the power and authority possessed by the mayor. Strong mayors are more ideally situated to exert influence and control.

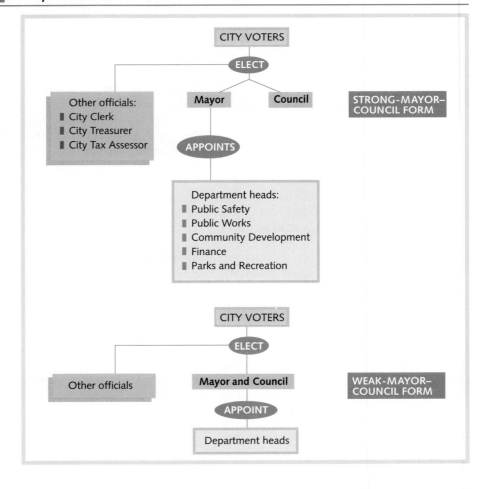

Mayor–council systems are popular both in large cities (where populations are greater than 250,000) and in small cities (with populations under 10,000). In large cities, the clash of conflicting interests requires the leadership of an empowered politician, a strong mayor. In small communities, however, the mayor–council structure is a low-cost, part-time operation. Large cities in which the administrative burdens of the mayor's job are especially heavy have established the position of general manager or chief administrative officer to assist the mayor.

City Commission Form   Under the city commission form of government, illustrated in Figure 10.4, legislative and executive functions are merged. Commissioners not only make policy as members of the city's governing body, they also head the major departments of city government. In other words, they are both policymakers and policy executors. One of the commissioners is designated as mayor simply to preside over commission meetings.

The commission form of government was created as a reaction to the mayor–council structure. Its origins can be traced back to the inability of a mayor–council government in Galveston, Texas, to respond to the chaos caused by a hurricane in 1900 that demolished the city and killed 6,000 people. Bowing to gubernatorial pressure, the Texas legislature authorized the creation of a totally new form of city government—a commission form—and by 1904, the new city government had entirely rebuilt Galveston.[23] The success of the commission led to its adoption first by other Texas cities (Houston, Dallas, Fort Worth) and then, within a decade, by 160 other municipalities (such as Des Moines, Iowa; Pittsburgh, Pennsylvania; Buffalo, New York; Nashville, Tennessee; and Charlotte, North Carolina). Its appeal was its ostensible reduction of politics in city government.

But almost as fast as the commission form of government appeared, disillusionment set in. One problem stemmed from the predictable tendency of commissioners to act as advocates for their own departments. Each commissioner wanted a larger share of the city's budget allocated to his or her department. Another problem had to do with politicians acting as administrators: Elected officials do not always turn out to be good managers. As quickly as it had

| FIGURE 10.4 | **City Commission Form of Government** |

Executive leadership is fragmented under a commission form of government. Each commissioner heads a department; together, they run city hall.

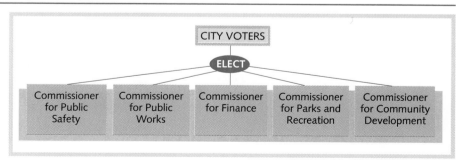

appeared, the commission form declined. By 1990, when Tulsa, Oklahoma, installed a mayor–council form in place of its commission system, only a few cities continued to use a commission structure. Notable among them was Portland, Oregon, with its modified commission form of government.

Council–Manager Form   The third city government structure, the council–manager form, emphasizes the separation of politics (the policymaking activities of the governing body) from administration (the execution of the policies enacted by the governing body). Theoretically, the city council makes policy, and administrators execute policy. Under this structure, the council hires a professional administrator to manage city government. Figure 10.5 illustrates this structure.

city manager

A professional administrator hired by a city council to handle the day-to-day operation of the city.

The administrator (usually called a **city manager**) appoints and removes department heads, oversees service delivery, develops personnel policies, and prepares budget proposals for the council. These responsibilities alone make the manager an important figure in city government. But add the power to make policy recommendations to the city council, and the position becomes even more powerful. When offering policy recommendations to the council, the manager is walking a fine line between politics and administration. Managers who, with the acquiescence of their council, carve out an activist role for themselves may be able to dominate policymaking in city government.[24] In council–manager cities, the two entities typically have a working understanding about how far the manager can venture into the policymaking realm of city government.[25]

FIGURE 10.5	**Council–Manager Form of Government**

The council–manager form of government places administrative responsibility in the hands of a skilled professional. The intent is to make the operation of city government less political.

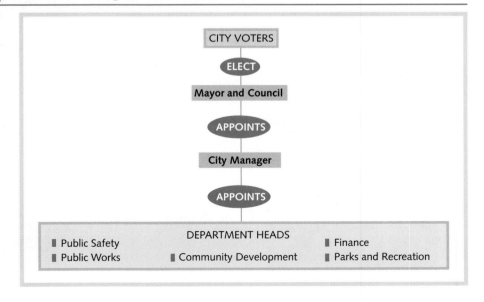

CITY VOTERS

ELECT

Mayor and Council

APPOINTS

City Manager

APPOINTS

DEPARTMENT HEADS

▌ Public Safety   ▌ Finance
▌ Public Works   ▌ Community Development   ▌ Parks and Recreation

Nearly one-half of U.S. cities use the council–manager form of city government. Among cities of 10,000 to 50,000 people, the council–manager structure predominates; it is also popular in homogeneous suburban communities and in the newer cities of the Sunbelt. Examples of large cities with a council–manager structure include Dallas, Phoenix, and San Diego.

Which Form of City Government Is Best?

Experts disagree about which city government structure is best. Most would probably agree that structures lacking a strong executive officer are generally less preferable than others. By that standard, the weak-mayor–council and the commission forms are less favorable. The strong-mayor–council form of government is extolled for fixing accountability firmly in the mayor's office, and the council–manager system is credited with professionalizing city government by bringing in skilled administrators. Yet strong mayor structures are criticized for concentrating power in one office; council–manager forms are taken to task for their depoliticization of city government. Thus, it is up to community residents to decide which form of government they want, and they have been doing just that. As the nearby *Debating Politics* box shows, Miami residents made some changes in their city government that are having a significant impact.

Toledo, Ohio; St. Petersburg, Florida; Fresno, California; and Spokane, Washington, have at least one characteristic in common: During the 1990s, they replaced their council–manager forms with a strong mayor–council structure. Wheeling, West Virginia, recently modified its charter to empower the mayor while retaining its council–manager form; Richmond, Virginia, switched from a weak-mayor structure to a strong-mayor form in 2004. In many other cities, structural reforms such as adding a chief administrative officer to a mayor–council system have created hybrid forms of government.[26] Not all proposed switches meet with success, of course. In Hartford, Connecticut, in 1993 and again in 2000, voters turned down a charter revision that would have empowered the mayor. In places as diverse as Dallas, Texas, and Dayton, Ohio, and in small communities as well, debate over the replacement of existing structures with newer, and hopefully better, ones continues. The best advice may be for a city to use whichever form of government works while remaining receptive to structural improvements.

Pressing Issues for Cities

The pressing issues in city governments these days include planning and land use, annexation, finances, and representation. Although the issues are discussed separately in the following subsections, they are frequently intertwined. For instance, decisions about land use can affect the city's finances; the annexation of new territory may alter representation patterns. Note that county governments also face similar pressures, although from different vantage points.

Planning and Land Use   Land is important to city governments for their economic and political well-being. City governments control land uses within their boundaries, frequently using a comprehensive plan (often called a general or

DEBATING POLITICS

Running Miami Like a Business

In 1997, Miami voters saved their city. Rallied by Hispanic supporters, Miamians turned back an effort to abolish the city and merge its territory with the surrounding county. Had they failed, Miami, a city of 350,000 in its 101st year, would have ceased to exist. It would have been an ignominious end to a proud city.

The Miami story is instructive. Beset by corruption and a $60 million budget deficit, the city was on the ropes in 1996. The city manager, city finance director, two commissioners, and a lobbyist had been indicted in a kickback scheme involving city contracts. (The manager and one commissioner were eventually sentenced to a year in federal prison.) The governor had appointed a financial oversight board to control city spending. Disgusted by these events, the Coalition for a New Miami began a petition drive to do away with the city. If successful, what had been Miami would become an unincorporated part of Dade County. Coalition supporters believed it would mean lower taxes and better local government. The Save Miami Political Action Committee launched a counteroffensive, advertising their anti-abolition message to the group most likely to be receptive to it: Hispanic voters. And the strategy worked: Voters defeated the ballot measure to abolish Miami by a large margin.

Although not inclined to put an end to Miami, voters were interested in redesigning the structure of the city. In that same election, they approved a plan to empower the mayor and to elect city commissioners from districts rather than at large. Since then, there has been some Miami-style political chicanery (a judge voided the mayoral election in 1998 after what he termed "a massive, well-conceived and well-orchestrated absentee ballot voter fraud"), but on the whole, things are looking up in city government. Reformers have been elected to the city commission, including one of the individuals who had founded the Coalition for a New Miami. The mayor, Manny Diaz, elected in 2001, made sweeping changes in the administrative structure of the city and in 2003 brought in a businessperson as city manager. The mayor's charge to the new manager, Joe Arriola, was to run the city like a business. Arriola ousted many of the key department heads in city government and hired replacements from the private sector. Performance measures were created to evaluate city agencies and department heads. The new director of the Department of Community Development, Barbara Gomez-Rodriguez, exemplifies the approach. Taking over an agency mired in debt, she negotiated a favorable loan repayment schedule with the U.S. Department of Housing and Urban Development. To try to get her department on a better financial footing, she has adopted standard business practices (some people might term them hardball tactics) for dealing with individuals and businesses slow to repay city loans. And in an effort to reduce bad debt in the future, she formed an all-volunteer committee of bankers, realtors, and developers to determine which loans should be made.

Miami's changed structure and new personnel have made a difference in a city worn down by scandal. But are business practices and policies effective models for city management? Should American cities be run like businesses? Or, is there something fundamentally different about a municipal corporation?

SOURCES: Peter T. Kilborn, "Miami Area's Mayors Ride a Volatile Political Wave," *New York Times* (April 17, 2000), p. A14; Jonathan Walters, "Miami, Inc.," *Governing* 17 (January 2004), www.governing.com/articles/1miami.htm.

---

master plan) to guide them. The plan typically divides the city into sections for commercial, industrial, and residential uses. In addition, a city might set aside areas for recreation and open space. For example, the general plan for Santa Barbara, California, designates portions of the city for parks, bikeways, and a bird refuge.

New York City enacted the first modern zoning ordinance in 1916; since then, cities have used zoning to effect land-use planning and control. Through zoning, the designations established in a city's plan are made specific. For example, land set aside for residential use may be zoned for single-family dwellings, multifamily units, or mobile homes. Commercial areas may be zoned for offices, shopping centers, or hotels. Industrial sections of the city are often separated into "light" and "heavy" zones. In addition, cities can overlay special zones onto existing ones. For example, cities bent on restoration of older sections of the commercially zoned downtown area may establish historic preservation zones. Once these zones are so designated, property owners are prohibited from tearing down old structures there and, instead, are encouraged to renovate them. A city eager to transform the appearance of a particular area may also create special zones so it can regulate architectural style or the height of buildings and thus achieve the right "look." Undesirable uses, such as pornographic bookstores and XXX theaters, are often clustered together in special adult entertainment zones.

Once set, zoning can be altered through applications for variances and rezoning, usually heard by a city's planning commission. A variance is a waiver of a zoning requirement such as a minimum lot size or a building height limit. Rezoning involves a change in zoning designation, either to allow more intense use of the land (an upzoning) or to restrict use (downzoning). Applications for variances and rezoning are often controversial. A study of fourteen years' worth of applications to upzone parcels in Wilmington, Delaware, demonstrated that community opposition played an important role in the outcome.[27] When community opposition existed, taking such forms as a protest by neighborhood organizations against an upzoning application, 70 percent of the applications failed. When no community opposition emerged, 80 percent of the upzoning requests were approved. Community resistance to the proposed construction of a Wal-Mart superstore in Inglewood, California, is the subject of the nearby *Breaking New Ground* box.

Zoning is ultimately a political exercise with economic consequences. Cities use zoning to promote "good" growth such as upscale residential areas and to limit "bad" growth such as low-income housing.[28] Some cities have engaged in a practice that became known as *exclusionary zoning*. For example, a city might restrict its residential zones to 4,500-square-foot single-family dwellings on five-acre lots. The resulting high cost of housing would effectively limit the potential residents to the wealthy. Court decisions have not only found exclusionary zoning illegal, they have also instructed local governments to engage in inclusionary zoning. The New Jersey supreme court led the way in its *Mount Laurel* decisions, in which municipalities in the state were ordered to provide housing opportunities for low- and moderate-income people. Few states have followed New Jersey's progressive lead, however.

annexation

The addition of unincorporated adjacent territory to a municipality.

Annexation Annexation has been a popular means of adding territory and population. In the past thirty years, many cities have found themselves squeezed by the rapid growth and incorporation of territory just outside city limits and hence beyond their control. What is worse (from a central city's perspective), some of these suburban cities have begun to threaten the central city's traditional dominance of the metropolitan area. People and jobs are finding suburban

BREAKING NEW GROUND

Wal-Mart Versus Inglewood: Score 1 for the City

Inglewood, California, a city of 112,000 in southern California, took on Wal-Mart, the world's largest company, in a battle of mammoth proportions. It began as a typical developer–city council encounter: Wal-Mart, looking for new urban markets to expand into, decided on this well-situated suburb of Los Angeles for its newest superstore. A sixty-acre vacant lot near a racetrack seemed a perfect Wal-Mart location, so the corporation went about getting the necessary approvals from the city for its plan, which also included development of shops and restaurants on the site. Inglewood officials, however, were not willing to give the corporation the go-ahead to build the megastore. The city council had concerns about environmental impact, traffic congestion, labor standards, and the effect on local small businesses. The mayor, however, supported the new commercial complex because of its potential to add jobs and improve the city's tax base.

Not accustomed to hearing "No," Wal-Mart responded to the rebuff by mounting a campaign to take the issue directly to the citizens. The corporation succeeded in collecting enough signatures to get the question on the ballot, and it spent more than $1 million to promote its passage. Legal wrangling over whether an initiative process could be used to usurp the power of the city council to issue building permits brought the California attorney general into the picture. Wal-Mart's public relations firm bombarded city residents with mail, telephone calls, and advertisements on radio and television. Besides touting the new jobs and increased tax revenue, Wal-Mart targeted its appeal to consumers, promising low prices.

Opponents, including organized labor, church groups, and community organizations, fought back. They organized the Coalition for a Better Inglewood, raised money, set up their own "vote no" phone banks, and took their Save Our Community from Wal-Mart campaign door-to-door. They contended that Wal-Mart pays low wages, offers minimal benefits, and fights employee attempts to unionize. They also argued that a Wal-Mart superstore would drain customers from locally owned shops and stores, which would close eventually, creating a net loss of jobs in the community.

The ballot measure would have exempted Wal-Mart from the city's planning, zoning, and environmental regulations. In many senses, it was a test case: If Wal-Mart was successful in Inglewood, it would open the door to similar tactics in other communities resistant to its plans. For example, in Contra Costa County, near San Francisco, voters had overturned a council-passed ordinance that would have banned the construction of superstores. In the end, the opponents of Wal-Mart were victorious in Inglewood: Voters rejected the ballot measure 60.6 to 39.3 percent. Wal-Mart, of course, moved on, searching for jurisdictions that might be a bit more enthusiastic about its presence.

SOURCES: John M. Broder, "Stymied by Politicians, Wal-Mart Turns to Voters," New York Times, nytimes.com (April 5, 2004); Sara Lin and Monte Morin, "Voters in Inglewood Turn Away Wal-Mart," Los Angeles Times, www. latimes.com (April 7, 2004); Stephen Kinzer, "Wal-Mart's Big-City Plans Stall Again," New York Times, nytimes.com (May 6, 2004).

locales to their liking and many have left the central city. To counteract this trend and to ensure adequate space for future expansion, some cities have engaged in annexation efforts. During one six-year period, cities added nearly 3.5 million acres of land via 45,000 annexations.[29]

Not all cities can annex, however. They run up against two realities: the existence of incorporated suburbs (which means the territory cannot be annexed) and the strictures of state laws. State governments determine the legal procedures for the annexation process, and they can make it easy or hard. Texas is a state that makes it easy for cities to annex and, not surprisingly, big Texas cities (in terms of population) have vast territories: Houston covers 580 square miles, San Antonio is 407 square miles, and Dallas is 342 square miles. And they continue to expand. Between 1990 and 2000, Texas cities annexed 1,126 square miles. And it is not just land that is being added—people are added to the total population. For San Antonio, annexations between 1990 and 2000 added 126,000 to the city's population.[30]

extraterritorial jurisdiction (ETJ)

The ability of a city government to control certain practices in an adjacent, unincorporated area.

In Texas, cities use their power of **extraterritorial jurisdiction (ETJ)** to supplement annexation. Under ETJ, they can control subdivision practices in unincorporated bordering territory. (The amount of territory varies from a half-mile for small cities to five miles for cities with over 250,000 people.) A Texas city can annex up to 10 percent of its territory annually without a referendum. The city simply has to provide adequate notice to the about-to-be-annexed residents. Houston has elevated this practice to an art form: It has annexed along major transportation arteries extending out of the city, thereby increasing its ETJ astronomically and reserving for itself vast territories for future annexation.[31]

Some states make it difficult for cities to annex. Cities may have to wait for landowners in an adjoining area to petition to be annexed. In some instances, a city bent on annexation will put pressure on landowners outside the city who use city services such as water or sewerage. Agree to be annexed, they say, or the price of the service may skyrocket or, even worse, the service might be curtailed.[32] Even when a majority of the landowners request annexation, referendum elections must be held if the proportion is less than 75 percent. State law may require that the annexation be approved by referendum by both the existing city and the area to be annexed. This stipulation is known as a dual majority, and it complicates the annexation process.

Some of the most prominent U.S. cities have rather confined city limits. For example, of the fifty most populated cities in the country, twenty-two control fewer than 100 square miles of territory. The most extreme cases are Newark, New Jersey (covering 23.8 square miles); Miami (35.6); Buffalo (40.6); San Francisco (46.4); and Boston (48.4).[33] In the older, established metropolitan areas, a central city has little room to expand because it is hemmed in by incorporated suburbs. Suburban areas incorporate—that is, become legal municipal entities—for many reasons. The threat of being annexed by a neighboring city frequently stimulates the creation of new cities.[34]

Large land grabs and strong-arm tactics have spurred a rethinking of the annexation process in a few states. Both California and Ohio have considered legislation that would empower counties and townships, respectively, as they contend with outreaching cities.[35]

Finances City governments, like other local governments, must balance their fiscal resources against their fiscal needs. Unlike the national government, however, these governments have to operate within the constraints of a balanced budget. As a result, they have become fairly creative at finding new sources of revenue in hard times.

One standard approach is to reduce the rate of growth in operational spending (expenditures related to service provision, such as city employee salaries). Another popular mechanism is to increase the level of fees and charges. For instance, a city might increase the cost of a building permit or charge more for health inspections at restaurants. It can also hike the cost of parking in a metered space or in a city-owned parking garage. (Commuting students at urban colleges with inadequate parking have probably marveled at how adept city officials are at the "make students pay" strategy.) Indeed, cities can boost revenues in several seemingly small ways. A city service that used to be free, such as a city park, may now have an admission fee. Cities can reduce their capital spending (expenditures for big-ticket items such as installation of sewer systems or the purchase of fire engines) and contract out services to private providers, for example, allowing a waste-disposal firm to collect residential garbage or a local charity to take over the operation of homeless shelters.

Cities and other local governments found the financial going tough in the early 2000s. Many faced a revenue-expenditure imbalance—in a negative direction. In 2002, city revenues, on average, grew by 2.2 percent, but city expenditures increased an average of 5.5 percent.[36] The primary explanation for the fiscal stress was the economic downturn, exacerbated by higher costs for city workers' health benefits and reductions in state aid. City governments responded by doing the predictable: increasing fees for services, imposing new fees and charges, reducing the municipal work force, and drawing down reserve funds. Figure 10.6 tracks the changes in city use of various fiscal tools. As these remedies began to take effect, the situation improved slightly in 2003, with revenue growth of 3.8 percent against an expenditure increase of 3.1 percent. The improvement in fiscal conditions should not mask an important reality: Many cities continue to struggle with stagnant local economies and insufficient revenue alternatives. For them, the effort to raise enough money to meet their citizens' needs remains a challenge.

at-large elections
Citywide (or countywide) contests to determine the members of a city council (or county commission).

district (ward) elections
Elections in which the voters in one district or ward of a jurisdiction (city, county, school district) vote for a candidate to represent that district.

reform movement
An early twentieth-century effort to depoliticize local governments through nonpartisan elections, at-large representation, shorter ballots, and professional management.

Representation   Representation in city government is another fundamental concern. How can citizens' preferences be represented effectively in city hall? In the colonial days of town meetings and civic republics, it was simple: A citizen showed up at the meeting hall, voiced his opinion, and the majority ruled. When this procedure proved to be unwieldy, a system of representative democracy seemed the perfect solution.

In city governments, city council members are elected in one of two ways: either at large or by districts (also called wards). In **at-large elections,** a city voter can vote in each council race. In **district (ward) elections,** a city voter can vote only in the council race in her district. From the perspective of candidates, the at-large system means that a citywide campaign must be mounted. With districts, the candidate's campaign is limited to a specific area of the city. As discussed in Chapter 11, the structural **reform movement** during the Progressive Era advocated at-large elections as a means of weakening the geographic base of political machines.[37] Candidates running in citywide races must appeal to a broad cross section of the population to be successful.

FIGURE 10.6 Revenue Actions, 1987–2003

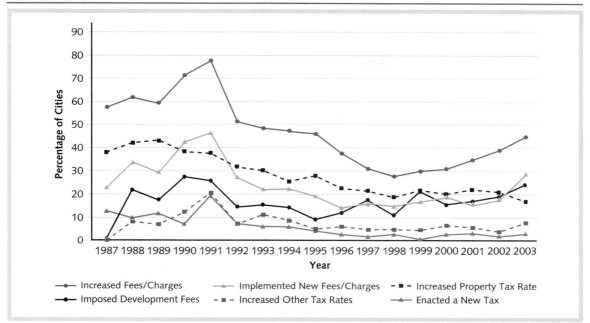

SOURCE: Michael A. Pagano, *City Fiscal Conditions in 2003* (Washington, D.C.: National League of Cities, 2003). Reprinted by permission of National League of Cities.

The use of at-large electoral systems has significant consequences. An in-depth study of almost 1,000 city council members across the country revealed that at-large members tend to be wealthier and more highly educated than council members elected from districts.[38] At-large council members also differ from district members in terms of their relationships with constituents. Council members elected at large devote less time to answering individual complaints and direct their attention to a citywide and business constituency.

Almost half of U.S. cities with populations of 2,500 or more use an at-large method for electing their council members, but the popularity of the method decreases as the size of a city's population increases. For example, only 15 percent of cities with populations above the half-million mark use at-large elections. This approach to city council representation is increasingly under attack for diminishing the likelihood that a member of a minority group can be elected. Research on more than 1,000 southern communities indicated that the abolition of at-large elections resulted in dramatic gains in black representation.[39] And the impact is not confined to the South. When New York City redrew city council district lines and increased the number of seats in 1991, the resulting council was composed of more African Americans and Hispanics than ever before.

Although research on the topic continues, studies have shown that changing the electoral system from at large to districts has other effects such as an overall increase in citizen participation in terms of greater attendance at council meetings, higher voter turnout, and a larger number of candidates.[40] However, these findings are not uniform. For example, a recent study of fifty-seven cities compared voter turnout in the two different electoral systems and found that turnout in at-large elections actually outpaced turnout in district elections by nearly six percentage points.[41] Furthermore, it is not altogether clear that changing to districts will translate into policy benefits for the previously underrepresented sectors of the city. Earlier research suggested that in terms of policy attitudes, there is really no significant difference between council members elected at large and those elected from districts.[42]

cumulative voting

Candidates compete at large and voters can cast as many votes as there are seats to be filled, either as a bloc for one candidate or spread out among several candidates.

Modified at-large voting is seen as an alternative to district elections in jurisdictions where minority candidates have met with electoral defeat. In **cumulative voting,** candidates run at large, and voters cast as many votes as there are seats to be filled. The voter may allocate these votes as he wishes, either as a bloc for one candidate or spread out among the candidates. In a community with a history of racially or ethnically polarized voting, the chance of minority-candidate success increases under a cumulative-voting arrangement. For example, when Alamogordo, New Mexico, adopted cumulative voting in the late 1980s, a Hispanic candidate who would have finished fourth in a standard at-large election placed third in total votes cast.[43] Because three seats were being contested, the difference between a third- and fourth-place finish meant the difference between winning and losing. Due to cumulative voting, Inez Moncada was elected to the Alamogordo city council. Nearly seventy local jurisdictions in four states use a cumulative-voting system.[44]

TOWNS AND TOWNSHIPS

The word *town* evokes an image of a small community where everyone knows everyone else, where government is informal, and where local leaders gather at the coffee shop to make important decisions. This image is both accurate and inaccurate. Towns generally are smaller, in terms of population, than cities or counties. And the extent of their governmental powers depends on state government. But even where they are relatively weak, town government is increasingly becoming more formalized.

How Do We Know a Town When We See One?

Towns and townships are general-purpose units of local government, distinct from county and city governments. Only twenty states, primarily in the Northeast and Midwest, have official towns or townships. In some states, these small jurisdictions have relatively broad powers; in others, they have a more circumscribed role.

town meeting

An annual event at which a town's residents enact ordinances, elect officials, levy taxes, and adopt a budget.

New England towns, for example, offer the kinds of services commonly associated with cities and counties in other states. Many New England towns continue their tradition of direct democracy through a **town meeting** form of government. At a yearly town meeting, residents make decisions on policy matters confronting the community. They elect town officials, pass local ordinances, levy taxes, and adopt a budget. In other words, the people who attend the town meeting function as a legislative body. Although the mechanism of the town meeting exemplifies democracy in action, it often falls short of the ideal, primarily due to the relatively low rate of citizen participation in meetings. Often, fewer than 10 percent of a town's voters attend the meeting. Larger towns in Connecticut and Massachusetts rely on representatives elected by residents to vote at the meetings.

New England towns, along with those in New Jersey, Pennsylvania, and to some degree Michigan, New York, and Wisconsin, enjoy fairly broad powers. In large measure, they act like other general-purpose units of government. In the remainder of the township states (Illinois, Indiana, Kansas, Minnesota, Missouri, Nebraska, North Dakota, Ohio, and South Dakota), the nature of township government is more rural. Rural townships tend to stretch across thirty-six square miles of land (conforming to the surveys done by the national government before the areas were settled), and their service offerings are often limited to roads and law enforcement. A part-time elected board of supervisors or trustees commonly rules the roost in townships. Some of the jobs in government may be staffed by volunteers rather than salaried workers. The closer these rural townships are to large urban areas, however, the more likely they are to offer an expanded set of services to residents.

Townships and the Future

The demise of the township type of government has long been expected. As rural areas become more populated, they will eventually meet the population minimums necessary to become municipalities. In 2000, for instance, residents of a Minnesota township decided to incorporate as a municipality to ward off annexation by a neighboring city.[45] Even in New England, questions of town viability have arisen. For example, many Connecticut towns with populations exceeding 15,000 have found it increasingly difficult to operate effectively through town meetings.[46] Accordingly, some are adding professional managers, whereas others are considering a shift to a strong-mayor form of government. Other towns face a different problem. Many are experiencing substantial population exodus and, in the process, losing their reason for existence. These towns may die a natural death, with other types of government (perhaps counties or special districts) providing services to the remaining residents. The question is: Do towns and townships make sense in contemporary America? Despite dire predictions, towns and townships have proved to be remarkably resilient. The U.S. Census Bureau counted 16,504 towns and townships in 2002, down only 125 from the 1997 figure. Most of the decline came in Midwestern states.

Towns and townships have not been idle while commentators speculated on their dim future. They formed an interest group, the National Association of Towns and Townships (NATaT), to lobby on their behalf in Washington, D.C. NATaT spawned a spinoff organization, the National Center for Small Communities, to provide training and technical assistance to towns. Financially, towns and townships benefited from General Revenue Sharing (GRS) funds distributed by the national government when those funds were still available. Since then, many small towns have embarked on ambitious economic development strategies: industrial recruitment, tourism promotion, and amenity enhancement.[47]

One observer has called for a triage strategy for allocating funds to small towns.[48] This approach would concentrate funds on towns with the prospect of survival, not on those that are either dying or flourishing. Taking a different tack, a political scientist and a state senator in Vermont teamed up to advocate redesigning their state government around a system of reinvigorated towns and regional governments they called *shires*.[49] In fact, they see towns and their grassroots governments as the last hope for democracy in the twenty-first century.

SPECIAL DISTRICTS

public authority

A type of special district funded by nontax revenue and governed by an appointed board.

Special districts are supposed to do what other local governments cannot or will not do. They are established to meet service needs in a particular area. Special districts can be created in three different ways. First, states can create them through special enabling legislation. Second, a general-purpose local government may adopt a resolution establishing a special district. Third, citizens may initiate districts by petition, which is often followed by a referendum on the question. Some districts have the power to levy taxes; others rely on user fees, grants, and private revenue bonds for funding. Taxing districts typically have elected governing boards; nontaxing districts—called **public authorities**—ordinarily operate with appointed boards.[50] The United States has approximately 35,000 special districts, and that number is increasing. In the ten-year period from 1992 to 2002, the number of special districts grew by nearly 3,500. As one might expect, the pattern of special-district creation (and abolition) varies from one state to another. For example, both Illinois and Indiana added 200 new districts from 1992 to 2002, while Maryland and Pennsylvania reduced their numbers.[51]

Not all special districts are organized alike. Ninety-one percent of them provide a single function, but the functions vary. Natural resource management, fire protection, housing and community development, and water and sewer service are the most common. Most states have other, state-specific districts, such as Colorado's mine drainage districts and tunnel districts or Florida's beach and shore preservation districts and mobile home park recreation districts. The budget and staff size of special districts range from minuscule to mammoth. Some of the more prominent include the Port Authority of New York and New Jersey, the Chicago Transit Authority, the Washington Public Power Supply System, and the Los Angeles County Sanitation District. Illinois and California have the highest number of special districts (3,145 and 2,830, respectively). Alaska and Hawaii have the fewest by far, with fourteen and fifteen, respectively.

Are Special Districts Needed?

Special districts overlay existing general-purpose local governments, and some question their necessity. The U.S. Advisory Commission on Intergovernmental Relations (ACIR) puts the question bluntly: "If general-purpose local governments are set up to perform a broad spectrum of functions and if they collectively cover practically every square foot of territory in a state, why [are] special districts needed at all?"[52] The answer has traditionally focused on the deficiencies of general-purpose local governments.[53] Three general categories of "deficiencies" are worth examining: technical conditions, financial constraints, and political explanations.

First are the technical conditions of a general-purpose local government. In some states, cities cannot extend their service districts beyond their boundaries. Moreover, the problem to be addressed may not fit neatly within a single jurisdiction. A river that runs through several counties may periodically overflow its banks in heavy spring rains. The problem affects small portions of many jurisdictions. A flood control district covering only the affected areas may be a logical solution. Problems of scale must also be considered. A general-purpose local government simply may not be able to provide electric service to its residents as efficiently as a special utility district that covers a multitude of counties. Finally, some states prohibit the jurisdictional coventuring that would allow counties to offer services jointly with other counties. For instance, operation of a two-county library requires that a special two-county library district be established.

A second set of deficiencies has to do with financial constraints. Local general-purpose governments commonly operate under debt and tax limitations. Demands for additional services that exceed a jurisdiction's revenue-raising ceiling or lead to the assumption of excessive debt cannot be accommodated. By using special districts, existing jurisdictions can circumvent the debt and tax ceilings. Special districts are better suited than general-purpose governments for service charges or user-fee financing, whereby the cost of the service can be directly apportioned to the consumer (as with water or sewer charges).

Technical and financial deficiencies of general-purpose local governments help to explain the creation of special districts, but political explanations shed even more light. Restrictive annexation laws and county governments with limited authority are political facts of life that encourage the use of special districts. For residents of an urban fringe area, a public-service district (which may provide more than one service) may be the only option. Some special districts owe their existence to a federal mandate. For example, national government policy has spurred the establishment of soil conservation and flood control districts throughout the country.

Once created, a special district may become a political power in its own right. In places where general-purpose governmental units are fully equipped legally, financially, and technically to provide a service, they may encounter resistance from special-district interests fighting to preserve the district.

Concerns About Special Districts

The arguments in favor of special districts revolve around their potential for efficient service provision and the likelihood that they will be responsive to constituents whose demands are not otherwise being met.[54] For the most part, however, scholarly observers look at special districts with a jaundiced eye. The most frequently heard complaint is that special districts lack accountability. The public is often unaware of their existence, so they function free of much scrutiny. And as research by Nancy Burns reminds us, the establishment of special districts is a costly political act.[55] Well-placed groups such as businesses, developers, and home owners' associations are among the beneficiaries of special-district creation. A new study of 100 airport and seaport districts found that those with an elected governing board were no more likely to be responsive to public preferences than those with appointed boards.[56]

One thing is certain: The proliferation of special districts complicates the development of comprehensive solutions to public problems. Consider the case of Harris County, Texas, where Houston is located. It has a grand total of 434 special-purpose districts. The presence of such an array of districts makes it difficult for general-purpose governments to set priorities. It is not uncommon for cities and counties to be locked in governmental combat with the special districts in their area. These governmental units tend to be turf-protecting, service-providing rivals. Special districts may actually drive up the costs of service delivery. A recent study of 300 metropolitan areas found that, compared with general-purpose governments, services provided by special districts have a higher per-capita cost.[57]

Cognizant of these concerns, state governments are looking more closely at special districts and the role they play in service delivery. Several have taken actions that give their general-purpose local governments more input into the state's decision to create special districts.

SCHOOL DISTRICTS

School districts are a type of single-purpose local government. They are a unique kind of special district and, as such, are considered one of the five types of local government. The trend in school districts follows the theory that fewer is better. Before World War II, more than 100,000 school districts covered the countryside. Many of these were rural, one-school operations. In many small towns, community identity was linked to the local schoolhouse. Despite serving as a source of pride, small districts were so expensive to maintain that consolidations occurred throughout the nation, and by 2002 the number of districts was less than 14,000. Nebraska exemplifies the trend. In 1952, there were 6,392 school districts in the state; by 2002, the state had only 575. Currently, the states with the highest number of school districts are Texas (1,089) and California (1,047).

Consolidating schools is a political hot potato, as the governor of Arkansas, Mike Huckabee learned. In 2003, Governor Huckabee proposed a consolidation plan that would eliminate school districts with fewer than 1,500 students.[58] In effect, it was an efficiency issue. The state supreme court had ruled that the school finance system was inequitable and that a remedy had to be designed. Since raising taxes was a political no-no, the governor offered his consolidation plan. However, the governor's plan meant eliminating two-thirds of the school districts in the state and merging them to create larger districts. Folks in the rural, small-town areas of Arkansas were displeased, to put it mildly. Governor

Huckabee's plan made for a lively legislative session in 2004, as lawmakers from affected areas fought to save their school districts.

School Politics

The school board is the formal source of power and authority in the district. The board is typically composed of five to seven members, usually elected in non-partisan, at-large elections. Their job is to make policy for the school district. One of the most important policy decisions involves the district budget—how the money will be spent.

School districts are governed by boards and managed by trained, full-time educational administrators. Like city governments, school districts invested heavily in the reform model of governance, and the average district has become more professional in operation in the past thirty years. An appointed chief administrator (a superintendent) heads the school district staff, the size of which depends on the size of the district. Finding the right person to take on the job of superintendent is crucial. Although some superintendents are home-grown, these days a superintendent's career path today typically takes her from one school system to another. For example, in 2002, Philadelphia's troubled school system hired as its new chief executive the superintendent credited with turning around the public schools in Chicago.[59]

During the 1970s, school districts were criticized for allowing professional experts to seize control of the educational system, thus reducing the governing function of school boards to mere rubber-stamping of administrators' recommendations. This accusation appears to be less true as time passes. The 1980s were a time of rediscovery of public education, leading to a repoliticization of school districts. Since the 1990s, the focus has been on reforming and restructuring public education.[60] Many of the new reforms feature decentralized decisionmaking such as school-based management, some increase the involvement of the private sector, and others enhance the role of parents.

School District Issues

School districts face myriad challenges. The burning issues in school districts range from student test scores to the dropout rate to the food that is served in school cafeterias, but one recurring central issue is finances. Although the relationship is a bit more complex than the old saying "you get what you pay for," it is widely agreed that children in well-funded school districts are better off than those in poorly funded ones.

Serious disparities in school funding, caused by great differences in the property taxes that provide most of the revenue, have led to the increasing financial involvement of state government in local school districts. State governments use an **equalization formula** to distribute funds to school districts in an effort to reduce financial disparities. Under this formula, poorer school districts receive a proportionately larger share of state funds than wealthier districts do. Although these programs have increased the amount of funding for education, they have not eliminated the interdistrict variation. Wealthier districts simply use the state guarantee as a foundation on which to heap their own resources. Poorer school

equalization formula

A means of distributing funds (primarily to school districts) to reduce financial disparities among districts.

districts continue to operate with less revenue. By 1990, this situation had prompted state courts in Montana, Texas, New Jersey, and Kentucky to declare their public-school finance systems unconstitutional. In those states, the legislatures struggled to design new, more equitable financial arrangements. Texas, for example, responded with a controversial property-tax sharing system. Michigan went even further by virtually abolishing property taxes for schools and substituting sales taxes and other revenues. Chapter 15 provides a close look at school administration, innovations in education, and school finances.

COMMUNITIES AND GOVERNANCE

Let us return to the governance issue that was raised early in this chapter and has been alluded to throughout: How do we know when a community is well governed? This chapter is full of examples of communities restructuring their governments in hopes of improving governance. Voters oust incumbents and elect new council members in a similar effort. Conflict over local government spending priorities continues. Local jurisdictions embark on innovative efforts to respond to their citizens' concerns.

A universally accepted set of criteria does not exist for evaluating the quality of governance. But efforts to create one have been made and three are highlighted here: the All-America City, the Government Performance Project, and Well-Governed City Elements. The All-America City designation is bestowed annually by the National Municipal League, a group that started during the reform movement. Only a few communities that embody what the league calls civic energy are selected for the award. Perhaps one key to good governance is energy.

Researchers from the Government Performance Project selected thirty-five major cities and conducted an extensive analysis of their management practices and performance. One category on which cities were graded was managing for results. Researchers wanted to get answers to these questions: Does the city have a well-articulated strategic plan? Does the city actively involve the public in the goal-setting process? Does it monitor its progress and use the results in policymaking? Collecting data from surveys and interviews, the researchers assigned grades to the cities (see Table 10.2).

Only Phoenix received an A; four cities received grades of A−: San Diego, Austin, Indianapolis, and Milwaukee. These five cities have well-developed visions for the future, performance measures and goals are linked, and citizen feedback is sought. At the other end of the grading scale were Buffalo (D+); New Orleans (D+); and Columbus, Ohio (D). These three cities have not had a commitment to strategic planning, they have not made regular use of performance indicators, and they have not engaged citizens sufficiently.[61] One of the likely outcomes of the grading process—which received widespread publicity— is that low-scoring cities will take a cue from their high-scoring counterparts and redouble their efforts.

| TABLE 10.2 | **City Grades: Managing for Results** |

CITY	GRADE
Anchorage	C−
Atlanta	B−
Austin	A−
Baltimore	B
Boston	C+
Buffalo	D+
Chicago	C+
Cleveland	C
Columbus	D
Dallas	B
Denver	B−
Detroit	B−
Honolulu	B
Houston	B−
Indianapolis	A−
Jacksonville	B
Kansas City, Mo.	B−
Long Beach	B−
Los Angeles	C−
Memphis	B−
Milwaukee	A−
Minneapolis	B−
Nashville	C−
New Orleans	D+
New York City	B
Philadelphia	B
Phoenix	A
Richmond	C+
San Antonio	B+
San Diego	A−
San Francisco	C
San Jose	C+
Seattle	B
Virginia Beach	B
Washington, D.C.	C+

SOURCE: "City Grades: Managing for Results," from Katherine Barrett and Richard Greene, "Grading the Cities," *Governing* 13 (February 2000): 36. Copyright © 2000 by Congressional Quarterly, Inc. Reprinted with permission.

Another attempt to isolate characteristics that could be related to governance has settled on seven elements.[62] According to this study, well-governed communities exhibit the following elements:

1. Tranquility among public officials—an absence of squabbles and bloodletting.
2. Continuity in office of top-level managerial officials—a stable corps of administrative personnel.
3. Use of analytical budgeting and planning processes—reliance on comprehensive, multiyear methods.
4. Participative management—less commitment to hierarchical models and more employee-oriented management.
5. Innovativeness—receptivity to new ideas.
6. Active public–private partnerships—a minimization of the traditional barrier between government and the private sector.
7. Citizen input into government decisions—the use of formal mechanisms to increase public involvement in government.

The last four items on the list provide a seedbed for taking a proactive approach. In other words, local governments that listen and experiment are local governments that lead.

The governance question goes back to Plato and Aristotle, and we are unlikely to resolve it here. But the approaches used in identifying All-America cities, in the grades of the Government Performance Project, and in elements of the well-governed city offer some guidance for continued discussion about government structure and function.

CHAPTER RECAP

- Theoretically, communities can be considered civic republics, corporate enterprises, or consumer markets. Legally, there are five types of local governments: counties, municipalities, towns and townships, special districts, and school districts. The United States has more than 87,800 local governments.
- Counties were created by states to serve as their local administrative extensions. Over time, they have taken on more functions and, especially in urban areas, they provide municipal-type services.
- The United States has more than 19,000 municipalities, or cities. The strong-mayor–council form of city government invests power in an elected mayor; the council–manager structure relies heavily on a professional administrator to run the city. The issue about which structure is better instigates much debate.
- Towns and townships are general-purpose local governments, like counties and cities. Twenty states, primarily in the Northeast and Midwest, have official towns or townships. Some have fairly broad powers; others, especially rural midwestern townships, offer more limited services. Many have predicted that towns and townships will gradually disappear as the nation urbanizes.

- Special districts are the most prevalent and at the same time the least under-stood of the five types of local government. They provide a service to an area that other local governments do not provide because of technical, financial, or political considerations. Natural resource management, fire protection, housing and community development, and water and sewer service are the most common special districts. Their financing varies: Some have the power to tax; others rely on user fees, grants, or bonds.

- The number of school districts has declined, because of mergers and consol-idations, to a current level of less than 13,000. School districts are typically governed by elected boards and managed by trained, full-time educational administrators. School politics can create rivalries as issues such as parental choice, neighborhood schools, and effective financing are debated.

- The public wants well-governed communities. Local governments redesign their structures in the hope of improving governance. Analysts continue to develop criteria such as managing for results in an effort to identify the best-performing localities.

Key Terms

metropolitan area *(p. 274)*

general-purpose local government *(p. 274)*

single-purpose local government *(p. 274)*

home rule *(p. 276)*

incorporation *(p. 281)*

charter *(p. 281)*

strong-mayor–council structure *(p. 281)*

weak-mayor–council structure *(p. 282)*

city manager *(p. 284)*

annexation *(p. 287)*

extraterritorial jurisdiction (ETJ) *(p. 289)*

at-large elections *(p. 290)*

district (ward) elections *(p. 290)*

reform movement *(p. 290)*

cumulative voting *(p. 292)*

town meeting *(p. 292)*

public authority *(p. 294)*

equalization formula *(p. 297)*

Surfing the Web

Most of the five types of government are represented by national associations, which have web sites: **www.naco.org** (National Association of Counties); **www.nlc.org** (National League of Cities); **www.natat.org** (National Associa-tion of Towns and Townships); **www.nsba.org** (for school districts, the relevant web site is that of the National School Boards Association).

To explore a specific school district, see **www.philsch.k12.pa.us** (the web site of the City of Philadelphia school district).

Special districts, by virtue of their specialized nature, tend to have function-specific national organizations. For example, the National Association of Conservation Districts can be found at **www.nacdnet.org.** A fifteen-county district, the Col-orado River Water Conservation District, whose web site can be found at **www. crwcd.gov,** is an example of an individual special district. The web site of one of the most famous special districts, the Port Authority of New York and New Jersey, is **www.panynj.gov.**

Over time, cities and counties have found that maintaining web sites is a good way to connect with the public. See the web site for Miami–Dade County at **www.miamidade.gov.** The web site for the city of Los Angeles can be found at **www.ci.la.ca.us;** the web site for the county can be found at **lacounty.info.** The web site for the largest county in Michigan is **www.waynecounty.com.**

You can find information about the Big Apple at **www.nyc.gov; www. cityofhouston.gov** and **www.cityofboston.gov** are web sites for the cities of Houston and Boston, respectively.

11

LOCAL LEADERSHIP AND GOVERNANCE

Community Power
The Elite Theory • The Pluralist Theory • New Haven: Is It All in the Approach? •
The Dynamics of Power

Local Executives
Mayors • City Managers

Local Legislatures
City Council Members: Old and New • Council Diversity • Councils in Action:
Increasing Conflict • Women on Local Governing Boards

Leadership and Capacity

A few years back, an article in the magazine *Governing* had a particularly provocative title: "Nobody in Charge."[1] The story went on to detail several examples of failed leadership in city governments such as those of Kansas City, Missouri; Cincinnati, Ohio; and Dallas, Texas. In each instance, the explanation was the same: the fragmentation of power. In such circumstances, elected and appointed officials vie for control in governmental structures that divide responsibility. The Kansas City case is illustrative. The mayor there had one priority, the city council had another, and the city manager still another. Moving in several directions, the city was essentially not moving at all. In Cincinnati, the city was said to bounce "from problem to problem," making "city government . . . a reactionary body rather than a proactive body."[2] And in Dallas, the replacement of at-large city council elections with a district system produced a highly factionalized, gridlocked council. These examples point to the importance of leadership in local government, or more precisely to the challenge of governance in its absence.

Leadership goes hand in hand with governance. It can make the difference between an effectively functioning government and one that lurches from one crisis to another. The terms that conjure up images of leadership in local government circles these days include *initiative, inventiveness, risk-taking, high energy level, persistence, entrepreneurship, innovation,* and *vision.* These words share a common element: They denote activity and engagement. Leaders are people who "make a difference."[3]

One of the popular labels for contemporary leaders is *entrepreneur.* How do you know an entrepreneurial leader when you see one in local government? You can identify such leaders by their advocacy of innovative ideas. They are the people "who actively seek opportunities for dynamic changes in policy or politics."[4] Some may occupy positions of power in local government; others may emerge from the ranks of ordinary citizens. Regardless of their background, they share a commitment to new ideas and a willingness to take risks. The spirit of entrepreneurialism is not limited to individuals—communities exhibit leadership too. At some point, on some issue, a jurisdiction may try something new; it may "think outside the box." Leading cities become models for other cities.

COMMUNITY POWER

Real questions about who is running the show in local government do arise. At the risk of sounding naive, we might suggest that "the people" run government; however, much of the evidence can persuade us otherwise. But we should not become too cynical, either. Citizen preferences do have an impact on public policy decisions.[5] Can we assume, therefore, that those who occupy important elected positions in government, such as the mayor and the city council, are in fact in charge? Are they the leaders of the community? These questions have interested scholars for a long time.

In sorting through the issue of who's running the show, we find that two theories predominate. One, the **elite theory,** argues that a small group of leaders called an elite possesses power and rules society. Conversely, the **pluralist theory** posits that power is dispersed among competing groups whose clashes produce societal rule.

The Elite Theory

One of the earliest expositions of the elite theory argued that any society, from underdeveloped to advanced, has two classes of people: a small set who rule and a large clump who are ruled.[6] The rulers allocate values for society and determine the rules of the game; the ruled tend to be passive and ill informed and cannot exercise any direct influence over the rulers. This division is reflected elsewhere in society. In organizations, for example, power is inevitably concentrated in the hands of a few people.[7] Given the pervasiveness of elite systems, should we expect decisionmaking in communities to be any different?

A famous study of power in the community given the name of Middletown (actually Muncie, Indiana) in the 1920s and 1930s discovered an identifiable set of rulers.[8] The researchers, sociologists Robert and Helen Lynd, determined that Family X (the Ball family) was at the core of this ruling elite. Through their

elite theory

A theory of government that asserts that a small group possesses power and rules society.

pluralist theory

A theory of government that asserts that multiple, open, competing groups possess power and rule society.

economic power, Family X and a small group of business leaders called the shots in Middletown. Government officials simply did the bidding of Family X and its cohorts.

Another widely read study of community power confirmed the basic tenets of elitism. Sociologist Floyd Hunter's study of Regional City (Atlanta, Georgia) in the 1950s and his follow-up research in the 1970s identified the top leadership— a forty-person economic elite—who dominated the local political system.[9] Hunter argued that an individual's power in Regional City was determined by his role in the local economy. Local elected officials simply carried out the policy decisions of the elite. To illustrate this point, Hunter compared the relatively limited power enjoyed by the mayor of Atlanta to the extensive power possessed by the president of a firm headquartered in Regional City, Coca-Cola.[10]

Assume for a moment that the elitist interpretations of community power are accurate; where do these interpretations take us? Do not be confused about the intent of an economic elite: They are not running the community out of a sense of benevolence. The following statement captures the larger meaning of elitism: "Virtually all U.S. cities are dominated by a small, parochial elite whose members have business or professional interests that are linked to local development and growth. These elites use public authority and private power as a means to stimulate economic development and thus enhance their own local business interests."[11] To many, this conclusion is disturbing.

The Pluralist Theory

The findings of the studies discussed above did not square with the prevailing orthodoxy of American political science: pluralism. Not everyone saw community power through the elitist lens, and many questioned whether the findings from Middletown and Regional City applied to other communities.

Pluralist theory views the decisionmaking process as one of bargaining, accommodation, and compromise. According to this view, no monolithic entity calls the shots; instead, authority is fragmented. Many leadership groups can become involved in decisionmaking, depending on the nature and importance of the issue at hand. Granted, the size, cohesion, and wealth of these groups vary, but no group has a monopoly on resources. Pluralism sets forth a much more accessible system of community decisionmaking than the grimly deterministic tenets of elitism do.

A study conducted by Robert Dahl in New Haven, Connecticut, challenged the sociologists' findings, particularly those of Hunter.[12] According to Dahl, decisions in New Haven in the 1950s were the product of the interactions of a system of groups with more than one center of power. Except for the mayor, a single leader was not influential across a series of issue areas, and influential actors were not drawn from a single segment of the community.

Further explication of the pluralist model revealed that, although community decisionmaking is limited to relatively few actors, the legitimacy of such a system hinges on the easily revoked consent of a much larger segment of the local population.[13] In other words, the masses may acquiesce to the leaders, but they can also speak up when they are displeased. Success in a pluralistic environment is determined by a group's ability to form coalitions with other groups. Pluralism, then, offers a more hopeful interpretation of community power.

New Haven: Is It All in the Approach?

New Haven, the setting for Dahl's affirmation of pluralist theory, has been examined and reexamined by skeptical researchers. Some of the debate between elitists and pluralists is a function of methodology—that is, the particular approach used in studying community power. Sociologists have tended to rely on what is called a **reputational approach,** whereby they go into a community and ask informants to name and rank the local leaders. Those whose names appear repeatedly are considered to be the movers and shakers. This approach is criticized on the grounds that it measures not leadership per se but the reputation for leadership. Political scientists approach the power question differently, through a **decisional method.** They focus on specific community issues and, using various sources, try to determine who is influential in the decisionmaking process. It is easy to see that the two different approaches can produce divergent findings.

Users of the decisional method claim that it allows them to identify overt power rather than just power potential.[14] In addition, it offers a realistic picture of power relationships as dynamic rather than fixed. Critics of the decisional method argue that when researchers select key issues to examine, they are being arbitrary. Also, a study of decisionmaking may ignore the most powerful actors in a community—those who can keep issues *off* the agenda, who are influential enough to keep certain issues submerged.[15] Table 11.1 reports the perceptions of members of a wide variety of citizen groups in seven large cities. Although 43 percent agree that business groups get what they want, their responses suggest, on balance, a relatively open local political system. In their view, city officials pay attention to interest groups and their demands.[16]

reputational approach

A method for studying community power in which researchers ask informants to name and rank influential individuals.

decisional method

A method for studying community power in which researchers identify key issues and the individuals who are active in the decisionmaking process.

TABLE 11.1	Citizen Groups' Assessment of Big City Politics

STATEMENT	PERCENTAGE AGREEING THAT THE STATEMENT IS A "GOOD" DESCRIPTION OF LOCAL POLITICS
Interest groups are active in city politics.	60
Business groups get what they want.	43
Elected officials oppose the aims of this organization.	39
Conflict erupts often in the policy area in which this organization is active.	32
Policy area in which this organization is active is marked by consensus.	25
City officials need not worry about interest groups.	10

NOTE: Members of a wide range of citizen groups in seven large cities were surveyed.
SOURCE: Adapted from Christopher A. Cooper and Anthony J. Nownes, "Citizen Groups in Big City Politics," *State and Local Government Review* 35 (Spring 2003): 109.

New Haven was found by Dahl to be a pluralist's delight. Convinced that the finding was affected by Dahl's methods, another researcher, G. William Domhoff, examined New Haven and emerged with a contrary view of the power structure.[17] He claimed that Dahl missed the big picture by focusing on issues that were of minor concern to the New Haven elite, and that Dahl's finding of an accessible decisionmaking process in which many groups were involved was not an adequate test of the presence of an elite. Domhoff investigated the urban redevelopment issue and discovered that the long-time mayor, whom Dahl had seen as leading an executive-centered coalition, was in fact being actively manipulated by a cadre of local business leaders. Domhoff contended that New Haven was not quite the pluralistic paradise it was made out to be.

The Dynamics of Power

The work of Hunter and that of Dahl remain significant, but neither elitism nor pluralism adequately explains who's running the show. In fact, some observers claim that "no single descriptive statement applies to community leadership in general in the United States today."[18] Not all communities are organized alike; even within a single community, power arrangements shift as time passes and conditions change. One group of political scientists, Robert Agger, Daniel Goldrich, and Bert Swanson, has argued that an understanding of community power requires an assessment of two variables: the means by which power is distributed to the citizens and the extent to which ideological unity exists among the political leaders.[19]

The effort of a Chicago growth coalition to promote the 1992 World's Fair offers an instructive example of how the power structure sometimes loses.[20] The 1992 Fair Corporation, a well-connected nonprofit group of economically powerful and socially prominent people, wanted to bring the 1992 World's Fair to Chicago. A world's fair produces value for a community, secondarily from the show and spectacle, but primarily because of the long-term development consequences. To bring the fair to Chicago, the group had to convince the city's political leadership of the event's importance. They were in the process of doing so when the political dynamics suddenly changed. A supportive mayor, Jane Byrne, was defeated, and the new mayor, Harold Washington, was indifferent to the project. The change in mayoral enthusiasm for the project was just the wedge that opponents of the fair needed. In the words of one commentator, "Chicago's new reform-minded black mayor and more open city council gave legitimacy to Fair critics."[21] Grassroots and political opposition intensified. Eventually, enough questions were raised that the state legislature refused to allocate the funds necessary to continue planning for the fair, and the 1992 Fair Corporation was forced to admit defeat. In this instance, power had shifted to a temporary coalition of forces.

Regime Theory   If the elite can be beaten in Chicago, is pluralism likely to triumph in communities across the land? Probably not. The penetration of the government's domain by private economic interests in American communities is deep.[22] Consequently, to understand the dynamics of power in a community,

regime

The informal arrangements that surround and complement the formal workings of governmental authority.

one must look to the **regime.** Political scientist Clarence Stone defines regime as "the informal arrangements that surround and complement the formal workings of governmental authority."[23] Stone uses the concepts of *systemic power* and *strategic advantage* to explain why community decisions so frequently favor upper-stratum interests.[24]

The starting point of his argument is that public officials operate in a highly stratified socioeconomic system with a small upper class; a large, varied middle class; and a relatively small lower class. According to Stone, "Public officeholders are predisposed to interact with and to favor those who can reciprocate benefits."[25] Two considerations define the environment in which public officials operate: electoral accountability (keeping the majority of the public satisfied) and systemic power (the unequal distribution of economic, organizational, and social resources). Decisionmakers are likely to side with majority preferences on highly visible issues, but on less visible ones, the possessors of systemic power—the upper stratum—will win most of the time. With their superior resources, they can set the agenda in the community and instigate (or block) change. In other words, they enjoy a strategic advantage. The nearby *Debating Politics* box focuses on an unusual source of power and influence in one southern community.

nonprofit organizations

Private sector groups that carry out charitable, educational, religious, literary, or scientific functions.

Nonprofit Organizations as Power Players   **Nonprofit** organizations have become increasingly important in communities. Many of these organizations have become fully integrated into the world of local government and politics. Four types of governmentally active nonprofit organizations can be identified:

- Civic nonprofits.
- Policy advocates.
- Policy implementers.
- Governing nonprofits.[26]

The first type, civic nonprofit organizations, plays a watchdog role, monitoring government and educating the public. A local citizen's league acts in this way, attending city council meetings and publicizing council decisions. Policy advocates, the second type, move beyond the provision of information to become active supporters of particular policies or programs. For instance, if an education advocacy group endorses year-round schools, it would lobby the school board vigorously in support of such a policy change. The third type of nonprofit organization, policy implementers, actually delivers services, often through a contract with a local government. For example, homeless shelters in many communities are operated by nonprofit groups supported by city funds, federal grants, and charitable contributions. Governing nonprofits, the fourth type, are different because they may work through or with local government but they also act independently. These nonprofits are the most powerful of the four types because they offer an alternative venue for decisionmaking. Chicago's 1992 Fair Corporation, discussed earlier, played this role with mixed results. Nonprofit organizations of all types have become omnipresent in localities throughout the nation.

Have nonprofit organizations upset community power structures? Policy advocates and governing nonprofits have the potential to reset agendas and effect real

DEBATING POLITICS

Who's Got the Power?

It all seemed so routine: a local hospital petitioning county government for permission to expand its facilities. But among the many opponents of the expansion attending the hearing was one unusual activist: Michael Stipe, lead singer for the band R.E.M. His presence at the hearing was one of several efforts by the band to block the hospital's plan. The band had made donations to a grassroots opposition group, Citizens for Healthy Neighborhoods (CHN) and had volunteered to foot the group's legal bills related to stopping the hospital.

The band's interest in local politics is both welcomed and resented in Athens-Clarke County, Georgia. Those who are on the same side of political disputes as the band are delighted with the musicians' activism. Those on the other side see the band as a big bully. R.E.M. was formed in Athens and played its first gigs there. The band's world headquarters are in the city and two members of R.E.M. still live in the Athens area. Driving their activism is their interest in preserving what they consider to be the special qualities of the community. Athenians who are more supportive of growth and development contend that the band is too aggressive in pursuing its agenda. In the case of the hospital expansion, both sides got some of what they wanted,

but not all. CHN was not able to stop the hospital's expansion but it was able to wrest some concessions. Under the hospital's revised plan, only ten homes would be razed, not sixty as originally proposed, historic buildings would be preserved, and the impact of traffic changes would be minimized.

Lead singer Stipe argues that the band acts as a check on the good-old-boy network of conservative politicians and developers. Their clashes are most intense when the issue on the table is historic preservation or environmental protection. R.E.M.'s wealth and reputation give it standing in the community. Many Athenians are less enthusiastic, however, about the band's role in local politics, especially its support of liberal causes. One of the Republicans on the city–county governing board put it this way: "The average citizen does not realize how much funding R.E.M. has put into political campaigns in Athens." She continued, "They have an attitude of ultimately trying to control what happens in Athens government." That's what community power is all about. All places have their own set of interest groups; seldom, however, do they include world-famous rock bands. Is R.E.M. a bully or a savior in local politics in Athens?

SOURCES: Tom Lasseter, "Rock Group Takes on Ga. Town's Political Network," *The State* (July 25, 1999), p. A15; Deborah G. Martin, "Reconstructing Urban Politics: Neighborhood Activism in Land-Use Change," *Urban Affairs Review* 39 (May 2004): 589–612.

---

change. Research on the city of Detroit offers some insight into the long-term impact of nonprofit organizations. Richard Hula and Cynthia Jackson-Elmoore studied the influence of two nonprofits created in the aftermath of Detroit's civil disturbances of the late 1960s.[27] For more than thirty years, these organizations, New Detroit and Detroit Renaissance, have been important players in the city's politics. Although they had a similar genesis—"both were born as an elite response to and fear of civil unrest"[28]— their styles and foci have varied. New Detroit has more of a social agenda, focusing on race relations and education reform. Detroit Renaissance, a smaller organization made up of the corporate elite from the Detroit area, has concentrated its energies on economic renewal. Both organizations have been active on the Detroit scene, advocating ambitious reforms and new policies over three decades. And although both organizations have enjoyed some successes, neither has been able to transform the local political agenda. Yet Hula and Jackson-Elmoore contend that the presence of New Detroit and Detroit Renaissance has had an important catalytic effect. When nonprofits join with local elected leaders, their impact increases. In other words, to become power players, nonprofit organizations must become part of the regime.

Hyperpluralism   The final word on community power structures has not been written. What is certain is that some interests, especially those of the economically powerful, seem to prevail more often than others. Two North Carolina cities provide contrasting examples. In Charlotte, the business elite drives broad-scale change in local education policy.[29] In Durham, four citizen groups with different ideologies and different racial compositions vie for influence in local education policy.[30] Different communities have developed different arrangements for governance. In some places, weak political leadership and a dispersed business elite have resulted in a condition called **hyperpluralism.** In hyperpluralistic communities, where many interests clash, competing groups cannot form coalitions. As a consequence, public policy may become incoherent and increasingly ineffective. In the 1990s, New Orleans, Philadelphia, and San Francisco were among the cities exhibiting signs of hyperpluralism.[31] The question of who's in charge remains an interesting one.

hyperpluralism

A condition characterized by a large number of groups and interests.

LOCAL EXECUTIVES

The mantle of leadership in local government falls most often on chief executives: mayors and managers. Although it is possible for chief executives to eschew a leadership role, they rarely do.

Mayors

Mayors tend to be the most prominent figures in city government primarily because their position automatically makes them the center of attention. Occasionally a city council member emerges as a leader on a specific issue or stirs up some interest with verbal attacks on the mayor (which many observers interpret as jockeying for position to run against the mayor at the next election). But for the most part, attention is drawn to the mayor.

A lot is expected of the mayor. In 2004, the city comptroller of New York described the incumbent mayor, Michael Bloomberg, positively: "He's hired a very talented group. He's run city services well. He's approached things in a balanced fashion." However, the comptroller continued. "But the mayor is not just a CEO. The mayor is an emotional leader, an inspirational leader, and in that regard I don't think he's done nearly as good a job."[32] A similar theme was echoed by Los Angeles City Councilman Bernard Parks as he mulled a bid for Mayor James Hahn's post. "There is a vacuum in leadership. This is a big city, a thriving city. The mayor's office doesn't make you a leader. You have to have a leader in the mayor's office."[33]

Differences Between Strong and Weak Mayors Chapter 10 explained some of the differences between strong and weak mayors. It is important to note that these labels *refer to the position,* not to the person who occupies it. A structure simply creates opportunities for leadership, not the certainty of it. True leaders are those who can take what is structurally a weak-mayor position and transform it into a strong mayorship. Some mayor–council systems have added a chief administrative officer to their structures, thus blurring the distinction between them and council–manager systems.[34]

A *strong-mayor* structure establishes the mayor as the sole chief executive who exercises substantive policy responsibilities. In this kind of structure, the position of city manager, someone who can expand an administrative role and become a policy rival to the mayor, does not exist. As an ideal type, a strong mayor is elected directly by the voters, not selected by the council; serves a four-year, not two-year, term of office; and has no limitations on re-election. She also has a central role in budget formulation, extensive appointment and removal powers, and veto power over council-enacted ordinances. The actual powers of a specific strong mayor may not include all these items, of course. The mayor of New York City, for instance, is a strong-mayor position but has a two-term limit and shares some appointment power with the city council. The more of these powers a mayor can exercise, the stronger her position is and the easier it is for her to become a leader.

A *weak-mayor* structure does not provide these elements. Its design is such that the mayor shares policy responsibilities with the council and perhaps a manager, and serves a limited amount of time in office. (In an especially weak-mayor system, the job is passed around among the council members, each of whom takes a turn at being mayor.) A weak-mayor structure often implies strong council involvement in budgetary and personnel matters. The variation in mayoral power is reflected in the mayors' remuneration—weak mayors receive token salaries. If a mayor in a weak-mayor structure is to become a leader, he has to exceed the job description.

Mayoral leadership was the subject of a recent discussion in the popular press.[35] An article entitled "The Lure of the Strong Mayor" argued that large, diverse communities grappling with complex problems are better served by a structure that fixes leadership and accountability in the mayor's office. In response, "Beware the Lure of the 'Strong' Mayor" contended that a too-powerful mayor could run amok, building political machines based on the exchange of benefits. Structural differences can indeed have consequences. It is important to remember, however, that individuals who work within structures are the essential factor. Leaders can make structures work for them (sometimes by performing minor surgery on the structure). As David Morgan and Sheilah Watson note, "Even in council–manager communities—where mayors have the fewest formal powers—by negotiating, networking, and facilitating the efforts of others, mayors clearly rise above the nominal figurehead role."[36] Consider the comment made by the mayor of Rochester, New York, a city that switched from a council–manager system to a strong-mayor form: "The bottom line is good people committed to good governance."[37]

Black Mayors   Black mayors were interesting in the past simply because there were so few of them, but today they are no longer rare. By the 1990s, black mayors headed more than 375 cities and towns across the country. (Approximately eighty are women.) Not only can you find black mayors leading cities where the population is predominantly black, you can find them in majority white cities, too. African American mayors remain a topic of discussion because of the different nature of the challenge they confront and the subtle shift in their orientation to it. Called by some scholars a new generation, these mayors consider themselves problem solvers, not crusaders; political pragmatists, not ideologues.[38]

For new-generation African American mayors, the focus tends to be citywide development issues rather than civil rights and empowerment of minorities.[39] According to Richard Arrington, former mayor of Birmingham, Alabama, "What black voters want now is a chunk of the city's commercial and economic development boom."[40] In many cities, new-generation black mayors have built coalitions among white voters so they can make a successful bid for public office. Table 11.2 lists big-city black mayors and the total percentage of the black population in the cities they lead.

Increased success by blacks in mayoral elections has led some observers to talk of **deracialization,** or the de-emphasis of race as a campaign issue in an effort to attract white voter support.[41] Instead of making racial appeals, candidates offer a race-neutral platform that stresses their personal qualifications and political experience.[42] In cities where the white electorate outnumbers the black electorate,

deracialization

The de-emphasis of race in politics, especially in campaigns, so that there is less racial bloc voting.

TABLE 11.2   Black Mayors in Big Cities, 2004

CITY*	BLACKS AS A PERCENTAGE OF CITY POPULATION	MAYOR
Philadelphia, PA	43.2	John Street
Detroit, MI	81.6	Kwame Kilpatrick
Columbus, OH	24.5	Michael Coleman
Memphis, TN	61.4	Willie Herenton
Washington, D.C.	60.0	Anthony Williams
New Orleans, LA	67.3	C. Ray Nagin
Atlanta, GA	61.4	Shirley Franklin
Toledo, OH	23.5	Jack Ford
Newark, NJ	53.5	Sharpe James
Birmingham, AL	73.5	Bernard Kincaid
Jersey City, NJ	28.3	Glenn Cunningham
Rochester, NY	38.5	William Johnson

*Cities with populations of 200,000 or more, listed in descending order according to size.
SOURCE: National Conference of Black Mayors, Atlanta, Ga., www.ncbm.org/50k_mayors.htm. Reprinted by permission of the National Conference of Black Mayors.

such as Columbus and Toledo (both in Ohio), neither Michael Coleman nor Jack Ford could have been elected without the support of white voters. Even in cities where white voters constitute a minority, they often control the electoral balance when two African American candidates square off in the mayoral race.

Deracialization works both ways. Some cities that have had African American mayors for many years have recently elected white candidates to the office. Gary, Indiana, which in 1967 was one of the first large cities to elect a black mayor, elected a white mayor three decades later. Baltimore, Maryland, led by an African American mayor for nearly fifteen years, elected a white mayor in 1999. Oakland, California (the subject of the *Breaking New Ground* box later in this chapter), has done the same. To win, white candidates in predominantly black cities have run campaigns focused mostly on service delivery, promising better services and lower costs.[43] Deracialization of local campaigns, and the manner in which a mayor elected by a multiracial coalition governs once in office, are compelling subjects for future research.

Do African Americans reap any economic benefits when a black mayor is governing the city? An earlier study has shown that the presence of a black mayor leads to increased minority employment in city government.[44] Later research suggests that the impact carries over into the private sector. Statistical analysis of twenty-eight large metropolitan areas indicated that black-owned firms in cities with black mayors fared better in the 1980s than black-owned firms in cities without a black mayor. The firms had higher total revenues, greater average sales revenues, and lower rates of business failure than their counterparts.[45]

Women Mayors More women are running for and winning local elective offices. The data from cities with populations of 30,000 or more are instructive. In 1973, fewer than 2 percent of the cities in that population range had female mayors. A quarter century later, the number of women mayors had increased to 202, or 21 percent, a level around which it has fluctuated. Fourteen women are at the helm of large U.S. cities (populations of 200,000 or more), as Table 11.3 shows.

Recent studies of female mayoral candidates have dispelled several electoral myths. For example, women do not appear to experience greater difficulty in raising money or gaining newspaper endorsements than men do.[46] Women mayors, however, do tend to be political novices. Few female mayors in Florida, for instance, had held elective office before their mayoral election; if they had, it was usually a city council seat. Other research indicates that mayors, regardless of gender, see their political environments similarly, which makes sense: Successful local politicians know their communities.

Sharon Sayles Belton, the female African American mayor of Minneapolis, Minnesota, offers an instructive story. In her first campaign for mayor in 1993, she crafted a platform that appealed to a broad spectrum of the electorate, regardless of sex or race. She cruised to victory with no discernible gender gap, and with 91 percent of the black vote and 67 percent of the white vote. However, rising crime rates and declining student test scores led to some dissatisfaction with her toward the end of her first term. In her bid for re-election in 1997, she faced a former city councilwoman—a white female Republican—who had

| TABLE 11.3 | Women Mayors in Big Cities, 2004 |

CITY*	MAYOR
Dallas, TX	Laura Miller
Portland, OR	Vera Katz
Cleveland, OH	Jane Campbell
Long Beach, CA	Beverly O'Neill
Kansas City, MO	Kay Barnes
Virginia Beach, VA	Meyera Oberndorf
Atlanta, GA	Shirley Franklin
Sacramento, CA	Heather Fargo
Tampa, FL	Pam Iorio
Lexington, KY	Teresa Isaac
Lincoln, NE	Coleen Seng
Plano, TX	Pat Evans
Glendale, AZ	Elaine Scruggs
Scottsdale, AZ	Mary Manross

*Cities with populations of 200,000 or more, listed in descending order according to size.
SOURCE: Center for American Women and Politics, "Fact Sheet: Women in Elective Office 2004,"
www.cawp.rutgers.edu/Facts/Officeholders/elective.pdf (May 25, 2004).

become a radio talk-show host. A tough campaign ensued, one with "unmistakable racial overtones," according to some analysts, but Mayor Sayles Belton won with 55 percent of the vote.[47] By 2001, when she ran for a third term, the bloom was off the rose. Minneapolis voters were in the mood for change, and Mayor Sayles Belton received only 35 percent of the vote, losing to political novice R. T. Rybak.[48]

Visionary Mayors For mayors to become leaders, they need to have vision; that is, they need the ability to identify goals for their city and achieve them, which is easier said than done. Three former mayors widely hailed as visionary when they were in office put their heads together recently to come up with a how-to list.[49] Their rules for creating and implementing successful city visions included several obvious items such as "borrow from everyone" and "build on existing strengths." But it also instructed mayors to market their vision on a human scale so that local residents and business interests can understand its relevance to them. Getting cooperation from the community goes a long way in bolstering mayoral leadership. But the immediate tasks of keeping the city running smoothly can cause some mayors to lose sight of the vision or, at the least, put it aside as they worry about potholes, garbage collection, and budget deficits.

Some have argued that the 1990s produced some of the most talented mayors ever to serve in the office. The mayor of New Orleans during that time, Marc Morial, contends that successful mayors blend vision with communications skills and, even more important, an ability to get results. With regard to the last item, it does not hurt for a mayor to surround him- or herself with talented people who share the vision. As a former Dallas mayor commented, "Mayors work in real time. You have to limit your agenda to the big stuff."[50]

City Managers

Progressive Era

A period in the early twentieth century that focused on reforming or cleaning up government.

City managers (as well as county administrators and appointed school superintendents) exemplify the movement toward reformed local government. Local government reform was a **Progressive Era** movement that sought to depose the corrupt and inefficient partisan political machines that controlled many American cities. To the reformers, local government had become too political; what was needed, they believed, was a government designed along the lines of a business corporation. To achieve their goals, reformers advocated fundamental structural changes in local government such as the abolition of partisan local elections, the use of at-large electoral systems, and the installation of a professionally trained city manager. Altering the structure of local government has had profound consequences for local government leadership. City managers—the professional, neutral experts whose job is to run the day-to-day affairs of the city—have become a force in their own right.

In the original conception, managers were to implement but not formulate policy. Administration and politics were to be kept separate. The managers' responsibility would be to administer the policies enacted by the elected officials—the city councils—who hired (and fired) them. But it is impossible to keep administration and politics completely separate. City managers are influenced not only by their training and by the councils that employ them but also by their own political ideologies.[51] When it comes to making choices, they balance professional norms, the politics of the issue, and their own predispositions. Hence, city managers typically end up being far more influential on the local government scene than their neutral persona might suggest. A case in point is the former city manager of Austin, Texas: Camille Barnett. As manager, she adopted a high-visibility role that, some argue, overshadowed the weak-mayor–council structure of this city of half a million people.[52] When the city council hired her successor, it opted for Jesus Garcia, an effective administrator in his own right, but someone with a quiet demeanor and lower profile. Oakland, California, has chosen a different path. Its council–manager structure was altered by strengthening the role of the mayor. Read about the Oakland experiment in the nearby *Breaking New Ground* box.

Managers as Policy Leaders As time has passed and more governments have adopted the council–manager system, the issue of whether the city manager should be a policy leader or a functionary of the city council has become paramount.[53] Should a city's policy initiation and formulation process involve a well-trained, highly competent administrator?

BREAKING NEW GROUND

Strong Mayor + Strong Manager = Strong City?

Oakland, California, the other big city on the San Francisco Bay, is engaged in a governmental experiment. In 1998, city voters approved a measure replacing their traditional council–manager structure of government with a modified strong-mayor structure. It is not a pure strong-mayor form because the city did not abolish the city manager's position. For a six-year period, Oakland was to operate with a governmental structure headed by a strong mayor *and* a city manager. City leaders hoped that its hybrid structure would produce doubly effective leadership. Link a powerful mayor and a skilled manager and the result should be a positive one, they contended. Blend electoral leadership with managerial leadership and voilà—the city moves forward. At least, that is how proponents of the idea envisioned it.

Now toward the end of the experiment, the results appear mixed. Some new ideas have taken root and flourished; others have faded away. And Oakland, with its history of machine politics and economic instability, is not the easiest city to lead. An earthquake in 1989 and forest fires in 1993 destroyed parts of the city. The quality of public schools is a perennial concern. Businesses and residents have fled Oakland and the city's image has suffered. In terms of race and ethnicity, the city is quite diverse. African Americans are the largest group (42 percent of the city's population); whites comprise about 34 percent. Approximately 17 percent of Oaklanders are of Hispanic origin; 16 percent are Asian/Pacific Islander; and 8 percent categorize themselves as "other." (The figures total more than 100 percent because racial and ethnic categories are not mutually exclusive.)

When the structural experiment was approved, critics warned that a strong mayor and a strong city manager would lock horns and that the result would be stalemate. Initially, the mayor, Jerry Brown, a former governor of California, and the city manager, Robert Bobb, a veteran administrator, fused their powers into "a formidable alliance for dramatic change." And change ensued: Entrenched city bureaucracies were restructured, new citywide policies were adopted, an aggressive economic development effort was launched, and the city's image brightened.

The relationship between the mayor and the manager began to fray in 2002 over plans to build a new downtown ballpark for the Oakland Athletics. Other problems related to dealing with budget shortfalls and service cutbacks arose. That same year, Mayor Brown announced that he was pleased with the trial run of the strong mayor/manager structure and offered a ballot measure that would make the hybrid structure permanent. He argued, "Diverse, complex cities need one decisive leader, accountable directly to the people." But city voters rejected his proposal by the narrowest of margins (50.3 to 49.7 percent) and the Oakland experiment began to unravel. In 2003, the mayor ousted Bobb (who was quickly hired as city administrator in Washington, D.C.) and replaced him with Deborah Edgerly, Oakland's finance director. In Mayor Brown's words, it was time for a change, for "new ideas and new blood." But for Oakland's bold experiment to continue past 2004, positive action by city voters is required.

SOURCES: Rob Gurwitt, "Mayor Brown & Mr. Bobb," *Governing* 13 (2000): 16–20; Evelyn Nieves, "As a Mayor, Jerry Brown Is Down to Earth," *New York Times* (February 11, 2000), p. A14; Eric Young and Steve Ginsberg, "Contract Lapses for Oakland City Manager," *San Francisco Business Times* (December 2, 2002), www.sanfrancisco.bizjournals.com; City of Oakland Proposed Measures, www.oaklandnet.com/government/measurex/MeasureCC.pdf (May 25, 2004).

The International City/County Management Association, the city managers' professional association (and lobbyist), says yes: The role of the manager is to help the governing body function more effectively.[54] The manager-in-training is taught that "the manager now is also expected to be a full partner in the political side of the policymaking process."[55] Ways in which the manager can assume a larger role in policymaking include proposing community goals and service levels; structuring the budget preparation, review, and adoption process so that it is linked to goals and service levels; and orienting new council members to organizational processes and norms. This approach has had the intended effect. James Svara, who recently surveyed officials of large cities, concluded that managers have become "more assertive in attempting to focus the council on long-range concerns and in shaping the tone of the policymaking process."[56]

One indisputable role for the city manager is as an information source for the busy, part-time city council. For instance, suppose that some enterprising college students are requesting a change in a city ordinance that prohibits street vendors. The council asks the manager to study the pros and cons of street vending. At a subsequent meeting, he reports on other cities' experiences: Has it created a litter problem? Does it draw clientele away from established businesses? How much revenue can be expected from vendor licensing fees? The manager then offers alternative courses of action (allow street vending only at lunchtime, restrict pushcarts to Main Street) and evaluates their probable consequences. In some councils, the manager is asked to make a formal recommendation; in others, his recommendation is more along the lines of "Well, what do you think?" At some point, a vote is called and the council makes an official decision.

Managerial Types Like mayors, city managers are not cut from one mold. The trick is to match the managerial type with the right community. Four general local managerial types have been identified:

- The *community leader,* who sees him- or herself as an agent for community change, as an innovator full of energy and idealism.
- The *chief executive,* the experienced community leader whose innovativeness and idealism have been tempered by pragmatism.
- The *administrative innovator,* an inward-focused manager who is interested in change within the organization by promoting technical and procedural improvements.
- The *administrative caretaker,* who values order and routine and who concentrates on the housekeeping functions of local government.[57]

For any of these administrators to be successful, he or she must fit the community. When managerial type and community style correspond, local government should function well; however, a perfect fit is difficult to achieve. City councils are replaced, local tax bases are disrupted, and managers shift their orientation toward the job. Communities search for the perfect manager; managers seek out the perfect community.

As noted earlier, one new trend is the hiring of professional managers in cities that do not use the council–manager form of government. Cities are adapting their structures to employ officials with titles such as managing director or chief administrative officer.[58] These individuals have the educational credentials and professional experiences of city managers, and their role in a strong-mayor city is limited to administrative matters. The city of Tampa, Florida, under its previous mayor, operated in this manner, as shown in the organizational chart in Figure 11.1. In the chart, mayoral authority and responsibility are denoted by the lines running from the box labeled *mayor*. With this structure, the mayor had direct responsibility for the police and fire departments, along with offices such as art and cultural affairs, the city clerk, and the development office. To assist the mayor in running some of the city's large departments, a chief administrative officer (CAO) was employed. The CAO supervised departments such as parks and recreation, public works, and water. But it remained a strong mayor system: The chief administrative officer served at the discretion of the mayor and reported to him. Wanting to handle things differently, Tampa's new mayor, Pam Iorio, abolished the position of CAO when she took office and reconfigured the agencies.

LOCAL LEGISLATURES

Local legislatures include city councils, county commissions, town boards of aldermen or selectmen, special district boards, and school boards. They are representative, deliberative policymaking bodies. In this section, we focus on city councils because that is where most of the research has taken place, but many of the points are also applicable to the other local legislative bodies. Although the ensuing discussion focuses on patterns across councils, it is important to remember that significant variations may exist from one city to another. For example, in some communities, council members receive high salaries, are assisted by clerical and research staff, and have no limits on the number of terms they can serve. In Chicago, for instance, city council members (called **aldermen**) earn more than $90,000 per year, have office staffs, and can serve an unlimited number of four-year terms. (To put it in perspective, the mayor of Chicago has an annual salary of $207,000.) In other places, council service is considered a volunteer activity, with members receiving no compensation whatsoever.

aldermen

A label used in some communities for members of a local legislative body, such as a city council.

City Council Members: Old and New

A former member of the city council of Concord, California, harkening back to an earlier time, commented: "When I first came on the city council, it was like a good-old-boys' club."[59] The standard description was that the city council was a part-time, low-paying haven for public-spirited white men who did not consider themselves politicians. Most councils used at-large electoral mechanisms, so individual council members had no specific, territorially based constituency. Council members considered themselves volunteers.[60] Research on city councils in the San Francisco Bay area in the 1960s found that these volunteer members were fairly unresponsive to public pressures and tended to vote according to their own preferences. In other words, there was not much representation going on.

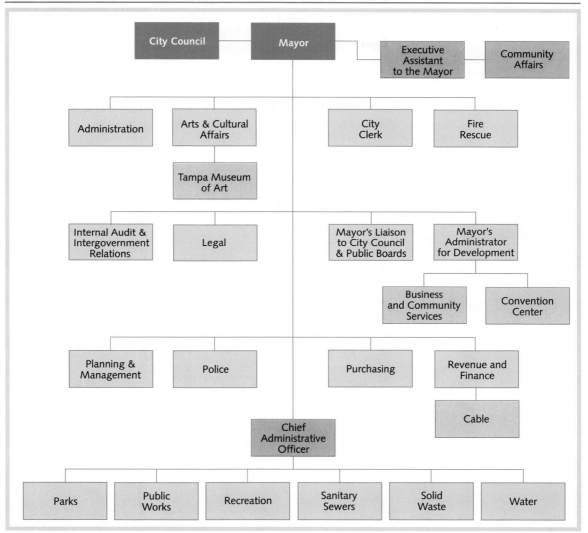

FIGURE 11.1 Organization Chart for the City of Tampa, Florida

SOURCE: www.ci.tampa.fl.us/departments (June 1, 2001).

Today, the circumstances have changed. City councils are less white, less male, and less passive than they were in the past. Now, city councilors are more engaged and active. Some of this change is due to modifications in the electoral mechanism such as the abandonment of at-large or citywide elections and the switch to district (or ward) elections. Figure 11.2 displays the district map for the Board of Supervisors of San Francisco, a city that recently made the change to districts. (San Francisco is a consolidated city–county jurisdiction; and its

board of supervisors

A label sometimes used, typically in counties, for the governing board.

legislative body is called a **board of supervisors.**) In many cities, including San Antonio, Texas, a council–manager city, only the mayor is currently elected at large. Other cities have chosen to retain some at-large seats while dividing the city into electoral districts. Houston, Texas, a strong-mayor city, is an example: Of the fourteen members of the Houston city council, five are elected at large and nine are elected from districts. (Table 11.4 shows the wide variation in both council size and number of members elected at large and from districts.) In cities across the nation, changes in election mechanisms signaled a change in council composition. More African Americans, Hispanics, and women serve on city councils than ever before, and they are taking their governance roles quite seriously.

| FIGURE 11.2 | **San Francisco's Districts** |

SOURCE: www.sfgov.org/site/bdsupvrs_index.asp?id=4385.

Council Diversity

Racial and ethnic minorities are making inroads into local politics in increasing numbers. In 2002, for example, 5,456 African Americans and 1,958 Hispanics served in elected city and county offices across the country.[61] (These figures do not include service on school boards, which account for approximately another 2,000 African Americans and 2,500 Hispanics.) And although Asian Americans accounted for just under 1 percent of locally elected officials, their numbers are also growing, especially in California localities. Despite the rise in minority representation, the percentages remain relatively low. Much research has been done on the impact of structural considerations—for example, the at-large election format, the size of the council, and the use of nonpartisan elections—on minority council representation.[62] Other factors such as the size of the minority group, its geographical concentration, and its political cohesiveness affect electoral

| TABLE 11.4 | City Councils of the Twenty Largest U.S. Cities |

CITY	2000 POPULATION	COUNCIL SIZE	NUMBER ELECTED AT LARGE	NUMBER ELECTED FROM DISTRICTS
New York	8,008,278	51	0	51
Los Angeles	3,694,820	15	0	15
Chicago	2,896,016	50	0	50
Houston	1,953,631	14	5	9
Philadelphia	1,517,550	17	7	10
Phoenix	1,321,045	8	0	8
San Diego	1,223,400	8	0	8
Dallas	1,188,580	14	0	14
San Antonio	1,144,646	10	0	10
Detroit	951,270	9	9	0
San Jose	894,943	10	0	10
Indianapolis	791,926	29	4	25
San Francisco	776,733	11	0	11
Jacksonville	735,617	19	5	14
Columbus	711,470	7	0	7
Austin	656,562	7	7	0
Baltimore	651,154	19	1	18
Memphis	650,100	13	0	13
Milwaukee	596,974	17	0	17
El Paso	563,622	8	0	8

SOURCES: Census 2000 Population Data, U.S. Bureau of the Census (May 2001); individual city web sites.

success. In general, a higher proportion of African American council members can be found in central cities that use a mayor–council structure and in southern cities with large black populations. Councils with higher-than-average Hispanic representation tend to be found in the Southwest and Far West and in larger central cities that use council–manager structures. Thus far, Asian representation has been clustered primarily in the Pacific Coast area in larger council–manager central cities. Native American representation is highest in small communities using commission structures in the southwestern and Pacific Coast areas of the country. The increase in nonwhite representation on councils has policy consequences. Data from 351 city council members show nonwhites pursuing a more liberal agenda than whites do.[63]

Given the finite number of council seats in any community and the fact that more groups are now clamoring for representation, two outcomes are possible: Minority groups may try to build coalitions, or they may opt for a more independent, competitive approach. Although temporary electoral coalitions have emerged in a few cities, racial and ethnic minority groups have remained largely separate.[64] Politically, it appears that inter–minority group competition is on the rise. Research in ninety-six cities demonstrates, for example, that an increase in the Latino population has a negative effect on black representation on city councils.[65]

Taking a break from the challenges of governing America's largest city, Mayor Michael Bloomberg (on the left) celebrates the 100th anniversary of Times Square.
SOURCE: Stephen Chernin/Getty Images.

Local governing boards in cities and counties are becoming more diverse in another way: The number of openly gay and lesbian elected officials is increasing. A 1999 estimate for local governing boards of all types placed the number at 120.[66] One study focusing on cities and counties that had anti-discrimination ordinances in place revealed several findings about the election of gays and lesbians. Based on that sample of jurisdictions, gay and lesbian electoral success was more likely in larger cities; in jurisdictions with higher numbers of nonfamily households (such as university communities); and in places with partisan, district election of council members.[67] The limited nature of the sample makes it difficult to generalize to all localities, but the research yields interesting findings about council diversity.

Councils in Action: Increasing Conflict

Earlier, when members of the council came from the same socioeconomic stratum (in some communities, *all* members of the at-large council came from the same neighborhood) and when they shared a common political philosophy, governing was easier. Members of the council could come together before the meeting (usually at breakfast in a restaurant near City Hall) and discuss the items on the agenda. Thus, they could arrive at an informal resolution of any particularly troubling items and transform the actual council meeting into a rubber-stamp exercise. No wonder that the majority of council votes were often unanimous; members were merely ratifying what they had already settled.

Intracouncil Conflict   Council members elected by districts report more factionalism and less unanimity than do their counterparts elected at large. Data from surveys of council members in 218 cities in 42 states shed more light on this question.[68] Policy conflict on councils revolves around three types of rivalries: development interests versus others, businesses versus neighborhoods, and tax cutters versus opponents. The growing tendency of cities to move away from complete reliance on at-large electoral mechanisms suggests that council conflict will rise in the future. Fifty-five percent of the city council members responding to a recent national survey reported that council member conflict was a serious source of frustration to them.[69] Ten years earlier, only 33 percent voiced a similar concern.

High levels of council conflict have other consequences. Research on city managers has shown a link between council conflict and managerial burnout.[70] Burned-out city managers perform poorly and often leave the city or the profession itself. To minimize the deleterious effect of conflict, budding city managers are encouraged to develop conflict-management skills to assist in their dealings with the council.[71]

The Chicago city council has historically generated intriguing cases of intracouncil conflict. A deliberative body as large as the Chicago council (with fifty members) and operating with a strong-mayor structure has several potential patterns of conflict.[72] In a *low-conflict* council dominated by a large voting bloc loyal to the mayor, the council acts as a rubber stamp for the mayor's proposals. Greater conflict is engendered in *fragmented councils* in which many small, loosely structured voting blocs contend for power. The instability of the coalitions requires that they be reassembled each time the council votes. Tremendous uncertainty results. A different pattern of conflict exists in *council wars,* in which two large factions—one pro-mayor, the other anti-mayor—battle. When Harold Washington served as mayor of Chicago during the 1980s, he could count on a large bloc of African American, Latino, and white reform aldermen for support. However, he could also expect a large bloc of primarily white ethnic machine aldermen to oppose every piece of legislation he proposed. Stalemate was the result. The lesson of Chicago is that the amount and type of conflict in a council affects its ability to make policy.

Battles with the Mayor Relationships between a city council and the mayor can be conflictual, to say the least. In fact, they can be downright hostile. A former mayor of Philadelphia did not pull any punches when he referred to the city council as "the worst legislative body in the free world."[73] As the new century opened, Birmingham, Alabama, and Salt Lake City, Utah, were two cities in which council–mayor dealings were rocky. In Birmingham, the retirement of a veteran mayor had opened the top job; Bernard Kincaid, an erstwhile city councilor, won the post in 1999. The council, led by an unsuccessful candidate for mayor, saw the change in leadership as an opportunity to reassert its authority. Thus, the council passed ordinances limiting the scope of mayoral power. The mayor vetoed the ordinances; the council overrode the vetoes; the mayor took the council to court.[74] The jockeying for power between Mayor Kincaid and the council continued until council elections in 2001 changed the composition of the council somewhat.

In Salt Lake City, the new mayor, Rocky Anderson, took several actions at odds with the city council when he assumed office in 2000. He vetoed several of the council's pet projects, and he took action unilaterally through executive orders when the council was indecisive on an issue. In the mayor's words, "You don't ask the council . . . you just do it."[75] And what does the city council in Salt Lake City think of the mayor's approach? One council member put it this way: "It's not smart to treat us with such disdain."[76] The result for citizens of Utah's capital city was a tense political situation.

Council–mayor conflict is not necessarily unproductive. Conflict is expected in a political system that operates on the foundation of separation of powers. Clashes between the legislative branch and the executive branch can produce better government. But when the disagreements between the council and the mayor escalate to the point of gridlock, effective governance is stymied.

Women on Local Governing Boards

Do women officeholders act differently from men and pursue different interests in public office? As the number of female officeholders in local government increases, this question becomes especially compelling. Nationally, women constitute 12 percent of county governing boards and 44 percent of school boards. Alaska and Hawaii consistently report female officeholding far above these national averages; Georgia and North Dakota are examples of states in which the proportion of women in local public office is substantially lower. In the South, a study of city councils in medium-size to large cities found that the percentage of councils without female members ranged from lows of 13 percent and 18 percent in Virginia and North Carolina, respectively, to highs of 70 percent in Arkansas and 73 percent in Alabama.[77] A national survey of city council members showed that, compared with males, female council members are much more likely to view the representation of women, environmentalists, abortion rights activists, racial minorities, and good-government organizations as extremely important.[78] In addition, men and women on the council see each other through different lenses. As Susan Adams Beck points out, "Men often express frustration that women ask too many questions, while women see themselves as well-prepared and think their male colleagues are often 'winging it.'"[79]

A review of the research suggests that women officeholders frequently differ not only from their male counterparts but also from one another. Four basic types of female political actors have been hypothesized:

- The traditional politician.
- The traditional liberal feminist.
- The caring humanist.
- The change-oriented feminist.[80]

Women who are traditional politicians articulate no particular gender differences and do not expect much divergence between men's and women's interests. Traditional liberal feminists, on the other hand, are concerned with what have been termed women's issues, such as abortion, rape, domestic violence, pornography, child care, and education. In addressing these issues, they work within the norms and practices of the established political system. Female officeholders of the caring-humanist type, though concerned with women's issues, place a higher priority on matters of social justice and ecological balance. They also tend to be somewhat estranged from the established order. And change-oriented feminists see sexism as a fundamental characteristic of our society and therefore have no interest in being assimilated into established male structures. Instead, they want to create a new order based on female sex-role expectations. Although all four types are represented among women holding local public office, most female officeholders have tended to cluster in the first two types.

LEADERSHIP AND CAPACITY

In the final analysis, the concept of leadership remains somewhat ephemeral. Regardless of the difficulty we might have in defining it precisely, it is a central, critical concern in local government. For example, Oshkosh, Wisconsin, a city of 63,000 people, has been hailed as a midwestern success story because of the rejuvenation of its declining economy. Replicating this success in other cities is a difficult task, though, because "so much is dependent upon the charisma, vision, skill, and commitment of particular business leaders, city politicians, and managers."[81] In other words, success depends on leadership.

Much is being made of a new pragmatism among America's big-city mayors, an orientation that is independent of race or ethnicity.[82] It is a back-to-basics approach to governing, one that emphasizes service delivery, balanced budgets, and working with the private sector to cure the city's ills. This new breed of mayor also seeks to build alliances with adjacent suburbs. Witness the pragmatism of Atlanta's mayor, Bill Campbell, who wanted to greet visitors coming to his city for the 1996 Olympics with a sign reading "Welcome to Atlanta—a real city with real problems and real people working real hard every day to solve them."[83]

At the same time, local governments are becoming more entrepreneurial. Local governments are confronting their problems and challenges by trying new ideas, exploring alternatives, and reaching out for solutions. New approaches do not necessarily work and therein lies the risk. But when they do, other places are quick to embrace them. As a result, local governments change and, one hopes, improve.

Although our focus has been on formal leaders in government, remember that leadership can be bottom-up; that is, leadership can flow from the grassroots into and perhaps even around government. An example comes from comprehensive community initiatives (CCIs). These efforts seek to build neighborhood capacity through various means, such as leadership training and organizational collaboration. Participants in CCIs share a sense of connectedness and a commitment to solve neighborhood problems. The results are tangible: a streetlighting project in Hartford, Connecticut; a scholarship program in Memphis, Tennessee; recreational activity grants in Detroit, Michigan.[84] Just as important is the empowerment of the grassroots participants who are, in fact, community leaders on a smaller scale.

CHAPTER RECAP

- Elite theory (a small group of leaders possesses power and rules society) and pluralist theory (power is dispersed among competing groups) have dominated the study of community power. Attention has been focused more recently on regime theory and the related concepts of systemic power and strategic advantage.
- Nonprofit organizations have become increasingly important in communities.
- Mayors tend to be the central figures in city politics and government, even if they operate in formally weak-mayor structures. One of the interesting features of mayoral politics is the deracialization of campaigns.
- City managers have become policy leaders. Even in cities without a formal city manager structure, chief administrative officers are being hired to take on some of the management responsibilities.
- City councils have changed from the good-old-boy clubs of the past. They are more active, they are more diverse, and more conflict occurs between city council members. One of the reasons for these changes is the switch from at-large, or citywide, elections to district (or ward) election of council members.
- Leadership is the ability to realize goals. It varies from one place to another, as a function of the situation. Leadership also comes from the grassroots.

Key Terms

elite theory *(p. 304)*
pluralist theory *(p. 304)*
reputational approach *(p. 306)*
decisional method *(p. 306)*
regime *(p. 308)*
nonprofit organizations *(p. 308)*

hyperpluralism *(p. 310)*
deracialization *(p. 312)*
Progressive Era *(p. 315)*
aldermen *(p. 318)*
board of supervisors *(p. 320)*

Surfing the Web

The association of mayors of cities with populations of 30,000, the U.S. Conference of Mayors, has a web site at **www.usmayors.org.**

Mayors in a single state frequently belong to a statewide organization such as **www.njmayornet.com** in New Jersey.

Specialized constituency groups often have their own organizations and web sites, as does the National Conference of Black Mayors at **www.blackmayors. org.**

The web site for the Center for American Women and Politics at Rutgers University, **www.rutgers.cawp.edu,** contains a wealth of data on women and politics.

Information about the city and county management profession can be found at the International City/County Management Association's web site: **www. icma.org.**

STATE–LOCAL RELATIONS

U rban sprawl, that is, new development on the outskirts of established cities, characterizes most metropolitan areas. Subdivisions and strip malls sprout up on land that was recently forests and farms. It costs a lot of money for government to provide infrastructure—streets, water and sewer lines, schools—to these new developments. Meanwhile, many inner cities are plagued by empty storefronts, vacant lots, and abandoned factories. In inner cities, the infrastructure is already in place. In 1997, the state of Maryland decided to do something about this trend. Calling sprawl "a disease eating away at the heart of America," the governor signed the Smart Growth Areas Act into law.[1] Simply put, the state rewards local governments that target new growth in areas that already have infrastructure, and it denies state funding for infrastructure projects that encourage sprawl. Several other states moved quickly to follow Maryland's lead. The following year Arizona adopted a Growing Smarter Act; by 2003, another twenty states had taken anti-sprawl actions of one sort or another.[2] A particularly ambitious plan was New Jersey's Blueprint for Intelligent Growth (BIG). Had BIG been adopted as originally drafted, huge portions of the Garden State would have been off-limits to additional development, much to the dismay of many local officials and builders.[3] Although the far-reaching anti-sprawl proposal was eventually pared down, it was clear that in New Jersey, as in many other places, state governments are reestablishing themselves as major influences in local governments' land-use decisions.

The relationship between states and their communities is often strained. On one hand, state government gives local governments life. States create the rules for their localities. (The nearby *Debating Politics* box provides a vivid demonstration of state power vis-à-vis localities.) On the other hand, state governments

DEBATING
POLITICS

Massachusetts Says "Adios" to Its Counties

Have you ever wondered whether a state would pull the plug on a local government? Look at Massachusetts and wonder no more. In June 1997, the Massachusetts House of Representatives voted 149 to 0 to abolish Middlesex County, one of the state's largest and most populous. The state paid off the county's debts and assumed control of its courts, jails, deed registry, and sheriff's department. You couldn't blame the other thirteen Massachusetts counties for being nervous. A spokesperson for the governor was quoted as saying, "It's the first nail in the coffin for county government." In 2000, another Bay State county, Berkshire County, held its final official meeting. Five counties had their functions taken over by state agencies, three counties became regional councils of government, and six counties were unchanged.

Admittedly, abolition of counties is a drastic move. Counties in Massachusetts date back to the colonial era. Why is the state taking such extreme measures? In the case of Middlesex County, the answer lies in the mismanagement and corruption that has marked the county government. In particular, the county's default on a $4.6 million loan for its hospital coupled with the county's $17 million debt

raised the state's ire. More generally, counties have become viewed as inefficient and obsolete, the white elephants of local government. Over the past twenty years, the state has slowly assumed the power of the county governments, which makes them appear as an unnecessary bureaucratic tangle. Although most county officials sought to defend their structures of government, others (including some in Middlesex County) welcomed the state's action.

The New England region is one in which counties traditionally had fewer responsibilities and functions. Thus, in the political landscape of the region, a state's termination of counties is less extreme than it would be in another region of the country. Will other states follow the lead of Massachusetts? Will the absence of counties produce new and different forms of regional governance? Or is Massachusetts making a mistake by eliminating a layer of government that provided a modicum of unity across villages, towns, and cities?

SOURCES: Don Aucoin and William F. Doherty, "House Votes to Pull Plug on Middlesex," *Boston Globe* (June 13, 1997), p. B12; John Laidler, "Altered State: The End of Counties," *Boston Globe* (February 9, 1997), p. B1; Jonathan Walters, "The Disappearing County," www.governing.com (July 5, 2000); League of Women Voters, "Massachusetts Government: County Government," www.lwvma.org/govcounty (March 31, 2004).

historically have not treated their local governments well. Over time, states have realized that mistreating their governmental offspring is counterproductive, and many have launched a sometimes uncoordinated process of assistance and empowerment of local government.

Capturing this evolution is the statement of the National Conference of State Legislatures (NCSL) Task Force on State–Local Relations: "Legislators should place a higher priority on state–local issues than has been done in the past. The time has come to change their attitude toward local governments—to stop considering them as just another special interest group and to start treating them as partners in our federal system."[4] Stronger, more competent local governments are an asset to state government.

Chapter 13 will address the financial relationship between state and local governments. This chapter examines broader issues for the two entities and related trends. Let us first consider the most fundamental issue: the distribution of authority between the state and its constituent units.

THE DISTRIBUTION OF AUTHORITY

Dillon's rule

A rule that limits the powers of local government to those expressly granted by the state or those powers closely linked to the express powers.

In essence, local governments are creatures of their states. Federal and state courts have consistently upheld the dependency of localities on the state since Iowa's judge John F. Dillon first laid down Dillon's rule in 1868. **Dillon's rule** established that local governments may exercise only those powers explicitly granted to them by the state, those clearly implied by the explicit powers, and those absolutely essential to the declared objectives and purposes of the local government. Any doubt regarding the legality of any specific local government power is resolved in favor of the state.[5] This perspective runs counter to the more Jeffersonian conception that local governments are imbued with inherent rights.[6]

In the words of the U.S. Advisory Commission on Intergovernmental Relations (ACIR), "State legislatures are the trustees of the basic rules of local governance in America. The laws and constitutions of each state are the basic legal instruments of local governance."[7] The ACIR statement denotes the essence of the distribution of authority between a state and its localities. It is up to the state to determine the amount and type of authority a local government may possess. As specified by Dillon's rule, localities depend on the state to give them sufficient power to operate effectively.

The Amount and Type of Authority

The amount and type of authority that states give their local governments vary widely. Some states grant their localities wide-ranging powers to restructure themselves, impose new taxes, and take on additional functions. Others, much more conservative with their power, force local governments to turn to the legislature for approval to act. Empowerment also depends on the type of local government. As noted in Chapter 10, general-purpose governments such as counties, cities, and towns have wider latitude than special-purpose entities like school districts. Even general-purpose governments possess different degrees of authority; counties tend to be more circumscribed than cities in their ability to modify their form of government and expand their service offerings.[8]

In general, states' regulatory reach is great. For example, states may regulate local finances (by establishing debt limits and requiring balanced budgets, among other approaches), personnel (by setting qualifications for certain positions, prescribing employee pension plans), government structure (by establishing forms of government, outlawing particular electoral systems), processes (by requiring public hearings and open meetings, mandating financial disclosure), functions (by ordering the provision of public safety functions, proscribing the pursuit of enterprise activities), and service standards (by adopting solid waste guidelines, setting acceptable water-quality levels). The preceding list makes it clear: The state capitol casts a long shadow.

Building codes offer an illustration of the variability of state–local authority. Researcher Peter May examined all fifty states to determine the amount of discretion allowed local governments to adopt and enforce building codes.[9] He found several different patterns. Twelve states (Kentucky and Michigan among them) played an aggressive role by imposing mandatory building codes on their local governments and overseeing local compliance. Thirteen states (including Indiana and Wyoming) had mandatory local codes but stopped short of state review or oversight. The rest of the states gave their local governments more leeway. In eight states (Iowa and Nebraska among them), local governments themselves decided whether to enforce the state building code. And seventeen states (including Delaware and Oklahoma) had no comprehensive building codes; thus, local governments were free to design and enact their own. The building code example underscores an important point: States vary in their treatment of local government.

Devolution (the shift in power from the national government to the states) has also occurred between states and their local governments. The more recently a state has adopted its constitution, the more likely the document is to contain provisions that strengthen local governments.[10] Many state constitutions set forth a provision for home rule (defined in Chapter 10). Although home rule falls short of actual local self-government, it is an important step in the direction of greater local decisionmaking.[11] And local jurisdictions tend to be extremely protective of whatever power they have wrested from state government. For example, the beleaguered Baltimore school system rejected a state plan to take over the schools in 2004 because, in the words of one official, "the solution to the problems in Baltimore city starts with Baltimore city."[12]

A State–Local Tug of War

Local governments want their states to provide them with adequate funding and ample discretion. Local officials are supremely confident of their abilities to govern, given sufficient state support. These same local officials express concern that neither their policymaking power nor their financial authority has kept pace with the increased administrative responsibilities placed on them by state government.[13] The recognition and correction of such conditions are the states' responsibility.

To learn more about the changes in state–local relations, the ACIR conducted a major survey of state laws, as of 1978 and 1990, in six categories: form of government, annexation and consolidation, local elections, administrative operations and procedures, financial management, and personnel management.[14] Two-hundred-and-one specific items were included in the ACIR survey, and the findings were instructive. On average, states have eighty-six local government laws on the books. Ohio has the most, with 113, followed by Florida and Montana with 112 each. States with the fewest local government laws tend to be located in the Northeast: Rhode Island and Vermont have forty-seven, and Connecticut has fifty-one. During the period from 1978 to 1990, states increased their regulation of local government by passing an average of sixteen new statutes or constitutional amendments. With the stroke of the same pen, they decreased their involvement somewhat by repealing an average of eight laws dealing with local government. Table 12.1 presents a selection of the laws that states have enacted with regard to the administrative operations and procedures of local governments.

As Table 12.1 shows, states are not at all reluctant to exercise power vis-à-vis their local jurisdictions. Consider these examples:

- Concerned that Florida cities might follow the example of Santa Fe, New Mexico, and require firms to provide higher minimum pay than the federal minimum wage, Sunshine State legislators passed a bill in 2003 to prevent local governments from doing so.[15]
- When state revenues fell below expectations in 2002, North Carolina's governor made up the difference by taking $200 million in tax money that had been earmarked for localities.[16]
- After a local jurisdiction used its power to take property in an aggressive way in 2004, Colorado lawmakers introduced bills designed to restrict localities' power in this area.[17]

A persistent theme runs through the preceding list items: state government can impose its will on local governments. These examples shouldn't suggest that states and localities are invariably at each other's throats. Plenty of examples of state–local partnerships exist, such as Florida's and Palm Beach County's joint effort to attract biotechnology industries. The county has purchased the land and is building a research facility ($200 million); the state is paying the facility's operating costs for seven years ($300 million).[18] Still, the relationship between a state and its local governments often involves conflict as each level tries to exert its will.

State Mandates

Although local governments generally want increased autonomy, state governments have shared their policymaking sphere with reluctance. Rather than let subgovernments devise their own solutions to problems, states frequently prefer to tell them how to solve them. For instance, when solid waste management became a concern in Florida, the state legislature's reaction was to require counties to establish recycling programs. Not only were counties required to initiate programs, they were ordered to achieve a recycling rate of 30 percent.[19] This kind of requirement or order is an example of a *mandate*. (The subject is discussed further in Chapter 13 in the context of state–local finances.) Unfunded mandates are a persistent source of friction between state and local levels of government.

From the perspective of state government, mandates are necessary to ensure that vital activities are performed and desirable goals are achieved. State mandates promote uniformity of policy from one jurisdiction to another (for instance, regarding the length of the public-school year or the operating hours of precinct polling places). In addition, they promote coordination, especially

---

| TABLE 12.1 | **Regional Comparisons and Changes in State Laws Governing Administrative Operations and Procedures of Localities** |

	REGION					
	SOUTH	WEST	NORTH CENTRAL	NORTHEAST	TOTAL	CHANGE SINCE 1978
	$N = 16$	13	12	9	50	
1. State law requires that all local government meetings at which official action is taken be open to the public.	15	13	12	8	48	+7
2. State law requires that local government records be open to public inspection at reasonable hours.	16	10	11	8	45	+15
3. State law mandates a procedure for adoption of municipal ordinances and/or resolutions.	11	11	8	3	33	+4
4. State law mandates a procedure for adoption of county ordinances and/or resolutions.	9	7	4	2	22	+8
5. State law authorizes initiative and referendum on local ordinances and/or resolutions.	3	11	9	3	26	+11
6. Local elected officials are subject to a state-imposed code of ethics.	8	7	3	3	21	+4
7. Sovereign immunity for local government torts has been waived by the state.	12	9	10	5	36	+4

SOURCE: U.S. Advisory Committee on Intergovernmental Relations, *State Laws Governing Local Government Structure and Administration* (Washington, D.C.: ACIR, 1993), p. 61.

among adjacent jurisdictions that provide services jointly (as with a regional hospital or a metropolitan transportation system).

Local governments see the issue quite differently. They have three basic complaints:

1. State mandates (especially those that mandate a new service or impose a service-quality standard) can be quite expensive for local governments.
2. State mandates displace local priorities in favor of state priorities.
3. State mandates limit the management flexibility of local governments.[20]

Table 12.2 provides some perspective on how those at the local level see the mandates issue. Based on a survey of local officials in Minnesota, the data in the table suggest that resistance to mandates is not uniform; that is, it depends on the policy area.[21] Mandates for infrastructure, public safety, and environmental protection, especially if funded at least partially by the state, are acceptable to local officials. But in areas such as recreation, economic development, and general government administration, a large subset of those surveyed believe that mandates are not appropriate. Recognizing that funding is one of the key considerations, many states have adopted **mandate-reimbursement requirements.** These measures require states either to reimburse local governments for the costs of state mandates or to give local governments adequate revenue-raising capacity to pay for them.

**mandate-reimburse-
ment requirements**

Measures that take the financial sting out of state mandates.

| TABLE 12.2 | **Minnesota Local Officials' Views on State Mandates** |

	MANDATES ARE APPROPRIATE . . .			MANDATES ARE NOT APPROPRIATE REGARDLESS OF STATE FUNDING
	. . . EVEN WITH NO STATE FUNDING	. . . IF THEY ARE PARTIALLY STATE FUNDED	. . . IF THEY ARE FULLY STATE FUNDED	
POLICY AREA				
Economic development	6	30	24	40
Environment	6	40	48	6
General government administration	6	32	26	40
Health services	2	25	44	2
Infrastructure	2	56	31	11
Public safety	2	47	37	10
Recreation	2	33	21	41
Welfare and human services	1	20	25	2

NOTE: The numbers indicate the percentage of Minnesota local officials responding to the survey who agree with each statement.
SOURCE: Lawrence J. Grossback, "The Problem of State-Imposed Mandates: Lessons from Minnesota's Local Governments," *State and Local Government Review* 34 (Fall 2002): 189. Reprinted by permission.

From their vantage point, local officials offer several suggestions for fixing the mandate problem. Three solutions supported by more than 80 percent of the respondents to the Minnesota survey are:

• The state should provide a clear statement of the rationale behind the mandate; in other words, the state should justify its action.
• Localities should be given greater flexibility in implementing the provisions of the mandate.
• Financial aid to local governments should be increased so that they can deal with mandates effectively.[22]

As might be expected, these solutions are substantially less popular with state officials. But certainly, more communication between state policymakers and local officials, especially at the outset, would reduce some of the friction generated by mandates. Allowing local governments more leeway in implementation, either through extension of time or variation in rules, would lessen the punch that mandates pack. Even more central to any type of mandate reform is adequate state funding of mandates. This action would go a long way toward improving state–local relationships.

STATE–LOCAL ORGANIZATIONS

Legal, administrative, and financial ties link state and local governments. Additional interaction occurs when state governments establish organizations such as local government study commissions and advisory panels of local officials. Among the most prevalent structures are task forces, advisory commissions on intergovernmental relations, and departments of community affairs.

Task forces tend to be focused organizations set up by the governor or the state legislature in response to a perceived local-level problem. If a state wants to investigate the ramifications of changing its annexation statutes, the legislature might create a task force on annexation and boundary changes or something similar. The task force would probably be composed of state and local officials, community leaders, and experts on the subject of annexation. First, the task force would collect information on how other states handle the annexation question; next, it would conduct a series of public hearings to get input from individuals and groups interested in the issue; finally, it would compile a report that included recommendations suitable for legislative action. Its work completed, the task force would then disband, although individual members might turn up as advocates when the task-force recommendations receive legislative attention. Task forces are quick organizational responses to local problems that have become too prominent for state government to ignore. A task force is a low-cost, concentrated reaction that undertakes specific tasks and, in some instances, actually influences legislative deliberations.

In an ongoing comprehensive effort at state–local cooperation, twenty-one states have created state-level *advisory commissions on intergovernmental relations* (*ACIRs*), modeled after the commission, now defunct, created by the U.S.

Congress in 1959. State-level ACIRs are designed to promote more harmonious, workable relations between the state and its governmental subdivisions. They are intended to offer a neutral forum for discussion of long-range state–local issues—a venue where local officials can be listened to and engaged in focused dialogue; conduct research on local developments and new state policies; promote experimentation in intergovernmental processes, both state–local and interlocal; and develop suggested solutions to state–local problems.[23] To prevent their recommendations from gathering dust on a shelf, many state-level ACIRs have added marketing and public relations to their list of activities.[24] Generally, state-level ACIRs return real benefits to local government. Whether in their narrowest form (as arenas for discussion of local issues) or in their broadest (as policy developers and initiators), ACIRs are useful to state and local governments. But their greatest impact occurs when they are given the authority and resources to do something more than simply discuss issues. Virginia's ACIR, for instance, has four primary duties:

- To provide a forum for the discussion of intergovernmental concerns.
- To conduct research and issue reports on intergovernmental topics.
- To resolve specific issues and problems as they arise.
- To promote needed policies.[25]

Another way in which states can generate closer formal ties with their local governments is through specialized administrative agencies. All fifty states have created *departments of community affairs (DCAs)* that are involved in local activities. They have different labels (Kentucky calls its DCA the Department for Local Government; Washington's is the Department of Community, Trade and Economic Development), but their function is similar: to offer a range of programs and services to local governments.[26] DCAs are involved in housing, urban revitalization, anti-poverty programs, and economic development; they also offer local governments services such as planning, management, and financial assistance. DCAs vary on several dimensions: their niche in state government, the sizes of their budget and staff, and whether they include an advisory board of local officials. Each of these dimensions contributes to the clout wielded by any DCA. For example, a DCA that has cabinet-level status (thirty-five of them do) is likely to be more influential than one located within another state agency (as is true in nine states) or within the governor's office (the case in six states). DCAs with bigger budgets and staffs should have more influence. The existence of an advisory board is problematic, however. Half of the DCAs have advisory boards, but few of them are active or effective in an array of local policy areas.[27]

Compared with state-level ACIRs, DCAs function much more as service deliverers and much less as policy initiators. Therefore, these two types of organizations tend to complement rather than compete with one another. Both function as advocates for local government, however, at the state level.

METROPOLITICS: A NEW CHALLENGE FOR STATE GOVERNMENT

State governments often find their dealings with local governments to be confounded by the side effects of urbanization. Regardless of which state we examine, its urban areas show the effects of three waves of suburbanization. An early wave occurred during the 1920s, when automobiles facilitated the development of outlying residential areas. Although the dispersion slowed during the Depression and World War II, its resurgence in the 1950s triggered a second wave, during which retail stores followed the population exodus. This so-called malling of America has led to the third wave of suburbanization: the development of office space beyond the central city.[28] This phenomenon is occurring nearly everywhere, from New York City to San Diego, from Milwaukee to Miami. One observer summed it up this way: "The American economy is rapidly becoming an 'exit ramp' economy, with office, commercial and retail facilities increasingly located along suburban freeways."[29] This third wave of suburbanization has caught the attention of state governments.

As a result of the transformation of American metropolitan areas, central cities have lost some of their prominence as the social, economic, and political focal points of their areas. People have moved to surrounding suburbs and beyond; businesses and firms have sprung up in the hinterlands; communities have formed their own service and taxing districts. The outward flow of people and activities has fundamentally altered metropolitan areas, which are now composed of "a series of relatively self-contained and self-sufficient decentralized regional units."[30] As noted above, these new boom towns are not simply residential but include business, retail, and entertainment activities. The de-emphasis of the central city suggests the need for changes in outmoded state government policy toward metropolitan jurisdictions. A serious concern is that rapid, unplanned growth is producing sprawl and fostering what are called shadow governments. A logical question is, What is state government doing while all of this is occurring? More than it used to, as we saw in the Maryland and New Jersey examples that opened this chapter.

Urban Expansion

Urban areas are mushrooming. New developments are cropping up on the outer reaches of city boundaries. *Washington Post* reporter Joel Garreau spent several years exploring the new developments on the urban fringes, places that he calls **edge cities**.[31] With their campus-style office complexes, shopping malls, and jogging paths, edge cities are the new frontier for an urbanized United States. The areas surrounding Phoenix, Honolulu, and Seattle offer interesting cases of governmental responses to growth.

edge cities
The new boom towns of office and retail developments on the outskirts of cities.

The Phoenix Area   Phoenix, which continues to be one of the fastest-growing large cities in the country, already has three full-fledged edge cities. Four growth hot spots are becoming the newest edge cities, and another five are antici-pated.[32] The map in Figure 12.1 shows their location. Phoenix was the first city in the United States to acknowledge these emerging urban centers officially in its planning process, thus suggesting that the growth areas will be targeted for public infrastructure investments—parks, libraries, government offices, hospitals—in anticipation of development rather than in reaction to it. Among city officials, the hope is that the state of Arizona will provide enough resources to help Phoenix prepare for the growth. As an initial step in the late 1980s, the legisla-ture commissioned a study of growth management strategies for the area. Its recommendations guided subsequent government actions until the Growing Smarter Act was adopted in 1998.

The Honolulu Area   Honolulu took an innovative approach in addressing the excesses of rapid urbanization on the eastern side of the island of Oahu. The state of Hawaii and Honolulu County joined forces to create a new municipality twenty miles from Waikiki Beach.[33] The new city includes waterfront resort ho-tels largely financed by Japanese investors, a defined downtown center, an indus-trial park, large residential neighborhoods, shopping centers, golf courses, and office buildings. Government officials and developers have tried to re-create the look of old Honolulu in the new city of Kapolei to avoid the high-rise concrete jungle that characterizes downtown Honolulu today. Of course, it is much easier to improve on the past when you have the luxury of starting from the ground up (quite literally in this case) than when you are confronted with years of accumu-lated land uses. Kapolei, which calls itself Hawaii's e-city, has proven to be a pop-ular place, attracting more than 70,000 residents in less than twenty years.

The Seattle Area   The state of Washington adopted a growth management act in 1990 that required its local governments to think seriously about land uses. Seattle reacted to the state's mandate with a master plan that called for the cre-ation of urban villages. According to the plan, Seattle's growth would be chan-neled into thirty-eight urban villages—namely, existing neighborhoods that contain a mix of residential and commercial development. The plan had a back-to-the-future feel to it. Ideally, each urban village would have "easily walkable neighborhood commercial centers; enough pedestrian traffic to support a di-verse collection of stores and businesses; less reliance on automobiles; conven-ient libraries, parks and community centers; the benefits to public safety of a lively street life."[34] In addition, areas outside the urban villages would be down-zoned; that is, growth restrictions would be imposed. Although the plan—originally 850 pages long—was the subject of much acrimonious debate and discussion, a scaled-down version was adopted by the city council in 1994. Ten years later, in its updated comprehensive plan, Seattle reemphasized its commit-ment to the urban-village concept as a growth management strategy.[35]

Urban Sprawl Versus Smart Growth

Population growth is, of course, something that states and localities desire. But the consequences of rapid and unplanned population growth test the capability

| FIGURE 12.1 | **Living on the Edge in Phoenix, Arizona** |

In the fast-growing Phoenix area, new work-play-sleep communities are springing up beyond downtown.

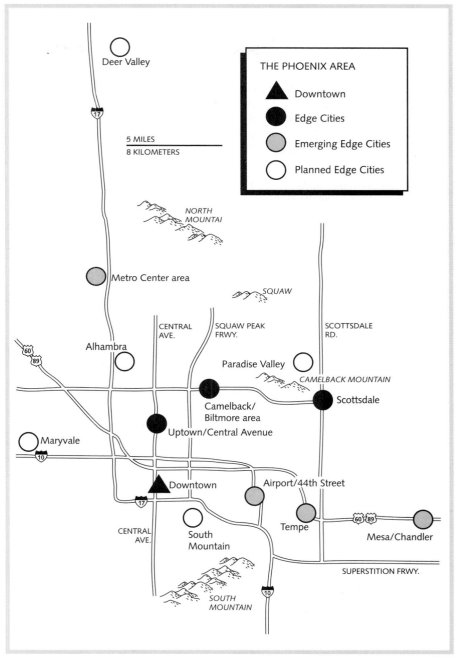

SOURCE: From *Edge City* by Joel Garreau, copyright © 1991 by Joel Garreau. Used by permission of Doubleday, a division of Random House, Inc.

of governments to provide services efficiently and effectively. As growth spills beyond city limits into unincorporated areas, as edge cities spring up along interstate highways, the result is often traffic congestion and overcrowded schools. Many states and localities have struggled to balance the benefits of new growth against the attendant costs.

urban sprawl

Development characterized by low population density, rapid land consumption, and dependence on the automobile.

Sprawling Growth   One of the hottest issues of the early twenty-first century is **urban sprawl,** a term that carries negative connotations. It refers to development beyond the central city that is characterized by low densities, rapid land consumption, and dependence on the automobile. It is often called leapfrog development because it jumps over established settlements. The exit-ramp communities mentioned earlier are a manifestation of sprawl. Urban sprawl is resource-intensive and costly, and it is also the subject of much political debate.

Las Vegas, Nevada, may offer the best contemporary example of a fast-growing, sprawling city. According to the city's statistics, "two hundred new residents arrive in Las Vegas every day; a house is built every fifteen minutes."[36] In the assessment of an official in the county's public works department, "Traffic is probably 100 times worse than it was 10 years ago."[37] Maintaining an adequate water supply is a persistent problem in this desert city. As human settlement pushes ever outward to lower cost land, local government is pressed to provide

impact fee

A charge levied on new development to offset some of the costs of providing services.

schools, parks, and roads. Growth has outstripped the infrastructure needed to support it. The mayor of Las Vegas proposed a $2,000 per house **impact fee** to mitigate the effects of growth, but the city lacked the authority to levy the fee; the Nevada legislature had to approve the proposal before it could take effect. Other places do not have the furious pace of development that Las Vegas has, but they face serious challenges related to growth nonetheless. Table 12.3 lists the concerns of five cities in different parts of the United States.

smart growth

Government efforts to limit urban sprawl by managing growth.

The majority of land-use decisions occur at the local level, and many states have begun to offer more guidance and provide localities with more tools to manage growth. The **smart growth** movement is an effort by governments to reduce the amount of sprawl and minimize its impact. One of the key aspects of these new smart growth approaches is a stronger link between land use and infrastructure planning. A Sierra Club report in 1999 rated Oregon, Maryland, Vermont, and Maine among the most effective states in comprehensive land use planning.[38] Tennessee and Wisconsin are two states that are fairly new to the ranks of growing-smart states.[39] Tennessee adopted legislation that requires local governments to establish growth boundaries, while Wisconsin promulgated uniform comprehensive planning requirements that protect farmland and open space. Not everyone, however, thinks that sprawl is so bad. In fact, to some, sprawl is simply the consequence of the unfettered workings of a free-market system.[40] Given a choice, they contend, Americans prefer a spread-out, car-centered lifestyle, a contention that has some truth.

Open Space   The relentless creep of urban sprawl has prompted reactions in many states and communities. For example, Ohio voters approved a proposal to dedicate $200 million to the conservation and preservation of natural areas,

TABLE 12.3	Growth-Related Challenges Facing Five Metropolitan Areas
METROPOLITAN AREA	**GROWTH-RELATED CHALLENGES**
Albuquerque, NM	Providing enough water to support growth.
	Conducting land-use planning in an area surrounded on three sides by federal and tribal land.
Atlanta, GA	Addressing an average daily commute time that is among the highest in the nation.
	Improving air quality in an area where ozone pollution exceeds the Clean Air Act standard.
Burlington, VT	Maintaining the area's rural character.
	Maintaining traditional downtown centers and villages.
Columbus, OH	Preserving farmland.
	Providing the water-sewer infrastructure needed to support growth.
Fresno, CA	Preserving prime agricultural land in the metropolitan area—which includes the highest-producing agricultural county in the nation.
	Maintaining an adequate water supply.

SOURCE: U.S. General Accounting Office, *Local Growth Issues—Federal Opportunities and Challenges* (Washington, D.C.: U.S. GAO, September 2000), p. 88.

open space, and farmlands. The Buckeye State is not alone: In 2000, 208 open space protection measures appeared on ballots throughout the country; 174 of them passed. These measures committed more than $7.4 billion for land conservation; much of it in the form of tax increases.[41] Two of the referenda involved the town of Fillmore in southern California. The community of 13,000 has been losing its orange groves to new housing and commercial developments. Concerned residents were able to place an initiative on the ballot that would require voter approval for development beyond the current city limits. It was called Save Open-space and Agricultural Resources (SOAR). City officials countered with their own less restrictive initiative: Vision 2020. Pundits characterized it as citrus groves versus Starbucks and sport-utility vehicles (SUVs).[42] The campaigns for and against the measures were intense and, in the end, *both* initiatives were defeated by voters. In the aftermath, Fillmore's city council decided to establish **greenbelts** on two sides of the town.

greenbelts
Open spaces in which development is limited.

States have been using public funds to purchase land, sometimes large tracts of land, to preserve as open space. Alabama has bought more than 47,000 acres of wooded land near Mobile, and Florida has purchased 18,000 acres west of Lake Okeechobee. States are assisted in their efforts by nonprofit groups such as the Conservation Fund and the Nature Conservancy. For instance, Maryland purchased 29,000 acres on the Eastern Shore; the Conservation Fund bought a similar amount.[43] Sometimes these lands have significant ecological value; in other instances, they provide a buffer from encroaching development.

Efforts to preserve open space confront a hard reality: A growing population creates demand for more housing, which in turn consumes open space. California presents the ultimate test, at least in terms of scale. By 2025, experts predict that another 18 million new housing units will be constructed in the Golden State.[44] While some of the new housing will replace existing structures, most of it will be built on what is now open space. Even though revenues for local governments will increase as a result of the development, costs of providing services will also rise and not necessarily commensurately. One study of Georgia counties found that for every $1.00 of revenue brought in by new housing developments, the cost of services was between $1.23 and $2.07.[45] Public education was the big-ticket item pushing up service costs. Only when commercial and industrial development complements subdivision growth do local governments typically enjoy a net revenue gain. But long-term questions of environmental degradation complicate cost-benefit calculations. As this discussion suggests, the entwined issues of growth and preservation are more complex than they appear.

Shadow Governments

shadow governments

Entities, especially unofficial ones, that function like governments.

As noted, edge cities are multiplying and new forms of governance are emerging. One of these new forms is called **shadow governments,** which may or may not be official government units but in many important ways behave as if they were. They levy taxes, regulate behavior, and provide services. Three types of shadow government exist: *private enterprise shadow governments,* such as home owners' associations; *public–private partnership shadow governments,* common examples of which are development corporations and business improvement districts; and *subsidiaries of conventional governments with unusual powers,* such as areawide planning commissions (see the discussion of regional coordination later in this chapter).[46] Shadow governments exist within the confines of state law, but most states have not taken an active role in overseeing them.

Estimates place the number of private enterprise shadow governments at about 150,000, the majority located in suburban areas. A condominium community provides an illustration. The property owners' association makes rules for residents (from the speed limit on community streets to the color of the condo), provides services (security, maintenance, landscaping), and assesses fees (based on the size of the unit). Residents typically vote for the board of directors of the association (in some instances, developers of the project retain seats on the board), and votes tend to be weighted according to the value of the housing unit. Owners with a greater financial investment have a greater say in the governing of the community, which is a far cry from the one-person, one-vote principle.

Shadow governments, especially the first two types, raise questions about matters of power and equity (but not about their efficiency because, by most accounts, they tend to operate fairly efficiently). The power issue centers on information, influence, and accountability. Shadow governments control information, restrict influence to those who belong or can pay, and have little public accountability. They are not subject to the same legal standards as are typical governments.[47] The equity issue addresses the class discrimination inherent in these governments. A poor family out for a Sunday drive may be able to traverse public streets in their ramshackle automobile, but if they turn their car onto a private street patrolled by private police, they are likely to be followed and perhaps even stopped, questioned, and escorted out of the neighborhood.

Whatever our uneasiness over power and equity issues related to shadow governments, their number is increasing. Shadow governments are especially popular in metropolitan areas, where in the words of one observer "local government boundaries are totally out of whack with the realities of economic geography or development patterns."[48] Their vaunted efficiency makes them a force to be reckoned with. Research on private enterprise shadow governments in California, Florida, and New Jersey showed each state taking vastly different approaches to their regulation.[49]

The social and economic changes in U.S. metropolitan areas have had a tremendous impact on urban governance. Urban expansion and shadow governments make up extended webs of interdependent jurisdictions. How can these places be governed best? Idealistic metropolitan reformers have called for regional government; more pragmatic observers have advocated regional coordination.

Regional Governance

regional government

An areawide structure for local governance, designed to replace multiple jurisdictions.

A **regional government** is a structure put in place because of the interdependence of proximate communities. Under a regional government, local jurisdictions give up some of their power and authority to a larger government in exchange for areawide solutions to local problems. State legislatures are important players in this process because, aside from the state constitution, they create the rules of the game. Their actions either facilitate or hinder local government reorganization into regional units.

city–county consolidation

The merger of city and county governments into a single jurisdiction.

City–County Consolidation In the United States, the closest thing to regional government is **city–county consolidation,** whereby area jurisdictions are absorbed into a single countywide government. Structure and function are unified. In a pure form of consolidation, one police department, one fire department, and one water and sewer system exist for the area. The functions of local government—public safety, public works, health and human services, community and economic development, and recreation and arts programs—are provided by a single jurisdiction. Thirty-two consolidated city–county governments exist in the United States. Some of these consolidated jurisdictions reflect political decisions of the nineteenth century, such as the combined city–county governments of Philadelphia, San Francisco, and New Orleans. Among the most prominent mergers of the past forty years are those in Indianapolis–Marion County, Indiana; Jacksonville–Duval County, Florida; and Nashville–Davidson County, Tennessee. Table 12.4 lists the consolidations that occurred in the past decade.

Regional government seems so rational, yet it has proven to be quite elusive. Voters usually defeat proposals to consolidate city and county government. During the 1990s, voters rejected the merger of Des Moines and Polk County, Iowa; Spokane and Spokane County, Washington; Wilmington and New Hanover County, North Carolina; and Knoxville and Knox County, Tennessee. Opponents of jurisdictional consolidation often include city and county governing boards, city and county employees, and taxpayer organizations. Support for merging

| TABLE 12.4 | **Recent City–County Consolidations** |

JURISDICTION	YEAR OF CONSOLIDATION
Augusta–Richmond County, GA	1996
Lafayette–Lafayette Parish, LA	1996
Kansas City–Wyandotte County, KS	1997
Louisville–Jefferson County, KY	2000

governments typically comes from the local Chamber of Commerce, real-estate developers, local newspapers, and civic organizations.[50]

To reformers, this lack of success is perplexing. The logic is straightforward: If small local governments in a metropolitan area merge to form a larger local government, two positive outcomes will occur. First, stubborn public policy problems can be tackled from an areawide perspective. For example, the pollution generated by City A that affects City B can be handled as a regional problem rather than as a conflict between the two cities. Second, combining forces produces *economies of scale* in service delivery. Instead of each jurisdiction constructing and operating separate jails, for example, one large regional facility can be maintained. Jail service can be provided at a lower cost to each participating jurisdiction. These outcomes are persuasive arguments for consolidation, and in 1996, two more city–county consolidations occurred: the city of Augusta and Richmond County, Georgia, merged, as did the city of Lafayette and Lafayette Parish, Louisiana. The following year, Kansas City, Kansas, and Wyandotte County consolidated, and in 2000, after rejecting consolidation on three previous occasions, voters approved the merger of Louisville, Kentucky, and Jefferson County.

Regional government does not always perform as expected. Research compared the taxing and spending policies of a consolidated jurisdiction with a comparable but unconsolidated area in the same state.[51] In Florida, both taxes and expenditures increased in consolidated Jacksonville–Duval County relative to those of unconsolidated Tampa–Hillsborough County. A study of pre-consolidation city and county budgets in Kansas City and Wyandotte County predicted only modest cost savings at best as a result of consolidation.[52] Another criticism of regional government is that it can be inaccessible and destructive of the hard-won political gains of minorities. Compared with a city or town government, regional government is farther away, both literally and figuratively. Residents of small towns fear the loss of identity as their community gets swept into bigger government. The effect on minority political strength, although not as obvious, is no less troublesome. Because the proportionate number of minorities may be lessened when jurisdictions are combined, their voting strength can be diluted. For instance, African Americans comprised 34 percent of pre-merger Louisville but only 19.5 percent of consolidated Louisville–Jefferson Metro Government.[53]

The successful consolidation votes in Georgia, Louisiana, Kansas, and Kentucky encourage reformers to push forward. One of the most interesting efforts underway in 2004 was in Buffalo, New York, where the county executive of Erie County proposed doing away with both city and county governments to create a new Greater Buffalo regional government.[54] This bold proposal came on the heels of the cash-strapped city's agreement to let the county take over its parks and its water system. Consolidation talk could be heard elsewhere, in Milwaukee, Wisconsin; Memphis, Tennessee; Fresno, California; Cedar Rapids, Iowa; and Tucson, Arizona. In each of these communities, merging governments is being promoted as a way to shake things up, and hopefully, lower costs. More rare than consolidation is secession, a topic discussed in the nearby *Breaking New Ground* box.

A City and Its Suburbs The former mayor of Albuquerque, New Mexico, David Rusk, after thinking long and hard about the relationship between a central city and its suburbs, jumped into the regionalism debate with this statement: "The real city is the total metropolitan area—city and suburb."[55] He uses the concept of elasticity (and inelasticity) to signify the ability of a city to expand its

BREAKING NEW GROUND

Killington, Vermont, Explores Its Options . . . in New Hampshire

Killington, Vermont, a place known as a skiing destination, may be heading down a slippery slope. At the annual town meeting in 2004, residents voted to explore the possibility of seceding from Vermont and becoming part of New Hampshire. To convey their seriousness, residents allocated $20,000 in the town's $2.5 million budget to get the secession movement underway. What fueled this unusual action? In a word: taxes. Killington residents were fed up with a Vermont tax system that, in their view, is inequitable, particularly with regard to funding for education. New Hampshire, their

neighbor to the east, looks inviting in comparison. Buoyed by the support of their fellow citizens, the leaders of the secession movement sought an audience with the governor of New Hampshire to pitch their idea.

The decision by Killington to pursue secession made financial sense. One economic study projected a tax savings of $10 million annually if the town joined New Hampshire. However, one logistical problem is that Killington is not on the Vermont-New Hampshire border; it is located twenty-five miles west of the Granite State. So, in effect, were it to join New Hampshire, Killington would be an out-of-state "island" in Vermont. Another problem is that any attempt to leave Vermont would have to be approved by the state legislature in the Green Mountain

state. The odds of that happening are slim to none.

Ultimately, what Killington residents really hope to accomplish with their bold exploit is to send a message to policymakers in the state capital, Montpelier. Threatening secession is an extreme action, but localities frustrated by state policies and actions have few tools at their disposal. And even if Killington's threat of secession is more bluster than reality, it will have attracted extensive media coverage to the issue of tax reform, and state policymakers will most certainly take notice.

SOURCES: Seth Harkness, "Killington Voters Opt to Leave Vt., Join N.H.," *Rutland Herald* March 4, 2004, p. 1; "Killington Residents Vote to Secede from Vermont," www.cnn.com (March 4, 2004).

city boundaries (or not). In a sense, a city's elasticity is its destiny. Elastic cities have been able to capture suburban growth; by adjusting their boundaries through annexation, they can keep pace with urban sprawl. Conversely, inelastic cities trapped in existing boundaries have suffered population loss and tax-base erosion, resulting in higher levels of racial and class segregation.

The solution offered is a familiar one: metropolitan government. But to be effective, the metropolitan government must include the central city and at least 60 percent of the area's population. The characteristics of the metropolitan area determine how this could be accomplished. In single-county metropolitan areas, empowerment of the urban county would effectively create metropolitan government, as would city–county consolidation. And in multicounty metropolitan areas, a single regional government could be created out of existing cities and counties. Obviously, the restructuring of local governments in these ways would engender substantial opposition; as Rusk contends, however, few alternatives are available to areas with low elasticity.

Put your ear to the ground and you can hear others beating a similar drum. A nationally syndicated columnist, Neal R. Peirce, has advocated the creation of citistates, a coherent urban whole formed from the central city and nearby communities.[56] The argument is simple: Since economies are essentially regional in nature, governance can (and should) be, too. As discussed earlier, however, regional governance has never been a popular alternative in this country. Overcoming traditional anti-regionalism sentiment will not be easy, but regional approaches may be necessary for effective competition in an increasingly global economy. Maybe the mayor of Missoula, Montana (population 57,000), said it best when he commented: "It is not possible for Missoula to understand itself, or its future, except in a regional context. The city draws its strength from the region."[57]

substate districts

Formal organizations of general-purpose governments in an area, intended to improve regional coordination.

Regional Coordination   Regional coordination is a variation on the regional government theme. **Substate districts,** usually called councils of government (COGs) or regional planning commissions, are examples. Substate districting does not involve a formal merger or combination of governments; instead, districts are loose collections of local governments designed to increase communication and coordination in an area. As noted earlier, they can become shadow governments. State governments were not active in the creation of substate districts; national government programs spurred their development. For example, the federal government requires states to create metropolitan planning organizations (MPOs) to coordinate transportation programs in urban areas.[58]

Although areawide planning is the most common activity of councils of government, they also perform other tasks. Member governments can turn to them for technical assistance (such as help in writing federal grant applications), professional services (planning, budgeting, engineering, legal advice), and information (economic data for the region).[59]

The impact of these councils has been less significant than their creators hoped, but they have had two positive effects. First, councils have elevated the concept of areawide policy planning from a pipe dream to a reality. They have been heavily involved in criminal justice, water quality, housing, and especially transportation planning. Second, councils have substantially improved the operational capacity of rural local governments by providing expertise to small local jurisdictions that cannot afford to hire specialized staff.

Some localities have taken a more informal route to regional coordination through service-sharing. In service-sharing, jurisdictions agree to consolidate specific services, cooperate in their provision, or exchange them. For instance, recreational facilities may be provided jointly by several jurisdictions, one government may rent jail space from another, or county residents may use the city library in return for city residents' use of the county's solid waste landfill. Service-sharing arrangements are popular because they hold the promise of greater efficiency in service delivery *and* they do not threaten the power and autonomy of existing jurisdictions the way consolidation does.

It's Up to the States   In many areas of the country, studies have found growing public enthusiasm for regionalism in its various forms. Researchers Larry Gerston and Peter Haas, in studying the San Jose area in California, have concluded that public concern about serious urban problems has generated new support for regional government. As they note, "With government boundaries and modern political problems increasingly not confluent, leaders and citizens alike must devise new schemes to overcome old jurisdictional lines."[60] One place that has done so is Portland, Oregon, where the city has joined with its suburbs and outlying jurisdictions to develop a regionwide vision for the future. The 2040 Plan, as it is called, aims at accommodating orderly growth while maintaining a desirable quality of life in the region. The planning process involved extensive public participation, including citizen surveys and public forums. In addition, the plan's backers launched media campaigns and offered free rental videos to acquaint residents with the proposal. The 2040 Plan is enforced by an elected regionwide council that works to secure the compliance of local governments.[61]

It would be erroneous, however, to assume that everyone everywhere is embracing regionalism. For instance, in southern California, surveys of the public report persistent negative attitudes toward regionalism.[62] In the final analysis, it is up to state government to provide a sufficiently supportive environment in which regionalism can take root.

STATES AND URBAN POLICY

If you have attended an urban policy conference recently, you would have heard the phrase *state government* used repeatedly. Many states have replaced some of their policies that had a negative impact on urban areas with urban-friendly programs. Michigan was one of the leaders when, in 1998, its Urban Caucus began a process of identifying state programs that hindered investment in central cities.[63] Since then, other states have followed suit. Three significant contemporary issues—housing, infrastructure, and new urbanism—are of particular interest in an urban environment. Let us consider each of these contemporary issues in terms of state–local interaction.

Housing Policy

For middle- and upper-income city residents, the housing market can be counted on to produce affordable units, but what is affordable to these residents is out of reach for low-income households. The mechanics of market economics effectively shut them out of the system. Low-cost housing does not generate the return that higher-cost housing does. As a result, governments have intervened to create incentives for developers to produce low-income housing units and, where incentives do not work, to become providers of housing themselves. One of the aims of the federal Housing Act of 1949 was "a decent home in a suitable living environment" for all Americans.

Over time, the national government has backed away from this goal and altered its approach to housing. In 1968, it was willing to become the nation's housing provider of last resort, but by 1982 the push was to deregulate and let market forces prevail. Modifications of national tax laws have had a negative effect on rental housing stock. Deliberate actions and inaction resulted in a decline in home ownership, an increase in the proportion of household income that is spent on housing, a decrease in the number of affordable rental units, an increase in the number of physically inadequate and abandoned structures, and an increase in the number of homeless people.[64]

In response, state governments have set up housing finance agencies, non-profit corporations have entered the low-income housing market, and local governments have adopted regulations to preserve their affordable housing stock. New Jersey, for example, mandated that all of its 567 communities provide their fair share of affordable housing for low- and moderate-income people. In some places, housing vouchers—a form of consumer subsidy that would open currently unaffordable housing to low-income residents—have been instituted. Another approach is for local governments to require developers to include a fixed proportion of affordable units in their market-rate projects as a condition for approval of a building permit. This approach works, however, only where developers are clamoring for access.

Connecticut has been particularly innovative in addressing its affordable-housing problem. As part of its statewide plan, the state conducted a housing needs assessment.[65] The bottom line is that "poor people don't make enough money to buy decent shelter at a price that the market can economically provide."[66] In a pilot program, Connecticut entered into mediated negotiations with local jurisdictions in a specified area to develop a fair-housing compact for the area. To encourage local jurisdictions to pursue the goals of the compact, it established a housing infrastructure fund to provide state financial assistance. As a result, thousands of new affordable housing units were constructed.[67] Connecticut's effort to address the scarcity of affordable housing has been emulated by other states.

Some local jurisdictions are also playing active roles. Montgomery County, Maryland, has been successful in generating affordable housing even as housing prices in the area have skyrocketed. The county requires developers to build low-cost housing in the suburban subdivisions they create.[68] In return for com-

density bonus

A provision that allows a developer to increase density (that is, build more homes) in a development in return for complying with a government regulation.

plying with this policy, developers receive a **density bonus** that allows them to build more homes than the zoning would have otherwise permitted. So-called moderately priced dwelling units (MPDUs) may look the same as other homes in the area, but they are sold (or rented) at below-market rates to lower-income people. The outcome has two positive effects: The county's supply of affordable housing increases, and neighborhoods become more economically diverse.

Infrastructure Policy

Infrastructure—public works projects and services—is the physical network of a community, that is, its roads and bridges, airports, water and sewer systems, and public buildings. Its importance lies in its connection to development; the simplest equation is, no infrastructure = no development. Infrastructure has become an issue in many communities because of its crumbling condition and the high cost of repair or replacement. For example, it will cost Baltimore nearly $940 million over fourteen years to fix defective sewer pipes and connections that discharge untreated waste into the Chesapeake Bay.[69] The price tag in Atlanta is even higher: $3 billion to overhaul its sewer system and upgrade its water-treatment facilities.[70] But the granddaddy of all recent infrastructure projects is the Big Dig in Boston: a $14.6 billion transportation project that, among other things, replaced an elevated highway with underground roads, bridges, and green space.

States take different approaches in financing local public works, and tradition is a powerful explanation of this behavior.[71] Generally, they are providing more financial support for local public works today than they did in the early 1980s, through grants, dedicated revenues (the money collected from a particular tax), loans, and bonds. States that have been particularly inventive in public works assistance include Pennsylvania, Massachusetts, Virginia, Wisconsin, and Wyoming.[72] Pennsylvania, for instance, allows cities to become financial partners in constructing roads to shopping malls and industrial sites. Massachusetts, through its Aquifer Land Acquisition Program, purchases property or development rights to protect public drinking-water supplies.

The stock of aging, sometimes unsafe infrastructure—coupled with declining federal aid for public works—has prompted states to cast about for solutions. In the area of transportation infrastructure, one approach receiving greater scrutiny is privatization. Nearly one-quarter of the states have allowed the construction of private toll roads. Private highway projects are criticized on two counts. Some argue that private roadways will produce a have/have-not distinction, with the affluent traversing pay roads and the poor being dispatched to congested freeways. Others claim that privatization offers a Band-Aid solution to the enormous transportation problems facing the nation. Despite these concerns, privatization remains an attractive option to governors and legislatures intent on holding down highway taxes.[73]

new urbanism

An anti-suburban, pro-small-town version of city planning.

New Urbanism

One of the most intriguing efforts at transforming the urban experience has its roots in architecture and urban planning. Called **new urbanism,** the approach rejects the suburban model of development in favor of a traditional small-town style. Proponents of new urbanism, especially Miami-based architects Andres Duany and Elizabeth Plater-Zyberk, have advocated what is essentially a high-density, pedestrian-friendly, environmentally sensitive design for communities.[74] In theory, residents of new urban places will acquire a sense of community and become engaged in civic life. One of the first experiments with new urbanism was the development of Seaside, Florida. (Movie buffs will remember it as the town where *The Truman Show* was filmed.) Another, called Celebration, has been created by the Walt Disney Company on 5,000 acres on the fringe of Orlando, Florida. It is a corporate-planned town with a private government.

The real test for new urbanism will be in an existing city, not in a geographically separate enclave. Can new urbanism work in a place plagued by social disorder and disinvestment? The answer to that question will not be known for years, and many observers are skeptical. An effort with some new-urbanism elements is taking place in Kansas City, Missouri, where a multiyear, grassroots strategic plan called FOCUS aims at redeveloping neglected neighborhoods.[75] The centerpiece is the conversion of Union Station into a science museum/multimodal transit center, complemented by a new entertainment center, hotels, and housing in the downtown area. San Diego, California, another city with pockets of new-urbanism development, has adjusted its building codes and zoning laws to accommodate the trend.[76]

So far, states have not taken new urbanism to heart. But as states seek ways to revitalize declining central cities, new urbanism may become a promising approach.

Seaside, Florida, designed with new urbanism principles in mind, is an idyllic beach town.
SOURCE: CORBIS.

STATES AND THEIR RURAL COMMUNITIES

When the local Dairy Queen closes its doors, a small town in rural America knows that it is in trouble. The Dairy Queen, like the coffee shop on Main Street, serves as a gathering place for community residents. Its demise symbolizes the tough times that a lot of rural communities face. In fact, some analysts argue that the major distinctions in regional economics are no longer between Sunbelt and Frostbelt, or East Coast and West Coast, but between metropolitan America and the countryside.[77] America's economy flourished in the 1990s, but several old rural towns in the Great Plains states became veritable ghost towns.

The places described above are examples of *declining communities,* suffering losses in both population and economic base. Typically, declining communities have had economies based on farming, mining, or manufacturing. But, not all rural areas are suffering. Three other community growth types can be identified from economic and demographic trends.[78] The opposite of a declining community is a *dynamic growth community,* where both population and economic growth are occurring. These places often have a locational advantage, that is, they are located closer to urban areas or coasts. A third type, *strain communities,* experiences population growth without proportionate gains in personal income. Over time, they may find themselves strapped to provide adequate public services to residents. Finally, in *preservation communities,* even though the population is stable or declining, personal income is on the increase. Without raising taxes, preservation communities can improve the quality of their public services and expand the range of services they offer. Yet even the more prosperous places face the real possibility that additional growth will disturb the community's rural flavor and identity.

The distressing news for declining communities is that, compared with the other types, studies have shown that their local leaders are the least supportive of administrative modernization and change.[79] Local governments in these communities are less capable of responding creatively to the problems they face. Consequently, the gap between places where dynamic growth is occurring and the declining communities is likely to increase. The fear is that this phenomenon will become self-perpetuating, until some communities simply disappear. Research on rural communities in the Midwest lends some credibility to this contention: The communities that have withstood economic downturns are those that have had the administrative capacity to identify and pursue opportunities. Macon County, Missouri, is an example. With "hard work, luck, and heads-up opportunism," Macon County transformed itself from a declining community into a dynamic growth community.[80]

What can state governments do to encourage the right kind of growth in rural areas? Short of pumping enormous amounts of money into the local economy, they can encourage the expansion of local intergovernmental cooperation, whereby small rural governments join together to increase their administrative capacity to deliver services and achieve economies of scale. Two state actions facilitate such cooperation. One is reform of state tax codes, so that jurisdictions can share locally generated tax revenues. Rather than competing with one another for a new manufacturing plant or a shopping mall, local governments can cooperate to bring the new facility to the area; regardless of where this facility is located, all jurisdictions can receive a portion of the tax revenue. A second useful state action is the promotion of statewide land-use planning. As one observer has noted, "Currently too many rural local governments engage in wasteful inter-community competition, mutually antagonistic zoning, and contradictory development plans."[81]

In 1990, a new federal initiative offered states a means of redesigning their rural development efforts. Concerned that existing rural programs were fragmented and only partially successful, the national government selected eight states for a pilot study in cooperation.[82] In those states, newly established rural development councils brought together—for the first time—federal, state, and local officials involved in rural development. Rather than mandating the structure of the councils and their agendas, the federal government assumed a hands-off posture and simply provided the necessary start-up funds. During the following years, each of the councils designed its own initiative aimed at specific conditions and problems confronting the state. Mississippi, for example, worked on a tourism and recreation project, South Dakota developed an on-line resource data base, and Washington undertook the issues of affordable housing and job retraining. The promise of these state-based interorganizational networks is substantial, and during the decade many successful projects were completed. Thinking optimistically, the federal government extended the initiative to another thirty states.

THE INTERACTION OF STATE AND LOCAL GOVERNMENTS

Constitutionally, state governments are supreme in their dealings with local governments. New York City, Los Angeles, and Chicago are large, world-class cities but even they have to follow the dictates of their respective state governments. Even so, power does not flow in only one direction. The political realities are such that these cities and their smaller counterparts influence what happens in their state capitols. Suffice it to say, the state–local relationship is subject to constant adjustment. A recent Governor's Task Force to Renew Montana Government, for instance, adopted several provisions aimed at diminishing the influence of the state in what are considered purely local issues.

Some issues or problems require a statewide, uniform response, while others are the particular concern of a single local jurisdiction. Consider the problem of drought, a condition that has affected most of the western states since 2000. Some areas of Colorado, such as Denver, have been especially hard hit. A local agency, Denver Water, is responsible for water management in the city; a state agency, the Colorado Water Conservation Board, has statewide authority. To address the drought problem, both agencies had to work together. The comments of a hydrologist capture the situation, "There needs to be a state coordinating mechanism, but it needs to be sensitive to the local context."[83] Thus, even with the constitutional superiority of the state, the state–local relationship is much more nuanced.

The words of New York Governor George Pataki are apropos: "As a former mayor, I know firsthand the importance of freeing our cities, towns, and counties from the heavy hand of state government."[84] But a governor has to engage in big-picture, statewide thinking, and it is awfully tempting to impose the state's will on those same localities. Thus, the state–local government relationship is not always harmonious. When San Francisco began issuing marriage licenses to same-sex couples in 2004, the state of California took the city to court. As the California attorney general said, "State law controls every aspect of marriage, leaving nothing to the discretion of local government."[85] But to the city by the Bay—and to other localities—that approach is just wrong.

CHAPTER RECAP

- States vary in the amount and type of authority they give their local governments. The general trend has been toward increased state assistance and empowerment of localities, but some states continue to keep their local governments on a short leash.
- The issue of mandates is a particularly contentious state–local matter.
- Three types of state–local organizations are common: task forces, advisory commissions on intergovernmental relations, and departments of community affairs.
- Urban sprawl has become a major issue in state–local relations. States have begun to adopt smart-growth laws that are designed to help localities manage growth.
- Regionalism continues to be advocated as a solution to many local problems. More jurisdictions are creating regional organizations to link their local governments.
- States continue to seek innovative solutions to challenging housing and infrastructure problems.
- New urbanism promotes a back-to-the-future community that appeals to a particular segment of the market.
- Rural communities come in many forms: dynamic growth, declining growth, strain communities, and preservation communities.
- Even as the interaction of states and localities becomes more positive, the tug of war between the two levels continues.

Key Terms

Dillon's rule *(p. 330)*
mandate-reimbursement requirements *(p. 334)*
edge cities *(p. 337)*
urban sprawl *(p. 340)*
impact fee *(p. 340)*
smart growth *(p. 340)*

greenbelts *(p. 341)*
shadow governments *(p. 342)*
regional government *(p. 343)*
city–county consolidation *(p. 343)*
substate districts *(p. 346)*
density bonus *(p. 349)*
new urbanism *(p. 349)*

Surfing the Web

The National Association of Regional Councils maintains a web site at **www.narc.org/.** It shows the differences and similarities of regional councils across the country.

The Association of Bay Area Governments' award-winning site can be found at **www.abag.ca.gov.**

The web site for the regional planning agency that deals with 184 cities and 6 counties in Southern California is **www.scag.ca.gov.**

For information on the activities of a state-level ACIR, see the Virginia ACIR at **www.acir.state.va.us.**

The Urban Institute's site for research on economic and social policy can be found at **www.urban.org.** It is a useful source of information on states and localities.

The Sierra Club presents its case against urban sprawl at **www.sierraclub.org/sprawl.**

To learn more about new urbanism, see **www.cnu.org,** the web site for the Congress of the New Urbanism.

Texas Rural Partners Inc., a rural development council, has a web site at **www.trdc.org.** Other states with rural development councils maintain web sites also.

STATE AND LOCAL FINANCE

Idaho Governor Dirk Kempthorne called it "the worst budget crisis among the states since World War II." Nevada's Governor Kenny Guinn asserted that his state's fiscal crisis was as "challenging as any period in [the state's] history." In Kansas, Governor Kathleen Sibelius told her constituents that they confronted "problems of historic proportions."[1] The depths of the budget holes states were looking up from in 2002–2003 are illustrated by the following (sometimes desperate) actions:

- Kentucky released 567 felons from state prisons, including a three-time bank robber.
- The governor of Missouri ordered workers to unscrew every third light bulb in state buildings to save on utilities.
- Teachers were forced to take on janitorial duties in Oklahoma public schools.

- In Idaho, towns held bake sales and auctions to pay teachers.
- The University of Nebraska eliminated 431 positions and cancelled financial aid for some 1,000 students.
- Texas dropped 275,000 children from health care coverage.
- Detroit offered to take 50 percent off unpaid traffic tickets and driving offenses for those miscreants who would come forward and pay.
- The public works department in Boise, Idaho, intentionally plugged delinquent taxpayers' sewer lines, causing vile backups.
- Many states and localities sold surplus property—from old fire trucks to scoreboards—on eBay.

Obviously, serious debt spawns creative and sometimes desperate thinking. This chapter deals with state and local finance: the politics and policies of taxing and spending. Finance is a topic of continuing, visceral interest in state and local jurisdictions, and the activities of taxing and spending are characterized by much change and experimentation. From taxpayer revolts to rainy day funds, the fiscal landscape has changed profoundly during the past thirty years. More change is certain as state and local governments strive to meet taxpayer service demands economically and creatively.

Students and their families protest cuts in education spending in California.
SOURCE: Stone/Getty Images.

THE PRINCIPLES OF FINANCE

A major purpose of government is to provide services to citizens, but providing services costs money: Equipment must be purchased and employees must be paid. Governments raise needed funds through taxes, fees, and borrowing. In a democracy, the voters decide what range and quality of services they desire and they register their decisions through elected representatives. Sometimes, when elected officials don't listen, voters revolt and take matters directly into their own hands.

Citizens in the eighteenth and nineteenth centuries expected few services from their state and local governments. The taxation of property was the major source of state and local revenue until the beginning of the twentieth century. Property taxes were augmented by business licenses, poll taxes, and various miscellaneous sources. As the scope and level of services rose in response to citizen demands, states and localities developed a wider array of revenue-raising methods, including taxes on income, merchandise sales, auto license plates, alcohol, tobacco, gasoline, and certain services.

Two basic principles describe state and local financial systems as they have evolved: *interdependence* and *diversity*. State and local fiscal systems are closely interlinked and heavily influenced by national financial activities. Intergovernmental sharing of revenues is a pronounced feature of our interdependent federal fiscal system. Yet our state financial structures and processes are also highly diverse. Though affected by national activities, their own economic health, and competitive pressures from one another, the states enjoy substantial autonomy in designing individual revenue systems in response to citizens' policy preferences.

Interdependence

Governments in the United States raise huge amounts of money. In 2002, the national government took in more than $2 trillion in revenues, and the states and localities collected about the same. Most of this money is **own-source revenue,** garnered from taxes, charges, and fees applied to people, services, and products within the jurisdiction of each level of government. Nonnational governments also benefit from **intergovernmental transfers.** The national government contributes about one-quarter of all state and local revenues; however, more than 60 percent of this federal money is passed through to *individual* recipients such as those receiving Medicaid. For their part, states pass on more than $220 billion to their cities, counties, and special-purpose governments.[2] Some states are economic powerhouses. California's $1.5 trillion economy is the fifth largest in the world, just ahead of France.

Local governments rely heavily on the states, and to a lesser degree on the national government, for financial authority and assistance. Only the states can authorize localities to levy taxes and fees, incur debt, and spend money. State constitutions and laws place many conditions on local government taxing and spending. As federal aid declined in importance, states increased their monetary support of local governments through state grants-in-aid and revenue sharing; they also assumed financial responsibility for activities previously paid for by localities—in particular, school and social welfare costs. The emergence of the

own-source revenue
Monies derived by a government from its own taxable resources.

intergovernmental transfers
The movement of money or other resources from one level of government to another.

states as senior financial partners in state–local finance has been challenged in some states (especially those without state income taxes) because of the need for large local tax increases to fund school improvements or local services.

Although federal grants to local governments have dropped (in constant dollars) since 1978, state–local finances continue to be linked closely to activities of the national government. For instance, when the federal government changes the tax code, it can wreak havoc on those thirty-five states that base their own income taxes on the federal tax code. Congress's repeal of the estate tax was expected to cost the states upwards of $5.5 billion over the next ten years.[3]

When national monetary and fiscal policies push the nation into a recession, state and local governments suffer most. This fact is sometimes recognized by Congress, which may send substantial amounts of **coun04cyclical aid** to the states and localities to help them recover from the ravages of recession. During the recession of 2001–2003, countercyclical aid was limited to $20 billion, with half of that earmarked for Medicaid costs.

coun04cyclical aid
A transfer of federal dollars to states and localities to counteract a downturn in the economic cycle.

Diversity

The second basic principle of state and local finance systems is diversity of revenue sources. Each level of government depends on one type of revenue device more than others. For the national government, it is the income tax; for the states, the sales tax; and for local governments, the property tax. But diversity triumphs among the states. Differences in tax capacity (wealth), tax effort, and tax choices are obvious even to the casual observer. (Some of these differences are illustrated in Table 13.1.) Most states tax personal income and merchandise

TABLE 13.1 **State Tax Collections and Percentage Distribution by Type of Tax, Fiscal Year 2003**

| | | DISTRIBUTION—PERCENTAGE OF TOTAL | | | | | |
	TOTAL ($)	GENERAL SALES & USE	INDIVIDUAL INCOME	CORPORATE INCOME	MOTOR FUELS	LICENSES	ALL OTHER
Alabama	6,368,026	26.7	33.0	2.7	7.9	6.8	22.9
Alaska	1,428,698	0.0	0.0	28.0	2.6	5.1	64.2
Arizona	8,456,739	46.4	27.2	6.4	7.1	3.0	9.7
Arkansas	4,911,035	36.1	31.9	3.8	8.3	4.5	15.5
California	90,453,746	26.9	49.3	7.6	3.5	4.3	8.4
Colorado	7,566,919	26.0	51.5	4.5	7.5	4.0	6.5
Connecticut	10,590,296	32.8	42.2	3.9	4.2	3.3	13.6
Delaware	2,174,440	0.0	33.1	9.5	4.6	39.1	13.7
Florida	24,938,748	59.0	0.0	6.4	6.9	6.2	21.5
Georgia	14,368,505	34.1	48.2	4.8	4.6	3.5	4.7
Hawaii	3,507,770	46.8	31.5	1.7	2.2	3.3	14.5
Idaho	2,558,098	30.6	40.3	5.6	8.1	9.7	5.8

	TOTAL ($)	DISTRIBUTION—PERCENTAGE OF TOTAL					
		GENERAL SALES & USE	INDIVIDUAL INCOME	CORPORATE INCOME	MOTOR FUELS	LICENSES	ALL OTHER
Illinois	23,150,229	27.3	33.1	9.6	5.9	7.9	16.2
Indiana	10,204,197	35.3	37.0	8.1	7.4	3.0	9.1
Iowa	5,158,780	34.0	36.6	3.2	6.9	9.6	9.6
Kansas	4,993,526	34.9	39.8	4.7	7.4	4.6	8.6
Kentucky	7,850,908	28.8	33.8	4.6	5.7	7.0	20.1
Louisiana	7,193,998	33.4	24.3	4.1	7.5	6.6	24.2
Maine	2,668,938	30.6	43.5	3.6	7.1	5.2	10.0
Maryland	10,785,695	24.5	43.8	4.6	6.4	3.7	16.9
Massachusetts	17,225,270	21.8	57.5	7.0	3.8	2.9	7.0
Michigan	22,263,874	34.7	30.5	9.4	4.8	5.5	15.0
Minnesota	13,534,585	27.9	43.6	5.4	4.5	6.0	12.6
Mississippi	4,749,481	49.0	21.8	4.4	8.5	6.4	9.9
Missouri	8,837,196	31.7	43.2	2.7	7.6	6.6	8.1
Montana	1,495,805	0.0	37.2	6.9	12.3	8.3	35.3
Nebraska	3,028,204	33.8	40.5	4.6	9.6	6.1	5.5
Nevada	3,832,227	53.5	0.0	0.0	6.5	9.7	30.3
New Hampshire	1,775,810	0.0	4.3	19.7	7.9	8.2	59.9
New Jersey	19,253,297	29.9	41.5	6.8	2.7	4.4	14.7
New Mexico	4,002,246	40.5	20.7	4.8	5.0	4.0	25.0
New York	44,855,582	19.6	59.0	7.1	1.1	1.9	11.3
North Carolina	15,625,133	22.1	48.2	4.6	7.7	6.1	11.2
North Dakota	1,231,049	27.6	17.3	5.1	9.1	7.7	33.1
Ohio	19,617,950	32.1	42.3	3.4	6.7	7.6	8.0
Oklahoma	6,341,714	24.2	35.9	2.6	6.3	12.7	18.2
Oregon	5,892,963	0.0	74.4	5.5	6.9	7.1	6.2
Pennsylvania	22,562,195	32.1	31.7	6.2	3.5	9.6	16.9
Rhode Island	2,243,295	31.0	41.4	3.5	5.8	3.9	14.4
South Carolina	6,147,594	40.5	34.6	3.1	6.6	6.3	8.8
South Dakota	977,469	52.7	0.0	4.4	12.4	14.3	16.1
Tennessee	7,821,984	57.3	2.5	8.6	9.9	11.2	10.4
Texas	29,422,936	50.0	0.0	0.0	9.4	12.8	27.9
Utah	4,065,364	36.4	41.9	4.0	8.0	3.5	6.1
Vermont	1,552,739	13.8	31.1	2.9	4.2	5.0	42.9
Virginia	13,085,329	20.2	55.2	2.8	6.5	4.1	11.2
Washington	12,679,410	63.6	0.0	0.0	5.8	4.9	25.6
West Virginia	3,422,875	27.1	29.8	6.3	6.9	4.5	25.4
Wisconsin	11,768,235	30.7	43.8	4.2	7.8	6.0	7.6
Wyoming	1,124,296	36.1	0.0	0.0	5.9	8.1	49.9
All states	559,765,398	32.1	37.1	5.7	5.4	5.9	13.9

SOURCE: Used by permission of The Tax Foundation, based on data from the Department of Commerce, Bureau of the Census.

sales, but a handful do not. A growing number of states operate lotteries and pari-mutuel betting facilities.

Some states, such as Alaska and Hawaii, tax with a heavy hand. Others, including New Hampshire, South Dakota, and Texas, are relative tax havens. Most fall somewhere in the middle. If the basic objective of taxing is to pluck the maximum number of feathers from the goose with the minimum amount of hissing, the wealthy states hold a great advantage because they can reap high tax revenues with much less effort than can poor states, which must tax at high rates just to pull in enough money to pay for the basics. Per-capita state and local tax revenues vary from $4,595 in Connecticut to $2,117 in Alabama. The U.S. average in 2002 was $3,100.[4] A fairly close relationship exists between state wealth (as measured by personal income) and tax burden. Table 13.2 shows how the states compare in state and local tax revenues, controlling for personal income. Joining New York and Hawaii as high-tax states are Wisconsin and Minnesota. At the low end of the scale are Alaska, Tennessee, New Hampshire, and Alabama. Tax levels can reflect factors such as citizen attitudes, population characteristics and trends, business climate, and the quality as well as quantity of government services. And taxes are only one method of plucking the goose. State and local governments increasingly rely on fees and charges for specific services provided. Examples include entrance fees for parks and recreation facilities, sewer and garbage fees, and motor vehicle fees.

tax capacity
The taxable resources of a government jurisdiction.

tax effort
The extent to which a jurisdiction exploits its taxable resources.

There is an important difference between **tax capacity,** the potential ability to raise revenues from taxes, and **tax effort,** the degree to which a state exploits its fiscal potential. High tax capacity is associated with high levels of urbanization, per-capita income, industrial development, and natural resources. But simply because a state has high revenue-raising capacity does not necessarily mean that it will maximize its tax-collecting possibilities. Indeed, many states with high revenue potential, such as Alaska and Wyoming, actually tax at relatively low rates, indicating low tax effort.[5] Tax effort depends largely on the scope and level of services desired by the people.

REVENUES

Although the state and local finance systems have their own strengths, weaknesses, and peculiarities, certain trends can be found in all of them. The property tax is increasingly unpopular. It is no longer a significant source of state revenue; however, its contribution to total own-source local coffers is still strong. User fees and other miscellaneous charges are gradually growing. States continue to depend heavily on the sales tax, but alternatives are being used more widely. In fact, tax diversification is an important trend in all state and local tax systems (see Figure 13.1 and Figure 13.2).

Criteria for Evaluating Taxes

Numerous criteria can be used to evaluate taxes. What one person or interest group likes about a tax may be what another dislikes. Nevertheless, most political

TABLE 13.2   **State/Local and Total Taxes by State,
As a Percentage of Personal Income, 2003**

STATE	STATE/LOCAL TAXES AS A % OF INCOME	STATE/LOCAL RANK	STATE	STATE/LOCAL TAXES AS A % OF INCOME	STATE/LOCAL RANK
Maine	12.2	1	Maryland	9.5	27
New York	12.0	2	Louisiana	9.5	28
Minnesota	11.0	3	Michigan	9.4	29
Rhode Island	11.0	4	Illinois	9.4	30
Connecticut	10.9	5	Kentucky	9.4	31
Hawaii	10.7	6	Colorado	9.3	32
Wisconsin	10.7	7	Arkansas	9.2	33
California	10.6	8	Missouri	9.2	34
Utah	10.6	9	Oklahoma	9.1	35
Ohio	10.3	10	Pennsylvania	9.1	36
Idaho	10.2	11	Montana	9.1	37
Vermont	10.1	12	South Carolina	9.0	38
Massachusetts	9.9	13	Oregon	9.0	39
Arizona	9.9	14	Virginia	8.9	40
Georgia	9.9	15	Nevada	8.9	41
Nebraska	9.8	16	South Dakota	8.5	42
North Dakota	9.8	17	Wyoming	8.5	43
Washington	9.8	18	Florida	8.4	44
New Jersey	9.8	19	Alabama	8.4	45
Kansas	9.8	20	Texas	8.3	46
New Mexico	9.7	21	Tennessee	7.7	47
Indiana	9.7	22	Delaware	7.3	48
West Virginia	9.7	23	New Hampshire	6.6	49
Mississippi	9.6	24	Alaska	5.5	50
North Carolina	9.5	25	U.S. average	9.7	
Iowa	9.5	26			

NOTE: Figures for the states exclude federal income taxes. The states are listed according to the amount of income they realize from state and local taxes; the state with the highest percentage from these sources is listed first.
SOURCE: Used by permission of The Tax Foundation, www.taxfoundation.org (accessed April 21, 2003).

FIGURE 13.1   Distribution of Total State Tax Revenue by Source, 2003

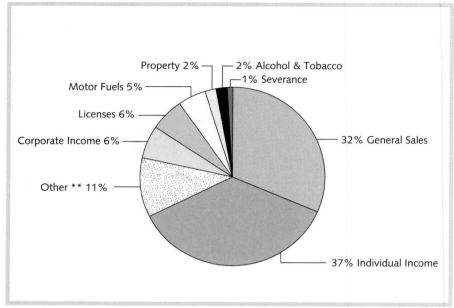

Property 2%
2% Alcohol & Tobacco
1% Severance
Motor Fuels 5%
Licenses 6%
Corporate Income 6%
Other ** 11%
32% General Sales
37% Individual Income

*Includes motor vehicle, hunting and fishing, alcoholic beverage, public utility, and occupation and business license fees.
**Includes insurance, estate and gift, and severance taxes, and nonlicense taxes on public utilities.
SOURCE: Used by permission of The Tax Foundation, www.taxfoundation.org.

scientists and economists agree that among the most important criteria are equity, yield, elasticity, ease of administration, political accountability, and acceptability.

Equity If citizens or firms are expected to pay a tax, they should view it as fair. In the context of taxation, equity usually refers to distributing the burden of the tax in accordance with ability to pay: High income means greater ability to pay and therefore a larger tax burden. Equity also has other dimensions such as the relative tax burden on individuals versus firms and the impact of various types of taxes on income, age, and social class.

regressive tax

A tax in which the rate falls as the base or taxable income rises.

Taxes may be regressive, progressive, or proportional. A **regressive tax** places a greater burden on low-income citizens than on high-income citizens. Thus, the ability-to-pay principle is violated, with the result that upper-income groups contribute a smaller portion of their incomes than lower-income groups do. Most state and local levies, including property and sales taxes, are considered regressive. For example, both low-income and high-income people would pay, say, a 5 percent sales tax. The latter will likely make more purchases and contribute more total dollars in sales tax, but at a lower percentage of their total income than the low-income individuals.

FIGURE 13.2   Total Tax Revenue for Local Governments, by Source, 2002

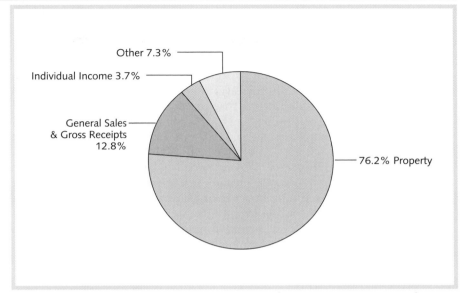

Other 7.3%

Individual Income 3.7%

General Sales & Gross Receipts 12.8%

76.2% Property

SOURCE: U.S. Census Bureau data, 2002, *Governing Sourcebook 2003* (supplement to *Governing* magazine), p. 36. Reprinted by permission of *Governing*.

progressive tax

A tax in which the rate rises as the base or taxable income rises.

A **progressive tax** increases as a percentage of a person's income as that income rises. The more you make, the greater proportion of your income is extracted by the progressive tax. Thus, those better able to pay carry a heavier tax burden than do the poor. The national income tax is a good example of a progressive tax. The more you earn, the higher your *income tax bracket*. Among the states, Montana's personal income tax is highly progressive, varying from 2 percent to 11 percent of taxable income, depending on the level of taxable income.

proportional (flat) tax

A tax in which people pay an identical rate regardless of income or economic transaction.

A **proportional tax,** sometimes called a **flat tax,** burdens everyone equally, at least in theory. For instance, a tax on income of, say, 10 percent that is applied across the board is a proportional tax. Whether you earn $100,000 or $10,000, you pay a flat 10 percent of the total in taxes. Of course, it can be argued that a low-income person is more burdened by a proportional income tax than a high-income person (as is true of the sales tax).

benefit principle

The principle that taxes should be levied on those who benefit directly from a government service.

Instead of ability to pay, some people advocate the **benefit principle.** Under this principle, those who reap more benefits from government services should shoulder more of the tax burden than people who do not avail themselves of service opportunities to the same degree. As a hypothetical example, it might be argued that parents whose children attend public schools should pay higher taxes for education than should senior citizens, childless couples, or single people without children. The benefit principle is the theoretical underpinning for user fees, which charge a taxpayer directly for services received.

Yield Taxes can also be evaluated on the basis of how much money they contribute to government coffers compared to the effort expended to collect them. The administrative and other costs of applying a tax must be taken into consideration when determining yield. Taxes that return substantial sums of money at minimal costs are preferred to taxes that require large outlays for moderate revenues. Income and sales taxes have high yields because they raise large sums of money at low expense. Property taxes, however, have lower yields because they are more expensive to assess and collect. Yield depends on base and rate. The broader the tax base and the higher the rate, the higher the yield. For example, a sales tax applied to all purchases yields much more than a sales tax on cigarette purchases, and a $1.00-per-pack tax produces more money than a 25¢ tax.

Elasticity This criterion is related to yield. Tax yields should be automatically responsive to changes in economic conditions, and revenue devices should expand or contract their yields as government expenditure needs change. Specifically, as per-capita income grows within the state and its localities, revenues should keep pace without increases in the tax rate. Tax reductions should accompany economic recession and declines in per-capita income so that citizens' tax burdens are not increased during hard times. The national income tax is considered to be elastic because revenues increase as individuals earn more money and move into higher tax brackets and decline as income falls. User fees, for example, generally do not move in tandem with economic conditions and are therefore considered to be inelastic.

Ease of Administration Taxes should be simple to understand and compute. They should also be easy to apply in a nonarbitrary fashion and difficult to evade. Income taxes are fairly easy to collect because most are deducted from paychecks and remitted to the state by employers. Local property taxes are difficult to administer because of the time and expense involved in regularly appraising property values and the inherent subjectivity of placing a dollar value on buildings and land. The sales tax is easy to administer at the time and place of sale, and nearly impossible to evade. (Exceptions to this rule involve out-of-state catalog and Internet sales, and consumers who cross state borders to avoid high sales taxes on merchandise, cigarettes, gasoline, and alcohol.)

Political Accountability Tax increases should not be hidden. Instead, state and local legislative bodies should have to approve them deliberately—and publicly. Citizens should know how much they owe and when it must be paid. For example, some state income taxes are silently hiked as wages rise in response to cost-of-living increases. After inflation is accounted for, taxpayers make the same income as they did before, but they are driven into a higher income bracket for tax purposes. This phenomenon, known as bracket creep, can be eliminated by **indexing** income tax brackets to changes in the cost of living.

indexing
A system in which tax brackets are automatically adjusted to account for inflation.

Acceptability The type and mix of taxes imposed should be congruent with citizen preferences. No tax commands wild enthusiastic applause, but some are less disagreeable than others. Tax acceptability varies from place to place depending on numerous factors, including equity implications and the perceived pain of paying. Large, direct payments, such as the annual property tax, inflict greater pain than small, frequently paid sales taxes. And a tax on someone else is always preferable. As Senator Russell Long of Louisiana put it many years ago, "Don't tax me, don't tax thee; tax that man behind the tree."

Major State and Local Taxes

The principal types of taxes are those on property, sales, and income. Various miscellaneous taxes also provide much-needed revenue for state and local governments.

Property Tax In 1942, taxes on personal and corporate property accounted for 53 percent of all state and local tax revenues. Today, they represent only 28 percent of tax revenue, and only 20 percent of all forms of revenue. States hardly utilize the property tax at all today (it accounts for only about 4 percent of their total revenues), but local governments continue to depend on this fiscal workhorse for three-quarters of all their own-source revenues. Other revenue sources have augmented the property tax so its proportionate contribution has diminished overall. As always, considerable variation exists from one state to another. States such as New Hampshire, which has no sales or income taxes, depend on property taxes for a high percentage of their total state and local tax revenues.

The best feature of the property tax is that it is certain; owners of property must pay it or the government may seize and sell their land, buildings, or other taxable possessions. But it has lost acceptability in recent years because it tends to be regressive, lacks political accountability, is hard to administer, and sometimes must be paid in a large lump sum. At first thought, it seems that property taxes cannot be truly regressive because only those people who own property pay taxes on it directly; however, renters pay property taxes indirectly through their monthly rent checks to the landlord. When property tax assessments climb, so do rental charges. Property taxes can also violate the ability-to-pay principle when housing values spiral upward, as they have done recently in Utah, Colorado, Oregon, and Arizona. Home owners on fixed incomes, such as retired people, discover with alarm that their annual property tax bills are rising sharply as housing prices escalate.

Just this sort of situation helped precipitate Proposition 13 in California, which was credited with kicking off a taxpayer revolt across the United States. In the Los Angeles and San Francisco Bay areas during the 1970s, property taxes doubled and then tripled in only a few years. Some senior citizens were forced to sell their homes to pay their property tax. Proposition 13 reduced property-tax bills by approximately $7 billion in the first year, and it imposed strict limitations on the ability of local governments to raise property and other taxes in the future. California dropped from the eighth-highest property-tax state to the twenty-eighth. This example illustrates the problem of political accountability: When property values rise to lofty heights, taxpayers' bills keep pace (unless they revolt), even though elected officials do not explicitly vote to hike property taxes.

Property taxes are difficult to administer and somewhat arbitrary. The process of levying an annual fee on real property (land and buildings) begins with a government assessor making a formal appraisal of the market value of the land and the buildings on it. Then property values are equalized so that similarly valued real estate is taxed at the same level. Time is set aside to make corrections and to review appeals on appraisals that the owner believes are too high. Next, an assessment ratio is applied to the property. For instance, houses might be assessed for tax purposes at 80 percent of market value. A rate is placed on the assessed value to calculate the annual tax amount. A house assessed at a market price of $100,000, and taxed at a ratio of .80 and a rate of $3 per $100 (30 mils), would produce a tax due of $2,400. Determining market value may seem fairly straightforward, but ultimately the appraised market value depends on the findings of the assessor, who may or may not be properly trained for the job or fully aware of conditions in the local housing market. Computer-assisted appraisals can remove some of the guesswork. Property can thus be underappraised or overappraised. For the sake of equity, property should be appraised regularly (for example, every five years). Otherwise, property that does not change ownership becomes increasingly undervalued.

Property tax systems are further criticized for exempting certain types of real estate and buildings. Government buildings such as hospitals and state offices are not taxed, even though they utilize police and fire protection, trash collection, and other local government services. Churches, synagogues, mosques, and related property used for religious purposes are also exempted in the vast majority of jurisdictions, as is property owned by charitable organizations. In some counties, as much as 60 percent of the property-tax base is exempted. States make payments in lieu of taxes (PILOTs) to help offset the effects of exemptions, but at rates below what local governments would have collected in tax payments.[6]

circuit breaker
A limit on taxes applied to certain categories of people, such as the poor or elderly.

In an effort to make property taxation more equitable and more in keeping with ability to pay, thirty-five states have enacted some form of **circuit breaker.** For instance, the property of low-income individuals is excluded from taxation in some states; others assign lower assessment ratios to the homes of senior citizens or set a top limit on the tax according to the owner's income (for example, 4 percent of net income). At least twenty-two states have truth-in-taxation laws that roll back property tax rates if appraised values rise rapidly. Most also offer homestead exemptions, in which owner-occupied homes are taxed at lower rates or assessed at lower values than are rental homes or business property. Massachusetts municipalities permit seniors to earn credits against their tax bills through public-service activities.

Despite such attempts to make the property tax fairer, differences in property values among cities, counties, and school districts still have important implications for the quality and distribution of services. Jurisdictions with many wealthy families, capital-intensive industries, or rapid construction growth can provide high levels of services with low tax rates, whereas areas with weak property-tax bases must tax at high rates just to yield enough revenue to maintain minimal services. For example, the tax rate is $4.55 per $100.00 of assessed value in Bridgeport, Connecticut, but only $0.67 in Denver, Colorado. Altering the unequal distribution of property values is essentially beyond the control of local governments. As a result, "wealthy suburbs remain wealthy, poor communities remain poor, and services remain unequal."[7] As discussed in Chapter 15, inequity in school funding has been the target of a growing number of lawsuits. In Michigan, the legislature significantly reduced taxes for public education and asked voters to substitute either sales tax increases or higher income taxes. Voters opted overwhelmingly for a 2¢ sales tax increase accompanied by a 50¢-per-pack cigarette tax hike. Dramatic property-tax-relief measures have also been adopted recently in South Dakota, Wisconsin, Idaho, and Texas. Because of a recent state supreme court ruling that its property-tax-funded public school system is unconstitutional, New Hampshire will probably be the next state to take drastic property-tax-relief measures.

Sales Tax   Mississippi was the first state, in 1932, to adopt this form of taxation. Others followed suit rapidly, and states currently collect more of their revenues today from the general sales and gross receipts tax than from any other source. It accounts for 33 percent of total state own-source taxes, just behind personal income taxes (34 percent). (Refer again to Figure 13.1.) Only five states do not levy a general sales tax: Alaska, Delaware, Montana, New Hampshire, and Oregon. State sales tax rates vary from 7.25 percent in California to 2.9 percent in Colorado. The national median is 5 percent. Some states, particularly those that do not have personal income taxes, are exceptionally dependent on the sales tax: Florida, Tennessee, and Washington derive approximately 60 percent of their own-source revenues from the sales tax.

The sales tax has remained in favor for two major reasons. First, citizen surveys have consistently shown that when a tax must be raised, voters prefer the sales tax. Although the reasons are not entirely clear, this tax is perceived to be fairer than other forms of taxation. Second, there is an abiding belief that high state income taxes depress economic development.[8] (As already mentioned, the property tax is widely detested.)

Thirty-three states authorize at least some of their municipalities and counties to levy local sales taxes.[9] When state and local sales taxes are combined, the total tax bite can be painful. In Alabama, the purchase of a $1.00 item requires up to 11¢ in sales tax. The rate on the dollar is 9.75¢ in Nashville, Tennessee. Sales taxes are almost always optional for the local jurisdiction and require majority approval by the city or county legislative body. Typically, states impose ceilings on how many pennies the localities can attach to the state sales tax; states also specify which sizes and types of local governments are permitted to exercise this option.

When applied to all merchandise, the sales tax is clearly regressive. Poor folks must spend a larger portion of their incomes than rich people spend on basics, such as food and clothing. Therefore, the sales tax places a much heavier burden on low-income people. Most of the forty-five states with a sales tax alleviate its regressive nature by excluding certain necessities. Twenty-eight states do not tax food, only five tax prescription drugs, thirty-one exempt consumer electric and gas utilities, and six exclude clothing.[10] New Jersey excludes paper products.

When the sales tax was extended to paper products in 1990, enraged Jerseyites mailed wads of toilet paper—some of it used—to legislators, who quickly rescinded the tax.

States can improve the yield of the sales tax by broadening the base to include services. In this way, more of the burden is passed on to upper-income individuals, who are heavier users of services. More than half of the states tax services such as household, automobile, and appliance repairs; barber and beauty shops; printing; rentals; dry cleaning; and interior decorating. Hawaii, New Mexico, and South Dakota tax almost all professional and personal services. However, two states moved too far and too fast with taxes on services. Florida and Massachusetts both broadened the base of their sales tax to services, only to have it repealed shortly afterward through lobbying efforts by the business community.

These setbacks are likely to be temporary. Services are the largest and fastest-growing segment of the U.S. economy. Eighty-five percent of new jobs are in services. As political journalist Neil Peirce asked, "How can one rationalize taxing autos, videocassettes, and toothpaste, but not piped-in music, cable TV, parking lot services, or $100 beauty salon treatments?"[11] Pet-grooming services, legal and financial services, and many others from landscaping to septic-tank cleaning are likely to lose their tax-favored status in years to come, when states are expected to extend sales taxes to services incrementally (thus fighting industry and lobbyists one at a time).

A big fight has erupted over state and local governments' right to tax an enormously promising revenue stream—electronic commerce on the Internet. Twenty-one states were levying taxes or fees on Internet access, data downloads, or goods purchased on the Internet. Then pressures from Internet interests, including servers (for example, America Online), media companies, and retail businesses, led Congress to pass the Internet Tax Freedom Act, which imposed a moratorium on taxing Internet access and on-line sales. State and local officials strongly opposed such limitations, estimating that it cost them as much as $15 billion in annual revenues in 2003 because Internet commerce is skyrocketing and more and more goods and services are bought electronically. Already states estimate that they forfeit $5 billion a year in uncollected taxes from interstate catalog sales. Only catalog sales to citizens living in the same state as a mail-order firm that has a presence in the state are now taxed. A rapidly growing number of states require citizens to declare and pay such sales taxes in their annual state income tax returns, usually to no avail because of the difficulty of enforcement.

Internet taxation is both complicated and controversial, and it has become a compelling issue for the states. A 1992 U.S. Supreme Court ruling blocked taxation of catalog sales on the grounds of violating the Interstate Commerce Clause, a ruling that has obvious applicability to taxing Internet commerce.[12] Congress has been tied in knots on the issue, as have the governors. No less than the fiscal integrity of state revenue systems is at stake. If states lose billions of dollars to a tax-free Internet, how will the gaping budget hole be filled? What about Main Street retailers whose prices are made less competitive by the amount of the sales tax? Yet it would be a heavy burden indeed for Internet vendors to comply with the tax laws of 7,600 taxing jurisdictions in the United States.

A compromise under active consideration (adopted by thirty-eight states as of 2004) is the streamlined sales tax, wherein each state would collapse all its local sales tax rates into one statewide rate, resulting in only fifty Internet tax jurisdictions.[13] This approach would have the added advantage of laying the foundation for taxing mail-order catalog sales. Seemingly a simple proposition, simplification of multistate sales systems has presented Zen-like conundrums such as: Are marshmallows food or candy? Are "fruit beverages" that contain only 10 percent juice a food or a soft drink?

Sales tax holidays have recently become popular. In 2003, nine states suspended the sales tax on clothing, computers, and shoes for anywhere from three days to one week before the start of school to help parents stretch their back-to-school dollars. Consumer response to this politically popular move has been positive, and additional states are considering sales tax holidays of their own. Critics, however, point out that retailers typically raise their prices during the sales tax holiday, thereby eliminating any real consumer savings.

Elasticity is not a strong point of the sales tax, although its productivity falls when consumer purchases fall and rises as consumers boost their spending. A few states have attempted to make the sales tax more responsive to short-term economic conditions by increasing it on a temporary basis, to make up for lower-than-anticipated revenues, then reducing it when needed monies are collected. A problem with these tactics, however, is that consumers tend to postpone major purchases until the tax rate falls.

The sales tax is relatively simple for governments to administer. Sellers of merchandise and services are required to collect it and remit it to the state on a regular basis. Political accountability is also an advantage because legislative bodies must enact laws or ordinances to increase the sales tax rate. And, as we have observed, the sales tax is the least unpopular of the major taxes.

Income Tax   Most states tax personal and corporate income. Wisconsin was the first, in 1911, two years before the national government enacted its own personal income tax. Forty-one states have broad-based taxes on personal income; two (Tennessee and New Hampshire) limit theirs to capital gains, interest, and dividends. Only Alaska, South Dakota, Florida, Texas, Nevada, Washington, and Wyoming leave all personal income untaxed. The latter three states also refuse to tax corporate income. Personal income taxes garner 35 percent of all state own-source taxes, and the corporate tax brings in 5.7 percent. Eleven states permit designated cities, counties, or school districts to levy taxes on personal income.

Six states tax at a flat rate, ranging from 2.8 percent in Pennsylvania to 5.0 percent in Massachusetts. State and local income taxes are equitable when they are progressive. This contingency normally entails a sliding scale, so that high-income filers pay a greater percentage of their income in taxes than low-income filers do. Most states do not levy a personal income tax on people whose earnings fall below a certain floor—say, $5,000. Overall, personal income taxes in the states are moderately progressive and are gradually becoming more so.

Personal and corporate income taxes are superior to other taxes on the criteria of yield and elasticity. By tapping almost all sources of income, they draw in large sums of money and respond fairly well to short-term economic conditions. Through payroll withholding, income taxes are fairly simple to collect. Also, many states periodically adjust income tax rates in response to annual revenue needs.

As mentioned earlier, political accountability can be problematic with respect to income taxes during periods of rising prices. Unless income tax rates are indexed to inflation, cost-of-living increases push salaries and corporate earnings into higher tax brackets. At least seventeen states have adopted cost-of-living indexing.

Miscellaneous Taxes   A wide variety of miscellaneous taxes are assessed by state and local governments. So-called sin taxes raise a small—but growing—percentage of all state revenues. All states tax cigarettes; the average tax per pack was 76¢ in 2004, after half the states hiked cigarette taxes to help balance their budgets. New Jersey discourages smokers with a $2.05-per-pack tax, boosting the price of some brands to over $8.00 per pack. Kentucky charges 3¢ per pack, and North Carolina 5¢; not surprisingly, both are tobacco-growing states. This startling disparity in prices has led to a flourishing trade in cigarette smuggling from low- to high-tax states. New Yorkers use Internet vendors or trek to Vermont or to nearby Indian reservations (where cigarettes are not taxed at all) to purchase their tobacco. North Carolina's low cigarette tax has fostered organized crime activity, including a Lebanese terrorist group that bought cigarettes by the case in Charlotte and trucked them for sale to Michigan. The proceeds were used to purchase arms and explosives in the Middle East.

Recently the states experienced the equivalent of winning the lottery. Over twenty-five years, a total of $246 billion from a court settlement with tobacco companies is expected to flow into state coffers. Ideally, the $8 billion per year should be used for public health and smoking prevention programs. But few strings are attached, and many states are spending the windfall on debt service or economic development initiatives. Some states, including Washington and Wisconsin, borrowed against future tobacco revenues to fill budget holes in 2002 and 2003.

Alcoholic beverages are also taxed in all fifty states, although rates vary according to classification: beer, wine, or spirits. Beer drinkers should steer clear of Hawaii, where the tax per gallon of beer is 93¢; frequent imbibers are invited to visit Missouri, where the tax is only 6¢ per gallon. (This low rate could perhaps be related to the fact that Missouri hosts the headquarters of Anheiser-Busch, the largest brewer in the country.) Ironically, as drinking and smoking have declined during the past few years, so have their tax-based revenues. Clearly, raising alcohol and tobacco taxes helps to curtail these habits. It has been suggested that marijuana and other recreational drugs be legalized so that they, too, can be taxed.

Though not a sin, gasoline also falls under the tax shadow. The highest state tax on gasoline in 2004 was in New York (32.35¢ per gallon). The lowest was in Georgia (7.5¢).[14] All states also tax vehicles and vehicle licenses.

Most states tax death in one form or another. Estate taxes must be paid on the money and property of a deceased person before the remainder is disbursed to the survivors. Eighteen states tax those who inherit assets valued at more than $675,000, which was the 2004 level set for the federal estate tax. Rates are generally staggered according to the value of the estate and relationship to the deceased. However, in 2005, a reduction—and proposed abolition—of what President Bush called the death tax may foretell a death knell for such state taxes as well, unless the states amend their estate tax laws.

Other miscellaneous sources of revenue include hunting and fishing licenses, business licenses, auto license fees, parking tickets, and traffic violation fines. Utah imposed a 10 percent tax on nude dancing clubs and escort services in 2004. One of the latest devices is the jock tax. Twenty-one states and several cities require professional athletes to pay a prorated income tax for games played in their jurisdiction. For highly paid baseball, basketball, and football players, the jock tax burns. San Francisco Giants' Barry Bonds had to pay a $2,143 jock tax to play in the 2003 All Star game in Chicago.[15]

User Fees

Setting specific prices on goods and services provided by state and local governments is one method that clearly pursues the *benefit principle:* Only those who use the goods and services should pay. User fees have been in existence for many years. Examples include college tuition, water and sewer charges, and garbage-collection assessments. Toll roads and bridges are coming back in fashion as well. Today, user fees are being applied broadly as state and especially local officials attempt to tie services to their true costs. Such fees are increasingly being levied on nonessential local government services, such as parks and recreation, libraries, airports, and public transit. The average American pays more than $1,340 a year in user fees.[16]

User fees offer several advantages. If priced accurately, they are perfectly fair under the benefit principle and they enjoy a relatively high level of political acceptability. But those people who do not have enough money to purchase the goods and services may have to do without—a circumstance that violates the ability-to-pay principle. A good case in point is higher education, which is shifting increasingly from state funding to tuition funding. (Fortunately, rebates, scholarships, fee waivers, and reduced-fee schedules mitigate ability-to-pay difficulties among low-income residents.) User fees are structured to yield whatever is needed to finance a particular service. An added benefit is that service users who do not live in the taxing jurisdiction must also pay the price, say, for a day in the state park. Elasticity may be achieved if the amount of the charge is varied so that it always covers service costs. In many instances, they can be levied without specific permission of the state.

Because service users must be identified and charged, some user fees can be difficult to administer. Political accountability is low because the charges can be increased without legislative action. However, a special advantage of user fees is that they can be employed to ration certain goods or services. For instance, entrance charges can be increased to reduce attendance at an overcrowded public facility, or varied according to the day of the week to encourage more efficient utilization. If the municipal zoo has few visitors on Mondays, it can cut the entrance fee on that day of the week by one-half.

An increasingly popular and specialized form of user charge is the local impact fee, or exaction, which requires private land developers to contribute roads, sewers, and other infrastructure as the price for local regulatory approval for development projects, such as subdivisions or factories. The cost of infrastructure is thus shifted to private firms and, ultimately, to those who purchase or use their buildings or facilities.[17] A related concept applied through a special sales tax on travel-related services is the travel tax. Here, taxes on lodging, rental cars, and other services paid largely by out-of-towners are imposed at rates averaging 12 percent. Table 13.3 rates various taxes and fees based on the six criteria discussed at the beginning of this section.

Severance Tax

For many years, states blessed with petroleum, coal, natural gas, and minerals have taxed these natural resources as they are taken from the land and sold. A fortunate few are able to export a substantial portion of their tax bite to people living in other states by including the cost of these taxes in their prices. However, in-state residents must pay the same tax rate as out-of-staters. A large majority of states (thirty-nine) place a severance tax on some form of natural resources, but just ten states collect 90 percent of all severance tax revenues. Taxes on oil and natural gas account for around 60 percent of total state revenues in Alaska. Wyoming brings in about 40 percent of its revenues from severance taxes on coal, oil, and gas (which may explain why these states are able to forgo personal income taxes). Several states are rather creative in applying the severance tax. Virginia levies the tax on pilings and poles; Washington, on oysters and salmon and other food fish; and Louisiana, on freshwater mussels.[18]

Severance taxes are popular in states rich in natural resources because they help keep income, property, and sales taxes relatively low. Severance tax revenues also help to pay for environmental damage resulting from resource-extraction

| TABLE 13.3 | Rating State and Local Taxes According to Six Criteria |

TAX	EQUITY	YIELD	ELASTICITY	EASE OF ADMIN- ISTRATION	POLITICAL ACCOUNTABILITY	ACCEPT- ABILITY
Property	C	B	C	D	D	D
Sales	D	B	B	B	A	B
Personal and corporate income	B	A	B	B	C	C
User fees	C	B	A	C	C	B

NOTE: A = excellent, B = good, C = fair, D = poor.

operations, such as strip mining. The major disadvantage is that a state economy too dependent on severance taxes can be damaged badly if the price of its natural resources declines, as Alaska experiences from time to time with depressed crude-oil prices. Even so, natural resources have been enriching for individual Alaskans. For more than twenty years, every resident of Alaska—man, woman, and child—has received a rebate from the state's $28 billion Permanent Fund. Checks totaled $1,107.56 per person in 2003, and they have been as high as $1,964. Established primarily with severance taxes on petroleum, the Permanent Fund's reserves are diversified through investments in office buildings, industrial complexes, stocks, and bonds.[19]

Gambling: Lotteries and Casinos

The lottery is an old American tradition; initially established in the 1600s, it was popular from the colonial days until the late 1800s. Lotteries flourished throughout the country as a means of raising money for good causes such as new schools, highways, canals, and bridges. But scandals and mismanagement led every state and the national government to ban so-called looteries. From 1895 to 1963, no legal lotteries were operated. Then New Hampshire established a new one, followed in 1967 by New York. Since then, forty more states have created lotteries.

Several factors account for the rebirth of "bettor government." First, lotteries can bring in large sums of money—around 7 percent of all state tax revenues in South Dakota in one recent year, for instance. Second, they are popular and entertaining. And they are voluntary—you do not have to participate. In addition, lotteries help relieve pressure on major taxes. In some states, net lottery earnings take the place of a 1¢ increase in the sales tax. Finally, state ownership of a game of chance offers a legal and fair alternative to illegal gambling operations, such as neighborhood numbers games or betting (parlay) cards.

But lotteries also have disadvantages. Lotteries are costly to administer and have low yields. Prize awards must be great enough to encourage future ticket sales. New games must be created to retain enthusiasm. Ticket vendors must be paid commissions. And tight (as well as expensive) security precautions are required to guarantee the game's integrity. As a result, lotteries generate only a small percentage of most states' total revenues, usually less than 3 percent of own-source income. The average yield for players is low as well: About 50 percent of the total revenues is returned to players in prize money. This amount is far below the returns of other games of chance, such as slot machines, roulette, and craps. Although many states earmark lottery proceeds for popular programs, especially education, parks and recreation, and economic development, the result is often a shell game. For instance, Florida's lottery officially benefits schools and colleges, but in reality lottery money simply *replaces* general-fund revenues rather than actually enhancing education funding.[20]

Lotteries can also be attacked on the grounds of equity and elasticity. Although the purchase of a ticket is voluntary and thus seemingly fair, studies indicate that low-income individuals are more likely to play. Participation is also higher among African Americans, males, older people, and those with low levels of education.[21]

The lottery, then, is a regressive way to raise revenues. Furthermore, lotteries also tend to encourage compulsive gambling. In recognition of this problem, some states earmark a portion of lottery proceeds for treatment programs. Lotteries are said to be inelastic because earnings are cyclical and generally unstable. Sales depend on factors such as the legalized gambling activities in neighboring states, the size of jackpots, and the effectiveness of marketing efforts.

Interstate lottery competition depresses profits, so all but two states (Hawaii and Utah) have adopted some form of legalized gambling, including pari-mutuel betting on horse and dog races, and gambling on riverboats, on Indian reservations, and at historical sites from the Old West such as mining towns. In a frantic quest for more revenues, many states have legalized casino gaming and gambling. Once restricted to Atlantic City and Las Vegas, casino gambling now occurs in twenty-three states, including operations on about 220 Native American reservations. Gambling establishments nearly blanket Minnesota and Mississippi. Touted as job producers, tourist attractions, and generators of higher sales and property-tax revenues, casinos share many of the same disadvantages as lotteries, including diminishing returns as new casinos open monthly across the country.[22] And little, if any, state revenue is derived from most tribal casinos.

Thwarting state-sponsored gambling activities are a growing number of illegal Internet gambling sites and, for coastal states, cruises to nowhere, in which the dice are rolled and black jack is dealt as soon as the ship enters international waters. Interactive systems permit couch potatoes to place bets over the Internet with their personal computers. Hundreds of illegal gaming sites, most of them from Caribbean Islands that can skirt U.S. prohibition and taxing authority, can be found on the Internet.

THE POLITICAL ECONOMY OF TAXATION

Spending

Taxes, above all, lead to spending. The principle of diversity in state and local finance is evident in terms of what state and local governments choose to do with their revenues. First, these governments spend a great deal of money. State and local spending has been ascending much faster than the gross national product (GNP) and the level of inflation. The functional distribution of spending varies from state to state. As indicated in Figure 13.3, education consumes the largest portion of total state and local spending, followed by social services, which includes public assistance, medical services, and health care.

Within each of these functional categories lies a wide range of financial commitments. For instance, higher-education expenditures in a recent year ran from 14.8 percent of total state and local spending in Utah to only 4.4 percent in New York. Alabama dedicated 16.5 percent to health care and hospitals, whereas Vermont set aside just 2.3 percent for the same purpose.[23] Such differences represent historical trends, local economic circumstances, and citizens'

FIGURE 13.3	Total State and Local Government Spending, by Service Delivered

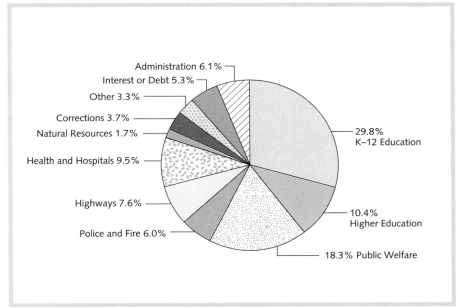

SOURCE: Expenditures for Current Operation, www.census.gov (accessed February 2, 2004).

willingness to incur debt to pay for services. Demographic factors also play a role. For instance, states with high populations of children invest more money in schools than do states with large proportions of senior citizens. Overall size of the state population also drives up expenditures for services such as water and sewer systems, street maintenance, and law enforcement. The largest expenditure gains in recent years have been registered in corrections and Medicaid. Swelling prison populations (including geriatric convicts), court-ordered changes in corrections practices, and tougher sentencing policies have propelled corrections spending upward at a rate twice that of other functional categories (see Chapter 16). Medicaid costs for indigents have also accelerated rapidly (see Chapter 17). Overall, state spending averaged an annual increase of 6 percent over the past two decades, but spending actually declined in 2003 as a result of revenue shortfalls.

One of the most difficult decisions for an elected official is to go on record in favor of raising taxes. The political heat can scorch even the coolest incumbent. But when revenues do not equal service costs and citizens do not want to cut services, raising taxes may be the only answer. Thirty-five states passed or seriously considered tax or fee increases in 2003 alone; however, most people do not want higher taxes. This dilemma is the familiar **tax–service paradox:** People demand new, improved, or at least the same level of government services but do not want to pay for them through higher taxes. For instance, the people of

tax–service paradox

Situation in which people demand more government services but do not want to pay for them through higher taxes.

Washington, in their collective wisdom, voted in a 1999 constitutional initiative to slice taxes. But the very next year, they passed another initiative to reduce class sizes and boost teacher pay—without, of course, providing any new money. Voters in a dozen other states have taken similar actions. As a former legislator put it, "I wouldn't say voters are stupid. But the same voter who wants unlimited services also does not want to pay for it. There is a disconnect."[24] Is it any wonder that user charges have become a popular option?

The tax–service paradox reflects a growing alienation between government and its citizens. The widespread belief that government at all levels—and particularly the federal government—has become too big and wasteful undoubtedly has some basis in fact. The size and responsibilities of state and local governments have grown dramatically during the past three decades, and waste and inefficiency have sometimes accompanied this growth. But the unwillingness of citizens to accept the inevitable reductions in services that follow tax cuts borders on mass schizophrenia.

Helping promote the tax–service paradox are the news media, which "commonly paint government with the broad brush of incompetence."[25] Prime-time television news capsules on "how government wastes your money" and typical reporting on actions of states and localities search for and emphasize the negative while ignoring the positive. Meanwhile, state and local government functions have become much more complex and technical, tending to make government more difficult to understand and to interact with.

State and local governments are responding to this near-impasse with outreach efforts designed to educate citizens about what their governments are doing for them and where their tax dollars are going. New York City's web site provides personalized tax receipts, showing what each citizen's tax dollars paid for. Local governments everywhere are striving to write their annual budgets in reader-friendly formats.[26]

political economy

Political choices that have economic outcomes.

Thus, the **political economy**—the set of political choices that frames economic policy—has become enormously perplexing for state and local officials. Several features of contemporary state and local economies merit additional discussion: the tax revolt, fiscal stress, and limited discretion in raising new revenues.

Tax Revolt

Taxpayer resentment of property taxes and changes in assessment practices, and the general perception that government is too big, too costly, and too wasteful, first took on a tangible form in 1978 with the passage of Proposition 13 in California. Between 1977 and 1980, eighteen states enacted statutory or constitutional limitations on taxing and spending by slashing personal or corporate income taxes, indexing their income taxes to the cost of living, and cutting the sales tax. In some instances, citizens took tax matters into their own hands through the initiative process. In other cases, state legislators jumped in front of the parade and cut taxes and spending themselves. The taxpayer revolt continued at a much slower pace during the 1980s and 1990s. Its legacy, however, remains enormously important. Public officials must work hard to justify tax increases; otherwise, they risk a citizen uprising and perhaps political suicide.

Indeed, the stirrings of new tax revolts are constantly in evidence. The prairie fire of tax revolt is not dead—only smoldering. Oregon voters fanned the tax-revolt flames in 2003 by soundly defeating a proposal to raise personal and corporate income taxes, choosing instead to accept prisoner releases, layoffs of state troopers, a shortened school year, and other serious budget-balancing measures. In desperation, the state legislature passed a plan to impose a three-year income tax surcharge. Angry protesters in Tennessee displayed their anti-tax fervor Volunteer State-style in 2001 by storming the capitol building, screaming insults at legislators, and hurling rocks.

Most state and local jurisdictions managed the fallout of the tax revolt reasonably well. Many of them held large budget surpluses that they utilized to ameliorate the immediate effects of **taxation and expenditure limitations (TELs).** TELs are restrictions on government taxing and spending, such as limiting the growth in spending to no more than the latest year's growth in per-capita income. For example, California had a $3 billion surplus with which it temporarily replaced property-tax revenues forgone by local governments. Only a handful of states followed California's stringent TELs, which cut property taxes by 60 percent. Massachusetts was one such state; approved on the general-election ballot in 1980, Proposition 2½ limited local property-tax revenues to 2½ percent of the total value of taxable property. Tax bills for Massachusetts home owners soon dropped by $1.3 billion. Nearly all states have some sort of property-tax restriction in effect, and many place limitations on other forms of taxation as well. Raising taxes now requires a constitutional amendment, voter approval, or an extraordinary legislative majority in quite a few states. States and localities have resisted reducing service levels, opting instead to rely less on the property tax and to find new sources of revenues, such as user charges.[27]

Political and economic consequences of the tax revolt have been studied in depth. In many cases, TELs have made state and local finance an extraordinarily difficult undertaking: Voters insist on passing spending mandates for education, law enforcement, or other popular programs while at the same time tying the hands of legislatures with restrictions on new revenue-raising. So far, TELs have not significantly reduced the size and cost of government, as had been advertised. Political and electoral influences are apparently more important in determining expenditures and size of government.[28] However, TELs have led local governments to depend more on the states and public officials to recognize the continuing need to measure the taxpaying public's pulse on tax issues.[29]

Fiscal Stress

During national and regional economic downturns, many state and local jurisdictions experience severe **fiscal stress:** They struggle to pay for programs and provide services that citizens want and need without taxing the citizens at unacceptably high levels. Many factors contribute to fiscal stress. Typically, adverse social and economic conditions, mostly beyond state and local government control, establish an environment conducive to financial problems. Older industrial cities are particularly vulnerable. Many jobs and manufacturing industries have been lost because of the gradual but compelling shift to a service- and

---

taxation and expenditure limitations (TELs)

Restrictions on state and/or local government taxing and spending.

---

fiscal stress

Financial pressure on a government from factors such as revenue shortfalls and taxing and spending limitations.

information-based economy and company relocation to the Sunbelt and foreign countries. In cities such as Detroit, Philadelphia, Pittsburgh, and New York, the exodus of jobs and firms has eroded the value of taxable resources (mostly property), yet citizens left behind have growing service demands.

Concentration of the poor and minorities in deteriorating housing, the shortage of jobs, high levels of crime, the illegal drug trade, homelessness, large expanses of blighted property, and related factors have produced crisis-level situations. Declining infrastructure also plagues older cities: Water and sewer lines, treatment plants, streets, sidewalks, and other components of the urban physical landscape are in dire need of restoration or replacement. The estimated amount needed to replace the Detroit metropolitan area's crumbling sewer system alone is an astounding $52 billion. Most of these problems, it should be noted, will require national government attention if they are to be addressed effectively. Special factors contributing to state fiscal stress include weak real-estate markets; declines in natural-resources prices; rapid increases in energy prices; unfunded federal and state mandates; and court-mandated and congressionally mandated spending increases in corrections, education, and other areas. The terrorist actions of September 11, 2001, erased travel and tourism dollars and cost state and local governments millions in police overtime pay and new security measures.

Political sources of fiscal stress typically compound the economic problems of older cities. Mismanagement of resources and inefficient procedures and activities are common complaints. Wage and benefits pressures from city workers and their unions have also driven up service-provision costs in some localities. Thus, service demands and the costs of providing services grow while taxes and intergovernmental revenues decline, a well-tested recipe for fiscal stress that evokes fears of bond defaults and even bankruptcy.

New York City offers a continuing, thirty-year-long case study of fiscal stress. People, jobs, and industry fled the city for the suburbs and the Sunbelt in the early 1970s, thereby reducing fiscal capacity. Yet public employees' pay and pensions grew to some of the highest levels in the United States, and welfare payments to the poor and a growing number of unemployed were generous. The tuition-free City University of New York (CUNY) had an enrollment of 265,000 students.

As revenues increasingly lagged behind expenditures, the city government played fiscal roulette with the budget and borrowed huge sums through municipal notes and bonds. Eventually it was poised on the brink of bankruptcy. Defaults on the city's bonds, notes, and other debt instruments seemed imminent. City officials cried out to the national government and New York State for help, but some people had little sympathy for a city that had lived beyond its means for so long.

Aided by national guarantees of new long-term loans, New York State and other large holders of New York City debt finally agreed to a bailout. Had this immense urban financial center collapsed, the fiscal shocks would have threatened New York State's economic stability and even resulted in serious fiscal repercussions for other states and localities throughout the United States.

The Big Apple once again risked being reduced to a seedy core in 1992. It faced a budget deficit of $3.5 billion, a mass exodus of jobs (100,000 within just three years), and the enormous cost of thousands of AIDS and crack babies. Seventy percent of the city's more than 2,000 bridges desperately needed expensive repairs, and water and sewer lines were rupturing regularly. Mayor David Dinkins responded with several actions, including massive city-employee layoffs, closure of libraries and clinics, and shutdown of 25 percent of the city's street lights. New York City's fiscal problems cannot be solved overnight. Its 235,000 employees and $30 billion operating budget serve 7 million people spread throughout five boroughs. The city itself is the area's biggest landlord. It owns television and radio stations, a huge higher-education system, and four hospitals. When Mayor Rudolph Giuliani took office in 1994, the operating deficit was pegged at $2.3 billion, and most of the country was enjoying economic growth. Giuliani, too, cut city employment and targeted various services for budget reductions. New York City continues to struggle with its vast fiscal problems with no relief in sight.[30] As the ashes of the Twin Towers cooled in late 2001, the new mayor, Michael Bloomberg, wrestling with a deficit of approximately $4 billion in his $43 billion budget, entertained the idea of a state takeover of city finances.[31] His so-called doomsday budget included tens of thousands of layoffs, significant service cuts, and large property-tax increases. The debt that New York City is still paying off from the 1970s had to be refinanced.

Most jurisdictions have not experienced the misfortune faced by New York City. The taxpayer revolt and fiscal stress notwithstanding, budgets have been balanced, payrolls met, and most services maintained. When necessary, state officials have swallowed hard, held their noses, and raised taxes. A national economic recovery beginning in 1992 spawned a nine-year period of nearly unprecedented economic growth, causing the state–local picture to improve rapidly. In 2000, state tax revenues had spurted beyond revenue estimates for seven years running in most states. Year-end treasury balances leaped, and everything seemed to be going right for most states, which were able to cut billions of dollars in taxes and also shore up rainy day funds (see below).

State officials know another recession is inevitable, and it will bring back fiscal pressures compounded by federal budget problems and reductions in grants-in-aid to states and localities. Evidence of an economic slowdown first appeared in 2001. In 2004, the state and local governments were still suffering what turned out to be their most serious crisis since the Great Depression. But most states managed to close their budget gaps as the national economy slowly recovered. Twenty billion dollars in fiscal relief provided to the states by the national government in 2003–2004 helped ease the budget strain. Officials quickly rediscovered how much easier it is to spend money than to cut back.

Recession notwithstanding, some states and localities face chronic fiscal shortfalls because of structural problems deeply embedded in their revenue systems. Structural imbalances result from tax systems developed for radically different state economies that existed fifty years ago and are now out of date.

Limited Discretion

TELs have placed ceilings on the rates and amounts of taxation and spending, thus limiting the discretion of the nonnational governments. Other constraining factors also keep state and local governments from falling prey to the temptation of taxing and spending orgies. An important one is interstate competition for jobs and economic development. High-tax states run a serious risk of having jobs, firms, and investments "stolen" by low-tax states.

Earmarking taxes for popular programs also limits state and local taxing and spending discretion. Earmarking is well established: Gasoline taxes have been set aside for road and highway programs since automobiles first left ruts in muddy cow pastures. What differs today are the levels of specificity and creativity in earmarking. Approximately 25 percent of state tax revenues are earmarked today, a proportion much lower than that of thirty years ago, but the number of dedicated purposes has grown markedly. Surpluses may accumulate in some dedicated funds, such as highways, while other important needs such as education or law enforcement are not sufficiently met. The hands of government officials are tied, however, because they cannot move the funds around. Cigarette buyers in Washington cough up millions of dollars each year to help clean up Puget Sound. Several states earmark penny increases in the sales tax for public education.

Financial discretion is partly determined by one's position on the fiscal food chain. The national government can essentially tax and spend as it wishes, subject only to its underdeveloped capacity for self-discipline. States must meet federal spending mandates for Medicaid, corrections, and other functions while somehow balancing their budgets each year. Local governments, in addition to suffering reductions in state aid during tough times in this game of "shift and shaft federalism,"[32] must comply with an increasing number of state spending mandates, even though their legal authority to raise revenues remains severely circumscribed in most states. In some ways, local governments are not masters of their own fiscal fate.[33]

MANAGING MONEY

Every state except Vermont is constitutionally or statutorily required to balance their operating budgets each fiscal year. In turn, the states require that local governments balance their budgets. Consequently, the reliability of revenue estimates is a vital consideration. Sometimes state and local government expenditures substantially outstrip revenues because government officials underestimated revenue, approved excessive tax cuts, or spent too much money, which happened in 2001–2003.

Estimating Revenues

Until fairly recently, state and local governments estimated their annual revenues simply by extrapolating from past trends. This approach works well during periods of steady economic growth, but it fails miserably during years of boom or bust. The states and most larger cities and counties are much more sophisticated today. Using computer software, they employ econometric modeling to derive mathematical estimates of future revenues. Economic forecasting firms and/or academics commonly assist or provide independent projections.

Econometric modeling places key variables in equations to predict the yield of each major tax in a fiscal year. A wide variety of variables are used, including employment levels, food prices, housing costs, oil and gas prices, consumer savings levels, interest rates, intergovernmental aid projections, and state and local debt obligations. Because state and local economies are increasingly linked to national and international factors, estimates often include measures for the value of the dollar, international trade and investment, and national fiscal policy.

Two critical factors determine the accuracy of revenue estimates: the quality of the data and the validity of the economic assumptions. Indeed, econometric modeling of state and local economies can be a voyage into the unknown. Data problems include difficulty in measuring key variables; periodic revisions of historical economic data, which require new calculations; and modifications in tax laws or fee schedules. But the major sources of error are the economic assumptions built into the models. The national economy may not perform as expected; energy prices may plummet or soar; natural or human disasters can disrupt state or local economic growth. Recessions are particularly damaging to fiscal stability because state and local taxes are highly sensitive to economic downturns.

Politics can also intrude into the revenue-projection process. For instance, politicians can purposely overestimate revenues so they can fund a popular new program. When projected revenues do not appear, implementation of the program may be delayed, but it now has official standing. Also, overestimates can defer cuts in politically sensitive programs or levels of public employment and help incumbents survive the next election. If revenue shortfall then reaches serious proportions, cutbacks are much more palatable than when the shortfall is a mere projection and elections are over for at least two years. Jurisdictions usually try to err conservatively by underestimating revenues because midyear cutbacks are painful and embarrassing for government officials, and also because a year-end budget surplus may be chalked up to good management.

Rainy Day Funds

Because a balanced budget is mandatory but estimation errors are inevitable, forty-seven states and many localities establish contingency or reserve funds. Popularly known as rainy day funds, these savings accounts help insulate budgets from fiscal distortions caused by inaccurate data or faulty economic assumptions; they are also available for emergencies. In years of economic health, the funds accumulate principal and interest. When the economy falters, governments can tap their "fiscal shock absorbers" to balance the budget and avoid imposing tax and fee increases.[34]

During the sunny days of the 1990s, the states filled up their contingency funds to 7.7 percent of total spending. Amidst the recessionary clouds of 2001–2003, they were forced to dip into these funds. The task of balancing the budget is especially daunting in local governments, given their lack of economic diversity, dependency on state taxes and financial aid, and sensitivity to economic dislocations. The departure of a single large employer can disrupt a local economy for years. So the potential advantages of such funds are numerous in the fragile fiscal context of cities and counties.

State and Local Debt

To deal with temporary revenue shortfalls and to finance expensive items that cannot be absorbed in the operating budget, governments borrow money, just as individuals use credit cards to make relatively small purchases that they will pay for when they receive next month's salary, or as they finance the purchase of an automobile or a house over a longer period of time. Borrowing is a major state and local government activity, amounting to a total debt of more than $1.452 trillion in 2003.

Temporary cash-flow deficits in the operating budget are alleviated through tax anticipation or revenue anticipation notes. Investors such as banks lend money to a government on a short-term basis (typically thirty to ninety days). In such cases, the loan is backed up by anticipated revenues from income, sales, and property taxes or other specified sources and is paid off as soon as the funds become available.

Other Financial Management Practices

State and local governments, of necessity, are becoming more knowledgeable about how to manage cash and investments. Cash reserves that once sat idly in non-interest-bearing accounts or a desk drawer are now invested in short-term notes, money market accounts, U.S. Treasury bills, certificates of deposit, and other financial instruments so that governments can maximize interest earnings. A majority of states have local government investment pools, managing billions of dollars in short-term assets. The process of spending and collecting monies is also manipulated to advantage. For example, large checks are deposited on the day they are received; conversely, payable checks are drawn on the latest date possible. In general, state and local financial management today resembles that of a large corporation instead of the mom-and-pop approach of years ago. After all, the nonnational governments spend and invest over $1.8 trillion annually.

The most important state or local investment is usually the public-employee pension fund. These retirement accounts comprise about $3 trillion in assets. In the past, they were conservatively managed and politically untouchable. Today, however, they tend to be invested in more aggressive instruments such as corporate stock. They also represent a tempting honey pot for financially strapped states, whose governors have dipped their hands in the funds and pulled out billions to balance the budget. They also are of enormous interest to investment firms. In Connecticut, former state treasurer Paul Silvester was convicted in 2000 of corruption charges for taking cash kickbacks in return for investing $500 million in state pension funds with certain investment firms.

State and local investments must not be managed too aggressively, as the case of Orange County, California, demonstrates. One of the nation's biggest (fifth-largest county) and wealthiest local jurisdictions, Orange County became the largest in history to file for federal bankruptcy in 1994. The county's financial nightmare commenced when its investment pool manager, Robert L. Citron, placed millions of dollars in financial instruments called derivatives. These instruments derive their value from underlying assets such as stocks, bonds, or mortgages. The derivatives' value changes when the price of the underlying assets changes. Orange County lost $1.5 billion when its derivatives, which were tied to interest rates, declined precipitously in value. In effect, Citron was borrowing money from stocks, bonds, and other assets to bet on the direction of interest rates. He lost, and so did Orange County's taxpayers.[35] Citron pleaded guilty to six felonies, more than 800 county employees were laid off, and $52 million was cut from social services. Orange County citizens lost faith in their local government.[36]

Long-Term Borrowing   Like corporations, state and local governments issue long-term debt obligations. (For governments, these obligations are incurred for typically five to twenty-five years.) Bonds are the most common form of long-term borrowing. Because of federal and state tax breaks for investors, the nonnational governments can finance bonded indebtedness at significantly lower rates than corporations can. Three conventional types of bonds—general obligation bonds, revenue bonds, and industrial development bonds—are used for long-term borrowing.

general-obligation bond
A debt instrument supported by the full financial resources of the issuing jurisdiction.

The principal and interest payments on **general-obligation bonds** are secured by the full faith, credit, and taxing power of the state or local jurisdiction issuing them. General-obligation bonds are used to finance public projects such as highways, schools, and hospitals. Lenders are guaranteed repayment as long as the bond-issuing government is solvent; defaults are nearly nonexistent, Orange County notwithstanding. In 1998, Pittsburgh broke new ground when the city began selling municipal bonds on the Internet. Billions in bonds are being sold electronically today to investors. Bypassing the middlemen, these transactions saved taxpayers millions of dollars.[37] Unfortunately, Pittsburgh's financial woes in 2003 led to downgrades in the city's credit ratings, accompanied by a devaluation of its municipal bonds.

revenue bond
A bond paid off from income derived from the facility built with the bond proceeds.

Revenue bonds are backed by expected income from a specific project or service; examples include a toll bridge, a municipal sewer system, or mortgage loans. Revenue bonds are payable only from the revenues derived from the specified source, not from general tax revenues. Because they typically represent a riskier investment than general-obligation bonds, they command a higher rate of interest.

industrial development bond (IDB)
A bond issued to fund the construction of a facility to be used by a private firm.

The **industrial development bond (IDB)** is a type of revenue bond. The payment of principal and interest on IDBs depends solely on the ability of the industry using the facilities financed by the bond to meet its financial obligation. If the user fails to make payments, creditors can seize and sell any real or personal property associated with the facility. Private interests, such as shopping malls or firms, are the primary beneficiaries of IDBs. Conventionally, these private-purpose bonds are issued by local governments to attract economic activity and investments; in fact, they are frequently used to furnish loans at highly favorable interest rates to small or medium-size firms.

Limits on Borrowing   The states and local governments owe their creditors about $1.5 trillion—about $5,151 per man, woman, and child in the United States. Almost all states place constitutional or statutory restrictions on their own and local government borrowing and indebtedness. Some have set maximum levels of indebtedness; others require popular referenda to create debt or to exceed specified debt limits. They tightly restrict local government debt, especially general-obligation bonds. (State-imposed constraints normally do not apply to revenue bonds.) The impetus for these restrictions came from a series of bond defaults in the 1860s and 1870s, and again during the Great Depression.

The bond market places its own informal limitations on debt by assessing the quality of bonds, notes, and other debt instruments. Investors in government bonds rely on Moody's Investors Service, Standard and Poor's Corporation, Fitch Ratings, and other investment services for ratings of a jurisdiction's capacity to repay its obligations. Criteria taken into consideration in bond ratings include existing debt levels, rainy day funds, market value of real estate, population growth, per-capita income, employment levels, and other measures of overall financial health and solvency. Highly rated bond issues receive ratings of *Aaa, Aa,* and *A.* Variations of *B* indicate medium to high risk. A rating of *C*, which California was fast approaching in its 2004 budget crisis, is reserved for bonds in immediate danger of default. The average interest rate on low-rated bonds usually exceeds that of top-rated ones by 1½ to 2 percentage points, which translates into a considerable difference in interest payments. Bond ratings tend to rise during periods of economic growth but can fall rapidly during recessions, driving up borrowing costs.

bond bank

A state-administered fund that aggregates local government debt instruments and sells them as a package at a reduced interest rate.

States can consolidate the bond sales of smaller municipalities and counties through a **bond bank.** These banks help provide increased management capacity to less-experienced local governments and save them significant amounts of money because of economies of scale.

STATE AND LOCAL FINANCIAL RELATIONS

Dollars and cents define state and local relations. Local governments today recognize that their financial future depends more on the states than on Washington, D.C.

An Uneasy Relationship

A conflicted relationship exists between states and local governments when it comes to money. The status of localities is not unlike that of an eighteen-year-old with a part-time job. Because he still lives and eats at home, he remains dependent on his parents. He fervently wants to assert his independence, but his parents often rein him in when he does. As long as he dwells in his parents' house, he must bend to their authority. If he misbehaves financially, he can expect parental intervention. Financial misbehavior in Flint, Michigan (including a budget deficit of $40 million in a city of only 125,000 people), led the state to take control of the city government in 2002. Officials in Breathitt County, Kentucky, were thrown in jail when they refused the state's order to raise taxes to pay off county debts.

Cities, counties, and other local governments will always live within the constitutional house of their parents, the states. They enjoy their own sources of revenue—property taxes, user fees, and business license fees—but they depend on the states for the bulk of their income. They suffer the frustration of having to cope with rising expenditure demands from their residents while their authority to raise new monies is highly circumscribed by state law. No wonder they turned to their "grandparent"—the national government—in the 1960s and 1970s to seek direct financial aid that bypassed the states.

The historical insensitivity of states to the economic problems of their cities and counties began slowly changing in the 1970s because reapportionment brought urban interests greater standing in state legislatures. Since that time, the states have had to assume an even more attentive posture because national aid to localities has not grown significantly.

The single largest source of local revenues is the state. About 40 percent of all state expenditures goes to local governments. Like federal grants-in-aid, however, state grants come with lots of strings attached. Most state dollars are earmarked for public education and social welfare. Other state assistance is earmarked for roads, hospitals, public safety, and public health. The result is that local governments have little spending discretion. During bad economic times, states have a tendency to push a portion of their own budget shortfalls down to their already struggling local governments. In 2001–2003, for instance, local officials had to decide whether to raise taxes, cut services, or both, as state-shared revenues and other aid was pared down.

Naturally, great diversity characterizes the levels of encumbered (earmarked) and unencumbered state assistance to local jurisdictions, much of which is related to the distribution of functions between a state and its localities. Highly centralized states such as Hawaii, South Carolina, and West Virginia fund and administer at the state level many programs that are funded and administered locally in decentralized states such as Maryland, New York, and Wisconsin. In states where taxation and expenditure limitations have hampered the ability of local jurisdictions to raise and spend revenues, the trend has been toward fiscal centralization. Greater centralization has also resulted from state efforts to reduce service disparities between wealthy and poor jurisdictions and to lessen the dependence of local governments on the property tax.

Table 13.4 shows the diversity in state aid to counties, municipalities, and townships, which varies from $1,952 per capita in California to $130 in Hawaii; the average is $1,175. This surprisingly large variation has been explored in empirical research by political scientists. It appears that the most important predictors of state aid to localities are centralization of functions (for example, more than 50 percent of Alaska's total aid is for education), state wealth (rich states provide more money than poor states do), fiscal need (fiscally stressed localities need greater state aid), and legislative professionalism (professional legislatures are willing to spend more on education, social services, and other local programs).[38]

What Local Governments Want from the States

What local governments want from their states and what they actually get may be worlds apart. Today, states and their local jurisdictions conduct nearly constant dialogue over financial matters. More and more often today, the states are

TABLE 13.4 **Per-Capita State Expenditures to Local Governments, Fiscal Year 2002**

STATE	PER-CAPITA PAYMENTS TO COUNTIES, MUNICIPALITIES, AND TOWNSHIPS	STATE	PER-CAPITA PAYMENTS TO COUNTIES, MUNICIPALITIES, AND TOWNSHIPS
California	$1,952	Illinois	975
Michigan	1,738	South Carolina	958
Wyoming	1,705	Nebraska	930
New York	1,656	Pennsylvania	927
Alaska	1,644	North Dakota	915
Minnesota	1,562	Oklahoma	899
Vermont	1,541	Utah	898
Wisconsin	1,532	Florida	893
New Mexico	1,354	Georgia	892
Arizona	1,182	Alabama	882
North Carolina	1,170	Colorado	876
Nevada	1,163	New Hampshire	862
Oregon	1,155	Montana	847
Mississippi	1,148	Louisiana	834
Ohio	1,141	Maryland	829
Indiana	1,114	Kentucky	816
Delaware	1,105	Missouri	814
Iowa	1,101	Texas	790
Washington	1,090	Tennessee	774
Kansas	1,065	West Virginia	750
New Jersey	1,033	Maine	720
Arkansas	1,028	Rhode Island	651
Virginia	1,019	South Dakota	597
Idaho	1,002	Hawaii	130
Connecticut	993	U.S. average	1,175
Massachusetts	988		

NOTE: Includes payments from the federal government, primarily state reimbursements for the supplemental security income program.
SOURCE: Rockefeller Institute of Government and U.S. Department of Commerce, Bureau of the Census.

recognizing and responding to local financial problems—subject, of course, to their own fiscal circumstances, citizen demands for tax relief, and their judgment about what is best for all state residents.

Simply put, what localities want most is *more money.* But they also want more control over how it is spent and the independent power to raise it. The tax revolt, reductions in federal grants-in-aid, and pressing infrastructure needs have left local jurisdictions in a financial bind. State governments must provide help, and in general they have done so. State aid for all local governments has grown every year since 1981, substantially outstripping inflation over that period.

Most increases in state aid are devoted to education, corrections, health care, and social services. Recently, however, states have been more willing to share revenues that cities or counties may spend as they desire. Many states distribute a portion of their tax revenues based on local fiscal need, thus tending to equalize or level economic disparities between local jurisdictions.[39]

The specific means for sharing revenues takes many forms. Most of the states make special payments in lieu of taxes to local governments where state buildings or other facilities are located. These buildings and facilities are exempt from property taxes but cause a drain on local services. Such payments are of particular importance to capital cities, in which large plots of prime downtown property are occupied by state office buildings.

In addition, local governments want the *legal capacity to raise additional revenues themselves,* especially through local option sales and income taxes. A share of gasoline, tobacco, and other tax benefits is greatly appreciated, as is the authority to impose impact fees on developers of residential property. The key is local option, whereby jurisdictions decide for themselves which, if any, taxes they will exact. More than two-thirds of the states have authorized an optional sales or income tax for various local governments, and some permit localities to adopt optional earmarked taxes. For example, Florida empowers its counties to place an accommodations tax on local hotel and motel rooms. Revenues are dedicated to tourism development projects. Local option taxes are attractive because they provide local jurisdictions with the flexibility to take action as they see fit in response to local needs. What protects citizens against "taxaholic" local legislative bodies in the aftermath of the taxpayer revolt is the state requirement that local tax hikes must be approved by the voters in a referendum.

Local governments also want *limitations on and reimbursements for state mandates* that require them to spend money. Through constitutional provisions, statutes, and administrative regulations, all states require localities to undertake certain activities and operate programs in accordance with state standards and rules. These mandates, which accumulate over the years, are similar to the strings attached to federal grants-in-aid (which also affect local governments), and they are just as distasteful to local governments as federal mandates are to states. Many state mandates are associated with local personnel policies, such as minimum wages, pensions, and safe working conditions. Others entail special-education programs, environmental-protection standards, and tax exemptions. Most are designed to achieve uniformity in the levels and quality of local government services throughout the state. Sometimes, however, state mandates appear to be nitpicking. Examples include requirements that public libraries carry a certain number of books per resident or that school buses be refueled daily, whether their tanks are empty or not.

Local governments believe that they should not have to both obey *and* pay, and that states should reimburse them for expenses incurred in carrying out such mandates. Many states have responded to this request. Forty-two states attach fiscal notes to any proposed legislation or administrative regulation or rule that involves local governments; these notes estimate the local costs of implementing the legislation. At least twenty states are required by law to go one step further and reimburse local governments in full for mandated expenditures. Seven states do not permit mandates to become binding until formally approved by their local governments.[40]

STATE AND LOCAL FINANCE IN THE 2000s

The fiscal and political travails of New York City are abnormal in certain respects, but overall they reflect common miseries that periodically afflict the great majority of large U.S. cities during bad economic times. In the past, the federal and state governments would have ridden to the fiscal rescue with economic assistance. But today their own financial problems rival those of the local governments. The national government, finally determined to keep its own budget in balance, has cut aid to the states, which in turn are pressured to contribute less to city and county coffers. The keys to surviving financial crises are intergovernmental cooperation, burden sharing, capacity building, and citizen comprehension of the basic tax–service relationship.

Long-term taxing and spending trends are being reconsidered by states and localities. They hope that the national government will continue to join them in facing up to the spiraling costs of Medicaid, corrections, and public education—burdens that should not be laid on the back of a single level of government. Mandates without money should be abolished in most instances. When mandates and program responsibilities are pushed to a different rung of the federal ladder, funds should follow. Local governments, particularly, need more revenue-raising authority and broader tax bases to pay for the services they deliver. Most states have been receptive to these principles; the federal government requires further education.

The need for increasing state and local capability and responsiveness by reinventing and reinvigorating government has perhaps never been greater. According to this approach, the financial structures and processes of state and local governments must be made more appropriate to the social and economic environment in which they operate, which includes a service-based economy; international markets; aging baby-boomers (the "gray peril"); and the changing gender, racial, and ethnic composition of the labor force. Special challenges to state and local governments are not being met sufficiently by present revenue systems.

Governments are obligated to be responsive to citizens, but they also need to educate taxpayers, who do not always grasp the relationship between taxes paid and services rendered. Resistance to new or existing taxes is fine, but truth-in-taxation campaigns must educate citizens that reducing or eliminating taxes may result in fewer services. It is also important that citizens and elected officials fully recognize that the current tax codes of the states are geared to yesterday's economy. They will need to be rewritten to capture revenues efficiently in a changing economic and demographic environment. Gradually, states are helping local governments reduce their dependence on property taxes. Several states are seriously considering extending the reach of their sales tax into services. Excessive reliance on one or two major taxes calls for a new, more diversified tax structure. Elected officials have the primary responsibility for taxpayer education, but often politics intrudes. However well-intended, campaign pledges for no new taxes do not help. Revenue decisions are difficult, but they are extraordinarily important for the well-being of governments and their citizens.

CHAPTER RECAP

- The two basic principles of state and local financial systems are the interdependence of the three levels of government and the diversity of revenue sources.
- Among the criteria for evaluating taxes are equity, yield, elasticity, ease of administration, political accountability, and acceptability.
- The major state and local taxes are those assessed on property, sales, and income. Other taxes and fees are also imposed.
- Legalized gambling and gaming also raise money.
- Taxpayer resistance has produced tax and expenditure limitations in many states, increased sensitivity of state and local officials to taxpayer preferences, and in some cases fiscal stress for governments.
- State and local governments estimate annual revenues and set aside money in rainy day funds for emergencies and contingencies.
- State and local financial relationships are characterized by sharing and cooperation, but also by conflict over mandates and limited local discretion.

Key Terms

own-source revenue *(p. 357)*

intergovernmental transfers *(p. 357)*

countercyclical aid *(p. 358)*

tax capacity *(p. 360)*

tax effort *(p. 360)*

regressive tax *(p. 362)*

progressive tax *(p. 363)*

proportional (flat) tax *(p. 363)*

benefit principle *(p. 363)*

indexing *(p. 364)*

circuit breaker *(p. 366)*

tax–service paradox *(p. 375)*

political economy *(p. 376)*

taxation and expenditure limitations (TELs) *(p. 377)*

fiscal stress *(p. 377)*

general-obligation bond *(p. 383)*

revenue bond *(p. 383)*

industrial development bond (IDB) *(p. 383)*

bond bank *(p. 384)*

Surfing the Web

The National Conference of State Legislatures' Principles of a High Quality Tax System are available for viewing at **www.NCSL.org.**

To check on the fiscal status of New York City, see its Tax Page at **www.ibo. nyc.ny.us.**

One of the best individual sites on state tax and budget information is that of the Texas State Comptroller at **www.window.state.tx.us.**

For current reports in developments, trends, and policy changes in state government finances, see the web site of the Center for the Study of the States at SUNY–Albany, **stateandlocalgateway.rockinst.org.**

Comparative state and local revenue, tax, and expenditure data may be found at the U.S. Census Bureau's web site (**www.census.gov**) and at the Tax Foundation's web site (**www.taxfoundation.org**).

See **www.taxsites.com** for general tax resources and official state tax sites.

14

ECONOMIC DEVELOPMENT

I n 2003, minivans and sport-utility vehicles began rolling off the assembly
line at a brand spanking new Nissan plant—not in Japan, but in Mississippi.
The state spent an estimated $360 million in job training, infrastructure im-
provements, and tax breaks to lure the automaker to the Magnolia State. Why
was the state willing to pay the big bucks? There are four related reasons. First,
Nissan's 5,000 jobs would generate $170 million in annual payroll. Second, the
state hopes that the Nissan plant will have a ripple effect; that is, that other industries will flock to the state. Third, Mississippi believes that winning Nissan
will add some much needed luster to the state's image. And last but not least,
if Mississippi had not come through with an attractive incentive package, its
neighbor to the east, Alabama, would have.[1] The motto for state economic development may be "You've got to pay to play."

economic development

A process by which a
community, state, or
nation increases its level
of per-capita income,
high-quality jobs, and
capital investment.

Attracting new investment like the Nissan facility is what **economic development** is all about these days. Capital investment, employment, income, tax base,

and public services—all are linked to economic development. And it is a competitive process, often pitting one state against another. State leaders are well aware of the stakes involved, as indicated in the salvo fired a few years back by New Jersey's governor: "No more losing our employers to job raids by low-tax states. New Jersey is open for business."[2] Resurgent state and local governments are pursuing economic development with a vengeance.

REGIONAL DIFFERENCES IN ECONOMIC PROSPERITY

The United States continues to be a nation of diverse regional economies.[3] When the headline in *USA Today* trumpets "Nation's economy soars," be assured that not all places are reaching the same heights. As economist Mark Crain noted, during the last three decades of the twentieth century, living standards (measured by real income per capita) in the United States increased by 50 percent.[4] However, this average figure masks a considerable range in the data: from a low of 28 percent in Alaska to a high of 64 percent in North Carolina. Even within regions, economies can vary. Detroit and Columbus are both located in the Midwest, but the largest city in Michigan and the largest city in Ohio are worlds apart economically. Different economic mixes of manufacturing, services, and retail employment mean different economic conditions. The effects of global economic restructuring coupled with a national recession hit states and communities hard in the early twenty-first century. Some places are doing better than others in adjusting to the new economic realities.

Remember that economies are dynamic; that is, economic momentum can slow down and speed up. The personal income growth in a state, the change in unemployment rates, and the level of population change are three indicators that can be combined into a useful index of economic momentum. The figures for the last quarter of 2003 showed Nevada and the two Dakotas at the top of the list, with Massachusetts and Michigan at the bottom.[5] The index for the same period in 2002 found Nevada, Alaska, and Rhode Island leading the way, with New York and Massachusetts at the end.[6]

Local economies are also dynamic. To illustrate, consider the cities of Denver, Colorado, and Salt Lake City, Utah, both of which boomed in the 1990s with surging high-tech and telecommunication industries. As the economy weakened in 2001, both cities were especially hard hit because technology and telecom firms began rounds of layoffs and closures.[7] The bloom was definitely off the economic rose—but only for awhile. Both cities began to rebound in 2004. As some cities decline, others surge. The nearby *Breaking New Ground* box discusses some cities that have become magnets for the creative class.

Figure 14.1 captures the varying economic fortunes of the states. The map shows the grade that states received from the Corporation for Enterprise Development (CfED), a nonprofit economic development organization. The CfED grades provide a snapshot of a state's economic health. Five factors went into the grade: employment, earnings and job quality, equity (income distribution), quality of life, and resource efficiency. Each of the factors is composed of between

BREAKING NEW GROUND

The Creative Class and Cool Cities

What's the hottest thing for cities these days? To be cool, that is, to be the kind of place that attracts well-educated, talented young professionals to its environs. Cool cities are magnets for the creative class, people whose work involves producing new ideas, new technology, or new creative content. And what are these individuals looking for in a city? They want a place with an opportunity-rich job market as well as desirable lifestyle features. The cool cities have these characteristics; their less cool counterparts do not.

Cool cities possess what Richard Florida calls in his book, *The Rise of the Creative Class,* the three T's: technology, tolerance, and talent. Their economies are knowledge-based, their policies promote social tolerance, and their communities nurture the arts and culture. Jobs are plentiful, gays and lesbians are welcomed, and the nightlife is lively. As a result, these cities are experiencing a brain-gain, that is, an influx of entrepreneurial, ambitious, and creative young people. And this trend has a snowball effect: More well-educated, mobile fun-seekers flock to cool cities. At the same time, cities lacking in some or all of the three T's are not keeping pace with the cool places.

Which large cities are the coolest? It depends on the criteria used. If it is creativity, then San Francisco is at the top, followed by Austin and San Diego. If it is the percentage of residents with college degrees, then Washington, D.C. is at the top, with Atlanta and San Francisco in second and third places, respectively. If it is the best place for singles then according to *Forbes* magazine, Austin leads, followed by the Denver-Boulder area and Boston.

Can cities that lack an abundance of cool characteristics appeal to the creative class? Cincinnati, Ohio, is an example of a city that is trying to do just that. It has developed a Creative City Plan that it hopes will make it more appealing to smart young people by enhancing amenities such as recreation, the arts, and entertainment. Cincinnati's reputation has been damaged by recurrent racial tensions and a provision in the city's charter that blocks the city council from passing anti-discrimination legislation that would apply to gays and lesbians. Efforts are underway to rectify both of these conditions. City leaders believe that attracting the creative class is the key to insuring Cincinnati's economic growth and prosperity. But can it compete with cities such as Seattle and Boston in attracting people with expertise in today's cutting-edge fields such as genome science, bioinformatics, and entrepreneurial management? The challenge for the not-yet-cool cities is substantial.

SOURCES: Karen Imas, "The Rise of the Creative Class," *State Government News* (March 2004): 12–13; Blaine Harden, "Urban Warfare," *Washington Post National Weekly Edition* (December 1–7, 2003): 6–7; Ross Atkin, "A Tale of Cool Cities," *Christian Science Monitor* (October 8, 2003): 11–13; Richard Florida, *The Rise of the Creative Class* (New York: Basic Books, 2002).

---

four to nine elements. For example, employment performance is measured by both long-term and short-term employment growth, the number of mass layoffs, and the unemployment rate.[8] A composite index like this one offers a more complete picture of a state's economic performance than simply relying on one or two items. States with grades of A or B have economies that performed substantially better than states with D and F grades did. A few years ago, the grades would have been different for many states. Overheated economies eventually cool off; chilly economies eventually thaw.

| FIGURE 14.1 | **Grading State Economic Performance** |

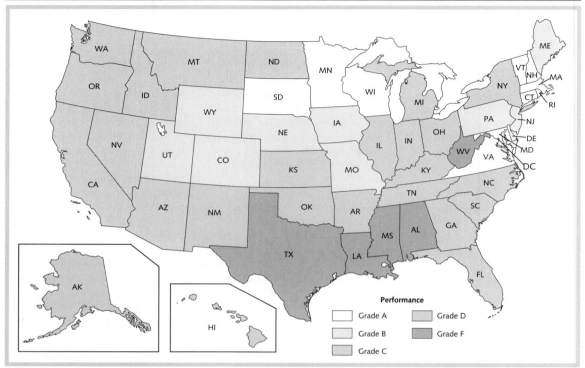

SOURCE: "2003 Development Report Card for the States," Corporation for Enterprise Development (Washington, D.C.: CfED, 2004);
www.drc.cfed.org/grades/indexes.

APPROACHES TO ECONOMIC DEVELOPMENT

Governments devise elaborate strategies *and spend a lot of money* to promote economic development within their boundaries. The approaches they use have evolved over time, but even some of the oldest tools remain viable today.

Early Approaches: First and Second Waves

Community efforts to spur economic development have a long history, but the first statewide program of industrial recruitment was created during the Great Depression. Mississippi, with its Balance Agriculture with Industry plan, made it possible for local governments to issue bonds to finance the construction or purchase of facilities for relocating industry. Other southern states followed suit, luring businesses from elsewhere with tax breaks, public **subsidies,** and low wages.[9] Called smokestack chasing, aggressive industrial recruitment had spread beyond the South by the 1970s. By the end of that decade, as states raided other states for industry, statistics showed that between 80 and 90 percent of new jobs

subsidy

Financial assistance given by a government to a firm or enterprise.

venture capital pools

Special funds earmarked for new, innovative businesses that cannot get conventional financing.

small-business incubators

Facilities that provide services aimed at nurturing start-up businesses.

enterprise zone

Areas of a community that offer special government incentives aimed at stimulating investment.

clusters

Geographically concentrated firms that compete and trade with each other and have similar needs.

came from existing firm expansions and start-up businesses, not from relocating businesses. About the same time, pressure from foreign competition intensified. Policymakers feverishly cast about for strategies that would spawn new businesses and keep state economies strong. These efforts began a new era, or second wave, in economic development. States established **venture capital pools,** created **small-business incubators,** and initiated work-force training programs in an attempt to support homegrown enterprise. Even with these new initiatives, many states continued to chase out-of-state industry.

Newer Approaches: Third and Fourth Waves

The 1990s saw a third wave gather strength. This wave represented "a rethinking of what government can do and cannot do, and how it can do it more effectively."[10] Second-wave programs, well-intentioned perhaps, simply did not have sufficient scale or focus to transform state economies. An **enterprise zone** (termed an empowerment zone by the Clinton administration), for example, may revitalize a neighborhood, but if an extensive network of such zones does not exist throughout the state, the overall impact is marginal. Third-wave efforts sought to correct some of the deficiencies of second-wave programs. One of the keys to the third wave was moving economic development programs from state agencies and into private organizations. Rather than directly supplying the program or the service, as it had done in the first and second waves, government would provide direction and seed capital.

The latest ripple flowing from the third wave is called **clusters.** It reconfigures the economy as clusters of firms that compete and trade with one another and have common needs.[11] By focusing on interconnections and working relationships among businesses, nonprofit organizations, and government, a state gets a better sense of its economic foundations.[12] Arizona pioneered the concept in its Strategic Plan for Economic Development. The state identified ten clusters ranging from food, fiber, and natural products to environmental technologies, to mining and minerals.[13] Each cluster has spawned an organization in which ideas can be shared, common strategies developed, and joint ventures negotiated. In Connecticut, the clusters are tourism, aerospace, and bioscience. To nurture and support its clusters, the Connecticut legislature redesigned the state's research and development tax credits.[14] High technology remains an important cluster in many places around the country despite the slowdown the industry experienced in the early 2000s.

Third-wave thinking continues to influence states and localities, but a fourth wave has already developed. Political scientist Susan Clarke and geographer Gary Gaile contend that a distinctively different set of strategies lies ahead.[15] This new set, or fourth wave, is more attuned to global markets, especially localities' use of trade and telecommunications to their economic advantage. The fourth wave is also more focused on human capital, that is, on educating and training its work force. Even as states and localities turn to these third- and fourth-wave approaches, however, they continue to use strategies from the first and second waves. How to pursue economic development remains a hotly debated subject.

A leading figure who has headed economic revitalization efforts in three states points to five key trends that are fashioning the future:

- The economic playing field is the world, not the neighboring county or state.
- The new infrastructure is technology and telecommunications.
- Regionalism provides an opportunity for states and others to work together. Boundaries are falling.
- Sustainable development strategies that recognize the interdependence of the economy and the environment are necessary.
- Successful economic development efforts are built on a high-quality work force.[16]

The Waves and Business Vitality in the States

The vitality of a state's businesses directly affects its economy. CfED measured business vitality across the fifty states, looking at the competitiveness of existing business and the level of entrepreneurial energy within the state. Each factor that it considered is made up of several items. For instance, entrepreneurial energy is derived from the number of new companies, the change in the number of new companies, new business job growth, technology industry employment, and the number of initial public offerings (IPOs) in the state.[17] Figure 14.2 displays the states' business vitality grades.

States with higher grades in business vitality have stronger economic engines than states with lower grades do. Their economies are diverse and competitive, new companies are starting up, and capital is being invested. There appears to be a link between economic performance (Figure 14.1) and business vitality (Figure 14.2): 66 percent of the states have scores on the two indexes that are within one letter grade. Three states—Massachusetts, Minnesota, and Virginia—have A's on both measures. Six states—Alaska, Hawaii, Mississippi, New Mexico, Oklahoma, and West Virginia—have low grades on both measures. About one-third of the states record substantially different grades when the focus shifts from economic performance to business vitality. South Dakota and Vermont slip from high grades to low grades when business vitality is considered, but Alabama, Illinois, and Texas improve greatly.

THE POLITICS OF ECONOMIC DEVELOPMENT

Economic development occupies a central role in campaigns for state and local elective office. Like reducing crime and improving education, it is a consensus issue: Everybody is in favor of it. Thus, each candidate tries to convince the voters that his or her approach to economic development will be the most effective. At both the state and local levels, candidates' campaign rhetoric typically emphasizes jobs and employment, as did the three leading candidates in California's 1998 gubernatorial primaries. Asked to identify their top priorities if elected, they responded, "sustaining and expanding economic growth," "providing every Californian the opportunity to share in our state's new prosperity," and "encouraging the success of free enterprise, capitalism, technological innovation, and small business."[18]

FIGURE 14.2	**State Business Vitality Grades**

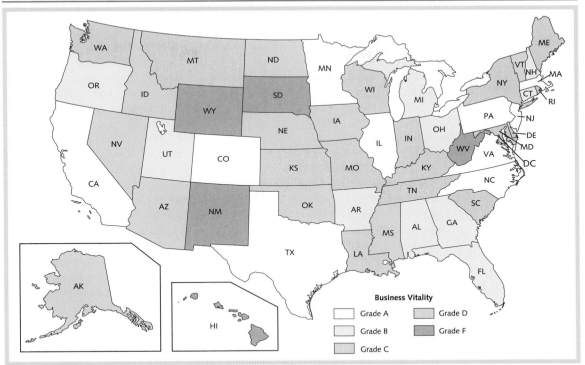

SOURCE: "2003 Development Report Card for the States," Corporation for Enterprise Development (Washington, D.C.: CfED, 2004); www.drc.cfed.org/grades/indexes.

Most states have created several mechanisms to implement economic development strategies.[19] Ideally, a state government should be internally united for its economic development effort, but several natural cleavages—partisan politics, legislative–executive disputes, and agency turf battles—make cohesion difficult. Because economic development is a central issue, it inspires a lot of political posturing. In the end, a state government with a unified, cohesive approach to economic development is likely to be more successful than a state without one.

As a state's top elected official and chief executive, the governor commonly takes the lead in economic development, creating task forces and blue-ribbon panels, such as Ohio Governor Bob Taft's Jobs Cabinet. These groups try to come up with fresh ideas and new tactics, maximizing the state's strengths and minimizing its weaknesses. This effort does not mean that states will not borrow a successful approach from another state. Once an economic development strategy is in place, the next challenge is implementation. During what we earlier referred to as the first wave of economic development strategies, the responsibility for implementation belonged to state agencies. Adherents to the third wave argue, however, that state agencies have not responded creatively and effectively to the challenges confronting them. Third-wave advocates want government agencies out of the economic development business, with more flexible, public–private hybrids or private-sector organizations as their replacements. Florida was the first state to replace its Department of Commerce with a public–private organization, which it named Enterprise Florida (or eFlorida).

Greater involvement by nongovernment organizations in providing economic development programs and services is risky. State governments have always had a complex relationship with the private sector. They must contend with demands from various interests, of which business is only one (albeit a powerful one). Nevertheless, state policymakers have generally tried to accommodate the demands of the business community. In fact, one persistent criticism of state legislatures is that they have been *too* receptive to the entreaties of business. Business leaders believe that because their success is central to a state's economy, they ought to be treated as a public interest rather than as a special-interest group.[20] A state may thus feel that it is less a partner than a prisoner. In response to the question "Who runs Massachusetts?" one state legislator responded: "The businesses that threaten to move out of the state. They have a chokehold on us."[21] This statement may be extreme in tone, but it conveys the frustration that some state officials feel about their government's relationship with business. It also highlights the skepticism with which many state policymakers greet calls for less government involvement in economic development. The subject of the *Debating Politics* box is offshore outsourcing, a topic of increasing salience for individuals and policymakers alike.

One successful partnership that has emerged in some states is the one between industries and universities. The Committee for Economic Development, a national group of prominent business executives and educators, identifies five ways in which states can facilitate these partnerships: through state-established centers, state grants to university research centers, research incubators, small-business development centers, and research parks.[22]

One emerging, potentially fertile area for industry–university collaboration is bioscience, especially stem-cell research. Minnesota was one of the first states to take action when it established a Stem Cell Institute and set up tax-free zones for bioscience companies; Wisconsin, another pioneer, has its nonprofit WiCell Research Institute. In 2003, legislatures in twenty-nine states considered seventy-one bills related to embryonic or fetal stem-cell research; five of them were enacted.[23] New Jersey passed legislation in 2004 that legalized stem-cell research in the Garden State and promptly budgeted $6.5 million a year through 2010 in support of it. California, where many biotech companies are located, had a massive spending initiative on its 2004 ballot. The California Stem Cell Research and Cures Initiative would spend a whopping $300 million a year for ten years. Stem-cell research could lead to significant advances in health but for states, the economic development benefits are just as—and maybe more—appealing. In the words of Missouri Governor Bob Holden, "Whether it's pharmaceuticals, biotechnology, or medical research—life sciences technologies will create the jobs of tomorrow.[24]

DEBATING POLITICS

Offshore Outsourcing: Globalization Grabs Some U.S. Jobs

It began as a trickle, a few firms shutting down operations in the United States and opening new plants in foreign countries. Borders became even more porous with the adoption of the North American Free Trade Act (NAFTA) and the rulings of the World Trade Organization (WTO). Over time, barriers that had kept foreign products out of domestic markets fell. As the process of globalization continued, more U.S. jobs were lost to countries with lower wages and fewer regulations. In India and Russia, for instance, wages for computer programmers average less than 10 percent of the wages for programmers in the United States. During the recession of 2001–2003, more than 15 percent of the 2.8 million American jobs lost were outsourced to other countries. Many of these jobs were white-collar service jobs. One forecast has the number of white-collar job losses reaching 3.3 million by 2015, although others contend that this estimate is based on faulty data. Even state governments have used overseas workers to provide certain kinds of services. Maryland, for example, hired a private firm to administer some of its welfare services through the firm's call centers in India and Mexico. It is no wonder that the issue of offshore outsourcing is generating intense debate.

To some, the reality is simple. As one southern governor said in his 2004 State of the State address, "We're in a global competition for jobs. We don't just compete with southern states anymore. We're now competing with the likes of China and India." This new reality has led to calls for slowing, even

prohibiting, the relocation of firms (and their jobs) to other countries. States cannot stop companies from moving their operations to foreign countries, of course, but states can cease to do business with them. For instance, in 2004, Michigan's Governor Jennifer Granholm signed two executive orders that prohibit the state from contracting with businesses that would outsource the work to foreign countries. But even as she acted, some state senators contended that the action would send Michigan "down a dangerous, protectionist path."

Is offshore outsourcing a dangerous trend? Does it raise red flags about the future competitiveness of the U.S. economy? Some commentators say yes. As one observer argues, "The U.S. gave away its agricultural knowledge, its education, its technology, its manufacturing jobs and is now giving away its IT [information technology] jobs." But Robert Reich, former U.S. secretary of labor sees it differently. He contends that, compared to the overall employment base of the United States, the number of positions being outsourced is relatively small. But as public policy expert Ron Hira notes, jobs are moving overseas at an accelerated pace. States and localities have an obvious interest in keeping jobs at home. Is offshore outsourcing something to fear, or is it simply the next stage in an evolving economy, something that states and localities will adjust to and learn from?

SOURCES: Jeff Finkle, "Grabbing While Holding On: Job Creation and Retention During the Recession," *Spectrum: The Journal of State Government* 77 (Winter 2004): 5–7; Ron Hira, "White Collar Jobs Move Overseas: Implications for States," *Spectrum: The Journal of State Government* 77 (Winter 2004): 12–14, 18; Laurie Clewett, "State of the States," *State Government News* (March 2004): 20; Kathleen Gray, "Governor Acts to Retain Mich. Jobs," *Detroit Free Press*, www.freep.com (March 22, 2004).

CURRENT INITIATIVES

State governments, aware that their economic development activities have appeared incoherent and even counterproductive to the outside world, have attempted to clarify their role. In doing so, many states have engaged in strategic planning. Economic sectors commonly targeted by states include travel and tourism, the arts, sports, and international trade.

Strategic Planning

strategic planning

An approach to economic development that emphasizes adaptation to changing conditions and anticipation of future events.

Strategic planning can be useful for several reasons, according to the National Association of State Development Agencies.[25] First, it produces an understanding of the state's economic bedrock. Second, it provides a venue in which public- and private-sector leaders can exchange perspectives and develop a consensus about the state's economic future. In addition, strategic planning moves the economic development issue from goal setting to implementation. Finally, it provides a mechanism for adjusting and correcting the state's actions to match emerging economic trends.

Wisconsin was one of the first states to engage in strategic planning for economic development. A twenty-three-member strategic development commission was established by the governor during a time of economic turmoil in the state that resulted mostly from the loss of industrial jobs. The commission's assignment was to analyze the Wisconsin economy and identify avenues for government action. Eighteen months and half a million dollars later, it produced its strategic plan. The focus was on preserving the existing job base, fostering new jobs, and adopting the ethos that "Wisconsin is first in quality."[26] More than 100 specific recommendations were included in the plan.

Since then, most states have undertaken strategic planning exercises. Georgia's State Strategic Plan is typical. Seven initiatives were singled out:[27]

- Attract new businesses and industries to the state.
- Assist existing businesses and industries.
- Promote Georgia businesses, products, services, and attractions.
- Provide technical assistance to all areas of Georgia.
- Enhance Georgia's economic infrastructure.
- Invest in research and development.
- Maintain a strong fiscal policy.

Georgia identified a series of actions intended to accomplish these goals. As with most strategic plans, the biggest hurdle is translating rhetoric into reality. But refer again to Figures 14.1 and 14.2: Georgia's grade in economic performance is a C; its business vitality grade is a B—not spectacular but better than average.

Ohio's strategic plan for economic development, called Ohio 2000/Ohio First, aimed at retaining existing jobs and attracting new ones. At its heart were programs that provide tax credits to businesses that create new jobs and purchase new machinery and equipment. For example, when LTV, a Cleveland-based steelmaker, decided to open a new $66 million steel-tube production facility in the state, it qualified for a tax-incentive package worth $8 million over a ten-year period.[28] LTV also received an 80 percent abatement of personal property taxes for ten years, valued at $2.97 million. Investments like LTV exemplified Ohio's strategic plan but even with the state's efforts, Ohio continued to lose manufacturing jobs. As of 2004, unemployment exceeded the national average in Ohio, and the state's overall economic performance was in the D range in Figure 14.1.

Many states have a less strategic economic development plan and use a more incremental, eclectic approach. The actual programs and tools that state and local governments employ to accomplish their economic development objectives are many and varied. Four that have maintained their popularity are travel and tourism, the arts, sports, and international trade.

Travel and Tourism

Travel and tourism are big business. According to National Conference of State Legislatures figures, spending by travelers accounts for 6.7 percent of the gross national product (GNP) and finances 6 million jobs, thus making travel and tourism the country's third largest retail industry.[29] To attract big-spending tourists, states spend big—and some states spend really big. At the local level, convention and visitors' bureaus, which are frequently the joint ventures of the Chamber of Commerce and city government, have been created to promote individual communities and their assets.

States are actively marketing the virtues of their coasts, mountains, Revolutionary War battlefields, national parks, regional cuisine, casinos—whatever might attract a tourist dollar. States develop advertising campaigns around a catchy slogan: You Could Use a Little Indiana, Kansas Secrets, or America Starts Here. As Iowa's tourism director noted, "We're looking for a type of kick-butt theme that gets on people's minds."[30]

For example, read how Maine is described in the state's Office of Tourism web site: "Maine is America off the beaten path. While most of the state remains as pristine as a primal forest, its villages offer a glimpse of contemporary New England life inextricably linked to the past. Geographically, culturally, and historically, Maine offers a bit of everything—from its famed rocky coast to western lakes and mountains, from quaint fishing villages to bustling outlet centers."[31] The images are appealing. Pennsylvania markets unusual attractions that it calls "downright quirky." Where else can one find the birthplace of the American pretzel industry or a museum devoted to Zippo lighters? One can spend a morning at the Crayola crayon factory's interactive center and the afternoon at the U.S. Weightlifting Federation Hall of Fame. The state's Office of Travel, Tourism and Film Promotion promises "memories that last a lifetime."[32]

Some states and localities are going after the foreign tourist, a pursuit complicated by the security measures in force since the September 11, 2001, terrorist attacks. Cumulatively, states spend more than $38 million annually in advertising and promotions designed to attract international travelers.[33] Some of the efforts are highly targeted. For example, South Dakota offered a special vacation package to German tourists who had seen the film *Dances with Wolves* and wanted to visit the locale.[34] International tourists shop, eat out, see the sights . . . and spend money. Before September 11, foreign visitors made up approximately 18 percent of New York City's tourists and generated 42 percent of total visitor spending.[35] After September 11, however, the number of foreign tourists dropped significantly, and the revenue effects were felt far beyond the Big Apple.

Travel and tourism are especially appealing because of the tax yield. Most states levy an **accommodations tax** (commonly referred to as a bed tax), and the money spent by travelers and tourists is also subject to state as well as local sales taxes. All in all, nonresidents contribute a significant sum to the tax base of tourism-rich locales. In fact, the tax sensitivity of tourists is much debated. At what point does the tax burden drive tourists away?

accommodations tax
A tax on hotel- or motel-room occupancy, with the revenues usually earmarked for tourism-related uses.

The Arts

Throughout the country, in medium-size to large cities, performing arts lovers (patrons of dance, opera, theater, and orchestra) are joining with business leaders to forge a coalition. Their intent is to use the arts as a development strategy. Promoting the arts as a development tool may not be as far-fetched as one might initially think.[36] Cities hope that, by sponsoring world-class concerts in acoustically perfect arenas, they can bring audiences of white-collar workers back to the city's center. Such events would also generate secondary spending by the audience (and participants) at restaurants, retail shops, parking garages, and hotels. And just as important, a new sense of liveliness and vitality would inspire the nightlife. In fact, the accessibility of community **amenities** such as the arts is a factor that frequently contributes to business-relocation decisions. Members of arts coalitions argue that company officials might look more favorably on their city if it regularly attracts Broadway shows and the Bolshoi Ballet. They point out that a successful performing arts center could stimulate additional physical development in the downtown area. Indeed, a community might invest in an arts strategy for many reasons.

amenities
Comfort and conveniences that contribute to quality of life.

In cities as large as Los Angeles and Dallas and as small as Eugene, Oregon, and Charleston, South Carolina, the performing arts have become a key development tool. The Performing Arts Center in Newark, New Jersey, makes the case for such a goal. After ten years of planning and construction totaling $180 million in public and private funds, the facility opened in 1997. Downtown Newark has not been the same since. A seedy and often scary section of downtown has been transformed into a glittering cultural area. The center, as part of an arts loop in the central city, serves as a symbol of rebirth. As former governor Christine Todd Whitman commented, "[P]eople are feeling a new sense of hope."[37] The psychic benefits are important, but so too is the economic impact, both direct and indirect. Nonprofit arts are said to be a $36.8 billion industry nationally. In New Jersey, the nonprofit arts sector is a $736 million endeavor.

The emphasis on arts as a development tool is not confined to the performing arts. Beaumont, Texas, a city of 119,000 residents located eighty-five miles east of Houston, sought to diversify its economic base (long dominated by petroleum and shipping) through the arts. The city has created its own version of an arts megablock with the construction of both an art museum and an energy museum and the restoration of a historic library on adjacent properties. These cultural projects stimulated not only economic diversification but also additional development in the downtown area.

Providence, Rhode Island, has undergone a similar revival in its downtown area. The city created an arts and entertainment empowerment zone that offers special tax breaks. Artists and performers who live in the one-square-mile area pay no state income tax on what they sell; their customers pay no sales tax on what they buy.[38] The city also offers tax incentives to property owners who convert old, unused buildings in the zone into residential units.

But the arts need not be highbrow to affect development. Popular culture—be it multiplex theaters, theme restaurants, sports arenas, or entertainment-oriented stores—is turning around many central cities.[39] Street art, especially sculptural displays, is another popular art form that many places have embraced. Chicago kicked it off with their colorful and clever Cows on Parade: 320 life-size fiberglass bovines. Cultural leaders in other cities took the idea and ran with it. There were pigs in Cincinnati, Ohio; horses in Lexington, Kentucky; geckos in Orlando, Florida; and cornstalks in Bloomington, Illinois. Clearly, the arts have become an important economic development tool.

Sports

Professional sports and big-league cities go hand in hand. Hosting a professional sports franchise is evidence that a city has arrived—that it is not simply a large city but a major-league city. Only fifty cities in the country host a top-level professional baseball, basketball, football, or hockey team. Smaller cities eagerly court minor-league teams to enhance the quality of life in the community.

Acquiring or retaining professional sports teams has become an important element in local economic development plans.[40] Denver and Miami, already home to professional football and basketball teams, had their multiple major-league status confirmed when major-league baseball selected them for new franchises. These two cities beat out four other finalists—St. Petersburg and Orlando in Florida as well as perennial contenders Washington, D.C., and Buffalo, New York. Denver and Miami had several factors in their favor, including geography, strong local support, and (in the case of Denver) secure stadium financing. St. Petersburg finally attracted a tenant for its publicly financed, domed stadium when the Tampa Bay Devil Rays took the field in 1998.

When the National Football League (NFL) expanded in 1993, it had bids from Baltimore, Maryland; Charlotte, North Carolina; Jacksonville, Florida; Memphis, Tennessee; and St. Louis, Missouri, on the table. Baltimore and St. Louis were sentimental favorites because both had been the home of NFL franchises in the past. When the league made its decisions, however, sentiment went by the boards: the Sunbelt contenders, Charlotte and Jacksonville, received the two new franchises. (Both Baltimore and St. Louis were awarded NFL teams subsequently; Memphians get their NFL fix from the Tennessee Titans [once the Houston Oilers] located 200 miles away in Nashville.) The Carolina Panthers play their games in a privately financed $160 million stadium; Jacksonville spent $121 million to renovate the Gator Bowl for the Jaguars. Although estimates of economic impact are hard to figure, the Panthers and the Jaguars pump millions of dollars into the economies of their regions.

Cities want professional sports franchises, but they don't come easily. In fact, ownership groups have to bid for franchises, typically through some sort of public subsidy. This subsidy usually comes in the form of below-market-rate leases and tax breaks for the stadium (depending on whether the facility is publicly or privately owned). City leaders defend these subsidies, arguing that the return, both economically and symbolically, is worth it. But the public is increasingly skeptical. In 1996, voters in Hamilton County, Ohio, approved a half-cent sales tax increase in support of new stadiums for their professional teams to "maintain Cincinnati as a major league city."[41] Within two years, however, projected costs were running $200 million more than anticipated, and the public was decidedly unhappy.[42] Even after the new stadiums opened in 2000 (football) and 2003 (baseball), controversy over the financial arrangements continued. In 2004, the county sued the NFL and the Cincinnati Bengals organization, claiming that it had been forced into a bad deal.

When public financial support is not forthcoming, team owners frequently threaten to relocate. The threat is a potent one, as Cleveland found out when their beloved Browns became the Baltimore Ravens. Baltimore, still smarting from the departure of the Colts in the 1980s, built a brand-new $200 million stadium for its new team. But owners are beginning to find their relocation options narrowing. When the owner of the Minnesota Twins threatened to move his team south after the legislature failed to come up with financing for a new stadium, he found a welcome mat but no cash. The electorate in North Carolina's Greensboro area turned down plans for a publicly financed baseball facility. In Rhode Island, which had hoped to become the new home of the New England Patriots, the governor concluded that the state could not afford to provide land and infrastructure, valued at $140 million, for the $250 million stadium complex.[43] Still, few politicians want their home-state team to relocate. Thus, in 2004, the governor of Minnesota, an opponent of stadium bills when he was a state legislator, proposed the construction of new stadiums for the Twins (baseball) and the Vikings (football). Governor Tim Pawlenty explained his flip-flop this way: "Bottom line: I don't want to lose the Twins or the Vikings on my watch."[44]

A study on the impact of sports stadiums on nine local economies found that the stadiums had negligible effects on jobs and development; instead, they diverted economic development from manufacturing to the service sector.[45] And a cost-benefit analysis of minor-league stadiums turned up negative.[46] But economic analysis is one thing; civic pride is another, which is why eight U.S. cities launched official bids to become the nation's choice to host the 2012 Summer Olympic Games. (New York City was selected by the U.S. Olympic Committee and is vying with sites in other countries to win the 2012 games.) Called by some the "world's largest economic development opportunity," the Olympic Games are the ultimate sports prize. The 1996 Summer Olympics in Atlanta produced an estimated $5.1 billion for Georgia's economy.[47] And the tax rev-

Cincinnati solidified its major league city status with the new Great American Ball Park, a $280 million stadium built mostly at taxpayer expense.
SOURCE: Jonathan Danol/Getty Images.

enues were put at $165 million. Those kinds of numbers help in creating a broad base of support for the Olympics. Opposition tends to be piecemeal and sporadic, intended to "divert development from a specific location or mitigate negative consequences."[48] Table 14.1 identifies instances of opposition to the 2002 Salt Lake City Winter Olympics. Environmental groups, neighborhood groups, taxpayer organizations, and citizen advocacy groups fought against certain aspects of the games and even enjoyed occasional successes. But there was no anti-Olympic coalition intent upon stopping the games. The very successful Winter Games brought international media attention to Salt Lake City (and to Utah) and long-lasting economic benefits.

International Trade

States are no longer content to concentrate on domestic markets for the goods and services produced in their jurisdictions—they are venturing abroad. States pursue international trade for two reasons. First, foreign markets can be important consumers of state goods. Second, foreign investors may have capital to commit to projects in a state. Thus, the promotion of international trade is a two-way street: State products are exported and investment capital is imported.

One highly visible means by which state governments pursue international markets and investments is through trade missions, in which the governor, top business leaders, and economic development agency officials make formal visits, most often to Europe and Asia. The state delegation exchanges information with representatives of the country's public and private sectors and establishes ties that members hope will lead to exports and investments.

TABLE 14.1   Opposition to the 2002 Salt Lake City Winter Olympics

YEAR(S)	TARGET OF OPPOSITION	TYPE OF ORGANIZATION	TECHNIQUES OF OPPOSITION	OUTCOME
1985–1989	Development in mountain canyons	Environmental	Publicity; negotiation with bid committee	Agreement to limit development included in referendum
1989	Diversion of sales tax for Olympic construction	Taxpayer	Publicity	Tax diversion approved in referendum
1991	Neighborhood site for skating oval	Neighborhood council	Negotiation with city officials	Site proposal withdrawn by mayor
1991	Spending sales tax money to construct venues	Taxpayer	Lawsuit; advertisements	Lawsuits dismissed
1992	Downtown site for skating oval	Neighborhood, religious, advocacy groups	Negotiations with mayor; public protest; advertisements	Site proposal approved by city council but eventually withdrawn
1995	Spending by city government on Olympics	Taxpayer	Petition drive for city initiative	Petition drive failed
1995–1996	Housing, Olympic committee appointments	Advocacy groups	Publicity; negotiation with Olympic and city officials	One new appointment to Olympic committee
1996–1997	Cross-country ski site	Environmental	Publicity; negotiation with Olympic and city officials	Site location process changed, new site selected
1996–1998	Development at site for downhill skiing	Environmental	Publicity; lawsuit	Federal legislation enacted
1999	Membership of Olympic committee	Advocacy groups, taxpayer	Publicity; petition drive	Structure of Olympic committee changed

State governments perform three important roles in export promotion: brokering information, offering technical support, and providing export financing.[49] As information brokers, states conduct seminars and conferences, sponsor trade shows, publish export handbooks, and offer individual counseling to American businesses. Oklahoma, for instance, has set up an international division in its economic development department to encourage export activity. One of its key functions is to identify export opportunities for Oklahoma's business firms.

Once an opportunity has been identified, the division provides technical support to help the relevant firm become more knowledgeable about the exporting process. Similarly, Delaware participates in trade events and provides trade leads to the state's businesses. In terms of the value of their exports, California and Texas lead other states by a wide margin.

Technical support is critical because U.S. firms may not be aware of the details involved in exporting: working with international banks, complying with another country's laws and regulations, securing the necessary licensing agreements, designing appropriate packaging for products, and the like. Thus, states conduct seminars like Delaware's ABC's of Exporting to inform businesses of the details. The unified European economic market has resulted in new rules for trading with Europe, and most states have set up offices in Brussels.[50] Export finance is also important because, without it, a state's information brokerage and technical support functions are weakened. The first state to tackle the export finance issue was Minnesota; it provides a firm with operating capital for the period between the signing of a sales agreement and the delivery of a product. In addition to working capital, some states offer insurance and export credit. The availability of financing converts the fantasy of exporting into reality.

State government is also involved in promoting the state as a place for foreign investment, although public sensitivity about foreign influences on the domestic economy necessitates a cautious approach. According to the U.S. Bureau of the Census, more than 5.6 million jobs are a direct result of foreign investment. (More than 10 percent of them are in California.[51]) Hawaii leads all states with 10 percent of its work force in foreign-owned businesses; Delaware and South Carolina follow with 8.9 percent and 8.7 percent, respectively. The value of foreign-owned property, plants, and equipment was over $1 trillion in 2000, with one-fifth of this investment located in two states: California and Texas. And while most people probably don't think of Montana in terms of international banking, the state's Foreign Capital Depository Act allows wealthy foreigners to stash their money and other assets in depositories overseen and regulated by the state.[52]

The enactment of foreign trade agreements such as the North American Free Trade Agreement (NAFTA) and the decrees of the World Trade Organization (WTO) add another dimension to the globalization of trade for states and localities. NAFTA gradually eliminates trade barriers and investment restrictions among the United States, Canada, and Mexico. NAFTA opens new markets to a state's industries, but it also puts pressure on those industries to remain competitive. States with a heavy reliance on low-wage, low-skill industries have the most to fear about a NAFTA-inspired job drain. The agreement also imposes new limitations and duties on state governments.[53] Under NAFTA, for example, states may no longer discriminate in favor of homegrown service-providing firms, nor can they restrict foreign ownership of land, unless these policies are specifically grandfathered into the agreement. The WTO picks up where NAFTA leaves off by, in effect, knocking down protectionism and opening borders throughout the world.

PERSISTENT QUESTIONS IN ECONOMIC DEVELOPMENT

A robust economy provides jobs for residents and revenues for governments. Therefore, economic health is a central public policy concern. Government actions intended to spark economic development are typically considered to be in the public interest.[54] Still, three questions in particular are associated with government involvement in the economy, and they pertain to the impact, the extent, and the fairness of government action.

Do State and Local Government Initiatives Make Much Difference?

Views about the impact of government actions on the economy diverge widely. Some studies suggest that many of the important factors that affect an economy are beyond the control of state and local governments.[55] Others contend that government action can greatly influence the fate of a local economy.[56] Both views contain a kernel of truth. One widely cited study of the location decisions of large firms found that a favorable labor climate and proximity to suppliers and consumers were important criteria to most firms.[57] Governments can affect the first factor but not the second. Also, states vary in the degree to which their economies are influenced by external forces.[58]

Questions about impact and return on investment continue to haunt state and local development officials. Can the actions of states and localities affect employment levels, income, and investment? Statistical tests suggest that the outcomes are both mixed and marginal. Research by political scientists Margery Ambrosius and Paul Brace has shown that, in some places, at some times, some economic development tools produce the intended outcomes.[59] A study of forty government-assisted development projects in ten medium-size cities reached similar conclusions.[60] Regardless of the modest results, however, governments continue to intervene in their economies. This behavior may rest in the political benefits of successful development projects to elected officials. Or it may be an outgrowth of business influence in public policymaking. Whatever the explanation, the behavior continues.

new economy
An economy based in global technology, as opposed to the old economy based in national manufacturing.

The comments of former Maryland governor Parris Glendening are apropos: "We are all having to learn new rules for the **new economy.** Under the old rules, states attracted businesses based on tax structures or incentive packages. But the high-tech companies that are the driving engines in this new economy can locate anywhere. They are motivated by the quality of the work force and the quality of life that is offered."[61] Thus, states may have to reorient themselves to fourth-wave thinking. Local–global links and investment in human capital may, in fact, make a difference.

Does Government Spend Too Much?

Some observers claim that government gives away too much in its pursuit of economic health.[62] This concern develops out of the fundamental relationship between a federal system of government and a capitalistic economic system.

Governmental jurisdictions cover specific territories, but capital is mobile, so business firms can move from one location to another. Because these firms are so important to a local economy, governments offer incentives to influence their location decisions. The impact of these incentives on firms' decisions is not clear, but most jurisdictions believe that they cannot afford *not* to offer them.[63] Concern is increasing, however, that competition among jurisdictions to attract business may be counterproductive and costly to government. As a consequence, citizens are beginning to look more closely at the **incentive packages**—tax breaks, low-interest loans, and infrastructure development—that their governments offer to business.

incentive packages
The enticements that state and local governments offer to retain or attract business and industry.

Examples of government concessions to the automobile industry abound—the Honda plant in Ohio, the Mazda facility in Michigan, the General Motors Saturn operation in Tennessee, and the BMW plant in South Carolina. The fundamental question is, How extensive should incentives be? The answer typically involves calculation of the return on the state's investment.

In one of the first big automotive deals in the late 1980s, Kentucky taxpayers provided an incentive package worth an estimated $325 million for a new Toyota assembly plant in the community of Georgetown.[64] Half of the state's costs ($167 million) were in the form of interest payments to purchasers of economic development bonds (the primary source of capital for the project). Land and site-preparation expenses were estimated at close to $33 million. Local highway construction absorbed $47 million in state funds; another $65 million was spent for employee training. Opposition to the incentive package came from local small businesses, unionized labor, and environmental protection advocates.[65] Their resistance was blunted, however, by a study predicting that the state would reap $632 million in taxes from Toyota and the industrial and commercial development that would follow.[66] The package was presented to taxpayers as a wise business decision. (Of course, the ten Toyota Camrys that the company gave to the community did not hurt, either.) Now widely acknowledged as a success story, the facility is credited with spurring the creation of an additional 460 motor vehicle-related firms that employ 88,000 people in Kentucky.[67] San Antonio hopes that the same kind of economic magic will happen there when Toyota's new Tundra truck-assembly plant begins production in 2006.

Jurisdictions compete for major investments such as automobile manufacturing facilities, and that competition has the effect of ratcheting up the value of incentive packages. When German automaker Mercedes-Benz announced that it was seeking a location for its first U.S. facility, more than thirty-five states expressed interest. Five states—Alabama, Iowa, Nebraska, North Carolina, and South Carolina—survived the winnowing process. Each state tried to outdo the others by offering generous packages of tax breaks and low-cost land. In 1993, Mercedes announced that Vance, Alabama, had been selected as the site of the $300 million facility. But the price that Alabama paid was a dear one. The state provided $92.2 million in land and facility construction costs, $77.5 million in infrastructure development, $60 million in training, and a twenty-five-year tax abatement. Estimates put the state costs at approximately $179,000 per job. The extravagant bidding for the Mercedes plant raised some eyebrows, but in the words of one Alabama economist, "the symbolism [of winning the Mercedes facility] may be as important as the direct economic impact."[68]

Concern about government overspending lingers, and it extends beyond the automobile industry. New York City, for example, has provided almost $200 million in tax breaks and utility concessions to keep the three major television networks in the city. And Tootsie Roll Industries and a Nabisco plant agreed to remain in Illinois after the state offered loans, tax exemptions, and job-training funds that totaled $52 million in value.[69]

But even as governments continue to offer these packages, they are becoming more savvy about the potential risks.[70] Concern that a government-supported development project might turn sour has led to imposition of **clawbacks.** Clawbacks require a subsidized firm that fails to deliver on its promises (regarding number of jobs, say, or amount of investment) to repay some or all of its subsidy. In this way, generous states and localities are not left holding the bag. Consider the case of United Airlines and its new maintenance facility in Indianapolis. To attract United to Indiana, the state offered the company a deal that included $300 million in assorted tax breaks . . . and several clawback provisions. When it failed to create the number of jobs the agreement called for, United Airlines had to return more than $30 million to the Hoosier state.[71]

Does Government Spend Fairly?

Traditionally, government involvement in economic development has taken the form of efforts to reduce costs to business. According to economic development professionals, the central business district, local developers, the local labor force, and existing business firms derive the greatest benefit from city-sponsored economic development activity.[72] As citizens began to ask *who* benefits, however, some state governments refocused their efforts toward direct investments in human resources. An outstanding illustration of this reorientation can be found in Arizona—a model of successful economic revitalization. At the top of the Arizona agenda for economic development are the goals of strengthening education, improving health care, and increasing skills training.[73]

Local governments have been especially active in expanding the concept of economic development beyond a narrow concern with business investment. Led by the pioneering efforts of San Francisco and Boston, some U.S. cities are tying economic development initiatives to the achievement of social objectives, an approach called **linkaging.** For instance, local governments have linked large-scale commercial development (office and retail buildings and hotels) to concerns such as housing and employment. This movement grew out of frustration over the disappearance of older low-income neighborhoods from revitalized, commercially oriented downtown areas.[74] The upscaling of formerly low-income neighborhoods—a process known as **gentrification**—displaces existing residents. With linkaging, developers are required to provide low- or moderate-income housing or employment to targeted groups or to contribute funding to programs that support these objectives. In return for the opportunity to enter a lucrative local market, a developer pays a price. This process has been called "the cities' attempt to share the profits of their prospering sectors with their poor."[75]

clawbacks

Requirements that subsidized firms repay some or all of the subsidy if they fail to deliver on their promises.

linkaging

A method by which local governments use large-scale commercial development projects to accomplish social objectives.

gentrification

An urban revitalization process that replaces low-end land uses with upscale uses.

Linkaging works best in cities with booming economies. But even in cities with more stable economies, local government can negotiate with developers for social concessions. In Richmond, Virginia, for example, city officials convinced developers to provide substantial minority participation in a major retail project in the downtown area. In return for city approval of a massive redevelopment project in Jersey City, New Jersey, developers agreed to reserve a certain percentage of dwelling units for low- and moderate-income individuals.

Some cities have taken a different tack in addressing the fairness issue: they have passed measures that increase the minimum wage in their jurisdictions. For instance, in 2003, San Francisco voters approved a ballot question that set the minimum wage at $8.50 an hour, or about 65 percent more than the federal minimum wage.[76] Other cities with relatively high costs of living, such as Santa Fe, New Mexico, have adopted similar increases in base pay. Although these actions are popular with workers, owners of small businesses such as restaurants are decidedly less enthusiastic. But supporters contend that without such increases, many people cannot afford to live in the city.

THE IMPLICATIONS OF ECONOMIC DEVELOPMENT POLICY

A healthy economy is central to the functioning of government. State and local officials know this and act accordingly. The slogan for Rhode Island's economic development campaign a few years ago sums up the attitude: "Every state says they'll move mountains to get your business. We're moving rivers."[77] The ad did not exaggerate: Rhode Island redirected two rivers as part of a $200 million redevelopment project in its capital city of Providence.

Yet when an observer steps back and ponders such strategies and deals, a degree of skepticism is inevitable. Could New York City have better spent the millions it committed to Chase Manhattan Bank to keep the financial institution from moving 4,600 office workers to New Jersey? The deal involved $235 million worth of tax abatements, discounted utilities, site improvements, and job-training tax credits over the next twenty years.[78] And which state really won when a division of Eastman Kodak turned down Maryland's $4.5 million package of subsidized land, tax breaks, and employee training in favor of Pennsylvania's $14 million deal? Some might conclude that corporations are staging raids on public treasuries. But many state and local government officials would argue that concessions for business serve an important function by creating jobs and generating economic activity, thus improving the local tax base, which in turn funds public services. Maybe the third and fourth waves of economic development will be characterized by more creative and productive efforts at achieving this outcome.

States and localities continue to experiment with an array of economic development programs, with varying results. A recent evaluation by CfED graded the states' capacity for future development. CfED focused on a state's resources (human, natural, financial, infrastructure) as well as on a category called innovation assets. Innovation assets measure the number of scientists and engineers, the amount of research and development spending in the state, the number of patents issued to businesses in the state, and so on. Figure 14.3 shows the states' grades. Typically the states with A's in development capacity were states that had scored A's in either economic performance or business vitality. (Refer again to Figures 14.1 and 14.2.) Massachusetts, Minnesota, and Virginia were the only states with straight A's on all three of CfED's report cards in 2003. Three states received the top grade only on this index: Oregon, Utah, and Washington. At the other end of the range were the states that received F's in development capacity: Alabama, Hawaii, Kentucky, Maine, and Mississippi. Low grades on development capacity raise questions about the direction of the states' economies.

Local economies are evaluated, compared, and ranked also. The magazine *Inc.* compiles an annual ranking of metropolitan areas using indicators of job growth and economic mix.[79] From these indicators, a list of the best places for business is compiled (Table 14.2). To make the comparisons more meaningful, the metro areas are grouped by size. Among large metro areas (places with a job base of 450,000 or more), Atlanta prevails, followed by the Riverside–San Bernardino area of California. In the medium-size metro area category (with a

| FIGURE 14.3 | **The Development Capacity of States** |

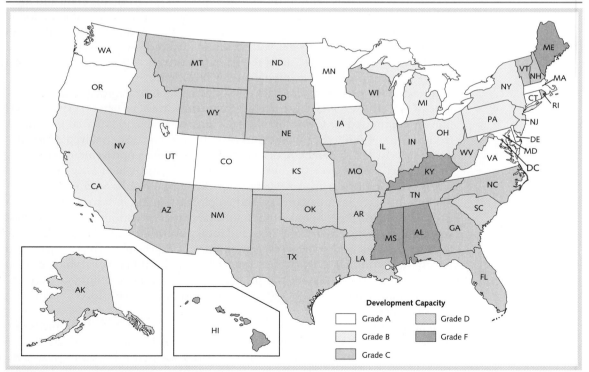

Development Capacity

- Grade A
- Grade B
- Grade C
- Grade D
- Grade F

SOURCE: "2003 Development Report Card for the States," Corporation for Enterprise Development (Washington, D.C.: CfED, 2004), www.drc.cfed.org/grades/indexes.

base of between 150,000 and 450,000 jobs), a pair of Wisconsin metro areas tops the list: Green Bay and Madison. The smaller metro area group (where the job base is less than 150,000) is led by Montpelier, Vermont, and Missoula, Montana. Perhaps the most notable characteristic, regardless of the category, is the regional variation in the best places for doing business.

As one might expect, states and localities scoring high on these rankings place far more value on them than their low-scoring counterparts do—at least publicly. But allowing for the inherent biases in the rankings, they certainly suggest that some communities are faring quite well in the economic development wars.

TABLE 14.2 **The Top Places for Doing Business in 2004**

LARGE METRO AREAS	MEDIUM-SIZE METRO AREAS	SMALL METRO AREAS
Atlanta, GA	Green Bay, WI	Montpelier, VT
Riverside–San Bernardino, CA	Madison, WI	Missoula, MT
Las Vegas, NV	Sarasota, FL	Casper, WY
San Antonio, TX	Fresno, CA	Rockland County, NY
West Palm Beach, FL	Bakersfield, CA	Sioux Falls, SD
Southern New Jersey	Reno, NV	Waco, TX
Fort Lauderdale–Hollywood–Pompano Beach, FL	Albuquerque, NM	Burlington, VT
Jacksonville, FL	Tucson, AZ	Dutchess County, NY
Newark, NJ	Vallejo–Fairfield–Napa, CA	Anchorage, AK
Suburban Maryland–D.C.	Modesto, CA	Manchester, NH
Orlando, FL	Stockton, CA	Bismarck, ND
Phoenix, AZ	Fort Myers–Cape Coral, FL	Bryan–College Station, TX
Washington, D.C.	Corpus Christi, TX	Danbury, CT
Tampa–St. Petersburg–Clearwater, FL	Syracuse, NY	Altoona, PA
San Diego, CA	Springfield, MO	Fargo–Moorhead, ND
Nassau–Suffolk, NY	Monmouth–Ocean, NJ	Las Cruces, NM
Richmond–Petersburg, VA	Westchester County, NY	La Crosse, WI
New Orleans, LA	Harrisburg–Lebanon–Carlisle, PA	Newburgh, NY
Austin, TX	Baton Rouge, LA	Albany, NY
Northern VA	Daytona Beach, FL	Medford, OR
Middlesex–Somerset–Hunterdon, NJ	Jackson, MS	Utica–Rome, NY
Miami–Hialeah, FL	Lancaster, PA	Lake Charles, LA
Orange County, CA	Portland, ME	Bristol, VA
Oklahoma City, OK	Boise City, ID	Fort Smith, AR
Albany–Schenectady–Troy, NY	Akron, OH	Enid, OK

SOURCE: Joel Kotkin, "Top 25 Cities for Doing Business in America," *Inc.* (March 2004): 93. Reprinted by permission of Gruner & Jahr.

Critics claim that competition for economic development is nothing more than the relocation of a given amount of economic activity from one community to another, with no overall increase in national productivity.[80] Mercedes-Benz was going to open a U.S. manufacturing facility anyway, the question was simply, Where? By playing states against one another, Mercedes-Benz was able to exact a subsidy of unheard-of proportions.[81] Many critics call for increased cooperation among non-national jurisdictions in their quest for economic development. However, this objective has been elusive at both the state and local levels. Frustration in Ohio led the legislature to pass a resolution asking Congress to step in and discourage states from raiding other states' industries. Similarly, Minnesota called on the federal government to eliminate the federal programs that are used to lure business from one state to another.[82] Counties, too, have found cooperation challenging. A National Association of Counties study of urban counties reported that only 5 percent frequently coordinated their economic development activities with other counties.[83] And a mere 19 percent indicated frequent coordination with cities located within their boundaries. Even when jurisdictions agree not to steal companies from each other, the agreements can unravel. Within months after signing a cooperative no-poaching pact, Miami-Dade, Broward, and Palm Beach counties in south Florida reverted to their old competitive behaviors.[84] Economic development has tended to be a singular proposition, with each jurisdiction pursuing its own destiny.

CHAPTER RECAP

- The economic performance of the states varies. Even in an individual state, its economic health changes over time. The same is true for localities: their economies are dynamic.
- Economic development has had four waves of different approaches or strategies. The first wave was characterized by smokestack chasing. The latest, or fourth, wave emphasizes globalization and human capital. Even now, states continue to use approaches from the earlier waves.
- The relationship between state government and the private sector can be complicated. Some states have begun to use public–private hybrid organizations in economic development functions.
- States have offered huge incentives to attract automobile manufacturers. But with trends showing a decline in manufacturing as a proportion of the job base, the emphasis is shifting toward research and technology. Many states have begun to invest in bioscience research.
- States have taken on many different economic development initiatives, including strategic planning, travel and tourism, the arts, sports, and international trade.
- Three major questions continue to surface with regard to government involvement in the economy: Do state and local government initiatives make much difference? Does government spend too much to attract and grow new business and to retain old business? Does government spend fairly; that is, does reducing costs for business come at a cost to other groups?

- Many organizations rank states and localities on aspects of economic development. In evaluating these rankings, it is important to consider the criteria used in their compilation.
- Economic development is a competitive activity, pitting one jurisdiction against others. Efforts are underway to foster more cooperative behavior among jurisdictions.

Key Terms

economic development *(p. 391)*
subsidy *(p. 394)*
venture capital pools *(p. 395)*
small-business incubators *(p. 395)*
enterprise zone *(p. 395)*
clusters *(p. 395)*
strategic planning *(p. 400)*

accommodations tax *(p. 402)*
amenities *(p. 402)*
new economy *(p. 408)*
incentive packages *(p. 409)*
clawbacks *(p. 410)*
linkaging *(p. 410)*
gentrification *(p. 410)*

Surfing the Web

The web site for the National Association of State Development Agencies at **www.nasda.com** provides up-to-date information on state activities and links to state agencies.

Two economic development organizations, one with a national focus, the other with an international emphasis, maintain useful web sites. These are the Corporation for Enterprise Development (CfED) at **www.cfed.org** and the International Economic Development Council at **www.iedconline.org.**

All states have a web presence in economic development, typically through a state agency. The comprehensive web site of Arizona's Department of Commerce can be found at **www.azcommerce.com.**

Explore a more targeted approach to economic development at **www.idahoworks.com,** which is a part of Idaho's Department of Commerce web site.

Other examples of states with less traditional economic development web sites are the state of Kentucky's new economy web site at **www.one-ky.com** and Enterprise Florida at **www.eflorida.com.**

A statewide organization devoted to local economic development is the California Association for Local Economic Development, **www.caled.org.**

www.newyorkbiz.com is the web site for the New York City Economic Development Corporation.

For economic development from a private sector perspective, check out the web site of Site Selection magazine at **www.siteselection.com.** It tracks new business activity around the nation.

EDUCATION POLICY

Nothing today commands the attention of governors, legislatures, and parents more than the condition of public education. Convincing evidence reports that too many students cannot read, write, and do math at grade level. Unqualified teachers, threats to personal safety, and crumbling school infrastructure also generate concern. In its much-cited report, *A Nation at Risk*, the National Commission on Excellence in Education lamented the erosion of the educational foundations of society "by a rising tide of mediocrity that threatens our very future."[1]

This critical statement appears to be supported by studies documenting the performance of U.S. students in comparison with students in thirty-one other industrialized countries. Despite much higher per-pupil spending on schools, scores in mathematics, science, and reading earned by U.S. fifteen-year-olds ranked poorly; only four participant countries performed worse than U.S. students in science and only five performed worse in math.[2] National surveys have discovered that the majority of U.S. adults cannot interpret a bus schedule or follow the major argument of a newspaper column. U.S. firms corroborate these horror stories with stories about their frustration in finding new employees who can read, write, and perform basic math functions. But the other side of the coin is that many school systems are doing an outstanding job of preparing youngsters for college and the work world, especially those public schools in middle- and upper-middle-class communities where funding is adequate and education is considered important. Much of the alleged crisis in public education is a product of demographics—poverty, single-parent families, and poor health and nutrition. These societal problems are factors that cannot be corrected by teachers or principals.

In the opinion of many Americans, education is the most important function performed by state and local government. The facts support this point of view. Education consumes more of state and local budgets than any other service. More than $374 billion is spent on elementary and secondary schooling by the states and localities. That translates to around $7,829 per pupil. The importance of education is also demonstrated by the sheer number of people involved in it. A majority of the U.S. population is either enrolled in an educational institution or employed in the system that delivers educational services. Citizens have high expectations for their schools, assuming that they will teach everything from good citizenship and driving skills to safe sex. Schools have served at the frontlines in the battle against racial segregation. To a great extent, the future of this country and its economy is linked to the quality of free public education.

In 2002, Congress overwhelmingly passed, and President Bush signed, a bill that promised to transform public education. The No Child Left Behind (NCLB) law, a $12 billion reauthorization of the Elementary and Secondary Education Act, saddled the states and their schools with significant new (and mostly unfunded) mandates, including mandatory and frequent testing and a stipulation that failing schools not making sufficient progress in any one of numerous student demographic categories would have to offer students a transfer and even private tuition. All teachers would have to be highly qualified within three years.

The broad goals of NCLB were admirable and widely accepted: that no child would be neglected and left behind in school, and that all would have an equal chance to succeed. But the devil was in the details of implementation. Teachers, principals, chief state school officers, governors, and state legislators soon howled like lost hounds as they became aware of their predicament. The costs of annual testing would amount to millions more dollars than what Congress was providing. Established, and demonstrably effective, state standards and testing programs would be overridden and replaced by cumbersome federal mandates. Local control of public education would be snatched away by federal regulations.

THE CRISIS IN EDUCATION

As the heated debate over NCLB illustrates, education policy has always been controversial and frequently proclaimed to be in crisis. For more than 100 years, policymakers, parents, teachers, and others have debated how schools should be organized and financed, and what should be taught. Our present, three-decade-long education crisis, however, is different in three respects. First, education policy must be constantly reformulated and altered if schooling is to be relevant and the United States is to remain a dominant player in the international sphere. In this sense, the crisis is now perennial. Second, improved analysis and data collection have provided a clearer picture of our specific shortcomings in education, and they have generated greater public awareness about them. Third, despite billions of additional dollars in state and local government spending in recent years, along with a spate of institutional and classroom reforms, the public perceives this education crisis to be worsening.

One seemingly straightforward sign of deterioration in the quality of schooling makes headlines in newspapers throughout the country each year: student performance on standardized college entrance exams. Scholastic Aptitude Test (SAT) and American College Test (ACT) scores on verbal and math sections dropped almost annually from 1963 to 1982, to levels below those existing at the time of the last declared crisis in education (see Figure 15.1). Following a

| FIGURE 15.1 | **Average SAT Verbal and Mathematics Scores, 1963–2003** |

Average SAT verbal and math scores began a prolonged period of decline in the early 1960s but turned upward in 1982. The current trend is positive.

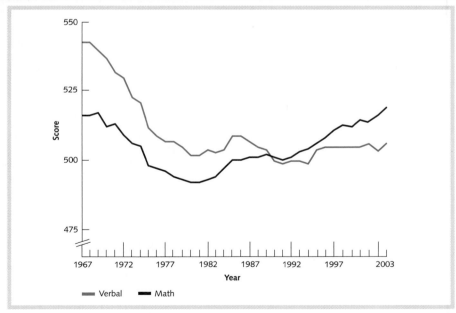

NOTE: Minimum 200, maximum 800 for each score. All scores have been recentered to match the 1996 College Board Scale.
SOURCE: College Board, www.collegeboard.org (2004).

brief rally during the mid-1980s, scores again began eroding slowly, then they stabilized. The trend since 1994 has been positive, especially in math.

Striking differences in SAT scores among the states reflect population characteristics such as race and ethnicity, immigration, poverty levels, and urban–suburban–rural population. But the greatest variation is accounted for by the percentage of high school students taking the SAT. Generally, the higher the percentage of high schoolers taking the test, the lower the state scores. A more comprehensive assessment of the quality of education in the states is found in Table 15.1, which grades them on five different measures not related to the SAT.

Is the U.S. education system failing? Or is perception more pessimistic than reality? Public opinion surveys reveal that Americans are mostly satisfied with their own public schools but highly critical of everyone else's. The media bombardment about public schools notwithstanding, standardized-test scores are advancing for all categories of students on the SAT and the ACT, and state scores on the National Assessment of Educational Progress (NAEP), given to eighth- and twelfth-graders, have also shown some improvement. Dropout rates have stabilized at about 5 percent a year, and students are staying in school longer.[3] But few would dispute that the U.S. education system suffers serious problems and needs much improvement. The most widely recognized policy problems can be reduced to four major variables: standards, students, teachers, and bureaucracy.

Standards

Schools have suffered from a malady that might be called curriculum drift. From the 1960s to the early 1980s, courses designed to teach basic verbal and mathematical skills were deemphasized and numerous nonessential topics became popular. For example, courses on the secondary school menu included self-awareness, who am I, skiing, sailing, love and marriage, and bachelor living. Most such subjects have since disappeared, only to be replaced by courses on slavery, the Holocaust, genocide, and the Irish potato famine—worthy topics, perhaps, but no substitute for the basics. To many critics, education sometimes seems to be aimed at helping students feel comfortable with themselves and have a good time rather than at teaching them basic skills and the ability to think analytically. Business, military, and university leaders complain about having to invest millions of dollars in remedial education before ill-prepared high school graduates are ready to work, serve in the armed forces, or study. They further lament the prevalence of social promotions.

Even more disturbing, millions of Americans are functionally illiterate—unable to perform simple tasks of reading, writing, comprehension, and mathematical computation. As a result, many students graduate from high school prepared for neither college nor the job market. The argument that the native intelligence of U.S. youth has declined has no basis, so considerable blame has been placed on vacillating educational standards for curricula and courses.

Students

Students themselves have not escaped criticism. Some choose to soften their curriculum with easy nonacademic courses rather than the basic English, math,

| TABLE 15.1 | **Summary of Grades by State** | | | | |

STATE	STANDARDS AND ACCOUNTABILITY	EFFORTS TO IMPROVE TEACHER QUALITY	SCHOOL CLIMATE	ADEQUACY OF RESOURCES	EQUITY OF RESOURCES
Alabama	B−	C	C−	C−	C−
Alaska	C−	D−	C−	C	C
Arizona	B	D−	B-	D	C−
Arkansas	C+	B+	C	C−	B
California	B	B−	C	C−	C
Colorado	B−	C	B−	C−	C−
Connecticut	B−	A−	B−	A−	D
Delaware	B+	C	B	B+	B+
District of Columbia	D−	D+	C−	NA*	NA*
Florida	A	C+	C	D+	C+
Georgia	B+	C−	C	B	D+
Hawaii	C+	D+	C	C	A
Idaho	C+	D	C+	C−	C
Illinois	A−	C	B−	C+	F
Indiana	A−	B	C+	B+	C
Iowa	F	C	B−	B	C+
Kansas	B−	C−	B−	B−	B−
Kentucky	A	B+	C	C	B−
Louisiana	A	B+	D	C−	C+
Maine	C	D	B	A−	D+
Maryland	A	C+	D	B	D
Massachusetts	B+	C−	C+	B−	D−
Michigan	B	D+	C	B+	C
Minnesota	C	D+	B	B	B
Mississippi	B−	C	D+	D+	C−
Missouri	B+	B−	B	C	C−

science, social studies, and foreign languages. Today's students are said to be poorly motivated and lazy in comparison to their predecessors. They are faulted for seeking instant gratification through television, video games, the Internet, drugs, alcohol, and sex instead of seriously applying themselves to coursework. In a typical year, nearly one half million students give up school altogether by dropping out.

Clearly, however, the legal and moral responsibility for providing direction to a young person's life rests with his or her parents. This responsibility includes encouraging the child to complete homework assignments and regulating televi-

STATE	STANDARDS AND ACCOUNTABILITY	EFFORTS TO IMPROVE TEACHER QUALITY	SCHOOL CLIMATE	ADEQUACY OF RESOURCES	EQUITY OF RESOURCES
Montana	D−	C−	C	C+	D
Nebraska	D	C	C+	B+	D+
Nevada	B−	C−	C−	D+	B
New Hampshire	C−	C−	B−	C+	D−
New Jersey	B−	C+	B−	A	D
New Mexico	B	C	C	C	B
New York	A	B	C	A	C−
North Carolina	B	B	C+	C	C
North Dakota	C−	D	C	C+	C
Ohio	A	B	C	B−	D+
Oklahoma	B+	B-	C	C	B−
Oregon	B-	C-	C	B-	B
Pennsylvania	B	C-	C	B	D-
Rhode Island	D	C-	B-	B+	D
South Carolina	A	A-	C+	B-	C
South Dakota	C+	D	C	C+	C
Tennessee	B	B-	C+	D+	C-
Texas	C+	C	C	C+	D+
Utah	C+	D+	C+	D	B-
Vermont	C	C	B-	A	C+
Virginia	B	B-	C	B-	D
Washington	C+	C-	C+	C	C
West Virginia	A	B-	B-	A	C+
Wisconsin	C+	D+	B	A	C+
Wyoming	D	D	B-	A-	C

*Because the District of Columbia does not have a state revenue source, it did not receive a grade for adequacy or equity.
SOURCE: *Education Week* by Editorial Projects in Education. Copyright 2004 by Editorial Projects in Education. Reproduced with permission of Editorial Projects in Education in the format Textbook via Copyright Clearance Center.

sion, video games, and Internet access. Researchers have found that U.S. children start the first grade with fewer academic skills than their Asian counterparts, whose parents give them a head start by regularly working with them at home before they enter school. Coaching after school helps Asian children maintain their early advantage. But U.S. parents tend to abdicate to the schools the responsibility for educating their children. Often parents have little choice; as a result of the high percentage of single-parent and two-worker households, parents have little time, and less energy, to spend helping their children. The shortage and expense of professional day care and after-school opportunities compound the problem.

Teachers

Teachers are the linchpins between students and the learning process. Effective teaching can bestow lifelong learning skills on fortunate students, and poor teaching can result in academic indifference among good students and dropping out for marginal students. One problem with teaching is that, for many years, the teaching profession has declined in terms of the quality of individuals who choose to enter it.

The gradual decline in the quality of teachers is partly due to changes in the nature of the work force and the elevated expectations for teachers. Until about forty years ago, most women had few job opportunities besides teaching, nursing, and clerical work. (And teacher contracts could preclude any meaningful social life, as you can see in Figure 15.2.) But in the mid-1960s, women began

---

FIGURE 15.2   Thou Shalt Not

THOU SHALT NOT

1922 Contract, Salisbury, N.C.

Miss_____ agrees:

1. Not to get married. This contract becomes null and void immediately if the teacher marries.
2. Not to have company with men.
3. To be at home between the hours of 8:00 pm and 6:00 am unless in attendance at a school function.
4. Not to loiter downtown in ice cream stores.
5. Not to leave town at any time without the permission of the Chairman of the Trustees.
6. Not to smoke cigarettes. This contract becomes null and void immediately if the teacher is found smoking.
7. Not to drink beer, wine, or whiskey. This contract becomes null and void immediately if the teacher is found drinking beer, wine or whiskey.
8. Not to ride in a carriage or automobile with any man except her brother or father.
9. Not to dress in bright colors.
10. Not to dye her hair.
11. To wear at least two petticoats.
12. Not to wear dresses more than two inches above the ankles.
13. To keep the classroom clean:
    (a) to sweep the classroom floor at least once daily.
    (b) to scrub the classroom floor at least once weekly with soap and hot water.
    (c) to clean the blackboard at least once daily.
    (d) to start the fire at 7:00 am so that the room will be warm at 8:00 am when the children arrive.
14. Not to wear face powder, mascara, or to paint the lips.

From "North Carolina Women: Making History" by Margaret Supplee Smith and Emily Herring Wilson. ©1999 by the University of North Carolina Press. Used by permission of the publisher. For more information, visit http://www.uncpress.unc.edu.

moving into traditionally male-dominated jobs in growing numbers. Even to-day, however, 79 percent of public-school teachers are women.

Academically gifted women who once would have chosen the teaching profession are now more likely to seek out higher-paying, more prestigious positions in government and the private sector. In their place, less able college graduates elect to become teachers, resulting in a severe shortage of qualified teachers in some states. In 2003, SAT scores for education majors averaged 965 versus 1026 for other subject majors.[4] Also reflecting the drop in quality of the teaching labor pool is that about 25 percent of those hired to teach each year lack the proper qualifications and preparation for the courses they teach.

Part of the blame must also be placed on university and college education schools that emphasize educational methodology courses, which teach prospective instructors how to teach rather than giving them substantive knowledge of their subject matter. Another reason it has been difficult to find good teachers is that, in some states, teaching remains a low-wage occupation, with the starting salary comparing unfavorably with starting salaries in other professional fields.

In an effort to help improve pay and working conditions, most teachers have joined unions such as the American Federation of Teachers (AFT) and the National Education Association (NEA). According to some critics, these unions have become part of the problem with public education because they further teachers' narrow self-interest instead of encouraging more effective schools and because they protect incompetents from being fired. Meanwhile, many of those who do become teachers quickly exit the profession—more than one-third of all teachers and one-half of those in urban schools quit their jobs within five years. Many discouraged teachers also feel that they are not valued or respected. The frustration of teaching is perhaps best illustrated by the responses of teachers when they are asked to identify the biggest problems inhibiting public-school children's ability to learn in their community. First on the list are lack of parental interest and support, students' lack of discipline, and use of drugs. Noisy, disruptive behavior by a handful of students, which is most likely in large schools in urban areas, spoils the learning environment for all. Teachers are assaulted in the classroom, and violent crimes occur on or near school grounds. Empty gestures by elected officials such as mandating posting of the Ten Commandments (Jackson County, Kentucky) or In God We Trust (Colorado) on classroom walls, requiring uniforms (New York City), or requiring students to address teachers as ma'am and sir (Louisiana) do not help. Teacher stress is augmented, especially in poor schools, by crumbling buildings, chronic supply and equipment shortages, overcrowded classrooms, and crushing paperwork burdens.[5]

Because of these and other dissatisfactions, severe shortages of teachers have developed, especially in the fields of mathematics, science, foreign languages, and special education. These shortages are exacerbated by teacher resignations and retirements. Meanwhile, the number of students is growing rapidly, while the number of teacher resignations and retirements grows. To accommodate the increased number of students, 2 million new teachers will be needed by 2009. Shortages are most severe in the booming Sunbelt. The acute teacher shortfall is forcing many school districts to hire unqualified, ill-prepared people simply to put a warm adult body in the classroom.[6]

Bureaucracy

Bureaucracy is under attack everywhere in government, and the schools are no exception. A strong case can be made that the country has too many school administrators, too many rules and restrictions imposed on teachers, and too few teachers. The ratio is as high as one nonteaching employee for every eight teachers in some districts. Critics say that school districts and their bureaucracies act like classic monopolies. They are guaranteed customers (students) and income (tax revenues), and they face little or no competition because parents have no choice about where to send their children to school. Critics also contend that problems are compounded by teachers' unions, which protect incompetent teachers from dismissal.

The results of these monopolistic school bureaucracies allegedly include a lack of accountability to parents and the community (and ultimately to students and teachers), unnecessary rules and red tape, inefficient use of human resources, and time constraints and odious mounds of paperwork for teachers. Like most bureaucracies, those in the schools are reactive and resistant to innovation and change. They are viewed as recalcitrant enemies of reform.

A scholarly debate has erupted over the bureaucracy issue. Some research finds that large, centralized bureaucracies with restrictive rules and red tape tend to reduce school effectiveness.[7] Findings of other political scientists show no significant effects of bureaucracy and that school bureaucracies tend to grow larger when schools perform poorly because administrators take actions to improve performance. In other words, bureaucracy does not harm school performance; rather, it is a rational response intended to arrest decline and boost performance by developing new policies and programs.[8]

Before reviewing the responses of the national, state, and local governments to these critical problems in public education, we look at how intergovernmental relationships in education have evolved.

INTERGOVERNMENTAL ROLES IN EDUCATION

The responsibility of establishing, supporting, and overseeing public schools is reserved to the states under the Tenth Amendment and specifically provided for in the state constitutions. Day-to-day operating authority is delegated to local governments by all states except Hawaii, which has established a unitary, state-run system. Ninety percent of U.S. primary and secondary school systems are operated by independent school districts, but cities, counties, towns, or townships run the schools in some states. Although local control is the tradition, the states have always been the dominant policymakers, deciding important issues such as the duration of the school year, curriculum requirements, textbook selection, teacher certification and compensation, minimum graduation requirements, and pupil–teacher ratios. The selection and dismissal of teachers, certain budget decisions, and management and operating details are carried out locally.

State involvement is growing substantially and is stronger than ever before, largely because of forceful actions taken to address the perceived education crisis. Centralization of state authority in education policy has always been greatest in the South, where poverty and race relations have called for high levels of state intervention. Conversely, the tradition of local autonomy is strongest in New England. But in the final analysis, it is difficult to identify a single important school policy issue today that is not subject to state, rather than local, determination.

State and Local Roles

More state involvement in the public schools has occurred because citizens and policymakers have lost confidence in the schools' ability to provide a quality education and because local school districts are increasingly unable to cope successfully with political and financial pressures. In several instances, local school systems have essentially lost their independence as the states have assumed full operational responsibilities—an especially likely outcome when the local school districts are unable to respond adequately to political and financial pressures. Several states, including Texas, New York, and Pennsylvania, have imposed the ultimate sanction on failing schools by assuming full operational responsibility or shutting them down entirely.

Political Pressures Political pressures rose to new heights in the 1960s when teachers, minority groups, and parents made new and controversial demands on their schools. As noted, teachers formed unions; they also sought to bargain collectively over salaries and working conditions. Minority groups wanted to desegregate all-white schools. Bilingual education became an issue in states with large Hispanic populations. And religious groups fought to keep prayer and Jesus in the classroom. None of this pressure has changed. As many local school boards wilted under the crescendo of demands, teachers, minority groups, parents, and other parties interested in education policy have more and more often taken their demands to the next highest political level—the governor, the state legislature, the courts, and the state board of education. In this way, school politics, once the province of local school boards and professional educators, has evolved into highly contentious interest group politics at the state level.

Financial Pressures The second factor behind state centralization has to do with increased financial pressures on the schools. Historically, schools have been funded mostly through revenues derived from a tax on property. A school district can assess taxes only on property within its local boundaries, so wealthy districts with a lot of highly valued residential and/or commercial property can afford to finance public schools at generous levels, whereas poor districts (even though they often tax their property at much higher rates than wealthy districts) tend to raise fewer dollars because of their lower property values. The consequence of such financial inequities is that some children receive a more expensive, and probably higher-quality, education than other children do, even though the parents of the advantaged group of children may contribute fewer tax dollars. Frequently, it is the children of the poor and minorities who fare the worst.

The states' assumption of financial responsibility for public schools has an important constitutional component. In the landmark case of *Serrano* v. *Priest* (1971), the California Supreme Court declared that inequalities in school-district spending resulting from variations in taxable wealth were unconstitutional. The court observed that local control is a "cruel illusion"; poor districts simply cannot achieve excellence in education because of a low tax base, no matter how highly property is taxed.[9] Therefore, education must be considered a fundamental interest of the state; in other words, the state must ensure that expenditures on education are not determined primarily by the taxable wealth of the school district.

Following *Serrano,* lawsuits were filed in other states by plaintiffs who sought to have their own property-tax-based systems declared unconstitutional. One of these cases, *San Antonio Independent School District* v. *Rodriguez* (1973), made its way to the U.S. Supreme Court. A federal district court had found the Texas school-finance system to be unconstitutional under the equal protection clause of the Fourteenth Amendment. However, the Supreme Court reversed the lower court, holding that education is not a fundamental right under the U.S. Constitution (it is not even mentioned).[10] The issue was thus placed exclusively in the constitutional domain of the states, which would have to rely on their own constitutions—and courts—to prevent arbitrary circumstances from predetermining the quality of a child's education.

Some forty-three state supreme courts have heard cases on educational financing; litigation is ongoing in approximately eighteen states. Nineteen states have determined that existing funding schemes were unconstitutional because they did not provide an adequate education for all children and have ordered equal funding for poor districts; New York, Arkansas, and New Jersey are the states most recently involved. A study of these cases found that courts declaring unconstitutional spending disparities and ordering greater revenue equity tend to have more liberal justices than courts that uphold school-finance systems and that these courts are most likely to be situated in states with a politically liberal populace. Thus, politics matters in explaining school-funding equity in the states.[11]

But all states have made efforts to equalize funding among school districts, usually by applying distribution formulas (the equalization formulas noted in Chapter 11) for state aid that take into account property values and property-tax effort in individual districts. Most increased state financing has been targeted to districts with low property values through foundation programs, which seek to provide all school districts with a minimum level of funding per pupil while furnishing extra financing to poor districts. State education allocations also take into account the number of special-needs students. In 1979, state aid to the schools exceeded local government contributions for the first time. Figure 15.3 displays the increasing state revenue contributions for public schools since 1920. Note that the federal portion, averaging only about 7.0 percent since 1970, increased a bit to 7.3 percent as a result of No Child Left Behind.

| FIGURE 15.3 | **Trends in Revenue Sources for Public Elementary and Secondary Education, 1920–2002** |

Elementary and secondary education has received the greatest portion of revenues from state government since 1979. The national contribution remains less than 8 percent.

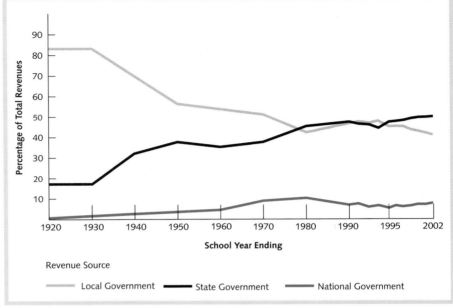

SOURCE: U.S. Department of Education, Center for Statistics, *Digest of Education Statistics*, 2003 (Washington, D.C.: U.S. Government Printing Office, 2003).

The Impact of Property-Tax Cuts Additional impetus to the state assumption of school costs was provided by Proposition 13 in California and by similar state legacies of the taxpayer revolt. Statutory and state constitutional limitations on taxing were typically aimed at the increasingly unpopular property tax. If public schools were to avoid such draconian measures as closing their doors in an effort to adjust to revenue shortfalls, the states had to increase their education contributions. For example, in California, where Proposition 13 followed *Serrano* v. *Priest* by seven years, the consequence was a severe erosion of local property-tax dollars for public education—in spite of the state supreme court order for more funds for poor districts. The local share of school funding dropped from 70 percent to 20 percent in 12 years,[12] and the state picked up the difference.

One state, Michigan, completely tossed away its property-tax-based school-financing system. Prompted by numerous voter defeats of proposed property-tax increases to fund public schools and the actual closure of one school system (in Kalaska), the Michigan legislature repealed all property taxes supporting the public schools. The legislature then gave voters a choice: increase the state sales tax from 4 percent to 6 percent and triple the cigarette tax, or raise the state income tax.[13] In a statewide constitutional referendum, voters picked the first option. Vermont replaced its school-funding system, which relied on local government for 70 percent of funding, with a statewide property tax that made the state's share more than 70 percent. An emerging trend is to let the voters decide how to fund education through referendums and initiatives, which occurred recently in Maine, New Mexico, and Arkansas.

These cases illustrate an important principle of education policy today: State centralization and control follow financial responsibility. A long tradition of local control of schools has been displaced in California, Michigan, Vermont, and elsewhere because state governments have become the prime education-policy decisionmakers. Local school districts in some states have become mere administrative appendages of the state government.

School Equity Although centralization of state control of education and efforts to equalize funding for poor districts have proceeded in all states and succeeded to some extent in most of them,[14] inequities continue to exist. A large proportion of state aid continues to be distributed according to the number of pupils in a district rather than on the basis of need. Anyone who compares a school in a wealthy suburb with one in a poor rural district or an urban ghetto cannot fail to be impressed by the differences in facilities and resources. Similarly, wealthy states can afford to allocate more money to schools than poor states can. This invidious geography of inequality is an advantage to those who live in a wealthy school district in a prosperous state.[15] Table 15.2 lists average state expenditures per pupil and teacher salaries.

Common sense tells us that money is related to the quality of schooling. Modern, well-designed buildings, up-to-date equipment, and the latest learning materials should enhance student achievement, as should a rich offering of honors and advanced placement (AP) courses. And schools that can afford to hire the best teachers and maintain low pupil–teacher ratios should be more effective than those with large classrooms and inexperienced or poorly prepared teaching staff. But research has revealed an astonishing paradox: There is no consistent, significant statistical relationship between school resources and student performance.

The first research to reach this conclusion was the so-called Coleman Report in 1966.[16] Sociologist James S. Coleman examined thousands of school situations and discovered that curricula, facilities, class size, expenditures, and other resource factors were not associated with achievement. He *did* find that the family and socioeconomic backgrounds of students influenced performance, with children of well-off, well-educated parents outperforming those brought up in less-advantageous surroundings, a finding supported in more recent research.[17] Also, black students performed better in predominantly white schools than in predominantly black schools—a finding that later served as the grounds for busing to put an end to school segregation. Coleman's staggering conclusions have been re-examined in more than 170 related studies. An extensive review of 120 of these studies determined that only eighteen found a statistically significant positive relationship between school expenditures and student performance.

TABLE 15.2	Expenditures per Pupil and Average Teacher Salaries, 2002–2003

SALARY RANK	STATE	AVERAGE SALARY ($)	EXPENDITURE PER PUPIL ($)	SALARY RANK	STATE	AVERAGE SALARY ($)	EXPENDITURE PER PUPIL ($)
1	California	56,283	7,244	27	Vermont	41,491	9,942
2	Connecticut	55,367	11,378	28	Arizona	40,894	5,197
3	New Jersey	54,158	11,103	29	South Carolina	40,362	7,403
4	Michigan	53,798	8,166	30	Florida	40,281	6,411
5	New York	52,600	11,515	31	Idaho	40,148	6,378
6	Massachusetts	52,043	10,691	32	Texas	40,001	7,152
7	Pennsylvania	51,424	8,331	33	Tennessee	39,677	6,048
8	Illinois	51,289	9,376	34	Missouri	39,292	6,819
9	Rhode Island	51,076	9,889	35	Iowa	39,059	6,974
10	Delaware	50,772	10,270	36	Kentucky	38,981	7,274
11	District of Columbia	50,763	13,355	37	Wyoming	38,838	9,232
12	Alaska	49,685	9,569	38	Maine	38,518	9,289
13	Maryland	49,677	8,124	39	West Virginia	38,481	8,722
14	Oregon	47,600	7,242	40	Utah	38,385	4,907
15	Georgia	45,533	8,238	41	Alabama	38,246	5,418
16	Ohio	45,498	7,518	42	Kansas	38,123	7,620
17	Indiana	45,097	8,307	43	Nebraska	37,896	7,203
18	Washington	44,963	7,516	44	Arkansas	37,753	5,789
19	Minnesota	44,745	8,628	45	Louisiana	37,300	6,698
20	Hawaii	44,464	7,455	46	New Mexico	36,965	6,857
21	Virginia	43,152	6,316	47	Montana	35,754	7,368
22	North Carolina	43,076	6,547	48	Oklahoma	34,877	6,829
23	Wisconsin	42,775	9,019	49	Mississippi	34,555	5,822
24	Colorado	42,679	7,428	50	North Dakota	33,210	4,773
25	New Hampshire	41,909	8,151	51	South Dakota	32,416	6,924
26	Nevada	41,795	6,128		U.S. average	45,930	7,829

SOURCE: Data from the National Education Association, *Rankings and Estimates: Update*, www.nea.org (Fall 2003).

The overall conclusion is that no strong or systematic relationship exists between them.[18] Oddly, however, school spending *does* appear to have a positive effect on the future earnings of school graduates, raising the possibility that resources have a delayed effect on students *after* they leave school.[19]

Thus, equity in school financing does not necessarily translate into equal effectiveness among schools, and boosting school spending does not necessarily generate superior student performance. Controlling for the effects of inflation, total national spending on K–12 education has grown significantly over the past two decades, yet measurable quality improvements have been only marginal, as shown by SAT scores and other tests and indicators. Obviously, money, however necessary, is not the only answer. Neither is financial equity. Exact spending equality among districts does not take into account the special needs of children in troubled urban districts or depressed rural areas, nor of English-language proficiency, physical limitations, and emotional disability. These realizations have shifted attention to education adequacy and outcomes rather than financial inputs.

The National Role

The federal government has traditionally played a minimal role in primary and secondary education, especially when compared with the governments of most other countries, where public education is treated as a national responsibility. The first grant of money for education came only in 1917, when the Smith-Hughes Act financed vocational education in secondary schools. Much later, the National Defense Education Act provided funds to improve math, science, and foreign-language education.

The national role was substantially enlarged during the 1960s and 1970s, primarily through the Elementary and Secondary Education Act (ESEA) of 1965. The ESEA established a direct national subsidy for education, providing funds to almost every school district in the United States. Amounts were allocated for library acquisitions, audiovisual materials, teachers' aides, and compensatory programs for children of poor families and for the mentally and physically handicapped. ESEA monies were originally distributed in accordance with a formula that favored wealthy states. Later, the formula was amended to the advantage of poor states. Parochial (religious) schools also benefit from ESEA funding, although no funds are provided for religious materials or courses or for teacher salaries. With each reauthorization of ESEA, Congress has taken the opportunity to pile on all kinds of mandates about how the money must be spent (examples include special education, desegregation, migrant education, gay rights, and gun control).[20]

The most recent reauthorization, No Child Left Behind (NCLB), is particularly onerous in its testing and performance mandates. Needless to say, the states and their school districts chafe under such restrictions. NCLB requires enormous new state and local education spending. Indiana estimated it would result in a 31 percent increase, and Maryland feared an increase of up to 49 percent.[21] A national government study estimated new state spending of $5.3 billion over six years.[22] The National Education Association claimed that NCLB would lead to one-fourth of all public schools being declared "failing," despite the fact that many of them have been indicating improvement over several years. A growing number of states and school districts, including Virginia, Iowa, New Jersey, and Tennessee, were seriously entertaining the option of walking away from NCLB and the federal money attached. With political pressure building from both sides of the partisan table, U.S. Secretary of Education Rod Paige relaxed some of the federal mandates and timetables in 2004. Congress, caught in the political whirlwinds of a presidential election year, postponed reconsideration of the issue.

During the 1960s and 1970s, the national government exercised policy leadership in education. The Head Start program helped prepare poor children for school and provided many of them with their first medical, dental, and nutritional care. Matching grants encouraged states and localities to experiment with other programs, and research findings, statistics, and new policy information were disseminated by the National Institute of Education and the National Center for Education Statistics. Other national entities furnished consulting and technical aid to local schools and state education departments. The national commitment to public schools received an important symbolic boost in 1979 with the creation of the U.S. Department of Education.

These new commitments brought the national share of total school expenditures from 4.4 percent in 1960 to 9 percent in 1980. Ronald Reagan unsuccessfully sought to abolish the U.S. Department of Education, but he did succeed in drastically cutting national aid to education. As shown in Figure 15.3, the federal government's proportion of education expenditures today is about 8 percent. Under President Bill Clinton, Head Start—demonstrated to be successful in several evaluations—was reauthorized and expanded to Early Head Start: all-day, all-year programs for low-income, at-risk infants and toddlers. Meanwhile, Clinton's Goals 2000: Educate America Act placed into statute five national education goals; as indicated in Table 15.3, results have been disappointing. Clinton's School to Work Act was aimed at helping states and school districts develop improved programs for high school students who do not go on to college. The Community and National Service Act established scholarships and tuition reimbursements for community service. The federal student loan program was overhauled to make college loans cheaper and easier to secure. New federal monies were also provided for school

TABLE 15.3	**Examples of National Education Goals for 2000 and Progress Toward Achieving Them**
GOAL*	**PROGRESS**
1. All children in America will start school ready to learn.	More children are starting school in better health and with stronger reading skills.
2. The high school graduation rate will increase to at least 90 percent.	The rate is 86 percent.
3. U.S. students will leave grades 4 and 8 having demonstrated competency in challenging subject matter.	Math scores have improved, and the percentage of high school graduates meeting goals has increased from 14 percent to 56 percent. Only about one out of four fourth- and eighth-graders meet program goals.
4. U.S. students will be first in the world in science and mathematics achievement.	U.S. students still place average or below average compared to students in other developed countries.
5. Every school in America will be free of drugs and violence and will offer a disciplined environment conducive to learning.	School violence and illegal drug use by students have diminished slightly.

*The nation's governors originally developed these goals in a slightly different form in 1989.
SOURCE: The text of Goals 2000: Educate America Act (1994); "Quality Counts," *Education Week*, www.edweek.org (January 2004).

modernization and construction, to improve technological literacy of teachers and students, and to promote charter schools. In 2002, the federal government aggressively asserted itself in the debate concerning the schools with NCLB, mandating higher standards and demonstrated performance or risk losing federal funds.

ACTORS IN EDUCATION POLICY

The proliferation of independent school districts in the latter part of the nineteenth century was accompanied by intensive politicization. School districts in both big cities and rural areas alike were as likely to hire teachers and principals on the basis of patronage as on the basis of professional competence. Reformers (mostly professional educators) struggled to remove partisan politics from the public schools by electing school boards on a nonpartisan, at-large basis, and by giving the primary responsibility for running school systems to professionals. These efforts were successful, but a new type of politics arose as teachers, school administrators, and state-level education actors began to dominate policy decisions as the "education establishment."

The Education Establishment

In the past, the members of the education establishment, often referred to as the education bureaucracy, tried to dominate school policymaking by resolving issues among themselves and then presenting a united front before legislative bodies and the governor. They constituted a powerful political coalition that managed to win substantial financial commitments to the schools. Because of the political pressures already mentioned, however, the education establishment is fractured today.

Teachers As noted, teachers had little power or influence outside the classroom until they began to organize into professional associations and unions. Before the 1960s, teacher organizations, particularly the NEA, focused their attention on school improvement rather than on the economic well-being of teachers themselves. Teachers and administrators maintained a common front before the state legislature. Gradually, however, a newer teacher organization challenged the dominance and docility of the NEA, especially in large cities. This rival organization, the AFT, openly referred to itself as a labor union and struggled to win collective bargaining rights for teachers. With the election of the AFT in 1961 as the bargaining agent for teachers in New York City, the teachers began carving a niche for themselves outside the cozy family of the education establishment. Both the NEA and the AFT lobbied for state legislation permitting collective bargaining in the late 1960s and 1970s and concentrated their efforts on winning better pay and working conditions for teachers. Today, approximately three-fourths of the nation's schoolteachers belong to one of these groups. However, many NEA locals, primarily in the southern and western states, still do not engage in collective bargaining either because they choose not to or because their state does not permit it. This key distinction between the two teachers' groups has prevented them from merging, although it has been seriously considered on many occasions.

Teacher militancy accompanied unionization. Strikes and other job actions disrupted many local school districts as teachers battled for higher pay, fewer nonteaching duties, and related demands. The explosion of teacher's unions forever fragmented the education lobby in most states as teachers sought to look out for their own interests rather than the interests of school administrators. Teachers remain the most powerful of education interest groups at the state level, although they regularly draw fire from citizens and other education stakeholders.[23] U.S. Secretary of Education Rod Paige referred to the NEA as a "terrorist organization" in 2004. Each year, the opening day of school must be delayed in some districts because teachers go out on strike over critical concerns such as pay and benefits, working conditions, and education quality issues.

Local School Boards Another member of the education establishment, the local school board, is a legislative body responsible for administering public education at the local level. About 15,000 of these local bodies exist in the United States. Local school boards are made up of laypeople, not representatives of the professional education community. Board members are elected by voters in independent school districts in most states, although some or all of them are appointed by local legislative delegations in several southern states.

The original American ideal of local control of public schools lodged its faith in local school boards, which were popularly elected and therefore responsive to citizens' opinions and points of view. In fact, their true authority has never equaled the myth of local control. Recently, the status and influence of local boards has reached low levels indeed. Some school boards have contracted with private entities to run their schools. Others (for example, in Chicago, Boston, Cleveland, and New York) have been rife with patronage practices and scandals. One critic recently called school boards "the worst kind of anachronism . . . ripe for corruption, as a springboard for aspiring politicians, and a venue for disgruntled former school employees to air their dirty laundry."[24]

School boards still determine school taxes and levy them on real estate in the district. They also continue to hire district superintendents of education and school administrators, approve teacher appointments, determine building and facility needs, set salary levels for certain personnel, and debate program needs. In fact, some local boards are criticized for trying to micromanage the daily minutiae of school operations instead of properly focusing on broad policy issues. These issues, however, are increasingly influenced by state standards and regulations. Local school boards often rely on their appointed school superintendents to make such decisions and in general furnish policy leadership.

The decline of school board power is also due to teacher collective bargaining, which often determines matters such as teacher compensation, working conditions, and even curriculum questions. In addition, local school boards suffer from deep public apathy, extremely low turnouts for board elections, and widespread ignorance of what such boards are supposed to be doing. About the only events that focus citizen attention on local boards are the occasional bond or tax referendum that proposes to raise property taxes in the school district, or vitriolic debates over conflicting goals and values such as school redistricting, funding equity, and student diversity.

Other Policy Actors   Also known as the state education agency, the state board of education (SBE) exists in all states except Wisconsin. It exercises general supervision over all primary and secondary schools. The SBE members are appointed by the governor or legislature in thirty-six states, elected in ten, or selected through some combination of processes.[25]

SBEs are administrative boards, but most of them also make policy and budget recommendations to the governor and legislature. With few exceptions, however, they are not significant policy actors. They tend to lack political clout, policy expertise, and public visibility. Like local school boards, state boards of education defer to the authority and expertise of another policy actor—in this case, the chief state school officer (CSSO). This person, known as the state superintendent of schools or the commissioner of education in some states, establishes and enforces standards for local school curricula, teacher certification, standardized student testing, and certain other matters and provides technical and other assistance to the schools. She or he may be appointed by the state board of education, popularly elected on a statewide ballot, or appointed by the governor. Although the formal relationship between the CSSO and the state board of education varies, nearly all CSSOs serve as executive officers and professional advisers to their state boards of education. Governors and state legislatures have increasingly provided policy leadership for the schools, so the influence of CSSOs has declined.

Yet another administrative creature, the state department of education, is responsible for rulemaking and for furnishing administrative and technical support to the CSSO and the SBE. It also administers national- and state-aid programs for public schools. The state department of education is almost exclusively the habitat of education professionals. State departments have grown in size, competency, and power. They have taken on the difficult job of monitoring state education reforms, and they have significantly increased their capacities for program evaluation, performance and measurement, and research.

The New Policy Leaders

Financial and political pressures on the education establishment, coinciding with a loss of public and business confidence in the schools, have fragmented the coalition of actors described above. Simultaneously, state-level education actors and business organizations have increased their interest in school issues and their capacity to respond to them, and governors and legislatures have added staff and augmented their ability to collect data and conduct research. The strengthened state departments of education are now handmaidens of the governors and legislatures. Education policymaking today orbits around state government rather than local education professionals, although the demand for, and tradition of, local control remains important. With NCLB, the national government has reestablished itself as an important education policymaker.

Governors The American people usually turn to their chief executives in times of crisis. Today, state chief executives are deeply involved in all major aspects of education policymaking. Education issues often receive considerable attention during campaigns, in State of the State addresses, and throughout a governor's term of office. Occasionally, education completely dominates governors' policy agendas. Generally, education policy remains the most important perennial issue in most states.

In formulating, lobbying for, and implementing education policy, the governors rely heavily on their staff. Many governors have special divisions of education. Staff members facilitate the flow of information to and from the governor's office and the desks of other key education policymakers. They analyze information from all levels of government, in and out of state, and from national organizations such as the National Governors' Association and the Education Commission of the States. They also draft proposed legislation, lobby legislators and education and business groups, and attempt to influence public opinion on education issues. The most successful governors have managed to weave delicate advocacy coalitions among all significant education policy actors to increase their chances of enacting substantial reform programs. (The nearby *Breaking New Ground* box briefly describes a reform program in Wisconsin.)

State Legislatures Legislatures have always had the final responsibility for enacting broad education policy and for implementing state funding of public schools. They were the leading state policy actors until governors upstaged them, but the critical policy battles are still fought on legislative turf.

BREAKING NEW GROUND

SAGE Students

The Student Achievement Guarantee in Education (SAGE) program is Wisconsin's contribution to improving student achievement in low-income schools. The comprehensive reform reduces student–teacher ratios to fifteen students per teacher in kindergarten through third grade. Participating school districts must sign contracts with the state to: (1) implement a rigorous curriculum; (2) extend school hours through enrichment programs before and after school; (3) systematically assess teachers, administrators, and professional staff and dismiss those who fail to learn and improve; and (4) collaborate with community organizations to make more recreational and social-service programs available in the school. Evaluations of SAGE students show that they outperform comparable students on every subject tested. Reduced class size results in fewer discipline problems, more individualized instruction, more frequent hands-on activities, and higher teacher job satisfaction.

SOURCE: Education Policy Studies Laboratory, "Class Size Reduction in Wisconsin: A Fresh Look at the Data," Arizona State University, www.asu.edu/educ/epsl/SAGE (September 2003).

Lobbyists for the education establishment are quite active in the statehouse, but their influence has diminished because issue conflicts have precluded a united front. Numerous other interests, including business, minority groups, the disabled, and the economically disadvantaged, also receive a hearing from legislators.

Although governors are the education policy leaders in most states, legislatures have expanded their capabilities. They have added their own education staff specialists, enhanced their research capabilities, and extended efforts to oversee the actions of governors and education agencies.

Courts Federal and state courts, especially the U.S. Supreme Court, are important factors in public education. They have issued rulings on several issues affecting students, such as censorship of school newspapers, personal dress and grooming standards, female participation in sports programs, student discipline, student drug testing, and school prayer. Federal courts imposed desegregation policies on public schools through a series of decisions beginning with *Brown* v. *Board of Education of Topeka* (1954), which declared that racial segregation violated the Fourteenth Amendment's equal protection clause.[26] Court-ordered busing to achieve school desegregation was mandated in *Swann* v. *Charlotte-Mecklenburg County Schools* (in North Carolina) in 1971 and in other decisions involving districts that had practiced government-approved racial segregation.[27] These decisions, and the subsequent busing, were highly controversial and contributed to white flight to the suburbs in many places. In some cities, such as Boston, Massachusetts, court-ordered busing led to violent protests.

Occasionally, the courts wield impressive policy influence. In 1990, the U.S. Supreme Court passed down a desegregation ruling with profoundly negative implications for American federalism. *Missouri* v. *Jenkins* was a suit brought against Missouri by a Kansas City school district and a group of minority students who claimed that the state was illegally maintaining segregated schools. The Supreme Court affirmed a lower-court ruling ordering Kansas City school-district officials to raise property taxes to fund a far-reaching and expensive desegregation plan, even though local citizens had rejected the plan six times in referendums. Civil rights groups heralded the decision, but local and state officials and various defenders of federalism assailed it as a tyrannical court pre-emption of local taxing power and "taxation without representation."[28] Federal Judge Russell Clark effectively seized control of the Kansas City schools, ordered local property taxes to be doubled, and imposed a grand design to integrate the schools while building quality education. Clark, who critics called the "poster child of the imperial judiciary," oversaw construction of thirty-seven new magnet schools to attract white residents into the nearly all-black school districts. Various schools had special features designed to attract students: Olympic-size swimming pools complete with underwater viewing rooms; professional-quality television, recording, and animation studios; a robotics lab; an arboretum; a planetarium; and a zoo; among other features. After spending $1.6 billion over a decade, the Kansas City schools reported a higher percentage of minority students than before (80 percent), rising dropout rates, and an unchanged test performance gap between black and white students.[29] Finally, the U.S. Supreme Court found Clark had exceeded his authority and reversed the earlier ruling.

Racial segregation of the schools remains just as serious and intractable a problem as it was more than forty years ago when *Brown* was decided. Clearly, busing has been a failure: Research confirms that more school segregation exists now than twenty years ago.[30] Racial and social disparities from housing segregation have created "islands of immunity" to school integration.[31] It appears that a tipping point is reached when nonwhite enrollment surpasses 25 percent, triggering white flight. Remaining behind are the children of poverty and color.[32] African Americans in particular continue to live in segregated housing and attend segregated schools. But with the endorsement of a conservative majority of the U.S. Supreme Court, many school districts, including Charlotte-Mecklenburg and Boston, have dismantled desegregation plans in favor of combining neighborhood schools with various "choice" options such as charter and magnet schools. On the positive side, however, is research indicating that blacks are now earning high school diplomas in nearly the same proportion (93 percent) as whites, after many decades of lagging behind.[33] Hispanic students, however, are still dropping out in numbers more than twice as high as African Americans and more than four times as high as white students.

State courts, too, have stimulated and even ordered changes in education policy. As we have noted, several state supreme courts have mandated school-finance reform to attain more equity in the funding of public education. State courts increasingly are being asked to resolve numerous legal disagreements spawned by education reforms. Individuals and groups representing minority positions can often capture the attention of top policymakers only through the legal system.

The Corporate Community   Of necessity, businesses have become involved in the public schools. Many high school graduates lack the basic skills and knowledge to tackle the demands of the contemporary workplace. Thus, some firms have developed their own training and education programs, often incorporating fundamental reading and writing skills.

To some members of the education establishment, business leaders are partly to blame for the sad state of the schools. Some industries based primarily on manual labor and unsophisticated skills historically opposed education reform as an unnecessary expense. Firms are also criticized for negotiating local property-tax breaks that deprive school districts of much-needed revenues, then complaining about the poor quality of education in those very districts they are starving financially. Today, however, most corporate leaders are vocal proponents of education improvement at all levels, from preschool to college. Even entry-level work has become technologically more demanding.

Corporate involvement encompasses a broad range of activities, from purchasing computers and supplies for local school and adopt-a-school programs to sponsoring opportunities in which students may concentrate on a specially designed curriculum in areas such as finance, tourism, or manufacturing, and then work in paid summer internships. Business leaders also try to influence the overall direction of public education by advocating performance-based accountability for school activities, decentralized school-management systems, and other reforms. Overall, the role of business varies from state to state, but in most locations its contribution is mostly rhetorical and episodic. Commercialization of the classroom is a growing problem. Product advertisements on Channel One, exclusive lunchroom franchises for soft-drink bottler and fast-food chains, and even advertising on school buses raises questions about the true interests of business in the schools.

Private Schools   The widespread presence of private schools, most of them church-sponsored, makes them influential policy leaders. They enroll approximately 11 percent of K–12 students nationwide. To their supporters, the superiority of private schools in providing quality education is taken on faith. Private schools may provide a superior education in some instances, but in others, private schools are inferior, or they are little more than "seg academies" used by parents to keep their children in predominantly white classrooms. Because private schools stand to reap substantial gains from voucher programs, they are strong supporters of this alternative to public schools.

EDUCATIONAL INNOVATION IN THE STATES

In the time since *A Nation at Risk* called national attention to the acute need for educational reforms, the states have responded on a large scale. Hundreds of task forces have thoroughly studied school problems and issued recommendations for resolving them. Many of these recommendations have been enacted into law as innovative programs to improve the quality of public education.

The states' share of school funding has risen dramatically. Many states have raised taxes specifically for aid to education. State support for schools jumped by more than 54 percent over a recent eight-year period.[34] A broad and powerful coalition of state and local elected officials, professional educators, parents, and business interests has been important in the reform drive. Improvement in education is a nonpartisan issue; Democrats, Republicans, and Independents agree that the economic future of the United States depends on the quality of schooling.

The states continue with incremental innovations in the four critical areas of standards, students, teachers, and the education bureaucracy. Every state has recorded remarkable program achievements in at least one of these categories, and a majority have implemented reforms in all four. But incremental reforms have not been bold enough to reverse the strong tide of school mediocrity in many troubled settings, opening up a growing demand for more far-reaching restructuring of public education.

Standards

Standards have been raised in almost every state. Curriculum and graduation requirements have been strengthened, instructional time and the length of the school day have been increased, steps have been taken to minimize overcrowding, and computer technology has been ushered into the classroom. Mississippi high school students receive instruction and assistance in assembling their own personal computers; in Maine, the state provides laptops to all seventh graders. Special programs have been developed to encourage gifted students in North Carolina, Illinois, Texas, and many other states. In North Carolina's School of Science and Mathematics, students on full scholarships balance academic work on topics such as DNA and fractals with weekly chores and community service.[35]

Minimum competency testing for basic skills has been another widely adopted reform. All states now test students at several grade levels to monitor progress in the basics, and at least twenty-four require students to pass a competency test (or exit exam) before graduating from high school. The tests can also be used to identify outstanding student achievement or to diagnose students who need remedial instruction. All states require school "report cards" to hold schools accountable for student performance. Successful schools and their teachers may receive financial rewards. Low-performing schools may be overhauled or even closed. Yet many teachers, parents, and students openly wonder if schools have gone overboard with frequent—and often intrusive—testing.

Elementary school students explore the Web in a public school classroom in Phoenix, Arizona.
SOURCE: Stone/Getty Images.

DEBATING POLITICS

Standardized Testing

Everyone reading this book is familiar with the SAT or ACT; most have taken one of these standardized exams to gain entry into an institution of higher education. One of these tests is required for most students. Standardized testing of students in grades 1–12 is now the norm as well. All states require standardized tests for various categories of students. Ohio even mandates testing for three- and four-year-old preschoolers!

No Child Left Behind requires states to test annually all students between grades 3 and 8 in reading and math, and, by the 2005–2006 school year, all students between grades 10 and 12 in math and English. Science is to be added in the upper grades beginning in 2007. Schools that fail to make required progress will be declared nonperforming and can lose their federal funding.

Proponents of the "standards and assessment" camp claim that:

- Standardized exams have the positive benefit of identifying underperforming students, schools, and school districts; corrections can be made in a timely manner.
- They encourage alignment of teacher objectives with statewide standards.

- Key subjects will be taught similarly across the state.
- Outperforming teachers and districts can be rewarded; underperforming ones can be penalized.

Opponents of annual standardized testing under NCLB argue the following:

- If resources follow performance, teachers will teach to the test. Some teachers and students may cheat.
- Standardized tests are expensive to develop, administer, and score. Indiana estimates its exit exam costs $442 million a year.
- Teachers must devote time to taking tests, drills, and practice for the standardized tests, leaving less time for teaching important, but untested, topics.
- Results can fluctuate randomly, making conclusions about progress or deterioration suspect.
- Superficial questions requiring little or no critical thinking or analysis do not enhance meaningful achievement.

Is "standards and performance" an issue best handled by state standards, school-district standards, or federal law? Which level of government should pay the financial costs for testing? Do the advantages of annual standardized testing outweigh the disadvantages?

The nearby *Debating Politics* box presents the arguments for and against standardized testing.

Year-round schooling is now required for more than 2.3 million students in some 3,100 public schools—a sevenfold increase during only six years.[36] Three-month summer breaks—the legacy of an agrarian economy in which children were needed to plant and bring in the crops—are being replaced with multi-tracking arrangements in which students and teachers are divided into several groups, or tracks. They attend classes for forty-five, sixty, or ninety days, then go on break for a two- or three-week intersession. Although the research remains inconclusive, year-round schooling may improve learning by ensuring that children keep their mental sharpness and do not forget much of what they have learned over the summer. It also saves money by maximizing the use of schools' buildings and resources. Certain problems must be addressed by schools and parents, however. For example, it is difficult to schedule maintenance on buildings and equipment, and extended schooling can interfere with sports and other extracurricular activities and disrupt family vacations and day-care arrangements.[37]

Students

Of course, students are the intended beneficiaries of the improvements and strengthening of standards. In general, expectations for student academic performance and classroom behavior have been raised. As noted, the trend for SAT scores has been moderately positive (refer again to Figure 15.1). Other standardized tests, such as the National Assessment of Educational Programs, have provided more positive indications of improvement. Great disparities remain, however, among states, suburban and urban districts, racial groups, and family-income categories.

One common-sense approach is to help prepare students better to begin school in the first place. The federal Head Start program is one such program, but states are helping to build first-graders' learning foundations through highly structured and innovative preschool programs. Such initiatives in Georgia, New Jersey, and Oklahoma improve childhood literacy and identify medical and social-service needs. Importantly, they also involve parents in the learning process. Children as young as three years are enrolled in some states.[38]

Course requirements for students to graduate from high school have been raised in forty-two states since *A Nation at Risk* was published. Students are required to take more upper-level math and science courses, and more students are enrolling in AP courses than ever before. In 1982, only 14 percent of public high school graduates had completed the core academic curriculum recommended in *A Nation at Risk;* today that figure approaches 56 percent.

outcomes-based or performance-based education

A reform that strives to hold schools, teachers, and administrators accountable for student performance, usually based on standardized test scores.

A national debate has developed on what has become known as **outcomes-based** or **performance-based education.** National standards, such as a national curriculum and achievement test on the basics for all students, is said to enhance school accountability by helping to determine levels of student knowledge, skills, and abilities, as well as curriculum and teacher development needs. Although almost everyone agrees that standards must be raised and many think that a national test is a good idea, moving beyond broad goals and relatively painless incremental changes is proving to be difficult. Negative reactions to the Bush administration's NCLB demonstrate that Americans support national standards, but they distrust the national government and fear federal intrusion into the schools. So far, national math standards have been agreed on and adopted by a growing number of states. But progress has not come easily or quickly on national standards for history or English, which are subject areas that can be politically loaded. For example, whose version of Columbus's voyage of discovery should be taught, the Europeans' or the Native Americans'?

Outcomes-based education is here to stay. With federal government encouragement, mandates, and monetary incentives, every state is developing or revising curricula to emphasize what children should know and be able to do regarding key subjects and testing them on that knowledge. By 2004, forty-eight states had specific standards in place for at least four core subjects, compared with only twenty-nine states just five years before. In about twenty-seven states, schools are rewarded or penalized financially for student performance.[39]

Student classroom behavior has been a target of reformers in many states. Strict discipline codes are being enforced, as are stronger attendance policies. In especially difficult school settings, police officers, closed-circuit television monitors, and other devices help maintain order. Most of the states that have adopted more stringent discipline policies in the past few years have made it easier for teachers to remove troublemakers from the classroom. More and more school districts are using zero tolerance policies to expel violent students, and they are implementing other violence-prevention programs. These programs teach conflict-resolution and anger-management skills to reduce fighting and offer anti-gang instruction to discourage gang membership. Some implement policies to reduce the incidence of bullying. Ironically, corporal punishment (paddling, usually) remains legal in twenty-three states and is still used (mostly in the Bible Belt states) to discipline unruly students.[40] High-profile school shootings such as that at Columbine High School in Colorado in 1999, and the resulting parental and student fear that it could also happen in local schools, have led to tightened security on school grounds.

Student drug testing became a hot issue in 2002, following a U.S Supreme Court decision that schools could perform drug tests on students participating in extracurricular activities.[41] Until that ruling, public-school students were presumed to be excluded from drug testing by the Fourteenth Amendment's protection against illegal search and seizure. Presumably, drug (urine) testing would identify trouble-prone students and send a message to those contemplating smoking weed or doing more serious substances. Hundreds of school boards across the United States began debating drug testing and what would be done with the results. Professional educators and health groups oppose drug testing, arguing that students engaging in extracurricular activities are less likely to use drugs, and that requiring screening as a condition of participation in sports, band, clubs, and other activities would deter students from participating. At a more fundamental legal level remains the matter of overcoming state constitutional provisions regarding privacy and illegal search and seizure. More court actions, this time at the state level, are likely.[42]

As a positive incentive, students who graduate high school with a B or better average in Georgia, New York, California, and several other states are guaranteed state payment of the full tuition at a state college or university, as long as they maintain a B average or better. Such scholarship programs have the added benefit of helping stem the brain drain of top students who attend college out of state and never move back. Incentives for regular, punctual attendance are being offered in many locales, including guarantees of a job or admission to college to all graduating seniors with a minimum grade point average and regular attendance. Taking a different tack, North Carolina revokes the driver's license of any high school student who drops out or fails to pass 70 percent of his or her courses. Naugatuck, Connecticut, fines truant students or their parents $25.00 a day. The goal, of course, is to keep in school some of the hundreds of thousands of students who drop out each year, at a huge cost in lost tax revenues and increased expenditures associated with welfare, unemployment, and crime.

Teachers

Of the many factors influencing student learning, the quality of the teacher in the classroom usually makes the greatest difference. Teachers have been the beneficiaries (or victims, depending on one's standpoint) of the most extensive and far-reaching educational reforms. They have universally welcomed higher pay, improved fringe benefits, and more opportunities for professional improvement. Smaller class sizes are particularly desirable, giving teachers more time to interact with each student. Voters agree with their teachers in Florida, having approved an initiative to cap class size at twenty-five in high school and at eighteen in grades K–3 by 2010. Class size has also been reduced by law in California, Nevada, and other states. Teachers have been much less pleased with paperwork requirements, performance appraisals, testing of teachers, and teacher merit-pay schemes.

Teacher salaries have basically tracked increases in the cost of living since the 1980s. Variations among the states continue to be rather pronounced, in response to differences in local cost of living, labor market conditions, and other factors (see Table 15.1). In 2003, teachers in California earned an average salary of $56,283; those in South Dakota averaged $32,416.

Teacher Shortages Because of retirements, attrition, and the spurt in public-school enrollment, critical shortages of qualified teachers, particularly for math and science courses, continue to exist in almost all states, and projections of the need for 2 million new classroom teachers by 2008 indicate even worse problems to come. The states are experimenting with several strategies to relieve teacher shortfalls. Most are taking steps to entice former teachers and education majors who are working in other fields back into the classroom, and nearly all have set up streamlined systems to certify noneducation majors. One particularly promising pool of new teachers consists of people who have retired early from military service, business, or government. Such nontraditional recruiting not only helps alleviate the teacher-supply problem but has the added benefit of elevating the quality and diversity of the teaching pool.

Several recent reports find that education problems stem from the failure to recruit, train, and retain good teachers. Some schools serve as retirement homes for the inept. Some teachers' colleges do an inadequate job of preparing teachers for the classroom. Some schools force teachers to teach out of their field of expertise and training. And once in the classroom, many teachers, especially in urban and poor rural schools, soon lose their enthusiasm and confidence in their own abilities when faced with at-risk children. States are taking steps to solve these and related problems. State education statutes and collective bargaining contracts are being modified to make it easier to dismiss teachers who should no longer be in the classroom. Teachers of at-risk students are receiving much-needed assistance. State teacher-licensing requirements are being tightened up to include longer classroom internships and mastery of material in the subject area they will teach. Gradually, schools are learning the importance of the mentoring of new teachers by experienced teachers. NCLB stipulates that all teachers in core student classrooms be "highly qualified." The exact meaning of this term remains vague, but states must demonstrate that teachers hold subject matter competence in their courses by 2005–2006.

Several states have experimented with merit-pay plans that seek to reward high-performing teachers with special pay increases. Career ladders, which promote outstanding teachers up several levels to higher job classifications, have also been tried. For various reasons—including budget cuts, teacher dissatisfaction with the plans, and a lack of union support—these initiatives generally have not been successful.[43] The current approach, used in California, Kentucky, and elsewhere, is to award teachers schoolwide bonuses when their school's standardized test scores exceed goals set by the state.[44]

Material incentives other than competitive salaries can be helpful in attracting and retaining teachers. Many states offer special scholarships, signing bonuses, or loans to attract college students into the teaching profession. The Massachusetts signing-bonus program offers $20,000 for new teachers. California's generous plan offers teachers a personal income tax credit of up to $1,500; a $10,000 bonus for earning board certification; $20,000 for graduate students who agree to teach in a low-performing school; and up to $11,000 in paid-up student loans.[45]

Bureaucracy and School Choice

school choice

A market-based approach to education improvement that permits parents and students to choose which school the child will attend. Examples include charter schools and voucher programs.

A single, boilerplate plan does not exist for reducing or avoiding the education bureaucracy, but all strategies hold one factor in common: **school choice.** Its most essential elements include a market-based, decentralized approach that permits individual selection of the school that the child will attend, while providing tax dollars to accompany the student to the chosen school. The expectation is that, in the scramble to attract tuition dollars, heretofore fossilized schools will try new ideas, offer new or specialized curricula, and take other steps to reinvigorate public education.[46] Schools unable or unwilling to adapt to and compete within the education marketplace would be forced to consolidate with more successful schools or close down altogether.

magnet school

A public school whose curriculum emphasizes a specialized area, such as performing arts or technology, to attract students from different ethnic and income groups.

Magnet Schools A common school-choice program, found in nearly all large urban school districts, is the **magnet school.** A form of public school, the magnet school offers specialized curricula to attract students from various backgrounds who share a common interest in areas such as dance, theater, science and technology, or foreign languages. Successful magnet schools help attract affluent children to the inner city and poor children to the suburbs. Related to magnet schools are **open enrollment programs** that permit students either to select schools inside the existing school district only or to choose any public school in the state. Within-district choice keeps resources and tax dollars in the same local jurisdiction. Between-district enrollment allows children to attend a school in a different district, perhaps many miles away. Open enrollment plans

open enrollment program

An option that permits students to attend a public school of their choice within a designated jurisdictional area. The intent is to increase educational options for all children.

are intended to increase educational opportunities for students regardless of race, ethnicity, or socioeconomic status.

Open enrollment is not without its problems, however. An important short-coming is that white and middle-class children tend to "choose" to flee inner-city schools for those in suburban or rural areas. An example of this "creaming effect" is found in Iowa. During the first three years of Iowa's experience with school choice, some 828 students, mostly white, decided to leave the Des Moines district. Such an outcome has obvious implications for racial and social-class balance in the schools. School-choice proponents claim that children of poor parents can also move to more desirable schools in the suburbs, but without special assistance, many poor children cannot afford transportation to outlying districts. This problem has been at least partially eliminated in states that help pay transportation costs for poor children. However, students still face the additional hurdle of gaining admission to their school of choice, which might be fully enrolled.

Charter Schools Charter schools enjoy great popularity and financial support from the federal government, state governments, and national teachers' unions. Unlike open enrollment programs, which provide greater choice among existing schools, charter schools expand the total number of school possibilities for parents to choose from. Charter schools are independent entities operating within the public-school system under charters, or contracts, that specify operating procedures and performance indicators. The charters are negotiated between their organizers and a sponsoring agency. The sponsor may be a local school board, teachers, parents, or other entity. Charter schools promise to deliver results in exchange for being unleashed from the bureaucratic chains of the educational establishment. Flexibility and innovation are their strong suits. Most design their own curricula, hire and fire teachers, and generally run their own show. Some feature a back-to-basics curriculum; others target high school dropouts or math and science whizzes. In actuality, however, their degree of autonomy varies widely, depending on the state authorizing legislation. Using public (mostly state) tax dollars to compete with traditional public schools, charter schools are intended to improve responsiveness to parents and enhance the quality of education throughout the jurisdiction.

Charter school laws have been adopted in thirty-nine states, and they are being actively considered in others. They are particularly popular in Arizona, California, and Texas. In 2003, some 2,700 charter schools were operating throughout the United States. The concept remains unproven, however, and teacher's unions and some school boards are skeptical of charter-reform efforts. Across the United States, a growing number of charter schools have been closed for various reasons, from poor performance to unsanitary health conditions.[47] Reliable evaluative research is only now appearing on how well they measure up.[48]

Voucher Plans In a voucher system, parents receive a certificate from the state or from their local school district that may be used to subsidize the tuition for a public, private, or religious school of their choice. The concept is quite similar to that of the G.I. bill and Pell grants for federal reimbursements to colleges and universities. Voucher legislation has been introduced in more than half the states, but as of 2004 they were operating only in Milwaukee, Wisconsin, Cleveland, Ohio, and Florida. Despite an early display of public enthusiasm for voucher programs, they have gone down to defeat in every state initiative and referendum. Support for using public money for private-school tuition was only 38 percent in 2003.[49] In addition to voter and legislative resistance, several state courts have proven to be less than friendly to voucher plans, having blocked them in Maine, Pennsylvania, and Vermont, among other states.

The Florida program, enacted on a small scale by the legislature in 1999, offers opportunity scholarships to students in chronically low-performing schools, permitting them to transfer to a better-performing public school or to any private school. The Florida voucher program was held unconstitutional by a Florida appeals court in August 2004.

The oldest, largest, and most-examined voucher experiment began in 1999 in Milwaukee. The Milwaukee school-choice program provides low-income parents with vouchers to send their children to private schools. It is used by about 11,000 low-income students, who receive about $5,800 each. The majority are enrolled in religious (mostly Catholic) schools.[50]

Formal evaluations of the Milwaukee program have become politicized by the highly controversial spending of public tax dollars for private schools. Separation of church and state became a volatile issue when the program was extended to religious schools. A state circuit court judge ruled that the inclusion of such schools was unconstitutional, but the decision was overturned by the Wisconsin state supreme court in 1998, thus permitting vouchers to be applied to parochial schools.[51] The court's reasoning was that the voucher money was going to parents, not to schools. The constitutional legitimacy of spending public money on religious schools was established under the federal constitution by the U.S. Supreme Court in 2002 in *Zelman* v. *Simmons-Harris et al.,* a decision heralded as the most important ruling on religion and the schools in forty years.[52] The Court's 5–4 majority concluded that Cleveland's plan offered "a genuine choice between religious and nonreligious schools," despite the enrollment of 96 percent of voucher recipients in religious schools.[53] Left undetermined is the constitutionality of such vouchers according to the other state courts.

Overall, it does appear that voucher programs have encouraged parents to participate more in their children's education and that parental satisfaction with schools has increased. And there is no shortage of voucher champions, chiefly among political conservatives and religious supporters.[54] But no one has yet determined whether vouchers have improved student achievement. In Milwaukee and Cleveland, the most thorough analyses to date indicate that school-choice students have not performed any better than similar nonchoice students.[55] Also undetermined is the effect of public spending for private schools on the quality of public schools. Will public schools improve so that they can compete with private schools, or will they become education hovels for the remaining poor children? Will vouchers truly benefit children of low-income families who, even with a voucher, still must come up with thousands of dollars annually to pay private-school tuition? Or will vouchers disproportionately help upper- and middle-income families? What will be the impact on racial and social-class segregation?

Privatization

Perhaps the most innovative restructuring plan of all involves turning over management and operation of the public schools to a private firm. Some fifty private firms managed more than 400 public schools in twenty-five states in 2003.[56] Edison Schools, Inc., operates for-profit schools in twenty-two states, including large contracts in Pennsylvania and Minnesota. One of the most interesting privatization experiments is in Philadelphia. Governor Mark Schweiker led a state takeover of Philadelphia's troubled school system in 2001. Forty-two failing public schools were transferred to seven outside administrators, including Edison, Temple University, and the University of Pennsylvania.[57] It is still too soon to assess the results in the City of Brotherly Love. Noteworthy failures in school privatization have occurred in Hartford, Connecticut, and Dallas, Texas, because of high financial costs and disappointing student performance. In the analysis by the U.S. General Accounting Office in 2003 comparing student test scores in public schools with privately run schools in six cities, results were mixed. Students in traditional schools did better on standardized reading and science tests in Cleveland and St. Paul, but did worse than test-takers in privately managed schools in Denver and San Francisco.[58]

Homeschooling

In addition to the large number of children enrolled in private schools (approximately 11 percent of the student population), it is estimated that up to 4 percent of school-age children are taught at home by their parents. Many homeschoolers are from religious families uncomfortable with the public school's performance or moral values. The homeschool curriculum, testing, and other factors are regulated by thirty-four states; no requirements exist in the other sixteen. Some states accommodate homeschooling by permitting selected public-school activities. For instance, Idaho public schools must allow homeschooled children to participate in any school activity, including sports.

Virtual Schools

Computer technology makes it possible for high school students to learn at home from long-distance teachers. California's Choice 2000 program enrolls middle school and high school students in a twenty-four-hour distance education program. The Florida High School, serving more than 10,000 students, is a Web-based high school that is structured around on-line learning. The virtual school, which is in its early stages of development, could be particularly appropriate for rural states with great distances between schools, such as Alaska and Wyoming. It has also attracted attention from charter schools. Unresolved issues with virtual schooling include test security, student performance assessment, parental involvement, and the effects of education without interpersonal interaction.

The Report Card on School Choice

Will the school-choice movement save the public schools or destroy them? Is the most salient issue the quality of education, or is it a desire for racial homogeneity and religious instruction?[59] Are parents truly capable and do they have sufficient information to make the best educational choices for their children?[60] Arguments are proffered from both perspectives. So far, relatively small numbers of students participate in school-choice programs. As a result, the data are insufficient, precluding proper assessment of student performance or possible unintended consequences of school-choice programs.

One thing is certain: School choice is highly controversial and, except for the charter- and magnet-school options, is perceived as a threat by almost the entire education establishment, especially teachers and school board members, who fear losing funding from reduced enrollment and being saddled with the most difficult, at-risk children. When school-choice proposals involve private schools, they are especially controversial. The U.S. Supreme Court ruling notwithstanding, constitutional issues concerning the separation of church and state are now taken to state courts, as they have been in Florida, Ohio, and Wisconsin. In short, public support of school choice is waning.

THE CONTINUING CHALLENGE OF PUBLIC EDUCATION

The states have linked their plans for economic and social development to excellence in education, and they are providing the sort of national direction and leadership once thought to be possible only through efforts of the national government. The vitality, innovation, and capability of the states are most prominent in education policy.

But we should not be overly generous in our praise. A wide gap separates policy enactment from policy implementation. Goals 2000 was not attained on time. And more time must pass before we can accurately gauge the consequences of new state initiatives and the federal NCLB. It will take a tremendous act of political will and much hard work to bring to fruition the state and national educational improvement goals.

The continuing problems in public education are manifold and daunting, and reform is extremely complex and elusive. For example, most experts agree that school resources are best expended in the classroom, yet mandates and other legal requirements force administrators and teachers to complete hundreds of reports and other paperwork each year. As education reform seemingly plods along, many frustrated parents opt for alternative arrangements. The number of private schools and the number of children instructed at home have grown tremendously. Meanwhile, during this crisis of legitimacy for the public schools, many thorny dilemmas persist. Students and teachers must learn how to utilize the Internet and other information technology productively, billions must be invested in much-needed building repairs and new construction, and the special problems of at-risk children in urban schools must be addressed more effectively.[61]

Putting state education reforms into practice requires the enthusiastic cooperation of many fragmented interests, including teachers, school administrators, superintendents, students, parents, and levels of government, each with their own interests and turf to defend. Triumph over this fractured policy subsystem will come only through civic action that mobilizes a vast array of public, private, and nonprofit actors and interests into a united front committed to reform over the long term—decades or more.[62] The unfinished portrait for educational excellence has been framed by governors, legislatures, the state education community, and the national government. The local schools must now fill in the details. And the states must encourage innovation and creative thinking at the local level while maintaining standards and accountability.

The national government has an important and legitimate role. State and local reform efforts are hobbled by childhood poverty, single-parent families, and other social problems that the national government can help address. And by funding and disseminating the results of research and experimental projects, the national government can elevate capacity and stimulate state and local innovation by state and local school districts. So far, NCLB has been perceived as exceedingly intrusive and costly. It certainly provides no final answer to the persistent problems of public education. If the incremental education reforms fail to move us toward these objectives, radical rethinking and restructuring of American public education may well be needed.

CHAPTER RECAP

- Education is the single most important—and most costly—function in state and local government.
- The public perceives a crisis in the public schools; criticism involves standards, student performance, teachers, and the education bureaucracy.
- The activities of state and local actors and the education establishment largely determine policy development and outcomes.
- Despite much political rhetoric in the past, the role of the national government in education policy has become more important with No Child Left Behind.
- The education establishment has fragmented, and the new key policy actors are governors, legislatures, courts, private schools, the business community, and the national government.
- A wave of education innovations in the states has raised standards, attempted to improve student retention and performance, hiked teacher salaries and benefits, and attempted to address a critical shortage of classroom teachers.
- The most controversial innovations have involved various school-choice programs, including magnet and charter schools and vouchers.
- The problems of reforming public education are multifaceted and complex, requiring the continual attention of government at all levels.

Key Terms

outcomes-based or performance-based
    education (p. 441)
school choice (p. 444)

magnet school (p. 444)
open enrollment program (p. 444)

Surfing the Web

For the National Report Card on state school systems, see **www.edweek.org.** This site may also be used to access informative articles on school reform in *Education Week.*

School-finance data are available from the National Center for Education Statistics at **www.nces.ed.gov** and on the U.S. Department of Education's web site at **www.ed.gov.**

State education agencies may be explored at **www.csso.org,** home for the Council of Chief State School Officers.

One of the best places to go for education-policy information and trends is the web site of the Education Commission of the States at **www.ecs.org.**

Teacher-salary data and education-policy analysis may be found on the American Federation of Teachers' web site at **www.aft.org** and at **www.nea.org,** the web site of the National Education Association.

Check out the Governance and Finance Institute web site for information on policy research, including charter schools, at **www.ed.gov/offices/OERI/ GFI/index.html.**

CRIMINAL JUSTICE

In 1990, New York City had been experiencing several years of a murder epidemic. During that year, 2,245 people were murdered in the city. Tourism activity dropped precipitously, the city's economy was weakening, and the city itself had become the butt of jokes on late-night talk shows. Something needed to be done and soon. By 2003, New York City's homicides numbered just 587—a rate well below that of nearly every other large U.S. city when population was taken into account.

How has the nation's largest city reduced the number of homicides and all other serious crimes at a nation-leading pace? In two ways: First, elected officials significantly bulked up the chronically underfunded law enforcement budget, permitting thousands of new police officers to be hired and much-needed new crime-fighting equipment to be purchased. Second, Police Chief Bill Bratton led the development of a new crime-fighting approach called COMPSTAT. Based on specialized crime units, precinct-level deployment grounded in daily statistical updates, and individual- and group-performance accountability systems, COMPSTAT helped New York City police attack criminal activity ranging from petty street crime (windshield cleaners harassing motorists for money) to the grave (drive-by shootings). Today, New York City–style policing is rapidly spreading across the country, having already been adopted successfully by Los Angeles, Baltimore, Philadelphia, New Orleans, and other large cities.[1]

Just over ten years ago, crime was seemingly out of control throughout the United States. As the case of New York City illustrates, however, a remarkable turnaround has occurred. The national violent crime rate has fallen to its lowest level since 1966. Property crime has dropped nearly as dramatically. A general decline in illegal drug use and trade accounts for some of the improvement. But these remarkable figures also indicate that states and local governments are re-

A police officer fires a Taser stun gun, which delivers a paralyzing electric shock at a range of fifteen feet. *SOURCE:* © Reuters/CORBIS.

sponding creatively and forcefully to the crime challenge and making significant headway in the fight against crime. More police officers on the streets, more criminals behind bars, fewer guns in the hands of violent criminals, community policing programs, and improved law enforcement technology receive much of the credit, along with an extended period of economic and employment growth.

HOW MUCH CRIME IS THERE?

Crime data are available from two major sources: the Federal Bureau of Investigation's (FBI's) *Uniform Crime Reports* and victimization surveys. The FBI's annual crime index, drawn from 17,000 state and local law enforcement agencies nationwide, covers four kinds of violent crime (assault, murder, rape, robbery) and four categories of property crime (arson, burglary, larceny, motor vehicle theft). It tracked a sharp increase in criminal behavior between 1960 and 1980, during which time the rate of violent crime tripled and that of property crime more than doubled. Beginning in 1981, the rates of both types of crime began to drop. During the 1980s, a seesaw pattern prevailed, with crime rates varying from year to year, but with no clear trend apparent. In 2000, the nation's crime rate fell for the ninth consecutive year, and violent crimes had fallen to 1966 levels. Criminal activity ticked upward slightly in 2001, but since then has resumed its decline.[2]

Paradoxically, a persistently high fear of crime exists in the face of a declining crime rate. Critics claim that television and newspapers emphasize dramatic and bloody crime stories to gain audiences, readership, and advertisers, and that television and movies pander to citizen fears with cops and robbers, murder and mayhem. Politicians have not escaped criticism either for their campaign bombast, simplistic sloganeering, and empty gestures.

The FBI's statistics are suspect, however—for three reasons. First, they reflect only those crimes reported to local police departments. It is estimated that only two out of every five crimes are officially known to the police. Second, some types of crime are more likely to be reported than others. In addition, police have an incentive to underreport crime to make jurisdictions appear safer than they are. Murders and auto thefts are almost always reported, whereas larceny and rape victims, whether out of embarrassment, fear, or other reasons, may remain silent. Third, the FBI's crime data include only eight types of criminal behavior. Most white-collar crimes and drug crimes are excluded, despite the fact that their numbers are growing. Thus, the index provides only a partial picture of actual criminal activity.

Because of these disadvantages, a second, more accurate approach to measuring crime is used. *Victimization surveys* scientifically poll approximately 76,000 residents of jurisdictions across the country, asking them whether they or members of their households have been victims of crime during a specified recent time period. Long utilized by large metropolitan areas and some states,

| FIGURE 16.1 | Crime Trends, 1973–2003 |

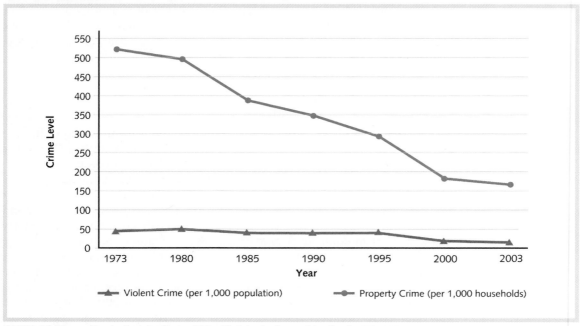

SOURCE: U.S. Bureau of Justice Statistics, *National Crime Victimization Survey, Crime Trends 1973–2003.*

victimization surveys have been conducted on a nationwide basis by the U.S. Bureau of the Census since 1973. Victimization statistics show identifiable patterns (see Figure 16.1). Men are more likely to be crime victims than women are, blacks more than whites or Hispanics, young people more than old, urban residents more than rural. According to the National Crime Survey, the true rate of crime is nearly two-and-one-half times greater than that reported by the *Uniform Crime Reports.* Yet even here, the rates of nearly all types of crime have declined markedly.

Prediction is problematic because we do not really know what causes crime. We can state authoritatively, however, that it is associated with certain factors. From a broad perspective, criminal activity is normally associated with economic recessions and joblessness. Crime is most likely to be committed by young males. Approximately half of the arrests for FBI index crimes in any given year are of males under the age of twenty.[3] Crime rates are higher in densely populated cities and states than in rural areas. Urban areas present more targets of opportunity, various sociocultural problems that promote criminal behavior, a better chance of escape for criminals, and a haven for gangs.[4] Crime also appears to be related to poverty, unemployment, marital instability, drug abuse (particularly of crack cocaine and methamphetamines), and race.[5] And some studies show that violence on television and in other popular forms of entertainment spawns aggressive behavior by the viewers.

But the issue is more complex than the studies cited above depict. Businesspeople are convicted of insider trading and other white-collar crimes on Wall Street that cost their victims millions of dollars. Some wealthy contractors rig bids on government construction projects and Pentagon defense contracts; some bankers embezzle money; some judges accept bribes; the occasional priest or minister sodomizes a child. The underlying causes of these and other sad cases cannot be attributed to economic deprivation, age, neighborhood, race, or the entertainment industry. Greed certainly contributes to many crimes; the origins of others remain unknown.[6]

Although reasonable people disagree about the causes of crime, most agree that law enforcement is not as effective as it should be in apprehending and deterring criminals. Fewer than 17 percent of all property crimes reported to the police are "cleared" by an arrest. For violent crimes, the record is better: approximately 47 percent.[7] Probably two-thirds of the arrests, however, do not result in a conviction or in any sort of punishment for the offender. Extrapolation from these somewhat rough estimates indicates that a criminal has only a slight chance—maybe one in a hundred—of being arrested and punished for a crime.

Throwing money at the problem does not seem to be the final answer; research has been unable to find a strong link between higher police expenditures on personnel and materials and a subsequent reduction in crime. Obviously, *how* the money is spent makes a difference. Most criminal activities cannot be prevented by law enforcement officials, and unreported crimes are very difficult to investigate. More prisons and longer sentences appear to have only a small effect on crime rates, as do gun control laws (see *Debating Politics* box). Factors that *do* appear to be associated with higher arrest rates, and lower crime rates as well, are related to the attitude and tactical deployment of police officers, as the New York City case indicates. Aggressive and active police work in responding to calls from citizens and in investigating criminal events seems to help, as does the use of one-officer instead of two-officer patrol units for a more widespread police presence.

Community policing is the popular terminology for a hands-on law enforcement approach. Typically, officers are assigned specific territorial areas of responsibility and encouraged to use their imagination and experience in fighting crime, a technique that also promises results. Police work with citizens and with relevant government and nonprofit organizations to identify problems and solve them creatively. If drug houses and junkies infest a community, the citizens and community police officer find a way to run them out. Minor troublemakers are dealt with before they become big-time offenders. To be effective, officers must add community organizing and social work to their law enforcement duties to make their assigned neighborhood one in which they would themselves like to live.

Political scientist James Q. Wilson developed the concept underlying community policing (and later the COMPSTAT approach) in a 1982 article with George L. Kelling entitled "Broken Windows." In the authors' words, "If a window in a building is broken and is left unrepaired, all the rest of the windows will soon be broken."[8] The message of a broken window is that no one cares. Of course, the metaphor doesn't apply only to broken windows but all manifestations of neighborhood decay, including public consumption of alcohol and

DEBATING POLITICS

Concealed Weapons Permits . . . Or, Will There Be Shootouts Over the Last Mustard Packet at Burger King?

Americans are of a decidedly mixed mind when it comes to guns on the street. On one hand, a national outcry against gun violence has been raised, based on the facts that firearms are the second leading cause of death for teenagers and young adults (surpassed only by motor vehicle accidents) and that hospital bills, emotional damage, and related problems from gunshot wounds cost society over $100 billion annually. At the national level, the Brady bill established a five-day waiting period and a criminal records check for handgun purchases. But in 1997, the U.S. Supreme Court ruled the Brady bill unconstitutional (see Chapter 2). Many states have gun-control laws that impose background checks, waiting periods, and other restrictions on individuals wanting to buy a handgun. Massachusetts, which has the strictest handgun laws, bans Saturday Night Specials and requires childproof locks on all guns sold in the state. And some states and localities, in efforts to get guns off the streets and out of houses, have sponsored gun-exchange programs in which cash, gift certificates, expensive sneakers, and even personal computers are offered in exchange for guns. (The next step, of course, is to determine what to *do* with the guns. Detroit, Boston, and Los Angeles have *resold* them, thus putting guns back on the street.)

Paradoxically, a trend has been to legalize the carrying of concealed weapons. Beginning with Florida in 1987, forty other states have passed such laws. Some of them impose safeguards, including those noted earlier, to keep guns out of the hands of criminals. In Texas, a concealed-weapons permit requires the applicant to take a proficiency exam and to undergo ten to fifteen hours of classes in sensitivity training and conflict-resolution techniques specifically designed to prevent verbal disagreements from becoming violent confrontations. In several states, gun owners may not take their "piece" into public buildings or establishments that serve alcohol. Other state laws, such as those in Florida, Mississippi, and Pennsylvania, contain minimal restrictions, permitting the issuance of permits to any adult who has not been convicted of a felony or who does not have a documented mental health problem.

Proponents of concealed-weapons laws maintain that they make law-abiding citizens safer by giving them a way to defend themselves against criminals and that they make streets and homes safer by encouraging prospective criminals to think twice before accosting a potentially armed citizen. Those against liberal gun laws fear that shootouts at traffic lights and on interstate highways could occur as a result of road rage, and they fear an increase in gun-related accidents involving children. Even the law enforcement community is divided. Some are convinced that weapons will deter crime and help vulnerable people protect themselves when police are not around. For other police officers, their worst nightmare is for armed shoppers to pull out their weapons and open fire at a purse-snatcher or shoplifter in a crowded Wal-Mart.

What do you think? Should anyone who so desires be permitted to carry a handgun on his or her person or in a vehicle? What restrictions would you impose? Should this dilemma be resolved by federal law or by state law? If you were hired as a consultant by the state of Florida or Pennsylvania to examine the impact of their gun laws on crime and on violence, how would you proceed? What potential pitfalls would you endeavor to avoid in your study?

SOURCES: Philip J. Cook and Jens Ludwig, *Gun Violence: The Real Costs* (New York: Oxford University Press, 2001); M.V. Hood III and Grant W. Neeley, "Packin' in the Hood? Examining Assumptions of Concealed Handgun Research," *Social Science Quarterly* 81 (June 2000): 523–37; John R. Lott and David B. Mustard, "Crime, Deterrence, and the Right to Carry Concealed Handguns," *Journal of Legal Studies* 26, no. 1 (1997): 1–68.

drugs, drug dealing, hookers on street corners, aggressive panhandlers, graffiti, and gang activity. Visual deterioration of a neighborhood leads to social degeneration. By preventing or correcting visible manifestations of neighborhood decline, or by "repairing" the "broken windows," neighborhoods will host fewer criminal activities, and positive forces can take root and flourish. Community policing and attention to "broken windows" appear to be at least partly responsible for the dramatic decline in violent crime in New York City, Boston, Fort Worth, and other large cities during the past few years.

Technological applications for crime fighting are developing rapidly and show much promise. Computer-based fingerprint identification systems and other data-sharing systems track criminals across multiple jurisdictions. Computer mapping of crime hot spots and trends, as pioneered by New York City's COMPSTAT, facilitates police planning and response by linking crime statistics to geographic information systems. Electronic-surveillance systems such as video cameras and acoustic sensors can detect crime activity and even identify a weapon type by the sound of the discharge. Commercial cell-phone translation services break through language barriers almost instantaneously. And DNA tests can positively match criminals to evidence found at crime scenes.[9]

Innovative activity by police agencies is on the rise. Imaginative and surprisingly effective sting operations have led fugitives to innocently turn themselves in to law enforcement officials. In Ohio, more than 100 fugitives showed up in person to collect a phony cash award from a class-action lawsuit, only to be handcuffed by waiting sheriffs' deputies. At New York's Riker's Island jail, fugitives who come to visit their buddies are commonly apprehended. As noted earlier, the application of advanced technology to crime is also on the rise. San Diego's bait-and-switch-off operation nabs car thieves who try to steal specially equipped vehicles. Once the thief breaks into the vehicle, police are notified electronically. Via remote control, police officers can lock the doors, close the windows, and turn off the engine. Audio monitors have the added benefit of recording the criminal's sometimes humorous verbal reactions to his plight.[10]

INTERGOVERNMENTAL ROLES IN CRIMINAL JUSTICE

The problems with the U.S. system of criminal justice cannot be attributed to a lack of human and material resources. More than 1.6 million employees work full-time in national, state, and local police and corrections agencies. Total state and local expenditures are more than $110 billion.[11]

The states and localities hold jurisdiction over more than 95 percent of all crimes that occurs in the United States. Municipal police departments carry much of the load of law enforcement, employing approximately 60 percent of all sworn police employees; counties employ 30 percent; and the state law enforcement organizations (highway patrol and special agencies) employ just over

9 percent.[12] These state and local entities enforce state laws and local ordinances. Federal crimes such as treason, kidnapping, and counterfeiting are dealt with by the FBI and processed through the federal courts and correctional system. The two systems are separate, but some cooperation occurs. For instance, the FBI and state law enforcement agencies exchange information such as fingerprints and details of the movements of fugitives, suspected terrorists, and drug smugglers; they also sometimes work together in criminal investigations, as they have in numerous drug busts and anti-terrorist activities.

Nine out of every ten dollars spent on police protection and corrections come from the coffers of state and local government—an illustration of the decentralized nature of criminal justice spending in the United States. The national government's resources are concentrated on its own enforcement and corrections agencies. However, Washington has provided certain forms of direct financial assistance to the states and localities.

Recent presidents talked tough on crime but delivered little in terms of new funding, with the exception of their multibillion-dollar war on drugs, which was highly touted but dismally ineffective. President Clinton and Congress did deliver a crime bill that provided $8.8 billion in grants to help state and local agencies hire "100,000 cops" and $7.9 billion to build more prisons.

Greater national involvement in state and local law enforcement appears necessary given the rise in new types of cybercrime; the growing economic, political, and global dimensions of organized crime and drug trafficking; the ever-present threat of terrorist acts; and the fact that criminal activities do not respect national, state, or local jurisdictional boundaries. States and localities can only do so much to combat the poverty, poor housing, inadequate education, and other social and economic conditions that are conducive to crime.

THE ONGOING CHALLENGE OF CRIME FIGHTING

As noted, the vast amount of dollars spent on law enforcement come from the coffers of states and localities. Congress provides plenty of rhetoric but relatively little material assistance. In the majority of jurisdictions, crime is under control and citizens feel relatively safe. But many jurisdictions, particularly in urban poverty areas, are victims of demographics. High poverty rates, dysfunctional families, free-flowing illegal drug markets, violent gangs—all these factors are invariably associated with high rates of crime. The hard-pressed police often find themselves simply trying to cope with the worst crimes. There is little opportunity for crime-prevention activities, and law enforcement agencies acting alone lack the capability to improve socioeconomic and other conditions conducive to criminal activity. As for politicians, it is easy for them to talk tough on crime. For the cop on the street, tough and immediate judgment calls must often be made: arrest or mediate in a domestic dispute? Call for backup now or deal with the situation first? Does this berserk moron have a gun?

What about suspicious behavior in a vehicle? Black men driving through a wealthy white neighborhood raise suspicions, but does stopping them without cause amount to racial profiling for "driving while black"? Such profiling of African Americans and Hispanics has been well-documented anecdotally and in several empirical studies,[13] but the tactic is highly questionable in terms of constitutionality and fundamental fairness. Perception of racial bias corrodes public faith and trust in the criminal justice system.

ACTORS IN CRIMINAL JUSTICE POLICY

There is a large cast of actors in state and local criminal justice systems. State policy leadership is exercised by the governor, who sets the tone for the pursuit of law and order through State of the State addresses, proposed legislation, and public presentations. During the past few years, few governors have not announced a new crime prevention and law enforcement program.

Besides being involved in judicial selection in several states, legislative bodies establish the structure of the legal system, decide which behaviors constitute a violation of law, and determine sentencing parameters, including the option of capital punishment. Legislatures tend to be responsive to citizen pressures on law enforcement issues, as demonstrated by recent legislative activity in areas such as gun control, the death penalty, and sentencing reform.

Law Enforcement Officials

The state attorney general formally heads the law enforcement function in most states; county and city attorneys and district attorneys generally follow the attorney general's lead. These positions call for a great deal of discretion in deciding whom to prosecute for what alleged crimes or civil violations. The prosecution of offenses is a politically charged endeavor, particularly when it is within the authority of people who aspire to higher political office. On the other side of the courtroom are public defenders and private defense attorneys, who try to get their clients declared innocent.

The state troopers (highway patrol), special state law enforcement divisions modeled on the FBI, county sheriffs, police chiefs, and local line and staff officers and civilian employees are also important. They are responsible for enforcing the policies decided on by elected officials and for carrying out the basic day-to-day activities connected with enforcing the law.

The Courts

State and local courts decide the innocence or guilt of defendants brought before them, based on the evidence submitted (see Chapter 9). In the great majority of cases, however, plea bargaining prevails and the case never goes to trial. Courts can also influence criminal justice through rulings that specify correct police procedures in criminal cases. U.S. Supreme Court decisions, in particular, have shaped the criminal justice process. The federal courts have the final word on cases in which the defendants claim that their federal rights have been violated by state or local law enforcement personnel. State courts handle alleged violations of state constitutional rights.

Critics have asserted that the Supreme Court under Chief Justice Earl Warren made it more difficult to convict criminals through decisions that expanded the rights of the accused. The first of these famous cases was *Gideon* v. *Wainwright* (1963), in which the Warren Court ruled that all accused persons have a constitutional right to be defended by counsel. If they cannot afford to pay an attorney, the state or locality must provide one free of charge.[14] The second ruling, *Escobedo* v. *Illinois* (1964), required that the accused be informed of the right to remain silent at the time of arrest.[15]

The often-cited case of *Miranda* v. *Arizona* (1966) further expanded the rights of the accused. It requires police officers to inform anyone suspected of a crime of the right to remain silent; the fact that anything said can and will be used against him or her in a court of law; and the right to be represented by counsel, paid for by the state if necessary.[16] Evidence obtained when the accused has not clearly indicated his understanding of these Miranda warnings or explicitly waived his rights is not legally admissible in the courtroom because it is considered a violation of the Fifth Amendment right not to incriminate oneself.

The Supreme Court cited evidence showing that before the *Miranda* decision, it was not uncommon for police to extract confessions from suspects by wearing them down through physical or psychological abuse, or misrepresenting or lying to them about their rights regarding self-incrimination and counsel. Many believed that *Miranda* would severely harm police efforts to obtain confessions and thereby result in some criminals going free. Post-*Miranda* research seems to confirm that confessions are now less likely to serve as the basis for convictions.[17] However, many accused criminals decline to exercise their *Miranda* rights and spill the beans anyway, maybe because they feel a strong sense of guilt or because they fail to comprehend the full implications of the warnings. And in the vast majority of cases, sufficient material evidence or testimony from witnesses can convict without a confession; law enforcement officers must simply work a bit harder to obtain it. In fact, although the Supreme Court threw out Miranda's confession, he was later found guilty because of the overwhelming physical evidence against him. Subsequent to the Warren Court, the Supreme Court has issued a series of decisions that narrow the scope of *Miranda*. Despite these rulings, the basic principles of *Miranda* have not been overturned and were indeed affirmed in the 2000 Supreme Court decision of *Dickerson* v. *United States*.[18]

The U.S. Supreme Court also influenced state and local criminal procedure in the case of *Mapp* v. *Ohio* (1961). Basing its decision on the due process clause of the Fourteenth Amendment, the Warren Court ruled that evidence obtained illegally by the police cannot be introduced in court.[19] This exclusionary rule extended the Fourth Amendment's protection from illegal search and seizure. The police must have a search warrant specifying what person or place will be searched and what will be seized. However, the Supreme Court later eased this requirement, particularly in circumstances in which the police were acting in good faith. Other Supreme Court decisions permit police to ask to search the belongings of auto and bus passengers without suspicion of wrongdoing, and to search all closed containers in a vehicle even when they have neither a search warrant nor probable cause to suspect that a particular container contains contraband.[20] Driver's license and driving-under-the-influence (DUI) checkpoints conveniently present police with such opportunities. But police cannot search people and their vehicles after merely ticketing them for routine traffic violations.[21] And police use of roadblocks and drug-sniffing dogs to search random motorists was held to be a violation of the Fourth Amendment prohibition against search and seizure if they are not based on a suspicion of wrongdoing or probable cause.[22] Similar types of constitutional questions are now being reviewed by the courts in cases involving electronic eavesdropping.

The Public's Involvement

Another participant in justice policy is the voting public. Citizens make demands on officials (the governor, legislators, judges, police, and so on) to conform to public opinion on crimes and criminals. Generally, the pressure is for more law and order, and it results in stricter criminal codes and correctional policies. Citizens also participate directly in the criminal justice system by serving on juries, which are selected from driver's license lists, tax returns, or registered-voter rolls. Most citizens consider it their public duty to serve on a jury from time to time, and such service does tend to be an interesting (if not always edifying) experience. Occasionally, a jury trial will drag out over a lengthy period; one of the longest was concluded in 1987, in Belleville, Illinois, after a forty-four-month marathon concerning liability for a toxic chemical spill. Attorneys for the losing party then announced that they would appeal.[23]

grand jury

A group of citizens appointed to determine if there is enough evidence to bring a person to trial.

Citizens also participate in criminal justice by sitting on grand juries. A **grand jury** (which is typically composed of twelve members) serves as a check on the power of the state or local prosecutor by considering evidence in a case, then deciding whether to indict the accused. Twenty states require a grand jury **indictment** for serious crime. In other states, it is optional, or a preliminary hearing of charges and evidence before a judge is used instead. Grand juries are usually organized on a county or district basis. In practice, they are inclined to rubber-stamp whatever course of action is recommended by the prosecutor. Rarely does one question the professional legal opinion of the district attorney or attorney general.

indictment

A formal, written accusation submitted to a court by a grand jury, alleging a specified crime.

An additional function of the grand jury is to act as an investigatory body for certain types of crimes, especially vice, political corruption, and organized crime. In this capacity, it is empowered to issue subpoenas for suspects and evidence that it wishes to examine. A statewide grand jury is most appropriate for criminal investigations because it can deal with activities that cross county or district boundaries. Among the states that provide for statewide grand juries are Arizona, Colorado, Florida, New Jersey, South Carolina, and Virginia.

Finally, the public may become involved in the criminal justice process by tackling crime on their own. Telephone and Web-based crime report lines, neighborhood complaints of prostitution, drug dealing, or gang activity, and similar actions to report "broken windows" help take a bite out of crime. Neighborhood watches and patrols help detect and deter criminal presence.

The Victim

The last influence on criminal justice policy is the one most frequently ignored in the past—the victim. Many victims are left psychologically, physically, and/or financially injured after a crime. States have responded to this sad fact by developing victim-compensation programs. These programs are typically administered by a board, which assesses the validity of victims' claims and decides on a monetary award to help compensate for hospital and doctor bills, loss of property, and other financial needs resulting from the crime. Maximum benefits, paid for in part by the federal Victims of Violent Crime and Their Families Act, usually vary from $10,000 to $25,000, depending on the state. Rarely is a victim made whole by these limited payments, but at least some assistance is provided to help the person deal with the various traumas of the crime. All states now permit use of victim-impact statements in court before sentencing a convicted criminal. The statements may include victims' and family members' views on how the crime has affected them, and their feelings about the crime and the accused. Most states and many counties now provide victim-notification systems so crime victims are made aware of their assailants' subsequent prison release. In Kentucky, victims can even call a toll-free hotline to check on a prisoner's status.[24] Finally, Megan's law requires notification of a community when a convicted sex offender moves into the neighborhood. (Megan was a seven-year-old girl who was sexually assaulted and murdered by a neighbor who had recently been released from prison after serving time as a sex offender.) At least thirty-five states post their sex offender registry on the Web.[25]

HOW POLICY PARTICIPANTS INTERACT: TWO POLICY AREAS

All states do not treat similar crimes in the same manner. The states' handling of crimes in two policy areas—victimless crimes and capital punishment—illuminates this point.

Victimless Crime

Prostitution, pornography, illegal drug use, music and movie pirating, and failing to wear seatbelts or motorcycle helmets are all examples of victimless crimes. Statutes enacted by legislative bodies define what constitutes criminal behavior, and public opinion usually influences what activities the legislatures treat as criminal. **Victimless crimes** are voluntary acts that violate the law but are perceived by some to present little or no threat to society. Up to 50 percent of all arrests in urban areas is estimated to include victimless crimes.

victimless crimes
Illegal acts that, in theory, do no one any harm.

Some people argue that such crimes should be wiped off the books because those who engage in these activities suffer willingly (if at all). A strong case can be made for legalizing, regulating, and taxing prostitution and drugs. People will pursue these activities anyway, the argument goes, so why criminalize a large portion of the population unnecessarily? Instead, why not get a little piece of the action for the public purse? State regulation of gambling helps diminish the role of organized crime in gambling, and regulation of prostitution could help prevent the spread of sexually transmitted diseases by requiring regular medical checkups for prostitutes. Almost every state permits some form of gambling, such as casinos, lotteries, bingo, and betting on horse or dog racing, but only Nevada has legalized and regulated prostitution. Finally, legalizing drugs promises to take the profits out of the drug trade and to reduce drug-related crime and corruption. About one-third of all new state prisoners have been convicted of drug-related crimes. The tens of billions of dollars spent by the United States on the war on drugs have resulted in a pathetic failure, leaving us today with just as many addicts, swelling prison populations, an enormously profitable importation and distribution system that lures young people and even grade-school children into the trade, and a great deal of drug-related violence. By shifting drug enforcement money and efforts to medical and psychiatric treatment of addicts and users, perhaps legalization would even lead to less addiction. Indeed, research indicates that treatment is seven times more effective in reducing the consumption of cocaine than is attacking its supply channels.[26]

In states where legislative bodies define the scope of criminal behavior broadly to include victimless crimes, an extra burden is placed on other actors in the criminal justice system. Prosecutors and law enforcement authorities find much of their time consumed by these relatively minor and nonthreatening activities when they could be concentrating on more serious crimes, such as murder, rape, and robbery. The courts must also spend a great deal of time on processing these cases. The legalization of victimless crimes would immediately shorten the dockets of prosecutors, police, and judges; render the process more manageable; and reduce the burgeoning prison and jail population. A less radical strategy is *decriminalization*—the prescribing of a minor penalty (usually a small fine) for certain crimes. For example, a handful of states and localities have decriminalized possession of small amounts of marijuana. Nine states (Vermont being the latest in 2004) have legalized the use of marijuana for prescribed medical purposes.

Opponents claim that *victimless* is the wrong word to describe these actions. For example, with the selling of sex, prostitutes and their clients can become infected with the HIV virus and other communicable diseases. It is not uncommon for prostitutes to commit other types of crime and endure serious emotional costs. Legalization of drugs such as methamphetamines, heroin, or crack cocaine might lead to a significant rise in addiction rates and require higher taxes for treatment and health care. And if legalization were selective (say, only marijuana, cocaine, and ecstasy were made available legally) new, more powerful designer drugs would likely debut on the market.

In practice, hard-pressed prosecutors often drop charges against perpetrators of victimless crimes, judges dismiss the least offensive cases or administer a small fine or a suspended sentence, and law enforcement personnel tend to look the other way when passing near a prostitute or a pot smoker. De facto decriminalization is the norm for many victimless crimes in much of the United States, especially in the case of prohibited sexual behavior between consenting adults, including sodomy, adultery, and the ever-popular fornication.

Capital Punishment

Capital punishment offers a second example of how states vary in their approach to crime. In this area, the interactions among individuals and institutions are critically important. Public opinion helps determine a legislature's propensity to enact a death penalty statute. Prosecutors must decide under what circumstances to seek the death penalty. Only juries can find a defendant guilty or innocent in a capital case. Judges must enforce the penalty of death, subject to lengthy appellate review. Governors have the power to commute a sentence of execution. And the federal courts have played an important role in determining the conditions under which a state can legally put a person to death for a crime.

Criminal executions were once commonplace in the United States. In colonial days, public hangings were considered appropriate for adulterers, religious heretics, blasphemers, and thieves. A total of 717 people were legally executed during the 1950s. But public opinion began to turn against capital punishment (only two individuals were executed in 1967), and so did the U.S. Supreme Court. In the 1972 case of *Furman* v. *Georgia,* a 5-to-4 majority held that the death penalty had been applied in a cruel, arbitrary, and racist manner by the states.[27] The Supreme Court expressly declared unconstitutional the capital-punishment statutes in Louisiana and North Carolina and implicitly invalidated similar laws in many other states. It held that death penalty laws could be valid only if used in accordance with correct procedures and standards and could be invoked solely for lethal crimes.

The Rehnquist Court has taken a somewhat less restrictive approach to capital punishment. In a 1987 case, again involving Georgia (*McCleskey* v. *Kemp*), the Court dismissed an allegation that the new death penalty statute was being utilized in a discriminatory way.[28] Since then, the Court has ruled that the use of the death penalty for those who committed crimes while juveniles (*Stanford* v. *Kentucky*) is not unconstitutional and it has limited federal court review of death penalties (*Herrera* v. *Collins* and *Vasquez* v. *Harris*).[29] In one seemingly bizarre 2003 case, the Court let stand lower court rulings that Arkansas could forcibly administer drugs to an insane murderer to render him sane enough to be executed.[30] However, the Court did ban the execution of a retarded murderer in 2002.

Several states voluntarily abolished capital punishment in the 1960s and 1970s. The majority, however, rewrote their statutes to conform with the Supreme Court's guidelines. Thirty-eight states have death penalty laws in place today (see Figure 16.2). These laws provide for execution by lethal injection (thirty-seven states), electrocution (nine states), lethal gas (four states), hanging (three states), or firing squad (Idaho, Oklahoma, and Utah). Some states permit more than one method of execution. Those supportive of the death penalty tend to have both a politically conservative population and a high murder rate. Some 3,500 inmates were languishing on death row in state penitentiaries in 2003. While statutes were being rewritten and clarified between 1968 and 1976, no executions were carried out. Since January 1977, however, 850 people have made the long walk from death row to the death chamber, more than 80 percent of them in the South. Texas is the leading executioner; the state used lethal injection to execute 286 people between 1976 and November 2002.[31]

Public opinion polls indicate that more than half of the American people still favor capital punishment, but a growing proportion favor life without parole instead. It remains a rather tedious and enormously expensive endeavor. The prisoners executed in 2002 had spent, on average, nearly eleven years on death row. The appeals process presents numerous opportunities for delay, and it is not unusual for an inmate, after languishing for a decade or more on death row, to escape the death penalty through the legal process. The price tag on death is shocking, averaging an estimated $2 million for each prisoner executed.

One troublesome aspect of the death penalty is that African Americans receive this form of punishment well out of proportion to their numbers. Although black people make up about 12 percent of the U.S. population, 34 percent of those executed since 1977 have been black, and 41 percent of death-row inmates are black.[32] Blacks who kill whites are significantly more likely to be sentenced to death. Less than 2 percent of those condemned to death since 1977 have been women, and very few women have been executed.[33] Under various U.S. Supreme Court rulings, states are required to write sentencing guidelines that consider factors related to the offender and the nature of the offense when deciding between a life sentence and death, yet the ultimate sentence must not

FIGURE 16.2	**States with Capital Punishment**

Most states permit capital punishment, although some have not actually carried out the death penalty for many years. For states that have allowed executions since 1977, the number executed is indicated in the map.

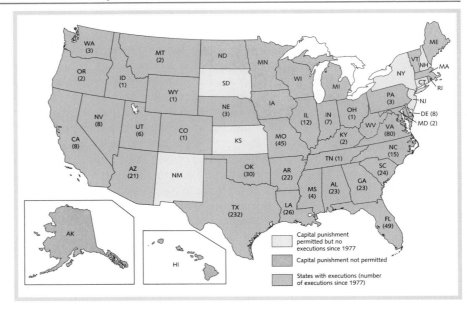

be idiosyncratic or capricious. Critics of the death penalty claim, however, that it is applied capriciously, from the decision of a prosecutor to ask the jury to determine that a given crime is a capital offense to the requisite review of a jury's death sentence by the state supreme court. The offender's race is definitely a consideration, as noted earlier. And according to one study, those who murder police officers, women, the elderly, or multiple victims are more likely to be sentenced to death, as are those who kill after a sexual assault or robbery.[34]

Obviously, a great deal of controversy continues to surround the issue of executing criminals. Researchers generally agree that if punishment is to discourage future criminal behavior, it must be swift and certain. Neither of these conditions is met by the death penalty in the United States. And few reasonable and informed people today argue that capital punishment acts as a deterrent, except in the specific case of the individual who is executed. Studies comparing homicide rates in states with and without death penalties either find no significant differences or that states with capital punishment actually have higher rates of homicide. Also disturbing is the fact that the personal characteristics of judges influence their decisions. Republicans are much more likely to vote for the death penalty, as are older judges and those with previous experience as a prosecutor.[35] In this sense, the death penalty resembles a lottery. Application of the death penalty can also be cruel and unusual punishment in more ways than one. Florida's "Old Sparky" overheated, causing flames and smoke to erupt from a leather mask worn by the unfortunate murderer, Pedro Medina. (This gruesome scene helped to convince Florida officials to replace the electric chair with lethal injection.) Perhaps most distressful of all aspects of the death penalty is the possibility that an innocent party might be executed.

Since 2000, the public has become increasingly ambivalent about the death penalty because of growing evidence of serious problems in the justice system. Studies found that two of every three death sentences are eventually overturned, usually due to errors by incompetent defense attorneys or evidence withheld by prosecutors and police officers. Calls for a moratorium on executions have grown louder. In 2000, Illinois Governor George Ryan, a proponent of the death penalty, halted capital punishment in his state and commuted the sentences of 167 death-row inmates to life imprisonment, citing the findings that thirteen death-row inmates were subsequently found innocent since 1977.[36] Concern is growing that innocent people are being put to death by states. DNA testing makes identification of a killer a statistical certainty when such evidence is available, and more states are demanding that DNA evidence be submitted before extinguishing a person's life.[37] Four inmates were exonerated and released from prison in 2004 in Illinois, two in Ohio, and one in each of four other states, all after being proven innocent by DNA testing.

On the side of those favoring the death penalty is the argument for the legitimacy of *lex talionis,* the principle that the punishment should fit the crime. According to this view, some crimes are so heinous that only the death of the perpetrator can balance the scales of justice and relieve the moral outrage of society. This argument for justice as retribution cannot be validated on empirical grounds; it is an ethical question that each individual must personally resolve.

CORRECTIONAL POLICY

A person convicted of a crime in a court of law becomes the object of correctional policy, which, as its name implies, aims to correct behavior that society finds unacceptable. It proposes to accomplish this daunting task in several ways. First, an offender should be punished, both for retribution and to deter future criminal behavior by the offender and by other potential criminals. Second, convicted lawbreakers should be rehabilitated so that they can become productive, law-abiding citizens after fulfilling the terms of their punishment. Third, criminals who represent a danger to society should be physically separated from the general public.

If correcting criminal behavior is the overarching goal of correctional policy in the states, we have a terrible policy failure on our hands. As already noted, most crimes do not result in an arrest. Even when an offender is detained by the police, she stands a good chance of avoiding conviction or incarceration. Thus, deterrence is a dubious proposition at best. Remember that the best way to prevent undesirable behavior is through swift and certain punishment. Those of us who quizzically stuck a foreign object into an electrical outlet in childhood received the shock of swift punishment. If we were foolish enough to try it a second time, we discovered that the punishment was certain. Only morons and masochists subject themselves to such abuse a third time. That is how our correctional policy would have to work if deterrence is to be achieved. But for various reasons, swift and certain punishment is improbable as long as we live in a humane, democratic society.

Rehabilitation was a correctional fad of the 1960s and 1970s that has largely been ignored since. The U.S. Department of Justice estimates that 67 percent of former inmates released from state prisons commit another serious crime within three years. It appears that prisons actually increase the likelihood that an individual will commit additional crimes when he is freed. Our state prisons have been called breeding pens for criminals. Instead of being rehabilitated, the first-time offender is likely to receive expert schooling in various criminal professions. Overcrowding, understaffing, physical and sexual brutality, gangs, and rampant drug abuse also make it unlikely that an offender will become a law-abiding citizen. Many schemes have been tried—counseling, vocational training, basic education, and others—but none have consistently been able to overcome the criminalizing environment of state prison systems.

Without doubt, most incarcerated offenders see deprivation of their freedom as punishment, and so retribution does occur. Just as surely, prison effectively removes undesirable characters from our midst. These two objectives of correctional policy are achieved to some degree, although cynics point out that sentencing tends to be rather inconsistent, and only about 50 percent of criminals serve at least half of their sentences before release. Most important, and contrary to the conventional wisdom, research consistently shows that state imprisonment rates are not significantly related to crime rates.[38] In fact, considering the notion of prisons as colleges for criminals, it might actually boost crime.

Sentencing

Sentencing reform has recently received a great deal of attention in the states. The inconsistency of criminal sentencing is obvious if we examine incarceration rates. In 2002, they varied from 790 inmates per 100,000 people in Louisiana to 137 in Maine (see Figure 16.3). Southern states tend to be toughest on crime: They are more than twice as likely as other states to convict people arrested on felony charges, and their sentences are more severe than those in other regions. As observed above, however, crime rates and incarceration rates are not closely related. Some states with relatively high rates of crime lock up fewer people than do other states with lower crime rates. One striking inconsistency is the extremely high lockup rate of African Americans in state and federal prisons: African Americans make up more than half of all such inmates but only about 12 percent of the nation's population. One out of every ten African American men is incarcerated today. This trend has been attributed to poverty and poor education, which drive up the black crime rate, as well as to the law enforcement focus on crack cocaine, which is found predominantly in the inner-city black commu-

FIGURE 16.3 **Prisoners in State and Federal Correctional Institutions, by State, as of June 30, 2002**

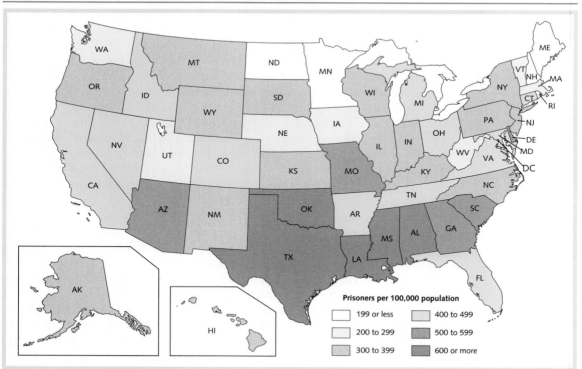

Prisoners per 100,000 population

199 or less	400 to 499
200 to 299	500 to 599
300 to 399	600 or more

SOURCE: BJS, *Prison and Jail Inmates at Midyear 2003*, U.S. Department of Justice, Office of Justice Programs (May 2004).

nity.[39] With more than 2 million prisoners, the United States has the highest incarceration rate in the world by far, averaging five to eight times higher than most industrialized countries.

indeterminate sentencing

Sentencing in which a judge exercises discretion when deciding on the number of years for the sentence.

Historically, state courts have applied **indeterminate sentencing,** whereby judges have great discretion in deciding the number of years for which an offender should be sentenced to prison. The offender then becomes eligible for parole after a minimum period is served. For instance, a ten- to twenty-year sentence for armed robbery will require the inmate to serve at least five years. After that time, he or she becomes eligible for parole, subject to the judgment of a parole board (usually appointed by the governor), which reviews the case and the prisoner's behavior in prison.

determinate sentencing

Mandatory sentencing that is determined by law, not a judge's discretion.

The recent trend has been **determinate sentencing,** in which offenders are given mandatory terms that they must serve without the possibility of parole. Under so-called truth-in-sentencing laws, about half the states require violent offenders to serve at least 85 percent of their sentences. Twenty-one states provide for the chilling sentence of "life without possibility of parole." Determinate sentencing is designed to reduce the sentencing disparity among judges. It also eliminates the need for parole. Inmates who stay out of trouble can be awarded "good time," which will deduct a limited amount of time from their prison terms.

Naturally, determinate sentencing keeps prisoners incarcerated for longer periods than indeterminate sentencing does. The generally punitive attitude that the public has taken toward criminals has helped stiffen not only the sentences awarded by judges but also the judgments of parole boards. Prison and jail populations have risen from 458 inmates per 100,000 persons in 1990 to 702 per 100,000 in 2002.[40] With over 2 million people incarcerated in federal, state, and local institutions, the resulting prison overcrowding is the nation's greatest crisis in corrections policy.

The situation is certainly not improved by the three-strikes-and-you're-out legislation that has been enacted in some twenty-six states. Such laws mandate tough sanctions for habitual felons who are convicted of a third violent or serious crime. In California, even a *minor* conviction can invoke a twenty-five-year to life sentence; one felon who stole a pizza in Redondo Beach is now doing twenty-five years. Another received fifty years to life for stealing videotapes from Kmart. The price tag for three strikes has been projected at billions of dollars annually for new prisons and their operating costs. New judges have to be hired and more courtrooms built to hear the increased number of jury trials. And despite the widespread media attention surrounding three-strikes laws in other states, they have rarely been used. Why? Because all states have long had statutes on the books that increase prison time for repeat criminals, so three-strikes laws have had little practical effect. States are rethinking mandatory minimum sentences for drug offenders. Connecticut, Louisiana, Maryland, Texas, and several other states have rolled them back, favoring drug treatment programs instead. California voters passed Proposition 36, an initiative in 2000 that mandates treatment rather than prison for first and second drug offenses. An estimated 36,000 drug offenders are eligible (drug dealers are exempted).

But more criminals *are* doing more time, and without some relief, prisons will be serving as expensive geriatric hospitals for relatively harmless criminals who are senior citizens. Already, states are grouping aging inmates within correctional facilities for their special health care needs as well as to protect them from younger, more violent inmates. The average yearly cost of housing a sickly, geriatric prisoner can run two to three times that of a younger, healthy inmate. Coupled with the "criminal menopause" that apparently afflicts felons in the twilight years, making them unlikely to commit a new crime, the rising costs are pressuring states to offer incarceration alternatives, such as parole, house arrest, and drug rehabilitation.

Prison Conditions

More than 2.0 million people are confined to state prisons and local jails in the United States. The number of prisoners has been growing by about 4 percent annually overall, and by as much as 12 percent in Vermont and 9 percent in Maine and Minnesota in 2003. Prisons are operating beyond official capacity in several states, but the construction of numerous new facilities has greatly reduced the problems of prison overcrowding.[41]

The Role of the Federal Courts   In the past, unsanitary living conditions, inadequate health care, high levels of violence, and inmate totals far exceeding the maximum intended capacity often went unattended by state correctional officials. The courts assumed a hands-off policy toward offenders once they were behind prison walls. The administration of state correctional systems was the sole responsibility of corrections officials.

But in a series of decisions, the federal courts applied the Eighth Amendment prohibition on cruel and unusual punishment and the Fourteenth Amendment provision for due process and equal protection of the laws to prison inmates. In addition, the Supreme Court permitted inmates of state and local facilities to bypass less sympathetic state courts and file suits alleging violations of their civil rights in federal courts. As a consequence of these various federal court rulings, the nature of correctional policy has been vastly changed.

Much of the litigation has concerned overcrowding. As more and more people were sentenced to prison, corrections officials responded by doubling, tripling, and even quadrupling cell arrangements. It was not unusual for inmates to be crowded together at the rate of one per ten square feet of floor space. Drastic improvements were long overdue in Arkansas and Alabama, for instance. At Arkansas's dreaded maximum-security institution, Cumming Farms, inmates were worked in the fields like slaves, ten hours a day, six days a week, in all types of weather. At night they slept in 100-man barracks. Homosexual rapes and other forms of physical violence occurred regularly. A federal lawsuit led to the finding that Arkansas's entire penal system was in violation of the Eighth Amendment. Recently, the adult prison systems of several states were being overseen by the national government under federal court orders. In 2002, fifty-two state prison facilities were subject to a more limited type of federal court order, mostly for overcrowding. State officials face the choice of balancing the stringent law-and-order approach sought by the public and elected representatives with court orders that sometimes seem to pamper inmates and turn convicted criminals out onto the streets to relieve overcrowding.

The intrusion of the federal courts into state correctional policy is quite controversial, particularly when they have taken over full operating responsibility or ordered increased state and local expenditures for prisons. Important questions concerning the proper division of power between the national government and the states have been raised, as have questions about the competence of federal court officials to run state prison systems. Some relief was provided by Congress in the 1995 Prison Litigation Reform Act, which greatly restricts the power of the federal courts to alter prison conditions and imposes a time limit on prison consent decrees.

State Response to Federal Orders However these important issues in federalism are ultimately resolved, the problem for most states has been producing more space for their growing prison populations and finding the money to pay for it. The only short-term alternatives are to release inmates, to sentence newly convicted offenders to something other than incarceration, or to find new space for lockup.

Prisons have become financial albatrosses, diverting state expenditures from education, highways, and social services. Most state prison populations have quadrupled over the past twenty years. State and local spending on prisons and jails, currently estimated at over $30 billion a year, rose at the startling rate of 15 to 20 percent annually from the late 1980s until 2002. Room, board, and care for one state prison inmate averages about $70.00 per day. An estimated 747,000 prison and jail guards must be paid. And each new prison bed space for the growing ranks of confined criminals costs up to $100,000.[42] Prison costs are also escalating as a result of health care inflation. Prisoners are a particularly unhealthy subset of the population: Most smoke, many are drug abusers, some have acute mental problems, and a troubling proportion have contracted the AIDS virus. There seems to be no easy end in sight for prison spending, because of "Murphy's Law of Incarceration": The number of inmates expands to fill all available space, or "if you build them, you'll fill them." However, the prison-building boom is tapering off because many new prisons have already come on line, prison admissions have diminished, and states have adopted alternatives to incarceration. The U.S. prison population grew at a slower rate in 2002 and 2003 than it had for some thirty years.[43]

Local jails have entered the litigation battlefield in increasing numbers. Almost every county and large municipality has a jail, and many have been the target of prisoner-rights lawsuits. The overcrowding and legal vulnerability of local jails, and their increasingly intimate links to state prison systems, have prompted states to mandate operational standards and to conduct inspections to enforce those standards. Alabama, Connecticut, Delaware, and three other states now have state-run systems. Other states have dedicated large sums of money to rehabilitating local corrections facilities.

POLICY ALTERNATIVES FOR STATES AND LOCALITIES

In addition to the immediate responses made necessary by federal court actions, states and localities are attempting to devise a more comprehensive approach to coping with the problem of prison overcrowding. Whatever their past failings, and for reasons of budget rather than conscience, they are demonstrating today an increasing propensity for experimentation and innovation. Three basic strategies are being employed to bring and keep inmate populations in line with institutional capacity: back-door strategies, front-door strategies, and capacity enhancement.

Back-Door Strategies

Back-door strategies include several methods for releasing offenders from prisons on probation or parole before they have served their full sentences. This strategy is the most conventional of the three, but some interesting innovations are being tested.

One of the less imaginative but nonetheless quite effective ways to deal with prison overcrowding is to grant early release. Most states have early-release programs in place, but the method of implementation varies. In some states, the governor or parole board simply lops off the last few months or weeks of sentences that are nearly completed, until the necessary number of inmates have left the prison. Other states apply a formula that predicts the likelihood that certain inmates, if released, will not commit another serious offense. For example, nonviolent offenders are freed before violent offenders, larcenists before burglars, marijuana users before heroin dealers, and so on. An inmate's personal characteristics, prison behavior, and work history may also be taken into consideration. Early release reduces inmate populations quickly, but public outcries are certain to follow if an offender released well before expiration of his sentence commits a highly publicized violent crime.

Ex-cons discharged without oversight and assistance are not likely to become model citizens overnight and entirely of their own will. Old habits tend to return. Today, felons incarcerated during the lock-'em-up mentality of the 1990s are returning home in record numbers—about 1,600 per day.[44] As observed above, 70 percent will become repeat offenders within three years, a problem that states and localities ignore at their own peril.

Despite fiscal problems, an increasing number of states are taking a close look at new reentry approaches for convicts to boost their chances for successful transition from behind prison walls to the streets. Job-related skills training, placement services, and alcohol and drug counseling (80 percent of ex-cons are released with substance abuse problems) are typical. New, more comprehensive programs are also receiving experimentation. Maryland's Reentry Partnership develops collaborative transition plans for inmates. The state corrections and parole division, local police and health departments, and community organizations work together to determine (with the prisoner's input) individual needs, including counseling, transportation, and housing. Caseworkers and a prisoner's advocate coordinate the services. Programs such as these are costly, but they are much cheaper than the average $23,000 per year to keep an inmate locked up.[45]

Conventional parole or probation is not very effective, although these programs account for three out of four individuals in the corrections population. In most states that utilize this technique, the parole officers (whose duty it is to keep up with the progress of parolees) are terribly overworked. It is not unusual for a parole officer to be responsible for 100 offenders—a nearly impossible task. Most probationers and parolees are supposed to receive substance abuse counseling, pay restitution to their victims, or comply with other terms of their release, but few do so. Around one-third of all state admissions consist of parole violators. In some cases, parolees escape supervision by moving to a different state.

Electronic House Detention A relatively new approach to parole takes advantage of technology to monitor parolees' whereabouts. Sometimes called *electronic house detention,* this technique requires released inmates to wear a transmitter (usually on the ankle) that steadily emits signals to a receiver in their home. Failure to detect a signal causes the receiver to contact a central computer automatically. The computer is programmed to know when the inmate is permitted to be away from home (usually during work hours). If an unusual signal appears, the computer prints out the anomaly for review by law enforcement officers. Removal of the transmitter also triggers an alarm at the central computer.

Electronic monitoring is an increasingly popular way to cope with prison overcrowding. It is cheaper than jail or prison, and it enables a working prisoner to pay her own share of the program and, in some cases, to repay the victim of the crime as well. But it is not appropriate for escape-minded individuals, who can simply walk away, perhaps to commit more crimes. (The receiver only registers the bracelet's presence or absence in the house—not specifically where it goes outside the house.)

Vocational Programs Another back-door strategy reduces the sentences of prisoners who participate in educational and vocational programs. These programs are intended to teach convicts skills that can help them obtain jobs once they are out of prison, and they have the added benefit of keeping inmates involved in productive, rather than destructive, activities while behind prison walls.

The idea of profiting from prison work has considerable appeal. In addition to using their time productively and learning marketable skills, inmates earn wages that can help defray the cost of their room and board, provide monetary restitution to victims, and fund savings accounts for the inmates to use after their release. Several programs have had encouraging results, including the making of stained-glass windows and restoring of classic cars by Nevada prisoners, baseball-cap manufacturing in Connecticut, saddle-making in Colorado, the sewing of everything from bed covers to Victoria's Secret lingerie in South Carolina, and the upgrading of secondhand computers for public-school classrooms by prisoners in Minnesota and other states.[46] Prison industries usually include more conventional activities like printing, metalworking, and basic manufacturing. South Carolina has used prison labor to build new correctional facilities, saving the state millions of dollars. Prison labor is not a bad deal for the inmates either. They get paid only 25¢ to $1.00 an hour, but they can earn time toward early release for each week they work.

Front-Door Strategies

The second basic strategy used to balance the number of prisoners with the supply of beds is the front-door approach, which aims to keep minor offenders out of prison in the first place by directing them into alternative programs.

creative sentencing

Sentencing in which the punishment matches the crime and the characteristics of the convicted person.

Creative Sentencing One front-door strategy is to grant judges more flexibility in determining sentences. **Creative sentencing** permits judges or community boards to match the punishment with the crime while keeping the nonviolent offender in society. An option that has gained increasing acceptance is community service—sentencing the offender to put in a specified number of hours cleaning up parks or streets; working in a public hospital; painting public buildings; or performing specialized tasks related to the person's professional expertise, such as dentistry or accounting.

Another option is to link the sentence to available prison space. This about-face from determinate sentencing is applied in an elaborate grid in North Carolina that helps judges balance the seriousness of a crime and the perpetrator's past criminal record with the number of beds available in the prison system. In determining the length of the sentence, the judge refers to the grid for minimum and maximum terms. Offenders must serve at least the minimum term without the possibility of parole. Nonviolent offenders such as petty thieves, embezzlers, and minor drug offenders are assigned to halfway houses, boot camps, drug treatment, or other programs.

Yet another strategy is for judges to assess fines in lieu of prison for relatively serious nonviolent crimes. A substantial fine, some argue, is just as strong a deterrent as a short stay in jail. So is the loss of a valued personal belonging. In Wake County, North Carolina, a juvenile court judge can confiscate a favorite item of clothing, a stereo, jewelry, or other possession from young larceny or breaking-and-entering offenders. Those convicted of the serious offense of child molestation in California can be given the choice of surgical or chemical castration. The first option removes some of the offending male equipment permanently. The second requires regular injections of a female contraceptive that reportedly shrinks male organs for as long as the drug is taken.[47]

A municipal court judge in Los Angeles provided an especially pertinent example for any renter who has ever lived in a substandard building ignored by the landlord. A Beverly Hills neurosurgeon who had earned the nickname Ratlord because of numerous city citations for health, fire, and building code violations in his four apartment buildings was sentenced to move into one of his own apartments for a term of thirty days. The apartment contained mounds of rodent droppings, an army of cockroaches, inadequate plumbing, faulty wiring, and other problems. Ratlord was fitted with an electronic anklet to ensure that he remained in his "cell" from 5:30 p.m. to 8:30 a.m. Permanent residents soon noted improvements in the building conditions.[48] Elsewhere, Arizona's tough slumlord law imposes fines and prison time on those who willfully neglect their properties and tenants, and Kansas City's Bad Apple program places slumlords in Landlord School where, among other inconveniences, they must face residents who relate their personal experiences and horrors of dwelling in revolting substandard units.[49]

Regional Restitution Centers Another front-door strategy used in Florida, Arizona, Georgia, and other states is the *regional restitution center* (also known as diversion centers), a variation on the standard work-release center. Nonviolent offenders are housed in restitution centers near their homes and work in the community during the day; they receive regular supervision. Their paychecks are turned over to center staff members, who subtract expenses for food and housing and distribute the remainder to the offenders' victims as restitution, to the court for payment of fines, and to the offenders' spouses and children for support. Anything left over belongs to the inmates.

Intensive Probation Supervision A third front-door strategy is *intensive probation supervision* (*IPS*). IPS is somewhat like house arrest because it is designed to keep first-time offenders guilty of a serious but usually nonviolent crime (for example, drunk driving or drug possession) out of state institutions. Those who qualify for the program face intense, highly intrusive supervision and surveillance for a prescribed period. Among other things, IPS requires face-to-face contacts between offenders and the IPS staff each week in the office, on the job, or in the home; random alcohol and drug testing and mandatory counseling for abusers; weekly employment verification; and an early nightly curfew (usually 8:00 p.m.). The program is basically self-supporting because probationers pay money into the program, in addition to the restitution they provide to their victims. The program has given prisons much-needed breathing space and saved a substantial sum of money for each offender diverted from prison.

A popular front-door approach to easing prison overcrowding is boot camps, or *shock incarceration*. Young (seventeen- to twenty-five-year-old) first-time felony offenders are given the option of serving their prison term or spending several months in a shock incarceration center, which resembles boot camp in the U.S. Marine Corps. In fact, former Marine drill instructors are often in charge. Those inmates who successfully complete the three- to six-month program win early release. Those who fall short are assigned to the regular prison population.

Shock incarceration is aimed at more than just relief of prison overcrowding. It is also intended to teach self-control and self-discipline to young people who come from dysfunctional homes or from selfish, undisciplined personal backgrounds. If shock incarceration has the long-term impact its advocates claim, it will keep thousands of young offenders from becoming recidivists; however, a growing number of skeptics are challenging the results of boot camps. Some camps are successful in reducing corrections costs and prison overcrowding, but only because boot-camp inmates are released sooner. Boot-camp dropout rates are high, and in most states the recidivism rate for graduates is only marginally lower than that for the regular prison population. Of course, dropouts and recidivists end up in prison, canceling any savings generated from boot camp. Savings are also canceled out when judges assign youths to boot camp instead of probation.

Inmate abuse and even deaths have been reported in boot camps in Arizona, South Dakota, and Texas. A review of Connecticut's program discovered gang infiltration, gambling, drug use, and other problems, leading the governor to close it down. Disappointing results have led several states, including Arizona and California, to close their camps.[50]

Capacity Enhancement

Capacity enhancement is the third major strategy for matching available prison beds with the number of inmates. Usually it entails construction of new prison facilities, which is indeed costly, but operating them is even more so. Some states have completed new facilities, but not been able to afford to staff and run them. Many taxpayers resent spending so much money on the care and feeding of criminals—although, ironically, they want convicted criminals to be locked up. Others oppose having a new prison located in their community. But poor, rural areas often perceive prisons to be a desirable form of economic development. A new prison typically brings 300 institutional jobs with 1,000 inmates. Prisons are supply-driven, and the flow of criminals is dependable. Prisons also purchase local goods and services. They pay sales taxes, water and sewer fees, and landfill charges. Also, because inmates are considered residents of local jurisdictions, their presence means more federal and state funding.[51]

The prison construction boom seems to have run its course for now. Texas built so many new prisons so fast that it had a surplus of about 20,000 county jail cells, which it proceeded to rent to states with too many prisoners. Several states, from Hawaii to Massachusetts, have sent nearly 4,000 inmates to the Lone Star State, at daily rates of as little as half those in states where the offender was sentenced.[52] Virginia has also leased cells to other states, bringing in $80 million in 2001. But Illinois, Michigan, and Ohio are closing prisons, primarily for financial reasons.[53]

Private Prisons One increasingly popular long-term capacity enhancement innovation is private prisons, or prisons for profit, an idea spawned from the near-hopelessness of many overcrowded state correctional systems. The private sector has long provided limited services and programs to prisons, including health care, food services, and alcohol and drug treatment. Privately operated prisons existed more than 100 years ago in Louisiana, New York, and a handful of other states, but they were closed down amid revelations of prisoner abuse.

Some 87,000 adults and juveniles are held in privately run correction institutions today in thirty-nine states and the District of Columbia.[54] These institutions include medium-security prisons in Virginia, Texas, Oklahoma, and Tennessee. The two largest prison-management firms, Corrections Corporation of America and Wackenhut Corrections Corporation, control 75 percent of the private corrections market. Private prisons have been built speculatively, with cell space offered on a first-to-pay basis across the states.

Despite its rapid growth throughout the 1980s and 1990s, prison privatization is a controversial idea. Those who support it claim that prisons built and operated by the private sector will save the taxpayers money. Because of less red tape, facilities can be constructed relatively quickly and cheaply. And because personnel policies are more flexible in the absence of civil service protections, operations are more economical. Most important, advocates claim, private prisons reduce overcrowding. Opponents of privatization, however, question whether firms can in fact build and operate correctional facilities significantly less expensively than state or local governments can. They believe that the profit motive is misplaced in a prison setting, where firms may skimp on nutritious food, health care, or skilled personnel to cut operating costs. A company whose business benefits from filling up cell space as soon as it is built might foster a lock-'em-up-and-throw-away-the-key approach. Such a firm might also lobby and contribute campaign dollars to legislators for stricter sentencing requirements and additional prisons.

Preliminary evidence on the economics of prison privatization is mixed. Most of the experimentation has involved juveniles, illegal aliens, and minimum- and medium-security offenders. The majority of studies indicate that cost savings have been marginal or nonexistent.[55] Corrections Corporation of America and other private prison firms have reported significant financial losses in recent years. And although overcrowded conditions may be relieved more promptly through privatization, the burden on the taxpayers appears to be about the same.

Who Should Be Responsible for Prisons? Although economic considerations are obviously important, constitutional and legal issues may ultimately be the undoing of prisons for profit. One of the basic questions is whether the delegation of the corrections function to a private firm is constitutionally permissible. The U.S. Supreme Court and state courts will have to determine not only whether incarceration, punishment, deterrence, and rehabilitation can properly be delegated but also who is legally liable for a private facility. The Supreme Court spoke on one such issue by declaring that private prison guards who violate inmates' rights are not entitled to qualified immunity—unlike public-sector guards.[56]

Another set of legal considerations concerns practical accountability for the day-to-day operation of jails and prisons. Who is responsible for developing operational rules, procedures, and standards and for ensuring that they are carried out? Who is responsible for maintaining security at the institutions and using force against prisoners both on a daily basis and in case of a riot? Who will implement disciplinary actions against inmates? What happens if prison employees strike? (Strikes by state correctional employees are illegal, but those by their private-sector counterparts are not.) What if the corporation hikes its fees substantially? Or declares bankruptcy because of financial mismanagement or a liability suit? Who is liable if prisoners are abused and have their civil rights violated by a firm's guards, as happened with Missouri felons doing time in a Texas prison run by a Mississippi company? Consider this case: In Texas, two men escaped from a private prison near Houston. They nearly made it to Dallas before they were caught. But Texas authorities couldn't prosecute because by breaking out of a private facility, the men had not committed an offense under Texas law. The men, who had been sent to the private facility from Oregon, could not be prosecuted for escape in Oregon because the event happened in Texas.

Economic and legal issues aside, perhaps the most important question is, Who *should* operate our jails and prisons? Legal scholar Ira Robbins suggests that we should remember the words of the novelist Feodor Dostoyevsky: "The degree of civilization in a society can be judged by entering its prisons." The state, after all, administers justice in the courtroom. Shouldn't it also be responsible for carrying out justice in the correctional facilities? Should profits be derived from depriving human beings of their freedom? With such questions in mind, legislatures in Illinois and New York have banned prisons for profit; Louisiana has placed a moratorium on new private prisons.

Does Prison Pay? The construction and operation of prisons is the fastest-growing budget item in many states, even faster than the growth of Medicaid. Yet every dollar sunk into correctional facilities is one less to pay for highways, social services, higher education, and the needs of children. Our priorities seem skewed indeed when we invest only $4,000 to $7,000 per year for a child's education while a prisoner costs tens of thousands of dollars each year to keep incarcerated.

Does prison pay by keeping repeat offenders out of action? Benefit-cost analyses comparing the costs of incarceration with estimated savings to society from foregone burglaries, larcenies, murders, and rapes do indicate a net benefit to society. Taking into account crimes not committed by inmates in Wisconsin, Piehl and DiIulio calculate "that imprisoning 100 typical convicted felons cost $2.5 million, whereas leaving them on the streets to commit more crimes would cost society $4.6 million." In a study of New Jersey, the same researchers confirm that "prison pays for most state prisoners," especially those who are either repeat or violent offenders who pose an immediate danger if released.[57]

Prison does not pay, however, for drug offenders, most of whom should be placed under supervision or substance abuse counseling, or released altogether. And it doesn't pay for offenders aged thirty or over, who are no longer high-risk individuals.[58] And as noted earlier, incarceration appears to have no measurable effect on the crime rate. States with the highest incarceration rates also have among the highest crime rates.

THE CONTINUING CHALLENGE IN CRIME AND CORRECTIONS

The idea of placing people in prisons to punish them with deprivation of their freedom was devised only 200 years ago. Until recently, brutality was the operating norm. Deliberately painful executions, maiming, flogging, branding, and other harsh punishments were applied to both serious and minor offenders. Misbehavior in prison was likely to be met with beatings or with more elaborate tortures such as stretching from ropes attached to a pulley in the ceiling or long confinement in an unventilated sweat box. By contrast, prison conditions in the states today seem almost luxurious. Inmates typically enjoy recreational activities; training and educational opportunities; the use of televisions, stereos, and videocassette recorders (VCRs) in their cells; and other amenities. Rules enforcement is also much more civilized and respectful of inmates' human rights. But a backlash is evident in some states. Surveys show that most citizens don't want criminals coddled.[59] They agree with former Massachusetts governor William Weld that prisons should offer "a tour through the circles of hell"—not the easy life. Today, shackled work crews can be seen along the highways of Alabama, Arizona, Florida, and Wisconsin. Law enforcement officials in Maryland, Wisconsin, and other states are requiring prisoners to wear stun belts instead of chains; these belts can be activated by an officer up to 300 feet away, triggering a blast of electricity sufficient to render the individual helpless.

Crime and corrections present major challenges to state and local governments. Certainly any long-term success will have to come from the recognition that all major components of the criminal justice system are interrelated to some extent. Thus, a broad approach to court, crime, and corrections is called for. That means beginning with the identification of at-risk children, creating a social welfare support system for them, providing alcohol and drug abuse rehabilitation for prisoners and minor offenders, and helping to repair families and communities that are lacking in resources. It means addressing homelessness, poverty, gangs, terrorism, and organized crime.

Some policies do seem to be driving down the crime rate. The aging of the U.S. population is an important factor, but so are community-based activities such as community policing, drug treatment, and citywide crackdowns on gang leaders and serial offenders. Before the states can fully cope with the challenges described in this chapter, we must understand such complex relationships more fully and attack the causes of crime as well as its effects.

CHAPTER RECAP

- Crime data are collected through the FBI's *Uniform Crime Reports* and victimization surveys. Both sources show a reduction in crime.
- Criminal justice is overwhelmingly a state and local government responsibility, with modest federal involvement.
- Key actors in criminal justice policy are law enforcement officials, the courts, the public, and victims.
- Victimless crimes and capital punishment are two policy issues that illustrate the variation in state approaches to criminal justice policy.
- Corrections policy deprives some criminals of their freedom, but little rehabilitation occurs.
- Policy alternatives for addressing prison capacity problems include back-door and front-door strategies and making additional prison cells available. Prison privatization is one controversial approach.
- Crime and corrections have become perennial challenges for state and local governments.

Key Terms

grand jury *(p. 461)*

indictment *(p. 461)*

victimless crimes *(p. 462)*

indeterminate sentencing *(p. 469)*

determinate sentencing *(p. 469)*

creative sentencing *(p. 474)*

Surfing the Web

Hundreds of law enforcement and corrections-related sites appear on the World Wide Web. A few of the more interesting include the Federal Bureau of Investigation (FBI) homepage at **www.fbi.gov** and the Police Guide at **www.policeguide.com.**

For community policing, see the Office of Community Oriented Policing (COPS) at **www.usdoj.gov/cops.**

Links to most major criminal justice policy issues are available at **www.corrections.com.**

Statistics on prison privatization can be found at **www.crim.ufl.edu/pcp.**

www.sentencingproject.org is a nonprofit organization that promotes alternatives to prison.

For corrections and sentencing data, and other valuable information, see **www.ojp.usdoj.gov/bjs/** and **www.ncjrs.org.** Another general source is the web address of the National Archive of Criminal Justice Data at **www.icpsr.umich.edu/NACJD.**

SOCIAL WELFARE AND HEALTH CARE POLICY

P overty in the United States has many faces. They include a Haitian immigrant in a Miami slum whose English is poor and whose prospects for a good job are bleak; an illegal Mexican immigrant in California who toils in the vegetable fields to earn money to send back to his family; a fourteen-year-old unwed mother in Detroit who has an eighth-grade education and no job skills; a high school graduate in Denver who was paralyzed in a skiing accident and may never be able to earn a living; a laid-off textile worker in Georgia with serious health problems that require expensive daily prescription drugs; and an eighty-five-year-old widow in Phoenix trying to make ends meet on her monthly Social Security check.

These images reflect some of the diversity of people who, for various reasons, need help coping with poverty or other burdens that afflict them either temporarily or permanently. Most of those who need assistance actively seek it through federal, state, local, and nonprofit social welfare and health care programs. Some do not receive government aid but choose to fight their battles themselves, some need temporary help until they can get back on their feet again, and some will be dependent on government assistance for the rest of their lives. Many of the poor work full-time jobs at low wages; others have never drawn a paycheck.

Welfare and health care reform programs are under way in every state today. While the federal government has been bogged down in a swamp of rhetoric and partisan mudslinging, the states have, with determination, embarked on a path of unprecedented health and welfare innovations. The growth in the states' capacity to design, develop, and administer such programs is remarkable. It is confirmation of their increased responsiveness to the problems besetting their citizens and their improved capability to address creatively and effectively some of the most difficult problems of our time.

THE MEANING OF POVERTY

Few cases of absolute deprivation exist in this country. The necessities of life—food, clothing, housing—are available to all through government programs and nonprofit organizations (the homeless represent a perplexing and painful exception). The extreme, life-threatening poverty found in Sudan or rural Bolivia does not occur here. Instead, poverty in the United States consists of relative deprivation: Some people are poor when their wealth and income are compared with those of the middle class.

The federal government uses a statistic called the *poverty line* to define poverty in quantitative terms. The line has been set at three times the amount of income necessary to purchase essential food. The official poverty line changes each year as the cost of food rises or (rarely) falls. In 2002, it was pegged at $14,480 for a family of three and at $9,359 for an individual.[1] The poverty line is important because it helps determine who qualifies for various forms of public assistance. More than 34.6 million "officially" poor people lived in the United States in 2002 (they constituted about 12.1 percent of the population). In Mississippi, 19.3 percent of the state's population is poor; in New Hampshire, 6.5 percent. In race and ethnicity comparisons, poverty rates ranged from 23.9 percent for African Americans and 21.8 percent for Hispanics, to 10.2 percent for whites. Overall, the U.S. poverty rate hit a twenty-year low in 1999, when national economic prosperity finally demonstrated a trickle-down effect. It has been rising since then because of greater unemployment and a weaker economy. Table 17.1 shows poverty figures for various categories of individuals.[2]

Measuring poverty is far from an exact science. Government statistics fail to account for regional cost-of-living differences, variations in states' ability and willingness to fund welfare programs, a decline in the inflation-adjusted value of the minimum wage, a significant change in consumption patterns, in-kind benefits such as food stamps and the earned income tax credit, and the value of off-

| TABLE 17.1 | **Who Is Poor?** |

INDIVIDUAL CHARACTERISTICS	PERCENTAGE BELOW POVERTY LEVEL	
	1994	**2002**
All Persons	14.5	12.1
White	11.7	8.0
Black	30.6	24.1
Hispanic	30.7	21.8
Asian or Pacific Islander	13.1	10.2
Children	21.2	16.7
White	16.3	13.4
Black	43.3	31.5
Hispanic	41.1	28.6
Asian or Pacific Islander	NA*	11.0
Senior citizens (65 years or older)	11.7	9.7

*Data not available (NA).
SOURCE: U.S. Bureau of the Census, www.census.gov/hhes/poverty/poverty02/table2.pdf (July 27, 2004).

the-books income and barter income earned by individuals. And the poverty line is based on relative food costs and preferences from the year 1963![3] It is widely acknowledged that the official poverty numbers significantly understate the actual degree of poverty. Poverty in America was once associated largely with old age, but this view is no longer true. The population has grown older and senior citizens have organized as a formidable interest group; higher Social Security benefits, federal programs such as Medicare, and age-based preferences in local property and state income taxes have eased elderly people's financial burdens. Today, only 10.4 percent of those age sixty-five and older are considered poor. The most alarming poverty victims are children: nearly 17 percent are poor. In the context of limited government resources, a generational reckoning is inevitable; society will have to decide how to allocate its resources between the old and the young. Already Social Security and Medicare outlays have grown rapidly as a proportion of federal spending.

Childhood poverty is related to a host of factors, one of which is called the feminization of poverty. This term refers to the incidence of poor, female-headed households, which now make up over half of all poor families. The United States leads the world in fatherless families. Almost two-thirds of all African American babies and one-fourth of all white babies are born outside marriage. And divorce rates remain high. Single mothers of young children must look for a job; if they want to stay home and take care of their children, they must rely on their families for help. If they find work, these single mothers must somehow contend with the serious shortage and high cost of day-care facilities. Their children often suffer from an unstable environment, undernourishment, material deprivation, sexual abuse, and violence. Poor children are at high risk for criminal behavior, drug abuse, mental illness, suicide, and teen pregnancy.

SOCIAL WELFARE AND IDEOLOGY

Intense debates over political ideology and values have always stormed across the social welfare policy landscape, resulting in confused policy goals, a faulty patchwork of programs, and perpetual crisis. Until recently, conservatives and liberals propounded starkly opposing points of view on the causes of poverty and the appropriate government response.

Conservatives, who generally believe in a restricted role for government, have tended to accept a modern version of the nineteenth-century view that "the giving of relief is a violation of natural law."[4] According to this viewpoint, the poor are victims of their own deficiencies. If they are to rise above poverty, they must hoist themselves up by their own bootstraps. From this perspective, the poor get what they deserve. Conservatives' traditional beliefs on government aid to the poor attack the social welfare system for interfering with the free market, discouraging more productive allocations of public funds, undermining the work ethic, encouraging immoral behavior, and creating a permanent "underclass" of dependent welfare recipients. Conservatives favor policies that discourage illegitimacy and teen pregnancy, promote individual responsibility, and cut welfare spending and dependency on public support.

For liberals, who generally believe in a broad and active role for government, poverty is a structural problem. People fall into poverty because of factors essentially beyond their control, such as inadequate schooling, poor parents, divorce, lack of jobs, various forms of discrimination, and the up-and-down cycles of a capitalistic economy. According to this view, people cannot help being poor; and so it becomes the responsibility of government not only to relieve their poverty through public assistance programs but also to provide the poor with the appropriate skills and physical environment to enable them to become self-sufficient.

What does the typical American think about welfare? Contrary to conventional wisdom, most Americans favor government efforts to help the poor and are willing to pay higher taxes to assist them. But people tend to make a distinction between the "deserving" poor and those who are not willing to work and be personally responsible for their behavior. Media reports and racial stereotyping contribute to the widespread—but erroneous—belief that most welfare recipients are African Americans who lack a work ethic and behave irresponsibly.[5]

The Origins of Social Welfare Policy

Social welfare programs developed later in the United States than in Western European nations. The U.S. programs in place today are also less uniform and less generous than those in Western Europe. These differences have been attributed to the federal system and especially to the competition among states for economic development. States attempt to create an attractive business climate characterized by low taxes and limited social program expenditures. This means less money for social services.

Our fragmented social welfare policy today is a reflection of shifting conservative and liberal control of Congress and the presidency, and the inherently controversial nature of redistributive policies—those that result in taking from one population group to give to another. Although its roots may be traced back to pensions for Revolutionary War veterans and their widows, the basic foundations of the welfare system were laid by the liberal Democratic administration of Franklin D. Roosevelt in response to the Great Depression of the 1930s. Private charity and state and local relief programs were completely inadequate for combating a 25 percent unemployment rate and a collapsed national economy. The federal government responded with massive programs designed to provide temporary relief through public assistance payments, job creation, and Social Security. Since the 1930s, competing political parties and ideologies have sewn together a patchwork of programs to help the poor and unfortunate. The most generous contributor was President Lyndon B. Johnson's War on Poverty programs during the 1960s. Johnson greatly expanded the budgets of existing welfare programs and initiated new, expensive efforts to attack poverty, such as the Economic Opportunity Act of 1965, which included Head Start (an educational program for disadvantaged children), the Job Corps, and community action programs. Some of the War on Poverty programs seemed to work, and others clearly did not. Generally, however, the Roosevelt and Johnson policies improved the lot of the poor.[6]

A Social Welfare Consensus

A social welfare consensus emerged among conservatives and liberals and led to a new coalition for reform in the late 1980s. Conservatives admitted government's responsibility to help the truly needy and economically vulnerable, and liberals saw the need to attach certain obligations to welfare and to address the behavioral dependency of the underclass. Behavioral dependency means that poor people become dependent on society for their economic well-being through their own choices, and it is a serious problem for this country's underclass, which is disproportionately young, male, black, and urban. Many of these people are school and societal dropouts—borderline illiterates with no job skills. A disproportionate number become involved in drugs and crime. Agreement exists that welfare dependency must be reduced so that people can get off the dole and on the job.[7]

This new consensus may reflect a common view of poverty, but disagreement about how to solve the problem persists. For example, which will most effectively encourage recipients to work: positive incentives or negative ones? Many agree that different types of poverty should be treated distinctively. For example, children, seniors, the disabled, single parents, working adults, and nonworking adults all have different needs. Many also agree that government should help those who can climb out of poverty through job training and other programs and that able-bodied welfare recipients have an obligation to seek and secure a job or perform public work.

Beyond these basic elements, the new consensus tends to unravel. Conservatives seek better behavior from the poor, admonishing them to complete high school, find employment (even at low wages), and either get married and stay married or not have babies and get off welfare. Liberals are more willing to utilize social programs to transfer government resources to the poor, with fewer conditions. Despite these differences, the social welfare consensus was broad enough to enable congressional passage of the Family Support Act of 1988. This law incorporated conservative principles of personal responsibility with liberal principles of poverty relief. Then, in 1996, President Clinton made good on his promise to end welfare as we know it by signing a law that eliminated the nation's largest welfare program, Aid to Families with Dependent Children (AFDC). In doing so, he also threw down an enormous challenge to state and local governments to assume the lead in helping the poor exchange welfare checks for paychecks.

CURRENT SOCIAL WELFARE POLICY

After the Great Depression, social welfare policy became primarily the responsibility of the federal government, with limited roles reserved to the states and localities. The states brought the various federal programs into action, administered them, and drew up rules to determine who was eligible for benefits. But with the 1996 welfare reform bill, entitled the Personal Responsibility and Work Opportunity Reconciliation Act (PRWORA), the federal government ceded a large portion of the policy field to the states and localities. Replacing AFDC was a new program, Temporary Assistance for Needy Families (TANF), which emphasized maximum state discretion. As a consequence, state and local governments are in the vanguard of innovation and program experimentation, even more so than in other public policy fields.

Dramatic variations among the states exist in levels of social welfare spending. New York spends $1,377 per capita on welfare—the highest in the United States. Alaska, Maine, and Minnesota follow with slightly over $1,000 in per-capita expenditures. The most stingy state is Kansas, at only $440, followed by Idaho ($471) and Utah ($480).[8] Some states pay relatively high benefits for one program, such as Medicaid, but relatively low benefits for another, such as General Assistance—the result of battles among various constituencies over a limited social welfare pie. States controlled by the Democratic Party tend to be more generous than Republican-dominated states, and strong party competition within a state drives up benefit levels. Political beliefs have an impact as well. The relationship between a dominant liberal or conservative ideology and state welfare spending levels should be obvious.

TYPES OF SOCIAL WELFARE PROGRAMS

Social welfare programs may be placed into two categories: public assistance and social insurance. Public assistance programs, such as food stamps or the Temporary Assistance for Needy Families (TANF) program, involve government payments of money or in-kind benefits to poor people who meet various qualifying criteria. Social insurance programs, such as Social Security, include recipient contributions (for example, the Social Security payroll tax) as well as government payments. Our concern in this chapter is primarily with public assistance programs.

The only way to get a basic understanding of complex intergovernmental social welfare policies is to examine the most significant ones individually. For purposes of discussion, we divide social welfare policies into three types: direct cash transfers, in-kind benefits, and social insurance (see Table 17.2). Most are public assistance, so-called "entitlement programs," meaning that these are government spending programs with eligibility criteria. If a recipient meets the criteria (age, income, and so on), she is entitled to the money.

TABLE 17.2   Major Social Welfare and Social Insurance Programs

PROGRAM CATEGORY AND NAME	NUMBER OF RECIPIENTS (IN MILLIONS)	WHO FUNDS	WHO ADMINISTERS	TOTAL EXPENDITURES (IN BILLIONS)
Direct Cash Transfer				
TANF	6.1	National	State	NA*
SSI	6.9	National	National, state	33.2
General assistance	NA*	State, local	State, local	2.9
In-Kind Program				
Food stamps	18.2	National	State, local	16.1
Medicaid	42.0	National, state	State, local	168.3
Social Insurance				
Social Security (OASDI)	39.7	National	National	425.2
Medicare	40.4	National, state	National, state	239.1
Unemployment compensation	7.4	State, private	State	32.4
Worker's compensation	2.1	State, private	State	11.2

*Figures were not available (NA).
SOURCE: U.S. Bureau of the Census, *Statistical Abstract of the United States*, 2003 (Washington, D.C.: U.S. Government Printing Office, 2003); www.census.gov.

Direct Cash Transfers

Direct cash transfers are welfare programs that directly convey money, in the form of government checks, to qualified recipients. Administrative arrangements vary by type of program. *Aid to Families with Dependent Children* was included in the Social Security Act of 1935 to furnish financial aid to poor children whose fathers had died. By 1996, however, AFDC payments went almost entirely (90 percent) to single-parent families in which the living father was absent.

AFDC was the most costly and most controversial social welfare program in the United States. Critics claim that it caused marriages to break up or to be consciously avoided; encouraged young, nonworking, unwed women to have babies; promoted migration of the poor to states paying higher AFDC benefits; and perpetuated dependency into future generations. No one professed fondness for AFDC, not even the recipients. As noted earlier, AFDC was abandoned in 1996 with passage of the new welfare reform act, PRWORA, which replaced AFDC grants to individuals with block grants to the states. The states in turn designed programs for promoting work and individual responsibility. The states receive vast new authority and flexibility for reinventing welfare, subject to certain federal requirements. States submit TANF plans outlining how the state will assist needy families with children and help prepare parents to become self-sufficient. The law stipulates that adults have two years to find a job without losing benefits and a lifetime limit of five years to receive benefits. Up to 20 percent of the state's welfare population may receive hardship exemptions for circumstances such as mental or physical disabilities. This "tough love" approach to getting people off public support also has a financial stick to move any recalcitrant states ahead. States that do not have at least 25 percent of their welfare recipients working at least twenty hours a week within a year can lose 5 percent of their block grants, increasing up to a maximum of 21 percent if future mileposts are not achieved.

Reaping sizable financial windfalls from the booming national economy of the late 1990s, the states combined TANF requirements with previously existing state welfare-to-work programs to drop welfare caseloads dramatically (by more than 80 percent in several states, and 51 percent nationwide). Most states were able to meet first-year program objectives. Many diverse options are being pursued by the states, including family caps that limit or eliminate additional payments for children born after a mother begins receiving benefits; time limits for aid cutoffs prior to the federally mandated maximums of two and five years; and individual development accounts, which permit recipients to establish savings accounts to pay for items such as college or technical education, a new home, or the start of a business. Most states provide some form of child-care assistance, job training, and transportation aid (so that workers can have a dependable way to get to and from their jobs). Some states use TANF funds to provide post-employment services to help clients keep their jobs and even win promotions.[9] States also vary in how they treat immigrants and citizens moving from other states, but in general they have been much more generous with immigrants than has the national government, even restoring benefits taken away by Congress. Following the initial years of success, the states are now hard-pressed to find jobs for the less able of the welfare population. The national recession of the early 2000s was damaging to job efforts. The states, however, believe that they are much better suited than the national government to handle welfare-to-work programs and that they will be successful. If they are not, however, much of the blame will be placed squarely on the backs of the states.

Supplemental Security Income (SSI) is financed and operated by the national government, except that state officials determine who is eligible for the program. Created in 1974, SSI combined three existing programs: Old Age Assistance, Aid to the Blind, and Aid to the Disabled. Its recipients are people who are unable to work because of old age or physical or mental disabilities and, increasingly since 1990, children with behavioral or learning disabilities.

General Assistance is a state and local program intended to help poor people who do not qualify for the other direct cash or in-kind transfer programs, such as the nonworking but physically able poor. State benefit levels vary greatly. Sixteen states do not offer the program at all, and several others have cut back severely on general assistance funding.

In-Kind Programs

in-kind program

The payment of a noncash social welfare benefit, such as food stamps or clothing, to an individual recipient.

In-kind programs provide benefits in goods or services, rather than in cash, as a way to address specific problems of poverty, hunger, illness, and joblessness. *Food stamps*—coupons that can be used to purchase food—are paid for by the national government. The program was established in 1964, and benefit levels are uniform throughout the United States. Both the working and nonworking poor can qualify with incomes of less than 130 percent of the poverty level.

Medicaid is a health care assistance program for the poor (SSI recipients automatically qualify). It is jointly funded by the national and state governments, and it is enormously expensive (more than $150 billion in 2003), constituting about 15 percent of state budgets. The Medicaid program provides free health care to uninsured poor people and is the principal source of assistance for long-term institutional care for the physically and mentally disabled and the elderly. It must be distinguished from Medicare, which grants health care assistance to those age sixty-five years or older. Since the inception of Medicaid in 1965, it has been wracked with scandals: Doctors, pharmacists, dentists, and other professionals have been charged with everything from performing unnecessary surgery and inflating fees to filing reimbursements for imaginary patients. Medicaid has also placed an increasingly onerous burden on state budgets.

Housing programs exist in several forms today. The Housing and Community Development Act gives Section 8 rent subsidies directly to the poor, who apply them to private rental units. States administer a portion of approximately 1.4 million subsidized apartment units; the U.S. Department of Housing and Urban Development administers the rest.

Other in-kind programs include numerous types of public assistance, such as the national school lunch program, Head Start, energy assistance for low-income families, legal services, supplemental food programs, family planning, foster care, and services for the physically and mentally disabled. National, state, and local participation depends on the specific program in question. Under TANF, states have great flexibility in offering in-kind aid to help move welfare recipients into jobs and keep them working. Examples include child-care services, job training, transportation, technical and college education, and workshops on how to find and keep a job. The diversity of in-kind programs is compelling evidence of the complexity of the poverty problem.

Since the 1996 policy reforms, welfare spending has shifted profoundly from cash assistance to in-kind services designed to help poor people acquire gainful employment and stay off government assistance. For example, 56 percent of the $25.4 billion in TANF dollars spent in 2002 was dedicated to noncash benefits.

Social Insurance

social insurance

A jointly funded benefit program made available by a government to its citizens as a right of its citizens.

Social insurance is distinguished from public assistance programs by the fact that recipients (or their relatives or employers) contribute financially through the Social Insurance Trust Fund, established by the Social Security Act of 1935. In effect, participants pay in advance for their future well-being. Although not generally considered to be a public assistance program, social insurance does help in the broad effort to relieve poverty. Contributions to social insurance come from Social Security payments by individual workers and by their employers.

Social Security (officially known as Old Age, Survivors, Disability, and Health Insurance) is run entirely by the national government and is paid for through a payroll tax on employers and employees. Monthly checks are mailed or sent electronically to retired people; to the disabled; and to the spouses and dependent children of workers who retire, die, or become disabled. It is the largest entitlement program.

Medicare provides federal health care and hospital benefits for people over the age of sixty-five in exchange for a monthly premium and copayments of medical expenses. It was created in 1965 through an amendment to the Social Security Act. Medicare costs have escalated rapidly as a result of the growing number of senior citizens and ballooning health care bills and prescription drug prices.

Unemployment compensation was mandated by the Social Security Act of 1935. It requires employers and employees to contribute to a trust fund administered by the states. Those who lose their jobs through layoffs or dismissals draw unemployment benefits for as long as thirty-nine weeks.

Worker's compensation is also part of the Social Security Act. Financed by employers and administered by the states, it establishes insurance for workers and their dependents to cover job-related accidents or illnesses that result in death or disability. Its cost, which is closely associated with the price of health care, has escalated rapidly.

Social welfare policy clearly demonstrates the interdependent nature of the federal system. The national government pays for and operates some programs on its own; Social Security is one example. State and local governments take care of general assistance. The states and localities perform key administrative roles in most social welfare efforts and serve as incubators for new ideas and programs, many of which have later been incorporated into national policy. The private and nonprofit sectors contribute through charities such as United Way agencies and institutions such as hospitals, clinics, nursing homes, and myriad community-based organizations. Contracting by all levels of government with nonprofits has made hidden partners of these nonprofit organizations, which increasingly attend to Americans' problems from cradle to grave.

STATE INNOVATIONS IN SOCIAL WELFARE

Public assistance policy today has two critical goals. One pertains to the well-being of children and of necessity the family. The other goal is to end welfare dependency. The respective roles of national, state, and local governments in these two policy goals are continually being sorted out. A perplexing array of welfare traps snares even the most carefully devised policy proposals (see Figure 17.1). Undeniably, however, the states and localities are the prime innovators in social welfare policy and the governments most responsive to the needs of the poor and disadvantaged.[10]

Saving the Children

Several important reasons explain the sad plight of children. Many children live with a single parent because of high divorce rates (almost half of all children experience a divorce during childhood), births to unwed mothers (some 33 percent of all infants), and irresponsible fathers who refuse to support their offspring (25 percent of custodial mothers receive none of the support due them). Even if single mothers have the necessary education or skills to secure employment, their children often must be placed in the care of older siblings or left on their own if family or friends cannot care for them. Opportunities for affordable, subsidized, or free day care are generally limited to Head Start and oversubscribed state-run and charitable programs. Finally, too many children are born not only into poverty but also into sickness. Because of inadequate diets, lack of health insurance, ignorance about prenatal care, drug abuse, and the spread of sexually transmitted diseases such as acquired immune deficiency syndrome (AIDS), many mothers give birth to premature, underweight, and sickly children. Some infants simply do not survive.

Children's issues have risen to the top of national and state policy agendas. Historically, the national government has addressed these problems, and it continues to do so today through programs such as Head Start, which provides preschool education and medical, dental, and social services for some 900,000 three- to five-year-olds. Head Start is a popular program that also promotes parental self-sufficiency. In addition, the states and some local governments have their own agendas. Some of the successful experimental programs to help children are likely to be adopted into national law in the future. But when more resources are devoted to children, welfare expenditures for adults and the elderly are likely to decline.

To deal with the growing problem of absentee fathers (97 percent of non-paying parents are male), the Family Support Act of 1988 requires the states to

FIGURE 17.1	Welfare Traps

The policy objective seems simple: Make welfare a reciprocal arrangement in which the poor must look for and accept a job in exchange for government assistance in preparing for work. If recipients refuse, they should lose their benefits. Welfare should offer a helping hand, not a lifetime handout. But many traps make achieving this seemingly simple objective both complex and elusive, and they present significant roadblocks to state policy innovation.

Trap 1: Some people *cannot* work. A large number of welfare recipients are simply incapable of holding down a job. Whether because of substance abuse, emotional problems, physical or learning disabilities, or other conditions, these people need long-term support for themselves and their children. It is not always easy to distinguish members of this group from the able-bodied.

Trap 2: Providing financial and other support may actually reduce the potential rewards of working. Taking even a low-wage job has forced nearly 1 million people to forgo the safety net of Medicaid, food stamps, and other programs.

Trap 3: The creation of community service or make-work jobs for the poor is opposed by labor unions and other groups that fear welfare recipients will displace workers in low-wage, low-skilled jobs, sending *them* onto the welfare rolls.

Trap 4: Special support for single-parent families can encourage divorce, separation, or out-of-wedlock births. If marriage or a job results in a loss of cash and in-kind assistance, why not stay single and unemployed?

Trap 5: Unless the government separates children from their parents and places them in foster homes, or other care facilities, help for poor children also means help for their parents. If welfare recipients are denied benefits for not working after two years, their children may suffer hardships. The denial of additional assistance for the single welfare mother's second or third child unfairly punishes the innocent child.

Trap 6: To get people off welfare and thus save money in the long run means spending money today. Most welfare reform proposals require spending for education, job training, child care, and related services. Failure to invest sufficiently can result in public assistance programs that are underfunded and doomed to fail. It is cheaper in the short run to send the poor their welfare checks. The long-run solution requires a large financial investment.

Trap 7: Bureaucracy can get in the way of compassion and good sense. The average length of a federal food-stamps form—which is designed by individual states—is twelve pages. Some run more than thirty pages. Confusing legalese and intrusive questions inhibit applications. Some states ask applicants to list the value of a burial plot, or what a child earns from cutting grass. Maryland requires applicants to list "deemor expenses" (perhaps some long-deceased attorney in Maryland knows what this means).

Trap 8: Welfare policy sets a double standard: It pushes the poor mother to exercise "parental responsibility" by leaving her children for a job to support them, yet the middle-class woman is praised for staying home to raise her children.

Trap 9: The typical job-training program requires that participants be job-ready, have a high school diploma, read at the eighth-grade level or higher, and provide their own day care and transportation. But the typical unemployed person has little or no work experience, has a tenth-grade education, reads at the sixth-grade level, has limited access to day care, and has no personal transportation. As a result, job training may not help.

Trap 10: Most new jobs are found in the suburbs, but the vast majority of the poor live in central cities. Low-income housing is not available or is rare in many suburbs, and many of the poor do not have access to reliable transportation.

SOURCES: The authors; also Kent Weaver, "Old Traps, New Twists," *Brookings Review* (Summer 1994): 14–21; Clare Nolan, "States Use Red Tape to Shrink Food Stamp Program," www.Stateline.org (August 14, 2000): 1–2.

withhold court-ordered child support payments from the wages of absent parents, even if the parent has not fallen behind in payments. States are also required to establish paternity, through blood tests and DNA techniques, for children born out of wedlock. The result is that more fathers are being held financially responsible for their offspring. The states now have additional authority to speed judicial and administrative procedures for obtaining paternal support, to establish guidelines for judges to determine the appropriate size of child support awards, and to monitor support payments. Many states use a "deadbeat dad" approach to publicize and prosecute delinquent fathers. The Family Support Act of 1988 borrowed heavily from state experience and innovations and was effectively promoted by the governors. Understaffed and unable to identify and rein in deadbeat dads across state lines, the states saw uncollected support payments leap to more than $30 billion in 1994. Since then, a huge national data base has been established; it is comprised of each person newly hired by every U.S. employer. States now can plug into the data base to track down deadbeat parents across state lines. Collection is growing rapidly as state computers connect with the federal computer.[11] State enforcement is more aggressive than ever. Michigan parents owing more than $40,000 in child support face up to four years in prison. Missouri revokes the professional licenses of doctors and other professionals for nonpayment of child support.

Day Care

The issue of day care for children of working and single parents has received a great deal of attention from the state and local governments, while the national government has struggled in vain to produce child-care legislation. Approximately 500,000 youngsters aged eleven and under are home alone each day from the time they return from school until a parent arrives. State and local governments are subsidizing day-care programs through tax breaks and are experimenting with various child-care arrangements under TANF. Nearly all states partly or fully fund child-care expenses for TANF recipients. States are also taking the lead in improving prenatal care, gradually reducing the nation's shameful infant mortality rate, which exceeds the rate of sixteen other industrialized nations. Certainly it is less costly to invest at the front end of a person's life than to try correcting medical and other ailments later.

Unmarried Teenage Mothers

The problem of unmarried teenage and preteen mothers is receiving growing policy attention. Teenagers and girls as young as eleven are highly likely to produce at-risk children (children more likely to experience school failure than other children). The rate of births to unwed mothers accelerated from 4 percent during 1950–1956 to 33 percent in 2002. Eighty percent of these children live in poverty. The annual taxpayer bill for aiding these almost certainly dysfunctional families is staggering. To conservative thinkers such as Charles Murray, "Illegitimacy is the single most important social problem of our time—more important than crime, drugs, poverty, illiteracy, welfare, or homelessness, because it drives everything else."[12]

The high teen birthrate perhaps represents a strong argument for greater use of counseling, contraception techniques, and abortion. Federal law prohibits using federal Medicaid funds for abortions for poor women unless their pregnancies are the result of incest or rape. Abortion is an extremely controversial "hot stove" issue in the states. State-paid abortions for poor women would undoubtedly reduce the number of illegitimate births and provide a family-planning option that is widely available to middle- and upper-class women. It would also save tax-payers the expense of supporting a substantial number of children born into poverty, perhaps with serious and costly health problems. But abortion is highly distasteful to many and sinful to pro-life advocates. To its most rabid opponents, it is grounds for assassinating physicians who perform abortions. The temper of the times is to be hard-nosed with all welfare mothers. Welfare moms who miss an appointment with an employment counselor or refuse to take a work assign-ment may forfeit their entire cash grant, food stamps, and medical insurance.

North Carolina targets middle-school adolescents who are at risk of sexual ac-tivity. Catawba County's Teen Up program, for example, provides classes in sex-ual abuse, sexuality, drug abuse, handling peer pressure for sex, and other topics for students identified by school counselors. Greensboro's Adolescent Pregnancy Prevention Program strives to teach sexual responsibility to males age ten to four-teen. Some communities provide teens with thirty-five-pound empathy bellies and crying dolls to provide some idea of what pregnancy and child-raising are like.

California, Delaware, Florida, and many other states are attacking teen preg-nancy by strengthening enforcement of long-neglected statutory rape laws. The goal is to discourage "sexual predators"—older males who prey on girls under the legal age of consent (fourteen years in Hawaii, eighteen in California and a dozen others, and sixteen in most states).

Improvement in the teenage birthrate has been recorded in most states. Fear of AIDS and other sexually transmitted diseases (STDs) has played a part in the decline, as have more reliable birth control techniques, including long-lasting implants and injections. More important, fewer teens are having sex. But the problem remains serious and perplexing. Teen pregnancy is a mother's recipe for lifetime poverty; it encourages dependency and greatly reduces career and life choices for the mother. It costs taxpayers billions of dollars for social welfare and health care support for the mother and child. The states are a beehive of exper-imentation and creative activity, but they have learned that a great chasm exists between establishing a new program and making it work effectively. Policy im-plementation, which political scientist Richard P. Nathan calls a "shadow land,"[13] is hindered by the complexities of our federal system, the waxing and waning of elected officials' attention, and the enormity of our social welfare problems. Government programs, no matter how well intended and desirable, sometimes cannot cause desired behavioral changes in target populations. The ravages of drugs, crime, and poverty; the lack of parenting skills; and low self-esteem place many Americans at risk of long-term welfare dependency. And once unmarried teens have given birth, it is an uphill struggle for public policy to help most of them become productive citizens.

TURNING WELFARE CHECKS INTO PAYCHECKS

Until the 1996 Welfare Reform Act, checks were handed over to AFDC recipi-ents, and little was required of them in return. The driving idea now is to help people find jobs and become independent. Jobs should produce more household income than AFDC did, along with improved self-images and self-reliance for recipients, and financial savings for taxpayers.

This is not a new idea. The Nixon administration's Work Incentive (WIN) program required employable AFDC recipients to register for work or for education and training courses aimed at making them more employable. But with the federal government in the driver's seat, WIN was a failure. Few recipients actually participated by doing public work (such as cleaning parks or painting government buildings). Some did get jobs, but they tended to be the most easily employable recipients anyway, and most jobs paid low wages, with few opportunities for advancement.[14]

Workfare was the centerpiece of the 1988 Family Support Act, whose major elements originated in and were developed in the states and were adopted at the national level at the insistence of the governors.[15] Under this federal legislation, the first major overhaul of welfare policy in over fifty years, each state was to implement the Job Opportunities and Basic Skills (JOBS) program. JOBS sought to combine job-related education, training, and services with the requirement that welfare parents obtain employment. States helped parents with child care and transportation costs. States were permitted to fashion their own approach to JOBS but had to match national government funds with a specified proportion of their own.

State JOBS experiments took place through federal waivers of statutory requirements. The purpose of such waivers, which were obtained by the states from the Department of Health and Human Services slowly and arduously (even under a sympathetic President Clinton), was to permit states and localities to test innovations for moving recipients into jobs. Among the waivers granted were those necessary to establish family caps, welfare time limits, and new techniques for preparing recipients for employment. When AFDC was replaced with TANF, the waivers became the building blocks of TANF.

The states have taken two different approaches to moving clients from welfare to work. With an eye to meeting required federal work-participation rates, many states adopted work-first strategies that stress immediate job searches. Others, more concerned about the long-term reduction of poverty, focus on helping recipients develop necessary job skills through education, training, and other preemployment preparation. TANF has evolved into additional efforts to help recipients retain jobs, earn promotions, and earn pay increases. Examples of work-first approaches are the widely praised Greater Avenues for Independence (GAIN) program in Riverside County, California, and Wisconsin Works. Minnesota has taken a quite different course toward reducing welfare roles and poverty. See the nearby *Breaking New Ground* box for a discussion of all three programs.

In a real change of direction, several states are privatizing all or most major components of public assistance programs. Private firms or nonprofit organizations are given contracts to process forms and applications in Arizona and elsewhere. Some county job centers in Wisconsin are run by private companies and nonprofits. Indiana has contracted out management of its entire TANF program as well as the food-stamps program.[16] About the only part of welfare that has not been privatized apparently is the determination of program eligibility.

BREAKING NEW GROUND

From Welfare Checks to Paychecks

The Greater Avenues for Independence (GAIN) program in Riverside County, California, has recorded more than 50,000 job placements, enabling many recipients to leave welfare altogether. GAIN is the nation's largest welfare-to-work program. It varies by county and is available statewide in California, and it contains several phases and options for recipients. If an initial assisted job search leads to nothing, the AFDC recipient is formally assessed and brought into a contractual arrangement that stipulates the obligations of the recipient and of the county administering the program. Education, training, and additional job searches typically follow. Transportation and child care are made available. If a job is still not to be had, the recipient must work in a public or nonprofit position designated by the county to earn a check. Once employed, GAIN recipients receive help to promote job retention and career advisement.

Wisconsin, long a leader in welfare reform under former governor Tommy Thompson, abolished AFDC two months before Congress did. By transforming the Badger State's welfare system into an employment assistance agency that, like GAIN, emphasized early employment, Wisconsin Works (dubbed W2) is making today's welfare recipients tomorrow's taxpayers. Transportation assistance, generous child-care benefits, health care subsidies, drug counseling, mental health services, job-access loans, and job-preparation and training programs are made available to unemployed welfare recipients. Those who cannot find a job must engage in community-service activities or employment-related training. Those who do not cooperate are cut off from support. This and earlier innovations in Wisconsin have resulted in an incredible 90 percent drop in Wisconsin's welfare rolls since the program began in 1987.

Minnesota's divergent path to welfare reform concentrates foremost on reducing poverty. Families are permitted to continue drawing welfare checks after they have commenced work. They are gradually weaned off welfare with a combination of work requirements and economic incentives. The result? Minnesota's welfare rolls dropped just 39 percent versus a national average of 53 percent. But a high percentage of recipients have found jobs, and positive family benefits have also been recorded, including improved behavior of children at home and in school, improved performance in school, a decline in domestic violence, and a slight increase in marriage rates among welfare couples.

SOURCES: www.riverside-gain.org; Richard P. Nathan and Thomas L. Gais, *Implementing the Personal Responsibility Act of 1996: A First Look* (Albany, N.Y.: Nelson Rockefeller Institute of Government, 1999); Clare Nolan, "Minnesota's Welfare Program Shows Dramatic Results," www.Stateline.org (May 31, 2000): 1–4; "A Jobs Program for Here and Now," *Governing* 10 (January 1997): 39; Steven Cohen, "What's Working? Lessons from the Front Lines of Welfare Reform," *Civic Review* 1 (July 1997): 7–9; U.S. Government Accounting Office, *Welfare Reform: Assessing the Effects of Various Welfare-to-Work Approaches* (Washington, D.C.: U.S. GAO, 1999), GAO/HEHS-99-179.

Many additional state and local efforts are under way. Individual development accounts, which encourage the poor to save, are in place in Oregon, Indiana, Illinois, and elsewhere. Baltimore, Boston, Denver, and other large cities require companies that do business with the city to pay their employees a living wage, which is set substantially above the federal minimum wage. As indicated by the welfare traps discussed in Figure 17.1, divine intervention in settling the welfare conundrum would not be unwelcome. State and local efforts to significantly reform welfare—courageous and well-intentioned as they may be—encounter enormous difficulties. Complicating factors abound in snarly webs.

For example, what should be done about welfare recipients who truly want but cannot find a job? And what about the 44 percent of TANF recipients who have physical or mental impairments?[17] Make-work or community service sounds promising, until one examines the costs of arranging, monitoring, and paying for it. What if a recipient is addicted to drugs and cannot hold a job? Detoxification and counseling are not cheap, but kicking the recipient off assistance could well result in a new enlistee in the ranks of criminals or the homeless. Evidence suggests that some welfare checks subsidize the drug trade. In effect, taxpayers have given money to some welfare recipients to purchase illegal drugs. New York, Kansas, Michigan, and other states now require their general-assistance recipients to undergo drug tests. Those testing positive must submit to treatment or forgo their monthly checks.

After sixty-one years of public assistance as an entitlement under AFDC, a new regime, grounded in work and self-sufficiency, is in place. Rapidly declining welfare caseloads in nearly every state (and nearly 60 percent nationwide) for 1996–2002 elated supporters of TANF and state and local innovators. But the early job placements essentially removed the better-educated and job-ready people from the welfare rolls. Those who simply do not want to work are also dropping off public assistance. Those still seeking a declining number of low-skill jobs are those with few employment skills, physical and emotional disabilities, and limited English-language abilities. As the national economy emerged from recession in 2004, the number of families living in poverty had increased. Counted among the newly unemployed were many former TANF recipients.

Not surprisingly, not all states have used TANF funds productively. Some, such as Colorado, Mississippi, and Arizona, have been accused of unlawfully or incompetently cutting clients off welfare. New York City's welfare-to-work program has been riddled with controversy and bureaucratic problems. And some states have transferred surplus TANF funds to transportation programs, property-tax reductions, and other purposes not directly related to reducing poverty, much to the irritation of federal overseers.

Fears of a race to the bottom, in which states seek to drive out the poor by cutting welfare benefits to the bare bone, and a magnet hypothesis, which predicted that poor people would move to states with relatively generous welfare benefits, have not been realized.[18] But unanswered questions and severe challenges remain for state and local governments: What happens as lifetime limits on cash assistance expire? Will more children be pushed into poverty? Will the numbers of homeless multiply? Are most of the newly employed in dead-end jobs that pay little and offer nothing in terms of advancement, or will former welfare recipients remain self-supporting? What happens to people who refuse to comply with work requirements and voluntarily drop out of welfare? Will the national government refrain from undermining state programs with new mandates? The 1996 welfare law was due for renewal in 2003, but Congress so far has punted on making tough political decisions by simply extending the existing law. And questions about the fairness of the welfare changes remain. Much is at stake in what is probably the greatest challenge to federalism since the Great Depression.

HEALTH CARE

A national debate has raged over health care reform since 1994, with little to show for it in terms of congressional action. The interest groups' hysteria and hand-wringing reach a fever pitch with each new proposal. Americans have learned a lot about the problems and politics of health care, along with a new vocabulary of health care terms (see Table 17.3). Meanwhile, as the national government continues to struggle with health care policy, the states have moved into the breach with innovative policies of their own, the results of which will serve as a road map for future national reform efforts.

The Problem

Nearly everyone agrees that, although the quality of health care technology in the United States is unsurpassed, the U.S. health care system is too expensive for all and dysfunctional for many. Costs have been soaring since the early 1980s. The nation's total annual health care bill exceeds $1 trillion, or 14 percent of the economy—by far the highest in the world. Medicare alone pays medical bills for more than 40 million aging citizens. Medicaid costs (funded by states at rates varying from 21 to 50 percent of total program costs) have skyrocketed and now consume 15 to 20 percent of state budgets. These costs include millions of elderly people in nursing homes, for whom taxpayers pay around $40,000 each per year. State and local government spending on public health and hospitals surpasses $127 billion annually.[19]

Expansions of eligibility for health care entitlement programs and price infla-tion drive up costs. So do fraud and abuse. For example, some physicians sell prescriptions for narcotics. Some nursing homes charge for services not pro-vided, and some home health care companies bill for nursing visits never made. (In some Florida nursing homes, patients in comas have been billed for speech therapy.[20]) In pill mills, a conspiracy of doctors, clinic owners, and pharmacists prescribe drugs and obtain government reimbursements, yet no drugs actually change hands. In a few publicized cases, illegal immigrants have come to the United States for expensive treatment, then left the country. All told, Medicare overpayments may run as high as 17 percent of all Medicare costs.[21]

Even though per-capita U.S. health care spending far exceeds that of other countries, a large portion of the population does not have health insurance. Con-sequently, the U.S. health care system is inferior to those of most other industri-alized nations; a recent ranking by the World Health Organization (WHO) placed the United States at a rank of 37 out of 191 countries. Uninsured Amer-icans must spend their personal resources to the point of bankruptcy before they can qualify for government aid through Medicaid. For many, a layoff or job change results in the loss of insurance coverage, meaning entire families court fi-nancial disaster. Others among the nation's 45 million working uninsured simply cannot afford to make monthly or quarterly insurance payments. When unin-sured, sick, or injured people take advantage of free government health care pro-grams, usually in hospital emergency rooms or free clinics, individuals with health

TABLE 17.3	An Essential Dictionary of Health Care Terms

Managed care: Involves several types of health plans that seek to contain costs by restricting the physicians and services that patients can access, promoting preventive health care, and capping hospital and physician payments. Managed care is available through health maintenance organizations (HMOs), consisting of gatekeeper physicians who direct patients to approved hospitals and other providers, and preferred provider organizations (PPOs), which are networks of approved doctors and hospitals.

Managed competition: Market-driven insurance plans that create incentives for competing insurance companies to provide health care services at low prices through negotiated fees.

Portability: The ability of individuals to take health care coverage with them wherever they work or live.

Single payer: A government agency administrating a health care system financed through taxes. This system is prevalent in Canada and several European countries. Examples in the United States include the federal Medicare program and Hawaii's state health care program.

Universal coverage: A national plan that offers comprehensive health care coverage to all citizens, typically through a national health insurance program. The concept has been proposed and debated in the United States since the turn of the twentieth century.

care insurance are the ones who pay. Doctors, hospitals, and others simply garner revenue lost from the uninsured through higher fees charged to those who can pay. The result is a two-tiered system in which the insured receive state-of-the-art health care and the uninsured experience health care services that are equaled or surpassed by those of some Third World countries.

Medical malpractice suits complicate the financial issues of health care policy. Physicians and other health care providers bemoan astoundingly high jury awards for pain and suffering, and soaring insurance premiums. Some doctors in New Jersey, Florida, and West Virginia have literally walked off the job in protest. Trial lawyers fight caps on jury awards and defend victims' rights to seek fair and just compensation for preventable medical mistakes. With no action forthcoming from Congress or the president, states are left to grapple with the issue, and a growing number have set limits on jury awards for "pain and suffering."[22]

If nearly everyone agrees that the U.S. health care system is broken, why doesn't Congress fix it? The answer is that the United States is ideologically and institutionally unable to develop a comprehensive solution acceptable to a sufficient number of interests. The current system richly benefits the health care status quo—hospitals, insurance companies, drug companies, and employers. Only a national health care crisis of extraordinary proportions will overcome the culture of incrementalism and interest group politics in this particular policy field.

Of course, health care problems endure and will be revisited by Congress. Meanwhile, managed care and managed competition are resulting in mergers and consolidation in the health care industry and monetary efficiencies as doctor, hospital, and pharmaceutical fees and prices are squeezed. But most of the juice is out of the orange, and state Medicaid costs are expected to grow at an average annual rate of 9 to 10 percent for the next five years. The states, frustrated

Thousands of people drive or take the bus to pharmacies in Mexico and Canada to save up to 70 percent on prescription drugs. *SOURCE:* Norma Jean Gargasz/Getty Images.

with delay in Washington and facing the immediate health care problems and costs of their own citizens, are busily engaged in reforming health care.

State Innovation

State efforts have aimed at expanding health care coverage to the uninsured, containing escalating costs (particularly of prescription drugs), and maintaining the quality of health care. All states are involved in some way in reforming health care, but each state has its own perspective on what is wrong with health care and its own approach to fixing it.[23] State actions are also guided by economics and special circumstances. For example, huge variations exist in state health care spending. Per-capita spending for health and hospitals varies from $939 in Wyoming to $130 in Vermont.[24] The Southeastern states present special health care problems because of the high prevalence of stroke. In the Southwest, especially Utah, tee-totaling, nonsmoking Mormons enjoy good health and help keep costs down. Florida's large aging population is a heavy consumer of nursing homes and other health care facilities, driving these costs up. Table 17.4 shows state health rankings. States that spend relatively high amounts per capita do not necessarily rank high on state health indicators.

State and local governments have always been concerned with the health of their citizens and indeed are delegated this responsibility in the U.S. Constitution. Colonial towns assumed responsibility for impoverished sick people in the 1600s, providing almshouses and medical treatment. Cities and counties, along with pri-

TABLE 17.4	State Health Rankings, 2002*

These rankings, from most healthy to least healthy, are based on various health indicators, including unemployment, smoking, availability of health services, and death rates.

1. New Hampshire	19. New Jersey	37. Texas
2. Minnesota	20. Idaho	38. Nevada
3. Massachusetts	21. Kansas	39. Kentucky
4. Utah	22. Indiana	40. Georgia
5. Connecticut	23. Pennsylvania	41. West Virginia
6. Vermont	24. California and Montana (tie)	42. New Mexico
7. Colorado and Iowa (tie)	26. Wyoming	43. Florida
9. North Dakota	27. Ohio	44. Tennessee
10. Maine	28. Maryland	45. Alabama
11. Wisconsin and Washington (tie)	29. Michigan	46. Oklahoma
13. Rhode Island	30. Alaska	47. Arkansas
14. Hawaii	31. Illinois	48. South Carolina
15. Nebraska	32. New York and Missouri (tie)	49. Mississippi
16. South Dakota	34. Arizona	50. Louisiana
17. Oregon	35. Delaware	
18. Virginia	36. North Carolina	

*Rank in order from most healthy to least healthy.
SOURCE: Kendra A. Hovey and Harold A. Hovey, *State Fact Finder 2003* (Washington, D.C.: Congressional Quarterly Press, 2003), Table I-3.

vate charities, built and operated public hospitals for the poor in the 1800s. Many states formally considered compulsory health insurance legislation before 1945.

Today, in the absence of systematic national government action, the states are hard at work extending quality health care protection to uninsured children and to the poor who are not currently covered by Medicare or Medicaid. North Carolina, Delaware, and a growing number of states now help the elderly pay for prescription drugs (see the nearby *Debating Politics* box). Some forty-three states have enacted patients' rights laws to help patients appeal the decisions of health insurers and sue their health care providers for poor service. States are trying to offer new coverage while controlling escalating health care costs. To implement significant health care changes and innovations, however, states must apply for and receive waivers of federal Medicare and Medicaid regulations. Most states, for instance, have received Health Care Financing Administration approval to convert their Medicaid recipients to managed-care programs. Several states are pursuing radical reform that would pool funds from Medicaid (which serves the poor) with funds from Medicare (serving the elderly and disabled) to care for dually eligible people, those who qualify for both. This group, composed

DEBATING POLITICS

Prescription Drugs and the Uninsured

Ensnarled in partisan battles and apparently rendered incapable of adopting significant health care reform by massive amounts of special-interest money, Congress has done little about rapidly rising prescription drug prices apart from a confusing and modest Medicare drug program for seniors in 2004. Approximately 70 million Americans do not have insurance coverage for prescription drugs, leaving many of them to do without or depend on the state or charity for financial assistance.

Maine broke the ice by enacting legislation to purchase low-cost prescription drugs for uninsured residents not poor enough to qualify for Medicaid assistance. By buying pharmaceuticals in bulk, Maine Rx lowers prices for pharmaceuticals to the benefit of qualified residents. Soon, most other states announced plans to institute programs of their own. Nine states have formed a regional nonprofit organization to negotiate lower drug prices and manage their prescription drug programs.

Perceiving a threat to the financial bottom line for pharmaceutical companies, the drug lobby—led by the Pharmaceutical Researchers and Manufacturers of America—has aggressively challenged these laws in federal court, spending an estimated $50 million in 2003 alone on state lobbyists and political influence. The drug lobby asserts that such laws are an unconstitutional constraint on interstate commerce and thus are in violation of the U.S. Constitution, expose patients to unnecessary risk, and violate Medicaid law.

Using massive purchasing power to ratchet down market prices differs significantly from the more conventional approach of state subsidization of prescrip-

tion drug purchases. And some states go even further. Vermont and California require pharmacies to provide Medicare clients with the same drug discounts mandated for Medicaid recipients. In some states, price controls on prescription drugs have been imposed. Oregon, Michigan, and Florida adopted a preferred-drug-list approach that has medical professionals evaluating and selecting equally effective but less expensive drugs for consumers. Vermont encourages its citizens to consider travel to Canada to buy drugs at 30 to 60 percent less than U.S. prices. Springfield, Massachusetts, established a program for city employees to purchase drugs in Canada. Texans and other southwesterners commonly take day trips over the Mexican border to register significant savings on prescription drugs. Indeed, the flow of U.S. citizens across borders has turned from a trickle to a full faucet flow.

How aggressively should state governments become involved in pricing decisions for prescription drugs? Should they set prices through mandatory controls or reduce prices through market leverage? Should the fifty states develop individual plans for helping the uninsured buy prescription drugs, or should one federal solution, such as an expanded Medicaid program, apply throughout the country? What about states and local governments openly encouraging or facilitating cross-border purchases?

SOURCES: Chris Mooney, "Remember the Maine," *The American Prospect* (September 2003): 18–19; Gardiner Harris, "Cheap Drugs from Canada: Another Political Hot Potato," *New York Times* (October 23, 2003), pp. 1–3; Maureen Cosgrove, "States Scrambling to Help Elderly with RX Costs," www.Stateline.org (February 9, 2000); Sandor M. Polster, "Maine Experiments with RX Price Law," www.Stateline.org (August 29, 2000).

of mostly low-income elderly and disabled people, accounts for only one-third of the total Medicaid population, but it makes up two-thirds of all Medicaid spending. Below we consider three states that have developed some of the most far-reaching health care reforms: Maine, Tennessee, and Maine.

Maine In summer 2004, Maine began enrolling uninsured residents in its trailblazing *Dirigo* (Latin for "I lead"). Within five years, some 160,000 people are expected to be signed up. *Dirigo* was the brainchild of Governor John Baldacci, who campaigned on the issue of universal health care coverage in his state. It will not come cheaply. First-year costs are estimated at $90 million. State contributions to *Dirigo* will be augmented by voluntary employer contributions and one-time federal money. Costs will be held down by price caps on hospitals and other health care providers and premiums paid by the uninsured or their employers. Individual premiums are based on a sliding scale, with low-income people paying less. As stated in the *Debating Politics* box in this chapter, Maine also uses the state's purchasing power to force drug companies to deeply discount prescription drug prices for the working poor, elderly, and others.

Tennessee Beginning in 1994, TennCare replaced Medicaid as the Volunteer State's health care program for the poor. The program was also extended to nonpoor, uninsured residents. More than 1.3 million Tennesseans have been enrolled, nearly all of the state's uninsured population. TennCare's managed-care, or HMO, approach involves twelve health care networks. Ten provide services regionally, and two operate statewide.

TennCare's unique plan pays each managed-care organization a set amount of money for each covered person who is enrolled. The money funds doctor visits, hospitalization, diagnostic tests, physical therapy, and all other standard health services. Participants share the costs based on a sliding scale that is based on their income. In this way, a strong incentive is provided to hold down medical costs by reducing waste and inefficiencies. Conventionally, doctors and hospitals have been rewarded financially by providing more services, whether necessary or not. For example, the more tests a doctor orders for a Medicaid patient, the larger the federal–state reimbursement. TennCare makes health care providers think carefully before ordering questionable services because their profits depend on keeping per-patient expenditures under the cost ceiling.[25]

This dramatic departure from health care business as usual emerged from a Medicaid-induced budget crisis in which Tennessee's inefficient system had become one of the most expensive in the nation. Few resources were available for other pressing needs, such as education and corrections. Former Governor Ned McWherter implemented TennCare through executive order, which was soon ratified by the legislature in the face of a frantic lobbying assault by physicians and various health care specialists who feared a loss of income.

Some operational and public relations mistakes have been made along the way, but nearly all previously uninsured people in the state are now covered. Medicaid costs, however, have been escalating in the 2000s by about 14 percent annually to $7.3 billion in 2003–2004. These rapidly rising costs raise serious questions about the long-term viability of the program as presently constructed. Major cost-trimming reforms were being considered in late 2004.[26]

Oregon Like other states, Oregon has extended Medicaid coverage to as many additional poor residents as is feasible. But unlike any other state, Oregon set up a system for rationing health care. A panel of laypersons and health care experts ranked 745 medical conditions, giving priority to potentially fatal but curable ailments such as appendicitis and bronchial pneumonia and to preventive-care services such as child immunization, birth control, and maternal care. Conditions for which treatments cannot cure or improve the quality of the patient's life came last: terminal AIDS and the common cold, for instance. The level of state medical funding would determine which conditions were treated and which were denied. Oregon's plan, like those of other states, could not be executed without federal approval. The idea of rationing—a health care triage system reminiscent of battlefield treatment—provoked a storm of criticism in Congress. Oregon's position was that it is better to provide many people with some care than to give a few people all possible care, no matter how expensive.

The first Bush administration pulled the plug on Oregon's plan in 1992 by denying the waiver of federal Medicaid requirements required for Oregon's law to take effect. The official reason given was that the plan conflicted with the federal Americans with Disabilities Act of 1990, which prohibits discrimination against individuals with disabilities (some disabilities would go untreated). The Clinton administration approved a revised bill for Oregon's plan in 1993. Since then, Oregon has had to ask for waivers from the federal Medicaid and Medicare Services offices for changes in its rating program, and has experienced numerous and frustrating delays. Oregon continues to be a trailblazer. In a state referendum, voters also approved a measure that legalizes medical marijuana (see the *Debating Politics* box in Chapter 2).

State Health Care Reform Moves Forward

Medicaid continues to burden the states financially. Despite the fact that state reforms, particularly managed care, have cut the rate of growth in Medicaid costs, this entitlement program now comprises the second largest portion of state expenditures, surpassing higher education. Medicaid costs are not the only serious problem. The ranks of the uninsured are increasing. Prescription drug prices are escalating. A disturbing and deleterious nurse shortage threatens the quality of medical care. The nursing-home industry is riddled with problems, as is care for the mentally disabled.

State health care reform must continue at a lively pace until Congress finally enacts universal health care coverage. Even then, states will be service integrators, implementers, and innovators in their classic "middleman" role in U.S. federalism, and meanwhile, they are clearing new trails that will inform and greatly influence future federal policymaking. The federal government could make the job of the states much easier by giving them greater authority or at least minimizing the conditions for federal waivers of state Medicaid changes. Another obstacle is the Employee Retirement Income Security Act (ERISA) of 1974, which amounts to a federal pre-emption of the states' authority to regulate employers' health care plans. The attendant waiver requirements are cumbersome and slow, thus inhibiting innovation. Greater flexibility is needed if the states are to be given a full opportunity to deliver health care services to their citizens. One after another, they are voyaging into the foreign land of health care reform. The least the federal government can do is provide a passport.

CHAPTER RECAP

- Social welfare and health care are major entries on the federal–state policy menu. The national government may own the restaurant, but the cooks who turn out the policy dishes are the state and local governments.
- Poverty in the United States is measured using a statistic called the poverty level.
- A social welfare policy consensus has yet to produce a coherent national policy, but the state and local governments are fully engaged in program design, experimentation, and administration.
- Programs to help poor children and to move adults from welfare rolls to payrolls have received special attention through state innovations.
- In the face of policy gridlock in Washington, the states are developing innovative approaches to providing affordable health care to all of their citizens.

Key Terms

direct cash transfer *(p. 488)*	social insurance *(p. 490)*
in-kind program *(p. 489)*	

Surfing the Web

The Joint Center for Poverty Research focuses on the causes of poverty and the effectiveness of policies aimed at reducing it. Their web site is located at **www.jcpr.org.**

For information on health care, see the Health Care Financing Administration's web site at **www.hcfa.gov.**

The Administration for Children and Families (ACF), within the U.S. Department of Health and Human Services (DHHS), is responsible for federal programs that promote economic and social well-being. Information about their programs can be obtained from their web site at **www.acf.dhhs.gov.**

Families USA is a nonprofit organization that works at the national, state, and local levels to achieve high-quality, affordable health care and long-term care for all Americans. Their web site, **www.familiesusa.org,** serves as a clearinghouse for information about the health care system.

For information on children's issues, see the Children's Defense Fund at **www.childrensdefense.org.**

For general information and links on welfare programs and initiatives, see **www.welfareinfo.org.**

ENVIRONMENTAL POLICY

The Political Economy of Environmental Protection
Public Opinion • New Approaches: Moving Toward Sustainability

Intergovernmental Relationships in Environmental Policy
The Recent National Role • Environmental Policy in the States • Green Localities

Dealing with Waste
Recycling Solid Waste • Managing Hazardous Waste • Storing Nuclear Waste

Two Challenges for Policymakers
Environmental Justice • Ecoterrorism

V isitors to downtown Chattanooga, Tennessee, can stroll the city's tree-lined Riverwalk and watch blue herons feeding along the shore. In the river, fish are jumping. Tourists board one of the city's seventeen electric shuttle buses for a ride to the Tennessee Aquarium, which features freshwater ecosystems. A bridge that once carried cars is now reserved for walkers, joggers, and cyclists. In the planning stages are a zero-emissions eco-industrial park and a grass-roofed convention center. Chattanooga, according to one environmentalist, is "a model for the nation and the world."[1] But what makes the Chattanooga story so compelling is that thirty-five years ago, the Environmental Protection Agency (EPA) called it "the dirtiest city in America."[2] The industries that lined the banks of the river had fouled the air and the water. New federal clean-air and clean-water regulations were adopted. Over time, some of the factories shut down; others modernized. Prodded by the Chamber of Commerce, the city underwent a period of intense self-study and emerged with a new vision for the future. The vision? Chattanooga would transform itself from a polluted wasteland to an ecologically sound community. Today, it is well on the way to doing so.[3]

Environmental policy in the United States is characterized by three features:

its intergovernmental nature, its regulatory focus, and (lately) its innovative design. The federal government is extensively involved in environmental policy, as are states and localities. These governments play different roles depending on the environmental problem and the era. The activity of government tends to be regulatory, that is, making rules and setting standards that affect the private sector, monitoring compliance, and imposing penalties. Finally, solutions to environmental problems are moving beyond the more traditional approaches and are becoming increasingly innovative and fresh. The rebirth of Chattanooga reflects all these features of environmental policy. As will be evident in the chapter, this policy area tests the capacity of states and localities to make smart choices for the future.

THE POLITICAL ECONOMY OF ENVIRONMENTAL PROTECTION

Environmental policy choices are made especially difficult by their economic implications. Control of pollution is a significant financial cost for many firms today. In the essentially nonregulatory era prior to the 1960s, this expense

This paper mill brought jobs to Mississippi, but it came with an environmental cost. The river is contaminated with dioxin, a byproduct of the paper-bleaching process.
SOURCE: Earl Dotter/Impact Visuals.

was either quite low or nonexistent. Increasing government regulatory intervention in industrial processes and outputs reflects the indisputable fact that market forces by themselves will not guarantee the protection of our health and the environment. Clean air and clean water are public goods that should be available to all of us, but polluters often have little economic incentive to stop polluting.

When left unregulated, most firms tend to maximize profits by minimizing costs—including the costs of environmental protection. Determining exactly what constitutes pollution or environmental degradation and deciding how stringently to regulate polluting activities have tremendous economic implications for firms and governments. Too much regulation could depress economic growth at national, state, and local levels; reduce employment; and even force some companies into bankruptcy. These concerns are not simply conjecture. A recent study has confirmed that, to some degree, states that imposed costlier regulatory burdens on the private sector experienced lower rates of new capital investment.[4]

The tradeoffs between economic growth and environmental protection spawn conflict and are evident wherever these important objectives clash. The 1990 Clean Air Act amendments, it is estimated, eliminated 15,000 jobs in the coal mines and cost U.S. industry $21.5 billion per year. When restrictions on logging were imposed on forests in the Northwest to save the habitat of the endangered spotted owl, timber interests forecasted the end of their industry. (Loggers sported bumper stickers on their trucks reading "Save a Logger—Eat an Owl.") Although their claims of doom were overstated, over 10,000 jobs in forest products had been lost within three years.[5]

Public Opinion

Research tells us that Americans generally support the goals of environmental protection. Public opinion polls indicate that most people are in favor of increased government spending for environmental protection and oppose efforts to weaken environmental standards.[6] This resounding endorsement weakens, however, when environmental protection is pitted against goals such as economic growth and adequate energy. When members of Earth First! square off against loggers in the forests of the Pacific Northwest, environmentalism becomes more than an abstraction. Environmental protection does not occur in a vacuum; achievement of its goals comes at a cost to other valued objectives.

Although support among the public for protecting the environment remains fairly strong, it has dropped since 1997. At the same time, the priority accorded economic growth has increased. Figure 18.1 shows the fluctuation in national public opinion from 1997 to 2003, as reported by the Gallup Poll. The polling question itself is called a forced choice because respondents with an opinion have to select either environmental protection or economic growth as a priority. Therefore, it requires the respondent to weigh the two options against each other. The question was worded in this manner:

With which one of these statements about the environment and the economy do you most agree—protection of the environment should be given priority, even at the risk of curbing economic growth (or) economic growth should be given priority, even if the environment suffers to some extent?[7]

As the graph in Figure 18.1 shows, the gap between the two priorities has narrowed considerably over time. The increased importance of economic growth can be attributed in part to the downturn in the nation's economy during the period. Even so, environmental protection continues to be a high priority because all of us are potential or actual victims of environmental problems. Polluted air, water, and land offend us aesthetically but, more important, they threaten the health and safety of ourselves, our children, and our grandchildren. People who drink contaminated water and breathe polluted air experience the costs directly. From a different perspective, all citizens must help pay the price of a safe and clean environment. We pay for a clean environment through the portion

FIGURE 18.1   **Changing Priorities in Public Opinion**

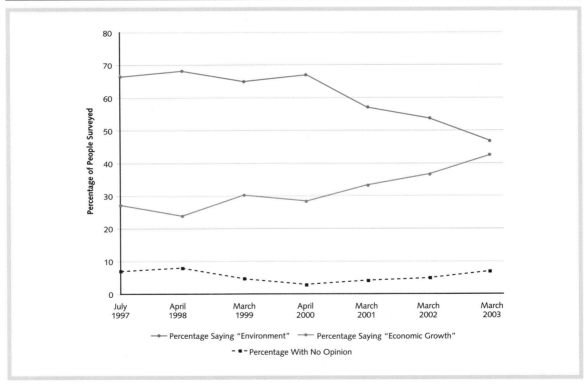

Source: *2003 Gallup Poll Social Series, The Environment* (Princeton, N.J.: The Gallup Organization, 2003), pp. 11, 30.

of our taxes that goes to government pollution-control efforts and through the prices we pay for goods, which include the cost of pollution control. The costs to consumers are especially heavy where the products of chemical companies, the auto industry, and coal-burning power plants are concerned. These industries have lobbied heavily against what they perceive to be excessive regulation. The nearby *Debating Politics* box features a new, controversial policy that is intended to improve relations between business and regulators: the **environmental self-audit.**

Because of the link between environmental protection and economic development, public policy is inevitably a compromise. Yet we should not forget how far environmentalism has come in thirty-five years. As proof, the U.S. Department of Commerce includes the degradation of natural resources in its calculations of the nation's gross domestic product (GDP).[8] Integrating environmental accounting with traditional economic assessments has long been a goal of environmentalists.

New Approaches: Moving Toward Sustainability

Government's role is to balance economic growth with environmental protection by regulating polluters. The political economy of environmental protection argues strongly for national domination of policymaking. Because states and local governments compete for industry (as discussed in Chapter 14), some jurisdictions might be tempted to relax environmental protection standards and thus influence a firm's decision about where to construct or expand a new manufacturing facility. National policies and standards can prevent the sacrifice of environmental quality in jurisdictions that seek growth and development at almost any cost. But concern about the high costs of traditional regulatory approaches has spawned some creative thinking about alternatives. This new thinking has moved in four directions:

- Changing production processes to limit the amount of pollution produced in the first place.
- Reducing exposure to pollutants rather than trying to eliminate pollution altogether.
- Exploring the tradeoffs between regulatory costs and environmental benefits to determine when an unacceptable imbalance exists.
- Replacing traditional administrative procedures with economic incentives and other market strategies with the hope of achieving both environmental protection and economic efficiency.[9]

It is not clear whether these new approaches will achieve what some of their proponents intend, that is, the marrying of environmental protection and economic development. The word often used to describe this marriage is **sustainability,** that is, an approach to economic growth that prevents harm to the environment.[10] But numerous studies have shown that as a nation's economy prospers, the public's concern over environmental quality increases.[11] These intertwined goals present continued challenges for policymakers.

environmental self-audit

A form of self-policing in which the regulated firm conducts its own review of its performance and voluntarily reports violations.

sustainability

The simultaneous achievement of economic development and environmental protection.

DEBATING POLITICS

Environmental Self-Audits: Industry Takes on a New Role

Environmentalists contend that industries have to be monitored by government agencies; otherwise, they will try to evade pollution regulations. That thinking also pervades most environmental-protection statutes. Industry has a different perspective: provide an incentive and we will monitor ourselves, thus saving government time and money. Environmental self-audits encourage firms to identify their pollution problems themselves and correct them voluntarily. Colorado was the first state to adopt such a law, largely as the result of an incident involving the Coors Brewing Company.

Coors brews 20 million gallons of beer a year at its Golden, Colorado, brewery. Several years ago, it discovered that it was emitting ten times more smog-forming volatile organic compounds (VOCs) into the air than permitted. Coors informed Colorado air-quality officials and promised to fix the problem. The state responded by imposing a $1 million penalty. Coors officials cried foul, claiming that they had been environmental good guys by telling the agency about the problem in the first place. (Colorado regulators contend that the agency had ordered Coors to check its VOC emission levels.) Regardless of the specifics (the fine was eventually reduced to $237,000), the stage was set for passage of a state law encouraging businesses to conduct voluntary pollution audits. If such audits turn up a problem, the firm is given immunity from penalties and the information is kept confidential.

By 2000, most states, including Idaho, Michigan, Ohio, and Texas, had versions of an environmental self-audit law on their books. On one side of the issue are many environmentalists for whom industry self-audits are akin to foxes guarding henhouses. Environmental activists are distressed that the law treats the self-reported violations as confidential. But some state environmental-protection officials defend environmental self-audits, arguing that sensible incentives are needed to encourage industry to acknowledge and correct its polluting ways. And the Environmental Protection Agency (EPA) eventually took a page from the states' book and adopted its own self-audit regulations, which they call self-policing. The popularity of self-audits with the firms themselves is undeniable. Since the EPA program began, hundreds of firms have self-reported thousands of violations. For example, in 2000, five telecommunications companies voluntarily disclosed and corrected 3,457 environmental violations that occurred at 1,122 of their facilities in forty-five states. After negotiations with the EPA, the companies paid a total of $329,426 in penalties for their admitted wrongdoing.

Are environmental self-audits a good idea? After all, the regulated interests themselves have a stake in the outcome. Do self-audits let polluters off the hook too easily? Or is distrust of industry outdated in today's state environmental agencies? With self-audits, are state agencies abdicating one of their primary responsibilities, that is, making sure that environmental laws are enforced?

SOURCE: Tom Arrandale, "Can Polluters Police Themselves?" *Governing* 10 (June 1997): 36–39; "Environmental Audits and Self-Disclosures," www.epa.gov.reg3ecej/audits.htm (December 2003).

INTERGOVERNMENTAL RELATIONSHIPS IN ENVIRONMENTAL POLICY

In the early days of the United States, government involvement in environmental protection was minimal at best. Natural resources were abundant, the country was developing, the future seemed limitless. The first government forays into the now-tangled jungle of environmental-protection policy began in the early 1800s with local ordinances aimed at garbage; human and animal waste; contaminated drinking water; and other unsanitary, health-endangering conditions in American cities. Local failures to contain and control such problems were punctuated by cholera and typhoid epidemics throughout the nineteenth century and into the early twentieth century. In 1878, a yellow fever epidemic caused 5,000 deaths and the exodus of another 25,000 fearful residents from Memphis, Tennessee. The population of that city dropped by more than half over a period of just two months.[12] Such episodes prompted the states to begin regulating conditions causing waterborne diseases, thereby redefining what had been a private problem into a problem for state government. By 1948, states had taken over responsibility for water-pollution control. Their early regulatory efforts were rather weak, however.[13]

The issue of water-pollution control shows the evolving centralization of federal government authority in environmental decisionmaking. Although the federal government acted to protect natural resources by setting aside land for national parks in the late nineteenth century, it paid little attention to environmental problems until after World War II. At that point, the forces of urbanization and industrial production began to draw attention to the national dimensions of environmental dangers. The initial federal statutory step into the policy field was the Water Pollution Control Act of 1948. Under the original version of this act, the national government assumed limited enforcement authority for water pollution. Since then, seven other major federal statutes or amendments have been enacted to address the problem. Under this overall statutory framework, the federal government pre-empted existing state and local water-quality standards and substituted national standards.

The reasons for this pre-emption are not difficult to understand. We have already noted that as states compete for economic development, they may be tempted to lower environmental standards to gain an edge over other states. In addition, because pollution problems are often cross-boundary (that is, they extend beyond a single jurisdiction), solutions can be difficult to design. Toxins dumped into a river upstream have deleterious consequences for jurisdictions located downstream. The failure of states to work together to solve shared environmental problems led to more involvement by the federal government.

Increasingly strong federal statutes also addressed the problems of air pollution, pesticides, and hazardous waste. By the late 1970s, the federal government had extended its authority to endangered species, strip mining, coastal zones, toxic substances, and many other areas. Thus, environmental protection was redefined as a national problem requiring national solutions. The national government does not operate alone, however; state and local governments play a significant role in implementing federal legislation.

States and localities speak with an important policy voice even in environmental fields that appear to be outside their sphere of influence. Take public lands as an example. Governed by Congress and managed by eight federal agencies, including the Bureau of Land Management, Forest Service, and National Park Service, the nation's 700 million acres of public lands make up almost one-third of the continental United States and more than 60 percent of the land area of four western states: Alaska, Idaho, Nevada, and Utah. These lands contain vast timber, petroleum, coal, and mineral resources. The states have an enormous economic stake in how these resources and their environmental implications are managed. The western states, in particular, have consistently sought a greater role in deciding how these resources are used, even insisting that much of the land be deeded over to the respective states.[14] The public lands issue is likely to intensify—several of the western state governors campaigned for office during the 1990s on a "West Versus Washington" platform.[15]

The Recent National Role

The lead agency in national environmental policy is the Environmental Protection Agency (EPA), which was created in 1970 as an independent regulatory body for pollution control. With its director appointed by the president, the EPA is faced with the task of coordinating and enforcing the broad array of environmental-protection programs established by Congress. To help with this task, the agency has decentralized much of its operation to ten regional offices located in major cities throughout the country. The scope of the EPA's responsibility can be overwhelming, involving regular interaction and conflict with other federal agencies, powerful private interests, and state and local governments. Its job is complicated by the tendency of Congress to pass environmental legislation that sets unattainable program goals and unrealistic implementation dates. Many deadlines for compliance with federal laws have been missed by the EPA, which lends ammunition to its critics on all sides.[16] Litigation brought by regulated industries and environmental groups has further ensnarled the agency, and a shortage of money and staff has plagued the EPA since the Reagan years.

An example of the scope of the EPA's responsibilities is water-pollution control. Every private and public facility that discharges wastes directly into water must obtain a permit from the EPA or, in some instances, from its state counterpart. The national government, through the EPA, establishes specific discharge standards. Day-to-day oversight and implementation, however, are performed by the states. In effect, the national government makes the rules and lets the states enforce them according to their own circumstances (a process known as **partial pre-emption**). The national government also disburses grants to state and local governments for the treatment and monitoring of water resources. Billions of federal dollars have been spent for the construction of waste-water treatment plants; millions more have gone for technical assistance and research and development.[17]

partial pre-emption
An approach common to federal environmental laws that requires states to apply federal standards.

A Democrat in the White House   When Bill Clinton and Al Gore (the latter an avowed environmentalist and author of *Earth in the Balance*) were elected in 1992, many assumed that a new wave of environmentalism would sweep the country. However, it did not work out quite that way. Although President Clinton signed a series of executive orders committing the United States to the goals of the Earth Summit, the administration was forced to retreat on its proposed changes to toughen public lands policy. A bill to elevate the EPA to a cabinet department was rejected by Congress. Other legislation, including reauthorization of the Superfund law and amendments to the Safe Drinking Water Act, stalled during President Clinton's first term. Although several factors contributed to the environmental stalemate, questions about the cost of pollution-control regulations and their impact on private-property rights raised new concerns. As Republican strength in Congress increased, support grew for the relaxation or repeal of many environmental-protection statutes. For instance, congressional Republicans championed the rights of landowners whose property was adversely affected by federal wetlands provisions and the Endangered Species Act. Environmentalists were put on the defensive, trying to maintain sufficient legislative strength to block the new initiatives. They were aided in this effort by public opinion that continued to support environmental protection.

President Clinton enjoyed some environmental successes during his second term, such as his executive order designating 1.7 million acres of southern Utah as a protected national monument and new rules reducing the amount of arsenic allowed in drinking water. The administration also put into place a new devolutionary performance partnership agreement (PPA) that allowed a state to combine its EPA funding into block grants that could be used for comprehensive statewide environmental problems.[18] Basically, states would have more power to set their own spending priorities. The idea was pilot-tested in North Dakota, New Hampshire, and Massachusetts with sufficient success to warrant its extension to other interested states. By 2003, thirty-eight states were involved in PPAs.

Republicans Retake the White House On taking office in 2001, the administration of George W. Bush made many bold moves regarding environmental protection. President Bush's first choice for director of the EPA, Governor Christine Todd Whitman of New Jersey, was greeted somewhat skeptically by environmentalists. On one hand, as governor, she had fought midwestern coal-fired plants that were polluting New Jersey's air. On the other, she had cut the state environmental-protection agency's budget for enforcement. Although groups like the Sierra Club did not endorse her selection, they did not oppose it either. However, Bush's choice for secretary of the Department of Interior, Gale Norton, was widely criticized by green organizations. Her background as a lawyer-lobbyist for polluting firms and for property rights groups raised concerns about her commitment to the department's mission. When Whitman resigned her EPA post in 2003, President Bush turned to another governor, Mike Leavitt of Utah, to head the agency. Like Whitman, Leavitt's gubernatorial record on environmental issues was mixed. For example, he exerted great effort to keep spent nuclear fuel from coming into Utah, but he also supported construction of a new highway through wetlands near the Great Salt Lake.[19]

In terms of environmental policy initiatives, the Bush administration fostered change. One of its first actions was to reject the Kyoto Protocol, an international agreement to reduce emissions of greenhouse gases that contribute to global warming. Next came a proposal to increase drilling for oil and natural gas on public lands, including the ecologically fragile Arctic National Wildlife Refuge. The regulations requiring environmental-impact assessments for highway and airport construction were weakened, as were restrictions on logging and mining on federal property.[20] New EPA rules to allow power plants, refineries, and industrial facilities to remodel without requiring them to reduce emissions of harmful pollutants were met with widespread opposition in the states. In fact, thirteen states and twenty cities filed suit challenging the federal government's action as a violation of the Clean Air Act.[21] A related proposal, the Clean Skies initiative, which aimed at cutting emissions from power plants by 70 percent by 2018, was more popular with states. It allows utilities to, in effect, buy and sell the right to pollute, as long as the aggregate amount of pollution does not exceed a predetermined level. An EPA program for which funding was increased during the Bush administration was the program that cleans up and redevelops abandoned industrial sites. Quite clearly, the Bush years signaled a new era in environmental policy.

Environmental Policy in the States

State and local governments have taken on greater responsibility for financing and operating environmental-protection programs and have become policy initiators. For example, Congress was gridlocked on acid rain legislation for years, but some states took unilateral actions to cut sulfur dioxide emissions within their borders (New Hampshire and New York were the first). Several states, including New Jersey and Ohio, passed legislation requiring firms to clean up hazardous wastes from industrial property before selling the property. Such legislation helps prevent companies from abandoning polluted sites that present health risks and leaving them for the states to clean up. California's far-reaching policies to improve the nation's worst air quality have become a model for other states and the national government. The Golden State also has led the way in its efforts to conserve water through, among other things, a statute requiring the use of water-efficient washing machines. Today, states have ventured forth on several environmental fronts, notably climate change. One-quarter of the states require utilities to use renewable sources for at least some of their power generation; New England states have agreed to roll back the production of greenhouse gases to their 1990 levels by 2010.[22] The bottom line: "States issue most of the permits, initiate most of the enforcement and compliance actions, and develop many of the innovative ideas for dealing with environmental issues."[23] The *Breaking New Ground* box explores the prospects of alternative fuels, an idea whose time has come.

States operate many of their pollution-control programs under the auspices of federal legislation and the EPA. They must develop and implement plans and standards under a host of federal laws. The Safe Drinking Water Act, for instance, requires local water systems to meet national standards for acceptable levels of contaminants such as coliform (a type of bacteria), asbestos, copper, and lead in their water supply. The Clean Air Act mandates the creation of vehicle inspection and maintenance programs for smog-stricken jurisdictions. State and local governments are closer to pollution problems and hence are best situated to address them on a day-to-day basis. The problem with this approach, according to states and localities, is that they have to pay a large portion of the costs themselves. Approximately 77 percent of the money in state environmental budgets comes from state revenues. Even the EPA acknowledged that the cost of federally imposed environmental mandates on state and local governments could bust their budgets, requiring millions of dollars of new spending.

BREAKING NEW GROUND

Driving Green: Environmentally Friendly Alternative Fuels

Imagine a day when you can drive into a "gas station" and fill up your car with a very different kind of fuel, maybe electricity, or hydrogen, or even fuels derived from agricultural waste. That day may not be as far off as you might think. The government, scientists, and automobile manufacturers have teamed up to explore a whole range of alternative fuels for vehicles. The impetus for this research comes from the need to shift from reliance on fossil fuels, such as petroleum products, to other energy sources that are less environmentally harmful. California, which has enacted stringent air pollution laws to deal with its smoggy skies, created several electric charging stations, even though by 2004, the electric car initiative had largely stalled. One promising recent effort in the state (and one that is popular in midwestern farm states) is the use of

ethanol, a fuel that is fermented from corn. Already on the road in California are an estimated 200,000 hybrid vehicles such as the Toyota Prius, which can run on ethanol or gasoline. At a super gas station in San Diego, for example, drivers have several fuel options: ethanol, diesel, biodiesel (made from recycled cooking grease), propane and natural gas (used primarily in buses), as well as three grades of unleaded gasoline.

The latest alternative fuel initiative coming out of the Golden State involves the use of hydrogen. California is considering a proposal to build a statewide network of 200 hydrogen filling stations along major highways and interstates. At the same time, the national government is funding research into hydrogen fuel cells. Many believe that if hydrogen-refueling stations are built every twenty miles or so, automakers will be more likely to produce hydrogen-powered vehicles, and consumers will be more receptive to buying them. But this bold move carries with it substantial risk: Scientists disagree on whether the mass-scale development of

hydrogen-fueled cars is even possible within the near future.

Meanwhile, at a factory in Missouri, a process called thermal depolymerization is turning turkey bones into light crude oil. In its first year, the plant is expected to produce over 7 million gallons of bio-derived oil, a modest amount compared to oil drilling but at a substantially lower environmental cost. Although we may not be gassing up our cars with turkey byproducts just yet, those Thanksgiving Day leftovers may have an entirely new use.

SOURCES: Miguel Bustillo and Gary Polakovic, "Governor Pushes for 'Hydrogen' Highways," *Los Angeles Times*, www.latimes.com/news/ local (January 20, 2004); Laurent Belsie and Mary Wittenburg, "Fuel from Foul," *Christian Science Monitor* (September 25, 2003), pp. 13–16; "Fill It Up with French-Fry Grease," *Christian Science Monitor* (August 6, 2003), p. 3; Matthew L. Wald, "Report Questions Bush Plan for Hydrogen-Fueled Cars," *New York Times*, www.nytimes.com (February 6, 2004).

State Spending to Protect the Environment Fiscally stressed states face hard choices about shifting expenditures, raising taxes, and imposing new fees to pay for environmental protection. In 2003, aggregate state spending on the environment and natural resources was $15.1 billion, down slightly from the preceding year.[24] This figure represents about 1.4 percent of total state spending, the lowest percentage in the past fifteen years. Table 18.1 shows how states allocated their environmental and natural resources expenditures for 2003 across different functional areas. The data in the table indicate that more money was budgeted for fish and wildlife programs (such as managing game and fish resources and enforcing related state laws) than for any other single expenditure category, followed by water resources programs. By far, nuclear waste programs, a primary responsibility of the national government, received the lowest levels of funding from states.

State Organizational Approaches States have established their own environmental-protection agencies and natural resource departments. The primary difference among the states in the structures of these agencies and departments is whether these functions are housed within a single large agency or assigned to different agencies. An example of the more comprehensive, single agency structure is found in Delaware's Department of Natural Resources and Environmental Control, composed of five divisions: Air and Waste Management, Fish and Wildlife, Parks and Recreation, Soil and Water Conservation, and Water Resources. Arizona separates functions across a Department of Environmental Quality, a Game and Fish Department, and a Natural Resources Division within the State Land Department. Different still are states such as Colorado, which combine environmental protection and public health in the same department.

In the mid-1990s, the leaders of state environmental-protection departments met in Phoenix to discuss common concerns and to create an organization to represent their interests. The result was the Environmental Council of the States (ECOS). By 2002, forty-nine states (Kentucky is the exception) and several

TABLE 18.1   State Budgets for Environmental Protection and Natural Resources

CATEGORY	AMOUNT (IN MILLIONS OF DOLLARS)
Water resources	2,187
Water quality	1,439
Drinking water	577
Marine and coastal	430
Forestry	1,598
Land management	1,091
Soil conservation	379
Mining reclamation	349
Pesticides control	225
Geological survey	179
Fish and wildlife	2,836
Hazardous waste	1,582
Solid waste	939
Nuclear waste	49
Air quality	1,280
Total	15,139

SOURCE: R. Steven Brown and Michael J. Kiefer, "ECOS Budget Survey: Budgets Are Bruised, but Still Strong," *ECOStates* (Summer 2003): 12.

territories had become members. ECOS is a nonprofit, nonpartisan association that has as its mission environmental improvement nationwide, with states as the driving force. The organization has three goals:[25]

- To exchange ideas, views, and experiences among members.
- To foster cooperation and coordination in environmental management.
- To articulate state positions on environmental issues to Congress and the EPA.

Ultimately, ECOS seeks greater decisionmaking authority for states vis-à-vis environmental policy. Acknowledging that state commitment to environmental protection varies, the amount of authority would vary also. States with an established track record would enjoy more leeway to design and implement their own programs; other states would not. Performance partnership agreements, mentioned earlier, are the first step in this direction.

State Commitment to Environmental Protection As noted earlier, states often face pressure from economic interests to weaken environmental regulations. Despite this pressure, at least some states have exceeded the guidelines set by the EPA to insure air quality. A survey of states found that nearly 30 percent had ambient air standards that went beyond the requirements of federal law.[26] What causes states to adopt more stringent regulations than EPA requires? The answer seems to lie in the strength of green groups, supportive public opinion, and the ability to convert this pro-environment political climate into legislative action.

States are often ranked on their environmental programs and performance. One rating system used state environmental conditions (such as the release of cancer-causing toxins) and state policies (such as environmental spending) to produce its comprehensive rankings.[27] The rating system found the greenest states to be Vermont, South Dakota, and Hawaii; the least green states were Louisiana, Alabama, and Indiana. Figure 18.2 categorizes the states into three groups, based on the rankings. Although regional variation exists within the best and middle categories, the states faring the worst are located in the South and Midwest. Montana, which lands in the middle category, might need to redouble its efforts to reach the best classification because the state constitution guarantees its citizens the right to a clean and healthful environment. A Montana supreme court ruling in 1999 reaffirmed the right.[28] Why are some states more committed to environmental protection than other states are? The explanation mirrors the reasons why some states exceed EPA regulations and others do not: the level of pro-green public opinion, the power of environmental interest groups, and the receptivity of policymakers to the issue.[29] These three factors are important determinants of a state's stance on environmental protection and natural resource conservation.

Green Localities

Local governments regularly take action to protect the environment and conserve natural resources. For instance, during 2003, Atlanta sponsored a tree-

| FIGURE 18.2 | **Green Rankings for the States** |

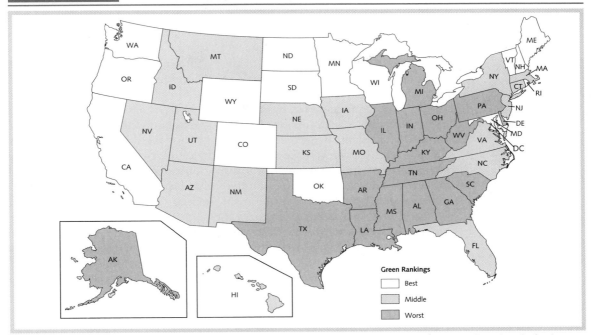

SOURCE: "Green Rankings for the States," from Chris Kromm, Keith Ernst, Jaffer Battica, *Gold and Green 2000* (Durham, N.C.: Institute for Southern Studies, November 2000). Reprinted by permission.

planting project for National Arbor Day; Kansas City, Missouri, promoted its Keep Kansas City Beautiful anti-litter campaign; the green power program in Riverside, California, offered classes on recycling and composting; Spokane, Washington, adopted a special tax in support of open space conservation. Meanwhile, New York City added 300 Toyota Prius vehicles—with a fuel efficiency rating of fifty miles per gallon—to its municipal fleet.[30] More than 100 cities joined the Cities for Climate Protection campaign to reduce the emissions of greenhouse gases. But even as cities and counties make decisions and allocate funds to protect the environment, they take plenty of actions that contribute to environmental degradation and natural resource loss. Think about the negative environmental consequences of a city government's approval of a developer's request to construct a new shopping mall at the city's edge. Natural resources are lost as the land is cleared of trees and vegetation, and wildlife habitat is destroyed. Once the mall opens, traffic congestion leads to polluted air; stormwater runoff from parking lots results in polluted rivers. As a city grows and develops, it produces a large **ecological footprint** in terms of its impact on the earth and its resources.[31]

Many cities have taken steps to become more green, that is, to soften the impact of their ecological footprint. Seattle is one such city, beginning with its

ecological footprint

The size of the environmental impact imposed on the earth and its resources.

1994 comprehensive plan, Toward a Sustainable Seattle. In functions such as land use, transportation, and housing, among others, the city set goals and adopted policies designed to make it more environmentally friendly. City departments were required to assess the environmental impact of their operations and devise ways of lessening that impact. Political scientist Kent Portney's research compared cities' commitment to sustainability and ranked Seattle at the top of the list, followed by Scottsdale, Arizona; San Jose, California; Boulder, Colorado; Santa Monica, California; Portland, Oregon; and San Francisco, California.[32] The approach taken by San Francisco is especially interesting: the city's 1997 sustainability plan identified several areas of concern such as air quality, biodiversity, climate change, and open spaces. For these areas of concern, specific indicators were developed to gauge the progress that the city has or has not made. For instance, the number of native plant species in parks is one indicator of biodiversity, as is the number of different bird species sighted.[33]

Some cities have become more green, such as the Minnesota communities that have begun to map and protect unspoiled ecosystems within their midst, but others have not.[34] Research on why some large cities are more green than others suggests that one explanation lies in the rate of population change. Growing cities, perhaps recognizing the threat that growth poses to natural resources and environmental quality, have adopted more green policies than non-growing cities have. Also, cities with a highly educated citizenry and with a Democratic electorate are more likely to enact pro-environment policies.[35]

DEALING WITH WASTE

One of the byproducts of modern life is waste of all varieties. Households, schools, hospitals, businesses, and factories produce massive quantities of waste daily. When garbage collectors in New York City went on strike several years ago, the towers of smelly refuse that piled up on city streets reminded New Yorkers how important this particular city service was. More threatening to public health and the environment are the toxic wastes generated by certain industrial processes, and the wastes associated with nuclear power. One of the challenges for government is finding better ways to manage all this waste.

Recycling Solid Waste

Vast amounts of household and industrial refuse are generated daily in the United States. Americans produce almost 370 million tons of garbage annually, or about 1.31 tons per person.[36] In general, states with more commercial and industrial activity tend to generate more solid waste than those with a more agricultural economy. Of the solid waste generated in a year, nearly 8 percent is combusted in waste-to-energy plants, another 27 percent is recycled or composted, leaving about 65 percent destined for landfills. Thousands of landfills were in operation in the 1980s; today there are about 2,300.[37] Many of them are so-called super dumps, where more than 500 tons of waste are disposed daily. (And, of course, some people use the "fling it out of the car" method of disposal. One study of America's highways found an average of 950 beer cans and bottles per mile.[38])

Like nuclear and hazardous waste, solid waste often brings out the not-in-my-backyard (**NIMBY**) syndrome. Everyone generates garbage, and lots of it, but no one wants to have it smelling over the back fence or threatening the well water. (There are some exceptions, of course, which has given rise to the term **PIMBY**.) The shortage of disposal sites has naturally driven up the price of land disposal in the dumps that still operate, and disposal fees have tripled in many localities during the past few years. Many cities must ship their waste hundreds of miles and across state lines to find an open dump site. For example, household garbage from suburban New York City communities may be transported to a dump in central Illinois or rural Virginia. One-quarter of the trash dumped in Michigan's landfills comes from other states or from Canada.[39] Burning trash in waste-to-energy plants once seemed the perfect solution: disposing solid waste and creating electrical power. But the high cost of building and operating these incinerators, especially as air-quality standards increased, has lessened their promise.

Recycling is a waste-management solution that makes good sense. Although estimates vary, approximately 38 percent of municipal solid waste is paper, another 12 percent is yard trimmings, and nearly all of these waste streams could be recycled.[40] Packaging and containers, often made of plastic, make up about one-third of municipal solid waste, and at least some of this waste could be recycled. Many states have aggressively tackled the mounting garbage problem by adopting statewide recycling laws, and a growing number of cities and counties have begun their own recycling efforts. In Portland, Oregon, residents separate recyclables into ten different categories—newspapers, magazines, cardboard, aluminum, plastic milk jugs, and so on—before city crews pick them up.[41] By 2002, the United States had more than 8,875 curbside collection programs.[42]

Recycling is not a panacea for the solid waste problem, however. It requires citizen cooperation if it is to be affordable, and some people simply will not cooperate. Recycling rates for aluminum cans and plastic soft drink bottles peaked at 63 percent and 41 percent, respectively. A city cannot refuse to collect non-participants' garbage without creating a public health problem. Another dilemma is the shortage of markets for recycled paper, aluminum cans, plastics, and other materials.

For some states, glutted markets and low prices for recyclables make it difficult to reach their recycling goals. Unable to sell the recyclable material, which instead piles up in warehouses, some localities resorted to paying brokers to haul it away. As a means of addressing that problem, states have stepped into market development—that is, they are enacting legislation and devising incentives to create a market for recycled goods. For example, when the demand for recycled newsprint fell, California and Connecticut passed laws requiring that publishers use a minimum amount of recycled content in newsprint.[43] Twelve states followed suit, and the market for recycled newsprint rebounded. Now, almost 60 percent of newsprint is recycled. These minimum content laws are just one alternative that states have in market development. Other approaches include sanctions (such as taxes on manufacturers based on their use of virgin materials),

NIMBY

Not in my backyard; the public desire to keep an unwanted facility out of a neighborhood.

PIMBY

Put in my backyard; a willingness to accept what others do not want, usually because of the economic benefit.

incentives (such as the provision of rebates to manufacturers using recovered materials), and exhortations (such as buy-recycled programs). Most state governments have adopted rules requiring or encouraging their agencies to purchase recycled paper products. A promising approach debuted in Minnesota in 2000 when the Sony Corporation agreed to fund a program to recycle any outdated Sony products owned by Minnesotans.[44] The program quickly spread to other states.

Approximately one-quarter of the nation's solid waste is recycled, but the figures are substantially higher (49 percent) in Maine and Oregon, and much lower in Montana and Wyoming (less than 10 percent). The explanation for why some states recycle at a greater rate than others is fairly straightforward: access and economics. In other words, recycling rates are higher in states that offer comprehensive curbside recycling programs and impose unit charges for refuse disposal.[45] Making recycling convenient for consumers and creating an economic disincentive not to do so stimulates recycling.

Managing the vast quantity of solid waste generated in our mass consumption, throwaway society is not easy. Recycling is an appealing option, but we cannot recycle everything. Some of the garbage must therefore be incinerated or deposited in a landfill. Every new waste technology has its own difficult issues, and the states and localities, with limited assistance from the federal government, are striving to deal effectively with the huge task of managing the country's garbage.

Managing Hazardous Waste

The image of garbage mountains rising above the horizon is disconcerting, to say the least. But solid waste is just one of several contributors to environmental destruction. Another insidious public health threat comes from hazardous waste—the poisonous byproducts of industrial processes. If these byproducts are toxic, corrosive, flammable, or reactive, they are considered hazardous. The industries that generate 90 percent of the hazardous waste in the United States are chemical and allied products, primary metals, petroleum and coal products, fabricated metal products, and rubber and plastic products.

Hazardous waste is more ubiquitous than most people realize. Pesticide residues, used motor oil, discarded cadmium batteries, used refrigerants, and paint sludge are hazardous leftovers that are frequently found in households and in so-called nonpolluting industries. It is no exaggeration to say that hazardous waste is all around us. Table 18.2 lists the five states where the largest amounts of toxic chemicals were released into the air, water, and ground in 2001. Ohio took the unwanted prize in toxic air emissions, Texas led in surface water discharges, and more toxins were released into the ground in Nevada than in any other state.[46]

The primary dilemma concerning hazardous waste is what to do with it. The discovery that wastes were not being properly or safely disposed of triggered government involvement; when hazardous liquids began seeping into people's basements from long-buried barrels, children playing in fields uncovered rotting drums of toxic waste, and motorists developed unusual skin rashes from pesti-

TABLE 18.2		State Leaders in Toxic Releases, 2001			
STATES LEADING IN TOTAL TOXIC AIR EMISSIONS	AMOUNT (IN THOUSANDS OF POUNDS)	STATES LEADING IN TOXIC SURFACE WATER DISCHARGES	AMOUNT (IN THOUSANDS OF POUNDS)	STATES LEADING IN TOXIC RELEASES INTO THE GROUND	AMOUNT (IN THOUSANDS OF POUNDS)
Ohio	121,341	Texas	26,008	Nevada	778,244
North Carolina	115,280	Indiana	20,134	Utah	745,779
Texas	102,741	Pennsylvania	18,741	Arizona	601,488
Georgia	92,020	Mississippi	12,965	Alaska	498,234
Pennsylvania	89,049	Louisiana	11,908	New Mexico	102,122

SOURCE: "Releases: Geography State Report," *TRI Explorer*, U.S. Environmental Protection Agency, www.epa.gov (July 2003).

cides sprayed along the roadway, government was called in. Some states feared that imposing tough new hazardous waste regulations would make them less attractive to industry. Others were concerned that tightening the laws for waste disposal would have the perverse effect of increasing the incidence of illegal dumping. A national policy initiative seemed preferable to state attempts at solving the problems.

The national government responded to the mounting crisis with two pieces of legislation: the Resource Conservation and Recovery Act (RCRA) of 1976 and the Comprehensive Environmental Response, Compensation, and Liability Act of 1980 (also known as Superfund). RCRA provides for cradle-to-grave tracking of waste and establishes standards for its treatment, storage, and disposal. Any firm that generates 220 pounds of hazardous waste per month (an amount that fills a fifty-five-gallon barrel about halfway) is covered by the law.[47] RCRA is considered partially pre-emptive because states have a degree of discretion and flexibility in implementation. Once the EPA is satisfied that a state program meets its standards and possesses adequate enforcement mechanisms, the agency authorizes the state to operate its own hazardous waste management program. Under RCRA, states can impose fines and hold individuals criminally liable for violating its provisions.

Superfund was passed in recognition of the fact that no matter how comprehensive and cautious hazardous waste management is in the future, the pollution of the past remains with us. Under Superfund, the national government can intervene to clean up a dangerous hazardous waste site and later seek reimbursement from responsible parties. Originally, the law contained a provision dubbed "polluter pays," which created a cleanup fund from fees levied on chemical manufacturers and the petroleum industry. These fees, which generated between $1 and $2 billion annually, allowed government to step in and begin the cleanup before all the complex legal issues were resolved. The cleanup fund provision expired in 1995, however, and affected industries have been successful in blocking its renewal. Thus, Superfund has become a program funded by taxpayers.

One of the first actions taken under Superfund was the identification of particularly troublesome sites in need of immediate cleanup, the National Priorities List (NPL). New Jersey was the state with the most sites on the list; Nevada had the fewest. One factor confounding the Superfund program is determining which parties—waste generators, waste transporters, site owners—are responsible for paying for the cleanup. Some of the firms that dumped toxic waste at these sites have gone out of business, and the hope of recovering any of the cleanup costs is remote. As time passed, frustration grew over the slow pace of remediation. Subsequent amendments to the law increased funding levels for the program (although Superfund expenditures peaked in 2001), and expanded the role for state governments in selecting cleanup remedies. In addition, EPA launched a new initiative to clean up and redevelop contaminated industrial sites, or **brownfields.** Many states have adopted their own mini-Superfund statutes that authorize them to conduct site assessments and initiate remedial cleanup actions or force a responsible party to do so. Many states have also passed laws making it easier to redevelop brownfields, adopted community right-to-know (about hazardous wastes in the area) statutes, and conducted household hazardous waste collection drives.

An issue that has bedeviled the states is disposing of hazardous waste. Disposal sites are locally unwanted land uses (**LULUs**). When efforts to find new disposal facilities are thwarted, states look beyond their borders for solutions. Some states and tribal governments have been willing to accept other states' hazardous waste for disposal, seeing it as a way to generate revenue. But even waste-importing states have their limits. At one point, Alabama banned hazardous waste importation from twenty-two states, an action that was struck down eventually by the federal courts. Alabama lawmakers responded with a fee schedule that taxed out-of-state waste at three times the rate of in-state-generated waste. The effect was dramatic: The quantity of out-of-state waste dropped by one-half, but the business still generated $30 million for the state treasury. Unfortunately for Alabama, the U.S. Supreme Court ruled in 1992 that the surcharge on out-of-state waste violated the interstate commerce clause. Regardless, efforts to block out-of-state waste will continue until solutions to the hazardous waste disposal problem are found. One eminently plausible, if partial, solution to waste-disposal dilemmas is to reduce the amount of waste generated in the first place. Less waste produced means less waste to dispose of.

Storing Nuclear Waste

Nuclear power was once thought of as a solution to the nation's energy problems, but it carries a heavy price: deadly, radioactive waste. The federal government plans to bury high-level nuclear waste, which retains its toxicity for hundreds of thousands of years, at Yucca Mountain, an isolated spot 100 miles northwest of Las Vegas.[48] The Bush administration has accepted the Department of Energy's recommendation to begin storing 77,000 tons of high-level waste at the site by 2010. This plan has generated a firestorm of protest from environmentalists and Nevada officials.[49] One concern is the rate of corrosion for the canisters in which the waste would be stored; another is the safety of shipping the waste to the site.

---

brownfields

Abandoned industrial sites with real or perceived environmental contamination.

LULU

Locally unwanted land use; a broad category of undesirable facilities such as landfills and prisons.

Low-level radioactive wastes (LLWs) are much less toxic in a relative sense because they break down to safe levels of radioactivity in anywhere from a few weeks or months to 300 years. LLWs are produced by commercial nuclear power installations (46 percent), nuclear-related industries (39 percent), and medical and research institutions (15 percent). The waste, much of it stored in fifty-five-gallon steel drums, includes items such as contaminated laboratory clothes, tools, equipment, and leftover bomb materials as well as bulk wastes.

The Low-Level Radioactive Waste Policy Act of 1980 made each state responsible for the disposal of the waste generated within its borders. States have the choice of managing LLWs within their own jurisdictions (that is, developing their own disposal sites) or entering into an interstate compact for out-of-state disposal. As expected, a few states have opted to handle the problem alone, but most have joined with their neighbors to forge a regional answer to the disposal question.

interstate compacts

Formal agreements among a subset of states, usually to solve a problem that affects each of the member states.

The use of **interstate compacts** to address the LLW problem was particularly inventive because nuclear waste disposal has historically been considered a federal responsibility. When interstate compacts are successful, they are a shining example of what the states can accomplish when left to their own devices.[50] Potential member states have to negotiate a draft compact that must be ratified by their legislatures and by Congress. Negotiations often break down as each state tries to get the best deal for itself, precisely the goal of each of the other participating states. By 2004, ten interstate LLW compacts had been formed; six states remained unaligned, preferring to go it alone. As shown in Figure 18.3, several of the compacts are decidedly nonregional in their composition. For example, the two Dakotas joined Arizona and California to form the Southwestern compact; Texas teamed up with Maine and Vermont to create the Texas compact.

The case of the Midwest compact demonstrates the hard decisions faced by all the compacts. The Midwest compact was one of the first to win congressional consent. Seven states were members; each agreed that it would take its turn to host a disposal facility for the entire compact. Weighing three factors for each state—the volume of LLW produced, the radioactivity of that waste, and transportation modes and routes—compact members selected Michigan as the first host state. Michigan spent several years evaluating the suitability of three possible disposal locations, only to reject all of them. The compact was no closer to a regional disposal site than it had been at the outset. In reaction, the other states booted Michigan out of the Midwest compact (Michigan is currently unaligned). Ohio, the runner-up to Michigan in the earlier state-selection process, became the host state.

NIMTOO

Not in my term of office; the desire by elected officials to avoid accepting LULUs while they are in office.

With compacts in place and host states selected, the next challenge is the actual construction of new disposal facilities. This step can be difficult because of the **NIMTOO** (not in my term of office) phenomenon. But time is of the essence because existing sites have begun to restrict access. For example, the Hanford, Washington, site accepts waste only from members of the Northwest and Rocky Mountain compacts and, beginning in 2008, the Barnwell, South Carolina, site plans to exclude waste from outside the Atlantic compact. As for other compacts, only California and Texas are slated to begin operations at their disposal facilities in the near future. In the meantime, generators are being told to store their waste on site or contract with private vendors for safe storage.[51]

| FIGURE 18.3 | **Low–Level Radioactive Waste Compacts** |

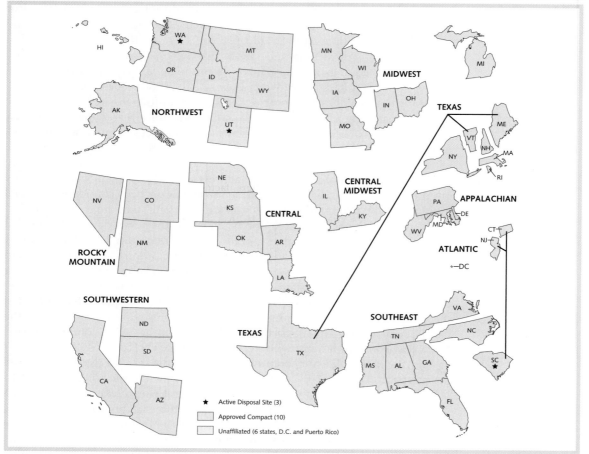

NOTE: Data as of December 31, 2000. Alaska and Hawaii belong to the Northwest Compact. Puerto Rico is unaffiliated.
SOURCE: Nuclear Regulatory Commission, www.nrc.gov/waste/llw-disposal/compacts.html (June 2003).

The lack of guarantees about the future consequences of nuclear waste disposal makes it a prospect both fascinating and frightening. Some observers predict that if California's power shortages of the early 2000s occur again—and
spread to other states—the demand for nuclear power will grow.[52] If so, the debate over disposal issues will intensify.

TWO CHALLENGES FOR POLICYMAKERS

Several challenges loom for those who are tangled up in the thicket of environmental policymaking. The growing influence of economic logic on environmental decisions is one; the widespread but shifting public support for

environmentalism is another. A problem that is only going to intensify is water shortages, a dilemma that already strains interstate relations in the West. The two challenges discussed below, environmental justice and ecoterrorism, will force policymakers to confront some disturbing realities of environmental policy.

Environmental Justice

In the early 1980s, protesters who fought vigorously against the dumping of polychlorinated biphenyl (PCB)-contaminated soil in a rural North Carolina county spawned a new movement: environmental justice. In general, the argument is that poor and minority communities suffer disproportionate exposure to environmental health risks. Two law school professors put the matter this way:

> People of color throughout the United States are receiving more than their fair share of the poisonous fruits of industrial production. They live cheek by jowl with waste dumps, incinerators, landfills, smelters, factories, chemical plants, and oil refineries whose operations make them sick and kill them young. They are poisoned by the air they breathe, the water they drink, the fish they catch, the vegetables they grow, and in the case of children, the very ground they play on.[53]

Research has found inequities in environmental policy.[54] For instance, one study of the relationship between race and the enforcement of environmental laws by the EPA showed that white communities received faster action and more satisfactory results than did minority communities.[55] One of the distinctive differences between areas that contain commercial hazardous waste facilities and those that do not is the proportion of minority residents.[56] Communities with these facilities tend to have double the proportion of minority residents than those without them. Other research, however, takes issue with contentions of environmental inequities. Statewide studies of Superfund site locations in New Jersey and hazardous waste facilities in South Carolina did not find statistically significant links to race or ethnicity.[57]

Concern over environmental justice has led several states to take action. For example, Arkansas passed legislation that discourages the location of high-impact solid waste management facilities within twelve miles of each other. Exemptions may be granted if specific benefits are provided to the host community in the form of jobs, fees, and improvements to infrastructure. In Louisiana, the Department of Environmental Quality was instructed to hold public hearings and make policy recommendations on environmental equity issues. Even the U.S. Department of Justice has gotten involved: The agency is reviewing state regulatory decisions that increase the environmental burden on minority communities.[58] It is clear that environmental justice will continue to be a salient topic for policymakers well into the future.[59]

Ecoterrorism

Environmentalists have long employed tactics such as civil disobedience as a way of attracting attention to their cause. For example, some have climbed trees in old-growth forests and become tree-sitters in an effort to keep loggers from cutting down the trees and destroying wildlife habitat. Others have locked arms and stood in highways to block trucks carrying hazardous waste into their communities. But those tactics pale in comparison to the actions taken by radical environmental groups such as the Earth Liberation Front (ELF). To members of this group, violence is an acceptable means of furthering their political objectives. To that end, they have vandalized new sport utility vehicles (SUVs) on dealership lots and set luxury homes on fire. These types of actions have been labeled ecoterrorism.

By 2003, reports from the FBI estimated the total number of ecoterrorism incidents at around 600, with property losses in the neighborhood of $50 million.[60] One of the first attacks occurred in 1998, when a new development in the Vail, Colorado, ski resort was burned to the ground. Ecoterrorists defended their actions as protecting the habitat for a threatened species, the Canadian lynx. Since then, their targets have expanded, as illustrated by the 2003 torching of a large condominium complex being built in an upscale San Diego neighborhood. At the core of the ecoterrorist agenda is opposition to the corporate sector and its profiteering. One of the ELF's goals is to "inflict economic damage on those profiting from the destruction and exploitation of the natural environment."[61] The ELF is a shadow organization, organized into autonomous groups that operate independently, with a remarkable capacity for attracting media attention.[62]

Legislators in several states have responded to these incidents by sponsoring bills that increase the penalties for property damage in the name of environmental protection. In Oregon, for example, legislators debated a new category of crime, **ecosabotage,** that could be prosecuted under the state's racketeering laws. If states do not take action on this issue, Congress may. In 2003, a bill called the Stop Terrorism of Property Act was introduced in the U.S. House of Representatives. Obviously, at both the state and national levels, policymakers want to crack down on zealous ecoterrorists. Caught in the middle are mainstream environmental groups that have publicly deplored the radical organizations but, by the same token, see these legislative measures as essentially anti-environmental.

ecosabotage

An action designed to inflict economic damage to those who profit at the expense of the natural environment; a tactic of ecoterrorists.

CHAPTER RECAP

- Public opinion shows support for environmental protection and economic growth; however, achieving one goal often comes at the expense of the other. Government's role is to balance the two objectives.
- The national government has been an important force in environmental protection. The recent performance partnership agreements and grants give states more power to set their own spending priorities.
- Environmental conditions and state programs vary from one state to another. A recent study found Vermont to be the greenest state, and Louisiana to be the least green.
- Many cities, such as Seattle, Washington, have embraced sustainability and have adopted green policies. Research shows that the explanation for this approach involves population growth, an educated citizenry, and a Democratic electorate.

- A tremendous amount of solid waste is generated daily in the United States. Although most of it is disposed of in landfills, recycling continues to be a promising approach.
- Two major federal programs, RCRA and Superfund, have set the hazardous waste management agenda. States play a major part in implementing RCRA, and they partner with the federal government in Superfund cleanups.
- Interstate compacts (there are ten) are used for the disposal of low-level radioactive waste.
- Two challenges facing contemporary policymakers are environmental justice and ecoterrorism. Although states have made strides in dealing with the former, they have just begun to confront the latter issue.

Key Terms

environmental self-audit *(p. 510)*
sustainability *(p. 510)*
partial pre-emption *(p. 513)*
ecological footprint *(p. 519)*
NIMBY *(p. 521)*
PIMBY *(p. 521)*

brownfields *(p. 524)*
LULU *(p. 524)*
interstate compacts *(p. 525)*
NIMTOO *(p. 525)*
ecosabotage *(p. 528)*

Surfing the Web

The official web site of the Environmental Protection Agency (EPA) is **www.epa.gov.** It is packed with information about the EPA's programs and initiatives.

The official web site of the Department of the Interior is **www.doi.gov.** It contains a wealth of information about the various activities of the agency.

All states have agencies devoted to environmental protection and natural resource conservation. See, for example, Oregon at **www.deq.state.or.us** and Ohio at **www.dnr.state.oh.us.**

A good place to track environmental protection policies, laws, and regulations is at **enviro2.blr.com.** This site is maintained by Business and Legal Reports, a firm that advertises itself as "making state environmental compliance easier."

For more information about environmental issues, contact the Sierra Club at **www.sierraclub.org,** the National Wildlife Federation at **www.nwf.org,** the Nature Conservancy at **www.nature.org,** and the Grassroots Recycling Network at **www.grn.org.**

To learn about the impact of pollution on the public, explore the web site of the Environmental Justice Foundation at **www.ejfoundation.org.**

REFERENCES

CHAPTER 1 NEW DIRECTIONS FOR STATE AND LOCAL GOVERNMENT PP. 1–23

1. Governor Janet Napolitano, "State of the State Address," January 12, 2004, Phoenix, Ariz.
2. Governor Tim Pawlenty, "State of the State Address," February 5, 2004, St. Paul, Minn.
3. Governor Arnold Schwarzenegger, "State of the State Address," January 6, 2004, Sacramento, Calif.
4. Governor Brad Henry, "State of the State Address," February 2, 2004, Oklahoma City, Okla.
5. Bruce Wallin, "State and Local Governments Are American, Too," *The Political Science Teacher* 1 (Fall 1988): 1–3.
6. Mike Sullivan, quoted in "Wyoming's Governor Signs Law to Restructure State Government," *Denver Post* (March 5, 1989), p. 8B.
7. "The Innovations in American Government Award," www.innovations.harvard.edu (January 28, 2004).
8. Beth Walter Honadle, "Defining and Doing Capacity Building: Perspective and Experiences," in Beth Walter Honadle and Arnold M. Howitt, eds., *Perspectives on Management Capacity Building* (Albany, N.Y.: SUNY Press, 1986), pp. 9–23.
9. "Grading the States 2001," *Governing* 14 (February 2001): 34; Grading the Counties, *Governing* 15 (February 2002): 28; and "Grading the Cities," *Governing* 13 (February 2000): 22–91.
10. Julie Bund and Gene M. Lutz, "Connecting State Government Reform with Public Priorities: The Iowa Test Case," *State and Local Government Review* 31 (Spring 1999): 73–90.
11. David M. Hedge, *Governance and the Changing American States* (Boulder, Colo.: Westview, 1998).
12. Gail Russell Chaddock, "Bush Education Law Transforming Schools," *Christian Science Monitor* (January 8, 2004), p. 3.
13. Terry Sanford, *The Storm over the States* (New York: McGraw-Hill, 1967), p. 21.
14. Quoted in Sanford, *The Storm over the States*.
15. John Herbers, "The New Federalism: Unplanned, Innovative, and Here to Stay," *Governing* 1 (October 1987): 28.
16. William A. Galston and Geoffrey L. Tibbetts, "Reinventing Federalism," *Publius* 24 (Summer 1994): 23–48.
17. Sheryl Gay Stolberg, "As Congress Stalls, States Pursue Cloning Debate," *New York Times,* www.nytimes.com (May 26, 2002).
18. Ann O'M. Bowman and Richard C. Kearney, *The Resurgence of the States* (Englewood Cliffs, N.J.: Prentice-Hall, 1986).
19. Sanford, *Storm over the States.*

20. Ann O'M. Bowman and Richard C. Kearney, "Dimensions of State Government Capability," *Western Political Quarterly* 41 (June 1988): 341–62; David R. Morgan and Kenneth Kickham, "Modernization Among the U.S. States: Change and Continuity from 1960 to 1990," *Publius: The Journal of Federalism* 27 (Summer 1997): 23–39.
21. Larry Sabato, *Goodbye to Good-time Charlie: The American Governor Transformed,* 2d ed. (Washington, D.C.: Congressional Quarterly Press, 1983).
22. Deil S. Wright, *Understanding Intergovernmental Relations,* 3d ed. (Pacific Grove, Calif.: Brooks-Cole, 1988).
23. James L. Garnett, *Reorganizing State Government: The Executive Branch* (Boulder, Colo.: Westview, 1981).
24. Alan Rosenthal, *Legislative Life: People, Process, and Performance in the States* (New York: Harper & Row, 1981).
25. Robert A. Kagan et al., "The Evolution of State Supreme Courts," *Michigan Law Review* 76 (1978): 961–1005.
26. Jacqueline Calmes, "444 North Capitol Street: Where State Lobbyists Are Learning Coalition Politics," *Governing* 1 (February 1988): 17–21.
27. Charles Strum, "Vanity for a Cause: States Expand Special Plates," *New York Times* (February 22, 1993), p. A8.
28. Penelope Lemov, "Balancing the Budget with Billboards and Souvenirs," *Governing* 8 (October 1994): 46–50.
29. Seth Mydans, "From Signs to Pistols, Cash-Short Cities Sell Past," *New York Times* (September 6, 1993), p. 6.
30. Tamar Lewin, "Battle for Family Leave Will Be Fought in States," *New York Times* (July 27, 1991), p. A6.
31. Russell L. Hanson, "Health Care Reform, Managed Competition, and Subnational Politics," *Publius* 24 (Summer 1994): 49–68.
32. Donald P. Haider-Markel, "Policy Diffusion as a Geographical Expansion of the Scope of Political Conflict: Same Sex Marriage Bans in the 1990s," *State Politics and Policy Quarterly* 1 (Winter 2001): 5–26.
33. Penelope Lemov, "The Workers' Comp Tug of War," *Governing* 10 (January 1997): 24–25.
34. Craig Savoye, "States Spare Residents from Telemarketers," *Christian Science Monitor* (December 22, 2000), p. 8.
35. William Celis III, "Unusual Public School Aiming to Turn a Profit," *New York Times* (November 6, 1991), p. B8.
36. David W. Winder and James T. LaPlant, "State Lawsuits Against Big Tobacco: A Test of Diffusion Theory,"

State and Local Government Review 32 (Spring 2000): 132–41.

37. Derek Cane, "States Sue Music Labels for Price Fixing," dailynews.yahoo.com (August 8, 2000).

38. Ann O'M. Bowman, "Horizontal Federalism: Exploring Interstate Interactions," *Journal of Public Administration Research and Theory* 14 (October 2004): 535–46.

39. Ann O'M. Bowman and Michael A. Pagano, "The State of American Federalism, 1993–1994," *Publius* 24 (Summer 1994): 49–68.

40. Governor George Voinovich, quoted in "Reassessing Mandates," *State Policy Reports* 11 (October 1993): 16.

41. Brad Knickerbocker, "States Take the Lead on Global Warming," *Christian Science Monitor* (October 10, 2003), pp. 1, 12.

42. John Kincaid, "The State of U.S. Federalism, 2000–2001: Continuity in Crisis," *Publius: The Journal of Federalism* (Summer 2001): 1–69.

43. Todd Sloane, "Governors Face Mounting Deficits," *City & State* 8 (November 4, 1991): 1, 20.

44. Don Boyd, quoted in "Overview," 2004 *State of the States* (Washington, D.C.: Pew Center on the States, 2004), p. 5.

45. John Holahan et al., *State Responses to 2004 Budget Crises: A Look at Ten States* (Washington, D.C.: The Urban Institute, 2004).

46. Bowman, "Horizontal Federalism," p. 17.

47. Thomas J. Lueck, "New York Vengeful over Neighbor's 'Raid,'" *New York Times* (October 11, 1994), p. C20.

48. Michael Johnston, "Right and Wrong in American Politics: Popular Conceptions of Corruption," in Arnold J. Heidenheimer and Michael Johnston, eds., *Political Corruption: Concepts and Contexts* (New Brunswick, N.J.: Transaction, 2002), pp. 173–91; see also, Richard T. Boylan and Cheryl X. Long, "Measuring Public Corruption in the American States, *State Politics and Policy Quarterly* (Winter 2003): 420–38.

49. Kenneth R. Gosselin and Christopher Keating, "Corruption Costs Jobs, Study Says," *Hartford Courant*, www.ctnow.com/news/local (February 25, 2004).

50. Jessica Garrison, Noam N. Level, and Patrick McGreevy, "Key Aide to Hahn Quits Amid Probe of Agencies," *Los Angeles Times*, www.latimes.com/news/local (March 26, 2004).

51. Kristin Collins, "Phipps Sent to Jail," *Raleigh News and Observer*, www.newsobserver.com/phipps (March 3, 2004).

52. Jerry Mitchell, "Diaz, Minor Plead Innocent to New Extortion, Bribery Charges," *Jackson Clarion-Ledger*, www.clarionledger.com/news (February 24, 2004).

53. "Table 2. Percent of Population by Race and Hispanic or Latino Origin, 2000," U.S. Census Bureau, www.census.gov/population/cen2000/phc-t6/tab02.pdf.

54. Rodney E. Hero and Caroline J. Tolbert, "A Racial/Ethnic Diversity Interpretation of Politics and Policy in the States of the U.S.," *American Journal of Political Science* 40 (August 1996): 851–71; Rodney E. Hero, *Faces of Inequality: Social Diversity in American Politics* (New York: Oxford University Press, 2000).

55. Genaro C. Armas, "Minority Groups to Swell by 2050," *The State* (March 18, 2004): A4.

56. Christopher Conte, "North of the Border," *Governing* 15 (January 2002): 29–33.

57. "Resident Population of the 50 States, the District of Columbia, and Puerto Rico," www.census.gov.

58. Adam Bell, "Utah Might Sue N.C. over Congressional Seat," *The State* (January 5, 2001): 7.

59. David Firestone, "Hurt in '90, Georgia Goes Out for Census," *New York Times* (March 15, 2000), p. A14.

60. Daniel J. Elazar, *American Federalism: A View from the States*, 3d ed. (New York: Harper & Row, 1984).

61. David R. Morgan and Sheilah S. Watson, "Political Culture, Political System Characteristics, and Public Policies Among the American States," *Publius* 21 (Spring 1991): 31–48.

62. Jody L. Fitzpatrick and Rodney E. Hero, "Political Culture and Political Characteristics of the American States: A Consideration of Some Old and New Questions," *Western Political Quarterly* 41 (March 1988): 145–53.

63. Keith Boeckelman, "Political Culture and State Development Policy," *Publius* 21 (Spring 1991): 49–92; Russell L. Hanson, "Political Culture Variations in State Economic Development Policy," *Publius* 21 (Spring 1991): 63–81.

64. James P. Lester, "A New Federalism: Environmental Policy in the States," in Norman Vig and Michael Kraft, eds., *Environmental Policy in the 1990s* (Washington, D.C.: Congressional Quarterly Press, 1994), pp. 51–68; Steven A. Peterson and James N. Schubert, "Predicting State AIDS Policy Spending," paper presented at the annual meeting of the American Political Science Association, New York City, September 1994.

65. Joel Lieske, "Regional Subcultures of the United States," *Journal of Politics* 55 (November 1993): 888–913.

66. Frederick M. Wirt, " 'Soft' Concepts and 'Hard' Data: A Research Review of Elazar's Political Culture," *Publius* 21 (Spring 1991): 1–13.

67. Emily Van Dunk, "Public Opinion, Gender and Handgun Safety Policy Across the States," paper presented at the annual meeting of the Midwest Political Science Association, Chicago, April 2000.

68. Elaine B. Sharp, "Introduction," in Elaine B. Sharp, ed., *Culture Wars and Local Politics* (Lawrence: University Press of Kansas, 1999), pp. 1–20.

69. Jonathan Walters, "Uncivil Disunion," *Governing* 17 (March 2004): 14.

70. Cecil Angel, "City Gives Tentative OK for Muslim

Prayer Calls," *Detroit Free-Press,* www.freep.com (April 21, 2004).

71. John Shannon, "The Return to Fend-for-Yourself Federalism: The Reagan Mark," *Intergovernmental Perspective* 13 (Summer/Fall 1987): 34–37.

72. Alan Ehrenhalt, "The Increasing Irrelevance of Congress," *Governing* 11 (January 1998): 6–7.

CHAPTER 2   FEDERALISM AND THE STATES
PP. 24–54

1. David B. Walker, *The Rebirth of Federalism,* 2d ed. (New York: Chatham House, 2000), pp. 19–38.

2. James Madison, *The Federalist,* No. 45, 1788.

3. Quoted in Richard Hofstadter, *The American Political Tradition* (New York: Vintage Books, 1948), p. 5.

4. Quoted in ibid., p. 9.

5. Ibid., pp. 9–10.

6. Richard H. Leach, *American Federalism,* No. 45 (New York: W.W. Norton, 1970), p. 1.

7. Charles S. McCoy, "Federalism: The Lost Tradition?" *Publius* 31 (Spring 2001): 1–14.

8. Quoted in Leach, *American Federalism,* p. 1788.

9. Walter Berns, "The Meaning of the Tenth Amendment," in Robert A. Goldwin, ed., *A Nation of States* (Chicago, Ill.: Rand McNally, 1961), p. 130.

10. Forrest McDonald, *States' Rights and the Union: Imperium in Imperio* (Lawrence: The University of Kansas Press, 2000). Walker, *Rebirth,* Chapter 2.

11. Hofstadter, *American Political Tradition,* p. 72.

12. *Santa Fe School District* v. *Doe,* 530 U.S. 99-62 (2000).

13. *McCulloch* v. *Maryland,* 4 Wheaton 316 (1819).

14. *Gibbons* v. *Ogden,* 9 Wheaton 316 (1819).

15. *Reno* v. *Condon,* 64120 S.Ct. 666 (2000).

16. *United States* v. *Darby,* 312 U.S. 100 (1941) at 124.

17. *National League of Cities* v. *Usery,* 426 U.S. 833 (1976).

18. *Garcia* v. *San Antonio Metropolitan Transit Authority,* 105 S.Ct. 1007, 1011 (1985).

19. Ibid. (O'Connor, dissenting.)

20. John C. Pittenger, "*Garcia* and the Political Safeguards of Federalism: Is There a Better Solution to the Conundrum of the Tenth Amendment?" *Publius: The Journal of Federalism* 22 (Winter 1992).

21. *U.S.* v. *Lopez,* 115 S.Ct. 1424 (1995). See Kenneth T. Palmer and Edward B. Laverty, "The Impact of *U.S.* v. *Lopez* on Intergovernmental Relations," *Publius* 26 (Summer 1996): 109–26.

22. *U.S.* v. *Morrison,* 2000 U.S. LEXIS 3422.

23. *Kansas* v. *Hendricks,* 117 S.Ct. 2072 (1997).

24. *Printz* v. *U.S.,* 521 U.S. 98 (1997).

25. *Coalition for Economic Equity* v. *Wilson,* No. 96-50605 (1997).

26. *Lee* v. *Harcleroad,* No. 96-1924 (1997).

27. *Hill* v. *Colorado,* No. 98-1856 (2000).

28. *Tahoe-Sierra Preservation* v. *Tahoe Regional Planning Agency,* S.Ct 00-1167 (2002).

29. *Nevada Department of Human Resources* v. *Hibbs,* S.Ct. 01-1368 (2003).

30. *Seminole Tribe of Florida* v. *Florida,* 116 S.Ct. 1114 (1996).

31. *College Savings Bank* v. *Florida Prepaid Postsecondary Education Expense Board et al.,* 98 S.Ct. 149 (1999); *Kimel* v. *Florida Board of Regents,* 120 S.Ct. 631 (2000).

32. *Federal Maritime Commission* v. *South Carolina Ports Authority,* No. 01-46 (2002).

33. Donald F. Kettl, "Potomac Chronicle: Tales of Devolution and the Flow of Power," *Governing* (August 1999): 10.

34. *Crosby* v. *National Foreign Trade Council,* 2000 U.S. LEXIS 4153.

35. *Sternberg* v. *Carhart,* 2000 U.S. LEXIS 4484.

36. *Lorillard Tobacco* v. *Reilly,* No. 00-596 (2000).

37. *Bush* v. *Gore et al.,* 00 S.Ct. 949 (2000).

38. Martha Derthick, "American Federalism: Half-full or Half-empty?" *Brookings Review* (Winter 2000): 24.

39. William H. Stewart, "Metaphors, Models and the Development of Federal Theory," *Publius* 12 (Spring 1982): 5–24.

40. Wright, *Understanding Intergovernmental Relations,* pp. 40–42.

41. Walker, *Rebirth,* Chapter 4.

42. Morton Grodzins, "Centralizing and Decentralization in the American Federal System," in Robert A. Goldwin, ed., *A Nation of States* (Chicago, Ill.: Rand McNally, 1961), pp. 1–3.

43. Richard S. Williamson, "A New Federalism: Proposals and Achievements of President Reagan's First Three Years," *Publius* 16 (Winter 1986): 11–28; Richard L. Cole and Delbert A. Taebel, "The New Federalism: Promises, Programs, and Performance," *Publius* 16 (Winter 1986): 3–10.

44. Timothy J. Conlan, "Federalism and Competing Values in the Reagan Administration," *Publius* 16 (Winter 1986): 29–47.

45. Ann O'M. Bowman and Michael A. Pagano, "The State of American Federalism 1989–1990," *Publius* 20 (Summer 1990): 1–25.

46. John Kincaid and Richard L. Cole, "Changing Public Attitudes on Power and Taxation in the American Federal System," *Publius* 31 (Summer 2001): 205–14.

47. Richard L. Cole, John Kincaid, Rodney V. Hissong, and Enid Arvidson, "Devolution: Where's the Revolution?" *Publius* 29, no. 4 (2001): 99–112.

48. Eliza Newlin Carney, "Power Grab," *National Journal* (April 11, 1998): 798–801; Christopher A. Mooney, "The Decline of Federalism and the Rise of Morality—Policy Conflict in the United States," *Publius* 30 (Winter 2000): 171–88.

49. Deil S. Wright, *Understanding Intergovernmental Relations,* 3d ed. (Pacific Grove, Calif.: Brooks/Cole 1988).

50. W. Dale Mason, *Indian Gaming: Tribal Sovereignty and American Politics* (Norman: University of Oklahoma Press, 2000).

51. Wright, 1988.

52. Neil MacFarquhar, "Ruling Like Solomon's Favoring New Jersey Splits Ellis Island in Two," *New York Times* (April 2, 1997), p. A21; "Ellis Island, New York–New Jersey," *The Hartford Courant* (May 27, 1998), pp. A1, A15; Bill McGarigle, "The Battle over Ellis Island," www.govtech.net (January 2000): 44–45.

53. Pamela M. Prah, "States Stuck with Federal $29 Billion Tab, NCSL Says," www.Stateline.org (March 10, 2004): 2–4.

54. Donald F. Kettl, "10th Amendment Turf War," *Governing* (October 1998): 13.

55. Carol S. Weissert and Sanford F. Schram, "The State of U.S. Federalism, 1999–2000," *Publius* 30 (Winter 2000): 1–19.

56. Derthick, "American Federalism," p. 27.

57. See Lamar Alexander, "Breaking Up the Arrogant Empire," *Madison Review* 1 (Fall 1995): 16.

58. See David B. Walker, "The Advent of Ambiguous Federalism and the Emergence of New Federalism III," *Public Administration Review* 56 (May/June 1996): 271–80.

59. John Kincaid and Richard L. Cole, "Issues of Federalism in Response to Terrorism," *Public Administration Review* 62 (September 2002): 181–92.

60. Frank J. Thompson, "Homeland Security: The State and Local Crucible," *Public Administration Review* 62 (September 2002): 18–20.

61. Marcia L. Godwin, "Innovations Across American States," paper presented at the 2001 annual meeting of the American Political Science Association, August 30–September 2, 2002, San Francisco, Calif.

62. Samuel H. Beer, "The Future of the States in the Federal System," in Peter Woll, ed., *American Government: Readings and Cases* (Boston: Little, Brown, 1981), p. 92.

CHAPTER 3   STATE CONSTITUTIONS
PP. 55–79

1. Dixie Roberts, "Alabamians Go by an Outdated Book," *New York Times*, www.nytimes.com/2002/02/25/opinion (February 25, 2002); David M. Halbinger, "G.O.P. Chief's Ideas for Raising Alabama," *New York Times*, www.nytimes.com/2003/06/04/national/04BAMA.html (June 4, 2003).

2. G. Alan Tarr, *Understanding State Constitutions* (Princeton, N.J.: Princeton University Press, 1999).

3. U.S. Advisory Commission on Intergovernmental Relations (ACIR), *State Constitutions in the Federal System*, A-113 (Washington, D.C.: ACIR, 1989), p. 2.

4. Donald S. Lutz, "The United States Constitution as an Incomplete Text," *Annals of the American Academy of Political and Social Science* 496 (March 1989): 23–32.

5. G. Alan Tarr and Mary Cornelia Porter, "Introduction: State Constitutionalism and State Constitutional Law," *Publius* 17 (Winter 1987): 5.

6. Donald S. Lutz, "Toward a Theory of Constitutional Amendment," *American Political Science Review* 88 (June 1994): 356; G. Alan Tarr, ed., *Constitutional Politics in the States* (Westport, Conn.: Greenwood Press, 1996), xv.

7. Donald S. Lutz, "The Iroquois Confederation Constitution: An Analysis," *Publius* 22 (Spring 1998): 99–127.

8. Daniel J. Elazar, "The Principles and Traditions Underlying State Constitutions," *Publius* 12 (Winter 1982): 11.

9. Quoted in Perry Gilbert Miller, "Thomas Hooker and the Democracy of Early Connecticut," *New England Quarterly* 4 (1931): 695.

10. Bruce Fraser, *The Land of Steady Habits: A Brief History of Connecticut* (Hartford: Connecticut Historical Commission, 1986), p. 10.

11. John Estill Reeves, *Kentucky Government* (Lexington: University of Kentucky, 1966), p. 7. As quoted in Penny M. Miller, *Kentucky Government and Politics* (Lincoln: University of Nebraska Press, 1994), p. 82.

12. Albert L. Sturm, "The Development of American State Constitutions," *Publius* 12 (Winter 1982): 61.

13. Ibid., pp. 62–63.

14. Paul G. Reardon, "The Massachusetts Constitution Makes a Milestone," *Publius* 12 (Winter 1982): 45–55.

15. David McCullough, *John Adams* (New York: Touchstone Books, 2001).

16. Quoted in James Bryce, "Nature of the American State," in Bruce Stinebrickner, ed., *State and Local Government*, 3d ed. (Guilford, Conn.: Dushkin, 1987), pp. 20–23.

17. Quoted in Thomas Parrish, "Kentucky's Fourth Constitution Is a Product of Its 1980 Times," in Thad L. Beyle, ed., *State Government: CQ's Guide to Current Issues and Activities 1991–92* (Washington, D.C.: Congressional Quarterly Press, 1991), p. 46.

18. U.S. Advisory Commission on Intergovernmental Relations (ACIR), *The Question of State Government Capability* (Washington, D.C.: ACIR, 1985), p. 36.

19. Council of State Governments, *The Book of the States*, Vol. 33 (Lexington, Ky.: Council of State Governments, 2000), Table 1.1, footnote (a).

20. David Fellman, "What Should a State Constitution Contain?" in W. Brooke Graves, ed., *Major Problems in State Constitutional Revision* (Chicago, Ill.: Public Administration Service, 1960), p. 146.

21. Sturm, "American State Constitutions," p. 64; see Christopher W. Hammons, "Was James Madison Wrong? Rethinking the American Preference for Short, Framework-Oriented Constitutions," *American Political Science Review* 93 (December 1999): 837–49.

22. David C. Nice, "Interest Groups and State Constitutions: Another Look," *State and Local Government Review* 20 (Winter 1988): 22.

23. Donald S. Lutz, "Patterns in the Amending of American State Constitutions," in G. Alan Tarr, ed., *Constitutional Politics in the States* (Westport, Conn.: Greenwood Press, 1996), pp. 24–27.

24. U.S. Advisory Commission on Intergovernmental Relations (ACIR), *A Report to the President for Transmittal to the Congress* (Washington, D.C.: U.S. Government Printing Office, 1955).

25. National Municipal League, *Model State Constitution*, 6th ed., rev. (New York: National Municipal League, 1968).

26. John J. Carroll and Arthur English, "Traditions of State Constitution Making," *State and Local Government Review* 23 (Fall 1991): 103–9.

27. *Gitlow* v. *New York*, 268 U.S. 652 (1925).

28. Thomas C. Marks, Jr., and John F. Cooper, *State Constitutional Law* (St. Paul, Minn.: West, 1988), p. 38.

29. Ibid., pp. 38–42.

30. Marks and Cooper, *State Constitutional Law*, p. 47.

31. Tarr and Porter, "Introduction," p. 9.

32. Stanley H. Friedelbaum, "The Complementary Role of Federal and State Courts," *Publius* 17 (Winter 1987): 48.

33. Council of State Governments, *The Book of the States 1990–91* (Lexington, Ky.: Council of State Governments, 2000), Table 1.3.

34. Albert L. Sturm, *Thirty Years of State Constitution-Making: 1938–1968* (New York: National Municipal League, 1970), pp. 27–28.

35. Cornwell, Goodman, and Swanson, *State Constitutional Conventions*, p. 81.

36. Robert F. Williams, "Are State Constitutional Conventions Things of the Past? The Increasing Role of the Constitutional Commission in State Constitutional Change," *The Hofstra Law and Policy Symposium*, Vol. 1 (1996): 1–26.

37. Janice C. May, "State Constitutions and Constitutional Revision: 1988–89 and the 1980s," *The Book of the States 1990–91* (Washington, D.C.: Council of State Governments, 1991), p. 25.

38. Quoted in U.S. Advisory Commission on Intergovernmental Relations, *State Constitutions in the Federal System* (Washington, D.C.: ACIR, 1989), p. 37.

39. Sturm, "American State Constitutions," p. 104.

40. W. Brooke Graves, "State Constitutional Law: A Twenty-five Year Summary," *William and Mary Law Review* 8 (Fall 1966): 12.

41. ACIR, *State Government Capability*, p. 60.

42. Richard H. Leach, "A Quiet Revolution: 1933–1976," in *The Book of the States 1975–76* (Lexington, Ky.: Council of State Governments, 1976), p. 25.

43. Terry Sanford, *Storm over the States* (New York: McGraw-Hill, 1967), p. 1983.

CHAPTER 4 CITIZEN PARTICIPATION AND ELECTIONS PP. 80–110

1. "Local Innovators," *National Civic Review* 89 (Summer 2000): 1–5.

2. Robert D. Putnam, *Bowling Alone: The Collapse and Revival of American Community* (New York: Simon & Schuster, 2000).

3. William E. Lyons, David Lowery, and Ruth Hoogland De Hoog, *The Politics of Dissatisfaction* (Armonk, N.Y.: M. E. Sharpe, 1992); Albert O. Hirschman, *Exit, Voice and Loyalty: Responses to Decline in Firms, Organizations, and States* (Cambridge, Mass.: Harvard University Press, 1972).

4. Henry E. Brady, Sidney Verba, and Kay Lehman Schlozman, "Beyond SES: A Resource Model of Political Participation," *American Political Science Review* 89 (June 1995): 271–94.

5. Richard Murray and Arnold Vedlitz, "Race, Socioeconomic Status, and Voting Participation in Large Southern Cities," *Journal of Politics* 39 (November 1977): 1064–72.

6. Virginia Sapiro, *The Political Integration of Women* (Urbana: University of Illinois Press, 1983).

7. Jan E. Leighley and Arnold Vedlitz, "Race, Ethnicity, and Political Participation," *Journal of Politics* 61 (November 1999): 1092–1114; Debra Horner, "Critiquing Measures of Political Interest," paper presented at the annual meeting of the Midwest Political Science Association, Chicago, Ill., 2000.

8. J. Eric Oliver, "City Size and Civic Involvement in Metropolitan America," *American Political Science Review* 94 (June 2000): 361–73.

9. Ibid.

10. Earl Black and Merle Black, *Politics and Society in the South* (Cambridge, Mass.: Harvard University Press, 1987).

11. Kim Quaile Hill and Jan E. Leighley, "Party Ideology, Organization, and Competitiveness as Mobilizing Forces in Gubernatorial Elections," *American Journal of Political Science* 37 (November 1993): 1158–78.

12. U.S. Federal Election Commission, www.fec.gov/pages/2000turnout/reg&to00.htm (April 22, 2004).

13. "Muslim Group Starts an Effort to Increase Voter Registration," *New York Times*, www.nytimes.com (February 23, 2002).

14. Brian Faler, "A Polling Site: Record Turnout," *Washington Post* (November 5, 2004), p. A7.

15. "Voter Registration Information," *The Book of the States 2000–01* (Lexington, Ky.: Council of State Governments, 2000), p. 169.

16. "Voter Registration Information," *The Book of the States 2004* (Lexington, Ky.: Council of State Governments, 2004), p. 278.

17. David Foster, "States Get Creative to Raise Voter Turnout," *Nation's Cities Weekly* (October 31, 1994): 10.

18. Margaret Rosenfield, "All-Mail Ballot Elections," Federal Election Commission (September 1995).
19. Priscilla Southwell and Justin Burchett, "The Effect of All-Mail Elections on Voter Turnout," *American Politics Quarterly* 29 (February 2000): 72–80.
20. "Methods of Nominating Candidates for State Offices," *The Book of the States 2004* (Lexington, Ky.: Council of State Governments, 2004), pp. 271–72.
21. John F. Bibby and Thomas M. Holbrook, "Parties and Elections," in Virginia Gray and Russell L. Hanson, eds., *Politics in the American States: A Comparative Analysis,* 8th ed. (Washington, D.C.: Congressional Quarterly Press, 2004), pp. 62–99.
22. Andrew Garber, "Veto Overhauls State Primaries with Montana-style System," *Seattle Times,* www.seattletimes.nwsource.com (April 2, 2004).
23. Alexandra Marks, "New York Wrestles with Its 'Party Machine' in Historic Vote," *Christian Science Monitor* (October 31, 2003), p. 2.
24. Priscilla L. Southwell, "Open Versus Closed Primaries and Candidate Fortunes, 1972–1984," *American Politics Quarterly* 16 (July 1988): 280–95.
25. Charles S. Bullock III, Ronald Keith Gaddie, and Anders Ferrington, "System Structure, Campaign Stimuli, and Voter Falloff in Runoff Primaries," *Journal of Politics* 64 (November 2002): 1210–24.
26. Peter L. Francia and Paul S. Herrnson, "The Synergistic Effect of Campaign Effort and Election Reform on Voter Turnout in State Legislative Elections," *State Politics and Policy Quarterly* 4 (Spring 2004): 74–93.
27. Dennis M. Anderson, "One Way to Run a Legislative Body: The End of an Era in Ohio," *Comparative State Politics* 15 (April 1994): 34–37.
28. Randall W. Partin, "Economic Conditions and Gubernatorial Elections," *American Politics Quarterly* 23 (January 1995): 81–95.
29. Council of State Governments, "Elections 2004," www.csg.org/CSG/States/elections/2004/gubernatorial.htm (November 5, 2004).
30. Kimberly L. Nelson, *Elected Municipal Councils: Special Data Issue* (Washington, D.C.: International City/County Management Association, 2002).
31. Brian F. Schaffner, Gerald Wright, and Matthew Streb, "Teams Without Uniforms: The Nonpartisan Ballot in State and Local Elections," *Political Research Quarterly* 54 (March 2001): 7–30.
32. "Wealthy Activists Bypass Lawmakers," *New York Times* (July 23, 2000), p. A10.
33. Arnold Fleischmann and Lana Stein, "Campaign Contributions in Local Elections," *Political Research Quarterly* 51 (September 1998): 673–89.
34. Luis Ricardo Fraga, "Domination Through Democratic Means: Nonpartisan Slating Groups in City Electoral Politics," *Urban Affairs Quarterly* 23 (June 1988): 528–55.
35. Christopher A. Cooper and Anthony J. Nownes, "Citizen Groups in Big City Politics," *State and Local Government Review* 35 (Spring 2003): 102–11.
36. David B. Magleby, "Taking the Initiative: Direct Legislation and Direct Democracy in the 1980s," *PS: Political Science and Politics* 21 (Summer 1988): 600.
37. Ibid., p. 602.
38. Elisabeth R. Gerber, ed., *Stealing the Initiative* (Upper Saddle River, N.J.: Prentice-Hall, 2001).
39. Caroline J. Tolbert, "Direct Democracy and State Governance Policies," paper presented at the annual meeting of the American Political Science Association, New York City, September 1994.
40. M. Dane Waters, "2002 Initiatives and Referenda," in *The Book of the States 2003* (Lexington, Ky.: Council of State Governments), pp. 281–85.
41. Jillian Lloyd, "A Circus Without Tigers and Lions . . . Oh My!" *Christian Science Monitor* (January 16, 2004), p. 3.
42. Shaun Bowler and Todd Donovan, "Economic Conditions and Voting on Ballot Propositions," *American Politics Quarterly* 22 (January 1994): 27–40.
43. "Broder Decries 'Lucrative' Ballot Initiatives," *Yale Bulletin and Calendar,* www.yale.edu/opa/v28.n26/story4.html (March 31, 2000).
44. Mark A Smith, "The Contingent Effects of Ballot Initiatives and Candidate Races on Turnout," *American Journal of Political Science* 45 (July 2001): 700–6. Caroline J. Tolbert, Ramona S. McNeal, and Daniel A. Smith, "Enhancing Civic Engagement: The Effect of Direct Democracy on Political Participation and Knowledge," *State Politics and Policy Quarterly* 3 (Spring 2003): 23–41.
45. Alana S. Jeydel and Brent S. Steel, "Public Attitudes Toward the Initiative Process in Oregon," *State and Local Government Review* 34 (Fall 2002): 173–82.
46. Elisabeth R. Gerber, Arthur Lupia, and Mathew D. McCubbins, "When Does Government Limit the Impact of Voter Initiatives? The Politics of Implementation and Enforcement," *Journal of Politics* 66 (February 2004): 43–68.
47. Valentina A. Bali, "Implementing Popular Initiatives: What Matters for Compliance?" *Journal of Politics* 65 (November 2003): 1130–46.
48. Paula D. McClain, "Arizona 'High Noon': The Recall and Impeachment of Evan Mecham," *PS: Political Science and Politics* 21 (Summer 1988): 628–38.
49. James P. Melcher, "Do They Recall?" *Comparative State Politics* 17 (August 1996): 16–25.
50. Joseph F. Zimmerman, *Participatory Democracy: Populism Revived* (New York: Praeger, 1986).
51. Jim Cleary, as quoted in "Fighting City Hall—and Winning," *The State* (May 26, 1987), p. 7A.
52. Thomas E. Cronin, "Public Opinion and Direct Democracy," *PS: Political Science and Politics* 21 (Summer 1988): 612–19.

53. Thad Kousser, "The California Governor's Recall," *Spectrum: The Journal of State Government* 77 (Winter 2004): 32–36.

54. Quoted in Daniel B. Wood and Mark Sappenfield, "California's Restless Dream," *Christian Science Monitor* (October 3, 2004), p. 8.

55. Kousser "The California Governor's Recall."

56. www.vote2003.ss.ca.gov/Returns/recall/mapN4.htm (April 20, 2004).

57. Jason White, "California Recall Unlikely to Be Repeated Elsewhere," www.Stateline.org (October 10, 2003), www.stateline.org/stateline.

58. Alan Greenblatt, "Total Recall," *Governing* (September 2003), www.governing.com (December 22, 2003).

59. U.S. Advisory Commission on Intergovernmental Relations (ACIR), *Citizen Participation in the American Federal System* (Washington, D.C.: ACIR, 1979).

60. Charles Mahtesian, "The Endless Struggle over Open Meetings," *Governing* 11 (December 1997): 48–51.

61. Neal Peirce, "Oregon's Rx for Mistrusted Government," *National Journal* 24 (February 29, 1992): 529.

62. Christopher Swope, "E-Gov's New Gear," *Governing* 17 (March 2004): 40–42.

63. Shane Harris, "Bridging the Divide," *Governing* 13 (September 2000): 36.

64. Stephen Knack, "Social Capital and the Quality of Government: Evidence from the States," *American Journal of Political Science* 46 (October 2002): 772–85.

65. Harry P. Hatry and Carl F. Valente, "Alternative Service Delivery Approaches Involving Increased Use of the Private Sector," in International City Management Association, *The Municipal Year Book 1983* (Washington, D.C.: ICMA, 1983), pp. 199–216.

66. Mary A. Culp, "Volunteering as Helping," *National Civic Review* 77 (May/June 1988): 224–30.

67. Jeffrey L. Brudney and Beth Gazley, "Federal Volunteerism Policy and the States: An Analysis of Citizen Corps," in *The Book of the States 2003* (Lexington, Ky.: Council of State Governments, 2003), pp. 516–22.

68. Evan J. Ringquist et al., "Lower-Class Mobilization and Policy Linkage in the U.S. States: A Correction," *American Journal of Political Science* 41 (January 1997): 339–44.

69. Rob Gurwitt, "A Government That Runs on Citizen Power," *Governing* 6 (December 1992): 48.

70. Tom W. Rice and Alexander F. Sumberg, "Civic Culture and Government Performance in the American States," *Publius: The Journal of Federalism* 27 (Winter 1997): 99–114.

71. Ibid., p. 113.

CHAPTER 5   POLITICAL PARTIES, INTEREST GROUPS, AND CAMPAIGNS   PP. 111–140

1. Mississippi Secretary of State, "2003 General Election Results," www.mississippi.gov (April 20, 2004).

2. "Mississippi Legislators Name Musgrove New Governor," dailynews.yahoo.com (January 4, 2000).

3. A. James Reichley, "The Future of the American Two-Party System at the Beginning of a New Century," in John C. Green and Rick Farmer, eds., *The State of the Parties*, 4th ed. (Lanham, Md.: Rowman & Littlefield, 2003), pp. 19–37.

4. Sarah M. Morehouse and Malcolm E. Jewell, "State Parties: Independent Partners in the Money Relationship," in Green and Farmer, *The State of the Parties*, 4th ed., pp. 151–68.

5. Kenneth Janda, Jeffrey M. Berry, and Jerry Goldman, *The Challenge of Democracy: Government in America*, 2d ed. (Boston: Houghton Mifflin, 1989), p. 304.

6. David Von Drehle, "Culture Clash: Geography, Technology, and Strategy Have Nurtured a Political Split," *Washington Post National Weekly Edition* (May 24–30, 2004), pp. 6–7.

7. James G. Gimpel and Jason E. Schuknecht, "Reconsidering Political Regionalism in the American States," *State Politics and Policy Quarterly* 2 (Winter 2002): 325–52.

8. Robert S. Erikson, Gerald C. Wright, and John P. McIver, *Statehouse Democracy* (New York: Cambridge University Press, 1993).

9. Malcolm E. Jewell and Sarah M. Morehouse, *Political Parties and Elections in American States*, 4th ed. (Washington, D.C.: Congressional Quarterly Press, 2001).

10. John H. Aldrich, "Southern Parties in State and Nation," *Journal of Politics* 62 (August 2000): 643–70.

11. Alan Greenblatt, "The Soft-Money Crackdown," *Governing* 17 (March 2004): 34–39.

12. Aldrich, "Southern Parties in State and Nation."

13. Robert E. Hogan, "Candidate Perceptions of Political Party Campaign Activity in State Legislative Elections," *State Politics and Policy Quarterly* 2 (Spring 2002): 66–85.

14. Ibid.

15. Christopher P. Gilbert and David A. Peterson, "Minnesota: Christians and Quistians in the GOP," in Mark J. Rozell and Clyde Wilcox, eds., *God at the Grassroots* (Lanham, Md.: Rowman & Littlefield, 1995).

16. Scott Pendleton, "GOP Religious Right Flexes Muscle in Texas," *Christian Science Monitor* (March 28, 1994), p. 2.

17. John F. Persinos, "Has the Christian Right Taken Over the Republican Party?" *Campaigns & Elections* 15 (September 1994): 21–24.

18. Frank J. Sorauf and Paul Allen Beck, *Party Politics in America,* 6th ed. (Glenview, Ill.: Scott, Foresman, 1988).

19. Scott Lasley, "Explaining Third Party Support in American States," paper presented at the annual meeting of the American Political Science Association, Washington, D.C., 1997.

20. Euel Elliott, Gerard S. Gryski, and Bruce Reed, "Minor Party Support in State Legislative Elections," *State and Local Government Review* 22 (Fall 1990): 123–31.

21. Richard L. Berke, "U.S. Voters Focus on Selves, Poll Says," *New York Times* (September 21, 1994), p. A12.

22. Thomas M. Holbrook and Emily Van Dunk, "Electoral Competition in the American States," *American Political Science Review* 87 (December 1993): 955–62.

23. Gary F. Moncrief, Peverill Suire, and Malcolm E. Jewell, *Who Runs for the Legislature?* (Upper Saddle River, N.J.: Prentice-Hall, 2001).

24. Charles Barrilleaux, "A Test of the Independent Influence of Electoral Competition and Party Strength in a Model of State Policymaking," *American Journal of Political Science* 41 (October 1997): 1462–66.

25. John F. Bibby and Thomas M. Holbrook, "Parties and Elections," in Virginia Gray and Russell L. Hanson, eds., *Politics in the American States: A Comparative Analysis,* 8th ed. (Washington, D.C.: Congressional Quarterly Press, 2004), pp. 62–99.

26. Everett Ehrlich, "Virtual Political Reality," *Washington Post National Weekly Edition* (December 22, 2003–January 4, 2004), p. 22.

27. Michael Slackman, "Voters Choosing None of the Above, and Parties Scramble, *New York Times,* www.nytimes.com (April 13, 2004).

28. Ibid.

29. J. P. Monroe, *The Political Party Matrix: The Persistence of Organization* (Albany, N.Y.: SUNY Press, 2001).

30. L. Harmon Zeigler, "Interest Groups in the States," in Virginia Gray, Herbert Jacob, and Kenneth N. Vines, eds., *Politics in the American States,* 4th ed. (Boston: Little, Brown, 1983), pp. 97–131.

31. Clive S. Thomas and Ronald J. Hrebenar, "2002 State Interest Group Power Update: Results and Tables," manuscript (June 12, 2003), pp. 1, 2.

32. "Top 15 Lobbying Organizations," *Minneapolis Star-Tribune,* www.startribune.com (September 28, 2002).

33. Thomas and Hrebenar, "2002 State Interest Group Power Update."

34. Zeigler, "Interest Groups in the States," pp. 111–19.

35. Sarah M. Morehouse, "Interest Groups, Parties, and Policies in the American States," paper presented at the annual meeting of the American Political Science Association, Washington, D.C., 1997.

36. Zeigler, "Interest Groups in the States," p. 117.

37. Clive S. Thomas and Ronald J. Hrebenar, "Toward a Comprehensive Understanding of the Political Party-Interest Group Relationship in the American States," paper presented at the annual meeting of the Western Political Science Association, Seattle, 1999.

38. Howard A. Faye, Allan Cigler, and Paul Schumaker, "The Municipal Group Universe: Changes in Agency Penetration by Political Groups," paper presented at

the annual meeting of the American Political Science Association, Washington, D.C., 1986.

39. Glenn Abney and Thomas P. Lauth, *The Politics of State and City Administration* (Albany, N.Y.: SUNY Press, 1986).

40. Jeffrey M. Berry et al., *The Rebirth of Urban Democracy* (Washington, D.C.: Brookings Institution, 1993).

41. Christopher A. Cooper and Anthony J. Nownes, "Citizen Groups in Big City Politics," *State and Local Government Review* 35 (Spring 2003): 102–11.

42. Virginia Gray and David Lowery, "A Niche Theory of Interest Representation," *Journal of Politics* 58 (February 1996): 91–111.

43. Donald P. Haider-Markel, "Interest Group Survival: Shared Interests Versus Competition for Resources," *Journal of Politics* 59 (August 1997): 903–12.

44. Clive S. Thomas and Ronald J. Hrebenar, "Interest Groups in the States," in Virginia Gray, Herbert Jacob, and Robert B. Albritton, eds., *Politics in the American States,* 5th ed. (Glenview, Ill.: Scott, Foresman/Little, Brown, 1990), p. 143.

45. "Lobbyists: Registration and Reporting," *The Book of the States 2004* (Lexington, Ky.: Council of State Governments, 2004), pp. 305–6.

46. Joyce Bullock, "State Lobby Laws in the 1990s," in *The Book of the States 1994–95* (Lexington, Ky.: Council of State Governments, 1994).

47. Virginia Gray and David Lowery, "Trends in Lobbying in the States," in *The Book of the States 2003* (Lexington, Ky.: Council of State Governments, 2003), pp. 257–62.

48. Alan Rosenthal, *The Third House* (Washington, D.C.: Congressional Quarterly Press, 1993).

49. Clive S. Thomas and Ronald J. Hrebenar, "Comparative Interest Group Politics in the American West," *State Government* 59 (September/October 1986), p. 130.

50. William P. Browne, "Variations in the Behavior and Style of State Lobbyists and Interest Groups," *Journal of Politics* 47 (May 1985): 450–68; Charles W. Wiggins, Keith E. Hamm, and Charles G. Bell, "Interest Group and Party Influence Agents in the Legislative Process: A Comparative State Analysis," *Journal of Politics* 54 (February 1992): 82–100.

51. Ron Faucheux, "The Grassroots Explosion," *Campaigns & Elections* (December/January 1995): 20.

52. Anthony J. Nownes and Patricia Freeman, "Interest Group Activity in the States," *Journal of Politics* 60 (February 1998): 86–112.

53. "Our Gang," *Campaigns & Elections* (December/January 1995): 9.

54. William P. Browne and Delbert J. Ringquist, "Michigan Interests: The Politics of Diversification," paper presented at the annual meeting of the Midwest Political Science Association, Chicago, 1987, p. 24.

55. Fred Monardi and Stanton A. Glantz, "Tobacco Industry Campaign Contributions and Legislative Behavior

at the State Level," paper presented at the annual meeting of the American Political Science Association, San Francisco, 1996, p. 8.

56. Frederick M. Herrmann and Ronald D. Michaelson, "Financing State and Local Elections: Recent Developments," in *The Book of the States 1994–95* (Lexington, Ky.: Council of State Governments, 1994), pp. 228–30.

57. Daniel M. Shea and Michael John Burton, *Campaign Craft: The Strategies, Tactics, and Art of Political Campaign Management* (Westport, Conn.: Praeger, 2001), pp. 75–98.

58. Geralyn M. Miller, "What the Candidates Had to Say," *Comparative State Politics* 20, no. 5 (1999): 13–28.

59. Cleveland Ferguson III, "The Politics of Ethics and Elections," *Florida State University Law Review* 25 (Fall 1997): 463–503.

60. Owen G. Abbe and Paul S. Herrnson, "Campaign Professionalism in State Legislative Elections," *State Politics and Policy Quarterly* (Fall 2003): 223–45.

61. *Campaigns & Elections* 9 (May/June 1988): 1.

62. Kris Axtman, "Que Es Esto? A Texas Debate in Spanish?" *Christian Science Monitor* (March 1, 2002), pp. 1, 4, 5.

63. Jerry Hagstrom and Robert Guskind, "Selling the Candidate," *National Journal* 18 (November 1, 1986): 2619–26.

64. Robert G. Berger, "The Homemade Home Video," *Campaigns & Elections* 12 (October/November 1991): 44–46.

65. Laurent Belsie, "The Surfing Majority? Candidates Expand Presence Online," *Christian Science Monitor* (March 4, 2003), p. 4.

66. Dan Balz, "Hispanic Executive Wins Tex. Democratic Gubernatorial Bid," *Washington Post* (March 18, 2002), p. A2.

67. Thad Beyle, "Governors: Elections, Campaign Costs, Profiles, Forced Exits and Powers," in *The Book of the States 2004* (Lexington, Ky.: Council of State Governments, 2004), pp. 145–56.

68. T. C. Brown, "2 Campaigns for Top Court Could Exceed $6 Million," *Cleveland Plain Dealer* (December 27, 2000), p. 1.

69. George Raine, "Political Ad Wars Expected to Be Costly, Nasty: Candidates' Spending Could Top $1.3 Billion in Races Nationwide," *San Francisco Chronicle,* www.sfgate.com (April 10, 2004).

70. Sarah M. Morehouse, "Money Versus Party Effort: Nominating for Governor," paper presented at the annual meeting of the American Political Science Association, Chicago, 1987.

71. Donald A. Gross and Robert K. Goidel, "The Impact of State Campaign Finance Laws," *State Politics and Policy Quarterly* 1 (Summer 2001): 180–95.

72. William E. Cassie and Joel A. Thompson, "Patterns of PAC Contributions to State Legislative Candidates," in Joel A. Thompson and Gary F. Moncrief, eds., *Campaign Finance in State Legislative Elections* (Washington, D.C.: Congressional Quarterly Press, 1998).

73. Ronald D. Michaelson, "Trends in State Campaign Financing," in *The Book of the States 2003* (Lexington, Ky.: Council of State Governments, 2003), pp. 270–80.

74. "Funding of State Elections: Tax Provisions and Public Financing," in *The Book of the States 2000–01* (Lexington, Ky.: Council of State Governments, 2000), pp. 229–32.

75. "Carter Reaches Signature Threshold, Will Run First 'Clean Election' Campaign for Governor," www.gp.org/press/states/me_04_10_02.html (April 10, 2002).

76. Kedron Bardwell, "Campaign Finance Laws and the Competition for Spending in Gubernatorial Elections," *Social Science Quarterly* 84 (December 2003): 811–25.

CHAPTER 6   STATE LEGISLATURES   PP. 141–171

1. Denny Heck, "Couch Potatoes Are Watching You," *State Legislatures* 24 (January 1998): 40–41; Christopher A. Cooper, "Media Tactics in the State Legislature," *State Politics and Policy Quarterly* 2 (Winter 2002): 353–71; "Legislatures Live," National Conference of State Legislatures, www.ncsl.org/programs/press/leglive.htm (March 29, 2004).

2. James N. Miller, "Hamstrung Legislatures," *National Civic Review* 54 (June 1989): 28–33.

3. "Bill and Resolution Introductions and Enactments: 2003 Regular Sessions," in *The Book of the States 2004* (Lexington, Ky.: Council of State Governments, 2004), pp. 120–21.

4. Ellen Perlman, "The 'Gold-plated' Legislature," *Governing* 11 (February 1998): 36–40.

5. Rich Jones, "State Legislatures," in *The Book of the States 1994–95* (Lexington, Ky.: Council of State Governments, 1994), p. 99.

6. *The Book of the States 2003,* various pages.

7. National Municipal League, *Apportionment in the 1960s,* rev. ed. (New York: National Municipal League, 1970).

8. *Baker* v. *Carr,* 369 U.S. 186, 82 S.Ct. 691 (1962).

9. *Reynolds* v. *Sims,* 84 S.Ct. 1362 (1964).

10. Timothy G. O'Rourke, *The Impact of Reapportionment* (New Brunswick, N.J.: Transaction Books, 1980).

11. Jeremy Buchman, "Save Me a Seat," paper presented at the annual meeting of the American Political Science Association, Washington, D.C., 1997.

12. Quoted in Alan Greenblatt, "The Mapmaking Mass," *Governing* 14 (May 2001): 21.

13. Sam Roberts, "Where Will Mappers of New Districts Draw the Line?" *New York Times* (March 23, 1992), p. B12.

14. William March, "Black Voters Win, Lose with Districting," *Tampa Tribune* (April 6, 1998), pp. B-1, B-5.

15. David M. Hedge, *Governance and the Changing American States* (Boulder, Colo.: Westview, 1998).

16. Ronald E. Weber, "Emerging Trends in State Legislative Redistricting," *Spectrum* 75 (Winter 2002): 13.

17. Michael A. Smith, "One Piece at a Time: The Role of Timing and Sequencing in Pivotal Politics," *Perspectives on Politics* 2 (March 2004): 85–89.

18. "Legislative Compensation: Regular Sessions," in *The Book of the States 2004*, pp. 94–96.

19. Ellen Perlman, "The Gold-Plated Legislature," *Governing* (February 1998): 40.

20. Peverill Squire, "Member Career Opportunities and the Internal Organization of Legislatures," *Journal of Politics* 50 (August 1988): 726–44.

21. Thomas H. Little, "A Systematic Analysis of Members' Environments and Their Expectations of Elected Leaders," *Political Research Quarterly* 47 (September 1994): 733–47.

22. Keith E. Hamm, Ronald D. Hedlund, and Stephanie S. Post, "Committee Specialization in State Legislatures During the Twentieth Century," paper presented at the annual meeting of the American Political Science Association, Washington, D.C., 1997.

23. Alan Rosenthal, *Legislative Life: People, Processes, and Performance in the States* (New York: Harper & Row, 1981).

24. Marvin Overby, Thomas A. Kazee, and David W. Prince, "Committee Outliers in State Legislatures," *Legislative Studies Quarterly* 29 (February 2004): 81–107.

25. Squire, "Member Career Opportunities."

26. Ibid.

27. Allen Ehrenhalt, "Putting Practice into Theory," *Governing* 14 (November 2000): 6, 8.

28. Peverill Squire, "Career Opportunities and Membership Stability in Legislatures," *Legislative Studies Quarterly* 13 (February 1988): 65–77.

29. Roy Brasfield Herron, "Diary of a Legislator," *Southern Magazine* 2 (May 1988): 31.

30. Eric M. Uslaner and Ronald E. Weber, "U.S. State Legislators' Opinions and Perceptions of Constituency Attitudes," *Legislative Studies Quarterly* 4 (November 1979): 563–85.

31. Donald R. Songer et al., "The Influence of Issues on Choice of Voting Cues Utilized by State Legislators," *Western Political Quarterly* 39 (March 1986): 118–25.

32. Uslaner and Weber, "U.S. State Legislators' Opinions," p. 582.

33. "Bill and Resolution Introductions and Enactments, 2003 Regular Sessions," *The Book of the States 2004* (Lexington, Ky.: Council of State Governments, 2004), pp. 120–21.

34. Smith, "One Piece at a Time."

35. Alan Rosenthal, "The Legislature as Sausage Factory," *State Legislatures* 27 (September 2001): 12–15.

36. Tom Loftus, *The Art of Legislative Politics* (Washington, D.C.: Congressional Quarterly Press, 1994), p. 76.

37. Ibid., p. 77.

38. Dawn Duplantier, "An Insider's View of the Legislative Process," *Texas Banking* (August 1997): 5–6.

39. David C. Saffell, "School Funding in Ohio: Courts, Politicians, and Newspapers," *Comparative State Politics* 18 (October 1997): 9–25.

40. "Getting from No to a Little Yes," *State Legislatures* 24 (January 1998): 18.

41. Citizens' Conference on State Legislatures, *The Sometimes Governments: A Critical Study of the 50 American Legislatures*, 2d ed. (Kansas City, Mo.: CCSL, 1973), pp. 41–42.

42. John Grumm, "The Effects of Legislative Structure on Legislative Performance," in Richard Hofferbert and Ira Sharkansky, eds., *State and Urban Politics: Readings in Comparative Public Policy* (Boston: Little, Brown, 1971), pp. 298–322.

43. Albert K. Karning and Lee Sigelman, "State Legislative Reform and Public Policy: Another Look," *Western Political Quarterly* 28 (September 1975): 548–52.

44. Philip W. Roeder, "State Legislative Reform: Determinants and Policy Consequences," *American Politics Quarterly* 7 (January 1979): 51–70.

45. Ann O'M. Bowman and Richard C. Kearney, "Dimensions of State Government Capability," *Western Political Quarterly* 41 (June 1988): 341–62.

46. Alan Rosenthal, "The New Legislature: Better or Worse and for Whom?" *State Legislatures* 12 (July 1986): 5.

47. Charles Mahtesian, "The Sick Legislature Syndrome," *Governing* 10 (February 1997): 16–20.

48. Charles W. Wiggins, as quoted in Andrea Patterson, "Is the Citizen Legislator Becoming Extinct?" *State Legislatures* 12 (July 1986): 24.

49. Representative Vic Krouse, as quoted in Patterson, "Is the Citizen Legislator Becoming Extinct?" p. 24.

50. Alan Rosenthal, "The State Legislature," paper presented at the Vanderbilt Institute for Public Policy Studies, November 1987; James D. King, "Changes in Professionalism in U.S. State Legislatures," *Legislative Studies Quarterly* 25 (May 2000): 327–43.

51. Jones, "State Legislatures," p. 99.

52. Richard Nathan, as cited in Kathe Callahan and Marc Holzer, "Rethinking Governmental Change," *Public Productivity Management & Review* 17 (Spring 1994): 202.

53. Stuart Rothenberg, "How Term Limits Became a National Phenomenon," *State Legislatures* 18 (January 1992): 35–39.

54. Joel A. Thompson and Gary F. Moncrief, "The Implications of Term Limits for Women and Minorities: Some Evidence from the States," *Social Science Quarterly* 74 (June 1993): 300–9.

55. Karen Hansen, "The Third Revolution," *State Legislatures* 23 (September 1997): 20–26.

56. Robert A. Bernstein and Anita Chadha, "The Effects of Term Limits on Representation: Why So Few Women?" in Rick Farmer, John David Rausch Jr., and John C. Green, eds., *The Test of Time: Coping with Legislative Term Limits* (Lanham, Md.: Lexington Books, 2003), pp. 147–58; Stanley M. Caress et al., "Effect of Term Limits on the Election of Minority State Legislators," *State and Local Government Review* 35 (Fall 2003): 183–95.

57. Gary Moncrief and Joel A. Thompson, "On the Outside Looking In: Lobbyists Perspectives on the Effects of State Legislative Term Limits," *State and Local Government Review* 1 (Winter 2001): 394–411; Joel Thompson and Gary Moncrief, "Lobbying Under Limits: Interest Group Perspectives on the Effects of Term Limits in State Legislatures," in Farmer, Rausch, and Green, eds., *The Test of Time: Coping with Legislative Term Limits*, pp. 211–24.

58. Daniel A. Smith, "Overturning Term Limits: The Legislature's Own Private Idaho?" *PS: Political Science and Politics* 36 (April 2003): 215–20.

59. Lucinda Simon, "Legislatures and Governors: The Wrestling Match," *State Government* 59 (Spring 1986): 1.

60. Governor Haley Barbour, State of the State Address, January 26, 2004.

61. Ted Strickland, as quoted in Simon, "Legislatures and Governors," p. 5.

62. "New Assembly Leaders Vow New Decorum," *San Jose Mercury News*, www.mercurynews.com (December 30, 2003).

63. Peter Eichstaedt, "No, No, Two Hundred Times No," *State Legislatures* 21 (July/August 1995): 46–49.

64. Gilbert K. St. Clair, personal communication, June 17, 2003.

65. Madeleine Kunin, as quoted in Sharon Randall, "From Big Shot to Boss," *State Legislatures* 14 (June 1988): 348.

66. Simon, "Legislatures and Governors."

67. Samuel K. Gove, "State Management and Legislative-Executive Relations," *State Government* 54, no. 3 (1981): 99–101.

68. Rosenthal, *Legislative Life*.

69. Dianna Gordon, "Virginia's JLARC: A Standard of Excellence," *State Legislatures* 20 (May 1994): 13–16.

70. Jerry Brekke, "Supreme Court of Missouri Rules Legislative Veto Unconstitutional," *Comparative State Politics* 19 (February 1997): 32–34.

71. Kathleen M. Simon and Dennis O. Grady, "Overseeing Rulemaking Discretion in the Resurgent American States," paper presented at the annual meeting of the American Political Science Association, San Francisco, 1996.

72. As quoted in Dave McNeely, "Is the Sun Setting on the Texas Sunset Law?" *State Legislatures* 20 (May 1994): 17–20.

73. Ibid.

74. William M. Pearson and Van A. Wigginton, "Effectiveness of Administrative Controls: Some Perceptions of State Legislators," *Public Administration Review* 46 (July/August 1986): 328–31.

75. Rosenthal, "The New Legislature," p. 5.

76. Rosenthal, *The Decline of Representative Democracy*, p. 85.

77. Alan Ehrenhalt, "An Embattled Institution," *Governing* 5 (January 1992): 28–33.

78. Dianna Gordon, "Theme for a Day," *State Legislatures* 30 (January 2004): 29.

79. Ibid.

CHAPTER 7   GOVERNORS   PP. 172–206

1. David Broder, "Governors Tackling Real-World Problems," *The News and Observer* (August, 12, 2001), p. D3.

2. Eileen Shanahan, "The Sudden Rise in Statehouse Status," *Governing* 9 (September 1996): 15.

3. Ann O'M. Bowman and Richard C. Kearney, *The Resurgence of the States* (Englewood Cliffs, N.J.: Prentice-Hall, 1986), p. 52.

4. For a more detailed discussion of the processes and results of the state government reform movement, see Bowman and Kearney, *Resurgence*, pp. 47–54.

5. Larry Sabato, *Goodbye to Goodtime Charles: The American Governorship Transformed* (Lexington, Mass.: Lexington Books, 1978), p. 13.

6. As quoted in George F. Will, "Ashcroft in 2000? He's Playing the Part," *Hartford Courant* (September 9, 1997), p. A24.

7. Jonathan D. Austin, www.cnn.com/2000/ALLPOLITICS (November 7, 2000).

8. Thad L. Beyle, "Election, Campaign Costs, Profiles, Forced Exits, and Powers," in *The Book of the States 2004* (Lexington, Ky.: Council of State Governments, 2004), p. 150.

9. Ibid.

10. Randall W. Partin, "Assessing the Impact of Campaign Spending in Governors' Races," *Political Research Quarterly* 55 (March, 2002): 213–24.

11. Thad Beyle, "The Governors," *The Book of the States 2003* (Lexington, Ky.: The Council of State Governments, 2003), p. 179.

12. Ibid., p. 180.

13. Beyle, 2003: p. 125; Richard G. Niemi, Harold W. Stanley, and Ronald J. Vogel, "State Economies and State Taxes: Do Voters Hold Governors Accountable?" *American Journal of Political Science* 39 (November 1995): 936–57; Robert C. Lowry, James E. Alt, and Karen E. Feree, "Fiscal Policy Outcomes and Accountability in American States," *American Political Science Review* 92 (December 1998): 759–72.

14. Elaine Stuart, "Roaring Forward," *State Government News* (January/February 1999): 9.

15. Sandor M. Polster, "Maine's King Makes Independence a Virtue," www.Stateline.org (November 30, 1999).

16. Sandor M. Polster, "Maine's King Makes Independence Work," www.Stateline.org (May 28, 2002): 1.

17. Ibid.

18. As quoted in Alan Ehrenhalt, "The Debilitating Search for a Flabby Consensus," *Governing* 9 (October 1996): 8.

19. Robert B. Gunnison, "Davis Says He Calls All the Shots," *San Francisco Chronicle* (July 21, 1999), p. A1.

20. Thad L. Beyle, "Being Governor," in Carl E. Van Horn, *The State of the States,* 3d ed. (Washington, D.C.: Congressional Quarterly Press, 1996), p. 88.

21. Michael Dukakis, as quoted in Thad L. Beyle and Lynn R. Muchmore, *Reflections on Being Governor* (Washington, D.C.: National Governors' Association, 1978), p. 45.

22. Deborah D. Roberts, "The Governor as Leader: Strengthening Public Service Through Executive Leadership," in Frank J. Thompson, ed., *Revitalizing State and Local Public Service* (San Francisco, Calif.: Jossey-Bass, 1993), pp. 41–67.

23. *The Book of the States 2004,* Vol. 36, Table 4.3.

24. Rochelle L. Stanfield, "Just Do It," *National Journal* 28 (March 30, 1996): 693–94.

25. Thad L. Beyle and Lynn R. Muchmore, "The Governor and the Public," in Beyle and Muchmore, eds., *Being Governor,* p. 24.

26. Lowry, Alt, and Feree, "Fiscal Policy"; Susan B. Hansen, "Life Is Not Fair: Governors' Job Performance Ratings and State Economies," *Political Research Quarterly* 52 (March 1999): 167–88.

27. Alan Greenblatt, "States of Frustration," *Governing* (January 2004): 28.

28. Jonathan Walters, "Full Speed Ahead: Remaking a State Through Ideology and Determination," *Governing* (November 2001): 44–51.

29. Alan Ehrenhalt, "Moving Mountains," *Governing* (December 2002): 36.

30. This exchange is cited in Rosenthal, *Governors and Legislators,* p. 18.

31. Thad L. Beyle and Lynn R. Muchmore, "The Governor as Party Leader," in Beyle and Muchmore, eds., *Being Governor,* pp. 44–51; Morehouse, *Governor as Party Leader,* pp. 45–51.

32. Alfred E. Smith, as quoted in George Weeks, "Statehouse Hall of Fame, Ten Outstanding Governors of the 20th Century," paper presented at the annual meeting of the Southern Political Science Association, Memphis, Tenn., November 1981.

33. John Wagner, "Hunt," *The News and Observer* (April 1, 2000), pp. 1A, 18A.

34. Tom McCall, as quoted in Samuel R. Soloman, "Governors: 1960–1970," *National Civic Review* (March 1971): 126–46.

35. Diane Kincaid Blair, "The Gubernatorial Appointment Power: Too Much of a Good Thing?" in Beyle and Muchmore, eds., *Being Governor,* p. 117.

36. Dennis Patterson, "Succession Changes Governors' Approach to Job," *The Daily Reflector* (November 14, 1999), p. B6.

37. As quoted in Coleman B. Ransome, Jr., *The American Governorship* (Westport, Conn.: Greenwood Press, 1982), p. 121.

38. *Rutan et al.* v. *Republican Party of Illinois,* 1110 S.Ct. 2229, 1990.

39. Thad Beyle, "The Governors," in Virginia Gray and Russell Hanson, eds., *Politics in the American States* (Washington, D.C.: CQ Press, 2004), p. 216.

40. Rosenthal, *Governors and Legislators,* pp. 11–12.

41. Beyle, "The Governors 1992–93," pp. 38–39; Dall Forsyth, *Memos to the Governor: An Introduction to State Budgeting* (Washington, D.C.: Georgetown University Press, 1997).

42. Charles Barrilleaux and Michael Berkman, "Do Governor's Matter? Budgeting Rules and the Politics of State Policymaking," *Political Research Quarterly* 56 (December 2003): 409–17.

43. Ibid.

44. E. Lee Bernick and Charles W. Wiggins, "The Governor's Executive Order: An Unknown Power," *State and Local Government Review* 16 (Winter 1984): 3–10.

45. James Conant, "Executive Branch Reorganization: Can It Be an Antidote for Fiscal Stress in the States?" *State and Local Government Review* 24 (Winter 1992): 3–11.

46. James K. Conant, "State Reorganization: A New Model?" *State Government* 58 (April 1985): 130–38.

47. Garnett, *Reorganizing State Government,* pp. 124–25.

48. Robert F. Bennett, as quoted in Flentje, "Governor as Manager," p. 70. For a description of failure in reorganization in Florida, see also Less Garner, "Managing Change Through Organization Structure," *State Government* 60 (July/August 1987): 191–95.

49. *The Book of the States 2003,* Table 4.3.

50. H. Edward Flentje, "Clarifying Purpose and Achieving Balance in Gubernatorial Administration," *Journal of State Government* 62 (July/August 1989): 161–67.

51. Thomas M. Holbrook, "Institutional Strength and Gubernatorial Elections: An Exploratory Analysis," *American Politics Quarterly* 21 (July): 261–71.

52. Richard C. Kearney, "How a 'Weak' Governor Can Be Strong: Dick Riley and Education Reform in South Carolina," *State Government* 60 (July/August 1987): 150–56.

53. Jay Barth and Margaret R. Ferguson, "American Governors and Their Constituents: The Relationship Between Gubernatorial Personality and Public Approval," *State Politics and Policy Quarterly* 2 (Fall 2002): 268–82; Nelson C. Dometrius, "Gubernatorial Approval

and Administrative Influence," *State Politics and Policy Quarterly* 2 (Fall 2002): 251–67.

54. Beyle, 2004, p. 206.

55. Kevin Sack, "North Carolina Incumbent Finds Recipe for Success," *New York Times* (October 14, 1996), p. A22; Rochelle L. Stanfield, "Just Do It," *National Journal* (March 30, 1996), pp. 694–95.

56. Kathleen Murphy, "Lame Duck Govs Offer Tips to Rookies," www.Stateline.org (November 13, 2002): 1–3.

57. See Thad L. Beyle, "Enhancing Executive Leadership in the States," *State and Local Government Review* 27 (Winter 1995): 18–35.

58. Matt Bai, "The Taming of Jesse," *Newsweek* (October 15, 1999): 38.

59. Jesse Ventura, *I Ain't Got Time to Bleed: Reworking the Body Politic from the Bottom Up* (New York: Villard, 1999).

60. Ventura, *I Ain't Got Time,* p. 179.

61. Jonathan Walters, "The Taming of Texas," *Governing* (July 1998): 18–22.

62. Charles Mahtesian, "The Conciliator-in-Chief," *Governing* 9 (December 1996): 28.

63. Barth and Ferguson, 2002.

64. Scott M. Matheson, with James Edwin Kee, *Out of Balance* (Salt Lake City, Utah: Peregrine Smith Books, 1986), p. 186.

65. See Paul West, "They're Everywhere! For Today's Governors, Life Is a Never-Ending Campaign," *Governing* 3 (March 1990): 51–55.

66. Beyle, (1995) "Enhancing Executive Leadership," p. 33.

67. David L. Martin, "Alabama's Governor Removed on Ethics Conviction: Implications for Other American States," *Comparative State Politics* 14, no. 3 (1994): 1–4.

68. As quoted in Alice Chasan Edelman, "Is There Room at the Top?" in Beyle and Muchmore, eds., *Being Governor,* p. 107.

69. Thad L. Beyle, "The Governors, 1992–93," *The Book of the States 1994–95* (Lexington, Ky.: Council of State Governments, 1996), p. 47.

CHAPTER 8 PUBLIC ADMINISTRATION: BUDGETING AND SERVICE DELIVERY PP. 207–242

1. H. George Frederickson, "Can Bureaucracy Be Beautiful?" *Public Administration Review* 60 (January/February 2000): 47–53.

2. J. Norman Baldwin, "Public Versus Private Employees: Debunking Stereotypes," *Review of Public Personnel Administration* 11 (Fall 1990–Spring 1991): 1–27.

3. See, for example, Theodore H. Poister and Gary T. Henry, "Citizen Ratings of Public and Private Service Quality: A Comparative Perspective," *Public Administration Review* 54 (March/April 1994): 155–59.

4. Harold D. Laswell, *Politics: Who Gets What, When, Where, How?* (Cleveland, Ohio: World, 1958).

5. Kurt M. Thurmaier and Katherine G. Willoughby, *Policy and Politics in State Budgeting* (Armonk, N.Y.: M.E. Sharpe, 2000).

6. Council of State Governments, *The Book of the States,* Vol. 36 (Lexington, Ky.: Council of State Governments, 2004), pp. 260–61.

7. Aaron Wildavsky, "Toward a Radical Incrementalism," in Alfred De Grazia, ed., *Congress: The First Branch of Government* (Washington, D.C.: American Enterprise Institute, 1966).

8. Aaron Wildavsky, *The Politics of the Budgetary Process* (Boston: Little, Brown, 1964), pp. 1–13.

9. Thurmaier and Willoughby, 2000; Glenn Abney and Thomas P. Lauth, *The Politics of State and City Administration* (Albany, N.Y.: SUNY Press, 1986), pp. 110–11, 115, 142–43; Rubin, *Class, Tax, and Power,* Chapter 6.

10. Charles E. Lindblom, "The Science of Muddling Through," *Public Administrative Review* 19 (Spring 1959): 79–88.

11. Janet M. Kelly and William C. Rivenbark, *Performance Budgeting for State and Local Government* (Armonk, N.Y.: M.E. Sharpe); Jonathan Walters, "Performance-Driven Government: Using Measures to Manage," *Governing* (January 2000): 69–73; Jonathan Walters, "Deeds, Data, and Dollars," *Governing* (November 2000): 98–102.

12. David K. Hamilton, "The Staffing Function in Illinois State Government After *Rutan,*" *Public Administration Review* 53 (July/August 1993): 381–86.

13. H. George Frederickson, "The Airport That Reforms Forgot," *PA Times* (January 2000): 11.

14. J. Edward Kellough and Sally Coleman Selden, "The Reinvention of Public Personnel Administration: An Analysis of the Diffusion of Personnel Management Reforms in the States," *Public Administration Review* 63 (November/December 2003): 165–76; Steven W. Hays and Richard C. Kearney, "Anticipated Changes in Human Resource Management: Surveying the Field," *Public Administration Review* 61 (September/October 2001).

15. Jerrell D. Coggburn, "Deregulating the Public Personnel Function," in Steven W. Hays and Richard C. Kearney, eds., *Public Personnel Administration: Problems and Prospects,* 4th ed. (Upper Saddle River, N.J.: Prentice-Hall, 2003), pp. 75–79.

16. See, for example, Kenneth J. Meier, "Representative Bureaucracy: An Empirical Analysis," *American Political Science Review* 69 (June 1975): 526–42; and Samuel Krislov and David H. Rosenbloom, *Representative Bureaucracy and the American Political System* (New York: Praeger, 1981), pp. 31–73, 75–107. But see also Kenneth J. Meier, "Latinos and Representative Bureaucracy: Testing the Thompson and Henderson Hypotheses," *Journal of Public Administration Research and Theory* 3 (October 1993): 393–414.

17. J. Edward Kellough, "Equal Employment Opportunities and Affirmative Action in the Public Sector," in Hays and Kearney, 2003, pp. 209–24.

18. *Hopwood v. Texas* (1996). 78 F.3d 932 (5th Cir; 1990) cert denied, 1996 WL 227009.

19. *Gretz v. Bollinger*, No. 02-516 (June 23, 2003); *Grutter v. Bollinger*, No. 02-241 F.3d 732 (June 23, 2003).

20. Mary E. Guy, "The Difference That Gender Makes," in Hays and Kearney (2003), pp. 256–70; Norma M. Riccucci, *Managing Diversity in Public Sector Workforces* (Boulder, Colo.: Westview Press, 2002).

21. Mary E. Guy, "Three Steps Forward, Two Steps Backward: The Status of Women's Integration into Public Management," *Public Administration Review* 53 (July/August 1993): 285–91; Will Miller, Brinck Kerr, and Margaret Reid, "A National Study of Gender-Based Occupational Segregation in Municipal Bureaucracies: Persistence of Glass Walls?" *Public Administration Review* 59 (May/June 1999): 218–29.

22. Sonia Ospina and James F. O'Sullivan, "Working Together: Meeting the Challenge of Workplace Diversity," in Hays and Kearney, 2003, pp. 238–55; Riccucci, 2002.

23. *Meritor Savings Bank v. Vinson*, 1986, 477 U.S. 57; *Teresa Haris v. Forklift Systems, Inc.*, U.S. Supreme Court. 92-1168 (November 9, 1993).

24. See M. Dawn McCaghy, *Sexual Harassment: A Guide to Resources* (Boston: G. K. Hall, 1985).

25. Selden, 2003.

26. www.bls.gov/news.realease/union2.t03.htm (accessed January 20, 2004).

27. See Richard C. Kearney, "Monetary Impacts," in *Labor Relations in the Public Sector*, 3d ed. (New York: Marcel Dekker Co., 2001), Chapter 6.

28. Joel M. Douglas, "State Civil Service Systems and Collective Bargaining: Systems in Conflict," *Public Administration Review* 52 (January/February 1992): 162–71.

29. Jeffrey S. Banks and Barry R. Weingast, "The Political Control of Bureaucracies Under Asymmetric Information," *American Journal of Political Science* 36 (May 1992): 509–24.

30. Abney and Lauth, *Politics of State and City Administration,* pp. 76–78, 178–81.

31. Charles Bullock and Susan MacManus, "Testing Assumptions of a Totality-of-the-Circumstances Test," *American Politics Quarterly* 21 (March 1993): 290–306.

32. Kenneth J. Meier, Joseph Stewart, Jr., and Robert E. England, "Politics of Bureaucratic Discretion: Educational Access as an Urban Service," *American Journal of Political Science* 35 (February 1991): 155–57.

33. Abney and Lauth, *Politics of State and City Administration.*

34. Jessica E. Sowa and Sally Coleman Selden, "Administrative Discretion and Active Representation: An Expansion of the Theory of Representative Bureaucracy," *Public Administration Review* 63 (November/December 2003): 700–10.

35. David Osborne and Ted Gaebler, *Reinventing Government* (New York: Penguin Books, 1993).

36. Keon S. Chi, Kelley A. Arnold, and Heather M. Perkins, "Privatization in State Government: Trends and Issues," *Spectrum: The Journal of State Government* (Fall 2003): 1.

37. Robert Jay Dilger, Randolph R. Moffett, and Linda Struyk, "Privatization of Municipal Services in America's Largest Cities," *Public Administration Review* 57 (January/February 1997): 21–26; Gerald T. Gabris and Douglas M. Ihrke, "Unanticipated Failures of Well-Intentional Reforms: Some Lessons Learned from Federal and Local Governments," *International Journal of Organization Theory and Behavior* 6 (February 2003): 195–225; George A. Boyne, "Bureaucratic Theory Meets Reality: Public Choice and Service Contracting in U.S. Local Government," *Public Administration Review* 58 (November/December 1998): 474–84.

38. Gary Enos, "We May Go Private," *Governing* 9 (November 1996): 40–41; Jonathan Walters, "The Welfare Bonanza," *Governing* (January 2000): 34–36.

39. See "Infrastructure Conference Report," *Governing* 9 (October 1996): 73; Lawrence L. Martin, "Public-Private Competition: A Public Employee Alternative to Privatization," *Review of Public Personnel Administration* 19 (Winter 1999): 59–70.

40. Dilger et al., "Privatization of Municipal Services," pp. 23–24; Boyne, "Bureaucratic Theory," pp. 475–80; Elliott D. Sclar, *You Don't Always Get What You Pay For* (Ithaca, N.Y.: Cornell University Press, 2000).

41. Pamela M. Prah, "E-Government Use Up 50 Percent, Survey Finds," www.Stateline.org (May 25, 2004): 1–3.

42. M. Jae Moon, "The Evolution of E-Government Among Municipalities: Rhetoric or Reality?" *Public Administration Review* 62 (July/August 2002): 424–33; Anya Sostek, "Bringing Sprawl to Life," *Governing* (December 2001): 31–32; Christopher Swope, "Working Without a Wire," *Governing* (June 2002): 32–34.

CHAPTER 9   THE JUDICIARY   PP. 243–271

1. W. John Moore, "In Whose Court?" *National Journal* (October 15, 1991): 2396.

2. Melinda Gann Hall, "State Judicial Politics: Rules, Structures, and the Political Game," in Ronald E. Weber and Paul Brace, eds., *American State and Local Politics: Directions for the 21st Century* (New York: Chatham House, 1999), pp. 114–38.

3. Henry Robert Glick and Kenneth N. Vines, *State Court Systems* (Englewood Cliffs, N.J.: Prentice-Hall, 1973), p. 19.

4. Ibid., p. 21.

5. Kevin Sack, "Where the Bench Orders Some Southern Comfort," *New York Times,* www.nytimes.com (January 29, 2002).

6. Brian J. Ostrom and Neal B. Kauder, eds., *Examining the Work of State Courts, 1998* (Washington, D.C.: National Center for State Courts, 1999).

7. Kenneth G. Pankey, Jr., "The State of the Judiciary," in *The Book of the States 1992–93* (Lexington, Ky.: Council of State Governments, 1992), p. 211.

8. Thomas R. Marshall, "Policymaking and the Modern Court: When Do Supreme Court Rulings Prevail?" *Western Political Quarterly* 42 (December 1989): 493–507.

9. Tod Newcombe, "Justifying the Process: Judicial Agencies Struggle to Learn the Art of Integration," www.govtech.net (April 1999): 56–59.

10. U.S. Advisory Commission on Intergovernmental Relations (ACIR), "State Court Systems," in *The Question of State Government Capability* (Washington, D.C.: ACIR, 1985), p. 191; see also Tracy Lightcap, "Issue Environments and Institutionalization: Structural Change in U.S. State Judicial Institutions," *The Justice System Journal* 24 (February 2003): 183–203.

11. American Bar Association, *Standards Relating to Court Organization* (New York: ABA, 1974), pp. 43–44.

12. Charles H. Sheldon and Linda S. Maule, *Choosing Justices: The Recruitment of State and Federal Judges* (Pullman, Wash.: Washington State University Press, 1997).

13. William Glaberson, "Court Rulings Curb Efforts to Rein in Judicial Races," *New York Times* (October 7, 2000), pp. A1–A4. Also see *Republican Party of Minnesota v. White,* No. 01-521 (2002).

14. Melinda Gann Hall, "State Supreme Courts in American Democracy: Probing the Myths of Judicial Reform," *American Political Science Review* 95 (June 2001): 315–30.

15. *Republican Party of Minnesota v. White,* No. 01-521 (2000).

16. Stephen Ware, "Money, Politics, and Judicial Decisions: A Case Study of Arbitration Law in Alabama," *Journal of Law and Politics* 15 (Fall 1999): 645–86; Madhavi McCall, "The Politics of Judicial Elections: The Influence of Campaign Contributions on the Voting Patterns of Texas Supreme Court Justices," *Politics and Policy* 31 (June 2003): 314–33.

17. Roy A. Schotland, "2002 Judicial Elections," *Spectrum: The Journal of State Government* (Winter 2003): 18–19.

18. Kathleen Hunter, "Money Mattering More in Judicial Elections," www.Stateline.org (May 12, 2004): 1–3.

19. As quoted in Sheila Kaplan, "Justice for Sale," *State Government: CQ's Guide to Current Issues and Activities, 1986–87* (Washington, D.C.: Congressional Quarterly Press, 1987), pp. 151–57.

20. See, for example, Henry R. Glick and Craig Emmert, "Selection Systems and Judicial Characteristics: The Recruitment of State Supreme Court Justices," *Judicature* 70 (December/January 1987): 228–35.

21. John Culver, "California Supreme Court Election: 'Rose Bird and the Supremes,' " *Comparative State Politics Newsletter* (February 1987): 13.

22. Steven D. Williams, "The 1996 Retention Election of Justice White," *Comparative State Politics* 17 (October 1996): 28–30.

23. Kathleen A. Bratton and Rorie L. Spill, "Existing Diversity and Judicial Selection: The Role of the Appointment Method in Establishing Gender Diversity in State Supreme Courts," *Social Science Quarterly* 83 (June 2002): 504–18.

24. Barbara Luck Graham, "Do Judicial Systems Matter?" *American Politics Quarterly* 18 (July 1990): 316–36; Mark Hurwitz and Drew Noble Lanier, "Explaining Judicial Diversity: The Differential Ability of Women and Minorities to Attain Seats on State Supreme and Appellate Courts," *State Politics and Policy Quarterly* 3 (Winter 2003): 329–52.

25. Melinda Gann Hall, "Electoral Politics and Strategic Voting in State Supreme Courts," *Journal of Politics* 54 (1992): 427–46; Melinda Gann Hall, "Toward an Integrated Model of Judicial Voting Behavior," *American Politics Quarterly* 20 (1992): 147–68.

26. Hall, "State Judicial Politics," p. 136.

27. James P. Wenzel, Shaun Bowler, and David J. Lanoue, "Legislating from the State Bench: A Comparative Analysis of Judicial Activism," *American Politics Quarterly* 25 (July 1997): 363–79.

28. ACIR, "State Court Systems," p. 190.

29. "New Questions About Rhode Island Chief Justice," *New York Times* (October 3, 1993), section 1, p. 22; "Ex-Top Judge Ends Rhode Island Appeal with a Guilty Plea," *New York Times* (April 30, 1994), section 1, p. 12; "Justice in Impeachment Inquiry Quits in Rhode Island," *New York Times* (May 29, 1986), p. A14.

30. Charles Mahtesian, "Supreme Chaos," *Governing* 9 (July 1996): 40–43.

31. Hall, "Electoral Politics and Strategic Voting."

32. Melinda Gann Hall, "Justices as Representatives: Elections and Judicial Politics in the American States," *American Politics Quarterly* 23 (October 1995).

33. See John C. Kilwein and Richard A. Brisbin, Jr., "Policy Convergence in a Federal Judicial System: The Application of Intensified Scrutiny Doctrines by State Supreme Courts," *American Journal of Political Science* 41 (January 1997): 145.

34. Gregory A. Caldeira, "Legal Precedent: Structures of Communication Between State Supreme Courts," *Social Network* 10 (1988): 29–55.

35. Law, "Accessing the Judicial System," pp. 168–80.

36. Gerald S. Gryski, Eleanor C. Main, and William J. Dixon, "Models of State High Court Decision Making in Sex Discrimination Cases," *Journal of Politics* 48

(February 1986): 143–55; Donald R. Songer and Kelley A. Crews-Meyer, "Does Judge Gender Matter? Decision Making in State Supreme Courts," *Social Science Quarterly* 81 (September 2000): 750–62.

37. Darrell Steffensmeier and Chester L. Britt, "Judges' Race and Judicial Decision Making: Do Black Judges Sentence Differently?" *Social Science Quarterly* 82 (December 2001): 749–64; Richard C. Kearney and Reginald Sheehan, "Supreme Court Decision Making: The Impact of Court Composition on State and Local Government Litigation," *Journal of Politics* 54 (November 1992): 1008–25.

38. John J. Scheb III, Terry Bowen, and Gary Anderson, "Ideology, Role Orientations, and Behavior in the State Courts of Last Resort," *American Politics Quarterly* 19 (July 1991): 324–35.

39. Mark L. Glasser and John Kincaid, "Selected Rights Enumerated in State Constitutions," *Intergovernmental Perspective* 17 (Fall 1991): 35–44.

40. www.ncsc.dni.us/Research/tcps-web (November 3, 2000).

41. Council of State Governments, *The Book of the States*, Vol. 35 (Lexington, Ky.: Council of State Governments, 2004), p. 247.

CHAPTER 10   THE STRUCTURE OF LOCAL GOVERNMENT   PP. 272–302

1. William Fulton and Paul Shigley, "Putting Los Angeles Together," *Governing* 13 (June 2000): 20–26; John H. Culver, "Reforming Los Angeles Government," *Comparative State Politics* 20 (October 1999): 41–44.

2. *2002 Census of Governments, Volume I Number 1 Government Organization* (Washington, D.C.: U.S. Census Bureau, 2002).

3. John Kincaid, "Municipal Perspectives on Federalism," unpublished manuscript, 1987.

4. Dennis Hale, "The City as Polity and Economy," *Polity* 17 (Winter 1984): 205–24.

5. Kincaid, "Municipal Perspectives," p. 56.

6. Council for Excellence in Government 2000, www.excelgov.org.

7. Victor S. DeSantis and Tari Renner, "Governing the County: Authority, Structure, and Elections," in Daniel R. Berman, ed., *County Governments in an Era of Change* (Westport, Conn.: Greenwood, 1993), pp. 15–28.

8. J. Edwin Benton and Donald C. Menzel, "County Services: The Emergence of Full-Service Government," in Berman, ed., *County Governments in an Era of Change*, pp. 53–69.

9. Christopher Hoene, Mark Baldassare, and Michael Shires, "The Development of Counties as Municipal Governments," *Urban Affairs Review* 37 (March 2002): 575–91.

10. Tanis J. Salant, "County Governments: An Overview," *Intergovernmental Perspective* 17 (Winter 1991): 5–9.

11. Barbara P. Greene, "Counties and the Fiscal Challenges of the 1980s," *Intergovernmental Perspective* 13 (Winter 1987): 14–19.

12. Tanis J. Salant, "Trends in County Government Structure," *The Municipal Year Book 2004* (Washington, D.C.: International City/County Management Association, 2004).

13. J. Edwin Benton, "The Impact of Structural Reform on County Government Service Provision," *Social Science Quarterly* 84 (December 2003): 858–74.

14. Beverly A. Cigler, "Revenue Diversification Among U.S. Counties," paper presented at the annual meeting of the American Political Science Association, New York City, 1994.

15. Alan Ehrenhalt, "Good Government, Bad Government," *Governing* 8 (April 1995): 18.

16. "County Grades at a Glance," www.governing.com/gpp/2002/gp2grade.htm (May 25, 2004).

17. "Counties Out of Date," *State Legislatures* 17 (March 1991): 17.

18. Jonathan Walters, "The Disappearing County," www.governing.com (July 5, 2000).

19. Douglas Yates, *The Ungovernable City* (Cambridge, Mass.: MIT Press, 1977).

20. Edward C. Banfield, *The Unheavenly City* (Boston: Little, Brown, 1968).

21. Susan E. Clarke and Gary Gaile, *The Work of Cities* (Minneapolis: University of Minnesota Press, 2000).

22. Joel Miller, "Boundary Changes 1990–1995," *The Municipal Year Book 1997* (Washington, D.C.: International City/County Management Association, 1997).

23. Robert Bradley Rice, *Progressive Cities* (Austin: University of Texas Press, 1977).

24. David R. Morgan, *Managing Urban America*, 2d ed. (Belmont, Calif.: Wadsworth, 1984).

25. James H. Svara, *Official Leadership in the City* (New York: Oxford University Press, 1990).

26. Victor S. DeSantis and Tari Renner, "City Government Structures: An Attempt at Clarification," *State and Local Government Review* 34 (Spring 2002): 95–104.

27. Brian M. Green and Yda Schreuder, "Growth, Zoning and Neighborhood Organizations," *Journal of Urban Affairs* 13, no. 1 (1991): 97–110.

28. Arnold Fleischmann and Carol A. Pierannunzi, "Citizens, Development Interests, and Local Land-Use Regulation," *Journal of Politics* 52 (August 1990): 838–53.

29. Mary Edwards, "Annexation: A Winner-Take-All Process?" *State and Local Government Review* 31 (Fall 1999): 221–31.

30. Rodger Johnson, Marc Perry, and Lisa Lollock, "Annexation and Population Growth in American Cities 1990–2000," *The Municipal Year Book 2004* (Washington, D.C.: International City/County Management Association, 2004).

31. Barry J. Kaplan, "Houston: The Golden Buckle of the

Sunbelt," in Richard M. Bernard and Bradley R. Rice, eds., *Sunbelt Cities: Politics and Growth Since World War II* (Austin: University of Texas Press, 1983), pp. 196–212.

32. Rob Gurwitt, "Not-So-Smart Growth," *Governing* 14 (October 2000): 34–38.

33. "Cities with 100,000 or More Population in 2000 ranked by Land Area," *County and City Data Book 2000*, www.census.gov/statab/ccdb/cityrank.htm.

34. Platon N. Rigos and Charles J. Spindler, "Municipal Incorporations and State Statutes: A State-Level Analysis," *State and Local Government Review* 23 (Spring 1991): 76–81.

35. Gurwitt, "Not-So-Smart Growth."

36. Michael A. Pagano, *City Fiscal Conditions in 2003* (Washington, D.C.: National League of Cities, 2003).

37. Tari Renner, "Municipal Election Processes: The Impact on Minority Representation," in *The Municipal Year Book 1988* (Washington, D.C.: International City/County Management Association, 1988), pp. 13–21.

38. Susan Welch and Timothy Bledsoe, *Urban Reform and Its Consequences: A Study in Representation* (Chicago, Ill.: University of Chicago Press, 1988).

39. Chandler Davidson and Bernard Grofman, "The Effect of Municipal Election Structure on Black Representation in Eight Southern States," in Davidson and Grofman, eds., *Quiet Revolution in the South* (Princeton, N.J.: Princeton University Press, 1994), pp. 301–21.

40. Alva W. Stewart and Phung Nguyen, "Electing the City Council: Historic Change in Greensboro," *National Civic Review* 72 (July/August 1983): 377–81.

41. Curtis Wood, "Voter Turnout in City Elections," *Urban Affairs Review* 39 (November 2002): 209–31.

42. Welch and Bledsoe, *Urban Reform and Its Consequences*; Jeffrey D. Greene, "Reformism and Public Policies in American Cities Revisited," paper presented at the annual meeting of the Southern Political Science Association, Atlanta, Ga., 2000.

43. Richard L. Cole and Delbert A. Taebel, "Cumulative Voting in Local Elections: Lessons from the Alamogordo Experience," *Social Science Quarterly* 73 (March 1992): 194–201.

44. Shaun Bowler et al., "Candidate Activities, Strategies, and Organization in U.S. Cumulative-Voting Elections," paper presented at the annual meeting of the American Political Science Association, San Francisco, 1996.

45. Melissa Conradi, "But Definitely Not St. Ventura," *Governing* 14 (January 2001): 16.

46. Dave Drury, "Town Meetings: An Enduring Image Changes," *Hartford Courant* (September 22, 1991), pp. A1, A10–A11.

47. Gary A. Mattson, "Municipal Services and Economic Policy Priorities Among Florida's Smaller Cities," *National Civic Review* 79 (September/October 1990): 436–45.

48. Thomas L. Daniels, "Rationing Government Resources Calls for 'Small-Town Triage,'" *Governing* 1 (March 1988): 74.

49. Frank Bryan and John McClaughry, *The Vermont Papers* (Post Mills, Vt.: Chelsea Green, 1989).

50. Kathryn A. Foster, *The Political Economy of Special Purpose Government* (Washington, D.C.: Georgetown University Press, 1997).

51. *2002 Census of Governments, Volume I Number 1 Government Organization*.

52. U.S. Advisory Commission on Intergovernmental Relations, *State and Local Roles in the Federal System* (Washington, D.C.: ACIR, 1982), p. 154.

53. John C. Bollens, *Special District Governments in the United States* (Berkeley: University of California Press, 1957).

54. Barbara Coyle McCabe, "Special District Formation Among the States," *State and Local Government Review* 32 (Spring 2000): 121–31.

55. Nancy Burns, *The Formation of American Local Governments* (New York: Oxford University Press, 1994).

56. Michael A. Molloy, "Local Special Districts and Public Accountability," paper presented at the annual meeting of the Midwest Political Science Association, Chicago, Ill., 2000.

57. Foster, *The Political Economy of Special Purpose Governments*.

58. Alan Ehrenhalt, "The Consolidation Divide," *Governing* 16 (March 2003): 6.

59. Michael Dobbs, "At the Heart of Reform," *Washington Post National Weekly Edition* (January 12–18, 2004), p. 31.

60. Clarence N. Stone, Jeffrey R. Henig, Bryan D. Jones, and Carol Pierannunzi, *Building Civic Capacity: The Politics of Reforming Urban Schools* (Lawrence: University Press of Kansas, 2001).

61. Katherine Barrett and Richard Greene, "Grading the Cities," *Governing* 13 (February 2000): 22–91.

62. Harry P. Hatry, "Would We Know a Well-Governed City If We Saw One?" *National Civic Review* 75 (May/June 1986): 142–46.

CHAPTER 11   LOCAL LEADERSHIP AND GOVERNANCE   PP. 303–327

1. Rob Gurwitt, "Nobody in Charge," *Governing* 10 (September 1997): 20–24.

2. Ibid., p. 23.

3. Jameson W. Doig and Erwin C. Hargrove, eds., *Leadership and Innovation* (Baltimore, Md.: Johns Hopkins University Press, 1987).

4. Mark Schneider, "Public Entrepreneurs as Agents of Change in American Government," *Urban News* 9 (Spring 1995): 1.

5. Martin Saiz, "Do Political Parties Matter in U.S. Cities?" in Martin Saiz and Haus Geser, eds., *Local Parties in Political and Organizational Perspective* (Boulder, Colo.: Westview, 1999).

6. Gaetano Mosca, *The Ruling Class* (New York: McGraw-Hill, 1939).

7. Robert Michels, *Political Parties* (New York: Free Press, 1962).

8. Robert S. Lynd and Helen M. Lynd, *Middletown* (New York: Harcourt Brace and World, 1929); Robert S. Lynd and Helen M. Lynd, *Middletown in Transition* (New York: Harcourt Brace and World, 1937).

9. Floyd Hunter, *Community Power Structure* (Chapel Hill: University of North Carolina Press, 1953); Floyd Hunter, *Community Power Succession* (Chapel Hill: University of North Carolina Press, 1980).

10. Hunter, *Community Power Succession,* p. 16.

11. Harvey Molotch, "Strategies and Constraints of Growth Elites," in Scott Cummings, ed., *Business Elites and Urban Development* (Albany, N.Y.: SUNY Press, 1988), pp. 25–47.

12. Robert Dahl, *Who Governs?* (New Haven, Conn.: Yale University Press, 1961).

13. Nelson Polsby, *Community Power and Political Theory* (New Haven, Conn.: Yale University Press, 1963).

14. Charles M. Bonjean and David M. Olson, "Community Leadership: Directions of Research," *Administrative Science Quarterly* 9 (December 1964): 278–300.

15. Peter Bachrach and Morton S. Baratz, "Two Faces of Power," *American Political Science Review* 56 (December 1962): 947–53.

16. Christopher A. Cooper and Anthony J. Nownes, "Citizen Groups in Big City Politics," *State and Local Government Review* 35 (Spring 2003): 102–11.

17. G. William Domhoff, *Who Really Rules?* (Santa Monica, Calif.: Goodyear, 1978).

18. Bonjean and Olson, "Community Leadership," p. 288.

19. Robert Agger, Daniel Goldrich, and Bert Swanson, *The Rulers and the Ruled*, rev. ed. (Belmont, Calif.: Wadsworth, 1972).

20. Anne B. Shlay and Robert P. Giloth, "The Social Organization of a Land-Based Elite: The Case of the Failed Chicago 1992 World's Fair," *Journal of Urban Affairs* 9, no. 4 (1987): 305–24.

21. Ibid., p. 320.

22. Ann O'M. Bowman, "Elite Organization and the Growth Machine," in G. William Domhoff and Thomas R. Dye, eds., *Power Elites and Organizations* (Newbury Park, Calif.: Sage, 1987), pp. 116–25.

23. Clarence N. Stone, *Regime Politics: Governing Atlanta, 1948–1988* (Lawrence: University Press of Kansas, 1989), p. 3.

24. Clarence N. Stone, "Systemic Power in Community Decision Making," *American Political Science Review* 74 (December 1980): 978–90.

25. Ibid., p. 989.

26. J. M. Ferris, "The Role of the Nonprofit Sector in a Self-Governing Society," *Voluntas* 9 (1998): 137–51.

27. Richard C. Hula and Cynthia Jackson-Elmoore, "Governing Nonprofits and Local Political Processes," *Urban Affairs Review* 36 (January 2001): 324–58.

28. Ibid., p. 326.

29. Stephen Samuel Smith, "Hugh Governs: Regime and Education Policy in Charlotte, NC," *Journal of Urban Affairs* 19, no. 3 (1997): 247–74.

30. Ramona L. Burton, "School District Mergers and Desegregation in North Carolina," unpublished Ph.D. dissertation, University of North Carolina, Chapel Hill, 1998.

31. H. V. Savitch and John Clayton Thomas, "Conclusion: End of the Millennium Big City Politics," in H. V. Savitch and John Clayton Thomas, eds., *Big City Politics in Transition* (Newbury Park, Calif.: Sage, 1991), pp. 235–51.

32. Elizabeth Kolbert, "The Un-Communicator," *The New Yorker* (March 1, 2004): 38–42.

33. Jessica Garrison and Patrick McGreevy, "Parks to File for Mayoral Race," *Los Angeles Times*, www.latimes.com (April 7, 2004).

34. Victor S. DeSantis and Tari Renner, "City Government Structures: An Attempt at Clarification," *State and Local Government Review* 34 (Spring 2002): 95–104.

35. Rob Gurwitt, "The Lure of the Strong Mayor," *Governing* 6 (July 1993): 36–41; Terrell Blodgett, "Beware the Lure of the 'Strong' Mayor," *Public Management* 76 (January 1994): 6–11.

36. David R. Morgan and Sheilah S. Watson, "The Effects of Mayoral Power on Urban Fiscal Policy," paper presented at the annual meeting of the American Political Science Association, New York City, 1994.

37. Thomas P. Ryan, Jr., as quoted in Jane Mobley, "Politician or Professional? The Debate over Who Should Run Our Cities Continues," *Governing* 1 (February 1988): 42–48.

38. W. John Moore, "From Dreamers to Doers," *National Journal* (February 13, 1988): 372–77.

39. Ibid., p. 373.

40. Richard Arrington, as quoted in Moore, "From Dreamers to Doers," p. 375.

41. Huey L. Perry, "Deracialization as an Analytical Construct in American Urban Politics," *Urban Affairs Quarterly* 27 (December 1991): 181–91; Nicholas O. Alonzie, "The Promise of Urban Democracy: Big-City Black Mayoral Service in the Early 1990s," *Urban Affairs Review* 35 (January 2000): 422–34.

42. Mary E. Summers and Philip A. Klinkner, "The Daniels Election in New Haven and the Failure of the Deracialization Hypothesis," *Urban Affairs Quarterly* 27 (December 1991): 202–15.

43. Charles Cohen, "Racial Politics Subside in Cities," *Christian Science Monitor* (November 2, 1999), p. 1.

44. Lana Stein, "Representative Local Government: Minorities in the Municipal Work Force," *Journal of Politics* 48 (August 1986): 694–713.

45. Timothy Bates and Darrell L. Williams, "Racial Politics: Does It Pay?" *Social Science Quarterly* 74 (September 1993): 507–22.

46. Several of these studies are summarized in Susan A. MacManus and Charles S. Bullock III, "Women and Racial/Ethnic Minorities in Mayoral and Council Positions," *The Municipal Year Book 1993* (Washington, D.C.: International City/County Management Association, 1993), pp. 70–84.

47. Jon Jeter, "In Minnesota, Political Views Change with Minority Influx," *Washington Post* (March 3, 1998), p. A1.

48. Rob Gurwitt, "Mysteries of Urban Momentum," *Governing* 15 (April 2002): 26–29.

49. "From Vision to Reality: How City Administrations Succeed in the Long Haul," www.civic-strategies.com (September 30, 2003).

50. "What Makes a Great Mayor?" Talk of the Nation, www.npr.org (December 10, 2003).

51. Clifford J. Wirth and Michael L. Vasu, "Ideology and Decision Making for American City Managers," *Urban Affairs Quarterly* 22 (March 1987): 454–74.

52. Alan Ehrenhalt, "The City Manager Myth," *Governing* 3 (September 1990): 40–48.

53. This subject is debated in H. George Frederickson, *Ideal & Practice in Council-Manager Government* (Washington, D.C.: International City Management Association, 1989).

54. Wayne F. Anderson, Chester A. Newland, and Richard J. Stillman II, *The Effective Local Government Manager* (Washington, D.C.: International City Management Association, 1983), pp. 45–73.

55. Ibid., p. 48.

56. James H. Svara, "Conflict and Cooperation in Elected-Administrative Relations in Large Council-Manager Cities," *State and Local Government Review* 31 (Fall 1999): 173–89.

57. Anderson, Newland, and Stillman, *The Effective Local Government Manager*, pp. 18–21.

58. H. George Frederickson, Gary A. Johnson, and Curtis H. Wood, *The Adapted City: Institutional Dynamics and Structural Change* (Armonk, N.Y.: M.E. Sharpe, 2004).

59. Larry Azevedo, as quoted in Alan Ehrenhalt, "How a Liberal Government Came to Power in a Conservative Suburb," *Governing* 1 (March 1988): 51–56.

60. Kenneth Prewitt, *The Recruitment of Political Leaders: A Study of Citizen-Politicians* (Indianapolis, Ind.: Bobbs-Merrill, 1970).

61. U.S. Bureau of the Census, *Statistical Abstract of the United States: 2003* (Washington, D.C.: U.S. Department of Commerce, 2003).

62. MacManus and Bullock, "Women and Racial/Ethnic Minorities in Mayoral and Council Positions," pp. 70–

84; Joshua G. Behr, *Race, Ethnicity and the Politics of Redistricting* (Albany, N.Y.: SUNY Press, 2004).

63. Bari Anhalt, "Minority Representation and the Substantive Representation of Interests," paper presented at the annual meeting of the American Political Science Association, San Francisco, Calif., 1996.

64. Manning Marable, "Building Coalitions Among Communities of Color," in James Jennings, ed., *Blacks, Latinos, and Asians in Urban America* (Westport, Conn.: Praeger, 1994), pp. 29–43.

65. Paula D. McClain and Steven C. Tauber, "The Urban Mosaic: Inter–Minority Group Relations in Urban Politics," paper presented at the annual meeting of the Southern Political Science Association, Atlanta, Ga., 1994.

66. Kenneth E. Yeager, *Trailblazers: Profiles of America's Gay and Lesbian Elected Officials* (Binghamton, N.Y.: Haworth, 1999).

67. James W. Button, Kenneth D. Wald, and Barbara A. Rienzo, "The Election of Openly Gay Public Officials in American Communities," *Urban Affairs Review* 35 (November 1999): 188–209.

68. Susan Welch and Timothy Bledsoe, *Urban Reform and Its Consequences* (Chicago, Ill.: University of Chicago Press, 1988).

69. James Svara, "Council Profile: More Diversity, Demands, Frustration," *Nation's Cities Weekly* 14 (November 18, 1991): 4.

70. James B. Kaatz, P. Edward French, and Hazel Prentiss-Cooper, "City Council Conflict as a Cause of Psychological Burnout and Voluntary Turnover Among City Managers," *State and Local Government Review* 31 (Fall 1999): 162–72.

71. William J. Pammer Jr., et al., "Managing Conflict and Building Cooperation in Council-Manager Cities," *State and Local Government Review* 31 (Fall 1999): 202–13.

72. Dick Simpson et al., "City Council Coalitions and Mayoral Regimes in Chicago from 1955 to 1995," paper presented at the annual meeting of the American Political Science Association, Washington, D.C., 1997.

73. Rob Gurwitt, "Are City Councils a Relic of the Past? *Governing* 16 (April 2003): 20–24.

74. Charles Mahtesian, "Mayor Deadlock," *Governing* 13 (February 2000): 10.

75. Alan Ehrenhalt, "Boldness Without Bluster," *Governing* 14 (December 2000): 8.

76. Ibid., p. 6.

77. Susan A. MacManus and Charles S. Bullock III, "Women on Southern City Councils: A Decade of Change," *Journal of Political Science* 17 (Spring 1989): 32–49.

78. Svara, "Council Profile," p. 4.

79. Susan Adams Beck, "Rethinking Municipal Governance: Gender Distinctions on Local Councils," in

Debra L. Dodson, ed., *Gender and Policymaking: Studies of Women in Office* (New Brunswick, N.J.: Center for the American Woman and Politics, 1991), p. 103.

80. Rita Mae Kelly, Michelle A. Saint-Germain, and Jody D. Horn, "Female Public Officials: A Different Voice?" *Annals of the American Academy of Political and Social Science* 515 (May 1991): 77–87.

81. Lurton Blassingame, "Frostbelt Success Story: Oshkosh, Wisconsin," *Journal of Urban Affairs* 9, no. 1 (1987): 37–46.

82. Jack E. White, "Bright City Lights," *Time* (November 1, 1993): 30–32; "Hell Is a Dying City," *The Economist* (November 6, 1993): 13–14.

83. White, "Bright City Lights," p. 32.

84. Robert J. Chaskin, "Building Community Capacity," *Urban Affairs Review* 36 (January 2001): 291–323.

CHAPTER 12   STATE–LOCAL RELATIONS PP. 328–354

1. Jayson T. Blair, "Maryland Draws Line Against Sprawl," *Boston Globe* (December 7, 1997), p. A26.

2. Christopher Swope, "McGreevey's Magic Map," *Governing* 16 (May 2003): 45–48.

3. Iver Peterson, "War on Sprawl in New Jersey Hits a Wall," *New York Times* (October 21, 2003), p. A15.

4. Steven D. Gold, "NCSL State-Local Task Force: The First Year," *Intergovernmental Perspective* 13 (Winter 1987): 11.

5. *Merriam* v. *Moody's Executors,* 25 Iowa 163, 170 (1868). Dillon's rule was first written in the case of *City of Clinton* v. *Cedar Rapids and Missouri Railroad Co.* (1868).

6. Jeffrey I. Chapman, "Local Government Autonomy and Fiscal Stress: The Case of California Counties," *State and Local Government Review* 35 (Winter 2003): 15–25.

7. U.S. Advisory Commission on Intergovernmental Relations, *The Organization of Local Public Economies* (Washington, D.C.: ACIR, December 1987), p. 54.

8. Joseph F. Zimmerman, *State-Local Relations* (New York: Praeger, 1983).

9. Peter J. May, "Policy Design and Discretion: State Oversight of Local Building Regulation," paper presented at the annual meeting of the American Political Science Association, San Francisco, Calif., 1996.

10. David R. Berman and Lawrence L. Martin, "State-Local Relations: An Examination of Local Discretion," *Public Administration Review* 48 (March/April 1988): 637–41.

11. Dale Krane, Platon N. Rigos, and Melvin B. Hill, Jr., *Home Rule in America: A Fifty State Handbook* (Washington, D.C.: Congressional Quarterly Press, 2001).

12. As quoted in Laura Vozzella and David Nitkin, "City Rejects State Plan, Offers Own School Loan," *Baltimore Sun* (March 9, 2004), p. 1.

13. R. G. Downing, "Urban County Fiscal Stress," *Urban Affairs Quarterly* 27 (December 1991): 314–25.

14. U.S. Advisory Commission on Intergovernmental Relations, *State Laws Governing Local Government Structure and Administration* (Washington, D.C.: ACIR, 1993).

15. "New State Law Bans City Minimum Wage," *Tampa Tribune,* www.tampatrib.com/floridametronews (June 5, 2003).

16. Alan Ehrenhalt, "Devolution's Double Standard," *Governing* 16 (April 2003): 6.

17. Alicia Caldwell, "High Court Pulls Reins on Eminent Domain," *Denver Post,* www.denverpost.com/cda/article (March 2, 2004).

18. Christopher Swope, "States Go for the Biotech Gold," *Governing* 17 (March 2004): 46.

19. Renu Khator, "Coping with Coercion: Florida Counties and the State's Recycling Law," *State and Local Government Review* 26 (Fall 1994): 181–91.

20. Jane Massey and Edwin Thomas, *State-Mandated Local Government Expenditures and Revenue Limitations in South Carolina, Part Four* (Columbia: University of South Carolina, March 1988).

21. Lawrence J. Grossback, "The Problem of State-Imposed Mandates: Lessons from Minnesota's Local Governments," *State and Local Government Review* 34 (Fall 2002): 183–97.

22. Ibid., p. 191.

23. Gold, "NCSL State-Local Task Force," p. 12.

24. Andree E. Reeves, "State ACIRs: Elements of Success," *Intergovernmental Perspective* 17 (Summer 1991): 13.

25. www.acir.state.va.us.

26. U.S. Advisory Commission on Intergovernmental Relations, *State-Local Relations Bodies: State ACIRs and Other Approaches* (Washington, D.C.: ACIR, 1981).

27. Ibid., pp. 38–40.

28. Anthony Downs, as cited in Joel Garreau, "From Suburbs, Cities Are Springing Up in Our Back Yards," *Washington Post* (March 8, 1987), p. A26.

29. Bruce Katz, "Smart Growth: The Future of the American Metropolis?" (Washington, D.C.: Brookings Institution, 2002), p. 2.

30. Jack Meltzner, *Metropolis to Metroplex* (Baltimore, Md.: Johns Hopkins University Press, 1984), p. 17.

31. Joel Garreau, *Edge City* (New York: Doubleday, 1991).

32. Joel Garreau, "Solving the Equation for Success," *Washington Post* (June 20, 1988), p. A8; Garreau, *Edge City,* p. 434.

33. Robert Lindsey, "The Crush on Waikiki Gives Birth to 2d City," *New York Times* (March 22, 1988), p. 8; www.kapolei.com (April 15, 2004).

34. Rob Gurwitt, "The Urban Village War," *Governing* 8 (December 1994): 54.

35. Ann O'M. Bowman and Michael A. Pagano, *Terra*

Incognita: Vacant Land and Urban Strategies (Washington, D.C.: Georgetown University Press, 2004).

36. William Fulton and Paul Shigley, "Operation Desert Sprawl," *Governing* 12 (August 1999): 16.

37. Ibid., p. 17.

38. "Land Use Planning," Sierra Club, www.sierraclub.org/sprawl/report99.

39. U.S. General Accounting Office, *Local Growth Issues— Federal Opportunities and Challenges* (Washington, D.C.: U.S. GAO, September 2000).

40. Christopher R. Conte, "The Boys of Sprawl," *Governing* 13 (May 2000): 28–33.

41. "More Than $7.4 Billion Committed to Open Space Protection," Land Trust Alliance, www.Lta.org/publicpolicy/referenda2000.htm; Katz, "Smart Growth."

42. Joseph Giordono, "California Sprawl Spawns Competing Ballot Initiatives," www.Stateline.org.

43. Bill Stoneman, "States' Big Land Deals," *Governing* 13 (December 1999): 42.

44. Daniel B. Wood, "Californians Raise Roof over New Housing," *Christian Science Monitor* (June 17, 2003), pp. 1, 4.

45. Christina McCarroll, "Measuring the Cost of Growth," *Christian Science Monitor* (February 6, 2002), p. 13.

46. Joel Garreau, "The Shadow Governments," *Washington Post* (June 14, 1987), p. A14.

47. Robert Jay Dilger, "Residential Community Associations: Issues, Impacts, and Relevance for Local Government," *State and Local Government Review* 23 (Winter 1991): 17–23.

48. Christopher Leinberger, as quoted in Libby Howland, "Back to Basics," *Urban Land* 46 (May 1987): 7.

49. Evan McKenzie, *Privatopia: Homeowners' Associations and the Rise of Residential Private Government* (New Haven, Conn.: Yale University Press, 1996).

50. Jered B. Carr and Richard C. Feiock, "Who Becomes Involved in City-County Consolidation?" *State and Local Government Review* 34 (Spring 2002): 78–94.

51. J. Edwin Benton and Darwin Gamble, "City/County Consolidation and Economies of Scale: Evidence from a Time-Series Analysis in Jacksonville, Florida," *Social Science Quarterly* 65 (March 1984): 190–98.

52. Gary Alan Johnson and Suzanne Leland, "Stealing Back Home: How One City and County Beat the Odds and Successfully Consolidated Their Governments," paper presented at the annual meeting of the Midwest Political Science Association, Chicago, Ill., 2000.

53. Alan Greenblatt, "Anatomy of a Merger," *Governing* 16 (December 2002): 20–25.

54. Robert J. McCarthy, "New Unified Government to Be Proposed," *Buffalo News* (February 11, 2004), p. 1.

55. David Rusk, *Cities Without Suburbs* (Washington, D.C.: Woodrow Wilson Center Press, 1993), p. 5.

56. Neal R. Peirce, *Citistates* (Arlington, Va.: Seven Locks Press, 1994).

57. Daniel Kemmis, as quoted in Neal R. Peirce, "Missoula's 'Citistate' Claim Marks a New Way to Define Regions," *The News & Observer* (July 1, 1993), p. 14A.

58. James F. Wolf and Margaret Fenwick, "How Metropolitan Planning Organizations Incorporate Land-Use Issues in Regional Transportation Planning," *State and Local Government Review* 35 (Spring 2003): 123–31.

59. U.S. Advisory Commission on Intergovernmental Relations, *State and Local Roles in the Federal System* (Washington, D.C.: ACIR, 1982).

60. Larry N. Gerston and Peter J. Haas, "Political Support for Regional Government in the 1990s," *Urban Affairs Quarterly* 29 (September 1993): 162–63.

61. Randolph P. Smith, "Region Idea Works, Oregon City Says," *Richmond Times-Dispatch* (October 30, 1994), pp. A1, A18.

62. Mark Baldassare, "Regional Variations in Support for Regional Governance," *Urban Affairs Quarterly* 30 (December 1994): 275–84.

63. Rob Gurwitt, "The Quest for Common Ground," *Governing* 11 (June 1998): 16–22.

64. Langley Keyes, lecture on "Rebuilding a Sense of Community," at the Urban Policy Roundtable, Boston, Mass., June 1988; Mara S. Sidney, *Unfair Housing: How National Policy Shapes Community Action* (Lawrence: University Press of Kansas, 2003).

65. Byron Katsuyama, "State Actions Affecting Local Governments," in International City Management Association, *The Municipal Year Book, 1988* (Washington, D.C.: ICMA, 1988), pp. 85–99.

66. Robert Kuttner, "Bad Housekeeping: The Housing Crisis and What to Do About It," *The New Republic* (April 25, 1988): 22–25.

67. *Beyond Shelter: Building Communities of Opportunity* (Washington, D.C.: U.S. Department of Housing and Urban Development, 1996).

68. Christopher Swope, "Little House in the Suburbs," *Governing* 13 (April 2000): 18–22.

69. Tom Arrandale, "Cities Take the Sewer Plunge," *Governing* 15 (August 2002): 24–25.

70. Tom Arrandale, "Atlanta to Spend Billions to Clean Water," *Governing* 16 (January 2003): 56.

71. Terry Busson and Judith Hackett, *State Assistance for Local Public Works* (Lexington, Ky.: Council of State Governments, 1987).

72. Ibid., p. 32.

73. Kirk Victor, "Paying for the Roads," *National Journal* (February 16, 1991): 374–79.

74. Hugh Bartling, "Private Governance and Public Opinion in a Company Town: The Case of Celebration, Florida," paper presented at the annual meeting of the Midwest Political Science Association, Chicago, Ill., 2000.

75. E. Crichton Singleton, "Kansas City Reborn," May 1998, www.e-architect.com.

76. Daniel B. Wood, "San Diego Reinvents Itself—and Gentrifies," *Christian Science Monitor* (February 26, 2004), p. 2.

77. DeWitt John, as quoted in William K. Stevens, "Struggle for Recovery Altering Rural America," *New York Times* (February 5, 1988), p. 8; Peter T. Kilborn, "Boom in Economy Skips Towns on the Plains," *New York Times* (July 2, 2000), p. A12.

78. Jim Seroka, "Community Growth and Administrative Capacity," *National Civic Review* 77 (January/February 1988): 42–46.

79. Ibid., p. 43.

80. Stevens, "Struggle for Recovery Altering Rural America."

81. Seroka, "Community Growth and Administrative Capacity," p. 45.

82. Beryl A. Radin et al., *New Governance for Rural America* (Lawrence: University Press of Kansas, 1996).

83. Christopher Conte, "Dry Spell," *Governing* 16 (March 2003): 20–24.

84. George Pataki, "Governor Pataki Offers $1 Billion Plan to Help Local Governments," Press Release, January 10, 1997.

85. Maura Dolan, "Lockyer Says S.F. Exceeded Its Legal Rights," *Los Angeles Times*, www.latimes.com/news/local/ (March 26, 2004).

CHAPTER 13   STATE AND LOCAL FINANCE PP. 355–390

1. Jason White, "GOVS Scramble for Soundbites to Decry Budget Crisis," www.Stateline.org (March 21, 2003): 1–4.

2. American Council on Intergovernmental Relations, *Significant Features of Fiscal Federalism,* Vol. 2 (Washington, D.C.: ACIR, 1998), Table 14.

3. Ivan Sciupac, "Federal Estate Tax Repeal Would Affect States," www.Stateline.org (March 16, 2001).

4. *Government Source Book 2003* (Washington, D.C.: CQ Press, 2004; supplement to *Governing* magazine), p. 31.

5. Robert Tannenwald and Jonathan Cowan, "Fiscal Capacity, Fiscal Need, and Fiscal Comfort Among U.S. States: New Evidence," *Publius* 27 (Summer 1997): 113–25.

6. David R. Berman, "State-Local Relations: Authority, Finance, Policies," *The Municipal Year Book 2000* (Washington, D.C.: ICMA, 2000).

7. Mark Schneider, "Local Budgets and the Maximization of Local Property Wealth in the System of Suburban Government," *Journal of Politics* 49 (November 1987): 1114.

8. Thomas R. Dye and Richard C. Feiock, "State Income Tax Adoption and Economic Growth," *Social Science Quarterly* 76 (September 1995): 648–54.

9. Council of State Governments, *The Book of the States 2003* (Lexington, Ky.: Council of State Governments), p. 350.

10. *The Book of the States 2004,* p. 339.

11. Neil R. Peirce, "Service Tax May Rise Again," *Public Administration Times* 11 (August 12, 1996): 2.

12. *Quill v. North Dakota,* 504 U.S. 298 (1992).

13. Laura Wilbert, "Taxing Times in Cyberspace," *New England Financial Journal* 3 (Summer 2000): 14–16; David C. Powell, "Internet Taxation and U.S. Intergovernmental Relations: From *Quill* to the Present," *Publius* 30 (Winter 2000): 39–51.

14. www.taxfoundation.org (July 19, 2004): 1.

15. www.taxfoundation.org/jocktax.html (March 2, 2004).

16. *State and Local Sourcebook* 2003 (Washington, D.C.: Governing Magazine, 2003), p. 37.

17. Jerry Kolo and Todd J. Dicker, "Practical Issues in Adopting Local Impact Fees," *State and Local Government Review* 25 (Fall 1993): 197–206.

18. Council of State Governments, *The Book of the States 2004* (Lexington, Ky.: Council of State Governments, 2004), Table 7.8.

19. Alaska Permanent Fund, www.apfc.org (March 1, 2004).

20. See Donald E. Miller and Patrick A. Pierce, "Lotteries for Education: Windfall or Hoax?" *State and Local Government Review* 29 (Winter 1997): 34–42.

21. See, for example, Mary Herring and Timothy Bledsoe, "A Model of Lottery Participation: Demographics, Context, and Attitudes," *Policy Studies Journal* 22, no. 2 (1994): 245–57.

22. U.S. General Accounting Office, *Impact of Gambling: Economic Effects More Measurable Than Social Effects,* GAO/GGD-00-78 (Washington, D.C.: U.S. GAO, April 2000).

23. Kendra A. Hovey and Harold A. Hovey, *State Fact Finder 2003* (Washington, D.C.: CQ Press, 2003), p. 240.

24. Timothy Egan, "They Give, but They Also Take: Voters Muddle States' Finances," *New York Times* (March 2, 2002), pp. 1–4.

25. Mark A. Glaser and W. Bartley Hildreth, "A Profile of Discontinuity Between Citizen Demand and Willingness to Pay Taxes: Comprehensive Planning for Park and Recreation Investment," *Public Budgeting and Finance* 16 (Winter 1996): 97.

26. Kathleen Murphy, "Oregon Rejects Tax Increase as States Set Ballot Fights," www.Stateline.org (February 4, 2004).

27. Alvin D. Sokolow, "The Changing Property Tax and State-Local Relations," *Publius* 28 (Winter 1998): 165–87.

28. James C. Clingermayer and B. Dan Wood, "Disentangling Patterns of State Debt Financing," *American Political Science Review* 89 (March 1995): 108–20.

29. James W. Endersby and Michael J. Towle, "Effects of

Constitutional and Political Controls on State Expenditures," *Publius* 27 (Winter 1997): 83–98; Daniel E. O'Toole and Brian Stipak, "State Tax and Expenditure Limitations: The Oregon Experience," *State and Local Government Review* 30 (Winter 1998): 9–16; Irene S. Rubin, *Class, Tax, and Power* (Chatham, N.J.: Chatham House, 1998).

30. Rob Gurwitt, "The Job of Rudy Giuliani," *Governing* 8 (June 1995): 23–27.

31. "Losing Control," *New York Times* (November 13, 2001), pp. 1–2.

32. Neal R. Peirce, "State Budget Disaster: Any Way Out?" *National Journal* (April 27, 1991): 1008.

33. Michael A. Pagano and Jocelyn M. Johnston, "Life at the Bottom of the Fiscal Food Chain: Examining City and Council Revenue Decisions," *Publius* 30 (Winter 2000): 159–70.

34. John E. Peterson, "Don't Forget Your Umbrella," *Governing* (October 2000): 70; Katherine Barrett and Richard Green, "The Gospel of Guidelines," *Governing* (September 1999): 68.

35. Sallie Hofmeister, "Fund Head Resigns in California" and "Too Many Questions, but Too Late," *New York Times* (December 6, 1994), pp. D1, D2.

36. Adam Pertman, "Orange County Officials Reap Bitter Fruit," *Boston Globe* (July 16, 1995), p. A6; Kevin P. Kearns, "Accountability and Entrepreneurial Public Management: The Case of the Orange County Investment Fund," *Public Budgeting and Finance* 15 (Fall 1995): 3–21.

37. Diane Kittower, "Taking Muni Bonds to the 'Net," *Governing* (July 2000): 82–83.

38. Beth Walter Honadle, "The States' Role in U.S. Local Government Fiscal Crises: A Theoretical Model and Results of a National Survey," *International Journal of Public Administration* 26, no. 13 (2003): 1451.

39. Keith J. Mueller, "Explaining Variation in State Assistance Programs to Local Communities: What to Expect and Why," *State and Local Government Review* 19 (Fall 1987): 101–7.

40. Joseph F. Zimmerman, "State Mandate Relief: A Quick Look," *Intergovernmental Perspective* 20 (Spring 1994): 28–30; Janet M. Kelly, "Institutional Solutions to Political Problems: The Federal and State Mandate Cost Estimation Process," *State and Local Government Review* 29 (Spring 1997): 90–97.

CHAPTER 14   ECONOMIC DEVELOPMENT
PP. 391–415

1. Christopher Swope, "Mississippi Signs on the Assembly Line," *Governing* 14 (January 2001): 62; "Mississippi-Nissan Synergy," *The Clarion-Ledger,* www.clarionledger/news/Nissan (May 23, 2003).

2. Christine Todd Whitman, as quoted in Tom Redburn, "2 Governors Split on Tax Strategies," *New York Times* (January 20, 1994), p. A20.

3. William R. Barnes and Larry C. Ledebur, *The New Regional Economies* (Thousand Oaks, Calif.: Sage, 1998).

4. W. Mark Crain, *Volatile States: Institutions, Policy, and the Performance of American State Economies* (Ann Arbor: University of Michigan Press, 2003).

5. "Index of State Economic Momentum," *State Policy Reports* (Washington, D.C.: Federal Funds Information for States, December 2003), p. 2.

6. "Index of State Economic Momentum," *State Policy Reports* (Washington, D.C.: Federal Funds Information for States, December 2002), p. 15.

7. Michael Janofsky, "Among 4 States, a Great Divide in Fortunes," *New York Times,* www.nytimes.com/2003/01/23/national (January 23, 2003).

8. "2003 Development Report Card for the States," Corporation for Enterprise Development, www.drc.cfed.org.

9. John Herbers, "A Third Wave of Economic Development," *Governing* 3 (June 1990): 43–50.

10. R. Scott Fosler, as quoted in Dan Pilcher, "Third Wave of Economic Development," *State Legislatures* 17 (November 1991): 34.

11. Mary Jo Waits, "Building an Economic Future," *State Government News* 38 (September 1995): 6–10.

12. William Fulton, "Making the Most of the Latest Buzzword," *Governing* 10 (February 1997): 68.

13. Waits, "Building an Economic Future."

14. Rob Gurwitt, "Cluster Power," *Governing* 13 (April 2000): 72.

15. Susan E. Clarke and Gary L. Gaile, *The Work of Cities* (Minneapolis: University of Minnesota Press, 1998).

16. J. Mac Holladay, "Trends That Strengthen Economies," *State Government News* 40 (August 1997): 6–7.

17. "2003 Development Report Card."

18. www.calvoter.org/98primary/statewide.

19. Committee for Economic Development, *Leadership for Dynamic State Economies* (Washington, D.C.: Committee for Economic Development, 1986), pp. 56–67.

20. Charles E. Lindblom, *Politics and Markets* (New York: Basic Books, 1977).

21. As quoted in Richard Reeves, *American Journey* (New York: Simon & Schuster, 1982), p. 46.

22. Committee for Economic Development, *Leadership for Dynamic State Economies*, pp. 73–77.

23. Ron Scherer, "States Race to Lead Stem-Cell Research," *Christian Science Monitor* (February 24, 2004), pp. 1, 10.

24. As quoted in Laurie Clewett, "State of the States," *State Government News* (March 2004): 20.

25. National Association of State Development Agencies, *The NASDA Newsletter* (January 21, 1987), pp. 1–7.

26. Ibid., p. 5.

27. Office of Planning and Budget, *State Strategic Plan 1997* (Atlanta, Ga.: Office of Planning and Budget: 1997), pp. 9–10.

28. "Anatomy of a Deal: The LTV Story," *Site Selection* (February/March 1998): 21–23.

29. National Conference of State Legislatures, *Travel and Tourism: A Legislator's Guide* (Denver, Colo.: National Conference of State Legislatures, 1991).

30. David Reynolds, as quoted in Charles Mahtesian, "How States Get People to (Love) Them," *Governing* 7 (January 1994): 47.

31. "Welcome to Maine," www.visitmaine.com (1998).

32. "Fresh Ideas Pennsylvania," www.state.pa.us/visit/html (1998).

33. "A Big Warm Welcome for Our Foreign Friends," *State Legislatures* 22 (March 1996): 7.

34. "Why Cities Love German Tourists," *Governing* 10 (July 1997): 46.

35. Jonathan Tisch, "Be Safe, but Don't Roll up the US Welcome Mat," *Christian Science Monitor* (August 13, 2003), p. 9.

36. J. Allen Whitt, "The Arts Coalition in Strategies of Urban Development," in Clarence N. Stone and Heywood T. Sanders, eds., *The Politics of Urban Development* (Lawrence: University Press of Kansas, 1987), pp. 144–56.

37. Christine Todd Whitman, as quoted in Carol Coren, "Profit in Nonprofit Arts," *State Government News* 41 (March 1998): 22–25.

38. Michael Janofsky, "Providence Is Reviving, Using Arts as the Fuel," *New York Times* (February 18, 1997), p. A8.

39. William Fulton, "Planet Downtown," *Governing* 10 (April 1997): 23–26.

40. Charles C. Euchner, *Playing the Field* (Baltimore, Md.: Johns Hopkins University Press, 1993); Michael N. Danielson, *Home Team: Professional Sports and the American Metropolis* (Princeton, N.J.: Princeton University Press, 1997).

41. Paul Cohan, "Supporting the Home Team," *State Government News* 40 (May 1996): 22.

42. Charles Mahtesian, "The Stadium Trap," *Governing* 11 (May 1998): 22–26.

43. Ibid.

44. Conrad Defiebre and Jay Weiner, "Pawlenty Unveils Plans for Stadiums," *Minneapolis Star Tribune,* www.startribune.com/viewers/story (March 16, 2004).

45. Rodd Zolkos, "Cities Blast Stadium Study," *City & State* 4 (April 1987): 3, 53. See also Kevin G. Quinn, Christopher P. Borick, and Paul B. Bursick, "The Stadium Game: An Empirical Analysis," paper presented at the annual meeting of the Midwest Political Science Association, Chicago, Ill., 2000.

46. Gary Enos and Rodd Zolkos, "Stadiums Ding Home Runs," *City & State* 8 (September 23–October 6, 1991): 1, 24.

47. Washington/Baltimore 2012 Regional Coalition, www.wbrc2012.org/.

48. Matthew J. Burbank, Charles H. Heying, and Greg Andranovich, "Antigrowth Politics or Piecemeal Resistance?" *Urban Affairs Review* 35 (January 2000): 334–57.

49. John Larkin, "States Spark Foreign Relations of Their Own," *PA Times* (June 1, 1992), pp. 1, 20.

50. Andreas van Agt, "Trading with the New Europe," *State Government News* 34 (December 1991): 20–23.

51. U.S. Census Bureau, "Foreign Direct Investment in the United States," *Statistical Abstract of the United States: 2003* (Washington, D.C.: U.S. Census Bureau, 2003), p. 806.

52. Garry Boulard, "Montana—Banker to the World?" *State Legislatures* 24 (April 1998): 24–27.

53. Conrad Weiler, "Free Trade Agreements: A New Federal Partner," *Publius* 24 (Summer 1994): 113–33.

54. Institute for Public Policy Studies, *Economic Revitalization in the City: A Sourcebook* (Philadelphia, Pa.: Temple University, 1985).

55. Richard S. Krannich and Craig R. Humphrey, "Local Mobilization and Community Growth: Toward an Assessment of the 'Growth Machine' Hypothesis," *Rural Sociology* 48 (Spring 1983): 60–81.

56. John M. Levy, *Urban and Metropolitan Economics* (New York: McGraw-Hill, 1985).

57. Roger Schmenner, "Location Decisions of Large Firms: Implications for Public Policy," *Commentary* 5 (January 1981): 307.

58. Paul Brace, *State Government and Economic Performance* (Baltimore, Md.: Johns Hopkins University Press, 1993).

59. Margery Marzahn Ambrosius, "Are Political Benefits the Only Benefits of State Economic Development Policies?" paper presented at the annual meeting of the American Political Science Association, San Francisco, Calif., 1990; Paul Brace, "The Changing Context of State Political Economy," *Journal of Politics* 53 (May 1991): 297–316.

60. Michael A. Pagano and Ann O'M. Bowman, *Cityscapes and Capital* (Baltimore, Md.: Johns Hopkins University Press, 1995).

61. Parris Glendening, "Smart Growth Tops Governors' Agenda," *Washington Post* (July 12, 2000), p. A14.

62. Terry F. Buss and F. Stevens Redburn, "The Politics of Revitalization: Public Subsidies and Private Interests," in Gary Gappert, ed., *The Future of Winter Cities* (Beverly Hills, Calif.: Sage, 1986), pp. 285–96.

63. Larry C. Ledebur and William W. Hamilton, *Tax Concessions in State and Local Economic Development* (Washington, D.C.: Aslan Press, 1986).

64. Eugene Carlson, "What's a Toyota Plant Worth to Kentucky? Possibly Plenty," *Wall Street Journal* (June 9, 1987), p. 37.

65. Ernest J. Yanarella and Herbert G. Reid, "Labor, Environmentalist, and Small Business Opposition to the Georgetown/Toyota Project: A Fragmented Challenge to State Economic Development and Multinational Capital," paper presented at the annual meeting of the

Southern Political Science Association, Charlotte, N.C., 1987.

66. Ibid.

67. Sujit M. CanagaRetna, "The Drive to Move South: The Growing Role of the Automobile Industry in the Southern States," *Spectrum: The Journal of State Government* 77 (Winter 2004): 22–24.

68. Mac R. Holmes, as quoted in Peter Applebome, "States Raise Stakes in Fight for Jobs," *New York Times* (October 4, 1993), p. A10.

69. Charles Mahtesian, "Romancing the Smokestack," *Governing* 8 (November 1994): 36–40.

70. Greg LeRoy, "Trends in State Business Incentives: More Money and More Accountability," *Spectrum: The Journal of State Government* 77 (Winter 2004): 15–18.

71. William Fulton, "The Clawback Clause," *Governing* 16 (October 2002): 72.

72. Ann O'M. Bowman, *The Visible Hand: Major Issues in City Economic Policy* (Washington, D.C.: National League of Cities, 1987).

73. David Osborne, *Laboratories of Democracy* (Boston: Harvard Business School Press, 1988).

74. Peter Waldman, "Cities Are Pressured to Make Developers Share Their Wealth," *Wall Street Journal* (March 10, 1987), p. 1.

75. Carol Steinbach, "Tapping Private Resources," *National Journal* (April 26, 1986): 993.

76. Mark Sappenfield, "Cities Try New Tactic to Boost Lowest Wages," *Christian Science Monitor* (November 13, 2003), pp. 1, 11.

77. "Taking Care of Business," *The Economist* (February 18, 1989): 28.

78. Neal Peirce, "Cities Must Learn When to Say No," *Houston Chronicle* (February 13, 1989), p. A12.

79. Joel Kotkin, "Top 25 Cities for Doing Business in America," *Inc.* (March 2004): 93.

80. Robert Goodman, *The Last Entrepreneurs: America's Regional Wars for Jobs and Dollars* (Boston: South End Press, 1979).

81. Charles J. Spindler, "Winners and Losers in Industrial Recruitment: Mercedes-Benz and Alabama," *State and Local Government Review* 26 (Fall 1994): 192–204.

82. Charles Mahtesian, "Resisting the Lure of the Smokestack," *Governing* 10 (May 1997): 76.

83. National Association of Counties, "Economic Development Survey: Urban Counties," unpublished report, no date.

84. Charles Mahtesian, "A Non-Poaching Peace Pact Is Under Fire in Florida," *Governing* 13 (May 2000): 88.

CHAPTER 15   EDUCATION POLICY   PP. 416–450

1. National Commission on Excellence in Education, *A Nation at Risk: The Imperative for Educational Reform* (Washington, D.C.: U.S. Government Printing Office, 1983), p. 1.

2. Diana Jean Schemo, "U.S. Students Prove Middling on a 32-Nation Test," *New York Times* (December 5, 2001).

3. National Center for Education Statistics, *The Condition of Education 2000* (Washington, D.C.: U.S. Department of Education, 2003), www.nces.ed.gov.

4. College Board, www.collegeboard.com (April 15, 2004).

5. Tiffany Danitz, "More Respect Please, Teachers Say," www.Stateline.org (May 31, 2000); Julia Steiny, "Too Many Kids," *Governing* (November 2000): 58–62.

6. John Silber, "The Correct Answer: Too Many Can't Teach," *The News and Observer* (July 8, 1998), p. A20.

7. John Bohte, "School Bureaucracy and Student Performance at the Local Level," *Public Administration Review* 61 (January/February 2001): 92–99; John E. Chubb and Terry Moe, *Politics, Markets, and America's Schools* (Washington, D.C.: The Brookings Institution, 1990).

8. Kevin B. Smith and Kenneth J. Meier, *The Case Against School Choice: Politics, Markets, and Fools* (Armonk, N.Y.: M.E. Sharpe, 1995); Kenneth J. Meier, J. L. Polinard, and Robert D. Wrinkle, "Bureaucracy and Organizational Performance: Causality Arguments About Public Schools," *American Journal of Political Science* 44 (July 2000): 590–602. Also see Robert Maranto, Scott Milliman, and Scott Stevens, "Does Private School Competition Harm Public Schools?" *Political Research Quarterly* 53 (March 2000): 177–92.

9. *Serrano* v. *Priest*, 5 Cal.3d 584 (1971).

10. *San Antonio Independent School District* v. *Rodriguez*, 411 U.S. 1 (1973).

11. B. Dan Wood and Nick A Theobald, "Political Responsiveness and Equity in Public Education Finance," *The Journal of Politics* 65 (August 2003): 718–38; Bill Swingford, "A Predictive Model of Decision Making in State Supreme Courts: The School Financing Cases," *American Politics Quarterly* 19 (July 1991): 336–52.

12. Robert B. Hawkins, Jr., "Education Reform California Style," *Publius* 14 (Summer 1984): 100.

13. William Celis III, "Michigan Debates What Tax Is Best to Pay for Education," *New York Times* (March 14, 1994), p. A12.

14. Michele Moser and Ross Rubenstein, "The Equality of Public School District Funding in the United States: A National Status Report," *Public Administration Review* 62 (January/February 2002): 63–72.

15. Douglas S. Reed, *On Equal Terms: The Constitutional Politics of Educational Opportunity* (Princeton, N.J.: Princeton University Press, 2001).

16. James S. Coleman, *Equality of Educational Opportunity* (Washington, D.C.: U.S. Government Printing Office, 1966).

17. Eric A. Hanushek, John F. Kain, Jacob M. Markman, and Steven G. Rivkin, "Does Peer Ability Affect Student Achievement?" *Journal of Applied Econometrics* 18 (September/October 2003): 527–44; available at www.edpro.stanford.edu/eah/papers/peers.aug01.pdf.

18. Eric A. Hanushek, "The Economics of Schooling: Production and Efficiency in Public Schools," *Journal of Economic Literature* 24 (September 1986): 1141–77.

19. See Gary Burtless, ed., *Does Money Matter? The Effect of School Resources on Student Achievement and Adult Success* (Washington, D.C.: Brookings Institution, 1996).

20. Martha Derthick, "American Federalism: Half-Full or Half-Empty?" *Brookings Review* (Winter 2000): 24–27.

21. William J. Mathis, "No Child Left Behind: Costs and Benefits," *Phi Delta Kappan* (May 2003): 680.

22. U.S. General Accounting Office, *Public Schools: Comparison of Achievement Results for Students Attending Privately Managed and Traditional Schools in Six Cities* (GAO-04-62) (Washington, D.C.: Government Printing Office, 2003).

23. Clive S. Thomas and Ronald J. Hrebenar, "Interest Groups in the States," in Virginia Gray and Russell L. Hanson, eds., *Politics in the American States: A Comparative Analysis*, 8th ed. (Glenview, Ill.: Scott, Foresman/Little, Brown, 2004). See Tom Loveless, ed., *Conflicting Missions? Teachers Unions and Educational Reform* (Washington, D.C.: The Brookings Institution, 2000).

24. Teresa Mendez, "School Boards: Democratic Ideal or a Troubled Anachronism?" *Christian Science Monitor* (October 21, 2003), p. 12.

25. Kenneth K. Wong, "The Politics of Education," in Virginia Gray and Russell L. Hanson, eds., *Politics in the American States: A Comparative Analysis* (Washington, D.C.: CQ Press, 2004), p. 362.

26. *Brown* v. *Board of Education of Topeka*, 347 I.S. 483 (1954).

27. *Swann* v. *Charlotte-Mecklenburg County Schools*, 402 U.S. 1 (1971).

28. John Clayton Thomas and Dan H. Hoxwroth, "The Limits of Judicial Desegregation Remedies After *Missouri* v. *Jenkins*," *Publius* 21 (Summer 1991): 93–108.

29. Paul Ciotti, "Kansas City Schools Show Money Can't Fix Everything," *Hartford Courant* (April 7, 1996), pp. D1, D4; Charles Mahtesian, "The Endless Court Order," *Governing* 10 (April 1997): 40–43.

30. Reed, 2001.

31. Reed, 2001.

32. Charles T. Clotfelter, "Public School Segregation in Metropolitan Areas," *Land Economics* 75 (December 1999): 487–504.

33. Mahtesian, "Endless Court Order"; Steven A. Holmes, "Education Gap Between Races Closes," *New York Times* (September 6, 1996), p. A18.

34. *Digest of Educational Statistics 2002,* Table 31; www.ncssm.edu (January 2, 2004).

35. Joseph Berger, "A State-Financed Boarding School Made Just for the Science-Deprived," *New York Times* (July 1992), p. B8.

36. *Ed Issues A–Z: Year-Round Schooling,* www.edweek.org (January 27, 2004).

37. Jodi Wilgorer, "Calls for Changes in the Scheduling of the School Day," *New York Times* (January 10, 2000).

38. Eric Kelderman, "Three States Lead in Preschool Programs," www.Stateline.org (February 19, 2004): 1–2.

39. Orlofsky and Olson, "The State of the State."

40. Jodi Wilgoren, "Lawsuits Touch Off Debate over Paddling in the Schools," *New York Times* (May 3, 2001), pp. 1–4; U.S. General Accounting Office, *School Safety: Promising Initiatives for Addressing School Violence* (Washington, D.C.: U.S. Government Printing Office, 1995).

41. *Board of Education of Independent School District No. 92 of Pottawatomie County et al.* v. *Earls et al.,* No. 01332 (June 27, 2002).

42. *Digest of Educational Statistics 2002,* Table 31; www.ncssm.edu.

43. Harry P. Hatry, John M. Greiner, and Brenda G. Ashford, *Issues and Case Studies in Teacher Incentive Plans* (Washington, D.C.: Urban Institute Press, 1994).

44. Jacques Steinberg, "Academic Gains Pay Off for Teachers and Students," *New York Times* (October 1, 2000).

45. Tiffany Danitz, "California Tries Landmark School Reform Plan," www.Stateline.org (July 27, 2000).

46. Chubb and Moe, *Politics, Markets, and America's Schools.*

47. See Winter, *New York Times,* 2003; Bryan C. Hassel, *The Charter School Challenge* (Washington, D.C.: The Brookings Institution, 1999).

48. Timothy Egan, "Failures Raise Questions for Charter Schools," *New York Times* (April 5, 2002), pp. 1–3; Diana Jean Schemo, "Nation's Charter Schools Lagging Behind, U.S. Test Scores Reveal," *New York Times* (August 17, 2004).

49. Center for Policy Alternatives, "Education: School Vouchers," *Policy Alternatives,* Washington, D.C., p. 85.

50. Ibid., p. 84.

51. Stephen L. Percy and Peter Maier, "School Choice in Milwaukee: Privatization of a Different Breed," *Policy Studies Journal* 24, no. 4 (1996): 657.

52. *Zelman et al.* v. *Simmons-Harris et al.,* No. 001751 (June 27, 2002).

53. Ibid.

54. See Paul E. Peterson, *The Education Gap: Vouchers and Urban Schools* (Cambridge, Mass.: Harvard University Press, 2002); Terry Moe, *Schools, Vouchers, and the American Public* (Washington, D.C.: Brookings Institution, 2001).

55. John F. Witte, *The Market Approach to Education: An Analysis of America's First Voucher Program* (Princeton, N.J.: Princeton University Press, 2000); Richard Rothstein, "Failed Schools? The Meaning Is Unclear," *New York Times* (July 3, 2002), pp. 1–2; Christopher Conte,

"The Boundaries of Choice," *Governing* (December 2002): 40–44; Kim Metcalf et al., *Evaluations of the Cleveland Scholarship and Tutoring Program, Summary Report, 1998–2001* (Bloomington: Indiana University, 2003).

56. U.S. General Accounting Office, 2003.

57. Jacques Steinberg, "At 42 Newly Privatized Philadelphia Schools, Uncertainty Abounds," *New York Times* (April 19, 2002), pp. 1–3.

58. Brian Gill, Michael Timpane, and Dominic Brewer, *Rhetoric Versus Reality: What We Know and What We Need to Know About School Vouchers and Charter Schools* (Santa Monica, Calif.: Rand Corporation, 2001).

59. Kevin B. Smith and Kenneth J. Meier, "Public Choice in Education: Markets and the Demand for Quality Education," *Political Research Quarterly* 48 (June 1995): 461–78.

60. Mark Schneider et al., "Heuristics, Low Information Rationality, and Choosing Public Goods: Broken Windows as Shortcuts to Information About School Performance," *Urban Affairs Review* 34 (May 1999): 728–41.

61. Clarence N. Stone, *Changing Urban Education* (Lawrence: University of Kansas Press, 1998).

62. Clarence N. Stone, Jeffery R. Henig, Bryan D. Jones, and Carol Pierannunzi, *Building Civic Capacity: The Politics of Reforming Schools* (Lawrence: University of Kansas Press, 2001).

CHAPTER 16   CRIMINAL JUSTICE   PP. 451–480

1. John Buntin, "Mean Streets Revisited," *Governing* (April 2003): 30–33; Shaila K. Dewan, "New York's Gospel of Policing by Data Spreads Across U.S.," *New York Times* (April 28, 2004).

2. U.S. Federal Bureau of Investigation, *Crime in the United States,* www.fbi.gov/ucr/htm#civs (2004).

3. See Federal Bureau of Investigation, *Crime in the United States* (Washington, D.C.: U.S. Department of Justice, various years).

4. Kevin B. Smith, "Explaining Variation in State-Level Homicide Rates: Does Crime Policy Pay?" *Journal of Politics* 59 (May 1997): 350–67.

5. William J. Wilem, *When Work Disappears: The World of the New Urban Poor* (New York: Alfred A. Knopf, 1996); Alex Piquero, John MacDonald, and Karen F. Parker, "Race, Local Life Circumstances, and Criminal Activity," *Social Science Quarterly* 83 (September 2002): 654–70.

6. Lee John Braithwaite, "Crime and the Average American" (Review Essay), *Law and Society Review* 27 (January 1993): 215–31.

7. Federal Bureau of Investigation, *Crime in the United States,* www.fbi.gov/ucr/civs (2002): Section III.

8. James Q. Wilson and George L. Kelling, "Broken Windows: The Police and Neighborhood Safety," *Atlantic Monthly* (March 1982): 29–38. See also Rob Gurwitt,

"Not By Cops Alone," *Governing* 8 (May 1995): 16–26.

9. *Crime and the Tech Effect,* special edition of *Government Technology* (April 2000).

10. Ellen Perlman, "Bait and Switch Off," *Governing* (February 2003): 16.

11. Harold A. Hovey and Kendra A. Hovey, *CQ's State Fact Finder 2003* (Washington, D.C.: Congressional Quarterly Press, 2003): Tables J-11, J-12.

12. Federal Bureau of Investigation, *Crime in the United States* (2003).

13. David A. Harriss, "The Stories, the Statistics, and the Law," *Minnesota Law Review* 84 (December 1999): 1–42; David Kocieniewski, "U.S. Wrote Outline for Race Profiling, New Jersey Agrues," *New York Times* (November 29, 2000).

14. *Gideon* v. *Wainwright,* 372 U.S. 335 (1963).

15. *Escobedo* v. *Illinois,* 478 U.S. (1964).

16. *Miranda* v. *Arizona,* 384 U.S. 486 (1966).

17. Richard Fowles, "Handcuffing the Cops? A Thirty-Year Perspective on Miranda's Harmful Effect on Law Enforcement," *Stanford Law Review* 50 (April 1998): 1055–1145; W. John Moore, "Shouting in the Dark," *National Journal* (February 12, 1994): 362–63.

18. *Dickerson* v. *United States,* U.S. 99–5525 (2000).

19. *Mapp* v. *Ohio,* 307 U.S. 643 (1961).

20. *Florida* v. *Bostick,* 115 L.Ed. 2d 389, 111 S.Ct. 2382 (1991); *California* v. *Acevedo,* 114 L.Ed. 2d 619, 111 S.Ct. 1982 (1991).

21. *Knowles* v. *Iowa,* 97–2597 (1998); *Wyoming* v. *Houghton,* U.S. 98–184 (1999).

22. *City of Indianapolis* v. *Edmond et. al.,* No. 99-1030 (2000).

23. "Free at Last, Free at Last," *Time* (November 2, 1987): 55.

24. Christopher Swope, "Kentucky Goes Statewide with Automated Victim Notification," *Governing* 11 (March 1998): 58.

25. www.parentsformeganslaw.com/htm.

26. C. Peter Rydell and Susan S. Everingham, *Controlling Cocaine: Supply Versus Demand Programs* (Santa Monica, Calif.: RAND Corporation, 1994).

27. *Furman* v. *Georgia,* 408 U.S. 239 (1972).

28. *McClesky* v. *Kemp,* 481 U.S. 279 (1987).

29. *Stanford* v. *Kentucky,* 57 U.S. Law Week 4973; *Herrera* v. *Collins,* 61 U.S. Law Week 3652; *Vasquez* v. *Harris,* 60 U.S. Law Week 3734; *Atkins* v. *Virginia* (2002).

30. *Singleton* v. *Norris,* 02-10605 (2003).

31. Death Penalty Information Center, www.deathpenaltyinfo.com (May 22, 2004).

32. Capital Punishment Statistics, www.ojp.usdoj.gov/bjs/cp.htm (July 27, 2004).

33. Ibid.

34. Melinda Gann Hall and Paul Brace, "The Vicissitudes of Death by Decree: Forces Influencing Capital

Punishment Decision Making in State Supreme Courts," *Social Science Quarterly* 75 (March 1999): 1368.

35. Hall and Brace, "Vicissitudes of Death," pp. 1136–51.

36. "Harmful Error," Center for Public Integrity (June 2003).

37. Ibid.

38. Robert H. DeFina and Thomas M. Arvanites, "The Weak Effect of Imprisonment on Crime: 1971–1998," *Social Science Quarterly* 83 (September 2002): 635–53.

39. *Prison and Jail Inmates at Midyear 2003* (Washington, D.C.: U.S. Bureau of Justice Statistics, 2004).

40. Ibid.

41. *Prison and Jail Inmates at Midyear 2003* (Washington, D.C.: U.S. Bureau of Justice Statistics, 2004).

42. Fox Butterfield, "With Longer Sentences, Cost of Fighting Crime Is Higher," *New York Times* (May 3, 2004).

43. *Prison and Jail Inmates at Midyear 2003* (Washington, D.C.: U.S. Bureau of Justice Statistics, 2004).

44. Buntin, 2003.

45. Christopher Swope, "Revising Sentences," *Governing* (July 2004): 38–41.

46. Ellen Perlman, "Rehab Programs Move Computers from Prisons to Schools," *Governing* 11 (May 1998): 52.

47. Greg Lucas, "Chemical Castration Bill Passes," *San Francisco Chronicle* (September 31, 1996), pp. A1, A8.

48. Judy Farah, " 'Ratlord' Sent to Live in Own Dump," *The State* (July 14, 1987): 1.

49. Elise Labott, "Slum Offensive," *Governing* (July 2000): 52–54.

50. "Death Puts Spotlight on Boot Camps," *The News and Observer* (July 8, 2001), p.15A; M. Peters, D. Thompson, and C. Zamberlan, *Boot Camps for Juvenile Offender Programs* (Washington, D.C.: Office of Juvenile Justice and Delinquency, 1997).

51. Fox Butterfield, "Study Tracks Boom in Prisons and Notes Impact on Counties," *New York Times* (April 30, 2004); Peter T. Kilborn, "Rural Towns Turn to Prisons to Reignite Their Economies," *New York Times* (August 1, 2001); Sarah Lawrence and Jeremy Travis, *The New Landscape of Imprisonment* (Washington, D.C.: The Urban Institute, 2004).

52. Sam Hose Verhovek, "Texas Caters to a Demand Around U.S. for Jail Cells," *New York Times* (February 9, 1996), pp. A1, A24.

53. Butterfield, January 21, 2002.

54. *Prison and Jail Inmates at Midyear 2003;* James Austin and Garry Coventry, "Emerging Issues in Privatized Prisons," U.S. Bureau of Justice Statistics (February 2001).

55. Anne Morrison Piehl and John J. DiIulio, Jr., "Does Prison Pay?" *The Brookings Review* (Winter 1995): 21–25.

56. *Richardson* v. *McKnight*, 138 L. Ed. 2d 540 (1997).

57. Anne Morrison Piehl and John J. DiIulio, Jr., "Does Prison Pay?" *The Brookings Review* (Winter 1995): 21–25.

58. James Austin, "Are Prisons Really a Bargain? The Use of Voodoo Economics," *Spectrum* (Spring 1996): 6–14.

59. Sarah Lawrence and Jeremy Travis, *The New Landscape of Imprisonment* (Washington, D.C.: The Urban Institute, 2004).

CHAPTER 17   SOCIAL WELFARE AND HEALTH CARE POLICY   PP. 481–505

1. Bureau of the Census, www.census.gov (June 16, 2004).

2. Ibid.

3. Louis Uchitelle, "How to Define Poverty? Let Us Count the Ways," *New York Times* (May 26, 2001), pp. 1–4; Jared Bernstein, "Who's Poor? Don't Ask the Census Bureau," *New York Times* (September 26, 2003), pp. 1–2.

4. Fred Block, Richard A. Cloward, Barbara Ehrenreich, and Francis Fox Piven, *The Mean Season: The Attack on the Welfare State* (New York: Pantheon Books, 1987), p. 92.

5. Martin Gilens, *Why Americans Hate Welfare: Race, Media, and the Politics of Antipoverty Policy* (Chicago, Ill.: University of Chicago Press, 1999).

6. John E. Schwarz, *America's Hidden Success,* rev. ed. (New York: W. W. Norton, 1988); Block et al., *The Mean Season.*

7. Raymond S. Franklin, *Shadows of Race and Class* (Minneapolis: University of Minnesota Press, 1991). See June O'Neill, "Can Work and Training Programs Reform Welfare?" and Robert Rector, "Welfare Reform, Dependency Reductions, and Labor Market Entry," *Journal of Labor Research* 14 (Summer 1993): 265–97.

8. Kendra A. Hovey and Harold A. Hovey, *State Fact Finder 2003* (Washington, D.C.: Congressional Quarterly Press, 2003), Table L-15.

9. U.S. General Accounting Office, *Welfare Reform: Progress in Meeting Work-Focused TANF Goals* (Washington, D.C.: U.S. GAO, March 15, 2001).

10. Marcia K. Meyers, Janet C. Gornick, and Laura R. Peck, "More, Less, or More of the Same? Trends in State Social Welfare Policy in the 1990s," *Publius* 32 (Fall 2002): 91–108.

11. Jocelyn Elise Crowley, "Supervised Devolution: The Case of Child-Support Enforcement," *Publius* 30 (Winter 2000): 99–117.

12. Charles Murray, as quoted in David S. Broder, "On Welfare: First, Tackle Teen Parents," *Hartford Courant* (June 28, 1994), p. C11.

13. Richard P. Nathan, *Turning Promises into Performance: The Management Challenge of Implementing Welfare* (New York: Columbia University Press, 1993).

14. See Charles Garvin, Audrey Smith, and William Reid, eds., *The Work Incentive Experience* (Montclair, N.J.: Allenheld, Osman, 1978).

15. John Herbers, "Governors Ask Work Plan for Welfare Recipients," *New York Times* (February 22, 1987), p. 30; Julie Rovner, "Welfare Reform: The Issue That Bubbled Up from the States to Capitol Hill," *Governing* 1 (December 1988): 17–21.

16. Penelope Lemov, "The Rocky Road to Privatizing Welfare," *Governing* 10 (July 1997): 36–37.

17. U.S. General Accounting Office, *Welfare Reform: More Coordinated Federal Effort Could Help States and Localities Move TANF Recipients with Impairments Toward Employment,* GAO-02-286SP (Washington, D.C.: U.S. GAO, 2001).

18. Richard M. Francis, "Prediction, Patterns, and Policy-making: A Regional Study of Devolution," *Publius* 28 (Summer 1998): 143–60; Jack Tweedie, "From D.C. to Little Rock: Welfare Reform at Mid-Term," *Publius* 30 (Winter 2001): 66–97.

19. Hovey and Hovey, *State Fact Finder 2003,* Table I–14.

20. Marilyn Werber Serafini, "Medicare Crooks," *National Journal* 29 (July 19, 1997): 1458–60; Malcolm Sparran, *License to Steal: Why Fraud Plagues America's Health Care System* (Boulder, Colo.: Westview Press, 1996).

21. Serafini, "Medicare Crooks"; Sparran, *License to Steal.*

22. Erin Madigan, "Medical Liability Debate Still Roaring in State Houses," www.Stateline.org (June 14, 2004): 1–4.

23. Marian Lief Palley, "Intergovernmentalization of Health Care Reform: The Limits of the Devolution Revolution," *Journal of Politics* 59 (August 1997): 657–79.

24. *Governing's State and Local Sourcebook 2003* (Washington, D.C.: Governing Magazine, 2003), p. 102.

25. See www.state.TN.US/tenncare/.

26. Penelope Lemov, "TennCare Tensions," *Governing* (July 2004): 56; "Second-Class Medicine," *Consumer Reports* (September 2000): 45; "Two Grand Experiments," *Governing* (February 2004): 80.

CHAPTER 18   ENVIRONMENTAL POLICY
PP. 506–529

1. As quoted in "Chattanooga on a Roll," *E Magazine* 9 (March/April 1998): 15.

2. As quoted in "Chattanooga on a Roll," p. 14.

3. Kent E. Portney, *Taking Sustainable Cities Seriously* (Cambridge, Mass.: MIT Press, 2003), pp. 185–93.

4. Richard C. Feiock and Christopher Stream, "Environmental Protection Versus Economic Development: A False Trade-Off?" *Public Administration Review* 61 (May/June 2001): 313–21.

5. Timothy Egan, "Oregon, Foiling Forecasters, Thrives as It Protects Owls," *New York Times* (October 11, 1994), pp. A1, C20.

6. Deborah Lynn Guber, *The Grassroots of a Green Revolution* (Cambridge, Mass.: MIT Press, 2003).

7. *2003 Gallup Poll Social Series, The Environment* (Princeton, N.J.: The Gallup Organization, 2003).

8. Robert D. Hershey, Jr., "Environmental Factors to Be Calculated in G.D.P.," *New York Times* (April 20, 1994), p. C2.

9. Walter A. Rosenbaum, *Environmental Politics and Policy,* 5th ed. (Washington, D.C.: CQ Press, 2002), pp. 12–13.

10. Portney, *Taking Sustainable Cities Seriously,* p. 9.

11. Lawrence S. Rothenberg, *Environmental Choices: Policy Responses to Green Demands* (Washington, D.C.: CQ Press, 2002).

12. John J. Harrigan, *Political Change in the Metropolis,* 5th ed. (Glenview, Ill.: Scott Foresman, 1993), p. 25.

13. J. Clarence Davies III, *The Politics of Pollution* (Indianapolis, Ind.: Pegasus, 1970), p. 121.

14. Rosenbaum, *Environmental Politics and Policy,* 5th ed.

15. Margaret Kriz, "Shoot-Out in the West," *National Journal* (October 15, 1994): 2388–92.

16. See U.S. General Accounting Office, *Hazardous Waste: Much Work Remains to Accelerate Facility Clean-ups* (Washington, D.C.: U.S. GAO, January 1993).

17. James L. Regens and Margaret A. Reams, "The State Strategies for Regulating Groundwater Quality," *Social Science Quarterly* 69 (March 1988): 53–69.

18. George Hagevik, "A New Way to Protect the Environment," *State Legislatures* 21 (June 1995): 28–31.

19. John Hughes, "On the Road to EPA Chief, Leavitt Stays in the Middle," *Christian Science Monitor* (August 20, 2003), p. 9.

20. Seth Borenstein, "Bush Has Made Big Changes Quietly," *The State* (January 27, 2003), pp. A1, A10.

21. Brad Knickerbocker, "Bush Takes Quiet Aim at 'Green' Laws," *Christian Science Monitor* (November 7, 2003), p. 3.

22. Brad Knickerbocker, "States Take the Lead on Global Warming," *Christian Science Monitor* (October 10, 2003), pp. 1, 12.

23. Environmental Council of the States, www.sso.org/ecos/ (October 15, 1998).

24. R. Steven Brown and Michael J. Kiefer, "ECOS Budget Survey: Budgets Are Bruised, but Still Strong," *ECOStates* (Summer 2003): 10–15.

25. Environmental Council of the States.

26. Matthew Potoski, "Clean Air Federalism: Do States Race to the Bottom?" *Public Administration Review* 61 (May/June 2001): 335–42.

27. The Institute for Southern Studies, "Gold and Green 2000," www.southernstudies.com.

28. Erin P. Billings, "Lay of the Land," *Missoulian* (November 1, 1999), p. A1.

29. Scott P. Hays, Michael Esler, Carol E. Hays, "Environmental Commitment Among the States," *Publius* 26 (Spring 1996): 41–58; see also Brad T. Clark and David W. Allen, "Political Economy and the Adoption of 'Everyday' Environmental Policies in the American

States," paper presented at the annual meeting of the Southwestern Political Science Association, Fort Worth, Tex., 2001.

30. Ann O'M. Bowman, "Green Politics in the City," paper presented at the annual meeting of the American Political Science Association, Philadelphia, Pa., 2003.

31. See the discussion in Portney, *Taking Sustainable Cities Seriously*, pp. 18–21.

32. Ibid., pp. 70–71.

33. Ibid., pp. 210–11.

34. Tim King, "Mapping Miniature, Unspoiled Plots of Land," *Christian Science Monitor* (September 4, 2003), p. 12.

35. Bowman, "Green Politics in the City."

36. Scott M. Kaufman et al. "The State of Garbage in America," *BioCycle* 45 (January 2004): 32.

37. Tom Arrandale, "Recycling's Reality Check," *Governing* 14 (October 2000): 54–58.

38. Kierstan Gordan, "The Can Man," *Governing* 14 (November 2000): 17.

39. Hugh McDiarmid Jr., "Michigan's Trash Heap Grows Larger," *Detroit Free Press*, www.freep.com (February 3, 2004).

40. Zachary A. Smith, *The Environmental Policy Paradox*, 4th ed. (Upper Saddle River, N.J.: Prentice-Hall, 2004).

41. Tom Arrandale, "Collecting More, Costing Less," *Governing* 7 (August 1994): 67.

42. Kaufman et al., "The State of Garbage in America."

43. Kathleen Meade, "Recycling That Pays $," *State Government News* 36 (October 1993): 28–29, 32.

44. Jim Motavalli, "Zero Waste," *E Magazine* 12 (March–April 2001): 27–33.

45. Christopher Borick, "Assessing the Impact of Solid Waste Management Initiatives in the American States," paper presented at the annual meeting of the American Political Science Association, Washington, D.C., 1997.

46. "Releases: Geography State Report," *TRI Explorer*, U.S. Environmental Protection Agency, www.epa.gov (July 2003).

47. Smith, *The Environmental Policy Paradox*.

48. U.S. General Accounting Office, *Yucca Mountain Project Management and Funding Issues* (Washington, D.C.: U.S. GAO, July 1, 1993).

49. "Criticism of Dump Mounts," *Las Vegas Review-Journal* (February 28, 2004): 1.

50. Anthony L. Dodson, "Interstate Compacts to Bury Radioactive Waste: A Useful Tool for Environmental Policy?" *State and Local Government Review* 30 (Spring 1998): 118–28.

51. Dianna Gordon, "Low-Level Waste Controversy," *State Legislatures* 20 (September 1994): 30–31.

52. Terry McDermott, "Nuclear Power May Rise Again," *Los Angeles Times* (February 9, 2001), pp. A1, A3.

53. Regina Austin and Michael Schill, "Black, Brown, Red, and Poisoned," in Robert D. Bullard, ed., *Unequal Protection* (San Francisco, Calif.: Sierra Club Books, 1994), p. 53.

54. James P. Lester, David W. Allen, and Kelly M. Hill, *Environmental Injustice in the United States* (Boulder, Colo.: Westview, 2001).

55. Deb Starkey, "Environmental Justice: Win, Lose, or Draw?" *State Legislatures* 20 (March 1994): 28.

56. United Church of Christ Commission for Racial Justice, *Toxic Waste and Race* (New York: United Church of Christ, 1987).

57. Susan Cutter, "Race, Class, and Environmental Justice," *Progress in Human Geography* 19 (March 1995): 111–22.

58. Tom Arrandale, "Regulation and Racism," *Governing* 11 (March 1998): 63.

59. Evan J. Ringquist and David H. Clark, "Issue Definition and the Politics of State Environmental Justice Policy Adoption," *International Journal of Public Administration* 25 (February/March 2002): 351–89.

60. Brad Knickerbocker, "New Laws Target Increase in Acts of Ecoterrorism," *Christian Science Monitor* (November 26, 2003), pp. 2–3.

61. Brad Knickerbocker, "Firebrands of 'Ecoterrorism' Set Sights on Urban Sprawl," *Christian Science Monitor* (August 6, 2003), pp. 2–3.

62. Robert J. Duffy, *The Green Agenda in American Politics* (Lawrence: University Press of Kansas, 2003).

INDEX